D1195372

ROMAN SOCIETY IN GAUL
IN THE MEROVINGIAN AGE

ROMAN SOCIETY IN GAUL

IN THE

MEROVINGIAN AGE

BY THE LATE

Sir SAMUEL DILL, M.A.

HON. LITT.D. DUBLIN, HON. LL.D. EDINBURGH, HON. FELLOW AND LATE TUTOR, C.C.C., OXFORD
LATE PRO-CHANCELLOR AND PROFESSOR OF GREEK IN QUEEN'S UNIVERSITY, BELFAST
AUTHOR OF
"ROMAN SOCIETY IN THE LAST CENTURY OF THE WESTERN EMPIRE"
AND "ROMAN SOCIETY FROM NERO TO MARCUS AURELIUS"

BARNES & NOBLE, Inc.
NEW YORK
PUBLISHERS & BOOKSELLERS SINCE 1873

77753

First published by Macmillan and Co. Ltd, London
in 1926

This edition published in 1966
by Barnes & Noble, Inc., New York
and George Allen & Unwin, Ltd, London
through special arrangement with
Macmillan and Co., Ltd, London

Reprinted, 1970

All rights reserved

Manufactured in the United States of America

PREFACE

THIS work, which occupied the last years of the life of the late Sir Samuel Dill, was virtually finished at the time of his death on May 26, 1924. It was intended by the author to complete a trilogy of studies of Roman Society, of which the two former, *Roman Society from Nero to Marcus Aurelius* and *Roman Society in the Last Century of the Western Empire* are well known.

Before he died he asked me to prepare for publication his final study of the period at which Roman Society is seen in Gaul in its decline and mergence with the more virile and barbaric forces of the Teutonic invaders. We had often discussed the scope and problems of the work, and I believe that in its arrangement and presentation his intentions have been in the main fulfilled.

Sir Samuel Dill was conscious of defects and repetitions in the work which would, no doubt, have been remedied had he lived. Some of these have been corrected ; in other instances I have allowed passages of power and interest to stand, at the risk of some duplication.

In the preparation of this book for the Press the assistance of Dr. L. C. Purser, Vice-Provost of Trinity College, Dublin, an old friend of the author, has been invaluable. The notes and references which are appended are due in the main to his learning and research. Without his aid the task of supplying authorities from so wide a field, with but little assistance from the manuscript, would have been one of insuperable difficulty.

v

My sincerest thanks are also due to Professor R. M. Henry, M.A., of Queen's University, Belfast, who has read and corrected the proofs and verified many references with scrupulous care. Without the aid of these two scholars and friends of the author I could not have completed a task which, in so far as it may have been successful, is a tribute of affection to the memory of one who typified to those who knew him, both in his scholarship and in his personality, the best traditions of classical culture.

C. B. ARMSTRONG.

S. COLUMBA'S COLLEGE,
RATHFARNHAM, CO. DUBLIN,
October 1925.

CONTENTS

BOOK I

THE HISTORICAL ASPECT

CHAPTER I

EVENTS IN GAUL FROM THE FALL OF THE WESTERN EMPIRE
TO THE ACCESSION OF CLOVIS

Causes of the fall of the Roman Empire in the West—Authorities scanty for affairs in Gaul—Summary of Gallo-Roman feeling—Early history of the Franks—The Frank name—Previous invasions of Brabant—The Salian Franks in Toxandria—Franks in the service of the Empire—Early Frank rulers in Gaul—Conquests and defeat of Chlogio by Aetius—Merovechus— Roman power vanishes from the Rhineland—Childeric, king of the Franks —His banishment—The Roman Aegidius appointed dux—The Syagrii— Military designs of Aegidius—His war with Theodoric and the Visigoths— His defeat and the restoration of Childeric—Subsequent campaigns of Childeric against the Visigoths—He assists the Gallo-Roman Syagrius, whose gallant struggle is unaided by Rome—Dangers of the Western Empire, the Vandals, Ricimer, the Burgundians, the Ostrogoths—Rome surrenders even the pretence of power in Gaul—Arianism the religion of the conquering races—Euric and the Visigoths—Deficiency of authorities for social life of the period—The *Lives of the Saints*—S. Geneviève— S. Rémi—S. Vivianus—S. Lupicinus—S. Gregory of Langres   Pages 1-39

CHAPTER II

EARLY FRANK AND BURGUNDIAN SOCIETY IN THE CODES

The unwisdom of generalisations on national characteristics—The evolution of the new nations from the German tribes—The Salian Franks in Toxandria—The Salic Code—The problem of its origin and composition—The society which it depicts is rural—Not unduly lawless, though often troubled by crime—Examples of its penalties—System of pecuniary compensation

—Its origin—Not inconsistent with the death penalty—Civil procedure—
Judicial procedure—The Rachimburgi—Appeals to Divine justice—Ordeals
—The combined oath—The villa of N.E. Gaul—The Burgundian Code—
A politic attempt of Gundobad to reconcile the Burgundian and Gallo-
Roman races—It reflects a civilisation more advanced than that of the
Salian Franks—No trace of legal superiority of the conquerors—Landed
property—Rural life and slave labour—Brigandage—Crimes of violence—
The protection of women—Judicial combat—Summarised view of the
Burgundian Code—Picture of a peaceful and happy land—Little trace of
the Church's power in this Code . . . . . Pages 40-76

CHAPTER III

THE CONQUESTS OF CLOVIS

Accession of Clovis—Favoured by the Church against the Arian Visigoths and
Burgundians—His conflict with Syagrius "rex Romanorum"—Battle
near Soissons; defeat of Syagrius and annexation of his kingdom—Few
signs of oppression by the conquerors—Coalescence with the Gallo-Romans
—Subsequent wars of Clovis—The siege of Nantes—Clovis and Chlotilde—
Their union favoured by the Church—Story of the wooing of Chlotilde—
The conversion of Clovis in A.D. 496 at the battle of Tolbiac—Defeat of the
invasion of the Alemanni—Baptism of Clovis—His motives—Feud of
Gundobad and Godegesil—Clovis invades Burgundy in A.D. 500—The
strategy of Aridius saves Burgundy for a time—Why Clovis permitted this
revival—Arian and Catholic powers—Frank and Visigoth in conflict at
last—Council of Agde, A.D. 506—S. Rémi sends Clovis as champion of the
Church—Battle of Vouglé and defeat of Alaric—Following up the victory
—S. Caesarius—His account of the siege of Arles—Theodoric and the
Ostrogoths decide to stem the Frank advance—The siege of Arles raised,
and Clovis retires northward—Ostrogothic occupation of Southern Gaul
Pages 77-105

CHAPTER IV

THE FRANK KINGSHIP AND COURT

The character and institutions of the Germans not immune from variation—
The Germans of Tacitus idealised—Their long wars must have caused great
changes in the German tribes—Growth of royal power through successful
war—Adaptation of tribal organisation to wanderings—Modification by
Roman civilisation and by the Church—The kingship the sole symbol and
organ of the Frank power—Theories as to its character too clear-cut—Its
politic adoption of Roman forms—Main characteristics in the sixth century:
(1) Hereditary, not elective. (2) Symbol of a peaceful fusion of two great
races. (3) Rests fundamentally on absolutism. (4) Supreme in every
department—Legislation autocratic—Powers of making war or peace—
A regular army, supplemented by the *levée en masse*—Difficulties in its
discipline—The kingly power reinforced by the "Merovingian legend"—
Hereditary principle paramount—Pretenders: (1) Munderic, (2) Chramnus,
(3) Merovech, (4) Gundobald—Taxation, especially the land tax—

Church lands sometimes exempted—Mode of collection—Were the Franks exempt ?—The evils of the despotism—Summary justice—Instances of Merovingian cruelty: Gailenus, Clovis, Mummolus, Leudastes, the physicians of Austrechildis—The king in council—Delegation of royal authority : the court a shadow of the Imperial courts—The career of a courtier—The great offices : Tribune, Referendary, Domesticus, Major Domus, Count—The Count's court, Mallus, and the Rachimburgs—Informal courts—Conflicting authority of Count and Bishop, *e.g.* Nonnichius, Nantinus, Leudastes—The Duke—The advantages and defects of the new system

Pages 106-154

CHAPTER V

THE SONS OF CLOVIS

The kingdom of Clovis divided between his sons Theuderic, Chlodomer, Childebert, and Chlothar—The tradition of conquest continued—Theuderic in Thuringia—523, invasion of Burgundy driven back—Revolt in Auvergne — 532, Childebert and Chlothar conquer Burgundy—Theuderic sacks Auvergne—Theudebert sent to invade Septimania—He succeeds his father Theuderic—The Franks intervene in Italy—Theudebald succeeds Theudebert in 547—On his death in 554 Chlothar annexes his realm, but soon has to defend it against the Saxons—Chramnus, son of Chlothar, intrigues with Childebert against his father—Death of Childebert, 558—Chramnus put to death in Brittany—Chlothar at his death sole king of the Frank conquests—His realm divided between his sons Charibert, Guntram, Sigibert, and Chilperic—After the death of Charibert, Sigibert holds Austrasia, Guntram Burgundy, and Chilperic Neustria—Sigibert marries Brunihildis, and Chilperic Fredegundis, after a short union with Galswintha, Brunihildis' elder sister—Galswintha's murder causes a blood-feud between Austrasia and Neustria—Characters of Sigibert, Chilperic, and Guntram—The rivalry of Fredegundis and Brunihildis—The struggle for the cities of Aquitaine—Triumph of Sigibert and his assassination—Merovech, son of Chilperic, marries the widowed Brunihildis—His treason and death—Struggle of Brunihildis against the Austrasian nobles—She is supported by Guntram—Guntram and Chilperic now the chief rivals, with the young Childebert a pawn in the game—Rigunthis — Chilperic assassinated—Union of Neustria and Burgundy—The conspiracy of Gundobald, a pretended son of Chlothar—He is backed by the Austrasian nobles and, perhaps, by Brunihildis—Guided by Guntram Boso, who soon deserts him—Supported by Desiderius (Chilperic's right-hand man) and Mummolus (Guntram's general)—Gundobald crowned at Briva—Guntram makes terms with Childebert, and unites Austrasia to Burgundy—Gundobald retires to Convenae—Its capture, 585, and death of Gundobald—Significance of his rebellion—Further attempts of the nobles—The pact of Andelot—Guntram Boso put to death—Futile expeditions against the Visigoths and Lombards—Tumultuous character of the Frank armies—Ravages of famine and disease—Deaths of Guntram, 596 ; Childebert, 596, and Fredegundis, 597—Final struggle of Brunihildis for Frank royalty, in the person of the boy Sigibert—Her capture and death—Chlothar II. left sole monarch of the Frank realms—Waning power of the Crown

Pages 155-212

BOOK II

THE SOCIAL ASPECT

CHAPTER I

THE ARISTOCRACY

Fate of the old Frank nobility—Sigibert, Chararic, Ragnachar—Clovis intended the new monarchy to be the sole political power—Antrustions the
only privileged class under the new monarchy—Gradual formation of a
new aristocracy of wealth and office—Gallo-Romans of senatorial rank in
episcopal and secular office—Parthenius, Celsus, Mummolus — Elevation
of low-born men—Andarchius, Leudastes—The landed nobility—Some
owing their position to donations of the king—Property forfeited by rebellious nobles—Heredity not secure except over transmitted property—A
new nobility in process of formation—Nobiles—Seniores—Leudes—The
new nobility feel their power—Intrigues of Austrasian nobles against
Brunihildis—Brunihildis's last effort against Austrasia and Theudebert—
610, defeat and murder of Theudebert—Brunihildis champions the young
Sigibert—Her failure and death—Her character typical of her age
                                                         Pages 213-234

CHAPTER II

THE LIFE OF THE COMMON PEOPLE IN THE MEROVINGIAN AGE

Rare glimpses of the life of the common people — Venantius Fortunatus—
"A typical country gentleman "—The roads—Journeys by water—The
dangers of travel—Freedom of communication restricted by wars—Trade
—Taxation of merchandise—The traders, Syrians and Jews—Anti-Jewish
legislation—Attempts for their conversion by Avitus and by Chilperic—
Scenes of everyday country life—Sabbath-breaking—Bee-keeping—Sport
—Disturbances of wars—Plague and famine—Poverty and profiteering
—Charitable relief—Hospitals—Arnulfus—Causes and types of disease—
The miracles of S. Martin's—Bubonic plague—Miraculous signs of its
approach—Doctors—Temporal *versus* spiritual aid—Surviving traces of
paganism—Life in the towns—Revival of the Curial system—Fortified
towns—Their independent wars—Street scenes—Shops—Dangers of town
life—Fires .   .   .   . Pages 235-267

CHAPTER III

MORALS

Difficulties of a general estimate—Gregory of Tours compared with Herodotus
—His estimate of the morality of his age—The ascetic view illustrated
by S. Patroclus and Bishop Nicetius—Contrast between the denunciations
of moralists and glimpses of general society—" The salt of Gallo-Roman
society "—The making of a solitary—Relative responsibility of Frank or
Gallo-Roman for the moral declension of the time—The mingling of the
races makes due apportionment impossible—The Aquitanian region—

Gregory treats Gaul as a whole and does not distinguish the two races—Difference of language vanishing—The conflict is rather of ideals than of races—The bad example of the house of Merovechus—Frequent contrast between the pictures of Fortunatus and Gregory—The dark picture of the Frank kings possibly exaggerated—But the treachery and cruelty of their family feuds unexampled—The wives of the Frank princes—Drunkenness—Loose morality in high places not reprobated by the Church—Morality of the clergy—And of the laity—Eulalius—Perjury common even in face of Divine penalties—Numerous instances—Guntram Boso—Rauchingus—Avarice—The journey of Rigunthis to Spain—Corruption and place-hunting—Plundering—Other tales of desecration and lawlessness—The feud of Sicharius and Chramnisind . . . . . Pages 268-307

CHAPTER IV

GREGORY OF TOURS AND HIS CIRCLE IN AUVERGNE

Sidonius and Gregory of Tours compared—Links between their lives—The family of Gregory—An episcopal house—Date of his birth—His grandfather Gregory, Bishop of Langres—The escape of his cousin Attalus—His uncle Gallus—Nicetius—Avitus of Clermont the friend of Gregory—Internal history of Auvergne in the decade before the birth of Gregory—His parents—St. Julian's of Brioude—An age which saw life darkly through the glass of superstition—Gregory's education—He experiences in 563 the healing power of S. Martin—The plague in Auvergne—Consecration as Bishop of Tours in 573—An enemy, the count Leudastes—His plot with Riculfus against Gregory—Synod of Braine, A.D. 580—Triumph of Gregory—Felix, Bishop of Nantes, another opponent—Guntram Boso and Merovech at Tours—Dangerous guests—A militant champion of orthodoxy against Arianism—Royal courts and royal visitors—A troubled year, 589—Ingeltrude—Election to the Papacy of Gregory the Great—Trial of Egidius of Rheims—Religious impostors—Gregory's pious devotion to S. Martin—His buildings and restorations—His " rustic style "—Variety of his life and value of his testimony—An atmosphere of miracle   Pages 308-351

BOOK III

THE ECCLESIASTICAL ASPECT

CHAPTER I

MONACHISM

An ascetic movement in paganism long before Christianity—Anchoretic and cœnobitic monachism — Anchorites not uncommon in the West in the sixth century—But community life and useful service more in accord with the Western temper—The foundation of religious houses—Motives various for retreat from the world—For security, for celestial reward, for purity—Monastic houses grow round the retreats of anchorets. Founders: S. Martius of Auvergne, Patroclus of Colombiers, Bracchio of Manat—

Endowment of monasteries—S. Carileffus—Monastic rules various—Weakness of discipline results in monasteries gradually coming under episcopal control—But general standard high for the age—Services of monasticism to the transition from the ancient to the modern world—Cassiodorus—The monks distinct from the secular clergy—For a long time laymen—Gregory the Great permits their ordination — S. Radegund's foundation, the convent of the Holy Cross at Poitiers—Venantius Fortunatus and his friends—His intimacy with Radegund—Meroveus, Bishop of Poitiers, looks with disfavour on the convent—His disapproval justified—Death of Radegund, 587—Scandals in the convent, 589—Chrotieldis leads a secession of forty nuns and appeals to the king against the conduct of the abbess—Efforts at settlement, finally successful—The fate of Chrotieldis—The state of affairs at the Holy Cross convent quite abnormal—Relation of the monasteries to the episcopal and royal power .   .   . Pages 353-394

CHAPTER II

SAINTS AND MIRACLES

Gregory's attitude to the miraculous is that of his age—He is the precursor of a great effort of systematic hagiography, the only literature of the time—The chasm which separates us from the early middle ages can scarcely be bridged by the historical imagination—The new theology of Gregory the Great—Tradition—The conversion of Europe for a long time superficial—The old anthropomorphism adapted to the new theology—An hierarchy intervening between God and man—Résumé of the theological system which was the basis of the mediæval Church—Parallelism of the earthly and heavenly hierarchies—The lost angels—The Devil—The unknown always attributed to supernatural causes—Epilepsy—The case of Landulfus—A brighter side to the picture—The saints—Pious imagination finds a refuge from the age in the enchanted world of their personal sanctity—Their lives the real literature of the day—Their charm—Romances of the forest—Artistry of the legends—A scientific explanation impossible—Miracle always expected and therefore constantly occurred—The attitude of the age to the miraculous—Natural growth of supernatural lore—The monastic biographers—Their credibility varies—Growth of hagiography from the sixth to the ninth centuries—Example in the life of S. Rémi—Sources of corruption or misrepresentation—The cult of the saints—Its materialism—Donations—A ludicrous or profane element in hagiography frequent—Relics—Their virtues for consecration and healing—Fierce contention for their possession—Sometimes used for unworthy ends—The old pagan instinct deep-rooted —Necromancers at Tours—Omens from nature—The credulity of the age not to be blamed .   .   . Pages 395-438

CHAPTER III

CHURCH LIFE

Growing wealth of the churches and monasteries—Forcible or fraudulent seizure of Church property—Its punishment by Divine justice—Or Councils—Taxes on Church property—Beauty of churches and services—Aspect and arrangement of churches—Hospitality and meals of the clergy—The

" hours " and services—Chapels and oratories—Their dedication and building—Decoration—Plate and jewellery—How guarded—The great shrines —The courts of S. Martin's—His miracles—Dependents of the great Churches, *matricularii* and *pauperes*—Rights of asylum—Merovech and Boso — Life of the refugees and mendicants — Abuse of the Church's sanctity and protection—Saintly ideals lowered by materialist superstition—Comparison of general moral tone of the French and Italian clergy—An indication in the Acts of Councils—Sexual laxity—Must not be presumed general—Scandals revealed by Gregory of Tours—Drunkenness —Plots and cabals—Clerical ambition — Incontinence—Minor offences— In spite of the decline of the Arian powers the fear of Arianism remains— Ingundis—Gregory's bitterness against Arianism—His debate with Agila and Oppila—Miracle confirms Catholicism—The Jews, penal legislation against—Yet treated generally with tolerance—Attempts for their conversion—Rationalist criticism—The interest of the West more practical than theological—Defects of the education of the upper classes—Literary output poor—Efforts after style . . . . . Pages 439-475

CHAPTER IV

THE BISHOPS

Peculiar powers and position of the Episcopate—The need of the age for statesmanship—Fitness of the bishops in general for their functions—Limitations on their power imposed by the Frank kings as regards elections and the summoning of Councils—Free from control in the spiritual sphere—Papal power scarcely recognised in Gaul in the sixth century—The Gallic Church under no patriarch or primate—Even the authority of the metropolitans circumscribed—Power of each bishop in his diocese almost uncontrolled— His power over his priests and other *clerici*—Results in an added temporal power—Laborious nature of their duties—Assisted by Chorepiscopi and, later, archpresbyters—The archdeacon—Episcopal elections — Power of the people in them—Their right of election sometimes delegated to bishops —The interference of the Frank monarchs—Council of 549 recognising the king as partner in the election—The case of Quintianus—Simony—Cato of Auvergne—Emerius of Saintes—The ordinary procedure preserved by Marculf—Appointment of courtiers and officials—The attractions of the office—Gregory of Langres—Bad bishops : Innocentius of Rodez, Bodegesilus of Le Mans, Eunius of Vannes—Trial of Praetextatus—Bertram of Bordeaux—Salonius and Sagittarius—The supreme importance of the Episcopate in the Merovingian age . . . . Pages 476-503

LIST OF PRINCIPAL ABBREVIATIONS USED IN NOTES AND REFERENCES . . . . . Pages 505, 506

NOTES AND REFERENCES . . . . . „ 507-542

INDEX . . . . „ 543-566

BOOK I

THE HISTORICAL ASPECT

CHAPTER I

THE FRANKS AND THE ROMANS : EVENTS IN GAUL FROM THE
FALL OF THE WESTERN EMPIRE TO THE ACCESSION OF CLOVIS

THE main purpose of this book is to collect what can be known
of the state of society in Gaul from the accession of Clovis
till the end of the sixth century. To the present writer the
material and moral condition of the Roman population after
the last shadowy forms of Roman administration had vanished
before the advance of the invaders has long seemed a subject of
absorbing interest. It is true that the great event which we
call the Fall of the Western Empire, though it is superficially
marked by the disappearance of the last holder of the Imperial
title, was not a sudden, cataclysmal change, effecting a radical
revolution in the material condition and moral tone of the old
population. It is now well known that the fall of the Imperial
system had been long prepared by the slow but deadly action
of fiscal and economic causes long before the disappearance of
Romulus Augustulus. Old augural science might find in the
twelve vultures which crossed the gaze of Romulus the forecast
of the fated term of Roman sway. But a detached philosophic
observer might long before the end have foreseen that the
Imperial system was drawing to its close from other causes than
an augural fate or the violent inroads of the peoples of the North.
Mysterious weakness at the centre of administration, increasing
taxes drawn from failing resources, unequal burdens, and hard-
hearted oppression of a single class, more and more unable to
bear them, till men were ready to abandon citizenship, home,
and freedom itself ; at Rome a nerveless, unarmed crowd who
resigned the defence of their frontiers to barbarian mercenaries ;

Rome itself for years at the mercy of German soldiers of fortune, who made and unmade Emperors at their will—these things of themselves would account for the fall of Rome. The pressure of the German tribes was indeed tremendous in the last years of the Empire. But it was a pressure which had been felt, with few intervals, from the days of Caesar, who clearly foresaw the danger of it. The invasions of the fifth century were not more serious in the weight of their onset than those of the third and fourth, which were repelled by Probus or by Julian. Why the earlier invasions failed and the later had permanent results which moulded all Western history is the great problem for the student of Roman society which the present writer has dealt with in a former work.

The period during which Imperial administration was melting away, and the new barbarian powers were beginning to organise themselves, is one of great interest, but, in the case of Gaul, it is illuminated only by scanty and feeble authorities. There is no contemporary history of the time properly so called. The Chronicles are vague, scrappy, and unsatisfying. Hagiography, when sifted, may furnish some materials of interest, but hagiography is often vitiated by an evident *parti pris*, and contemporary lives of great Churchmen were often recast and redacted, with liberal additions, by later hands in the eighth or ninth centuries. The letters of Sidonius Apollinaris, with all their euphuism and depraved rhetoric, are an invaluable revelation of society in a Gallo-Roman district before its final abandonment by the Empire; but Sidonius had no worthy successor. We wish to know so much, and we can know so little, of one of the most momentous periods in European history. Great events in Italy and great movements in Gaul are going on simultaneously, and are certainly related and interacting. But our fragmentary information leaves endless room for conjecture as to their connexion, and offers little certainty of conclusion. While Frank and Visigoth are pressing on to the Loire and preparing the final struggle at Vouglé, the central Imperial authority is paralysed by the Vandal sea power and the jealous tyranny of Ricimer, the ceaseless influx of German war bands into Northern Italy, and the blackening thunder-cloud of the Ostrogothic advance. In Gaul the old fabric of Roman administration has gone to pieces, and only a shadow of it remains in the little kingdom of the Syagrii at Soissons. The impotence of Rome to save the great province of the West is only made more glaring by the fruitless missions of Licinianus and S. Epiphanius. The Gallo - Romans were divided, a gallant remnant fighting hopeless battles in Auvergne or on the Loire against Euric, and a mass of Romans who have lost faith in Rome and are ready to accept and to serve Burgundian or Visigothic power. Even the Church, which has smarted under the intolerance of an Arian prince, lends itself to an arrangement which will make him master of one of the last patches of Roman territory in Provence. The absence of military virtue in the Gallo-Roman population has indeed purchased at a great price for many of them com- parative tranquillity and security on their ancestral estates. The family of Sidonius probably enjoyed for generations a peace- ful life in the glades and gardens of Avitacum. An ancestor of Gregory of Tours, who was an infant in the year of Attila's invasion, served the Burgundian kings as Count of Autun for forty years, and died in 540, as Bishop of Langres when the Franks were masters of Gaul to the mouth of the Rhone. And the genealogy of many a count or saint reveals the existence of large numbers of Gallo-Roman aristocrats, especially in Bur- gundy and Aquitaine, who were in undisturbed possession of their hereditary estates.

When Clovis, then a boy of sixteen, succeeded to the chieftain- ship of the Merovingian Franks in 481, his tribe had been firmly settled in Brabant for nearly a century and a half. But before their settlement the Franks had a long and tumultuous history. Around the origin of a race endowed with such brilliant energy, so passionately eager for distinction, and, in its great leaders, conscious that it was predestined to a great future, in what was eminently a mythopœic age, legend was sure to gather. The chroniclers of the eighth century are content with nothing short of a Trojan origin for the Franks to match that of the Roman race. The first Franks, as the story ran, had fought at Troy, and, with Priam as their chief, had migrated to some region to the north of the Euxine. They had been the champions of Rome against the Alan hordes in the marshes of the Palus Maeotis. One section established themselves on the Danube. Another, after long wanderings, at length emerged in a district on the Rhine, where they built a city bearing the name of Troy.

In the third century, Roman geographers give the name Francia to the country on the right bank of the Rhine stretching from Nimegen to Coblentz. From the days of Tacitus it was occupied by the Sicambri, Chamavi, Bructeri, Chatti, and Chauci. The Sicambri, both in prose and poetry, are identified with the Franks ; and the tribe of the Salian Franks first come into the light of history in the country to the east of the Yssel, which was also the seat of the Sicambri. But the Frank name covered other tribes than the Salii. The origin of the Frank name has been a subject of controversy. But it is now generally agreed that it is a common designation of a fluctuating confederacy of tribes on the Weser and Lower Rhine in Westphalia, Hesse, and Brunswick, among which the Salii or Sicambri became the most famous. This formidable league, under the Frank name, first appears in Imperial history in the reign of Gallienus (253), when the first of the great invasions swept over Gaul and across the Pyrenees, and left its mark in the ruins of Tarraco and Lerida. The Roman generals of that gloomy time, Postumus and Probus, performed prodigies of valour and strategy in the effort to roll back the German hordes. Probus twice inflicted on them a crushing defeat, and relegated a band of Frank warriors to the shores of the Euxine, where, according to legend, their ancestors had originally found a home after the fall of Troy. Is there not possibly a connexion between their deportation by Probus and the Trojan romance of the Merovingian chronicler ? The exiles returned by sea to their old home on the Weser and the Rhine, after plundering on their voyage rich cities in Asia Minor, Greece, and Sicily.

For two generations after Probus, with hardly an inter- mission, the Franks were harrying the districts on the Meuse and the Lower Rhine. Again and again they occupied Batavia. Sometimes they are crushed and driven back. Sometimes they treat with the Romans, receive settlements in Gaul, and even accept new chiefs appointed by the Emperor. The chronicle of those years merely repeats with wearisome monotony what we read of the condition of that region in Caesar and Tacitus. The island of Batavia, surrounded by the Rhine, the Meuse (Vahal), and the sea, before Caesar's time had been occupied by a band of Chatti. In Caesar's time the lands of the Menapii, where the Franks finally settled (in the fourth century), were overrun by two tribes, Usipetes and Tencteri, flying before the advance of the Suevi. The Sicambri had come to terms with Augustus and again with Tiberius, and received from them leave to settle on the left bank of the Rhine. Thus from the earliest times that region must have been Germanised, and the invaders of Batavia and Toxandria were plundering or annexing the lands of their kindred in the fourth and fifth centuries. The Franks were notorious in the fourth century for ferocity and faithlessness, and neither force of arms nor diplomacy could check their encroachments. In 341 and 342 the Franks were conquered and brought to terms of peace by Constans. But the peace was short-lived. Within ten years a great host of Alemanni and Franks swarmed across the Rhine, sacked and burnt many flourishing cities, including Cologne and Trèves, and probably established themselves in fertile lands on the Meuse. The extraordinary military genius of Julian, with a comparatively small force, threw back the invasion and recovered the Gallic bank of the Rhine from Strasburg to Cologne. In 358, in a third campaign, he advanced to attack the Franks and Chamavi between the Scheldt and the Rhine. There, in the district called Toxandria, he found the Salian tribe established at Tongres where, according to Ammianus Marcellinus, they had in former times established themselves on Roman territory. Tongres then is the first settled home of the Franks in Gaul ; and in that region we may lay the scene of that social life which we shall find described in the Salic Code.

In these years of Frank invasion, we learn, both from Ammianus and the Fasti, that great numbers of the Franks were in high office in the Palatine service. Frank soldiers of fortune rose to be Masters of the Cavalry, Counts of the Largesses, even to the Consulship, as colleagues of an Emperor. Richomer, the friend of Symmachus, and in high command under Gratian and Theodosius, Arbogastes, Master of the Forces, who led again and again Roman armies against his own race, and who actually raised Eugenius to the purple, Merobaudes, colleague of the Emperor in the Consulship, Bauto who was colleague of Arcadius and father of the Empress Eudoxia—such names as these reveal an ambition and capacity which in the last quarter of the fourth century could make the Frank a power at the centre of the Empire as well as on the Rhine and the Meuse. Arbogastes had in two or three campaigns driven back the

Franks and made peace with them. Frank warriors fought under
him for Eugenius in the battle on the Frigidus, where the short-
lived Emperor and his Frank lieutenant both came to a tragic
end. And it is curious that the last stand of paganism in the
battlefield should have been made by the leader of a race which,
within a hundred years, was destined to be the one Catholic
barbarian power in Europe, and to win Burgundy and Aquitaine
from Arian masters.

In the last years of the century, the stately verse of Claudian
celebrates the peace which Stilicho granted to the prostrate
Sicambri and Franks and many another tribe, a peace by
which the Franks were engaged to guard the Rhine. In the
storm which burst on the Rhineland in the last days of 406 they
were staunch to the Empire, and drove back the Alemanni, but
were themselves defeated by the Alans. The confusion and
horror of that time is mirrored in the fragments of a lost historian
preserved by Gregory of Tours. Franks are fighting for Rome
against Vandals and Alemanni and other Franks are sacking the
Roman towns. Four times between 409 and 415 the city of
Trèves was captured, burnt, and despoiled by Frank armies ;
and that in the very years when Gaiso, a Frank, held the offices
of Count of the Largesses and Master of the Forces at Rome.
The pressure became so severe that Aetius, the greatest Roman
general of the time, had to exert all his force to drive the Frank
raiders from the valley of the Moselle.

The first king of a Frank tribe in Gaul, known to tradition,
is Chlogio, the son or successor of Theodemir. Gregory tells us
that the first *king* was unknown and that the great authority for
that time, Sulpicius Alexander, only speaks of *duces*, like those
three chiefs Genobaudes, Sunno, and Marcomer who headed the
great invasion of 388, devastated the fertile lands, and threatened
Cologne. Of the legendary Pharamond there is no trace except
in Prosper's chronicle. The Franks of Chlogio had been settled
in Toxandria for generations and certainly at Tongres since 358.
Chlogio is said to have had his seat at Dispargum, which probably
lay between the modern Brussels and Louvain. He soon began
to press forward to the south-west, occupied Cambrai after de-
feating the Romans, and established himself on the Somme.
About the year 447, at some distance to the north of that river,
while the Franks were feasting at the wedding of one of their

chiefs, they were surprised by a Roman force under Aetius and Majorian. This attack on Cloghio is only known to us from the inflated poetry of Sidonius. What the effect of it was on the rising Frank power is left uncertain. It is probable that Chlogio had for the time to abandon his new conquests between the Scheldt and the Somme, but there is nothing in the poem of Sidonius to indicate that the Salii were driven from their homes at Tongres which they had occupied with the consent of Rome since the campaigns of Julian in 358. On the contrary, it would seem that they were left undisturbed in 447, as the price of a friendship which in the following years was more than once displayed. Chlogio died in 448, after a reign of twenty years. He was succeeded by Merovechus, whose birth is surrounded in the chronicle with the proper air of miracle and mystery. The mystery is deepened by a tale in the Byzantine historian Priscus, and the ingenious hypotheses founded on it. It matters little to us whether Merovechus was the son of a sea god or the second son of an unnamed Frank chief, with the flowing yellow hair of his race, whom Priscus had seen at Rome suing for the support of Aetius against his elder brother.

The reign of Merovechus is only a faint, shifting patch of cloud-land. But in that reign one of the greatest events in history occurred, the invasion of Gaul in 451 by Attila. In the great battle of Châlons, among the countless tribes of Central Europe, there were Franks from beyond the Rhine. But the genius and dæmonic energy of Aetius, aided by Avitus and Tonantius Ferreolus of Auvergne, had mustered in an incredibly short time another army of German tribes, many of whom had served under the standards of Rome. And among them, almost certainly, were the Salii of Merovechus from Tongres. That they fought in a manner worthy of their race is not hard to see even in the bald narrative of Jordanes. In a dim combat on the night before the great battle 15,000 Frank warriors fell fighting against the Gepidae, who were in the van of the Hun army. Whether Merovechus was at their head, the chronicles do not tell us. But, remembering the numbers of brilliant Franks who in those times held the highest places in the Roman service, and that Merovechus himself had probably been at Rome and been fascinated by Aetius, the greatest captain of Rome, we can well believe that the Salian chief was at the head of his tribe. In the

three years following the Hun invasion Aetius was murdered by
Valentinian III., and the Imperial assassin and debauchee himself fell by the hand of Maximus. Every sign of weakness at
the centre encouraged the hordes of barbarism to make a fresh
effort to gain " a place in the sun ". On the Scheldt, the Meuse,
and the Lower Rhine, the withdrawal of the Roman troops in
406 had left that region without a garrison. Following on half
a century of German incursions across the Rhine, the Hun
invasion of 451 must have left faint traces of Roman power in
the Rhineland. The Ripuarian Franks held both banks of the
river from the Lippe to the Lahn. The Burgundians in a quiet
advance, or "penetration", had become masters of the region
along the Saône and Rhone. The Visigoths were steadily annexing all Western Gaul up to the Loire. The Salian Franks, although
probably weakened by their losses at the battle of Châlons,
renewed the advance of Chlogio's reign, and had probably
reached Tournai when Childeric became chief of the tribe.
Immediately to the south of the new Salian conquests there lay
a little patch of territory along the Aisne and Seine, with its
capital at Soissons, where, for a quarter of a century, Aegidius,
a Gallo-Roman who became a shadowy Master of the Forces
under Majorian, and his son Syagrius, maintained the lingering
tradition of Roman power in Gaul.

Childeric became head of the Franks in 458. His career is
one which romantic tradition has done its worst or its best to
translate into myth—the tribute of a loyal and credulous age to
the father of the great conqueror of Gaul. And the tradition is
various and variously expanding. Yet that there is a kernel of
historic fact under all tales of romantic fancy can hardly be
doubted. The tale in Gregory of Tours is more sober and less
embroidered with charm of legend than the story in Fredegarius.
The young Frank chief, with the daring and sensuality of nearly
all his race, had, by his amorous excesses, at the very outset of
his reign, aroused the angry disgust of a people who, even in
their rudest times, jealously guarded the honour of their women.
Childeric narrowly escaped death and fled for refuge to the court
of Bisinus, the King of Thuringia, leaving a faithful friend behind
to mollify the anger of the Franks, and, by a concerted signal, to
inform Childeric when he might safely return. On the deposition of Childeric, the Franks, according to Gregory and Frede-

garius, had unanimously elected Aegidius to be their chief. But another chronicle describes his elevation as a hurtful and ill-advised measure. It may have been the result of a Gallo-Roman intrigue, working on a section of the tribe who, in the previous reign, had come under Roman influences. For eight years Aegidius reigned over the Salian Franks, when "the friend" had so far succeeded in bringing them back to their old allegiance that they even demanded the return of their native chief to his hereditary place. There is nothing at all incredible in Gregory's narrative. He apparently knows nothing of, or has carefully avoided, the poetic and romantic details accumulated in Frede-garius. He does not give the name of Childeric's "faithful friend", nor does he describe the subtle arts by which he is said to have made the rule of Aegidius appear crushing and detestable. All this is developed with suspicious rhetoric by the later chronicler, who actually carries the Frank chief to Constantinople in the reign of the Emperor Maurice, at the end of the following century. It is evident that in later years the reign of Childeric became more and more surrounded with an aureole of myth. Indeed, some have gone so far as to deny historical value to any Frank tradition before Clovis. In particular, the compulsory abdication of Childeric, and the recognition by a German tribe of a Roman chief in Aegidius, has been pronounced incredible. The simple narrative of Gregory makes this scepticism rather difficult. Nor is there anything really at that time to discredit such a tale. In that age of confusion Franks had often fought under Roman leaders, as Romans had often served under Franks. At this very time a Sueve was Master of the Roman Armies at Rome. A Burgundian prince, Gundobad, succeeded him, and carried his Imperial title back to his kingdom on the Rhone. The combined efforts of Roman, Frank, and Visigoth to save the civilisation of Gaul from the Hunnish hordes in 451 showed that Roman and German could act together for a common purpose, with little regard to distinctions of race. And it is quite possible that the Frank tribe, newly settled at Tournai, and with vague and far-reaching ambitions, may have been ready, when from internal weakness they felt the need of a strong ruler, to adopt as their chief the man who was the great bulwark against the aggressive Visigoths. Whether the position of Aegidius was undermined by the arts of Childeric's friends

working on the sentimental attachment of Franks to the chief
of their tribe, or by fiscal oppression of the Imperial type,
exercised by Aegidius, must be left to each inquirer to decide, if
he can, for himself. It has also been suggested that as, about
the date of Childeric's return, a great invasion burst on the
Rhineland, he may have been borne back on its tide and at its
head to his old place.

Majorian on his death left two lieutenants who, for a few
troubled years, asserted the power of old Roman character in
the weltering chaos around them. Marcellinus defeated the
Vandals, set up an independent state in Dalmatia, and swept
their galleys from the Adriatic. Aegidius, his friend and colleague,
and bound to him by a common hatred of Ricimer, the barbarian king-maker, became Master of the Forces, and took up
the task of Aetius in Gaul. He was probably grandson of that
Afranius Syagrius who was Consul in 382, and from whom also
was descended Tonantius Ferreolus, a friend of Sidonius and
Prefect of the Gauls in 453. The Syagrii were a great Gallo-
Roman family, possessing estates probably in the neighbourhood
of Soissons, and also in Burgundy. They were one of those
great houses in which, during the Imperial period, high office
was practically hereditary, at a time when high office meant
almost regal power. Some of its cadet members, as the force of
the Empire waned and receded, seem to have buried themselves
in their rural domains ; others appear to have lived in close
intercourse with the Teutonic invaders, mastered their language,
and adapted themselves to their ways of life. A rare glimpse
such as that which we catch of the Syagrii helps us to understand that the " Invasions " were often really far less subversive
of the old social order than we might at first suppose, and how
a century after they have run their course, old Gallo-Roman
families are still in secure possession of the estates of their
ancestors, and, instead of giving prefects to the service of the
State, are furnishing great prelates to the service of the Church.
But the ascendancy of the Syagrii was quite exceptional. For
more than a generation, and even some years after the fall of
the Empire of the West, they held the valley of the Seine and
the plain of Central Gaul up to the walls of Troyes and Orleans
in the name of Rome, but really as independent kings. The
little kingdom of Aegidius was like an island amid the German

conquests, which, by the year 480, had partitioned the greater part of Gaul. The Visigoths, seated at Toulouse, were practically masters of all the territory from the Loire to the Pillars of Hercules. The Burgundians, in a steady, quiet advance, had established themselves on the banks of the Rhone and Saône up to the foot of the Alps. The Salian Franks, as we have seen, had pushed their conquests to the valley of the Somme. It illustrates the immense strength and prestige of old Roman character and civilisation that the little kingdom of Soissons should have made itself a power to be reckoned with, and should, by skilful diplomacy or military force, have maintained its independence so long.

A *grand seigneur* and country gentleman, Aegidius was for half-a-dozen years the solitary champion of Rome between three powerful German tribes, and practically cut off from Rome. He bore, it is true, the title of *magister militum*, and had been the trusted lieutenant of Majorian. When Majorian, after the loss of his fleet at Cartagena, returned to meet his doom at Tortona, Aegidius was left in command of the Roman troops in Gaul. The death of his master and the arrogant tyranny of Ricimer called him to the duty of revenge. But, before he crossed the Alps to accomplish it, Gaul had to be left tranquil in his rear. He had to quell, or make terms with, Visigoths and Burgundians, with Bretons on the Loire and Franks on the Somme ; or, rather, as it turned out, he had to band together Franks, Bretons, and Burgundians to check the ambition of the Visigoths freshly aroused since the death of Majorian. The Bretons had fought for Rome against Attila, and had supported her sometimes in conflicts with the Visigothic forces south of the Loire. The Burgundians, who had joined the Visigoths in their campaign against the Sueves in Spain, seem by this time to have abandoned the alliance, and to be ready to support the Imperial officers. But it was even more important to secure the tranquillity or the active support of the Franks, his warlike neighbours to the north, who had just come under the sway of the young chief Childeric. But Childeric's vices, as we have seen, led to his expulsion and exile, and the mysterious election of Aegidius as King of the Franks.

All the plans and ambitions of Aegidius, as we have seen pointed to an expedition across the Alps to overthrow the despotic power of Ricimer. It might have been thought that a more subtle policy would have led Theodoric, the Visigothic king, to allow the Gallo-Roman to carry out his original design, leaving the field clear for a fresh Visigothic advance in Gaul. But, for some reason which the meagre chronicles of the time leave unexplained, Theodoric suddenly renounced the peace which he had been forced to make with Majorian, and prepared to seize the great Roman cities at the mouth of the Rhone which were the oldest seats of Roman power in the Province, and formed the last link between it and the Empire. The attack developed rapidly, and fell first on Narbonne. Probably Theodoric had been encouraged in his designs by treacherous overtures from leading Gallo-Romans. It is clear that in these years some men of this class, seeing the steady advance of the German power, and disgusted with the weakness of the Imperial administration, which was ready to abandon its provincial subjects, preferred to come to terms at once with the conquerors. Among these was one, Count Agrippinus, who held high office at Narbonne, and now threw open the gates of the town to the forces of Theodoric. He pressed on to lay siege to Arles, which was held by the forces of Aegidius. Apparently the town was in danger of capture when Aegidius sallied forth with such energy and, according to legend, with the aid of S. Martin, that he utterly routed the besiegers. Of the many glorious exploits performed by him against the Visigoths, which are vaguely celebrated by Priscus, only one other has been faintly preserved by tradition. Theodoric despatched his brother Frederic against the Bretons, who apparently could muster considerable forces on the Loire. The Gallo-Roman general went to succour his allies, and inflicted a decisive defeat on the Visigoths, who fell in great numbers, along with their general.

This prosperous and hopeful campaign of Aegidius comes to a mysterious end in the year 463. In that year there occurred a great invasion of Franks and other tribes, from beyond the Rhine, in which Cologne and Trèves were overwhelmed and desolated. Great numbers of Romans were slaughtered, and, according to one tradition, Aegidius, who had hastened up with his army, only escaped by flight. It is more than probable that Childeric, after four or five years of exile, may have organised and inspired this invasion of the Rhineland, and may, by means of it, have been restored to the headship of his tribe. The chronicles are vague and embody different traditions. But the

most probable is that preserved by Fredegarius, " that Childeric
was restored with the unanimous consent of the Franks, that he
had many combats with Aegidius, and finally cut him to pieces ".
But the end of the great Gallo-Roman chief is wrapped in mystery.
He died in 464.   And it is much more probable that he died in
battle against Childeric than that the two reigned for some time
in placid unanimity, as Gregory would have us believe.   Childeric
survived Aegidius seventeen years.   And even, from the dim
light of the chronicles, we can faintly see that his reign was one
of struggle, not of victorious advance.   That was reserved for
his great son.

Any one who has tried it knows how hopeless is the attempt
to reconstruct a definite narrative of those years from the
cramped and confused chronicles of the time.   What we should
wish to know particularly is the part which Childeric and his
Franks played in what is evidently a severe struggle on the
Loire from Orleans to Angers.   The scanty and enigmatical
record of it is to be found in a chapter of Gregory of Tours in
which, deserting Frank legend, he seems to be heaping together
scraps from Roman chronicles or traditions.   From that mysterious passage, according to the acutest interpretation, we may, if
we must, extract the following result :

Childeric fights a battle at Orleans, which is probably that in
463, already referred to, in which Frederic, the brother of the
Visigothic King, was attacking the Breton allies of Rome and was
utterly defeated.   In this battle the Franks were almost certainly
supporting the Romans against the Goths, who, in their advance,
were threatening Roman and Frank alike.   The Saxon, Odovacer,
seems to be a free lance, looking chiefly for plunder, and possibly
instigated by Ricimer to embarrass the Romans of Soissons in
their conflict with the Visigoths.   The expulsion of the Bretons
from Bourges refers probably to the expedition of the Breton
chief, inspired by Anthemius against the Visigoths.   After the
Visigothic victory over the Bretons, they have to meet the
onslaught of a Roman army under Count Paul, who has Franks
fighting on his side against the forces of Theodoric, aided by a
contingent of Saxons under Odovacer.   In these engagements
Count Paul is slain, Childeric comes upon the scene to support
the Roman cause, and secures the town of Angers.

In this conflict we can only dimly discern that Romans and

Franks are leagued in an effort to stay the northward advance
of the Visigoths.   The champion of Rome was almost certainly
Syagrius, the son of Aegidius, and the leader of the Franks is
Childeric, now established at Tournai.   Franks and Romans now
saw that they had a common enemy in the Visigothic King who
was rapidly and decisively wiping out the last traces of Imperial
power in Southern Gaul.   As Frank and Roman, twenty years
before, had fought side by side against the Hun, so might they
now combine to repel a foe in whom the old Teutonic force had
been organised and disciplined by contact with Roman civilisation for more than half a century.

It was a gallant struggle, but the Imperial power in Gaul
was doomed and already expiring.   No effective help could
come from the Imperial centre to the failing remnant who still
clung to the Roman name on the Seine or in Auvergne.   Great
forces of economic and financial decay were undermining the
majestic fabric of the Western Empire.   Though they were
probably little noticed even by the keenest observers of the
time, still men were losing faith in the Empire which could no
longer defend its citizens, and which continued its cruel exactions
to the very last.   Many, revolting from the mingled weakness
and greed of Imperial functionaries, were at last ready to come
to terms with the new barbarian power and even to lend Roman
skill and experience to its service.   Moreover, all the news from
Italy in those years must have been profoundly depressing to
the most ardent Roman patriots.   And we must remember
that, in spite of all the confusion of the time, which may be
easily exaggerated, news spread fast and far.   Communication
on the great roads was still, as we see now and then, rapid and
easy.   Travelling merchants, private couriers, priests and monks
on ecclesiastical missions, or great nobles and proprietors hurrying
to look after some distant estate, or that mysterious, " divine
rumour " which, in every age from Homer or Herodotus has
sped with miraculous speed—all these may well have almost
anticipated the telegraphic and simultaneous news of our time.
A well-informed Gallo - Roman at Soissons, Tours, or Toulouse
might well begin to lose that faith in Roman destiny which had
held fast for so many centuries.

There were manifestly great external forces which were
hastening to the fatal term of Imperial sway.   No reflecting

man could ignore the menace of the Vandal fleets, the jealous ambition and unscrupulous arts of Ricimer, or the restless movements of the tribes on the Danube, Rugian or Sueve, or, above all, the Ostrogoth, which threatened alike the capitals of East and West. Never was the enormous importance of " sea power " more vividly displayed than by the Vandal fleets in the last years of the Western Empire. Genseric was a commanding personality, who combined a wide outlook with an insatiable cupidity, an inscrutable diplomatic cunning with the old barbarian ruthlessness. This is the judgement of Jordanes, who, in his condensed and penetrating analysis of Genseric's character, if not in his Latin, for once faintly approaches the power of Tacitus. Every island or seaside town was for years liable to sudden raids. Sicily, Sardinia, and the Balearic Isles, Spain, Liguria, the coasts of Campania or Lucania, the shores of the Adriatic and the Cyclades, were all visited by the Vandal corsairs. The whole trade of the Mediterranean was long at their mercy. In 455 the Vandal fleet anchored in the Tiber, and the Imperial city was for fourteen days given up to plunder. The Vandals carried back to Africa untold wealth and, a prize to Genseric perhaps even more precious, the Imperial ladies, Eudoxia, the widow of Valentinian III., with her two daughters, who, as hostages, enabled the Vandal King for years to put pressure both on Rome and Byzantium. By his possession of Placidia he was able to dictate the choice of her fiancé, Olybrius, for the throne. His diplomacy had urged on Attila to his invasion of the Western provinces, and, at a later date, he applied similar pressure to the Ostrogoths in Pannonia, and to the Visigoths in Aquitaine. Roman generals and statesmen, both of the East and West, realised the enormous danger from the Vandal command of the sea, and, singly or united, they, again and yet again, mustered all their strength to crush it. Majorian had done so by superhuman effort, but, by the sinister fortune which dogged all his efforts, or by treachery, his fleet was captured at Cartagena. Some years later, in the reign of Anthemius, the Eastern Empire threw all its strength into an expedition under Basiliscus, aided by Heraclius and Marcellinus, the hero of many a fight against the Vandal, one of the last great champions of Rome ; but the guile and ruthless energy of Genseric gave him a victory which once more left him unchallenged master of the seas.

C

Along with the Vandal sea power, in hastening the fall of the Western Empire, must be reckoned the baleful ascendancy of Ricimer. The murder of Majorian, whose reign was the last hope or illusion of old Roman sentiment, was the real close of the Western Empire. Henceforth it was at the mercy of German chiefs, who for a few years made and unmade shadowy emperors, till the principate of the Caesars merged in the barbarian kings of Italy. Ricimer was the first of that series of German military chiefs which culminated in the reign of Theodoric the Ostrogoth. In birth Ricimer was not unworthy of the great place which he held for eleven years. His father was sprung from a princely house among the Sueves. His mother was a daughter of Wallia, who founded the Visigothic monarchy in Aquitaine (Toulouse (418)). By his sister's marriage with Gundiac of Burgundy he was uncle of Gundobad, who became his lieutenant and successor at Rome, and who returned from his elevation or his exile to overthrow his brother Chilperic II. Thus Ricimer was no mere barbarian adventurer, but, in native rank, the equal or superior of the greatest Roman nobles. And, like others of his class, he added to his claims of birth a record of military service which few of the unwarlike Roman senators could boast. He belonged to that school of soldiers formed by Aetius which produced Aegidius, Majorian, and Marcellinus, who from the Rhineland to Dalmatia had, with barbarian forces, revived for a brief space the military energy and prestige of Rome. Ricimer was one of the new Teutonic noblesse in the service of the Empire. They were dangerous rivals to the native Roman aristocracy who, whether in Gaul or Italy, as a rule, had little taste or skill for war, and, in a time of momentous changes, which demanded all the old Roman " virtue ", were hypnotised by the charm of a failing and perverted literary culture. These degenerate Romans, for the most part, lived in a world of illusions, trying to revive a past which was gone for ever, feeding their vanity with feeble imitations of great literary models, or with the titles of great magistracies whose effective power had long vanished. The new barbarian leaders represented a different world, often of cruel reality, which held in germ the forces of the future, although the noblest of them still felt an awe of the great shade of Rome and were proud to wear the insignia of her ancient offices.

Ricimer was one of the ablest of this class. Commanding

immense barbarian forces cantoned in the passes from Noricum, personally proud of his own native rank, and disdaining even Roman dress, this Sueve soldier of fortune rose to the Roman rank of Count, Master of the Forces, and, finally, to the Patriciate, the greatest place under the Emperor. He lived through the reigns of five emperors, two of whom he raised to the purple, four of whom he dethroned, or did to death. For six years, between the fall of Majorian and the accession of the " Greek " Emperor, Anthemius, he really wielded the forces of the Empire, under the name of his creature, Libius Severus, and, for an inter-regnum of many months after the wretched Severus had died by poison, Ricimer possessed the substance of Imperial power, without even a shadow of constitutional authority. He, more-over, broke the formal concord of East and West, and seemed determined to isolate Italy. In reading the strange tale of the last years of the Western Empire, we cannot help asking, why a man so able and ambitious, who never scrupled at any treachery to remove an obstacle to his ambition, did not openly claim that Imperial place which he disposed of at his pleasure. He was a true barbarian to his inmost core. He hated Majorian as a Roman of the old breed, thwarted him in his efforts, incited dis-affection against him, and probably contrived his death. He was the implacable foe of Aegidius and Marcellinus, the last true soldiers of Rome, and, probably, by secret intrigue added fuel to the ambition of the Visigothic King to master the great prefecture of the Gauls. Why did not a man of this character at once proclaim himself Emperor of the West ? We can only say that in the five centuries of the Empire, only once did a barbarian leader assume the Imperial place for a moment, Maximin, in 235. Some mysterious awe or scruple kept the most daring and capable of German chiefs from usurping a title which was often apparently within their grasp. It might have been better for the Roman world if Ricimer had nerved himself to seize the great prize, instead of exerting his personal power as a Mayor of the Palace. As it was, his combined cowardice and ambition, his jealousy and treachery, rendered his power a constant danger, and a source of distracting weakness both in the capital and the provinces. There were some in Gaul who still clung passion-ately, in spite of all appearances, to the faith in Roman greatness, and who were ready to defend the last corner of Imperial territory in Auvergne or on the Seine. Let us imagine the cruel doubts and fears which must have tortured a Roman senator in his villa at Narbonne as the news from the capital came day by day in vessels arriving from Ostia or Puteoli. What must he have felt about the death of Majorian surrounded by sinister rumour, the equally mysterious end of Severus, the feuds of Anthemius and Ricimer, culminating in the barbarian's siege and capture of Rome, with all the horrors of famine and slaughter, and then the failure of the great expedition against the Vandals, starting with such prosperous omens and ending in ignominious ruin. The descent of Olybrius, the short-lived successor of Anthemius, from the great Anician house, and his marriage with a daughter of Valentinian, would not disguise from our Gallic observer the ominous fact that he was really the nominee of Ricimer and Genseric. The Western world was now absolutely in the power of the Sueve, the Vandal, and the Visigoth. The Burgundians, as we have more than once noticed, were often involved in the confused fighting of those years. Their kings had occupied the lands up to the Alps with some sort of title as Roman officers. In the division of the land about 456 they had been on the whole fair and considerate to their Roman " hosts ". Their King, Gundicar, had fallen fighting for the Romans against Attila. Yet his two sons, Gundiac and Chilperic I., gave devoted service to Theodoric, the Visigoth, in his campaign against the Sueves in Spain. It is probable that the commanding personality and prestige of Aegidius detached them from the Visigoths, and won their support for the Roman cause in Gaul. This alliance was renewed and strengthened in the reign of Anthemius. By this time Burgundy was divided among four kings, Gundobad, Godegesil, Chilperic II., and Godomar, the sons of Gundiac. But the partition did not last long undisturbed. Chilperic and Godomar combined to drive out their brothers and seize their kingdoms. Chilperic II. became the sole ruler, and fortunately we have a glimpse of Burgundy as it was under him in the letters of Sidonius. The King was an Arian, but his wife, by race a Gallo-Roman, was a devoted Catholic, and a fast friend of the saintly Patiens of Lyons. In spite of the Arianism of the Burgundian kings, it is fair to say that they left their female relations perfectly free in their Catholic devotions. Clothilde, who became the Queen of Clovis, was a daughter of Chilperic II., and, as every one knows, was almost fanatically devoted to the Catholic faith. The dim sketch which Sidonius gives us of the secular side of Chilperic's court is far from pleasing. The King seems to have been jealous and restless and despotic. The Gallo-Romans in Burgundy were far more numerous and far richer and more cultivated than his compatriots ; and, in the confusion of the time, there was a corrupt and degenerate class eager for plunder and ready to flatter the King, or betray men of their own race. Perhaps Chilperic's suspicions and alarms were not without good grounds. His banished brother Gundobad had gone into exile at Rome, and, evidently daring and able, had attached himself to Ricimer, who was then at the height of his fortune. He had won Ricimer's favour and risen at a bound to the rank of "Patrician". On the death of Ricimer, Gundobad, for a short space, succeeded to his power, and had the doubtful distinction of raising the obscure Glycerius to the purple. After that brief appearance on the Imperial stage Gundobad answered the call of events in Burgundy, and returned there in 473, probably with some Italian troops. He is the " new prince " alluded to by Sidonius, who soon made his presence felt and took his revenge for his exile. Burgundy had no love for the suspicious, overbearing Chilperic. A war broke out between the brothers of which we only know the ghastly end described in brief cruel words by Gregory. " Gundobad had his brother slain by the sword : his queen drowned with a stone round her neck : he sent Chilperic's two daughters into exile, of whom the elder, Chrona, entered the 'religious life' : the younger was Clothilde."

In the year 471, which saw the sack of Rome by Ricimer and the death of Anthemius, the young Theodoric, son of Theodemir, King of the Ostrogoths, returned from the Eastern court, after ten years' detention as a hostage. The Ostrogoths in Pannonia had long been hard pressed by many powerful tribes. They had fought many bloody battles. The country had been devastated, and no longer sufficed for their support. The boy of eighteen, who was destined to govern Italy with extraordinary skill and tact for thirty-three years, gave the signal for the advance of his people into new lands. One horde under his father, Theodemir, invaded Macedonia. To his brother Videmir was assigned the invasion of Italy, at the moment when, within a few months, Anthemius, Olybrius, and Ricimer had vanished from the scene, and the Empire was in the hands of Glycerius, the creature of the Burgundian Gundobad, and very unequal to deal with such an emergency. He met the invaders with diplomacy backed by bribes. They were advised to seek a settlement beside their kinsmen in Southern Gaul, and they carried across the Alps the impotent mandates of the Emperor. Videmir joined his forces with those of Euric when the Romans of Auvergne were making a last desperate stand against the Visigoths. We can dimly discern what the bishop of Auvergne and his kinsman, the chivalrous Ecdicius, behind their crumbling battlements, must have felt at this cowardly and selfish betrayal by the Emperor of a great province, in the vain effort to save a power that was beyond salvation, and that did not deserve it.

Julius Nepos came to the throne with the support of the Eastern Empire, and aroused a flickering hope in Gaul as "supreme in arms and character". Once more the Imperial puppet revealed to the anxious patriots of the West how baseless were their hopes. Once more the craven Emperor sacrificed his faithful subjects in Gaul to a mere dream of security at home. The quaestor Licinianus was despatched to treat with Euric, and to confer the empty dignity of Patrician on the heroic defender of Auvergne. The experienced diplomat found that words availed nothing against ambition backed by force. Face to face with the menace of fresh invasions from the North, the feeble Emperor could not denude the Italian frontier to send an Imperial force to Gaul. By the advice of a council at Milan, Epiphanius, Bishop of Pavia, was sent to try the effect of ecclesiastical rhetoric on the Arian King. Ennodius does his best for the credit of the episcopal envoy, and would have us believe that his mission was a triumph. Unfortunately it ended in the cession of Auvergne to Euric, in which a commission of four Catholic bishops bore an unenviable part. To save the shadowy hold of Rome on a fragment of the great province, the Imperial agents abandoned their last devoted subjects and confessed the final impotence of the Empire. The shameful surrender of the gallant remnant who, wasted by famine and disease, still guarded the walls of Clermont is bitterly described in the words of Sidonius : "Facta est servitus nostra pretium securitatis alienae ". The " safety " so purchased was a strange illusion. The distracted Senate and the nerveless Emperor were at the mercy of Orestes, the new Master of the Forces, the former secretary of Attila, who with a motley host (from the Danube) was encamped at the gates of Rome, preparing the transient appearance of the last shadowy Emperor. With the retirement of Ecdicius from a hopeless conflict, the last illusions of the most devoted Gallo-Romans must have melted away. In the ranks of Christian enthusiasm, faith in Rome, face to face with the fresh forces of barbarism, had long been growing faint and doubtful. And now the most idealist dreamer among the dilettanti senators of Aquitaine and Auvergne must have seen that the Imperial power in Gaul was gone for ever, and that the future of Gaul was in the hands of the new Teutonic kings. In both Gaul and Italy the " inbelles Romani " had to accept the fate of an old, overripe civilisation which did not realise that in a world of urgent problems, eager ambition, and not very scrupulous force, the future does not belong to the dignified, selfish aristocrat, the literary trifler, or the ascetic recluse. The stately aristocrat had for two generations enjoyed literary antiquarianism and luxurious social life, only slightly and occasionally disturbed by incursions of the German tribes. For two, and even three, generations bishops and monks and hermits, some of them born perhaps in the reigns of Honorius or Valentinian III., had lived in their dreams of miracle and sanctity, through invasions of Hun and Vandal and Frank, and some of them were destined to see Clovis the master of Gaul. Both the worldly aristocrat and the hermit of the Vosges or Auvergne have left few traces of their feelings about the momentous events of the time. With very different interests and rules of life, they were probably all alike indifferent to the future of their country. But, while they were absorbed in dreams of literary euphuism or selfish sanctity, men of ruder and more masculine force were working, unembarrassed by tender scruples, to replace the chaos or void of Roman administration by a new order. Jordanes tells us in brief, rugged phrase that Euric, the King of the Visigoths, perceiving that the Empire was tottering, reduced Arles and Massilia under his sway, inspired by the advice of Genseric, who by urging the Ostrogoths to attack the Eastern Empire, and the Visigoths to occupy the Western provinces, hoped to secure his own hold on Africa. Euric probably little needed such incentives from the Vandal. He was strong and ambitious. He knew the hopeless state of Italy

under the heel of successive leaders of a great German army
nominally in the service of Rome. The diplomacy of Licinianus
and the clerical rhetoric of Epiphanius probably only aroused
his contempt. They certainly did not turn him from his purpose. When Roman officials were deserting their posts or playing
the traitor, like Arvandus, when, even in heroic Auvergne, there
was a party urging surrender to his generals, what was a strong
King of the Visigoths to do but to consolidate and organise the
conquered territory, and restore in some sort the peace and
order which had vanished ? Euric could be despotic and ruthless. He was a bigoted Arian and intolerant, as all men are in
ages of profound convictions. The hatred between Arian and
Catholic, which is luridly illustrated in the Vandal conquest of
North Africa, and which sometimes emerges in the pages of
Gregory of Tours, was then the more intense because it sprang
from a conflict of races as well as a conflict of religious belief.
In the last years of the Western Empire the three great tribes
of invaders, Ostrogoth, Visigoth, and Vandal, were Christians of
the Arian faith, while the people of the lands which they had
overrun were devoted to the Catholic Church. It might have
seemed probable at the end of the fifth century, on a calculation
of forces, that the religion of Europe was destined to be Arian.
Euric was an enthusiastic sectary, interning bishops, or keeping
sees vacant for years. But his sectarian zeal, while it did credit
to his sincerity of conviction, showed a lack of statesmanship, in
view of the growing intensity of Catholic asceticism and the growing power of the bishops. The banishment of Sidonius for a time
from his diocese was a confession that episcopal leadership was
a formidable force. The appointment of the Catholic Count
Victorius as Governor of Auvergne showed a certain prudent
inclination to conciliate the people of the district. And the
scene in which Victorius bent over the death-bed of Abraham,
the hermit from the East, reveals the power of the spiritual movement which was the most potent influence of that age. Euric
was a commanding figure, and, according to Sidonius, the ramifica-
tions of his name and influence had spread throughout all the
German tribes, and even, if we may believe it, to the remotest
East. He had conquered the Sicambrian ; the Burgundians
suppliantly begged for peace at his hands ; the Ostrogoth lived
under his patronage ; the Parthian Arsaces humbly begs to hold

his throne as tributary ; and the weakness of the Tiber claimed succour from the potentate of the Garonne. It is thus that the lawless verse of Sidonius magnifies the power of Euric after he had restored the bishop to his lands and see. There is doubtless here a ludicrous exaggeration of Euric's power. Yet a more prosaic chronicle seems to confirm a part of the panegyric of Sidonius. At any rate, Euric had before his death made himself master of all Spain, and of Provence and the great cities of Arles and Marseilles. It remained for Odoacer to make a formal cession of the whole prefecture of the West and to sever it finally from the centre of the Empire. Had Euric lived a few years longer, he might not improbably have overwhelmed the nascent Frank monarchy at Tournai, and carried his dominion to the Scheldt and the Meuse. He died two years before the accession of Clovis, and fifteen years before his conversion and baptism by S. Rémi. Under Euric's weaker son the Visigoths of Aquitaine had to pay heavily for his father's sincere intolerance. Yet in the dim confusion of the time, even in 481, it would have needed supernatural prevision to predict that of all the German tribes the only one which was destined to enduring dominion was the little band of Frank warriors who followed Clovis to the front after the battle of Tolbiac. If Euric had accorded to the Catholic Church the toleration and respect which Theodoric paid to it in Italy, it is possible that, even under Alaric, the Visigothic power in Aquitaine would not so easily have succumbed to the onslaught of the Franks.

Meanwhile, ordinary Gallo-Roman life probably went on as it had done for generations before the Visigoths appeared at Toulouse, or the Franks at Cambrai, and Church life was even less disturbed by the great upheaval. We can see or infer that the great landholders and senators, although they may have had to share their estates with a Gothic or Burgundian guest, on the whole maintained their rank and wealth. We can trace a long line of bishops at Clermont or Tours who followed one another in tranquil succession from the time of S. Martin. We can see that Church building, even on a great scale, was not suspended ; that a splendid basilica replaced the Church of S. Martin ; that another was erected at a great centre of miracle and devotion at Brioude. Yet the social condition of Gaul, as a whole, from the final cession of Auvergne to Euric down to the

triumph of the Franks at Vouglé, lies in deep shadow. A
bundle of letters which should tell us, in some sort, how the
mass of people were living (on the Seine, the Loire, or the
Garonne), and what were their anxieties or regrets, would be of
priceless value to the historian who is not content to be a mere
chronicler.   Unfortunately, the last glimpse of the light we long
for comes to us in the last letters of the Bishop of Auvergne in 479.

Many of the older friends of Gregory of Tours were born
before the fall of the Western Empire, and must have witnessed
the great changes which followed the disappearance of the
Imperial administration in Gaul.   But even the keenest and
most cultivated minds in the fifth century were little conscious
of the momentous revolution which was going on around them,
and even less alive to the duty of leaving some record of their
experience to posterity.   Gregory of Tours, or his father, had
talked with aged hermits, some of whom might have seen the
bands of Childeric on the Loire, or Gundobad returning to claim
the throne of Burgundy, or Clovis pressing on the rear of the
Goths after Vouglé.   But the life of the hermitage, like the life
of the château, made men deaf to the noises of the great world
of combat and action, and indifferent to the common life of
their time.   And yet it is curious that for a few scattered and
tantalising glimpses of that everyday life we must go to hagiography.   It is true that, despite their religious and psychological interest, the lives of the saints have only a slight historical
value.   They were generally written for religious comfort and
edification, by men who, from training and habit of mind, knew
and cared nothing for those canons of evidence which are
necessary to secure severe historical accuracy.   An original life
of a saint was often recast, in later centuries, with many additions and conventional details which recur with suspicious
frequency.   Old traditions were handled with a freedom which
was justified to the redactor by a spiritual motive or effect.
Traits and incidents are freely transferred from one life to
another : and, more excusably, the narrative is coloured by
reminiscences of Biblical story.   Yet when criticism has passed
its harshest judgement, to any one eager for vivid facts of social
life, hagiography has a strange fascination, and sometimes gives
him just what he seeks.   The novels and romances of the last
century will be a great source for the future historian of society

in the Victorian Age.   And so, the Lives of the Saints may be used, in the absence of better material, for traits of contemporary society in the fifth and sixth centuries.   These glimpses are, it is true, only seldom and casually vouchsafed to us.   They come fitfully at long intervals, in the desert of conventional legend. But the natural, unconsidered way in which the external setting of spiritual life is revealed inspires a degree of faith that here we have a fragment of the original record, a solid substratum on which has been piled a mass of legend and miracle by pious fancy.

In the effort to fill a lamentable void we have selected three or four saintly lives of that age which may perhaps shed a few feeble rays on the dim common life of the latter part of the fifth century.   One such is the Life of Saint Geneviève of Paris. In its present form it probably dates from the first quarter of the eighth century.   Grave difficulties are raised by its reference to the episcopate and passion of S. Dionysius, and the foundation of the famous Church dedicated to him.   And yet we cannot help feeling that here and there we are carried back to the days of the early Frank monarchy.   Saint Geneviève lived for eighty years, and may have died shortly after the year 500.   As an infant she received the prophetic benediction of S. Germanus in 429, when he passed through Paris with Lupus of Troyes, on his way to quell the Pelagian heresy in Britain.   When the rumour of Attila's invasion reached the banks of the Seine, and the people began removing their valuables to safer places, in the face of violent mobs, and at the risk of her life, she exhorted them to trust to the protection of Christ, and prophesied that Paris would be saved from the terrible Hun.   The monkish biographer has, unfortunately, more than once displayed a contempt for chronology.   S. Geneviève was not the founder of the famous shrine of S. Dionysius, where lie the remains of so many of the French kings.   And so we must reluctantly abandon as a romance of the cloister that scene in which the swineherds report that they have discovered a quarry from which the lime, hitherto sought in vain, might be drawn for the building of the new basilica.   Nor can we confidently accept the tale that Childeric at Paris, out of reverence for the saint, once set free the prisoners whom he had condemned to death.   It is doubtful whether Childeric was ever master of Paris, and the

ten years' siege of the city has a suspicious flavour of many
other reminiscences of the tale of Troy which meet us in the
early annals of the Franks. Yet such legends need not compel
us to reject the more sober part of the narrative. Such a
sceptical method would play havoc with many historic lives.
We may pass by the tales of wonder and miracle which followed
every step of the virgin's career. If such a life in the fifth
century—a period of luxuriant mythopœic fancy—had not
contained miracles, we might well suspect that it was the work
of a much later and more prosaic age. But we can, with
pleasure, gather some grains of fact from the glimpses of rural
scenes on the Marne, the Aube, or the Loire, through which the
saint passed on her sacred missions. We can follow her in her
voyages on the Seine to Troyes, landing here and there, and
gathering supplies of corn to relieve the famine-stricken people
of Paris. Sometimes her passage is blocked by the fall of a
tree across the channel. Sometimes her boat is in danger of
being swamped by a sudden squall. Or again she faces the
vicissitudes of a passage down the Loire from Orleans to
Tours. The general impression we get from these narratives is
that of passing through scenes of peaceful industry in quiet
country. The woodman is felling trees for a new basilica. The
harvesters in a field on the Marne are threatened with a sudden
rainstorm, which opportunely is averted by prayer and miracle.
But the common troubles of life, of course, are not wanting. We
meet the Tribune of Arcis-sur-Aube, whose wife had been seized
with paralysis, or the *Defensor* of Meaux, who craved a cure for
his deafness. There is not a word about any social upheaval, or
panic spread by forays of Frank bands on the war-path, or
battles with the Visigoths on the Loire. The element of tragedy
is found in the crowds of the sick, the blind, the palsied, the
epileptic, supposed to be possessed by evil spirits, who thronged
around the saint at each landing-place, or in the cloisters of
S. Martin's at Tours, begging and receiving marvellous deliverance from their ills. For many generations such tales of
wondrous power will have far more interest, even for the
educated class, than the momentous social and political revolution which was opening a new future for the Western world.
There is not a word in this Life of the victories of Clovis over the
Roman Syagrius and the Visigoths of Alaric. Yet S. Geneviève

may probably have lived to see the early triumphs of the Franks, and Clovis installed at Tours or Paris.   All we are told of them is that, out of reverence for her and at her prayer, the great Frank conqueror released prisoners under punishment for their crimes, and, in her honour, began the basilica of the Apostles, which was finished by his Queen, Clothilde, and in which all three repose.

In the Lives of other saints of the same time who rose to celebrity there is unfortunately little which tends to illuminate the course of events or the social life of the people.

The saint is often of noble stock, trained in a feeble tradition of literature or rhetoric at the neighbouring school.   His family life in early youth seems to be safe and placid, with hardly a sign that new German governments are taking the place of Imperial functionaries, or that life and property are in more danger under the new régime than under the old.   Of course it would be unsafe to found too much positive inference on the silence or *insouciance* of a class who were avowedly turning away from all worldly things and becoming more and more absorbed in the life of the spirit.   And there is at least one of these biographies in which the writer found it impossible to escape from all notice of events in which the saintly subject bore a commanding part.

The Life of S. Remigius, the great Bishop of Rheims for three-quarters of a century, by Hincmar, his successor in the ninth century, undoubtedly offers a tempting mark to destructive criticism.   There was an original Life which was followed by Gregory of Tours, and from which Fortunatus made some extracts for an abbreviation, containing little but tales of the saint's miracles.   In the violation and plunder of the Cathedral of Rheims in the time of Charles Martel, the original Life was destroyed by damp, vermin, or human hands, except a few scattered leaves of the MS., which were collected by Hincmar, and worked up with extracts from other old books and floating popular tradition.   Among these old histories were undoubtedly those of Gregory and Fredegarius and the Frank chronicles which we still possess.   But these authorities almost certainly drew from an original Life, in which the conversion and baptism of Clovis, through the influence of S. Remigius, and the extension of the Frank conquests to the Seine and the Loire, must have held a prominent place.   But Gregory, in his other works, shows that he knew much more of the life of Clovis than he has given in his history. The early career and achievements of the Frank conqueror, with which the life of S. Rémi was so closely involved, must have been celebrated and prolonged in popular tradition and Frank saga. Such sources in that age teemed with wonders that appealed to the imagination of the people and were the natural and expected setting of great lives. If historians are content to accept the main facts of the conversion and baptism of Clovis, in spite of the descent of the mystic dove bearing the cruise of the holy oil, we may be permitted to glean some facts of social life from the same source.

S. Rémi was a contemporary of S. Geneviève, although he outlived her probably by more than twenty years. Rarely has any man lived to see so many great events. His long life extended from 437, the year when King Chlogio routed the Roman troops, seized Cambrai, and pushed his raids, or conquests, to the Somme, down to the year 533, more than twenty years after the death of Clovis, and a very few years before the birth of Gregory of Tours. He and Principius, Bishop of Soissons, were probably brothers, sprung from a family of rank in the district of Laon. It was a circle possessed with all the intense religious spirit of the time, which saw the life of man constantly surrounded by diabolic arts or the ministry of angels. And so the birth of the great Churchman who was destined to win the Frank race for the Catholic faith was heralded by omens and prophecy of the true Biblical type.

His miraculous birth, foretold by the monk Montanus, is related at great length. His training in letters is dismissed in a formal sentence. Though inclined in early youth to the solitary life, his aspect and manners, which could be stern and commanding, and, on occasion, winning and gentle, marked him out from the first as one fitted for high place in Church or State. Without regard for the Canons, he was called to the vacant bishopric of Rheims in his twenty-second year by the unanimous voice of the people, which was confirmed by the decision of the bishops of the province with equal unanimity. That was the very year when Aegidius, Master of the Forces, was elected chief of the Salian Franks, in the room of the young Childeric, banished for a time to Thuringia. There is no mention of this event in the Life of S. Rémi. We are only told that the Romans held the

lands from the Rhine to the Loire, under the chieftainship of
Aegidius, and that a Frank host in those days stormed and burnt
the cities of Cologne and Trèves. Those must have been stormy
times on the Moselle and Rhine when fresh German hordes were
pouring into Champagne. And yet Rheims seems to have known
nothing of the wanton barbarity with which its ancient fane has
been marred and desecrated by the degenerate descendants of the
invaders of those days. The youthful bishop seems to have been
tranquilly performing his pastoral duties, visiting the remote
churches of his see, or, as a preacher, making a name which had
reached Auvergne in the last years of Sidonius Apollinaris. But
the surest testimony to the bishop's power and fame is the
tradition of the many miracles which he performed, the only
side of his activity which his biographer, Fortunatus, thought
worth recording, and that which struck the imagination and
aroused the awe and wonder of Clovis and his pagan Franks. It
is perhaps hardly to be regarded as a miracle that, with his love
of birds, a cloud of sparrows should come down to perch upon
his hand and gather up the remains of a banquet he was giving
to his friends. He could cast out unclean spirits, give sight to
the blind, and raise the dead to life. The fame of his wonder-
working power spread throughout Gaul, as far as the capital of
the Visigoths. A maiden of noble birth, one perhaps related to
King Alaric, was possessed by a demon which resisted all spiritual
powers. She had been taken in vain to the tomb of S. Peter, and
her tormentor had defied the efficacy of the most potent of the
local saints. The " ancient enemy " at last, under constraint of
most solemn adjuration, proclaimed that the evil spirit could
only be expelled by the prayers of S. Rémi. She was conveyed
on the long journey to his presence by an embassy charged with
letters to him. The saint reluctantly, and only in obedience to
the entreaties of the people, at last drove out the demon. But,
unfortunately, in the agony of deliverance, the girl expired, and
a second miracle was needed to restore her to life.

It is strange that so many miracles of that age are wrought
for very trivial and selfish purposes. Again and again we hear,
in that land of the bounteous vine, that a stinted supply of wine
is marvellously replenished. And one such feat of S. Rémi
deserves a slight notice, not because it refilled the cellar of a
country house, but for a glimpse which the story gives of the

life of a country house in those days. On one of his circuits the bishop, in passing an estate at Thugny in the Ardennes, while the reapers were at work in harvest time, went up and addressed them, and ordered them food and drink. His cousin, who was the owner of a neighbouring estate, happened to be passing at the time, and begged him to honour her house with a visit. On their arrival, her steward, like Caleb Balderston in Scott's novel, knowing that there was no wine in the cellar, whispered a hint to his mistress which reached the ear of the bishop. Assuring his cousin that she need have no anxiety, on the pretext of inspecting the gardens and buildings, he found his way to the butler's quarters, shut himself in the cellar, and, by prolonged prayer and the holy sign, won an ample supply for the dinner-table !

But the Life of S. Rémi has, besides such rather trivial tales, much to satisfy or tantalise the serious historian of great events, evidently drawn from authentic chronicles, or from yet living and trustworthy tradition, which will be dealt with in a coming chapter. We shall hear of the Alemannic war, and its consequence in the conversion and baptism of the victor, the death of Aegidius, the succession of Syagrius and his overthrow by Clovis in his irresistible advance. We shall see the Frank king first at Soissons, then at Paris, then pushing his conquests to the Loire and preparing his onslaught on the feeble King of the Visigoths, and his conquest of Aquitaine. We shall hear also of the victory of spiritual power over wild, untamed character. We shall see a Catholic bishop, with no material force at his command, by strength of will and the sense of a lofty mission, mastering the young impetuous chief of the pagan Franks, and, with the gentle aid of the pious Queen, along with the glamour of miracle, winning him from paganism to be the champion of the Church. We may well believe that, in the first onset, many churches were desecrated and plundered. But the personality and supernatural power of S. Rémi were a potent spell to check the predatory instincts of the Franks. Passing along the *Via Barbarica*, which ran close to the episcopal city, the Frank chief did not enter it himself, but, without his knowledge or command, a band of his warriors, breaking away from discipline, once raided the town and carried off the ornaments and holy vessels of the altar. The army was on its march to Soissons, and there the booty was brought together to be divided as usual by lot. The King had received a message from the bishop begging that one sacred vessel might be restored, and now appealed to his warriors to make him a special gift of one sacred urn. In spite of the insolent defiance of one young Frank, it was enthusiastically granted to Clovis and restored by him to the cathedral.

S. Rémi had large paternal estates, and, like other bishops of the time, he was shrewd and diligent in adding to the revenues of his see. Whether we accept all the details of his acquisitions or not, it seems clear that he obtained large grants of land from the Frank conqueror for the church of Rheims. Once Clovis promised to assign to him all the lands which the bishop could go round during the king's mid-day sleep. It is curious that the tenants seemed to have preferred to remain under the King's lordship. One impious miller refused absolutely to be included in the new church domains and his mill met its proper fate. The wheel began to turn backwards — and from that day no mill-wheel could ever be got to work upon the spot. Whether the saint abused his wondrous power for worldly ends we cannot tell. But his pious biographers believed it. Religious zeal has often, in the history of the Church, cloaked very worldly greed and ambition, and the contrast of corporate worldliness with personal sanctity is one of the enigmas of religious history. S. Rémi disposed in his will of great estates, with their serfs and slaves. He left much to the church of Rheims, which he had loved and guarded for seventy-four years. The sacred robes and vessels passed to his successor in the see, and, above all, the silver vase which had been used in the baptism of Clovis and which was the gift of the illustrious convert. Bequests of vine-yards, woods, meadows, and serfs are left to his brother Principius and his nephew Lupus, who became successive bishops of Soissons, with the grant of freedom to certain serfs on the episcopal estates. Specified provision is made for the clergy of every grade, and for the poor *in matricula*, who lived on the alms of the faithful. Vineyards and slaves are bequeathed for the repose of S. Rémi's soul in those very districts of Cerny and Vaudresse where the guns are, as these words are written, thunder-ing towards the plateau of Laon. It is all very business-like and minute : the name of every little vineyard and its keeper, the coloni and their wives, are all set down with scrupulous

D

precision. Even his house linen is not forgotten, and his swine
are to be divided between the bishop Lupus and the priest
Agricola. With the accustomed critical dogmatism this document is pronounced to be an elaborate forgery of the eleventh
century. We would fain believe that we have here a precious
picture, in legal form, of the charming district which is now
being reduced to dust by the new barbarians.

Many churchmen and hermits of those days seem to have
lived to a marvellous old age, and S. Rémi was ninety-six at his
death. He had seen the early rise of the Frank monarchy, the
fall of the Western Empire, the extinction of the last traces of
Roman sway on the Aisne and the Seine, the conquest of southern
Gaul by Clovis. For more than twenty years he saw Gaul
divided under the sway of the sons of Clovis. He saw the
kingdom of Burgundy annexed by the Franks. And in his very
last years he saw Theuderic and Chlothar returning from their
slaughterous campaign in Thuringia. He almost lived to see the
birth of Gregory of Tours. Miracle had attended him through
his long life and added to his imperious strength. And, as
always in such days, miracles issued from his tomb. There
were many known to Hincmar. One is described by Gregory, a
better authority, with minute, picturesque detail. In the year
546 the bubonic plague was carried to Arles from the ports
of Africa. The people of Rheims were panic-stricken at the
rumours of its progress. Their one refuge was the tomb of
S. Rémi. Around it they kept vigil, with chants and hymns.
Then, arranging the pall that covered it, as over a bier, they
bore it in procession around the city. The pestilence, we are
told, reached the borders of Rheims, but was checked at the
precise spot to which the sacred relic had been borne.

The life of another somewhat obscure saint who lived in the
early manhood of S. Rémi casts a little light on the society of
Aquitaine under Theodoric II. S. Vivianus (or Bibianus) was
the son of a citizen of Saintes who remained a pagan, and
would never to the end of his life accept baptism. The saint's
mother was a devout Christian, and from his sixteenth year he
came under the peculiar care of Bishop Ambrosius, who watched
over his training in sacred letters and his preparation for the
priesthood. On the death of Ambrosius he was unanimously
elected his successor by the voice of both clergy and laity, and

reluctantly assumed the office. It was a time of great social trouble and financial stress, which may have been due to the drain on the Visigothic treasury caused by the campaigns in Spain and against Majorian and Aegidius at Arles in 461–463. At any rate the people of the bishop's diocese, one and all, both nobles and commons, were suffering from intolerable taxation. Their property and their persons were being seized, in default of payment ; and the Visigothic power was imitating only too faithfully the cruel fiscal tyranny which did so much to hasten the fall of the Western Empire. The Bishop of Saintes, like the Bishop of Auvergne, a few years later, and indeed like all the great bishops of the time, felt that he was the temporal as well as the spiritual guardian of his flock, and he set out on a journey, long for those days, to expostulate with Theodoric. Bibianus was now an old man, and he made a slow journey in a waggon drawn by oxen. When at length he reached Toulouse he found a lodging in a poor inn in the outskirts of the town, and fortified himself by frequent prayers in the shrine of the Blessed Martyr Saturninus. In the night the oxen which had borne him were stolen ; but the audacious brigand was mercifully pardoned by the bishop. That stately gentleman, Theodoric, hearing of his arrival, courteously invited him to dine at the palace with some of his brethren. But at the banquet, by a piece of narrow-minded and ill-bred rudeness, Bibianus declined to drink wine with the Arian king. And only a vision of the night, or, more probably, the good nature of Theodoric, saved the bishop from unpleasant consequences. We can well understand the scene from the picture of the great knightly Goth sketched in the letters of Sidonius. Bibianus, in spite of his rudeness, succeeded in his mission : the fiscal debtors of Saintes were released ; and the monastic biographer, like all his kind, attributes their deliverance to the wondrous powers of the Catholic bishop, rather than to the tolerant clemency of the heretic king. We may note that the district of Saintes was then being harried by Saxon pirates, who were probably the same bands as those mentioned by Sidonius, and engaged in fierce battles with Franks and Bretons from Angers to Bourges. There were traders from the Levant in those days at Saintes as there were in the days of Gregory of Tours at Orleans and Paris. Certain disgusting relics of the saint were carried away by a trader to be enshrined in

Eastern lands and worked wonders of healing. At Saintes a basilica rose over his tomb, which was finished by Bishop Leontius and his wife Placidina, a great - granddaughter of Sidonius Apollinaris. Fortunatus has celebrated the splendour of gold which was lavished on the roof.

About the very time when Bibianus was visiting Theodoric at Toulouse, the Lives of the Saints give us a glimpse of the state of Eastern Gaul under the Burgundians. That people which crossed the Rhine in 415 had in twenty years pushed their settlements to Metz and Toul, and after being thrown back by Aetius in 436, had quietly established themselves, with Imperial sanction, on the Saône and Isère by 456. But the woody solitudes of the Jura were attracting crowds of other settlers fleeing from the world. The letters of Sidonius speak of those who had " celestial habitations " in that romantic region bordering on the country of the Alemanni. The lives of some of these anchorets have come down to us. Two were probably born in the district of Vosges. But there is not a hint of the ravages of war or of the settlement of Burgundian " guests " on the lands of Romans, which certainly took place in their youth. They were the earliest pioneers of solitary asceticism in the region which stretches from the forests of the Jura to the northern shores of Lake Leman. In a wooded glade near a stream, with a small open patch for culture to supply their few wants, amid solitudes never broken save by some wandering hunter, the visionaries made their home of prayer. Yet, in some strange way, rumours of their severe sanctity and strange, occult powers spread fast and far, and such numbers, eager for a life like theirs, flocked around them, that the hermits had in the end to organise the crowd into spiritual communities. They had to build huts, cut down the woods, clear the rough land for crops, to provide bare means of life. Energy and zeal soon supplied more than the stinted anchoret's fare, and, with growing luxury, there soon came the usual train of monastic troubles, when practice gave the lie to profession. The abbot's cares were divided between those who should never have left the " world " and were eager to return to it, and those who were ready to wreck all natural powers of mind or body by a frenzied self-torture. But the external and economic story of these monasteries on Lake Leman is to us, for the present, more

interesting than the melancholy tale of the vices, or the strained
efforts for superhuman sanctity, which are the same in all ages
of the monastic life. The monks were skilful and energetic
farmers. The woods were cleared and fresh land was broken in.
The stream was skilfully diverted or dammed to turn the mill-
wheel. Yet there came times of scarcity, when the corn supplies
of the old year were spent before the next harvest could
be garnered. It was either to obtain relief in such straits
or, according to another account, to defend the poor against
official tyranny that, about the year 453, Lupicinus, the abbot
of Romainmôtier, set out for Geneva to make an appeal to
Chilperic, the Burgundian king, or, as he is also styled, the
" Patrician ". The oppressor was plainly one of those Roman
servants or sycophants of the new German power, whose mingled
treachery, venality, and truculence are depicted by Sidonius
about this time. This arrogant official, in the presence of
Chilperic, charged the monk with having predicted, ten years
before, utter ruin from the coming of the Burgundians. The
undaunted monk boldly accused him and his tribe of having,
by their cruel oppression of the poor, shaken the authority of
Rome, vested in " her skin-clad lieutenant ", and foretold that
the " new guest " might not spare their acres. The king was
moved by the bold sincerity of the abbot's words, and offered
the monastery a grant of lands and vineyards which were in the
end commuted for a yearly subsidy of grain and wine with 100
aurei in gold. The monks were also troubled by the raids of the
Alemanni, who blocked their access to a neighbouring supply of
salt ; and the monastery was compelled henceforth, with great
delay and some danger, to draw their supplies from the shores
of the Mediterranean.

The sympathetic reception of the unknown abbot of the Jura
by an Arian German king is a pleasant episode ; but it does
not surprise any one who knows something of the inner story
of the time. The Burgundians were known to their Roman
neighbours as a jovial, good-humoured race who, as we shall
soon see, made their intrusion among their Gallic hosts as little
galling and disturbing as possible. The so-called barbarian
conquest of the West was, to a great extent, a process of infiltration, or of " peaceful penetration ", far more insidious and
effective than open overthrow in the field. The victims for

whom Lupicinus pleaded were feeble folk deprived of their property and freedom by Roman agents applying all the heartless pressure of the old administrative tyranny of the Imperial treasury in the service of the new German chief. But the Burgundian Code is an authentic record of an effort to create a system of equal rights as between the two races. And many a dim record of the time reveals the fact that great Gallo-Roman families continued undisturbed and influential for generations under their new rulers, often transferring to the service of the Church the prestige and devotion which in an earlier time would have been given to the State.

One such career, preserved in shadowy outline, illustrates the relations of Roman and Teuton in Eastern Gaul. But it is tantalising, because, while it bridges the momentous interval between the middle of the fifth century and almost the middle of the sixth, the ecclesiastical biographer is so occupied with miracles and traits of ascetic sanctity that he almost ignores the great secular events of the time. Gregory, the great-grandfather of Gregory of Tours, sprang from an ancient senatorial stock with estates at Dijon and Autun, and he was the ancestor of a line of bishops two of whom occupied the throne of S. Martin at Tours. He was a slightly younger contemporary of S. Rémi. He was born a little before 450 and died about 540. He received a good education at one of the centres of Roman culture in Gaul, where the tradition of the Gallic renaissance of the days of Ausonius probably still lingered. At a very early age he entered public life in the service of the Burgundians, and for forty years, from the accession of the Emperor Anthemius to the year before the Frank victory at Vouglé, he filled the office of Count of Autun. His worldly experience in those years when Syagrius and Ecdicius of Auvergne were striving to save the last remnant of Imperial power in Gaul must have been as rich as that of Sidonius Apollinaris. And yet not the faintest record of it has come down to us through his descendant, the Bishop of Tours, whose mother Armentaria must have often talked with her grandfather in his home at Dijon. We only know of those years from Fortunatus, who made the tour of Gaul a few years after the death of the older Gregory. On the death of his wife he resigned official and worldly life and, though he never ceased to be a great aristocrat, he practised the severest rules of asceticism.

The aristocrat at those times easily and often became the prince bishop, and in 507 Gregory was called by the popular voice to the Episcopate of Langres, which he held for thirty-two years. He saw the fall of the Western Empire, the settlement of the Burgundians on the Saône and Lake Leman, and their subjugation by the new Frank conquerors. His name is subscribed to the Councils of the time. In the Council of Orleans in 538 it is significant that he is represented by a presbyter. Coming to Langres soon after, at the time of Epiphany, he was seized with a fever and died in his ninety-second year.

These sketches, drawn from hagiography, are offered to the reader as almost the only available material for forming some faint picture of social life in Gaul for the seventy years between the reign of Honorius and the death of Clovis. Scanty and broken as they are, they infuse a little blood and life into the shadowy ghosts of chronicles, and illuminate an age and a society which else had been dark indeed.

CHAPTER II

THE purpose of this chapter is to frame some conception of the character and social life of the Franks and Burgundians from the time of their first settlement in Gaul till the conquest of Gaul by Clovis. It is not an easy task, for many reasons, to get a clear view of any of the German tribes at that period of convulsion, and after many years of wandering and war. The facile generalisations which attribute certain vices or virtues to Frank, Vandal, or Burgundian, like similar judgements of national characteristics in our own day, may be the result of limited or hasty observation, and very precarious. Among the same race there were probably the most startling contrasts according to social grade and the chances of experience. There could not be much in common between a polished Frank who had risen to be Master of the Forces, or even to the Consulship at Rome in the reign of Honorius, and the rude chief of a band from the forests of Thuringia which, in the beginning of the fifth century, stormed in among the Curiales of Trèves at one of their banquets. There could not have been much in common between a Burgundian prince who had been colleague of Ricimer in making and unmaking emperors, and a good-humoured, jovial Burgundian man-at-arms who had settled on a Roman farm to enjoy hunting and good cheer in the Vosges. Nor shall we gain much light from earlier pictures of German character and society in Caesar or in Tacitus, or from German critics of them, whose erudition is always obedient to an unfaltering faith in German strength and virtue in all ages, and whose picture of the German character in the first century is often about as trustworthy as that of the

American Indians in Fenimore Cooper. This is not the place to compare the German character and social life as depicted in Caesar or Tacitus with that of the invading tribes in the fifth century. The Germans of the time of Arminius were certainly not the spotless heroes of romance who float before the imagination of the modern German professor, although his analysis of their tribal institutions may be characteristically exact. Nor did their descendants carry with them into the regions they conquered all the institutions and instincts of freedom which they enjoyed in their old homes in the first century. There is a great gulf between the Germans of Tacitus and the fierce, faithless Frank of Gregory of Tours, living under a military monarchy which dominated a vast territory.

In the long interval, German character and institutions had been profoundly affected by the rough and varied experience of three centuries of war and migration. How could any national character or institutions remain unchanged after wandering from the shores of the Baltic to the shores of the Euxine, from the Danube to the Rhine or Rhone, at one time serving in Roman armies against their own countrymen, at another storming Roman cities and overrunning Roman provinces ? Romantic patriotism may dream of an unchanged German character and polity. But this patriotic romance is not history. There were in fact immense changes brought about by the conquest. The petty German tribe, in its small district, in old days could have frequent meetings to manage its own affairs. It was now dispersed over a vast new territory in which meetings were impossible. The chief, surrounded by his band of warriors, personally attached to him, became in Artois or Burgundy a great landowner with tenants and serfs. German chieftainship or royalty changed its character profoundly. The King was no longer a military chief : he was lord of a wide territory which still retained a long tradition of Roman administration, and he appropriated such authority as might be drawn from the titles, powers, and insignia of the empire. In carrying out his new task of administration he was obliged to use the trained skill of Roman lawyers and administrators. And, above all, he had to recognise and use the great new power of the Catholic Church, that " ghost of the Roman Empire, sitting on the grave thereof ".

Therefore, in trying to know the character of the Franks in

the first quarter of the fifth century, we must seek for information as near as possible to the sources of the period, and without the prepossessions of Teutonic patriotism. The Franks were pro-verbially a faithless race, and certainly the character of many of the Merovingian kings and nobles, in the record of the Bishop of Tours, would seem to justify the charge. Like all barbarian tribes driven from their old seats perhaps by mere hunger, they were greedy and rapacious, with an incalculable ferocity which often seemed to defy all thoughts of mercy or prudence. Yet a great race which has done great things should not be finally judged by its behaviour in moments of the delirious excitement of rapid conquest following years of penury and hardship. It should be estimated rather by the social system which it strives to organise when the struggle is over, and when it has to address itself to the task of ordering a community on the lines of peace and justice.

As we have seen, the Frank race by the middle of the fifth century had been long settled in Flanders and North-eastern Gaul. We find them at Tongres, Cambrai, and Cologne. But that section of the race with which we are more nearly concerned is the Salian tribe settled in the modern Limberg and Brabant. They had had a home in Toxandria since the days of Julian, for more than one hundred years. They found themselves in a region which, for four centuries from the reign of Tiberius, had been to a great extent Germanised, either by Imperial policy or unauthorised incursions from beyond the Rhine. As a con-sequence of the frequent passage of Teutonic bands across the great river, which almost ceased to be an effective boundary of races, the Franks of North-eastern Gaul and Flanders were more purely German in tone, character, and institutions than the Burgundian and Visigothic invaders of the east and south. They had come less under the spell of old Roman civilisation, and they were still pagan, although they were destined to become the sole champions of the Catholic Church among all the great German tribes who had overrun the Western Empire. Nothing shows more vividly the magical power of the Church in fashioning the future of Europe, than that this German race, which to the last remained most pagan, followed Clovis to the font at Rheims, crushed the Arian powers of Burgundy and Aquitaine, and in the last years of the eighth century revived the glory of the Christian Empire in Charlemagne.

In seeking the sources of Western institutions in the wreck of the Western Empire, no documents are so illuminating and precious as the codes of those tribes which took its place. And the code of the Salian Franks has a peculiar interest, because in some of its clauses it seems to go back to a time when the Salian Franks were still on German soil, while it underwent successive redactions in the time of Clovis and his successors, even down to Charlemagne. Our main purpose being to extract from this code some authentic knowledge of the early social condition of the Franks on the eve of their conquest of Gaul, we are little concerned with the critical and thorny questions which have gathered around it, and which have deeply divided the learned world. The law is preserved in a good many MSS. of the eighth or ninth centuries, which exhibit many variations of phrase and arrangement. The majority of these MSS. are entirely in Latin ; three contain what are called the Malberg glosses in German. Yet, contrary to apparent probability, the German redaction implies a later date than anything in the purely Latin versions, and refers to an " ancient law " of which the Latin know nothing. The law is never mentioned by the earlier Frank chroniclers Gregory or Fredegarius, and it is only in the *Gesta Francorum* that we hear that, while the Franks were still on German soil near the mouth of the Rhine, after the election of Pharamond, their law was framed by four sages, Wisovast, Wisogast, Arogast, and Salegast, representing four cantons of the tribe. Some of the MSS. open with a prologue or preface giving the same tradition with variations. They agree in glorifying the strength, beauty, and valour of the Frank race, now converted to the Catholic faith, although its ancient law was framed in the days when it was still pagan, yet inspired by God with the desire of justice and piety. It was afterwards, in the light of the true faith, amended by the illustrious Clovis, Childebert, and Chlothar. The preface is of course the work of a late pious copyist full of the grandeur of the conquering Merovingians, who were true sons of the Church. But it also preserves a popular tradition that the floating legal customs and maxims of the Franks had been formulated while they were still pagans on German soil. There are also indications in the law, in its later redactions, that the Franks had pushed their conquests to the Loire, and the institutions of the Catholic Church are recognised and guarded. Further, the contents of the law reveal that it belongs to a time when the Franks were settled in an agricultural life among a Roman population, who are treated as of inferior status, though not with any glaring injustice. Moreover, the tariff of composition for crimes and losses, in its high scale of pecuniary compensation, can hardly represent the social state of an old German tribe beyond the Rhine. It rather implies a relatively high standard of wealth in a people leading a prosperous life of settled industry. There are many strata, as it were, in the various MSS. down to the close of the eighth century. But it is certain that they do not contain all the " old law " to which they sometimes refer. It is, however, clear that there were ancient legal rules in force in the tenth and eleventh centuries of which there is no trace in the Latin MSS. which we possess. Yet in some MSS. there are embodied Teutonic words and formulæ which, according to some critics, may be survivals from that ancient trans-Rhenane source, although this is strenuously denied. Any conclusion on these points, we believe, must be far from dogmatic. A great authority on ancient law in the last century laid it down that " the *Leges Barbarorum* are not rude enough to satisfy the theory of their purely barbarous origin ", and that the record has not come down to us of more than a fraction of the legal rules in force among the German tribes. He further thinks that a considerable element of debased and undigested Roman law " clothed with flesh and muscle the scanty skeleton of barbarian usage ". " The codes of the barbarians, archaic as they seem, are a compound of true primitive usage with half-understood Roman rules, very different from the refined and subtle jurisprudence of Justinian."

Looking at these questions as a whole, we may be justified for our practical purpose in this chapter in coming to the following conclusions :

1. That in the Salic Law we have a rather chaotic mass of old Frank legal usages, which was first redacted and codified, perhaps early in the fifth century, in Toxandria, where the Salii had been firmly seated since the campaigns of Julian. It was probably drawn up by some Roman ecclesiastic or jurisconsult and modified and adapted to the condition of the Salian tribe settled, more or less peaceably, among a conquered people of a higher civilisation.

2. Only a very sceptical critic will refuse to see traces of old German usage, and the code bears the marks of all archaic codes from the days of Solon. It is an enumeration and recital of customs already in force, and therefore it is wanting in the order and tone of scientific jurisprudence. It deals with actual, concrete facts, without regard to general principles of law.

3. It ignores, or takes for granted, political and judicial institutions which lie in the background of its enactments.

4. It is essentially a penal code for the repression of prevalent crimes. It is almost entirely silent on procedure for their detection, exposure, and punishment. An immense proportion of the enactments deal with multifarious rustic thefts, acts of violence, mutilation, and outrage or insults against women. The Ripuarian Code, which is probably of later date, embodying the customs of the Austrasian Franks, displays an advance in civilised jurisprudence by a more extensive civil code, a greater prominence of the regal power, and a tone of more scientific generalisation, as opposed to a bald registration of ancient legal usage.

It may be assumed, then, with a certain confidence, that, in spite of later redaction, the Salic Law remains, though fragmentary and incomplete, still a truthful picture of the mingled Frank and Roman society in Belgic Gaul in the fifth century. And in this picture the first thing that strikes us is that it is a thoroughly rural society : towns are hardly mentioned. Yet this rustic society, in spite of much violence and crime, is organised and civilised in a fashion which, externally at least, very much resembles a remote countryside in England in the days of our grandfathers. There were estates of various size (*villae*), with land under every kind of culture—arable land, vegetable gardens, vineyards, and orchards. There are meadows and forest pastures, with herds of oxen, sheep, swine, and horses, tended by their keepers. It is not hard to revive in imagination, even from the bald rough Latin of the Salic Law, many pleasant scenes of rural life. One may call up the picture of comfortable granges on the Scheldt, the Lys, or the Meuse, in the fifth century, with their courtyards, surrounded with barns and offices, or the cottages and allotments of the slaves and coloni. Hard by there will be the mill and workshops, in which many degrees of skilled labour are supplying the wants of the household or the farm.

There will also be seen the apple orchard, fruit garden, and bee-hives, all carefully tended, hawks on the perch, and hounds eager for the chase. The fields of the home farm are evidently fenced with hedges, which are often broken through by wandering herds. There are many signs, as we should expect in such a region, that water is never far off : eel nets are often stolen, and boats at the ferry are stealthily taken to the other side, without the owner's leave. There are the favourite sports of country life so dear to the Frank race and their kings. And the penalty for the theft of dogs or hawks shows that the Frank or Roman gentleman was jealously protected in his amusements.

In all these peaceful scenes there are singularly few signs of war or warlike preparations. But there are many signs of internal disorder, lawlessness, and insecurity. The picture has been described as that of a gross and violent society, in which private rights were in constant jeopardy. And it is quite true that much of the greed, and violence, and capricious crime shadowed forth in the Salic Law may find a parallel in the pages of Gregory of Tours. Yet we should remember that this is essentially, and almost exclusively, a penal code, and a code mainly criminal should not be taken to represent the average habitual life of a community. The criminal legislator has naturally nothing to say of the mass of quiet, law-abiding people whom he is striving to protect. If the number and enormity of the crimes enumerated by the Salic lawgivers represented a general state of society, it would be difficult to account for the evidently solid and prosperous rural life of which the code supplies abundant indirect evidence. And the strenuous severity of the lawgiver to crime may be the measure of the moral force which all law must have behind it.

Yet it must be admitted that the chances and dangers to which life and limb and property were then evidently exposed do not offer a pleasant picture. Out of a total of 343 crimes dealt with in the Law, 150 are cases of theft, of which 74 are thefts of domestic animals ; 113 articles deal with crimes of violence, 30 being various forms of mutilation, and 24 outrage or insults to women. The theft of all the live things that surround a prosperous farm — bulls, cows and calves, horses, sheep-dogs and watch-dogs, sheep, goats and swine, hawks and bees—is the subject of many enactments with varying degrees of fine or compensation. Thus a theft of fowl may be atoned for by 3 *solidi*, while a bull of the royal herd is rated at 90. The penalty for stealing a hive of bees within an enclosure will be 45. The same is the compensation for the theft of a trained house-dog or a hawk on its perch, whereas that for a sheep-dog, or a hawk on a tree, is only 3. The theft of horses is atoned for in various degrees, from 3 for a foal to 90 for a stallion belonging to the prince. In the case of the abduction of slaves, the compensation ranges from 35 *solidi* for an ordinary slave to 70 for a skilled vine-dresser, carpenter, or huntsman. But the value of what is stolen is only one of the circumstances taken into account. There are other considerations which determine the penalty, *e.g.* the numbers of the pens from which the theft was made ; whether stolen bees or fruit trees were inside or outside an enclosure ; whether stolen flax or hay was carried off on a waggon or on the back of the thief ; whether a stolen horse belonged to a private person or to the King. In fact, the law-giver, laying down no abstract principle, seems to have tried to embrace every variety of offence, and graded the penalties according to the value of the thing stolen, the status of the owner, and the greater or lesser audacity of the culprit.

The articles on crimes of violence are rather less numerous than those on theft. But they are perhaps more interesting, as a picture of the time on its darker side. They also show curious variations in the penalties attached to them. It costs as much to attack a country house (*villa*) and kill the men and dogs of the household as to set fire to a house in which the inmates are asleep, but far less than the murder of a guest (*conviva*) or courtier (*antrustio*) of the King, or the murder of a pregnant woman. The life of an ordinary Frank is reckoned worth double that of a Roman ; while that of a king's guest or courtier counts many degrees above either. If a Roman robs a Frank with violence, the composition is more than double that for a similar offence committed by a Frank. The lawgiver has evidently an eye to " man power " and population in his varying penalties for the murder of girls and women, according to their capacity for child-bearing. One of the heaviest penalties, 600 *solidi*, is for killing a pregnant woman. Less than a third of that avenges the murder of the girl before puberty, or of the woman whose hope of offspring is past. Abortion is heavily punished. The virtue of women, even of the servile class, is jealously guarded. Even with consent, the seducer is heavily mulcted. Debauchery of slave girls is more indulgently treated, unless they are *ancillae regis*. But if the seducer is a slave, he may be punished by castration. The first stealthy assaults on female honour are warded off by an ascending scale of compensations. To touch the breast of a woman costs a man three times as much as an amorous clasp of the hand. To call a woman a harlot costs a man eight times more than to call a Frank warrior " a hare ".

This recital does not exhaust the recital of crimes of violence and disorder, more or less serious, which it would be tedious to give in full. We can see that fences were violently broken down, and herds of animals were let loose in meadows, vineyards, or fields of growing crops. On the other hand, straying beasts without a keeper, which have been impounded, are to be restored uninjured. But there are many other signs of lawlessness, robbery with violence, assaults with poisoned arrows, the serving of poisoned drinks, bribery of assassins, murder of slaves. There are traces of free men being kidnapped and sold abroad. Men were thrown into wells or into the sea, or their remains were burnt or covered with boughs in the woods. People might be attacked on the roads, or in their own houses in the country by bands of bravoes gathered for the purpose, each of whom, it is pleasant to read, was liable for a heavy compensation ; or a banquet might sometimes be a scene of slaughter, and probably often was. There is an article on wounding and mutilation, which in many cases must have been deliberate, and which, if frequently perpetrated, would brand any race as hopelessly savage. The penalties are graduated, to all appearance, according to the importance of that part of the unfortunate man's body which has suffered. The loss of an ear, a tooth, or a little finger counts for only a third of that of a thumb or a nose, or a fourth of that of an eye. Castration or cutting out the tongue is punished as heavily as killing a Roman farmer. The tale in Gregory of Tours about Guntram Boso, a great Austrasian noble, plundering a grave at Metz may show us that the enactments in the Salic Law against the desecration of tombs were necessary. The penalty for such crime is one of the heaviest, and the culprit might be made an outlaw. On the other hand, we may be inclined to sympathise with the man who, like Quentin

Durward, took down a poor victim from the gibbet, or rescued an impaled head from the ignominy of exposure.

To these crimes, more or less ghastly, we may find a foil in others which, if not innocent, still have a charm of ordinary freakish criminality. To jump on a horse on urgent occasion without leave from the owner, or steal the bell of a swineherd, or pilfer from a well-stocked garden some grapes or apples, or to carry off a tame stag or an eel net, or use a boat without the owner's leave, seem to be hardly offences in some codes deserving the penalties assigned to them. These are trivial things, but they have a certain value in shedding a flash of light on the life of an obscure time. And it is the common peaceful life of the country about Liège and Courtrai and Tournai in the early fifth century which we have desired to revive and depict. The crime and gross scandal and outrage will find many parallels in Gregory of Tours. But behind it all there seems to be a life of prosperous well-doing which, though often invaded by violence and greed, is still stable and happy. The most striking feature of the Salic criminal legislation is the system of pecuniary compensation for almost every offence. This has given birth to very various theories as to the state of society which it represents. Some regard it as an importation of old German custom into Gaul. The satisfaction in money paid to the injured person or his family is, according to this theory, a mitigation of the blood-feud, a recognition of the right of private vengeance, unchecked by the power of the State. Other theorists, pointing out that the system goes far beyond that which is described in the Germany of Tacitus, treat it as a comparatively late development. To the poor and avid Frank of the fifth century, it is said, a round sum in cash was a heavier penalty than that death which constant peril had taught him to despise. It also offered to the injured something more tempting than the barren satisfaction of revenge. Psychological considerations such as these are a dangerous substitute for historic evidence, and there are certain broad facts which may suggest another conclusion.

It is undoubtedly true that in the Germany of Tacitus a " whole family " (*universa domus*) might accept satisfaction for the murder of a relative in a certain number of cattle. And this was regarded as a wholesome method of mitigating the ferocity of the vendetta. But it is also certain that at that time death

E

was inflicted, by hanging or drowning, on the coward, the deserter, or the effeminate. It may also be pointed out that the Burgundian Code awards capital punishment, not only for murder, but for violent robbery, adultery, the theft of slaves, horses, or oxen. The Visigothic Code is equally severe. And even in the Salic Law, when it is closely examined, the conciseness only conceals the existence of fiercer penalties than any pecuniary loss. The death penalty in many cases evidently lies in reserve, or else what is the meaning of the recurring phrase *de vita sua componat* ? This is the alternative which lies before the man who has not means to pay the composition. It amounted, for example, to 1800 *solidi* for the murder of an *antrustio*, with concealment of the crime.   How could an assassin, unless of the highest rank and wealth, discharge such an obligation in money ?   But the Salic Law is very far from being a complete and exhaustive code.   The chronicles and the hagiography of the age leave no doubt that men accused of crimes, even those falling short of homicide, were not seldom condemned to death by Merovingian judges and hung.   King Guntram once found that his chamberlain had been violating the forest laws in the Vosges.   He allowed a judicial combat between the chamberlain's grandson and the keeper of the chase.   Both fell dead, and the accused man fled to take refuge in a neighbouring shrine.   Before he could reach the asylum he was, by the King's orders, seized and stoned to death.   In Gregory's Miracles of S. Martin, a thief condemned to crucifixion is only saved by a miraculous whirlwind which overturns the tree on which he hung.   In another case, Becco, a Frank man of rank, condemned a serf of S. Julian's at Brivate to death for the theft of a hawk.   The *saevitia judicum* is, in the Lives of the Saints, constantly mitigated by the entreaties or the supernatural powers of great saints and churchmen.   It is to be feared that the Salic Law is not to be interpreted as a code of mercy, even if the mercy seems to take the form of pecuniary composition.

The probability is that the system of composition is a growth from three different roots. 1. Old German custom allowed or encouraged it in the case of homicide. 2. Roman law authorised pacts between the parties in cases of theft and incendiarism, and even estimates the amount according to social grade. 3. The Church made a great effort in the sixth century to soften the lot of condemned prisoners, and to deprecate the sentence of death on malefactors even guilty of heinous crime. Great bishops and obscure hermit-saints alike expend their pity and their prayers on behalf of those convicted of the most atrocious outrages. And the powers of the unseen world, which they have at their command, will often defeat the obduracy of a worldly or conscientious magistrate by striking off the chains of a man who had been a danger to society.

The influence of the Church, which was steadily growing, must have had an enormous effect in reducing the number of capital sentences in that age. A bishop was once deposed by the authority of a council for having assented to a sentence of death. Murderers, adulterers, and robbers, condemned by the secular courts, if they took shelter in a consecrated place, were safe from the grasp of human law, unless after a solemn oath by their captor that they will not suffer death or any corporal punishment. Thus the crime is best atoned for by pecuniary composition with the injured party. On the spiritual side, according to prevailing belief, the criminal has been urged on to crime by some malign power. His crime is a misfortune, which may be wiped out by confession and penitence. The chance of Divine pardon must not be taken from him. The men who taught this doctrine were generally Gallo-Romans, not men of the Teutonic breed just redeemed from paganism. And the German kings and lawgivers gave full effect to the ecclesiastical view on the subject of capital punishment and the right of asylum, even in the case of slaves. The Burgundian Law ordains that the criminal who has taken refuge shall compound for his life by a payment fixed by the injured party. In a Frank decree, a slave refugee is to be restored to the master on promise of pardon. The Bavarian Code lays it down that no crime is so grave that, from reverence for God and the saints, it should not be pardoned, since the Lord has said, " to him that forgiveth, it shall be forgiven ".

It was these influences which tended to stimulate the system of allowing pecuniary composition for crime. It has been suggested that under the Empire the inability of the provincial governors to cope with all the criminal administration of a vast region may have led, with their tacit connivance, to a growing practice of secret arrangements of this kind. And it is certainly curious that the Burgundian Code of 501 emphatically forbids, under penalties, such clandestine compositions without the forms of open trial, and implies that the custom had become general in that part of Gaul which probably remained most under the influence of Roman tradition. One of the earliest capitularies of the Frank kings prohibits secret composition for theft, and requires the presence of a judge. There can be little doubt that, under the influence of the bishops and great churchmen, the practice came to be more and more recognised as a means at once of saving a soul from death, and restoring harmony between families at feud. Thus we are told of a great noble of Auvergne that, having committed many crimes, he had been plunged in debt by the amount of his compositions, and had been compelled to pledge his wife's ornaments and jewels. On the other hand, we find a man taunted with having enriched his family by the same means. And it may well be believed that avidity and greed had a larger share in popularising the system of pecuniary satisfaction for criminal, or even accidental, injury.

Moreover, the Government, as well as private persons, had a pecuniary interest in sanctioning the system. For out of every composition the local count was instructed to keep one-third, which was called *fredus*, and divided between him and the King. These fines became a most important part of the royal revenue.

Civil procedure occupies but a small space in the Salic Code, but it is an interesting and important part. The article entitled *Reipus* is a distinct relic of the time when wives were bought. It deals with the case of a widow who is sought in second marriage : the suitor has to appear before the *mallus* summoned by the presiding magistrate, the *tunginus* or *centenarius*, with three witnesses, and to pay over 3 *solidi* and 1 *denarius* to the next of kin, in a descending order of seniority. There is another chapter laying down the rule of inheritance to the Alod or paternal property. Personal property goes equally to males and females ; the whole of the landed property passes only to the male. In some MSS. of the Code this is called *terra salica*, and the phrase has given birth to ambitious theories of conquered lands held by military tenure. There is no trace of benefices held on military service in the Salic Law. If *salica* is a genuine reading, it means the land attached to the *sala*, or hall, *i.e.* the whole paternal estate, which is rendered by the word *aviatica* in the Ripuarian

Code. Two or three articles undoubtedly embody a record of old German symbolic usage. The composition for some kinds of homicide, as we have seen, was for those days enormous, and the culprit must have often found it impossible personally to discharge it. The debt then became a debt of his family. And, in order to assert their obligation, he had to go through a symbolical form, probably of great antiquity. Entering his homestead with his paternal and maternal relatives, he gathered some earth or dust from the four corners of the room in his right hand. Then, standing on the threshold, he took some of the earth in his left hand, and threw it over the shoulders of his three nearest kindred, who were thereupon rendered liable. But a man might naturally wish to escape from so serious an obligation, and provision is made for such a case. He must appear before the *mallus* duly summoned, and breaking four rods of poplar or alder over his head, cast them down in the assembly, declaring that he cuts himself off from all legal tie with his family. But if he is thus relieved of an onerous obligation, he also cuts himself off from all rights of inheritance. It is clear that in these picturesque symbolic usages we are carried back to remote ages in regions beyond the Rhine.

It is often said that the Salic Code is tantalising by its omissions or scanty information on matters of great importance. Yet we should remember that it was drawn up for an immediate practical purpose, not to satisfy the antiquarian curiosity of a distant age. Of the political system of the Salian tribe we learn nothing. The King is seldom mentioned, although his servants, guests and courtiers, and his herds and horses are protected by heavy penalties against violence. Of his powers and prerogatives, we only hear that any person defying the decision of a local court may be summoned to the presence of the King. There is absolutely no trace of a hereditary noble class. The only social grades known to the law are freemen, whether Frank or Roman, freedmen, and slaves. The class of Leudes, so frequently referred to in Gregory of Tours, is never mentioned in the Code. On the other hand, men *in truste regis*, or *antrustiones*, and *convivae regis*, are frequently mentioned, and their safety is protected in a manner corresponding to their rank. Yet the *antrustio* might originally be of any social grade or race, provided he was *ingenuus*. He might even have been a *puer regis*.

But as one who had sworn fealty to the King, and one guarded
by the royal faith, he held, of course, a high position.   In return
for loyalty and good service he had his reward in royal gifts
or in maintenance at the King's table.   The *antrustio* had his
own train of followers who were called his *arimannia*, bound to
equal loyal service to himself.   The only great official mentioned
in the Code is the *grafio*, the *comes* of Gregory of Tours.   He was
the civil and military governor of a canton, with manifold
responsibility.   But, as the supreme judicial authority in his
district, he is constantly called *judex*.   Of the other high officers
in the Merovingian age, *dux, referendarius, domesticus,* etc.,
there is no trace in the Salic Law.   These great officials, whose
rank presupposes a monarchy with extended sway, could hardly
have found a place under a Salican chief whose territory may
have hardly reached the Somme.

The conciseness and reticent practical aim of the Salic Code
is nowhere more striking than in its slight references, or its silence,
as to the composition and procedure of its judicial tribunals.
Of course these were long and well known to those for whom the
law was framed.   And the curt, bald mention of *mallus, grafio,
tunginus,* and *rachimburgi* in the Law may be amplified and
vivified by materials from the record of judicial proceedings in
Gregory and in the legal documents of the following age.   They
must not be amplified and distorted, as they have often been,
by *a. priori* theories founded on conceptions of German society
before the Salii had crossed the Rhine.   Historical accuracy
should not be sacrificed to fanatical patriotism.

The Salic Law recognises broadly two degrees of jurisdiction.
There is first the supreme judicial authority of the King.   If a
man refuses to submit to the judgement of the inferior court (or
mallus), he is required to appear before the King, on pain of
confiscation of his whole estate.   And accusations may at once
be made before the royal tribunal.   Of the proceedings before
that tribunal the Salic Code tells us nothing, although, as we shall
see, much may be gathered from later authorities.   The inferior
local court is the *mallus*, a term around which much controversy
has raged.   When the Code is coldly and dispassionately examined,
it is clear that the *mallus* is simply the court or tribunal of the
count, or *grafio*, or the *tunginus*.   It is certainly not the
assembly of the free men of the canton in arms, as the warlike

Teuton professor would have himself and us believe. No honest, unprejudiced criticism can extract such a conclusion from the language of the Law. Supreme judicial power belongs to the King, or his officer, the count or *grafio*. The count, as ruler of a district in the King's name, has many functions, but he is constantly called *judex*, and his judicial functions were probably the most important. We see him in the history of Gregory of Tours, often making a progress through his district to hold his courts. We see also that, in urgent criminal cases, he can judge alone, and inflict punishment in a summary way. But he is always subject to certain rules of a salutary kind, in the interest of pure and unsuspected administration, which may be partly of Teutonic origin, and partly a tradition of the Roman Law. The *grafio* or count sat as judge in the *mallus* with doors open to all. This court is the successor of the old *conventus* which surrounded the Roman provincial governor on the judgement seat, or of the armed gathering of the Teutonic tribe around the Princeps in the Germany of Tacitus. The count has also assessors sitting with him, called *rachimburgi* or *idonei*, or *boni homines*, who have important functions. Much arbitrary and *a priori* theory has been spun around the name Rachimburgi, with the object of magnifying the judicial power of the people at the expense of the *grafio*. Now the Salic Law gives no explanation of the name Rachimburgi. It assumes them. It certainly gives no countenance to the theories that they were all the freemen of the canton, for, in certain cases in the Law, the *rachimburgi* are few in number, seven or twelve ; still less that they are the warriors of the canton, since the Salic Law is essentially framed for a peaceful agricultural population. Nor is there any proof that they were elected by the freemen in certain numbers. They could not have been men of the poorer class, since they are liable for an illegal decision to an extremely heavy fine. The function imposed upon them implies education and power of interpreting the law. The terms by which they are described in legal documents, *idonei, boni homines, viri magnifici*, certainly seem to designate men of substance and social consideration. There being no evidence that they were popular representatives or nominees of the King, the conclusion is forced on us that they were designated by the *grafio* out of the assembled notables for each occasion. And, silent as the Salic Law is on such matters, one passage seems to make this clear, in which the count is required to " gather about him seven Rachimburgs, solvent and capable men ". The count was probably often a military man, with no expert knowledge of the law, and perhaps little knowledge of the social character of his district. And he might well feel the need of the assistance of men possessing both kinds of knowledge, who could examine the witnesses with some information as to their character and refer the case to the precise clauses of the law bearing on it. They are also said to judge and decide the cause, and are subject to rigorous penalties for failure in their duty. It has been maintained, in the interest of a theory of purely popular jurisdiction, that the decision lay entirely in their hands, and that the count's part in the proceedings was merely formal, that of presiding and pronouncing the decision of the Rachimburgs. And the Law leaves his relation to his assessors rather obscure. But other authorities seem to support the conclusion that, although the count might often defer to the judgement of the Rachimburgs, and tacitly accept it, he is still an authoritative constituent member of the court, and does not stand apart as a powerless official merely registering or publishing its decision. In some formulæ the proceedings are said to take place in the presence of the count and the " other Rachimburgs ", words which seem to imply that he is reckoned as one of them, in examination of witnesses and in the final decision. The Salic Code, however, leaves little doubt that the count is the centre of judicial power in his district, and this is confirmed by later authorities. But his duties were manifold, and it might sometimes be impossible for him to be present at the *mallus*. In such cases he would be represented by the *tunginus* or *centenarius* as his deputy, or, apparently, the Rachimburgs might hold a court by themselves, just as the King's court might hold a sitting without the presence of the King. In four clauses of the Salic Law the *tunginus* or *centenarius* presides over a court. In three of them the questions relate to the law of the family ; the fourth deals with a question of debt. One of these concerns the *reipus* of a widow on remarriage ; in one version the case comes before the *tunginus*, in another before the *grafio*. The safest conclusion seems to be that the count, as representing the King, who is the fountain of justice, is supreme over all causes in his district. The Law describes him as engaged in the service of

the King, and, as being one of those *in truste domini*, the composition for his murder is 600 *solidi*, *i.e.* threefold more than that
for the murder of an ordinary freeman. With regard to legal procedure also, the Salic Law is wanting
in completeness. Of the two kinds of evidence, oral and docu-
mentary, there is no reference to the latter, which is required
by the later Ripuarian Code. The witnesses are summoned by
the parties, not by the court. They are required to attend the
mallus on the appointed day, subject to a penalty of 15 *solidi* if
they neglect the citation, and to tell what they know of the facts
upon oath. A fine of the like amount is the penalty for false
evidence. But after the direct evidence had been given and
sifted by the *rachimburgi*, the proof may have seemed inadequate,
or the judges may have been wanting in skill to interpret it.
In such failure, the most natural resource in those days lay in
an appeal to the judgement of God. It is curious to observe in
an age almost pedantically scrupulous about legal forms, which
were probably a tradition from the Imperial jurisprudence, side
by side with these an implicit faith in a Divine judgement ever
ready to decide the most trivial questions of worldly interest by
inflicting physical suffering or death on the perjured litigant.
The reader of Gregory of Tours or the Lives of the Saints will not
wonder at the call on the heavenly powers to decide a question
of ownership or crime. If they deign to refill an empty oil
flask or supply fresh wine for thirsty reapers, they may surely
be expected to guard the purity of justice by their powerful
sanctions. In an age of wild impulses, still imperfectly tamed,
the fear of the Unseen Judge was a powerful stay of civic order
which was still unstable at the best. Superstition, as Plutarch
taught, lowers the ideal of God and degrades the character of
man. And yet in that age of materialist religion it provided a
salutary, though often ineffectual, check on the instincts of
greed and falsehood.

The ordeal of boiling water, the ordeal of the cross, judicial
combat, and compurgation, were the various modes of appealing
to the Divine judgement in the absence or uncertainty of human
testimony. Of these only the first and the last are recognised
in the Salic Law. They are probably the most extra-judicial
means of proof, and certainly come down from early Teutonic
usage. The ordeal of the extended arms is probably of Christian

origin. The judicial duel first appears in the Code of Burgundy
and then in that of the Ripuarian Franks. By the Salic Law
the *rachimburgi* may, in default of clear proof of innocence,
require a man to plunge his hand in boiling water or submit to
the composition which is prescribed in his case. If the hand
emerges uninjured, the man's innocence is proved. If a defendant charges the witnesses on the other side with perjury,
he may be called on to submit to the same ordeal, and if he
escapes unharmed, each of the false witnesses has to pay 15 *solidi*,
the same penalty falling on himself if his hand does not endure
the test. But physical nervousness or conscious guilt might
often make a man shrink from the chance of torture. And in
that case the law permitted him, subject to the consent of the
other side, to " redeem his hand " by a composition proportioned
according to the composition for his offence.

The other appeal to God in the Salic Law is the oath of
compurgation. This must not be regarded as forming part of
a strictly judicial proceeding. It was, in its origin and in its
forms, a religious act. It was founded on the firm belief that
perjury would not go unpunished, even in this world, and many
an instance can be culled from Gregory of Tours of men falling
dead as they left the altar with a perjury on their lips, or dying
within a few months. The combined oath was resorted to when
ordinary proof had failed to satisfy the court. The idea that
the " *conjuratores* " came to the trial at the beginning to support
a friend or kinsman by their presence is not supported by the
authorities. Nor are they ordinary witnesses summoned (*mallati*,
manniti) to the *mallus* in ordinary course. A passage in the
Salic Law runs thus : " If a Roman is charged with having
robbed a Frank, and has no certain proof, he may release himself
from the charge by means of 25 *conjuratores*, *i.e.* men who will
together with him take a solemn oath that he is innocent. If
he is unable to find such persons, he must either submit to the
ordeal of boiling water or be judged liable for 62 *solidi*." In
other similar clauses the number of *conjuratores* varies from
20 to 65. It appears from these clauses that the ceremony of
the combined oath was resorted to when formal judicial proceedings had failed to elicit the facts, and, duly performed with
the prescribed number of *conjuratores*, it at once relieved the
defendant from the charge under which he lay. It is further to

be observed that such a method of release was open to a Roman as well as to a Frank. From the Ripuarian Law and the judicial formulæ of the time we discern fuller and more explicit information than that conveyed by the Salic Code. It appears that the combined oath was appealed to not only in cases of alleged crime, but in civil causes, to determine a question of free birth, or of succession to an estate. Sometimes, as when personal status or freedom was involved, the Law required that the nearest relatives of the party involved should join him in the oath, inasmuch as such a question affected the family as a whole. In other cases they had to be *similes*, *i.e.* men of the same social condition, or neighbours, or actual eye-witnesses of the facts in dispute. But the Salic Law recognises that sometimes it may not be easy to find the required number, and accordingly an interval of as many as forty-two days may be allowed for their assembling. It is also recognised that it may be impossible to produce the required number. Even if a man whose life was at stake, or who had a direct pecuniary interest in the result, were ready to perjure himself, he might not find it so easy to produce twelve, twenty, or sixty persons who, with little or no personal interest at stake, would be equally willing to incur the possible, or even probable, judgement of God and the saints on those who invoked them to witness to a lie. For the proceedings were surrounded by all the circumstances calculated to arouse the conscience and impress the religious imagination. It was no ordinary conventional oath which was required. Although the phrase in the Ripuarian Law, " *In haraho conjurat* ", is obscure, it is clear from other authorities and other passages in that Code itself that the scene of the ceremony was a church. There, in a church designated by the court, and on an appointed day, the party implicated, along with the required number of *conjuratores*, appeared, and with hands laid on the altar they all took the required oath by the holy place and the guardianship of the saints whose relics lay beneath. The act was attested and recorded by those present in a solemn form, which in many cases has come down to us, and which enables us to fill in details that are omitted in the Salic Law. If, on the contrary, the party concerned failed to appear at the time and place appointed, the fact was recorded, and his cause was *ipso facto* lost. It will now be clear that the combined oath was a religious rather than a judicial act, although it was performed by judicial order. Just as in the ordeal, it is an appeal to the judgement of God, with the risk of heavy punishment for daring falsehood.

It has been said that the Salic Code was framed for a peaceful agricultural society only disturbed by thefts of cattle, raids on quiet granges, or private blood-feuds and violent assaults. That is generally true, and it is somewhat surprising if we recall that in the years when the Code was drawn up the Salic tribe, so far as fragmentary tradition allows us to see, were steadily advancing to the south-west, and that their early kings were men of war. But when they came to settle on the fertile lands on the Scheldt and Moselle, their chief object must have been to secure a tranquil, prosperous life beside their Gallo-Roman neighbours. They were a keen and greedy race, fully appreciating the possession of lands and flocks and herds, and eager for such wealth as these could yield. But a closer inspection of the Law will show that war is only in the background, and that the tribe is a race of warriors. Thus the manumission of a *lidus* (vassal) in the field costs the offender 100 *solidi*. The killing of a freedman in the field is punished by threefold composition, and an enormous penalty is imposed for the murder of a king's *antrustio*. To reproach a man with having thrown away his shield in battle is also severely dealt with.

But in the Law the Franks are chiefly seen in their farms and country houses (*villae*). The *villa* of North-eastern Gaul in the fifth century is Roman, not Teutonic, in name and meaning. Alike in classical Latin and in that of Sidonius Apollinaris, it means a country house or farm. And in Merovingian Latin, *villa* and *ager* are often synonymous. It was, in fact, the old Gallo-Roman estate before the conquest, which corresponds to the modern château and village and rural commune in one. Everything points to an unbroken continuity from the Gallo-Roman to the Frank régime on rural estates, and the very name of the ancient *villa* is in many instances perpetuated in the names of modern villages and communes, some of them evidently derived from the names of Roman masters, while others are probably of German origin, although in some cases even these may be older than the invasions of the fifth century. It is noteworthy that the term *vicus* never occurs either in the Salic or the Burgundian law. In Gregory of Tours, and in private instruments of sale and donation in that age, *vicus* repeatedly stands for *villa* as the domain of a private master. There are indeed *vici* which were evidently villages or groups of cottages inhabited by serfs and tenants, but they were almost always included in the limits of the great estate, and formed a part of its organisation. In the French laws, as in the charters of this period, the *villa* is a property, generally of one person, bought or sold or donated, with everything included in its territorial limits, and even its population of freemen, slaves, and coloni. The centre of this rural domain is the lord's mansion, the old *praetorium* of Roman writers, like the Avitacum or Prusianum of the letters of Sidonius.   Around it were grouped various buildings, the mill and granary, the oil- and wine-presses, and rooms for all domestic arts and manufactures, along with the quarters of the serfs.   The enclosure is described as a yard or court (*curtis*). Around lay the arable land, the woods and meadows of the lord's peculiar domain, and further off, the farms of free tenants held on payment of rents or stipulated service.

The term *villa* occurs several times in the Salic Law. In one case there is penalty for a violent attack on another man's *villa* in which doors are broken open, the dogs killed, and the inmates beaten and plundered. There is more than one reference to a stranger's coming to settle in a *villa*, and it appears that this could only be done by the King's express permission or the unanimous consent of those already in occupation. From this it has been concluded that the social organisation of the *villa* is that of the mark, and that it was a community holding assemblies and making or enforcing bye-laws for its internal government. There is not a word in the Law to support this theory. It merely says that if one or more of the original occupiers object to the incursion of a stranger, he must withdraw, and the objector is provided with a legal remedy if he obstinately refuses ; and it is to be noted that the rubric of the emended law implies that the *villa* is the property of one man. But even those who see in this a survival of the mark system, are obliged to admit that, as regards land holding, that system had passed away. With the growth of population, the improvement in the methods of tillage, and the growing skill and ambition

of some farmers as compared with others less capable and
energetic, the common system was bound to give way to separate
and permanent ownership. The old system, already profoundly
changed, could not survive the conquest and the settlement on
lands owned and organised for centuries under Roman law.
How the Frank conquerors came into possession of their farms
or estates in Flanders and Gaul remains a matter of mystery or
of learned theory. It may have been in some cases the result of
gradual settlement and infiltration, going on for generations ;
in others, of fierce and sudden seizure, or of peaceful and amicable
partition of the revenue of estates, as in Burgundy, between the
invaders and the old owners. There is no record of any formal
division of lands among the conquerors. But public lands
belonging before the conquest to the Roman fisc may have been
granted by Clovis or his sons to their leading warriors, as in
hagiography they are said to have been granted to great churchmen. In any case there seems to be little trace of any hard and
cruel treatment of the old Gallo-Roman proprietors. If they
suffered, their complaints have not come down to us, and the
story of great houses in Sidonius and Gregory of Tours leaves
the clear impression that they felt little change in their material
fortunes in the convulsions of the fifth century.

The Burgundian Code is a more satisfactory and fruitful
source for a picture of society in Gaul after the fall of the Western
Empire than the Salic Law. Its date and authorship can be
more definitely ascertained. Although it probably gives effect
to an older body of custom or prescription, it is a distinct body
of legislation issuing from a known political authority within the
limits of tolerably certain dates, and it has for its principal
object the regulation of the relations of Gallo - Romans and
Burgundians, and, in a separate Code, the relations of the
Romans among themselves. For there are two bodies of Burgundian laws. The *Liber Constitutionum*, under the authority
of Gundobad and Sigismund, is a law for both the German
invader and the old population. The *Lex Romana*, like the
Lex Alarici, for the Visigothic kingdom, is for the dealings and
controversy of Gallo-Romans among themselves. The former of
the two codes conveys the legal commands of the Burgundian
kings : it issues from an existing political power. The *Lex
Romana* is an abbreviated and edited record of Roman Law,

derived from the Theodosian Code and the commentaries and opinions of the great jurists.   It follows the order of " titles " in the *Liber Constitutionum*, and was probably compiled by order of Gundobad from purely Roman sources after the issue of his own code for both populations.   But the question of priority has little interest unless to illustrate the conflicting conclusions which German scholars can draw from the same materials.

The same diversity of view is seen as to the composition and date or dates of the other Code, which we may distinguish as the Burgundian.   According to Gregory of Tours, it was issued as a politic measure of conciliation to win the support of the Roman population when the Burgundian power was threatened by the Franks about the year 500 B.C.   Some modern critics would throw it back some years, 480–490, soon after Gundobad had returned from Rome and regained his throne in Burgundy. There are definite dates, *e.g.* 502, 517, 523, indicated in the Constitutions themselves.   There are also references to *constitutiones parentum*, and to civil suits pending in the year of the Hun invasion, 451.   There are also laws correcting or supplementing earlier enactments, *i.e. novellae.*   And there is a body of *constitutiones extravagantes*, which either contain remnants of earlier enactments or others later than Gundobad's reign.   The Preface evidently was composed at two different dates, and refers to two publications, one by Gundobad, the other by Sigismund.   We shall probably find the safest conclusion, though one far from certain, if we hold modestly that Gundobad issued the first edition about 501, that a second, with additions and amendments, appeared in 517, and that further additions were made as late as 523.

When the Burgundian Code was first issued by Gundobad, his people had been for more than three generations on Gallic soil.   They had crossed the Rhine in the great invasions of the beginning of the fifth century.   In 438 they had pushed their advance as far as the modern Metz and Toul, where they were thrown back for a time by the fiery energy of Aetius.   A few years later they had resumed their progress, and by 443 they had established themselves on the Isère.   Of a milder nature than most of the German tribes, their chiefs seem to have been readier to cultivate peaceful relations with the Empire, and the Empire, in its growing anxieties and waning force, was equally willing to enlist them as its officers and defenders, and to welcome their people as its " guests ". And so the Burgundians, along with the Visigoths of Aquitaine, lent the support of their warriors to withstand the cataclysm of the Hun invasion in 451. A few years afterwards, 456, the Burgundians had moved on to the region of the Saône and the territory of Lyons, in the reigns of Gunderic and Chilperic I. It was when they were settled in that region of the Saône and Rhone that Gundobad, a very able prince, with peculiar experience of the Roman world, tried to consolidate and harmonise the discordant elements in his realm by a code of laws.

Gundobad was the grandson of Gundicar, who had fallen in the battle of Châlons, and was one of four brothers who were at perpetual feud. One of them, Chilperic II., the father of Queen Clothilde, seized the sole sovereignty, and banished his brothers Gundobad and Godegesil. Gundobad, who was a nephew of Ricimer, found an asylum and high place at Rome in the last years of the Western Emperor and was raised by his uncle Ricimer to the patriciate in the reign of Anthemius, and on the death of Ricimer succeeded for a brief space to his power. But the recovery of his rights in Burgundy seemed more alluring than the precarious position of regent of the falling Empire. On his return he dethroned and murdered his brother Chilperic and banished Chilperic's daughters, Chrona and Clothilde. His brother Godegesil shared his power. The Burgundians, like the Gothic tribes, were devoted Arians, while their Gallo-Roman neighbours were Catholics. And, although the Queen of Chilperic and his two daughters were Catholic devotees, Gundobad, as Gregory records, withstood stoutly all the dialectic and diplomacy of Bishop Avitus.

As in Aquitaine so in Burgundy, there was a great conspiracy engineered by the Church in favour of the Frank powers. Godegesil seized the chance to invoke the aid of Clovis against Gundobad, and for a moment succeeded. But the end of the struggle was fatal to him, and although Gundobad had for a time to stoop to be a tributary of Clovis, by force of will and diplomacy he shook off the yoke, and secured the independence of Burgundy for more than a quarter of a century. Probably the most effective means of re-fortifying his power was the Code which he had framed, as Gregory says, to prevent the official oppression of his Gallo-Roman subjects. For it must have been clear to a man of great ability like Gundobad, who must have learnt many lessons during his exile at Rome, that he must come to terms with the old provincials of his realm. They were far more numerous than his Burgundians, who, like the Visigoths and the Franks, were a mere fraction of the Gallo-Roman population. Moreover, the Romans still possessed great landed wealth and had a monopoly of that intellectual culture which, although decadent, had still a strange power over the young barbarian races. Just as in Auvergne and Aquitaine, there must have been a large number of the senatorial class living on their villae, with broad estates cultivated by serfs and tenants. This class was bound together by a collective pride of race, official rank, and culture, which might be an invaluable support if friendly, or a serious danger if it became sullen, offended, and disloyal. The recent troubles had revealed that Franks were fighting in the army of Godegesil, along with Romans of the senatorial class. Gundobad saw that the danger must be met by statesmanship and politic concession. And he could command the services of Roman jurisconsults in framing a code which should secure pure administration and establish a rule of equal justice between the two races.

Unlike the Salic Law, the Burgundian Code is a body of formal legislation framed by skilled jurists like the accomplished Leo, who lent his legal skill to Euric at Toulouse. Gundobad or Sigismund frame their enactments "by and with the advice and consent" of their grand council, inspired by "the love of justice and the desire to secure the welfare and peace of their peoples". The administrative and judicial service is numerous and organised in various ranks of great dignitaries—counts, councillors, domestics, and mayors of the royal house, chancellors and counts of cities, whether Burgundian or Roman, and deputy judges. The Preface sets forth the benevolent purpose of the king to secure the just and incorrupt treatment of every class of his subjects by means of laws regulating causes between Burgundian and Roman, and another code for suits between Romans according to Roman law. All judges and officials of every rank are sternly forbidden to solicit or receive any gift or promise of recompense for a decision. The judge proved guilty of accepting a bribe, even if his decision is just, may be punished with death. Illegal or negligent decisions, even without any taint of corruption, and the wilful refusal or delay of judgement, render the offender liable to a heavy fine. The emphasis and fulness with which official corruption or negligence is condemned seem to show that there was much to amend in official conduct in Gundobad's realm.

In the authoritative tone of a supreme civil power the Burgundian Laws, like those of the Ripuarian Franks, show a marked difference from that of the Salic Law, which is mainly a record of legal custom, more or less ancient. Moreover, the enactments of the Burgundian kings seem to reflect the tone and structure of a more civilised and advanced society, in which social relations are more complex and various. They are more precise, and at the same time display a wider outlook and a more reflective and scientific jurisprudence. While civil enactments and procedure occupy only one-sixth of the compass of the Salic Law, in the Burgundian they have nearly one-half assigned to them. A large number of these deal with wills, succession to property, contracts, donations, married women's property, and on the form of some of these articles the influence of Roman law may be clearly seen. The penal code is about equally divided between crimes of violence and offences against property. And here another important difference from the Frank laws may be noticed. In the Salian law pecuniary compensation is almost universal : other punishments are almost unheard of. In Burgundy, besides the pecuniary sanction, there are many and various punishments for crime, some of them even harsh and cruel. This, however, it has been observed, does not prove a less civilised social tone, but rather the reverse. The Burgundian legislator, in fact, is striving to abolish the vindictiveness of private conflicts by making the State the avenger of personal wrongs. And so he deals out a greater variety of penalties, and sentence of death is frequent, while the apparently growing practice of clandestine composition, without the cognisance of a judge, is restrained.

There is hardly a trace of German ideas or institutions in the legislation of Gundobad. He has no resemblance to the old German chief, surrounded by his assembled warriors. His type and model is the political authority wielded by the Emperor or the great Praetorian Prefects. Like the Emperor, he is sur-

rounded by a council of grandees and high officials to advise and
assist him. Almost from their first appearance in Gaul the
Burgundian kings had borne the character of great Roman
officers, Prefects, Patricians, or Masters of the Forces, rather
than chiefs of a German tribe. And the residence, during his
exile, of Gundobad at Rome must have cultivated in him the
instinct for civilised government on the Roman model. Sidonius
seems to regard his Burgundian neighbours as friendly and good-
natured conquerors. And we derive the same impression from
the Burgundian Code. In this Code, it is true, there are three
social grades sharply marked off from one another, especially
in the different value attached to human life in each, the
noble, the bourgeois, and the lowest class. But there is
absolutely no trace of the legal superiority of the conquerors
which is stamped on the face of the Salic Law. The life of a
Gallo-Roman is as sacred and valued as high as that of a
Burgundian. Again and again it is laid down that precisely the
same rules hold for the two races. A Roman litigant, who seeks
the patronage of a Burgundian, loses his suit, and the Burgundian
who grants his support in such a case is fined. If a Burgundian,
when asked for hospitality by a passing traveller, seeks to impose
him on a Roman neighbour, he is made to pay for his churlish-
ness and arrogance. Burgundians are forbidden to intermeddle
in litigation between Roman landholders in questions of boundaries. Any forcible and quarrelsome entry into another's house,
whether German or Roman, is liable to the same fine. A Roman
girl who marries a Burgundian without her parents' consent,
shall lose any rights of inheritance from them, an enactment
clearly aimed at overbearing conduct by a Burgundian wooer.

But the justice and fairness of the invaders is perhaps most
clearly manifested in the regulations as to landed property.
The partition of estates between the conquerors and the conquered is never alluded to in the Salic Law. It is more than
doubtful whether any wholesale assignment of Gallo-Roman
estates to Franks ever took place. Many of the Frank warriors
of Clovis had by gradual infiltration acquired properties in
Belgic Gaul to which they returned after the conquest. Clovis
probably made over to leading warriors, as benefices, public lands
which had belonged to the Roman government. In other cases,
lands may have passed by purchase into Frank hands, like the

holding of Paulinus, of the "Eucharisticos", at Bordeaux. There
was probably great variety and confusion in the land settlement
under the various incursions of the German tribes. In Burgundy
there appears to have been a peaceful division by which the
Burgundian was accepted as a *hospes* and co-proprietor with the
old Gallo-Roman owner. This is treated as an established fact
in the law. The proportion of two-thirds of the land and one-
third of the slaves which the Burgundian " guest " may hold is
definitely laid down, and further demands and encroachments
are forbidden. One half of the woodland and orchard is secured
to the Roman holder. But part of the estate was often held in
common. In such a case either of the joint owners could
demand an equal division of it. The Burgundians appear to
have had little taste for country life, and frequently to have
wished to sell their share of the common holding. In such
cases, the law requires the vendor to sell by preference to his
Roman partner, who might thus restore the original integrity
of the estate. Another enactment dwelling on the growing tendency of the Burgundians to alienate their allotments, confines
the right of sale to the man who has more than one holding.
Finally, it is clear from another law that the partition of Roman
estates was not finally closed with the settlement of the Germans
in the country, but was still proceeding from time to time at the
beginning of the sixth century. The Code puts a final term to
this process, and places beyond question all existing tenures.
The object of the legislator throughout is, while guarding the
position of Burgundian settlers, to protect also the rights of
Romans against fresh encroachments, and to promote harmony
and community of interest between the two peoples.

The Code gives a picture of a rural society untroubled by
war, and although occasionally disturbed by private acts of
greed or violence, on the whole, securely settled on firm lines.
The arable lands, meadows, and vineyards are all marked out,
fenced, and held in private ownership. There is not a trace of
lands held or tilled in common by the people of a district. Even
the woods are held in private ownership. For there is a law
permitting a farmer who does not happen to have wood on his
holding, to cut timber for his uses in a neighbour's forest, with
the exception of pines and fruit trees. It is evident that in yet
unappropriated land between two estates, fresh land is being

taken into cultivation, with equal rights to both proprietors, and new vineyards are being planted in forest clearings. Some estates, and especially the royal manors, were of an extent with which we are acquainted in the Theodosian Code. They are farmed by coloni and slaves, and managed by *actores* or *conductores*. It would rather dimly appear from one enactment that the lives of these agents were often in danger, and that there had been delay and uncertainty in bringing the malefactors to justice. The law is now made severe and decisive ; any freeman, Burgundian or Roman, who kills an agent, unless under necessity of self - defence, is to be heavily fined. If a slave commits the crime, without the cognizance of his master, he is condemned to death. Another clause makes it evident that the agent often provoked his fate by his own violence. The character of these agents we know was often low and untrustworthy, and the law reveals more than one possible cause of feuds and disputes with them. For instance, runaway slaves were often harboured and concealed by the agents of other estates, whether with or without the privity of their master, and several enactments minutely provide for the punishment of this offence and for the interception of fugitives.

Just as in the time before the conquest, labour of all kinds is chiefly carried on by slaves, who, indeed, generally in the ancient world, represent our free labouring and artisan classes. The value of slaves, as we learn from the tariff of composition for killing them, varied greatly according to their different aptitudes and industries. Thus an ordinary agricultural slave or swineherd was rated at 30 *solidi*, a carpenter at 40, a smith at 50, while the value of a slave skilled to work in gold or silver, ranges from 100 to 200. The rewards for intercepting the escape of servants so valuable are high, and also the penalties for sheltering them or helping with food, or directing them on their flight. And it is little wonder that the Burgundian slave should try to escape from his thraldom. For not to speak of their hard, unrewarded toil, under agents whose character we have described, their offences were punished with a disproportionate cruelty. A theft of cattle, which a freeman could compound for by paying three times their value with a fine of 12 *solidi*, if committed by a slave, was punished by 300 strokes of the club. If a freeman knocked out the teeth of another in a quarrel, the assault was atoned for in cash according to the rank of the injured person. If a slave were guilty of such an act, he lost a hand, while a similar assault on a slave cost only 2 *solidi*. In assaults on women, the *ingenuus* could compound in money : the slave for similar offences might receive 200 blows of the club, or even be put to death. If a slave inveigled a girl of free birth into marriage, both had to die. In the dry concise prescriptions of these laws, we can almost see these poor wretches trying to escape from their miseries on their masters' horses through the woods of the Jura, into the country of the Alemanni ; sometimes plundering on their way, sometimes asking for bread or to be helped across a river, or offering their service to the agent of a remote estate. Yet many of them were men of skill and business capacity who often established themselves in some trade, as goldsmiths, tailors, or shoemakers, with the consent of their master and probably to his profit. For the master in such cases is made responsible for money borrowed by the slave tradesman.

There is a pleasant realism in the Burgundian Code which will stimulate even sluggish imaginations. The features of country life are pretty much the same as those which we have observed in Toxandria among the Salian Franks. Cattle and bees and horses are being stolen from prosperous farms. Herds of swine are breaking into cornfields and vineyards, or they are straying far and are impounded. But the farmer who detains them is liable for compensation, if notice is not sent to the owner, and for all loss to him during their detention if he has not been informed. Horses and draught animals were constantly straying, and no one was bound to stop them. But if a man found them damaging his property, after due notice, in three days he might drive them away. It is interesting to note that such strayed animals are no longer, as required by former laws, to be handed over to the king's *pueri*, who appear often to have abused their trust, and to have appropriated the animals which they were bound to return to their owner.

In such a society, with numbers of fugitive slaves and broken men roaming through wild country, and in the absence of any organised rural police, it is not surprising that brigandage was common. It is the same condition of society as that depicted in the Theodosian Code, the letters of Symmachus, and the poems of Ausonius. If highwaymen exercised their craft near the gates of Rome or Bordeaux, as they did in the fifth century, they would have as free a hand certainly on the roads to Geneva, Dijon, or Lyons in the year 500. Even the royal messengers, engaged in levying the dues of the courts, were not exempt from the danger of assault and plunder by these desperadoes of the road. In such cases threefold satisfaction is exacted. But, with a curious candour, the royal jurist reminds his wandering officers that they must not themselves be guilty of illegal demands. The financial servants of the kings of Burgundy, like those of the last emperors of the West, evidently knew how to add to their salaries in collecting the dues of the state. That brigandage, in spite of all the menaces of the law, was still rampant appears from a *novella*, probably of Sigismund (and later than the clause xxiv. of the Lex Romana). In this enactment, not only is the robber himself liable to death for his crime, but his wife and his sons, above the age of fourteen, as being almost certainly privy to his crime, are adjudged to be the slaves of the plundered man.

With the organisation and external appearance of a tolerably advanced civilisation, the peoples of Burgundy, in the fifth century, were evidently prone to personal quarrels and acts of impetuous violence. And it is noteworthy that an earlier enactment against such offences is sometimes repeated and strengthened. Almost every kind and degree of violence is catalogued with exhaustive ingenuity. The grade of the culprit and of the injured party, the part of the body injured, the amount and manner of the force employed—all these details, with other circumstances, are to be considered in graduating the punishment. Merely to draw a sword by way of menace is naturally punishable at such a time. Blows with stones, clubs, or fists are atoned for according to the social grade of the injured party by a fine or composition for each blow. A single blow of a slave's fist incurs 100 strokes of the cudgel. To seize a freeman by the hair with one hand costs 8 *solidi*, with both hands, 10. Cutting off a woman's hair, or knocking out her teeth are rightly punished with severity. But one cannot help wondering how the victim of one of these outrages could be trusted to notice or remember all these minute particulars, whether the assailant used one hand or two, or whether the assailant was a freeman.

petty trader, or a slave. Certainly the judges had a difficult
task set them to deal with the evidence of excited people on such
bewildering details.

The Burgundian law is honourably characterised by a chivalrous care for the honour and purity of women of rank. It may
be doubted whether the most modern legislation in this field has
quite reached the same level. In some of these enactments the
influence both of the Roman law and the Catholic Church can
be clearly traced. Still, the whole tone as to the status of women
shows that the Germans of the conquest cherished the ideal of
female purity, which was one of their distinctions in the eyes of
Tacitus. The ravisher of a girl, if he is unable to pay the composition, is to be handed over to her parents to be dealt with,
probably in no very gentle fashion. The slave who violently
attempts a free woman's chastity, is capitally punished ; if the
girl has consented to her seduction by a slave she shares his
fate. The virtue of the slave girl is jealously guarded both
against freeman and fellow slave. The latter might receive 150
strokes for his offence. The incestuous adulteress became a royal
slave. Both the man and woman caught in adultery might be
put to death. A woman divorcing her husband is punished in
the old Teutonic way described by Tacitus. A man may not
divorce his wife, except for one of three causes recognised in
Roman law, viz., adultery, witchcraft, or the violation of tombs.

There are other sections of the code on donations, inheritance,
and women's property after second nuptials which bear many
marks of a highly civilised and orderly society, and, here and
there, the impress of Roman jurisprudence. The old law of
equal succession of sons, and, failing male heirs, of the right of
the daughter, is reaffirmed. The succession in case of intestacy
is regulated. The practice of arbitrarily cutting off a son from
his rights of inheritance is sternly reprobated. The power and
suggestion of the Church are seen in the provision that a daughter
who has taken the veil inherits one-third of the patrimonial
estate. The " undutiful " freedman, in accordance with Roman
law, may be recalled to his former state of servitude. Loose
practice with regard to attestation of wills, donations, and
manumission is corrected. And the lawgiver requires either full
documentary record of the transaction, or the presence of seven
or five witnesses after the Roman precedent. There is one

article of the Code which reveals the care that in those days was
necessary as to the truth and weight of evidence. It is one of
the few with a definite date, and was given at Lyons, on May 28,
according to the Consul, of the year 502. In his preamble, the
king says that the law has been called for by the growing practice
of " tendering oaths on matters which were uncertain, and of
constant perjury on things known ", and he legalises and regu-
lates the " judgement of God in combat ", as a substitute for the
discredited ceremony of compurgation. And, in order to bring
home to the would-be perjurers that, after all, perjury may be
expensive, the witnesses on the losing side in the judicial combat
have to pay a heavy forfeit. This is one of the few passages in
the laws reminding us that the Burgundians were warriors as
well as farmers. A great authority of the last century maintained that " judicial combat " was in its origin simply an early
effort to regulate the violence of private vengeance, when pecuniary composition had failed, and the idea of its being an appeal
to the judgement of God to decide a cause in which human testimony had failed was a later theory of the mediaeval Church.
However that may be, the words of this law, *Deo judicante*,
leave no doubt as to the view of the lawgiver of 502.

The purpose of this chapter is not to make an exhaustive
examination of the German codes. That would occupy a
volume. Our object rather is to draw from these dry records
of legal custom or enactment whatever may enable a curious
inquirer into social history to form some conception of the
everyday life in Gaul on the eve of the Frank conquest. We
have been so much accustomed to sounding phrases about the
sweeping advance and ruinous devastations of the invaders of
the Empire, that the real condition of the conquered Romans is
apt to be ignored or misunderstood. The chronicles of the time
are curt on such subjects and unsatisfying, compiled by men
who had no wide outlook on the world, with very scanty and
imperfect sources of information, and no critical instinct or
training. The Romans, who might have left some fuller and
truer record of the time, from various causes, are strangely silent.
It is a marvel that at one of the greatest crises in the history
of man, when young nations were struggling to their birth from
the expiring agonies of Roman civilisation, none of the cultivated
race found the inspiration to describe this period of transition in

any worthy way. Therefore the later inquirer has to make the best of fragmentary glimpses of that time of change. And it is the temptation of the scholar, meditating on such very vague and unsubstantial materials, to exaggerate the certainty of con- clusions, and to erect theory and hypothesis into real historical fact. The one great check on such laudable, but often reckless, reconstruction of an obscure past, is the solid, although limited, and sometimes obscure, evidence of the legal documents which have come down to us. In concluding this rapid survey of the Burgundian laws, we have ample evidence that, in spite of many signs of violence, cruelty, and cupidity among the population, the rulers were making an effort to carry on the great Roman tradition of social justice and order. Their great object was to guarantee purity and fairness in administration, and absolute equality of the two races in the eye of the law, to crush the still exuberant forces of greed and violence, and, by a rigid term of prescription, to give fixity and security of tenure and to limit litigious strife. The Code is a gratifying testimony at once to the enduring tradition of Roman justice and to the humanity and fairness of the invaders. It is true that life in Eastern Gaul was not quite idyllic in those days. There was much crime and violence throughout Burgundy in general, as there was in the royal house. But on the mere evidence of a criminal code one may easily paint too dark a picture of any period of history. We are always too apt to seize on startling facts emerging in sharp sudden outline from the grey monotonous level of ordinary existence, to exaggerate their importance, and frame rash generalisations on what is merely sporadic and exceptional. People are constantly doing this about our own times. Un- fortunately it can be done with more impunity about a distant past whose relics may be few and only preserved by the strange caprice of time. In all ages the criminal law-maker has generally to deal with a minority who are only restrained by fear of punishment, not with the great mass who quietly and uncon- sciously conform to conventional rules or to deep-seated and hereditary moral sentiment. We should think not only of what a code condemns, but of the moral tone behind it which dictates and gives force to its mandates. And after all, these laws, as we rise from their study, leave on the mind the impression that Burgundy was generally a peaceful and happy land. There is a prevailing air of prosperous industry or genial sport over those villae where meadow, rich cornfield, and vineyard, all well enclosed, ran up to the virgin forest, in which herds of swine fattened on the oak-mast, or the hunter trapped the wolf or chased the stag and wild boar. The vineyards, famous for so many centuries, were spreading in forest clearings, and their wealth was carefully guarded day and night. But all fences and guardianship could not ward off the invasion of vagrant herds and excited horses breaking into the fields, and followed by their anxious keepers. Towns and villages are never mentioned, although of course there were flourishing cities on the rivers and lakes. Inns there were none. But the traveller, whether a simple stranger or officer of the court, could by law claim hospitality and forage for his team, under a heavy penalty for churlish treatment by the insolent agent on a remote estate. Or at nightfall a fugitive slave might crave a meal and a night's shelter, or even lawlessly seize and mount a horse in the paddock, or unmoor the boat at the ferry and take it to the other bank. The peace of the remote grange would now and then be ruffled by the rumour of a travelling merchant plundered by outlaws on the great road, or of a sudden fire spreading over the autumn cornfield, or of the murder of a steward by the slaves on a lonely estate. Or again there would be gossip about some quarrel between a Roman and a Burgundian farmer as to their proper shares in the cornland or woodland. Perhaps they came to blows dealt savagely. But in the end the cause came peaceably before the count on his progress. There might be talk that he was under the influence of a great German noble in the neighbourhood, or that a present from a Roman patron had opportunely arrived at his quarters. But such things after the issue of these laws became dangerous.

There is in this code little trace of the growing power of the Catholic Church, which is so marked in the Ripuarian and Visigothic Codes. In Burgundy the old Arian heresy still made a bold front against even great prelates like Avitus. Gundobad stoutly withstood all his blandishments and dialectic, although in the royal family there was a serious defection from the creed of the tribe. Therefore we do not expect to find that the Church has had much share in moulding the laws of Gundobad or the customs of his ancestors. There is only one article, probably issued in the reign of Sigismund, and redolent of the Acts of

Councils at that time. It condemns any Jew who assaults a
Christian in any way to the loss of his hand or a fine of 87 *solidi*.
If he raises his hand against a priest of Holy Church, the crime
must be atoned for by death and the forfeiture of the culprit's
estate to the Crown. The rest of the code is, perhaps fortunately,
free from religious inspiration of this kind. Nor is there any
sign of the ascetic movement, as yet spontaneous and unorganised,
which in the reign of Chilperic II. had already begun to penetrate
the solitude of the Jura, and create those " divine abodes " of
which we shall hear more in a later chapter.

CHAPTER III

THE CONQUESTS OF CLOVIS

CLOVIS, according to the Chronicle, was the offspring of an amour of the Thuringian Queen Basina with her exiled guest the Frank Childeric, who had fascinated her. And the annalist might well have added to the tale of his lawless birth that he was a great and illustrious warrior. Although an eminent historian, for the moment forgetting the perspective and dignity of history, has called him a "brutal ruffian", a more cool and sedate judgement must recognise in Clovis the greatest of the Merovingians, and a great maker of history. At the age of fifteen Clovis succeeded to the chieftainship of a small tribe settled amid an alien population. The future of the tribe was dim and precarious. Childeric, it is true, had shown energy and ambition, had pushed his conquests to the Somme, and borne a part in great conflicts in the Loire. But the Salian Franks were still settled about Tournai. Syagrius, as *Rex Romanorum*, still held sway in the region from Soissons to Troyes. The Burgundian king, Gundobad, who had, on his return from Italy, made away with his brother, Chilperic II., now, with the title of Roman Patrician, was master of the territory along the Saône and Rhone. His brother Godegesil ruled the shores of Lake Leman. Alaric, the Visigoth, reigned over an immense territory from the Loire to the Straits of Gibraltar. The Franks at Tournai were only a small band, probably not exceeding 6000 warriors. But the energy of Childeric, and the effective part which he had taken in campaigns against the Visigoths on the Loire, must have created an impression that the Franks were a force to be reckoned with. And the Church in Gaul seems to have perceived very early the chance of using the

Franks against her heretical foes, the Visigoths and Burgundians.
It is difficult now to conceive the fear and hatred which Arianism
then inspired in orthodox Catholics. But the fears and anti-
pathies had some cause. There was a time when it seemed
possible that the creed of Arius might be that of the western world.
The Franks were the only German tribe which had escaped the
taint of heresy. It is true they were still pagan at the accession
of Clovis, and devoted to their old German gods. But such
paganism could not spread among the Gallo-Roman population.
And there seemed to the churchmen to be greater hope of con-
verting a pagan than an Arian. As early as 481, probably before
the death of Childeric, and fifteen years before the conversion
and baptism of Clovis, the terror of the Franks and the intrigues
of the Church had penetrated into Burgundy. In that year,
Aprunculus, the bishop of Langres, was detected by Gundobad in
a plot for calling in the Franks, and he had to fly to Auvergne,
where he became the eleventh bishop of that diocese. A few
years later, two bishops of Tours, Volusianus and Verus, were
suspected of similar intrigues by the Visigoths, and driven into
exile. It is possible that the far-sighted policy of the Roman
clergy aroused and even anticipated the ambition of Clovis. If
a Burgundian bishop, perhaps in the year in which the boy
Clovis came to the throne, could venture to engage in a conspiracy
to call in the Franks against the Burgundian kings, it is probable
that he had behind him the sympathy of the Gallo-Roman
Catholics, who viewed with alarm the predominance of the
heretical German powers in Gaul and were readier to trust
their religious liberty to a pagan Frank than to a Euric or Alaric.

Syagrius had maintained an independent sway in his little
kingdom of Soissons for seventeen years from the death of his father
Aegidius. On his career, except its disastrous close, the Chronicle
is provokingly silent. As to the means by which he guarded
such an isolated position, surrounded by Burgundians, Franks,
and Visigoths, we can only make dim conjecture. The district
which included the cities of Amiens, Beauvais, Rheims, and
Troyes, was in Caesar's time known for its fertility and dense
population, and could put 50,000 warriors in the field. The
Syagrii had ancestral estates at Soissons; Aegidius held the highest
rank in the imperial hierarchy; his son, from being Patrician, was,
on the fall of the Empire, accorded the title of *Rex Romanorum.*

The king of the Burgundians in theory reigned by the same title as the king of the Romans at Soissons. It is very probable that Syagrius is the same as the Syagrius of the letters of Sidonius, who is, half ironically, complimented on his knowledge of the German language and German ways. Such a man, with all the pride and strength of Roman culture, and a great family tradition, might well impress the imagination of races who were still under the spell of Rome. And with Roman arms and discipline, he may have had at his command a military force of better quality than the "loose bands of volunteers or mercenaries" with which Gibbon assumes, although doubtfully, that he had to face the onslaught of the Franks. At any rate, Syagrius accepted the challenge of Clovis to an appointed field of battle in the year 486, when Clovis had been only five years chief of the tribe at Tournai and Arras. Reinforced by the Franks of Ragnacarius at Cambrai, Clovis overwhelmed the Romans in battle, perhaps at Nogent, ten miles north of Soissons. Syagrius fled for refuge to the court of Alaric at Toulouse. His surrender was demanded under a threat of instant war, and, the Visigothic Government, "with their usual timidity", to use the words of Gregory, handed over the fugitive, who, after a short imprisonment, was executed by the command of the Frank king. Here we see the arrogant self-confidence of Clovis, and the weakness of the race which within twenty-one years was to be shattered on the field of Vouglé.

Clovis took over the realm of Soissons, and probably some of his leading warriors obtained estates in that fair region on the Marne and Seine. But it is strange that, as to the land settlement of Clovis after the conquest, the authorities are absolutely silent. The Burgundian and Visigothic conquerors had generally taken over from one-third to two-thirds of the Gallo-Roman farms or estates. The transference was strictly, and not unmercifully, regulated by law. The German might perhaps by choice accept his allotment in wild or forest, leaving the arable portion to the Gallo-Roman "host", or he might offer to purchase a property from the Roman owner. Paulinus of Pella tells us that, when he had lost everything in the first storm of the Visigothic invasion at Bordeaux, he was astonished to receive from an unknown German the price of a piece of his ancestral estate. The absence of any record of an orderly legal assignment of lands to the Frank conquerors has led to the conclusion that the invaders, dispersed over the country, seized by force whatever lands they coveted. It is quite possible that, in the confusion of the times, here and there such violent annexation of estates may have occurred. But there is nothing in our authorities which tends to show that such usurpation was general. The story of the vase of Soissons, in the distribution of the spoils of conquest, shows how sternly Clovis could restrain the reckless cupidity of his followers. He was bound of course to find for his principal warriors a settled home, and some reward for their toils in war. But it is to be remembered that the members of his tribe, at the date of his baptism in 496, probably did not exceed 6000 men, and that some of his Franks would probably return to their original farms or estates in Belgium. Moreover, succeeding to the power of the Imperial Prefect, he had public or vacant lands at his disposal from which grants could be made without loss or damage to private owners. Clovis was a statesman and organiser as well as a warrior. He had to respect the feelings and rights of a Gallo-Roman population, which was highly civilised, and far more numerous and skilled in the arts of life than his Franks.

The years following his first conquests, judging from the organisation bequeathed to his sons, and of which we have a full picture in Gregory of Tours, must have been busy years with Clovis. And there can be little doubt that Clovis wished to win the contented allegiance and good-will of his new subjects. The theory, born of the French Revolution, that the mass of the old Gallic people had been from the first crushed by the arrogance and exactions of the original conquerors, and by the French noblesse who were descended from them, is now seen to be a figment inspired by a political purpose and without any historical foundation. The Gallic people, after the conquest, were never subjected to the degradation and cruel exactions which precipitated the Revolution. There is hardly a sign that the Gallo - Roman population felt themselves impoverished and oppressed. Certainly there was no oppression by a Frank aristocracy of birth, such as the Revolutionary theory assumed. Under the early Frank kings there was no Frank aristocracy, in the sense of hereditary rank. The only aristocracy, as shown in another chapter, was the circle of official dignitaries, surrounding and advising the king, who made and could unmake

them ; a class, moreover, which included from the first men of
the conquered race. In the fratricidal wars of the sons and
grandsons of Clovis the Gallo-Romans served loyally in the
Merovingian armies, and, although they far outnumbered the
Franks, they never once rose against their conquerors. The
two races seem to have speedily coalesced in social and political
union, with no sharp lines of division. The reader of the Lives
of the Saints will remember many cases of Gallo-Roman families,
living in secure possession of their ancestral estates, and following
the routine of social life which is pictured in the letters of
Sidonius Apollinaris. The kingly power, which was the only
power in the sixth century, was exerted equally over both races.
In Gregory of Tours, although there are many tales of fierce
passion and violence, there is hardly a trace of hatred and friction
in the social relations of the two races.   If, here and there, the
Frank Code displays the pride of a conquering race, *e.g.* in fixing
a lower wehrgeld for a Roman than for a Frank, the Roman not
less decidedly and successfully maintains the claims and influence
of the old civilisation of the Empire.   And the Franks readily
adopted and assimilated what was left of the ancient culture.
The German kings, even such masterful rulers as Euric and
Theodoric, had to rely on Roman advisers in the problems of
administration.   And we may be sure that Clovis had also to do
so.   The problem of bridging over the gulf between the new
régime and the old, in judicial procedure and provincial administration, was one that surpassed the skill and experience of the
Frank chief.   The old municipal organisation was, in some of
its features, left unchanged.   Proofs are not wanting that the
Curia retained many of its powers under the Visigoths, Burgundians, and Franks, and that Romans of high rank still gladly
accepted its membership.   Some great Romans, in the perilous
period of the invasions, may have retired for safety to strongly
fortified castles.   But in the time of Clovis and his sons they
seem to have taken their part in public life, both in Church and
State.   The great Churchmen, from the first, were generally of
Roman race.   And Roman names appear with growing frequency
in the great offices of State.   The list would be a long and tedious
catalogue if it were fully recited from the Chronicle.   A few
instances may be given in illustration.   In the reign of Theudebert,
only twenty-four years after the death of Clovis, two Romans,

Asteriolus and Secundinus, stood high in the favour of the king. They were both clever and accomplished men and steeped in the old rhetorical culture of the Roman schools, and one of them was sent as envoy to the Eastern court. In the same reign another man of Gallo-Roman birth, Parthenius, had the dangerous task of imposing fresh taxes on the Franks, and, in spite of the protection of the Church, was stoned to death with the utmost ignominy for his devotion to the Frank king. Of the dukes and counts who were appointed to lead armies or administer municipal districts, with the full confidence of the king, a large number could be enumerated who were evidently of Gallo-Roman birth. In Burgundy, under King Guntram, Romans rose to the highest office. One Celsus, a man, as he is described, tall and strong, of copious powers of speech, and learned in the law, attained the patriciate. Another Roman, Amatus, followed him, and he was succeeded by the greatest of them all, Mummolus, who, by bribery, displaced his own father, Peonius, a count of Auxerre, and, with great strategic genius, threw back the Lombards in three great invasions between 572 and 575.

The chronicler tells us that many wars and victories followed the triumph over Syagrius. But we have no details of these struggles, which were probably long and precarious. In only one case have we a glimpse of light in a conflict in which the Franks seem to have met a decided check. The tradition of it is preserved in a chapter of Gregory's *Glory of the Martyrs*. The Franks of Clovis had been besieging the city of Nantes for sixty days without success. Suddenly, at the dead of night, a procession emerged from the basilica, clothed in white and carrying flashing torches ; and then as suddenly disappeared. At the sight, a panic fell on the Frank army, and, when morning broke, it had fled. Procopius, in a passage, unfortunately, of doubtful reading, seems to refer to the same struggle, and relates how the Armoricans (or Arborychans) defended themselves so stoutly that the Franks were obliged to come to terms with them. It would have thrown a valuable light on the Frank settlement if the terms of this compact had come down to us. But the vague tradition shows at least that the conquest was not always an easy one, and that diplomacy had sometimes to come to the aid of force.

Chilperic II. of Burgundy, who was unpopular and surrounded by intrigue and suspicion, after a fierce conflict, was dethroned and put to death by his brother Gundobad, on his return from Rome. He left two daughters, who, at an Arian court, were devoted to the Catholic faith. Chrona, the elder, embraced the religious life. The second, Clothilde, equally devout, and famous for her charm and fascination, lived in retirement at her uncle's court at Geneva. The Burgundian kings were Arians, but of a milder type than the Vandal and Visigothic kings : they do not appear to have persecuted their Catholic subjects. The Catholic bishops, Patiens and Avitus, held high place and influence at court, could freely debate the doctrine of the Trinity in the presence of the king, and were directors of the queen and princesses. Bishop Avitus seems to have been on intimate terms with Gundobad and even to have thrown a veil over his crimes. Embassies were often passing between the court of Burgundy and Clovis in those years, and tales of the beauty and strong sense of Clothilde were soon carried to his ears. Nor is it improbable that pious intrigue was employed to give a Christian bride to the young pagan conqueror on whose future so much depended for the Church. We have seen that as early as 481, in the reign of Childeric, Aprunculus, bishop of Langres, had been banished by Gundobad for taking the lead in a movement for handing over Burgundy to the Franks. It would not be astonishing, if we knew all the facts, to discover that S. Rémi, in concert with his brethren of Burgundy, had a part in arranging a happy union which might also help to win the Frank race to the cause of Christ. The wooing of Clothilde is only curtly told by Gregory. A much fuller and more romantic tale is given by Fredegarius, who probably resided in Burgundy in the first half of the seventh century. Clothilde and her sister were living at Geneva, engaged in works of charity. They appear to have been carefully secluded, so that the emissaries of Clovis were never permitted to get a sight of the fair princess. At last the Frank king despatched one of his trusted Roman subjects, named Aurelian, disguised as a beggar with a wallet on his back, to find his way into Clothilde's presence, and Clovis gave him his ring to show her as a pledge of his faith. The royal ladies were used to comfort needy strangers with alms and hospitality, and, as Clothilde knelt to wash the supposed beggar's feet, he bent down and whispered in her ear a message from Clovis, offering to make her queen of the Franks, and he gave her the ring as pledge. She rejoiced, we are told, with exceeding joy, and rewarded the envoy with 100 *solidi*. Then placing her own ring in his hands, she bade him return to his master with all speed and tell him to seek her hand from her uncle Gundobad. She added, with strange prudence, that haste was necessary, for a certain Aridius would soon arrive from Constantinople, whose counsels might be fatal to the alliance. Clovis, struck with admiration of the practical sense of Clothilde, followed her advice. Her uncle, who had a fear of the Frank power, readily gave his consent, and Clothilde was formally betrothed in the fashion of the Franks, at a formal *placitum* at Chalon. Her carriage, with all her treasure, was escorted by a band of Frank warriors. On the way, hearing that Aridius had arrived, Clothilde ordered the Frank officers to place her on horseback, in order to make the journey with greater speed. Her instinct was true. Aridius had at once warned his master that this alliance might be the beginning of trouble for Burgundy, since the young queen was sure to demand vengeance on Gundobad for the murder of her father and her brothers. An armed Burgundian force was soon upon her track ; but the princess had already reached the border of the two realms, and, as she passed it, with a ruthlessness strange in one so beautiful and pious, she ordered her escort to lay waste the country for twelve leagues, and, when it was done, she gave thanks to Almighty God that she had seen the beginning of the vengeance for her slaughtered kindred. This was the tale which was afloat in Burgundy about the wooing of Clothilde, and, through the haze of popular romance, we can dimly discern that there were two parties in that kingdom, one favouring alliance with the new Frank power, the other, with good reason, mistrusting it. And it is surely significant that Clothilde had been living at the capital of her uncle Godegesil, who, within six or seven years, had made a secret pact with Clovis. Thirty years afterwards, Clothilde is said to have inspired her sons to crush the independence of Burgundy. Although she began and ended her life as a pious recluse, she was regarded in her time as a far-seeing statesman, guided alike by policy and an undying passion for revenge.

Of the charming tales of the early years of Clovis' reign, his birth and wooing, his conversion and baptism, who can divine the sources or vouch for the authenticity ? The only reply is the subjective impression of the critic. Gregory and the chroniclers tell us nothing of the sources from which their narrative is drawn. The critic is thrown back on the style and time of the narrative. In one passage it may have the curt, arid style of a meagre chronicler such as Prosper or Idatius. In another, it seems to break out into the vivid colouring of a song or epic on heroic deeds. Or again, we may suspect that we have the record of a Roman cleric, with the rhetorical training of his time. From such a hand surely must have come the story of the conversion of Clovis. It was certainly a Roman rhetorician from whom Gregory drew the appeal of S. Rémi : " Mitis depone colla, Sicamber ; adora quod incendisti, incende quod adorasti ". Gregory had enough of the old culture to wish to decorate his page with this antithetic rhetoric : he certainly had not enough to invent it. Of the wooing of Clothilde, and her romantic journey to the court of Clovis, the picturesque details are drawn from Fredegarius, who compiled his Chronicle between 613 and 643, that is more than three generations from these events and one hundred years from the death of Clothilde. The narrative of Fredegarius, according to the best critics, is often drawn from popular tradition which was afloat in Burgundy in his time. The details are so minute and dramatic that they appear to come from eye-witnesses and contemporaries. Nor should we contemptuously discredit such oral tradition. Without oral tradition, great tracts of history would be a blank. How much of the Persian wars in Herodotus, and of the events preceding them for more than fifty years, could have come down to us in any other way ? The tradition in families who have borne a part in great events, and the simple vivid recollection of common people, especially in the ages when written or printed record was almost unknown, may be often faulty and inaccurate ; but in its broad lines it is a precious treasure which should not be contemptuously flung aside. After the triumphs of the Frank house during one hundred years, and the glorious part which the queen of Clovis had borne, we may be sure that the tale of her early years would be preserved and revived, probably with the decorations of popular legend, in the region of her birth.

Probably long before Clovis had come under the charm of Clothilde, he had dimly felt the commanding power of the Church in intercourse with the great bishop of Rheims. In his marches along the " Barbaric way ", he must often have met S. Rémi, and been restrained by his counsels from violent deeds. The Frank warriors, it is true, in the first excitement of the conquest, had pillaged the churches and had not even spared the Cathedral of Rheims. But the king, by the advice or warning of the bishop, restored the famous vase in defiance of an angry warrior at Soissons. Clovis, although like all his race indulging in lawless amours, felt a strong, pure love for his wife, along with a deep respect for her intellect and sagacity. But he still remained a pagan. When the young queen desired her firstborn to be baptized according to the rites of her own faith, her husband reluctantly consented, and listened patiently to a long sermon from his wife, such as might have been delivered to Roman pagans, two hundred years before, by S. Augustine. If she ever spoke in such a strain, Clothilde had evidently learnt her lesson from some pedantic priest who knew only the heathen beliefs of his Roman ancestors. The scandals of classical mythology are flung in the face of a man who believed in Odin, Frieda, and Thor. The king was unmoved by the clerical rhetoric. And when the little Ingomer died a few days after his baptism, Clovis not unnaturally reproached his wife with having submitted to a fatal rite a child who should have been kept true to the gods of his race.

Yet the king, with startling indulgence, permitted a second boy, Chlodomer, to be baptized. Again the child sickened, and the father's fears and reproaches were renewed. But, this time, the infant was saved by the mother's prevailing prayers. Still, for three years after his marriage, Clovis remained staunch in his ancestral faith till in 496 an event occurred which, in its religious consequences, had a far-reaching effect on history. In 496 the Franks had to face a great invasion of the Alemanni, who held the east bank of the Rhine, along the valleys of the Maine and the Neckar and the region of the Black Forest. They were following on the track of the Franks, and pressing across the Rhine to gain a settlement in the wealthy plains of Gaul. The Alemanni made their heaviest onslaught on the district of Cologne, and a few miles west of that town the two armies met

in stubborn battle on the field of Tolbiacum. Even the seasoned
soldiers of the Franks for a time could not withstand the shock,
and all seemed to be lost when Clovis, recalling the lessons of
Clothilde and her priests, with eyes raised to heaven implored
the aid of Jesus, the God of Clothilde, and vowed that if He gave
him the victory, he would believe in Him and be baptized in His
name. The king of the Alemanni fell in battle, and this had
probably as much to do with their defeat as the sudden conversion of Clovis. The Alemanni, left leaderless, gave up the
struggle, and the larger number became subjects of Clovis. An
obstinate remnant retired to Rhætia to be under the protection
of the great Theodoric. Clovis returned to tell Clothilde of the
victory which he had won by the invocation of Christ. She
immediately summoned S. Rémi to confirm the still wavering
devotion of her husband. The Frank king, who was no despot,
had to be wary in the face of his pagan tribe. The bishop had
a secret meeting with Clovis, at which he pressed him with the
" word of eternal safety ". Clovis was willing to accept the
counsel for himself : but he knew that he must also try to draw
his people away from the gods to whom they were blindly devoted.
Divine grace had anticipated his appeal, and his whole people
proclaimed that they had flung away their " mortal gods " and
were ready to "follow the God whom Remigius preached". The
clerical tradition has not unnaturally, in the excitement of an
historical event, overrated the unanimity and enthusiasm of the
Franks in adopting the new faith. Only about half his warriors
followed Clovis to the font. Even after 1400 years we have seen
in our own day a recrudescence of Teutonic loyalty to the " old
German God ".

The pontiff, full of joy at the triumph of the Church, made
stately preparations, in which the Catholic Church has always
been so skilled, to celebrate an event so momentous as the
baptism of the Frank conqueror. And miracle at once began
to consecrate his power. His baptism was heralded by a
miraculous light, a divine voice, and an odour of marvellous
sweetness breathing through the sanctuary. When the priest with
the holy chrism was, owing to the press of people, unable to
approach the baptistery, a dove of snowy whiteness alighted with
the ampullula on his back. The great historic ceremony was
ordered with a pomp and splendour worthy of the occasion, and

is described by Gregory with unusual richness of colour. The " new Constantine " advanced to the sacred laver along aisles hung with pictured tapestry, while fragrant odours, as of Paradise, breathed around. The baptism of Clovis was felt all over the Catholic world to be no ordinary event, one pregnant with immense consequences for the future of the Church. An obscure barbarian chief, fighting for his own hand, sprang at once into the position of the consecrated champion of Catholic orthodoxy against the other German races whose sway had threatened Western Europe with the blight of Arian heresy. Congratulations poured in upon him. The newly elected Pope, Anastasius, sent a special envoy with a letter in which he thanked God for having provided such " a helmet of salvation for the Church " against the assaults of deadly foes. Avitus, bishop of Vienne in the kingdom of Burgundy, who had probably moulded the religious character of Clothilde, and who vainly strove to make a convert of her uncle Gundobad, wrote in a similar strain : " Your faith is our triumph : every battle you fight is a victory for us ". This was an ominous voice coming from a powerful bishop of Burgundy. It was the first loud signal of a vast clerical conspiracy to install the new sons of the Church in Burgundy and Aquitaine.

The motives and feelings which determined Clovis to become a Christian were probably very mixed. His invocation of Jesus in the stress of battle was inspired by the hope that Jesus would give him the succour which his ancestral gods had denied. That materialist motive is not to be imputed to the king as one peculiarly selfish : it penetrates the whole religious sentiment of the time in its attitude to God and the saints. It was the old pagan theory of religion, and to some extent that of the Old Testament, nor unknown in later times, that the Heavenly Powers will reward their faithful servants with temporal blessings, and that they will infallibly punish any wilful neglect to pay them due honour. Prayer and worship are regarded in fact as a kind of barter with the Deity. Clothilde for three years had preached the doctrine that the old gods could give no help or prosperity to their most loyal worshippers. S. Rémi fortified his royal disciple with visions of an empire in succession to that of Rome, which should be the inheritance of the Merovingian race. But the promise is only to the true believer in the Trinity, as defined by Councils. This is the lesson derived from the history of his time by Gregory of Tours. After narrating the conquests of Clovis, he opens his Third Book with a theological lesson. The confessors of the Holy Trinity have won the battle : the Arian heretics have had their reward in ruin in this world and the next. Clovis is master of Gaul : Alaric, the son of the persecuting Euric, has, like Arius, the founder of his heresy, sunk to endless perdition. The Arian kings of Burgundy have lost their country along with their souls. No valour or patriotic statecraft can save a prince from the doom that awaits the slightest lapse from the dogma of Nicaea.

To a religion with such a conception of God, the pagan Clovis found little difficulty in giving his allegiance. Jesus was a stronger Odin : the God of the Old Testament was a God of battles, and took part with His votaries in all their struggles and rewarded them with solid blessings. And yet one may have a doubt whether mere selfish calculation was the sole inspiration of the conversion of Clovis. In spite of his conquests, his position was not an easy one in the conflict of religions. He had to face a real danger and he knew it. The paganism of the Franks was bound up with all their national memories and old associations, and it died hard. According to the tradition only 3000 of his warriors accepted baptism along with Clovis : the rest forsook him for another chief. At Cologne and Cambrai there were two other tribes who were still firmly pagan. And, far into the sixth century, pagan shrines and monuments attracted crowds of devotees, especially in the region of north-eastern Gaul. Towards the end of that century a man from Trèves on a voyage to Italy found that he was the only Christian on board. Paganism was anathematised again and again by the Councils of the sixth century. Therefore the Frank king's abandonment of his old religion, while his power was still unstable, was an act of courage, even if it was also a stroke of ambition. Clovis was often cruel and faithless, like the men of his race and time. But he was not without some generous impulses, and could reverence a virtue superior to his own. He listened to the monitions of S. Rémi even in his pagan days. And his affection for his wife was a powerful influence in working his conversion. Even Gibbon admits that he was inspired by a " transient fervour " when he yielded to the religion of the Crucified. According to

Fredegarius, the tale of the Passion of Christ, when it was told him, roused him to such fury that he exclaimed, " If I had been there with my Franks, I would have avenged His wrongs ". We may be sure that at a court in those days where the queen was a devout Catholic, tales of miracle would be freely circulated, and invest the Christian faith with weird or romantic attractions for a rude untutored spirit. And, in a great leader of men of different races, whose task it was to organise and govern as well as to lead in battle, there may have been some desire to find the secret of that strange strength which, in an age apparently of mere material force, could calmly cultivate the recluse, saintly virtues, and hold its own against worldly power, which could be so gentle without weakness, so strangely imperious without arrogance. And a rude soldier who was called to rule over a race with ancient Christian traditions, might well accept the creed which had moulded them, although his own conduct might fall far short of its ideals.

The brothers Gundobad and Godegesil were joint rulers of the regions along the Saône to the Rhone, and of the district of Massilia. They were both Arians, but they were continually at feud. Godegesil, who probably had the support of the leading Gallo-Romans and the Catholic clergy, opened communications with Clovis to seek his aid in dethroning Gundobad, with a promise to hold the realm of Burgundy as tributary to the Franks. In the year 500, Clovis invaded Burgundy and marched on the famous fortress of Dijon. Gundobad, who had secured the doubtful support of his brother, advanced to meet the Frank army. An engagement was fought on the river Ouche, in which Gundobad, deserted by his treacherous brother, was routed and fled through the marshes to the distant Avignon. Godegesil seemed to have his reward in an easy composition for sole possession of the realm and retired to Vienne. The Frank king, having reinforced his army, pressed on to the south to crush the forces of Gundobad, after the manner of Frank armies, devastating the country on his march. It seemed that Avignon could not long hold the Franks at bay, and Gundobad trembled for his fate. In his despair at the incursion of " these barbarians ", he had recourse to a Gallo-Roman of rank, named Aridius, probably the same man who had warned him against the union of Clothilde with Clovis. Romans of rank had always immense

influence in Burgundy either by strategic or diplomatic skill, and
Aridius, a man of rank, ability, and statesmanlike prudence, was
equal to the crisis. With the approval of Gundobad, he secured
a passage into the Frank lines as a feigned deserter, and was
warmly welcomed by Clovis, to whom he professed boundless
devotion. The cultivated Roman gentleman imposed on simple
warriors by his brilliant conversation, his energetic counsels, and,
strange to say, by his apparent honesty and good faith. He
appealed to Clovis not to detain his army in the siege of a place
so strong, or in destroying the fruits of a region which was now
practically his own. Why not try the surer and less expensive
methods of diplomatic craft ? " Impose an annual tribute on
Gundobad, and, if he should refuse the terms, let him take
the consequences." The terms, of course, were accepted by
Gundobad, and the Frank army retired, leaving, however, a
contingent of 5000 to strengthen the forces of Godegesil. It is
needless to say that Gundobad, having soon rallied his forces,
forgot all about the promised tribute, and marched on Vienne.
The siege was hard pressed, famine threatened, and Godegesil
had to send away some of the inhabitants to husband his supplies.
Among those expelled was the engineer who was in charge of the
aqueduct of Vienne. In those days the aqueduct was often a
point of danger to a beleaguered fortress. The engineer guided
the storming party through the fatal passage and broke through
the obstructions with which he was familiar ; the gates were
opened, the garrison was surprised, and all was lost. Godegesil,
with an Arian bishop, fled for asylum to an Arian church, but
the Burgundian king would not respect even Arian protection,
and Godegesil was slain. His Frank auxiliaries were spared by
special orders of Gundobad, and sent in exile to Toulouse. The
Roman senators and Burgundian supporters of Godegesil were
massacred. Gundobad, undisturbed by Clovis, had a reign of
sixteen years, though the tribute was never paid. Gundobad
had learnt the lesson of the invasion and of the weakness of
Burgundy from divisions and intrigue. The Burgundian Code,
which he issued soon afterwards, and which, as we have seen, is
singularly fair to the conquered Romans, undoubtedly secured
his position and prolonged his reign.

It is difficult, perhaps, to unravel the web of intrigue which
undoubtedly lay behind these puzzling events. Godegesil was

playing a purely selfish part and ready to sacrifice the independence of his country, if he could be sole viceroy of the Franks.
Gundobad was probably an honester man, and had also been
trained by long experience in Rome in the secrets of statecraft,
which included a politic deference to the Church. He was on
friendly terms with bishop Avitus, who wished for the victory of
the Franks, and yet, in one of his letters, he seemed to promise
Gundobad security if he would " obey the law of God ", that is,
if he would turn Catholic. Gundobad replied that he " could
not worship three Gods ". Yet, yielding to the persuasion of
Avitus, he sanctioned a disputation between the clergy of the
rival sects on the Feast of S. Just. It had the usual result of
such discussions where both parties are equally convinced and
equally intolerant. The orthodox bishops assured Gundobad
that his dangers could be easily averted if he would only accept
the Catholic faith. Gregory says he feared his Burgundian
subjects. It is possible that he shrank rather from making an
insincere profession of what to him was an idolatrous faith.
Why Clovis allowed Gundobad to crush Godegesil and reassert
his independence is a mystery, so far as our authorities go.
Visigothic influence in support of Gundobad may have had some
effect on his policy. It is also a probable conjecture that the
attitude of the great Theodoric, who could threaten from Rhætia
the flank of a Frank army, and whose daughter was married to
Sigismund, the heir to the Burgundian throne, may have
suggested to Clovis a policy of caution. For, in those years,
Theodoric was a mighty force all over the West. Hardly seven
years had passed since the capture of Ravenna and the death of
Odoacer. Yet in that short space Theodoric had woven, by
diplomacy and marriage alliances, a vast network of international
influence from Thuringia to Carthage. He was brother-in-law
of Clovis, and of the Vandal king. The king of the Visigoths
and the heir of Burgundy were married to his daughters. His
niece was wife of Hermenefred, the king of Thuringia. It seemed
as if a great league of the Arian conquerors, Visigoth and
Burgundian, Vandal and Ostrogoth, might have checked the
advance of the new champion of the Catholic Church. Theodoric
probably had some such object in view, and would gladly have
forwarded it by a peaceful diplomacy. But the Arian powers
had not the solid organised unity of the Catholic Church.

History shows that the inevitable tendency of non-Catholic opinion is to sporadic division and individualism. Freedom of thought and indifference to the collective opinion of the past necessarily generate a temper unfavourable to combined action in questions of religious belief. Theodoric and Gundobad were tolerant sectaries. In fact, the finest formula of religious toleration comes from Theodoric, the Ostrogoth. The Vandal and Visigothic kings had been the most ruthless persecutors who could have had little sympathy with the temperate policy which Theodoric pursued towards the Church in Italy. Moreover, the Arian powers could not command that trained and supple diplomacy, represented by men like Epiphanius of Pavia and Avitus, which could so powerfully influence even heretic chiefs. The superior organisation of the Catholic clergy gave them an incalculable power in the great events of that age. United in belief, still more united in devotion to their order and to spiritual authority, maintaining constant communication with one another, and fully informed as to the character of great potentates and the feelings of their subjects, they were a subtle, secret, and almost irresistible force. The bishop of a remote and obscure diocese might return from a church council in the fifth or sixth century with the latest and most authentic information as to great movements and great princes, of whom he had only heard before a distant, uncertain rumour. The Arian clergy, as ambitious and as intolerant as the Catholic, had not the same compact organisation binding them together for common aims. They had no conception of a world-wide city of God, absorbing all individual energy and ambition, consecrating its members to a common purpose, above all inspired with the feeling that the future belonged to the Catholic church.

The history of the years between the Burgundian war and the battle of Vouglé is obscure. In 503 or 504, although Gregory gives no hint of such a campaign, it would appear from the letters of Cassiodorus that the Alemanni had once more challenged the Frank, and had been defeated and hard pressed. A section of this people had taken refuge in the province of Rhætia, under the protection of Theodoric, and the great Ostrogoth, who mistrusted the ambition and energy of his brother-in-law, is said to have warned him against pushing his attacks on the Alemanni too far. Theodoric was also watching with

anxiety the growing danger of a collision between Visigoth and
Frank on the Loire, which was in those years becoming more
and more probable to keen observers. The conflict was precipitated quite as much by the Catholic sentiment and the intrigues
of the higher clergy as by the energetic ambition of Clovis. The
action of the higher clergy in Aquitaine against their Arian
rulers was more clear and decided than that of their brethren in
Burgundy. In Burgundy the church, on the whole, was fairly
treated ; the royal house, since the time of Sidonius, had been
divided between the two faiths. But the persecutions of Euric
had embittered the Gallo-Roman Catholics of Aquitaine. The
news of the conversion of Clovis, as we have seen, ran through
the Catholic world, both East and West, with electric speed, and,
along with the fame of the conquests of Clovis, must have
aroused unrest and hope in the Catholics of south-western Gaul.
Clerical intrigue against the hated heretic power of Toulouse
immediately received fresh impetus. The honour of opening the
secret campaign belongs to Volusianus, seventh bishop of Tours.
Soon after 496 he was, on suspicion of treachery to the Visigothic power, deposed from his see and sent into exile in Spain.
He was rewarded by Catholic sentiment with the honours of
martyrdom. Alaric, or his advisers, fully aware of the growing
restlessness of his Roman and Catholic subjects, attempted a
liberal and conciliatory policy. The *Breviarium Alarici*, compiled from the Theodosian Code and the *responsa* of the great
jurists, was a statesmanlike effort to satisfy the Gallo-Roman
population and place the two races on a footing of legal equality.
In 506, with Alaric's sanction, the thirty-four bishops of his
kingdom met in council at Agde, and opened and closed their
session with prayers for the king. It has been suspected, not
without reason, that the council was perhaps quite as much
occupied with plans for smoothing the way for a Frank conquest
of the south, as with questions of doctrine or discipline. Some
of its members soon gave a curious illustration of the sincerity
of their prayers for Alaric. Quintianus of Rodez, in a quarrel
with some of his flock, was charged with plotting to betray the
province to the Franks. The Visigoths resolved to put the bishop
to death. He succeeded in making his escape and took shelter
with Eufrasius, bishop of Auvergne, who endowed him with
lands and vineyards. About the same time, Verus, eighth

bishop of Tours, who succeeded Volusianus, was deprived of his
see and driven into exile, because his loyalty was suspected by
the Visigothic government. Another bishop, Galactorius of
Béarn, actually armed some of his flock, and took the field to
support the advance of Clovis. But, before he had gone far,
he was surprised by the Goths and killed in battle. There
can be no doubt that the chronicler is right in saying that
many of the Gallo-Romans ardently wished to have the Franks
as masters.

Four years before the battle of Vouglé, Alaric became alarmed
by the constant victories of Clovis over neighbouring peoples.
The Thuringi had been among the many allies of Euric, and their
kings were connected with the Visigothic house by intermarriage.
The victory over Syagrius had brought the Franks to the Loire.
The campaign of 499 against Burgundy, although Gundobad had
for the time saved himself by becoming a tributary of Clovis,
was evidently only the prelude to a final conquest of his country.
With those menacing portents before his eyes, and also still
further alarmed by the warnings of Theodoric, who surveyed the
field of Western Europe with a far, penetrating gaze, the weak
Alaric sent envoys to Clovis in 503 to propose a friendly conference. The two kings met on an island of the Loire, and, with
much conviviality, pledged themselves to amity. The friendship
was not very deep or sincere. Theodoric, watching the course
of events with a keen eye, had tried to avert a conflict which
he felt might be disastrous to the Goths. His Quaestor Cassiodorus was instructed to send warnings to the Teutonic kings in
Gaul, and even to the chiefs of the Heruli and Thuringi, urging
them to listen to counsels of peace, as coming from an old man.
Theodoric warned his son-in-law especially that the Visigothic
race, although it had humbled Attila, had since that effort lost
something of its warlike energy in long years of peace. To
Clovis he spoke, almost in tones of menace, bidding him beware
of turning a friendly adviser into a foe. And the other barbarian
powers were advised to combine against a race whose lawless
energy threatened them all alike. Why the warnings of Theodoric were not followed up by any effective action is an unexplained mystery. It has been suggested, with some probability, that Gundobad's active support of the Frank invasion,
by interposing a barrier between Italy and Aquitaine, made the

advance of an Italian army in Alaric's support precarious and difficult. It is also possible that the rapidity of the Frank advance across the Loire left no time for Theodoric himself to appear in the field.

The army of Clovis started with the assurance of divine favour which, in those days, was worth more than military strength. Clothilde advised him to win the divine favour by the foundation of a great shrine in honour of the Holy Apostles. S. Rémi, now the most trusted adviser of Clovis, sent him forth with the benediction of the Church, and assured his coming triumph. S. Rémi had previously warned Clovis to honour the priests of God, by obeying whose counsels his government would be secure. The king followed this advice in the letter and the spirit. Stern orders were issued against any attempt to plunder churches or monastic houses. The territory of Tours and the holiest shrine in Gaul, were especially protected from any violence. The respect of Clovis for the saint of Tours was amply rewarded. The king wished to have some omen of victory, and sent envoys with presents to entreat S. Martin's help. As they entered the basilica at the hour of service, they caught the words of the antiphone : " Praecinxisti me virtute ad bellum et supplantasti insurgentes in me subtus me et odientes me disperdidisti ", and returned with the inspiring news to the king. When the Frank army could not find a crossing over the swollen Vienne, a stag of marvellous size entered the waters and revealed a secret ford. As Clovis was lying in his tent near Poitiers, a globe of fire issued from the church of S. Hilary, and shed a miraculous radiance over the king's quarters. Ten miles from Poitiers, the armies met. Alaric probably intended to play a waiting game, but prudent counsels were set at naught by the impetuous self-confidence of his troops. The nobles of Auvergne, with the son of Sidonius at their head, displayed great gallantry on the Visigothic side, and left many dead upon the field. But it is probable that the Gallo-Roman soldiers of Alaric, in general, were not very staunch in a conflict with the new Catholic power for whose advent, according to Gregory, they had been praying. The clerical chroniclers, who regarded miracles as more important than strategy, give us hardly any incidents of a conflict on which the future of Gaul depended. We only know that Alaric was slain in single combat by the hand of Clovis himself, and that Clovis was only saved from the lances of two cavaliers of the Goths by the temper of his corslet and the speed of his horse.

After the victory the Frank army then divided and took two different routes to the south. One, under Theuderic, the eldest son of Clovis, marched through Eastern Aquitaine to Albi and Rodez. Then turning north he entered Auvergne, where he joined forces with the Burgundian Gundobad in a campaign to annex the cities in the Rhone valley and on the Durance. Little resistance seems to have been offered to their advance. But, like all the Frank armies of the time, they left a trail of ruin and misery behind them. Town and countryside were plundered and desolated, and the inhabitants of whole provinces were carried off into captivity. The march of Theuderic was checked at last by the walls of Arles, behind which the flying Goths had taken refuge. Meanwhile Clovis had occupied Bordeaux, where he passed the winter. Thence he advanced to Toulouse, from which he bore away part of the treasure of the Visigoths. Another part was stored in the city of Carcassonne, which had been fortified with all the skill of Roman engineers, and which was all through the Middle Ages regarded as an impregnable fastness. The sacred vessels of Solomon's Temple, which had been carried off, along with the spoil of Rome, by Alaric in 410, and whose value was exaggerated by general rumour, fascinated the imagination of the Franks, always eager for plunder. Clovis probably valued the stronghold rather as a strategic point to command Southern Aquitaine.

The siege of Arles by the Franks, under Theuderic, and the Burgundians stands out in vivid detail in the Life of S. Caesarius, a contemporary document of great value, illuminating social life and events which, without it, would be obscure. S. Caesarius was born at Chalon-sur-Saône about 469, and at eighteen, after some years of youthful licence, received the tonsure from Bishop Silvester. The attraction of the monastic life at Lérins was powerful in those years : and Caesarius determined, against the wishes of his family, to join that community. His craving for ascetic perfection and a spiritual idealism, which set at naught the life of the world, soon attracted the notice of Porcarius, the abbot, who appointed the young monk to preach in his own place, and to serve the office of *cellarius*. But, under a superior whose vigilance and energy were slackening with age, the discipline of the great house had begun to show signs of laxity. Luxury and secret self-indulgence were creeping in, and the severe discourses of the young preacher, along with the restraints which, as cellarer, he could impose, excited something like a mutiny. Caesarius was deposed from his office. His own severity of self-discipline, and, perhaps, the vexation caused by malice and failure, undermined his health, so that his superior thought it well that he should go to consult the famous physicians of Arles. Firminus, belonging to a consular house, which was connected with the family of Magnus Felix, a friend of Sidonius Apollinaris, and with Ennodius, the Bishop of Pavia, received Caesarius into his household, and placed him under the tuition of Pomerius, a professor of rhetoric then in high repute. The artificial pomp of Roman rhetoric, which had so sadly degenerated from the art of Cicero, had no attractions for the serious mind of Caesarius, whose main object was to strike home to the consciences of simple people. Aeonius, Bishop of Arles, to whom Caesarius was introduced by his aristocratic friends, discovered that he was a native of Chalon, and indeed a relative of his own. He claimed him from the monastery of Lérins, ordained him to the priesthood, and sent him to restore the discipline of a monastic house in the neighbourhood. Soon afterwards, feeling that his own end was near, and that ecclesiastical discipline needed a stronger hand, Aeonius commended Caesarius to the Visigothic king as his successor. In his thirty-third year, Caesarius reluctantly became bishop of the see of Arles; many another monk of Lérins, *e.g.* Lupus of Troyes and Faustus of Riez, had risen to episcopal rank in the preceding generation. Caesarius was a powerful and searching preacher, consoling, alluring, or threatening. He told his colleagues in the ministry, as he felt for himself, that they must ever carry in their minds the warning —" Woe unto me if I preach not the Gospel ". He urged on all to attend diligently the regular offices, and restrained the growing practice of leaving the church after the Gospel in the Mass ; and he enjoined that the laity should take a part in the chanting, both in Greek and Latin. He was specially devoted to the care of the sick and poor and of captives taken in war ; and he obtained from Alaric a liberal grant for the relief of such distress. In the midst of his devoted ministry, he was delated by one of his own secretaries to the Gothic king as having engaged in a plot to bring Arles under the Burgundian power. Undoubtedly, all through Aquitaine, such suspicion was in the air. The Visigothic court had good reason to distrust the loyalty of the Catholic bishops and their flocks ; and Caesarius was relegated, by a mild punishment, to a formal exile at Bordeaux. The extinction of a fire in that city by his prayers, as people said, along with clear proof of his innocence, led Alaric to restore him to his see. On his return he was met by a great concourse of the citizens of Arles, headed by the clergy, who led him back in procession, with crucifixes and candles and psalmody. His false accuser had been, in accordance with the stern justice of the Visigothic Code, sentenced to death by stoning. But the culprit was saved from his fate by the intercession of the charitable bishop whom he had tried to ruin.

Caesarius was engaged in organising a religious house for women under his sister Caesaria ; and the buildings were already begun when the Frank and Burgundian army appeared before the walls in the year 508. Arles, like the other great cities of Southern Gaul in those days, was divided in its sympathies. A strong party, with the Catholic clergy at their head, beyond a doubt looked eagerly for an opportunity of shaking off the yoke of an Arian power, although the bishop always preached the evangelical principle of rendering obedience to all just commands of the powers that be. On the other hand, the Visigoths had a strong party in their favour, in which the Jews, from their wealth and numbers, formed a powerful element. For both in Italy and in Gaul, at that time, the Jew was always inclined to support the Arian Goth against the Catholic Church. The Gallo-Roman Catholics of Arles apparently were unable to make any open attempt to aid the Frank besiegers. But it can hardly be doubted that there was a secret intrigue for the betrayal of the city into their hands. One night a young priest let himself down from the battlements by a rope, and entered the Frank lines. The biographer of Caesarius tells us that he was animated merely by the levity of youth, and a wish to escape captivity. Unfortunately he was a compatriot and kinsman of Caesarius, and the Visigoths and their Hebrew partisans not unnaturally came to the conclusion that the young priest was an intermediary between the bishop and the generals of the besieging force. A furious crowd, maddened by the suspicion that they, with their

wives and children, were being handed over to the tender mercies
of a Frank army by a clerical clique, swarmed around the clergy
house, dragged forth the bishop, and handed him over to be
strictly confined till they should decide whether he should be
flung into the Rhone, or immured in the castle of Ugernum,
which stood outside the walls. His house was occupied by the
heretics, but the legend soon spread that a Goth, who presumed to
occupy the bishop's bedchamber, had been smitten by the hand
of God, and had died on the following day. The bishop was
placed in a pinnace to be carried to Ugernum ; but all efforts
to move the boat from the bank were in vain, and Caesarius
was once more confined in the government house, while his
followers long remained uncertain about his fate. But another
act of treachery turned the scale in his favour. A Jew, who was
keeping his watch as sentinel, tied a letter to a stone, and tried
to fling it into the Frank lines. It fell short, and next morning
was picked up by a Visigothic soldier, during an interval when
the enemy had somewhat fallen back. In this letter a certain
point in the defences was indicated where the Franks might
effect an escalade, and, as a reward for this betrayal, it was
stipulated that, in the sack, the persons and property of the
Jewish inhabitants should be spared. " Thus was the fiendish
cruelty of the race, hated both by God and man, exposed in
open day." The Catholic party seized their advantage and the
bishop was released " like another Daniel from the den of lions ".

Meanwhile Theodoric, the Ostrogothic King of Italy, who had
mysteriously failed to support the Visigoths at Vouglé, was now
alarmed by the victories of the Franks, and, in a stirring general
order, mobilised his troops in the early summer of 508, to save
the Visigoths in Southern Gaul. The headlong advance of the
Franks to the Rhone brought them dangerously near to the Alps
and the frontier of Italy, and Italy was drawn into the fray.
One column of the Italian army under Tulum crossed the Maritime Alps and stormed the bridge over the Rhone. Another,
commanded by Mammo, in the following year penetrated by a
different route into the valley of the Durance, and threatened
the Burgundian besiegers of Arles in their rear. The details of
the conflict are obscure. The final battle beneath the walls, in
which the Goths were under the leadership of Count Ibbas,
resulted in a total defeat of the besiegers who, according to

CHAP. III THE CONQUESTS OF CLOVIS 101

Jordanes, left 30,000 dead on the field. The Gothic army returned with a crowd of captives, many of whom were ransomed
by Caesarius with unsparing generosity. The treasures bequeathed by Aeonius, his predecessor, were devoted to this charitable work. Even the holy vessels of the altar went to the
melting-pot. Long afterwards there could be seen the marks
left on column and arch by the axes with which precious ornaments and memorials had been torn away to swell the ransom.
In reply to critics who were troubled by such use of holy things,
Caesarius used to say that it were better the Holy Mysteries
should be celebrated with earthenware than that men should
remain in bondage. A few years after the siege, the good bishop
had the chance of displaying similar lavish charity. In the year
after he founded the religious house, of which his sister Caesaria
was abbess, he fell once more under suspicion of disloyalty to
the Gothic power, which was by this time securely established
at Arles. He was conveyed, under military escort, to defend
himself at Ravenna before Theodoric. The exuberant rhetoric
of hagiography constantly arouses suspicion. Yet it can hardly
be doubted that the charge against Caesarius originated in a
clique at the Ostrogothic court, and that it was dissipated when
Theodoric, with his profound knowledge of men, was brought
face to face with one whose interests were purely spiritual, and
yet who was a commanding power. Instead of questioning the
bishop's good faith, Theodoric, with his stately politeness,
sympathised with Caesarius on the hardships of the journey
which had been needlessly imposed on him, and made kindly
inquiries about the fortunes of Arles and his own Goths who had
been left to garrison it. The accusers were sternly rebuked for
their insult to a man so evidently innocent. On returning to his
inn, Caesarius received from the king a silver dish of 60 pounds
weight and a sum of 300 *solidi*. The city was crowded with
captives carried off in the late war from Burgundy and Provence,
who invoked the bishop's aid to procure their release. Within
three days the presents of Theodoric had been sold and numbers
of captives were ransomed and sent back to their native place.
Theodoric applauded the deed of mercy, and the example of the
king was of course obsequiously followed by crowds of courtiers.

The great defeat of the Franks and Burgundians under the
walls of Arles threw back the Frank advance in the south and

saved a remnant of Gaul for the Visigoths. Septimania, the
strip of coast-land extending from the Rhone to the eastern end
of the Pyrenees, was left in their possession, with a capital at
Narbonne. Theodoric annexed to his Italian dominions the
territory south of the Durance from the Alps to the Rhone,
and thus had an easy access to Spain, where he controlled the
feeble administration of his grandson, Amalaric, the son of
Alaric, who had escaped from the field of Vouglé. At this
moment Theodoric seemed to be recovering much of the territory
of the Western Empire. He had asserted his power over Rhaetia,
Noricum, and Pannonia. And now he had established a hold on
the richest lands and cities of Southern Gaul, and a commanding
influence in the Spanish peninsula. But it may be doubted
whether he was thinking so much of reviving the glory of Roman
sway in the West, as of checking the advance of the Franks,
whose energy and ambition were a serious menace.

His generals followed up their victory at Arles by an energetic
pursuit of the retreating besiegers. The Burgundians were
driven back on the Durance. Ibbas pressed the pursuit of the
Franks from the Rhone with the object of compelling Clovis to
raise the siege of Carcassonne, near the borders of Septimania.
With the eye of a strategist Clovis, perceiving that the campaign
in the south was lost for the time, raised the siege of Carcassonne,
and fell back to the north. The generals of Theodoric did not
follow him further. Theodoric was not the man to imperil vast
interests by attempting to drive the Franks back beyond the
Loire. He contented himself with guarding Septimania for the
young Visigothic king. By his annexation of the lands from the
Alps to the Rhone, the Franks and Burgundians were shut out
from the great seaports on the Mediterranean, and a free passage
was left for Theodoric's troops and couriers across the Pyrenees.
The relief and reorganisation of the province evidently occupied
his thoughts much in the years following the victory at Arles.
The old prefecture of the Gauls was no more. But Theodoric
sent a Vicar named Gemellus, evidently of Roman race, to restore
peace and order. An edict exhorted the provincials to put off
the barbarism and violent spirit which they had learnt under
Visigothic rule, and to return to the mildness and equity of
Roman administration. They might now, without fear of spoliation, bring out their hoarded wealth. To these counsels Theodoric

added practical proof of sympathy with the distress which the presence of three armies had spread along the Rhone. The devastation of a region so richly endowed by nature had caused an immense destruction of life and property. Even the cold, bald record of the savagery of conquest in the fifth century must shock the most languid imagination. Theodoric, who had seen for many years, on the Danube or the Po, the cruel tragedy going on before his eyes, and who, beyond any man of his time, warrior as he was, hated the atrocities of war, and longed for the old " Roman peace ", applied his principles to the reorganisation of the province on the Rhone. His officials were to display the magnanimity and incorruptible purity of the great age. They were to relieve distress, and so act that the people might be glad to have been conquered. And, for himself, he at once remitted the " tribute of the 4th Indiction " (510–511) to those districts that had been ravaged. The commissariat of his army was to be supplied from the stores of Massilia, which were drawn from Italy. Massilia was the special care of the Ostrogothic king. The glory of its Greek culture of 1100 years had sadly faded, and it had lost its proud pre-eminence. Theodoric restored its ancient privileges, and gave it a great official who was specially charged to protect the poor against the powerful. The commander of the Ostrogothic troops at Avignon is warned that they must offer no violence to " our new subjects ", and that they must remember that Italian troops are there to restore civil order and not to oppress. The people of Provence must have bitterly regretted the policy which a few years afterwards led Witigis to hand them over to the tender mercies of the grandsons of Clovis.

Our information about the close of the Frank campaign in Aquitaine is deplorably scanty. Clovis, when he raised the siege of Carcassonne and withdrew towards the north, is said to have taken some fortresses, such as Angoulême, which were still held by Visigothic garrisons. Detachments, according to one tradition, were left in Bordeaux and Saintonge. He had won four-fifths of Gaul. If his dominion did not extend to the Pyrenees, it probably embraced the greater part of the two Aquitaines. In Lower Novem Populana, to the south of the Garonne, Frank domination was probably established, since the bishops of Auch, Bazas, and Eauze were present at the Council of Orleans, which was convened in 511, by the authority of Clovis.

The forms of administration were little changed. Frank or Gallo-Roman officials replaced those of Visigothic race. But municipal life went on externally pretty much as before the conquest. Yet the moral effect of the conquest must have been profoundly felt by the population of Aquitaine. Vaunted as Catholic Christians, who came with sacred omens and the benediction of the Church to end the reign of accursed heretics, the Franks, as they did for generations, gave a curious example of their superior Christianity. Yet we may be sure the ecclesiastical chroniclers have dealt gently with the barbarous ferocity of these new sons of the Church. Here and there, indeed, the lands of a famous abbey, or a church guarded by relics, might be spared. But as a rule, the Frank army, living on plunder, and wantonly destroying what they could not use, left a trail of massacre and ruin behind them. Innumerable captives were swept from the countryside to be sold as slaves, and even priests and monks were carried off. In 510, three years after the battles in the south, the glut in the slave-markets was so embarrassing that Clovis left the fate of his prisoners to the decision of the bishops. The Visigothic kings had been disliked as heretics, but their rule had, on the whole, been mild and just, and Aquitaine for a generation had enjoyed peace and security. The savage devastation spread by the Frank armies must have left a deep impression on the feelings of the province. In the two following generations it was destined to have frequent experience of the same lawless ferocity in the struggle between the sons and grandsons of Clovis for the cities and rich lands of the south.

Clovis on his return to the Loire stopped at the city of Tours. There he received from the Emperor Anastasius the honours of Patrician, and, perhaps, of Consul. The Eastern Empire still strove to maintain a shadow of sovereignty over Gaul, as it did over Italy in the days of Odoacer and Theodoric ; and the German kings, even when they had a Roman province at their mercy, guarded and dignified their power by the magic of old Roman titles. Odoacer and the kings of Burgundy were proud of the title of Patrician. Theodoric gladly received about the same time the *ornamenta* of Imperial office from Constantinople. Such dignities might have a very different meaning to the Roman emperor and to the German king ; but new and unstable power was glad to fortify itself with the spell of immemorial tradition.

Clovis, who appears in the Chronicles as a rather brutal conqueror, probably possessed some qualities of statesmanship which
the chronicler could not understand. His assumption of Imperial
dignities as he entered Tours in triumph was probably a stroke
of state-craft. He had conquered a great population which had
been Romanised for centuries, and which was proud of the
Roman name. In those regions his Franks could only have been
dotted here and there in feeble bands. The mass of the Gallo-
Roman population in the south, still retaining the impress of
Roman culture, never took kindly to Frank rule. The clergy,
whose chief ministers were, and long remained, chiefly men of
Roman descent, were the one class who, from hatred of the
Arian Visigoths, welcomed the new Catholic power. They had
intrigued for Clovis, and helped him on his march with omen,
benediction, and miracle : and they must have gladly seen
their coming champion wearing the insignia of the old prefect
of the Gauls. The Church welcomed the Frank conqueror to
the holiest city of Gaul with the stately pomp which in all ages
she has known so skilfully to arrange. It was more than a
century since the great apostle of Gaul had been laid to rest on
a sacred spot on the Loire, which is still marked by an oratory.
Thence his successor in the see of Tours transferred his remains to
a chapel which he built close to the city. Perpetuus, the sixth
Bishop of Tours, thinking this chapel too mean for such a memory,
swept it away, and in 473 raised a great basilica. In that
sanctuary, in the year 510, Clovis was proclaimed Patrician and,
in the name of the Emperor, invested with the purple tunic, the
mantle, and diadem. Then he mounted his horse and rode
through the town, flinging largess of gold and silver to the crowd.

In another chapter we shall attempt to ascertain and describe
the real meaning and basis of Frank kingship as borne by him
and his descendants.

CHAPTER IV

THE FRANK KINGSHIP AND COURT

THE scene at Tours when Clovis was invested with the dignity and insignia of an Imperial magistrate naturally suggests an inquiry into the character of Frank kingship in the fifth century. Many things have conspired to make this a difficult question. The social institutions of the German tribes attracted the notice of a great number of historians from Polybius to Ammianus Marcellinus for a period of over five hundred years. During that time the German race had known many vicissitudes of fortune, alternately invading and invaded, engaged in tribal wars or restless migrations, bursting on the frontier defences of the Empire, crossing the great rivers again and again, taking service under the eagles to fight their own countrymen, or cantoned peaceably on Roman soil. It is clear that no institutions or national character could remain stable and unchanged under the strain of such varying fortunes, and that the reports of historic observers at different times will show a corresponding variety. The barbarian codes were committed to writing after the invasions, although, as we have seen, they have embedded in them many relics of the more ancient legal customs and social traditions of the German tribes. Obviously great caution and a scrupulous critical conscience are needed in the use of such distant and multifarious sources to interpret the institutions which grew up after the conquest, whether under Clovis or the Ostrogoth Theodoric. Much as we owe to the researches in this field of German scholars, a candid student cannot help feeling that the erudition and ingenuity of these learned men is constantly vitiated by a *parti pris*, a patriotic determination to find everything essentially Teutonic. Because the Franks were Germans, their whole organisation of Gaul, and particularly the power and status of their kings, followed the lines of the *Germania* of Tacitus, or even of a legendary tradition older than Tacitus. The German character and social institutions of the first century are discovered, with slight modifications, in the Gaul of the sixth century, after the German tribes had gone through the changes and disintegration of four hundred years of war and wandering.

Four hundred years had passed since the *Germania* of Tacitus was written. It is indeed one of the most precious sketches of ancient society that we possess. And Tacitus, whose father was Procurator of Gallia Belgica, and who probably had held that office himself, had evidently first-hand sources of information. His penetrating genius also gives immense value to the facts which he had accumulated. But, with all reverence for Tacitus, one or two reservations must be made by the scrupulous inquirer. Tacitus was a severe moralist, living in the most abandoned period of Roman history. He has branded the vices of the great with eternal infamy, and especially the abuse and degradation of Imperial power. In a society of nomads and shepherds in the woods of Germany, his imagination seemed to discover a virgin virtue, as yet untainted by the vices of a depraved culture. He had discovered a popular freedom resting on warlike instinct, a mild-tempered kingship resting on ancient descent and popular reverence, a general atmosphere of freedom, finding a vent for pent-up and eruptive energy in military adventure under tried and adored chiefs. Tacitus had evidently gathered the facts about the social and political life of the German tribes with interest and care. But an intense and passionate idealist, as he was, could hardly describe them without a certain colouring from his own moral tone. The Germans of Tacitus are therefore perhaps as idealised as the Mohicans of Fenimore Cooper. Moreover, it is clear that there were wide differences between the institutions of different tribes. Some were monarchical. Some had no king, but were ruled by the *principes*, who were elective magistrates. Where kingship exists, it is expressly stated that its powers are very limited and indefinite ; it is a place rather of honour than of power. It is not a military office. For the chiefs to command in warlike expeditions are specially chosen, and have their own staffs of " companions ", sworn to fight for them to the death. Nor is the kingship a hereditary office, but elective from one of the noble houses of the tribe.

Long before the great migrations or invasions, in the days of Caesar and the days of Tacitus, there were constant wars among the tribes of Germany. Caesar says that some tribes had surrounded their frontiers with a devastated region as a proof of their valour and a security against sudden invasion. In Tacitus we see tribes often expelled from their old seats or absorbed by others. The Batavi had been a branch of the Chatti before they were driven by intestine feuds into Roman territory. The Chatti, true predecessors of the Prussians, believe only in war and the glory of slaughter : they have no settled homes or lands or any peaceful instincts. The Bructeri have been invaded and wiped out by the Chamavi and Angrivarii. The Cherusci earned the repute of folly and weakness by indulging a too peaceful temper. The Marcomanni expelled the Boii, and, by superior valour, maintained a threatening front along the Danube, under their powerful kings, till the time of the Antonines. In all these incessant wars there must have been immense social and political changes. Tribes secure in sequestered regions may have led a peaceful rural life of farming and hunting, while others were always on the war-path. Some were often visited by Roman itinerant merchants, or contributed recruits to Roman armies. There was no centralised German state with uniform institutions to justify the sweeping generalisations of modern scholarship. There must have been, of course, some settled agriculture and pastoral industry to ward off famine. But it must have been generally feeble and ineffectual to provide for the wants of a growing population. The fear of famine, the unrest born of deadly ennui, the passion for combat and adventure, sent the young bloods of a tribe on raids for plunder or in quest of new settlements in more favoured regions. In these expeditions, the king, unless he had special gifts for war, was not necessarily the leader. The king was chosen from a noble clan to a generally peaceful and ornamental dignity. For leadership in war, the Germans chose a man noted for his courage and military gifts. The idyllic scenes of peaceful pastoral life, with graded ranks, finding a voice in free assemblies, were left far behind, often for ever, by these war bands which for three centuries ranged from the Baltic to the Euxine, from the Danube to the Rhine. How could old social institutions and political authority escape profound and permanent change, when the warlike section of a tribe had quitted its old home, under a chosen warlike chief, surrounded by his " companions " devoted to him to the death ? The ancient spirit of the race, its boldness and pride of freedom, no doubt, survived, and may even have taken a keener edge from military pride and common adventure. The war chief, chosen for great qualities, and served by a devoted staff, if he justified his choice by success, necessarily rose to a power which the old Teutonic king, however noble and honoured, could never claim, unless he were a great warrior like Maroboduus, who with a disciplined army of 70,000 men wielded for a time despotic power along the Danube, till he was overthrown by Arminius fighting in the name of liberty.

Still deeper changes were wrought when the German war bands, after many vicissitudes, overran some province of the Empire, deposed the Roman rulers, and settled permanently on the lands which they had seized. The orthodox German theory is that, in doing so, they imported, with little change, the institutions and social spirit of the Germany of Tacitus, idealised by patriotic learning. The immense interval of 400 years, during which the conquering tribe had been cut off from its early home, had adapted its organisation to its wandering life, and the vicissitudes of constant warfare, are ignored or forgotten. It is also forgotten that the small band of warriors had, in the end, settled among a population highly organised and civilised, penetrated for generations by Roman traditions, and far outnumbering their conquerors. Nor is it often remembered that the conquered peoples had submitted to the ascendancy of a highly organised Church, whose higher clergy were often men of commanding and statesmanlike ability, and filled with the spirit of the regime which was passing away, and an ambition to assert the authority of the Church. The German chiefs nearly always felt a certain awe and reverence for that Imperial power which they had sometimes fought and sometimes served. The very name of Rome cast a spell on the greatest of them, Alaric, Theodoric, and Clovis ; and they were often eager to wear the titles and insignia of a once world-wide sovereignty. They found themselves in the midst of a Romanised population, with many old families possessing great estates and a long tradition of culture and of service in high office. The people at large were indeed untrained to war and unable to meet such seasoned warriors as the Germans. But they were a great population accustomed to skilful government ; and the problem of setting up a new administration for a large territory must have severely exercised the minds of the German chiefs even in the first flush of victory. To come to terms with the conquered people, to utilise what was left of the old officialdom in the deserted prefecture, and above all to enlist to their aid the power and influence of the clergy, this was the manifest policy of the conqueror. His military force must assume the show of a legitimate succession to Imperial authority, gather up the threads of the old administration, and conciliate the moral support or the acquiescence of his new subjects.

In this policy, it seems to the present writer that the early Merovingians achieved a striking success. The full conquest of Gaul had indeed taken about half a century from the accession of Clovis. But the Gallo-Romans offered little resistance except for a brief space in the little kingdom of Syagrius. The great task of the early Frank kings was the overthrow of the two other Teutonic powers in Gaul, the Burgundian and the Visigoth. Henceforth, although there was plenty of fighting in Gaul or beyond the frontiers, it was between the Merovingians themselves or in conflicts with the Thuringi, Saxons, or Lombards. There were some few risings, but they were momentary outbursts of discontent at oppressive taxation, not serious attempts to overthrow the Frank monarchy. The mass of Gallo-Romans seem never to have thought of challenging the power of the Frank kings. The Franks, under the glamour of the Merovingian legend, never as a body attempted to assert that old German liberty which they had enjoyed 400 years before in their old home. The Gallo-Romans, under the sway of Imperial officers, had never had a taste of political freedom or a share in administration. They were contented with the " Roman peace " and prosperous lives. The Franks in their long wanderings and wars had lost their old nobility, and even the memory of those old free gatherings of their armed warriors of which we read in Tacitus. The one institution which held all the population together, Frank or Roman, which was moulding them into a nation, and the sole symbol and organ of its power, was the kingship.

The character of Teutonic royalty after the invasions has been debated with great force and learning, but sometimes with more patriotic prejudice than scrupulous critical judgement. Some have discovered in the power of the Frank kings the image of the German royal power in Tacitus, which was limited and tempered by election and by the prestige of a great noble class, and the vigorous freedom of the assembly of warriors. Others regard it as a military chiefship, fortified by military obedience through generations of struggle and wandering, confirmed by the glory of conquest, and finally remoulded and inspired by the tradition of Roman despotism ; the Frank king, entering on his new realm, took over the powers which had been vicariously wielded by the Praetorian Prefect. Others again, following a middle course, hold that Roman principles of government developed and extended the power of the Teutonic kings, without altering its essentially German character.

The weakness of such theories is that they are too theoretical. Their authors are too much under the influence of *a priori* ideas or patriotic ideals, and pay too little attention to the facts, as handed down to us, of an age of transition, convulsion, and chaos. It was not an age either guided or to be explained by the neat, clear-cut formulae of the political philosopher. It was a time when force was predominant, although it might be tempered by some statesmanlike prudence in the face of a vast and conquered population : a time in which strong personality and the prestige of victory gave a man a wide discretion in organising a new government. It may well be doubted whether Clovis, or any of his Franks, ever had had a glimpse of that settled life of old Germany described by Tacitus and idealised by modern scholars. The living traditions in their minds were of long wanderings from the Euxine to the Seine, and constant fighting under " long-haired " chiefs. Their greatest chief, at first only one of several Frank kings, had defeated Syagrius, the last representative of Roman power in Gaul. He had crushed the Thuringians in a great battle. He had scattered the Visigoths at Vouglé and pushed his advance to the Mediterranean. His authority had grown with his successes. The booty of wealthy and long-settled provinces had enabled him to reward his more important followers, and provided him with ample resources. He finds a country long skilfully administered under Roman principles of government. He wisely continues the Roman tradition, as far as possible, and probably takes over many of the staff of the prefecture. But his Franks, although redoubtable warriors, are only a small band, amid a vast population steeped in the traditions of Rome. It was a stroke of policy to present himself at the end of his conquests, in the holy city of Tours, bearing the insignia and prestige of the ancient offices of Patrician and Consul. His kingship might be originally German : for that he probably cared little. But it had become a greater and more impressive title since he had swept down to Carcassonne and returned to be invested by priestly hands with the Roman chlamys and the Oriental diadem before the altar of S. Martin's. Rude soldier as he was, Clovis probably felt, like Alaric and Theodoric, the magical glamour of the city which, along with Jerusalem and Athens, seems to have an unfading power of fascinating the minds of men. And, as a shrewd practical statesman, Clovis had to face the problem of organising the government of a wide territory. The great majority of his future subjects were Roman in tradition and sentiment.

Hence the proud, self-willed Frank assumed the title of *vir illustris* which the prefect had borne. The Frank king has the name *princeps* in Gregory of Tours, and the Ripuarian Code. His treasury is called *fiscus* in the Salic Code. His house is the *sacrum palatium*, and he is addressed, or describes himself, in those terms of exaggerated reverence of the Lower Empire, *Gloria Vestra, Sublimitas,* and *Serenitas.* His edicts often, in the tone of the later Theodosian Code, proclaim the king as an earthly Providence, watching over the safety and quiet of his subjects. These things may to us seem trivial or absurd. But, at that time, they represented a statesmanlike policy, probably inspired by Gallo-Roman advisers, to smooth the period of transition, and win the allegiance and support of the Roman population. We cannot imagine a German king of the old breed disguising himself thus in the cast-off habiliments of the last shadowy emperors.

But now, leaving this field of rather futile controversy as to the foundations of Frank monarchy in a vanished past, let us try to ascertain from our sources what were its actual claims and powers in the sixth century, and how, either personally or by delegation, it provided for the government of its subjects. In the first place, the Frank monarchy was hereditary and not elective. There is no trace in the codes or chronicles of the election of a Frank king. Clovis succeeded Childeric without question, and the Merovingian succession lasted unbroken till the eighth century. The heir, even when an infant, could count on the unwavering loyalty of the people and the nobles. *Mihi solium regni debetur* is the watchward of the house. The famous pact of Andelot, drawn up with all legal precision, assumes the right of sons to succeed their father. Guntram, without legitimate heirs, assigns the succession to his nephew Childebert. In spite of vice and weakness, the race of the long-haired kings had a powerful hold on the allegiance and imagination both of Franks and Romans. Men might murmur against them ; they might, in sullen discontent, transfer their allegiance from one Merovingian ; they might flock to the standard of Gundobald, the adventurer from Constantinople, who claimed to be a son of Chlothar I., but they never revolted against the house of Merovechus. The appeal of Guntram from the steps of the altar in the church of Orleans expressed their feeling to their kings : " The kings were their defenders ", although the defence sometimes took a curious form. The royal power is a hereditary estate, the succession being regulated, not by constitutional enactment, but by the law or custom of private inheritance. Hence females are excluded, and the inheritance is divided equally among the sons of the dead king. The new king assumes his place as of right, or, if an infant, is presented by some powerful noble to the assembled people as their rightful lord. Thus on the murder of Sigibert, his son Childebert II., then only four years of age, was proclaimed by Duke Gundobad in Austrasia. There is no hint of free election ; but according to old German, and perhaps Roman, ways, there was a formal ceremony of installation and the oath of allegiance was taken by the subjects. It was a solemn form, like the enthronement of a bishop. It was the ceremonious recognition of a ruler whose position was already assured. The ceremony in ancient Germany was accompanied by the elevation of the designated chief on a shield, amid the acclamations of his warriors. Only three instances of this ceremony are found in Gregory of Tours. When Sigibert of Cologne had been done to

I

death Clovis his cousin was, by this form, confirmed in the chiefship of the tribe. In the same fashion, Sigibert, the son of Chlothar, received the allegiance of the Neustrian Franks, on their desertion of his brother Chilperic in 575. So also the ill-fated pretender Gundobald Ballomer was borne upon the shield round the streets of Briva. It will be observed, however, that in these three cases the person so honoured was not succeeding in natural order of descent, but was replacing another branch of the race. But in the ordinary succession of their kings, the Franks had forgotten the power they had possessed 400 years before. The Gallo-Romans under the Empire had never known such power ; their rulers were appointed by Imperial choice. And so they accepted the rule of Clovis and his race with as little question as they had accepted that of the prefect of the Gauls. The title *Rex Francorum*, borne by the Merovingian dynasty, is apt to be somewhat misleading. It was undoubtedly a proud reminiscence of a conquering race, but it speedily came to designate the monarchs of both races happily destined to blend in one great nationality. The idea of some writers of the time of the Revolution that the mass of the Gallic people were beaten down and crushed into servitude by a small band of Frank warriors, who founded the great feudal houses, has been triumphantly shown to be a figment of political hatred and inspired by a political purpose. If there was on the one side the pride of conquest and high military spirit, there was on the other the equally exclusive pride in the Roman name and long tradition. The conversion of Clovis and his Franks, however spiritually shallow it may have been, was really a turning point in history. It enlisted the princes of the Church on the side of the Frank monarchy in every diocese, gave the King skilled and educated advisers who knew better than any others the needs and feelings of the Gallic people, and, through their sacred ministry, were a bond between Roman and Frank. The Roman Church carried on in the spiritual sphere the higher traditions of the Empire.

Under all these influences, after the first confusions and violence of conquest, the Gallo-Roman population seem on the whole to have been treated in a spirit of fairness and conciliation by Clovis. The land tenure seems to have been as little as possible disturbed. Here and there in the heat of conquest there may have been cases of spoliation and violence. But there is no trace of the partition of estates such as was clearly enforced under the Burgundian and Visigothic kings. Clovis, coming into possession of the treasures of the Roman fisc, together with the booty which always falls to a victorious invader, had ample means of rewarding his leading followers ; and he had the derelict lands which belonged to the Imperial government in Gaul to distribute. Moreover, a population probably dwindling in the barbarian raids and inroads of a hundred years, must have left great tracts open for new settlers. The Franks of Clovis, as we have seen, had been long settled in Belgium, and many, when they were disbanded after the wars of conquest, would probably return to their farms in Brabant, of which we have glimpses in the Salic Law. Everything goes to show that, long after the noises of the invasion had died away, numbers of Gallo-Roman families were enjoying undisturbed the lands of their ancestors. It would be difficult to discover any sign of hate and bitterness between the two races. Gallo-Romans of high position held their place in municipal councils in Aquitaine and Auvergne, and wielded great authority in their native province, where they were often appointed by the King to the office of Count, with large powers, judicial, financial, and military. From their monopoly of legal and official knowledge, Romans were welcomed in the offices of the "Palatium", where long-tried experience and administrative tact and skill were of essential importance in smoothing the difficulties of a critical period of transition. Out of fifty-four Counts mentioned by Gregory and Fortunatus, forty-two have Roman names. Although the Gallo-Romans, from the long tranquillity of the "Roman Peace", had little of the military spirit, still the finest military skill and instinct in great crises was occasionally found in Romans such as Mummolus and Desiderius. Above all, it is to be remembered that for a long period Gallo-Romans had almost a monopoly of the episcopate. In the lists of the councils of the sixth century pure Roman names are far the most numerous. And the power and prestige of great bishops of Gallo-Roman race, Remigius of Rheims, Germanus of Paris, Gregory of Tours, can hardly be exaggerated.

We have thus, to all appearance, a process going on of peaceful fusion of the two races. In no epoch of history is the better and nobler side of human nature totally obscured. Yet in wild times force must always assert itself, if society is not to dissolve in chaos. And in spite of all wild antiquarian idealism, the power of the Merovingian monarch was naked absolutism, often exercised with brutal cruelty. Popular assemblies with any traditional constitutional powers were never held. The gathering on the Field of Mars, as it was held by Clovis, or by the Ostrogoth Theodoric, once a year, was a military review. It was no longer the assembly of German freemen to deliberate on the fortunes of their tribe. The word *populus*, suggestive of democratic power, when it occurs in our authorities, means, as a rule, simply the inhabitants of a district, not a political body. And popular rights have been so completely absorbed in regal supremacy that the adjective *publicus*, strange as it may seem, has come to mean " royal ". From the day when Clovis cut down with his battle-axe at Soissons the French warrior who disputed his right to the famous vase, the authority of the Merovingian house was practically arbitrary and undisputed in peace or war. The Salic Law in one prologue is attributed to four rather mythical jurists across the Rhine. But in other MSS., Clovis, Childebert, and Chlothar are the authors of extensive alterations and additions, of their mere will, to ancient customs of their people. There is not a hint in the Salian or Ripuarian Codes that they rest on the will of the people. In the latter code it is distinctly stated that King Theuderic chose certain sage men, learned in the law, and commanded them, under his dictation, to write down the laws of the Franks, altering whatever was of pagan tone in accordance with Christian law.

It would be futile to attempt to discover any clean-cut definition of the powers of the Frank kings, legislative, financial, judicial, or military. It was an age of transition in which the old was melting into the new, and any idea of constitutional checks was unknown. In the wreck of old institutions only two figures emerge with unchallenged authority, the King and the Bishop. In that age of boundless license and untamed self-will, in which the finer ideals here and there existing were over-shadowed by the selfishness of avidity or the brutality of revenge, these two, in their several spheres, stood out with strong, self-assertive and unquestioned authority. When Avitus, the famous bishop of Vienne, was striving to persuade Gundobad, the King of Burgundy, to accept the Catholic faith, and the King shrank from doing so from fear of his Arian subjects, the bishop

met his doubts with the formula of absolutism : " Tu es
caput populi, non populus caput tuum ". That was the feeling
of King Guntram when, on a Sunday at mass in the church of
Orleans, he claimed the allegiance of the people as their sole
stay and " defender ". In the codes we need not expect to find
any such definite assertion of the King's power. It is taken
for granted in several enactments. Those *in truste regis*,
his immediate retainers at court, have a higher *wehrgeld* attached
to their persons than men of the highest rank outside the circle.
Offences against any of the King's servants are more heavily
punished than those committed against ordinary freemen. The
King's summons to the host or to the performance of any
public service is treated as beyond challenge ; and any act of
disobedience, save on grounds of sickness, involves a heavy fine.
Any proved act of disloyalty to the King is punished by composition for the offender's life, and the confiscation of his estate.
The " law of majesty " of old Roman times was still a living
force, as Baddo, one of Fredegundis's emissaries sent to murder
King Guntram, was made to feel. Even Aegidius, the powerful
bishop of Rheims, only obtained his relief from the charge of
high treason by skilful diplomacy backed by gold.

In every department of administration, on an examination
of our records, the royal power will be found to be omnipresent
and supreme. We have seen how the kings supplemented of
their own authority the enactments of " legal sages ". The
mass of legislation under the Merovingians was issued in the
same style of autocratic authority. These enactments are
styled edicts, decrees, or constitutions, often framed after models
in the Theodosian Code. They begin with the lordly words :
" *Jubemus, statuimus* ", etc. ; but they are hardly ever described
as *leges*, because *lex* was a half sacred, antique term of
reverence, reserved for the Roman code or old customary Frank
legislation. But the edicts and decrees of the King have all the
force and effect of law ; and as the edicts of the Roman emperors
were fashioned in consultation with jurists and high officials of
the Imperial Consistory, so the decrees of the Frank kings were
discussed and beaten into shape in councils (*placita*) of the realm,
with the aid of the *proceres* and *optimates*. But, in the end, the
legislative power and responsibility belongs solely to the King.
The great check on the power of the German kings in the time

of Caesar or Tacitus lay, as in Homer's days, in the assembled warriors of the tribe, instinct with the idea of personal freedom and manhood, and the group of nobles, some of them with as proud a descent as their King. But all these checks had lost their power when the tribe, after absorbing other tribes, or itself absorbed, had, after generations of wandering, found itself in victorious occupation of the coveted lands of the West. Its King was now a military chief who had led it to victory and whose commands, as in battle, had to be obeyed without question. The old, forgotten Folkmote was no longer a possible institution, when the conquerors were widely scattered over many leagues of territory. Their old noble class had lost many of its chiefs in battle, or by the hardships of campaigns, and the feeble remnant were dispersed on estates far apart. As the King's power grew, a new class of courtiers and officials was forming and gaining administrative power, dependent on the King's will and bound by gratitude and self-interest to support and aggrandise his power. That new aristocracy will in the end challenge and undermine it, but that day was not yet.

The old Teutonic assemblies of the tribe were absolute in determining questions of peace or war. The new German kings in Gaul or Italy levied war or made peace solely by their own will. Clovis might appeal to his warriors on the eve of an expedition against the Visigoths and arouse their new Catholic enthusiasm to drive out the Arian heretics from Aquitaine. But his sons and grandsons, when they launched expeditions against Thuringians, Saxons, Lombards, or Visigoths, were evidently unchecked by any popular control. The King's orders went forth to his Dukes and Counts to call out the fighting men of their districts on a certain day. The King was said, in recurring phrase, to "put his army in motion". There might be murmurs of discontent; there might be malingering; but the man who disregarded the *bannus* of the King made himself liable to a penalty of 60 *solidi*, which in those days to a poor man was a very heavy fine, and which the provincial authorities were not slow to exact. The army of Clovis, composed of about 6000 Franks, and the Roman troops taken over after the defeat of Syagrius, formed a regular army which had been long under arms; hardened by danger and highly trained, it must have been a formidable force. Whether his sons retained

a like force it seems impossible to affirm.   But there is nothing
to show that the Merovingians of the second generation possessed
a regular army on a permanent footing, or permanent garrisons
to guard the frontier.   This is a singular fact.   For during the
sixth century there were few years in which the country was not
convulsed by intestine conflicts or preparation for foreign expeditions.   The kings were constantly fighting one another or hurling
their forces against other German tribes.   For all those operations they seem to have had to rely on a *levée en masse*, raised in
obedience to the King's sole and arbitrary order.   Sometimes, if
the hostilities had only a limited range, only the men of a neighbouring province would be called out, as when Sigibert, in his
attack on Arles, employed the men of Auvergne, or when
Chilperic summoned the troops of Poitiers and Tours for his
expedition against the Bretons.   There appear to have been no
legal limits to the military powers of the King.   There would
seem to have been no fixed limit of age or length of service for
the soldiers.   Men could be sent anywhere, to Thuringia, Italy,
or Spain.   There was no organisation for military training.
There was no regular pay or organised commissariat.   In many
districts, especially south of the Loire, the Franks must have
been few in number, and therefore Gallo-Romans must have often
far outnumbered them in a levy from such districts as those of
Poitiers, Bourges, or Auvergne.   How these tumultuary armies,
sometimes of 100,000 men, were armed and got into any military
order, at very short notice, must remain a mystery.   Where did
the subordinate officers come from, who are the backbone of
modern armies, and essential to any kind of discipline ?   Apparently the Count, along with his officials, headed the men of his
canton when in the field.   But where had the Count obtained his
knowledge of war ?   And the men under his command were not
only the higher and more intelligent class of large farmers and
proprietors, who might have some instinct for discipline and the
use of arms.   It is clear from Gregory of Tours that small cottiers
and tenants, even the men who are called *pauperes* and *juniores
ecclesiae*, on occasion, were not exempted from service in the
army.

  The higher commanding officers must have had a trying task
in getting such an army, or rabble, in motion for its objective,
and in maintaining order on the march.   These officers, Patricians,

Dukes or Counts, were apparently often men of Roman race, and how they got the knowledge required for command is mysterious, since the Gallo-Romans, during many generations, had generally lost all taste or aptitude for war. One can hardly conceive Sidonius or most of his literary friends commanding a corps in one of the Frank armies, although Ecdicius of Auvergne proved himself a gallant cavalier, and the Arvernian nobles fought well at the battle of Vouglé. And some of the most brilliant generals in the sixth century were of Gallo-Roman race : Celsus, Desiderius, and above all Eunius Mummolus, who repelled successive invasions of the Lombards, and finally lent his genius to the ill-fated effort of the pretender Gundobald. But however they were commanded, the Merovingian armies, wanting as they were in morale and discipline, often got beyond any control, and became more dangerous to their friends than to the enemy. They were defeated by Saxons, Lombards, and Huns. In his war with Chilperic, Sigibert in 574 had to invoke the aid of a horde of Germans from beyond the Rhine, whom he found it impossible to control. The Frank armies were often seized with a general panic and fled homewards in utter disorder. Or, setting out for an expedition to Italy, they would hopefully begin by plundering and devastating part of their own territory, as when the army of Childebert II. in 590, starting on a campaign against the Lombards, under the command of twenty dukes, speedily left a trail of pillage and massacre behind them in the plains of Metz. Famine and gross indulgence alternately spread disease among their ranks, and only a broken remnant ever returned to their homes in Gaul. The commanding personality of Clovis had severely checked the predatory instincts of his army in his campaign against the Visigoths in 510. But two generations later, in 585, when his grandson Guntram sent an army to drive the Goths from Septimania, the army became so utterly demoralised that Guntram called his generals to account. And their impotent defence was that their forces would respect no authority, human or Divine. The Frank king was theoretically, in modern German phrase, an all-powerful war lord. But the address of Guntram to his generals in the church of S. Symphorian betrays, under all its high-sounding menaces, a strange sense of weakness.

The King was absolute in theory, and generally in practice. He could order a whole population to his standards, and they

generally obeyed. But once in the field, these tumultuary armies
not only sometimes defied their officers in their rage for rapine ;
they sometimes even challenged or questioned the supreme
authority of the King. When, in 532, Chlothar and Childebert
were meditating the invasion of Burgundy, they sought the aid
of their brother Theuderic in the expedition. Theuderic refused, because he was at the time bent on punishing the defection
of Auvergne, which had declared for Childebert. But Theuderic's
warriors threatened to forsake him if he did not join in the
expedition of his brothers. With them it was a question of the
larger booty, and Theuderic secured the obedience of his men by
promising them the rich plunder of Auvergne, a promise which
was amply and cruelly fulfilled. One other instance of military
insubordination may be given. In 556, King Chlothar was
irritated by the failure of the Saxons to pay their promised
tribute, and levied an army to invade their territory. In order
to avert the invasion, the Saxons made successive offers successively rising, until at last they tried to propitiate the invaders
by a promise of all their goods and half their territory. Chlothar
was naturally, as a responsible chief, ready to accept such terms
at once. But his army would hear of nothing but measures of
extreme severity. And at last they actually dragged the King
from his tent, and, under threats of death, forced him to lead
them forward on an expedition which ended in the failure that
his military prudence could foresee.

These military risings inspired by rage for plunder did not,
however, seriously shake the foundations of the King's authority.
The arbitrary and even savage assertion of their power (of which
we shall presently see some glaring examples) never for generations seems to have weakened the hold of the Merovingian race
on the mass of their subjects, whether Frank or Roman. The
Merovingian family had some secret spell which guarded them
and gave them a longer permanence than was conceded to other
conquering German tribes. The Visigoths had the evil custom
of murdering their kings. If Frank kings were murdered, it was
by the will of some rival of their house. The appeal of Guntram
in the church at Orleans in 585, that his house should be guarded
from violence and extinction as the sole defenders of the people,
was powerful and probably effective. It was a startling appeal
for loyalty from a family stained with all the crimes of Pelopid

legend. It seemed like setting wolves to guard the fold. And yet this would not represent the facts and sentiment of the time. The man in supreme authority over a great people, a Nero or a Caligula, may be guilty of the most revolting atrocities to a small circle surrounding him, while to the vast mass of his subjects he may not only seem, but really be, a guardian and just ruler. Men, especially in unquiet times, feel so deeply the need of leadership and order, and the effective symbols of it, that they will often endure to be governed by a figure-head or a monster. The experience and traditions of both races in Gaul tended to foster obedience and respect for authority. They had their long tradition of allegiance to the Emperor or his representative, the prefect, even although the one might be a feeble Honorius and the other a monster like Arvandus. The tale of the " long-haired kings " ran back into mists of legend and linked them with heroes of Troy and forgotten chiefs in wars on the Danube. Whatever else the Frank chiefs had been, they had always been gallant fighters, and they had led their tribe at last to victory and fruitful conquest. The conquests of Childeric and Clovis had made a wandering band of warriors masters of Gaul and Western Germany, and shed new lustre on the line of Francion and Merovechus. These exploits, chanted round the watch-fires, invested the ruling house with an imaginative halo which is the surest power of kingship.

Clovis inherited his chieftainship from at least three generations of kingly ancestors, and his line continued in unbroken succession till the middle of the eighth century. During all that time the Frank people never rose against their royal house, in spite of many provocations. The Franks who refused to become Christians with Clovis deserted him indeed, but they put themselves at once under another Merovingian, Ragnachar of Cambrai, and they afterwards returned to Clovis. The division of the territory among brothers, again and again, with ever-fluctuating boundaries between the kingdoms, caused the transference of allegiance from one to another : but it was always from one Merovingian to another. If a Merovingian king was left the solitary representative of his house, he assumed the sole sovereignty of all the Frank realms without challenge. The sacred law of royal inheritance which, amid the jealous and unscrupulous aristocracy, so often guarded the rights of an infant king, had calamitous results in the long minority of so many kings, which did so much to weaken the monarchy. But although the hereditary title of the house was so secure against popular attack, the principle of divided inheritance of sovereignty created danger in the house itself. A district around Soissons, through its leading (*fortiores*) men, asked Childebert II. to give them his son, then four years old, as their king. And more than once the kings had to face the claims to equal rights of real or pretended members of their family. These claims may sometimes have been legitimate, for the sexual connections of the early Frank kings were of Oriental laxity ; they had their harems. And "legitimate" and "illegitimate", in such a household, became doubtful terms. In the period covered by this book there were at least four claimants to a share in sovereignty, and all claimed on the strength of their Merovingian descent. They all had some support, but all failed in the end. In the reign of Theuderic I. one Munderic, who claimed to be his blood relation, boldly asserted his equal right to a share in the sovereignty, and Theuderic, by inviting him to a conference, seemed to give some recognition to his claims. But the conference was declined, and Theuderic had to face an armed revolt. Munderic threw himself into the strong fortress of Vitry, which Theuderic found it impossible to take by force. He therefore allured his enemy from his shelter by a sworn pledge of safe conduct which he intended to violate. Munderic perpetrated the folly of trusting a Merovingian. On coming forth he was at once beset, but when he fell he left a pile of enemies around his corpse. A more formidable attempt was that of Chramnus in 555. He was the son of one of the many wives of King Chlothar. He bore the title of Rex and was appointed Viceroy of Auvergne, where he made himself detested. He deposed the Count, insulted and menaced the bishop, and outraged the modesty of high-born maidens. Not content with convulsing Auvergne, he laid plans, with the support of his uncle Childebert, to seize the southern possessions of his father, and vested himself in a monarchy of Aquitaine and Auvergne. It was an anticipation of the attempt of Gundobald a generation later. Chlothar was engaged in a desperate campaign against the Saxons. But his two other sons, Charibert and Guntram, were ordered to march against their rebellious brother. The armies were about to engage when a thunderstorm came on which delayed the battle. Chramnus circulated a rumour that Chlothar had fallen in battle with the Saxons, and his two brothers fell back on Burgundy. Chramnus pressed upon their heels and took Chalon by siege. At Dijon, laying the sacred books upon the altar, he sought by the *sortes biblicae* to learn his fate. Prophet, apostle, and evangelist were equally menacing. Still he pressed on, entered Paris, and joining hands with Childebert overran the region from Rheims to the Rhine. The death of Childebert at Paris was fatal to the ambitions of the rebellious son of Chlothar. Chlothar returned from his campaign in Germany, took over all the realm and treasure of his brother, and seems to have even pardoned for the time his traitorous son. But Chramnus was incurably disloyal. He broke out again and fled to raise the standard of revolt in Brittany. Chlothar, like another David, advanced against another Absalom, mourning and weeping. Chramnus and his Bretons were routed ; he was captured with his wife and daughters ; and, by order of his father, they were all burnt alive in a peasant's cottage. It was a ghastly crime, but it gives us the measure of the peril which a powerful monarch felt might threaten him from a member of his own house.

Twenty years later Chilperic, the son of Chlothar, had to meet a similar but less serious conspiracy. Merovechus, one of his three sons by Audovera, having been ordered to lead an expedition against Poitiers, suddenly deserted his command and betook himself to Rouen, ostensibly to visit his mother there. His real object was to marry his widowed aunt, Brunihildis, the Queen of Austrasia, by whose beauty he had been fascinated. The wooing was short : the ceremony was performed by the bishop Praetextatus, who had "taken the young prince" from the sacred font, and was blindly devoted to him. The guilty pair, on the approach of Chilperic, took refuge in a church of S. Martin. But that placable monarch was easily reconciled to them, although he carried off his son to Soissons. Presently, an army under Godinus, an Austrasian general, appeared under the walls, and a battle was fought which proved disastrous to the invaders. When Chilperic reflected on the sudden invasion from Champagne coupled with the union of Merovechus and the Austrasian queen, he could only come to one conclusion. It was all a daring plan to drive him from the throne and to unite

Neustria and Austrasia under the sway of Merovechus and Brunihildis. The suspicion was amply confirmed by the subsequent
conduct of Merovechus, and by the revelations at the trial of
Bishop Praetextatus.

The fourth, and not the least serious, rising against the Frank
monarchy was that of Gundobald, who claimed to be a son of
Chlothar. Its importance in the history of the time is so great
that it has been treated at length in another chapter. The
pretender was probably, as he claimed to be, a real son of the
Merovingian house. Though perhaps personally insignificant, he
was supported with great treasure by Maurice, the Eastern
emperor, and by the intrigues and secret diplomacy of the nobles
of Austrasia. The object of the plot is rather obscure. But it
seems to have been designed to wipe out the monarchies of
Burgundy and Neustria, and to found a single Frank monarchy
embracing Aquitaine and the three Frank kingdoms of the north,
in which the nobles of Austrasia should have a dominant influence.
Great generals supported Gundobald, but his career was a short
one, and his effort was stamped out in blood under the walls of
Convenae. Not one of these assaults on the Merovingian
monarchy came near to success. There was no strong popular force
behind them, and the leaders were all crushed with ruthless energy.

The only popular risings which caused momentary anxiety
were due to the burden and the supposed injustice of taxation.
The people might indignantly demand the reduction of a tax ;
but they seem never to have questioned the King's supreme power
of taxation. And wherever we hear of taxes being levied, it is
by sole command of the King, who appoints the collectors
(*descriptores*) to make the assessments and draw up the registers.
Yet it seems highly probable that the Merovingians in the
main lines of their financial administration followed the Imperial
system which they found established or decaying in Gaul. In
the main the Imperial organisation of customs and market dues
seems to have been retained, with little alteration. The Roman
names of the taxes and of the officials who collected them, are
the same far into the early Middle Ages. Customs and tolls which
were collected under the Empire were maintained or raised by the
Frank kings ; sometimes granted to a bishop of Tournai, or
remitted in favour of the abbey of S. Denis. It is clear from
one document that the old custom-houses were still kept up at

Marseilles, Arles, Toulon, Avignon, Valence, Vienne, Lyons, and Chalon. A capitulary of Charlemagne's time requires the ancient *telonea* to be still exacted from traders at ports and bridges. The Imperial rule that all officers, agents, and couriers of the government could demand lodging and entertainment on their routes was not relaxed by the German kings. It is sternly enforced in the Burgundian and Ripuarian Codes, and in an edict of Charlemagne.

The great source of Imperial revenue which, in its weight and the mode of collection, did so much to precipitate the fall of the Empire, was the land tax, called *tributum*, or *census publicus*. The lists were drawn up, with full particulars of acreage, mode of culture, and yield, by *descriptores* or *peraequatores*. The heavy charge of collection was laid on the members of the municipal *curia*, who were responsible for the amount so levied. The nature of their task and the tragedy of their fate may be read in 192 enactments of the Theodosian Code. From the technical terms and descriptions in many of our authorities, Gregory of Tours, the Lives of the Saints, and the Acts of Councils, it appears probable that the land tax of the Empire was, as a general system, retained by the Frank kings. The great authority on the subject is a resolution of the Council of Auvergne, in 535, in the first generation after the conquest, which was intended to guard landed proprietors in one Merovingian realm, invaded, as they were often were, by another of the race. The words *debita tributa* seem to refer to an old customary tax of the Empire. It is evident that this tax under the early Merovingians was a great resource of revenue entirely at the command of the kings, and raised or lowered at their will, with some deference or submission to the difficulties and feelings of their subjects.

It seems almost impossible to determine the scale or amount of the tax on land levied by the Frank kings. King Chlothar about the year 544 levied a tax of one-third of their fruits from estates of the Church. And his demand was resisted only by Injuriosus, the Bishop of Tours, who by fierce maledictions compelled Chlothar to abate it. The only other indication of the amount of the tax is in the account of Chilperic's fresh exactions in 580, by which it was fixed at one amphora of wine to half an acre (*iugerum*). One of the ablest and most judicious German writers on this period, in an elaborate calculation, comes to the conclusion that this was far from an exorbitant demand, and that the Merovingian land tax was much lighter than the Roman had been. It is to be noted that Chilperic imposed other taxes on lands and the serfs employed in their culture. As to the mode of levying the land tax the authorities are equally scanty and obscure. Only one, relating to a *descriptio* of Childebert in 587, throws a doubtful light on the problem. A revision of the census of the district of Poitiers was demanded by the bishop. It was decided that, while the assessment made in the preceding reign must stand, due consideration should be given to the fact that in the interval many deaths had taken place, and that the burden now often fell on widows and orphans and impoverished persons. M. de Coulanges contends that in this passage of Gregory we find a clear continuation of the system of the Empire by which the levy on each estate was proportioned to the number of tenants and serfs on it ; and that on an estate where the population of tenants had been reduced by death, justice required a revision of the assessment to be made. It seems very doubtful whether this ingenious explanation of the words of Gregory will bear examination. For it was the lord of the estate who had to pay the tax, and the object of Childebert's revision was to relieve the widows and orphans of men liable for payment who had died. It is hard to believe that the *pauperes* and *infirmi* whom the King's officers were directed to relieve of the burden were the bereaved families of cottiers and serfs.

But whatever may have been the weight of the tax, it is clear that again and again in the sixth century the people found it too heavy, and the most despotic kings felt obliged to order a revision of the census rolls, or even their public destruction. It is curious that more than once the taxation under Chlothar I., a man of the most vicious life and fiendish cruelty, is appealed to in later times apparently as a standard of fairness and justice. Three or four years after his death a new levy by the Frank kings aroused such discontent that S. Aridius hastened to the court in order to plead for its abatement. In 580 Chilperic ordered a fresh revision of the census rolls, with greatly increased taxation. The immediate result was that many, being unable to meet the demands of the tax-gatherers, abandoned their lands and emigrated to other realms. The people of Limoges, incensed by fiscal cruelty, rose in revolt and would have put the royal referendary to death but for the interposition of the bishop,

Ferreolus. But the census rolls were seized by the mob and given to the flames, a defiance which was fiercely punished, even by the torture and crucifixion of priests and abbots who had borne a part in the revolt.

A few months later than these tumults, when the terrors of the plague had fallen on the royal house and Chilperic and his children were stricken, Queen Fredegundis, for once humbled by the Divine vengeance, " in a late penitence ", as the chronicler says, appealed to her husband to put an end to their cruel exactions, and to pay heed to the sighs and tears of the orphans and widows of those whom they had plundered and crushed. The cellars and barns, she says, are full to overflowing. Their treasure chambers are packed with gold and silver and all sorts of jewels and lordly wealth. Smiting her breast, the impetuous and guilty Queen ordered the census rolls of her cities to be cast into the flames, and appealed to Chilperic to imitate her example and restore the scale of taxation established by Chlothar, which Chilperic had enormously and oppressively raised. Chlothar II. made an attempt to increase his revenue by a fresh levy, but was forced to exempt from it the diocese of Tours by the determined opposition of Gregory the bishop, who showed that Tours had, " *pro reverentia S. Martini* ", enjoyed immunity in the reigns of Chlothar I., Charibert, and Sigibert. The agents of the fisc produced a register containing an assessment of the lands of Tours, which had probably been drawn up in the reign of Chlothar, before that monarch had been persuaded to do honour to the see of S. Martin. But the bishop proved that this document could not have come from the royal archives, but must have been a municipal copy surreptitiously kept by some of the citizens, and now treacherously produced to avenge himself on an enemy in one of the sanguinary feuds which then afflicted Tours.

Such exemptions of church lands or districts consecrated by the memory of a saint were not uncommon in that age. The Merovingians, however gross their personal conduct, yielded to none in religious reverence, or rather fear of the wrath of supernal powers. For their rapacity was sorely tempted by the growing wealth of the Church, of which Chilperic used, probably with justice, to complain. And we have seen a king attempting to claim one-third of the Church revenues for his treasury. But the bishops could powerfully guard the treasures of the Church by the menace of Divine vengeance on him who laid a sacrilegious hand on the gifts of the faithful.   The appeal, as in the case of Tours, protected not only the immediate property of the shrine, but that of the people of the district, who thus gained an exemption at the cost of the general tax-paying public of the realm. Auvergne was equally favoured by the pious Theudebert, who, probably owing to the far-spread fame of S. Julian, remitted all the tribute due from Church property in that region.   In the year 590 Childebert II. made a remission of Arvernian tribute on a large scale to all the churches, the monastic houses, and to the clerical class generally.

The passage which records the pious act of Childebert also throws some light on the mode in which the tax was collected. It appears that the collectors in Auvergne were at this time ruined by a growing difficulty in obtaining payment of the tribute, caused by the minute subdivision of estates which had been going on for generations.   Those officers bear the name *exactores*, which their predecessors of the Empire had borne. And, like them, they are not direct agents of the government, but private middlemen who are held responsible for the total amount of the levy to the Treasury.   The reform of Childebert II. seems to have provided that in future the collector should not be ruined by the tardiness of the proprietors in paying the sums for which he was responsible to the count.   For it was one of the count's principal duties to remit every year to the Royal Exchequer all the dues and taxes imposed on his district.   Thus he stood in the same relation of responsibility to the King as that in which the *exactores* stood to him.   And in both cases there must often have been anxiety and risk.   The count had probably to make his payment to the Treasury regularly on a certain day.   If he had not then received the amount due, he was compelled to advance it at his own risk.   Unless he was a rich man he would then have to resort to the money-lenders, who were probably in that age often Jews.   A tragic tale in Gregory reveals all the details of one of these transactions at Tours.   Two Jews, with two Christian partners, had advanced on bonds the amount of the tribute to Injuriosus, an ex-Vicar, and Eunomius, the ex-count. Armentarius, the head of the money-lending firm, came to Tours to claim payment, and was promised an immediate settlement

K

with full interest, and, along with his partners, he accepted an invitation to a banquet, where they were killed by the servants of Injuriosus and their bodies were flung into a well, where they were discovered by the relatives of the murdered men. The matter came before the local courts. The complainants failed to produce sufficient evidence, and as they declined to accept the oath of innocence from Injuriosus, the case was carried up to the King's presence. But as no documents were forthcoming and the accusers failed to appear, after three days Injuriosus returned to his home. It is significant that a tribune, who was probably a collector (*exactor*) of the tax, was rumoured to be privy to this crime, as he also was in debt to the Jew.

The question whether the Frank proprietors were exempt from the land tax has been long debated with a confidence and dogmatism hardly justified in the uncertainty and scantiness of our authorities. Theoretically, and *a priori*, the exemption of Franks, in the first years of the conquest, might appear to be natural. The conquerors might probably claim and obtain freedom from the burden. And when the King made grants out of the public lands, which had not been on the Roman register for taxation, they may probably for the time have continued exempt in the hands of the new private owner. And just as some great bishops obtained relief for their dioceses, so a powerful Frank may have now and then won his exemption on the ground of great services. But although all this is possible, and even probable, it cannot be proved from the extant authorities. On the contrary, it is clear from two passages in Gregory that the Franks of Austrasia had borne the burden in the reign of Theudebert, and that, although some Neustrian Franks had enjoyed immunity in the reign of Childebert I., they had been deprived of it by Chilperic. Frequently in the Chronicles and the Lives of the Saints we hear that a new levy of taxes was ordered for all the *civitates* of the realm, and no hint is given of any express exemption for men of Frank race. Yet these edicts issued by Chilperic must have embraced districts such as Tournai, an old home of the Salian Franks, where they must have remained a majority of the population. And in the cases where Gregory speaks of a revision of the census, he never hints at any distinction between Roman and Frank. The conclusion of Löbell, one of the sanest of historical critics, seems the most probable approach to the facts. It was not an age of definite rights, fixed by express agreement or legal formula. There is no trace of a general formal exemption of the Franks from fiscal burdens, although it is probable that many of them did actually enjoy such freedom. But, as the power of the Merovingians became more consolidated and confident, and Romans rose to higher status in Church and State, the kings strove to establish an equality of the two races, and we have seen two kings imposing the land tax on the Franks.

Unfortunately the Frank absolutism which we have tried to describe in its various aspects often in the judicial sphere enforced its will by the most inhuman means, by exquisite torture or cruel execution, without the pretence of legal forms. From the day when Clovis, flushed with victory, did to death his near kinsmen at Cologne and Cambrai, the record of his house, from one generation to another, is stained with blood and foul treachery. His son Theuderic planned to kill Chlothar, his brother, in a campaign across the Rhine; and Chlothar and Childebert put to death the orphaned sons of their brother Chlodomer, fallen in battle against the Burgundians. Such a race, clothed with autocratic powers, and unchecked by any other recognised authority, popular or aristocratic, had free play for its despotic instincts where crime was in question, and especially crime against themselves. In legal jurisdiction, as in legislation and the control of the army and the treasury, it is now clear that the Frank kings in the sixth century had practically unlimited power, and they claimed it in their edicts. These documents give the most sweeping powers to *comites* or *judices* to investigate and punish crime in the King's sole name, with stern warnings against venality or injustice; and the *judex* appears to have frequently inflicted extreme punishment, in spite of the merciful entreaties of the bishop. The count might be surrounded on the bench by great churchmen and magnates of the district—and no doubt they could advise, expostulate, and plead for milder punishment—but the *judex* had behind him the King's authority, and his decision was supreme and final. In the Lives of the Saints holy men often intercede for the accused; sometimes they prevail for mercy, sometimes their entreaties are in vain. But it is always clear that the royal judge can accept or reject their appeals in virtue of his delegated authority. That the Church had decided opinions as to the *saevitia judicum* is often picturesquely illustrated by the miracles wrought to mitigate it, even towards the worst criminals. Yet in this sacred sentiment is there not, in an age of brutal force and selfishness, a fine tradition of Him who was gentle to publicans and harlots, and who threw the screen of His pity around her who was taken in adultery ?

But judicial power, unrestrained by any popular check, was often summary, arbitrary, and even cruel. Probably, in an age of fierce impulses and unchastened character, the judge had no choice between laxity and severity. Society had to be held together, even at a great cost to individual safety and liberty ; crime had to be kept down without fear or favour, and the count or *judex* always knew that he had the King's authority, expressed in formal edicts, at his back.

In a great number of cases in the Chronicles and the Lives of the Saints we see the count or *judex* dealing most summarily with a criminal, without even the form of a trial. Thus Count Becco ordered a servant of S. Julian's to be crucified for the supposed theft of a lost hawk. Thus Count Leudastes cast into prison as a runaway slave a free artisan visiting S. Martin's for a cure. The judges are enjoined to administer justice according to law, and never to accept or solicit bribes for their decisions. But their first duty is to suppress crime, and to do it ruthlessly. In one decree the judge is ordered to put to death at once any man guilty of rape. In another, when the count hears of a robbery, he is at once to go to the house of the criminal, and, if he is a man of low degree, he is to be hanged on the spot ; if he is a Frank, he will be tried before the King. And we constantly see the order acted on. At Vermandois, a priest, who had had his horse stolen, informed the count, and that zealous officer at once apprehended the guilty man, put him in prison. and on his confession condemned him to the gibbet. M. de Coulanges rightly draws attention to the fact, which cannot escape an unprejudiced student of the authorities, that, in these and many other cases, there is not a hint of any popular control in the administration of justice. The commission of the count, issued by the Royal Chancery, and the constant exercise of uncontrolled authority, leave no doubt that the judicial system of the Merovingians paid slight heed to old German ideas of justice. It was not an age governed according to ancient precedents and formulæ, but one demanding rough and ready action to meet the problems of a society which was remaking itself.

The *judices* or counts wielded a delegated authority, although it was often exerted, and intended by the King to be exerted on necessary occasion, with sole despotic decision. But the King was the ultimate source of this authority, and the King was, and claimed to be, " over all causes supreme " ; and his was the final court of appeal. This court is constantly described as being in " his presence ", or in " his palace ", wherever that " palace " for the time may have been, at Paris, Soissons, or Metz, or in one of the many *villae* or country houses among which the Frank kings were constantly moving. Sometimes the chronicler represents the King as acting as sole judge with supreme judicial authority, and that even in civil cases as to property. But the most striking examples of sole decisions of the King are in criminal cases, especially in cases of dangerous treason (*crimen majestatis*), where, in those days, the treacherous plot or disloyal act needed to be speedily and signally avenged. Thus Guntram ordered the execution of the sons of Magnacharius, who had cast abominable imputations on his queen Austrechildis, and he confiscated all their property. A Frank named Chundo was summoned before the King for unlicensed hunting in the royal chase. The King at first dealt with him judicially, for Chundo was allowed trial by combat. When his champion was defeated, the culprit tried to take sanctuary in the Church of S. Marcellus, but was seized by Guntram's orders, bound to a stake, and stoned to death. Three Franks of the highest rank, who were detected in a plot against Childebert, were at once executed by the King's command. Clovis and his descendants never hesitated to assert their omnipotence in council or in the field ; and irresponsible power, uncontrolled by any settled traditions of ordered freedom, will often assert itself or defend itself by savage cruelty. The catalogue of such enormities is too long and monotonous to be told in detail, but one or two specimens may be taken to represent a ghastly series. In 575 Sigibert, one of the few estimable members of his race, when his brother Chilperic seemed to be at his mercy, was suddenly struck down at his *villa* at Vitry by two assassins armed with poisoned daggers by Fredegundis, Chilperic's queen. Chilperic, whose doom seemed almost sealed, celebrated his restoration to power by ordering one of Sigibert's adherents, a Goth named Sigila, to be exquisitely tortured with red-hot instruments, and torn limb from limb. When Merovechus, Chilperic's rebellious son, after many romantic adventures, was at last driven to earth among the Morini, being hard pressed by his pursuers, in order to avoid falling into his father's hands, he begged his faithful squire, Gailenus, to despatch him by the dagger. Gailenus obeyed, and Chilperic in hot haste arrived only to see his son's dead body. He at once ordered the hands, feet, and nose of Gailenus to be cut off, and the poor victim of loyalty to a Merovingian died under accumulated tortures. Under Chilperic's eyes, and presumably with his consent, Queen Fredegundis perpetrated the most revolting atrocities, unchecked either by form of law or human feeling.

Clovis, the son of Audovera, the queen whom Chilperic had discarded, became an object of fear and hatred to his stepmother, and not altogether without cause. He had used reckless language about his prospects of succession, and cast aspersions on Fredegundis, which were probably coloured and perverted by designing reporters. Clovis was said to have cast eyes of desire on one of Fredegundis's maids : such a thing was not improbable in a Merovingian household. But the mother of the girl was charged with having used spells and dark arts to make away with the two young stepbrothers of Clovis, in order, of course, to secure for her daughter a place which the equally low-born Fredegundis had won. The Queen felt that her reign was challenged. The girl was impaled before the windows of Clovis. Her mother, under exquisite torture, confessed her guilt. Clovis was summoned, stripped of his arms and the proper dress of his rank, and brought in bonds before the Queen. She was eager to discover from him whether a great conspiracy lay behind. Clovis confessed that he had strong support. He was relegated to the royal villa of Noisy on the Marne, where he died, either by suicide or assassination. His mother, Queen Audovera, also perished by a cruel death. The woman whose daughter had attracted the eyes of Clovis was burnt alive. It was thus that the Merovingians dealt with their subjects and their kinsmen in the year of grace 580.

The same lawless cruelty is seen in the treatment dealt out by Fredegundis to the witches of Paris and their patron Mummolus, the prefect. A third son of Fredegundis, when little more than a year old, was carried off by the plague. A rumour reached the Queen's ears that the boy had been done to death by magic arts, and that Mummolus was privy to the crime. Women suspected of weird arts were seized and, under torture, confessed that they had devoted the child's life for that of Mummolus, the prefect. They were broken on the rack, or died under other awful tortures. Mummolus was stretched on the wheel and flogged with a triple lash till those who wielded it were exhausted ; and splinters of wood were driven under the nails of his feet and hands. At last, a mere wreck of a man, he was placed on a wagon and driven away to die at Bordeaux, the place of his birth. The same determined cruelty is seen in the ghastly death inflicted on Leudastes. Leudastes is a type of the cynical immorality and greedy ambition of the time, shameless, false, and arrogant. In a stormy career of strange vicissitudes he had earned the hatred of Fredegundis. Presenting himself before the Queen one Sunday at Mass, he was driven out with contempt into the streets, and then set upon and wounded by the Queen's servants and thrown into prison. Orders were given that he should be carefully tended by the doctors, but only to prepare him for prolonged torture. He expired under brutal violence and indignities inflicted by order of the Queen.

King Guntram, like Chilperic, is a complex and puzzling character. He was the least despotic and the most generous of his family. He could be genial and good-humoured on occasion, and he was evidently a popular ruler. But he was selfish and faithless, forming alliances and forsaking his allies in rapid succession, and in lawless cruelty he could match any of his race. He had married Marcatrudis, daughter of the duke Magnacharius. This lady was said to have poisoned Gundobad, a son of Guntram by a concubine, and was divorced. She was succeeded by a waiting woman named Austrechildis, and the sons of Magnacharius, in avenging their sister, did not spare Austrechildis's reputation. Guntram, without any legal formality, put them to death and confiscated their estates. Queen Austrechildis, in that dreadful year, 580, was smitten with the plague, and when she was on the verge of death she bound her husband by a solemn oath to put to death her two physicians, whose drugs, as the ignorant fierce woman firmly believed, had hastened her end. When her obsequies had been duly performed, Guntram calmly and faithfully observed his promise to the letter.

In these examples of arbitrary cruelty by the Merovingians there is no trace of judicial proceeding, but only personal passion or the desire of vengeance, unrestrained by law. At the same time we must not ignore a more tempered and regular procedure in the royal courts. While the King could decide a cause by his sole will, as a matter of fact, in giving judgement, he is often seen surrounded and advised by a numerous council, composed variously of bishops, *optimates* or *proceres*, counts, *domestici*, referendaries, and other officers of the household, resembling our Privy Council. But it is to be observed that the members of this council were nearly always men holding office by royal choice and favour. And their decisions are not given by their own right and in their own name ; their judgement is given in the name and authority of the King. Of course, just as in later times, this may be often a loyal fiction. When a boy king of six years loftily declares his will, we may be sure that he speaks in the name of mature councillors who for the time are acting for him and gilding their decisions by his prestige. Probably the King was at times prevented from attending his council by other engagements. In one curious case he actually retires at the request of one of the litigants. In such cases the decision was really that of the *proceres*, etc. But in the extant documents it is always pronounced and issued by the King, by his sole and supreme authority. The royal court must have dealt with a wide range of business, both criminal and civil. It received appeals from the decisions of counts and lower judges. But matters both civil and criminal might be brought at once before the King ; or the King, on information reaching him, might summon the parties to his presence, without the intervention of any lower jurisdiction. Both in the codes and the royal edicts counts and governors are threatened with extreme penalties for corruption or abuse of their powers, and the court before which these officials could be impeached was the court of the Palace. It was also the court before which all causes where a bishop was a party were brought for adjudication.

The King was thus absolute in theory, and supreme in all departments of administration, civil, military, or judicial. But no man, however despotic in temper and ambitions, could personally cope with the multifarious business of a great realm; and the most powerful monarch needs many hands and eyes, even in the rudest stage of political development, to assist him in the tasks of government. The mode in which the Frank kings organised the central or provincial administration of Gaul after the conquest is a subject of great interest, and the study of it must excite a certain surprise that a band of rude warriors should, in so short a time, have created a system which, in spite of faults and vices of administration, aimed generally at the good of the subjects and a settled order. But Clovis may have had around him some Frank chiefs who had served in Roman armies, mixed in the society of the capital, and imbibed something of the spirit which had organised the Imperial order. And bishops of Gallo-Roman race, who had long experience both of civil and ecclesiastical government, would certainly bear a part in the reconstruction; and, of course, a deep-seated tradition of old German institutions, which, at least in tone and sentiment, survived many years of wandering from the old homes of the race, cast its colour over the new structure of society. The Franks, with all their fierceness and pride of race, still must have had a prudent sense of the practical difficulty of ordering anew a great society, disorganised by invasion and the collapse of ancient authority, yet instinct with the tradition of a civil order which had for centuries prevailed from the Channel to the Mediterranean.

The court of the Merovingians is a kind of shadow or reflection of the court of the Roman Emperors. Its very name, *Palatium*, recalls the centre of the Imperial regime. It designates not only the residence of the sovereign, but also the seat of government; and a great number of the *palatini* are not only courtiers in attendance, but political officers whose work may lie sometimes in the bureaux of the Palace, sometimes in seats of provincial administration. The Frank kings had their chief place of residence at Paris or Soissons or Metz. But they had many *villae*, or country seats, among which they were continually moving either for the pleasures of the chase or to obtain fresh supplies for their numerous households, without the cost and difficulty of transport. Wherever they may be, for the time their residence is the " Palace ", in the political sense as a centre of authority and administration. It is probable that after the conquest the

Frank kings took over the bureaux of the Praetorian Prefect. with their hierarchy of officials, very much as the permanent civil service in modern countries remains unchanged on a change of ministry, or even after a revolution. The official titles and offices of the Empire often reappear at the Frank courts. The Palace is still " sacred " as in the reign of Constantine or Theodosius. The great courtiers are still *viri illustres* and *magnifici*. Many of them in a long *cursus honorum* pass their whole lives in the Palatine *militia* from early boyhood to old age. They are *nutriti* or *convivae* or *amici regis*, titles which had not only a ceremonial but a very real value in the enactments of the Code. Although mere talent or audacity sometimes found a career at court, yet the young candidates for the King's service were generally drawn from families of wealth and social rank, whether Frank or Gallo-Roman. The youthful aspirants to office were " commended " to the King and enrolled in a *corps des pages*, to be trained under royal tutors in the fading literature of the decadence, in religious doctrine and practice, in arms and the arts which go to form the administrator or the courtier. The court schools were excellent in intention, and probably formed many skilled officials and polished men of the world, although the record of many of the referendaries, dukes, and counts whom they trained may leave a doubt as to their influence on character.

It would be tedious to go minutely through the long list of officers who were either in personal attendance on the King, or who carried on the various departments of administration. The relative importance of the court officials and their precise duties are not definitely ascertained. The *cursus honorum*, traced in a poem of Fortunatus, describes Conda, one of his patrons, as rising by gradual ascent from the tribune's place to that of count, then to that of *domesticus*, and finally to the crowning dignity of *conviva regis*. The tribune in Gregory of Tours appears to have been a collector of taxes. He had also probably to assist the count in his other functions. The *referendarius*, a title of the Byzantine Empire, possessed great power and consideration under the Frank kings and is frequently mentioned in Gregory and Fortunatus. His duty was to present documents for the royal signature and to countersign them. He also naturally had the custody of the great seal. But he was occasionally employed in

provincial administration, as when one Marcus, referendary of
Chilperic, was sent to Limoges to arrange a new land tax, when
there was serious popular clamour. Gregory and Fredegarius
also sometimes mention the *camerarius* or *thesaurarius*. These
officers had the custody of the Royal Treasury, in which were laid
up not only the bullion, coin, and jewels, but the census lists
and other records pertaining to the revenue. The *domestici* are
a puzzling class of officials ; but it is clear that they have important powers and status. The title comes down from the
household of the Emperors of the West ; but in the sixth
century it has changed its meaning and its functions. The
domestici are no longer a bodyguard of the sovereign, nor do
they embrace a large class of various functionaries. They have
become, in one section, controllers of the royal estates, and in
another of the services of the Palace, probably exercising a purely
financial authority over royal tenants and servants. Such an
office of financial importance to the State was bound to acquire
a great and commanding authority. In the gradation of offices
the *domesticus* ranks above count and referendary, although he
cannot claim equality with duke. The importance of such an
office may be realised by forming a conception of what a royal
villa meant. We can see in Sidonius what the country seat or
manor of an aristocrat of the fifth century was. Around the
great house there was a small town, with every grade of rural
household and industry, ploughmen, shepherds, vine-dressers,
cooks, and bakers ; and a crowd of other skilled workers, carding
wool, spinning, weaving raiment for the household and tenants, in
fact carrying on, for a single small society, most of the arts and
manufactures which are now concentrated in our great towns.
When the *villa* was a royal estate, with all the demands of a
luxurious court and a crowd of servants and dependants, an
official who was responsible for its management was bound to
gain large powers and high rank. And such would appear to
have been the position of the *domesticus* in the sixth century.
The office of *major domus*, which rose to such commanding
authority in the following century and finally overthrew and
replaced the Merovingian monarchy, occupies only a small space
in our period. It is mentioned only three times in the works of
Gregory of Tours. The origin of the office is as obscure as its
destiny was splendid. It is claimed as of old Teutonic origin,

and the office certainly existed, with varying functions, at the courts of the Vandal, Burgundian, and Ostrogothic kings. With more probability it is traced to a Roman source. In great Roman houses of the time of S. Jerome the rustic population of a senatorial estate was controlled by a *major domus* with almost despotic power. The precise name does not occur in the list of imperial officers of the Palace ; but the office itself existed under the title *cura palatii* or *praepositus palatii*, and had been held by Aetius in the household of Valentinian III., and by Narses under Justinian. The slight notice of the *major domus* in Gregory of Tours, who knew so intimately the interior of the Frank court, would seem to indicate that the office was comparatively unimportant, with little promise of the commanding authority which it assumed soon after his time, especially in the realm of Austrasia. It was still probably quite subordinate, and far inferior to that of *domesticus*. But once installed as master of such a household, the *major domus* of the Austrasian court, like the great freedmen of the early Emperors, would steadily develop into a great political officer, a Minister of the Interior, interpreting the King's will from having close access to him, and in the end wielding a power only second to the King's. The control of finance, which is the centre of political power, would enable personal ambition to extend a theoretically limited authority till it covered the whole field of administration. It is in the troubled period which lies beyond the limits of this work, in the last years of Brunihildis, that the mayors of the Palace are seen coming to the front in the conflict between the Austrasian nobles and the throne.

Of all the great officers under the Merovingians in the sixth century those whom we meet most frequently in the Chronicles of the time are the count and duke. They were primarily members of the palatine service, and in countless documents they appear in the enumeration of the magnates who surrounded the King in council. Some of them probably never left the precincts of the court, and held high palatine offices such as that of the *comes palatii* or *comes stabuli*. But they were generally engaged in the civil or military administration of provincial districts.

In the fifth century the prefecture of Gaul had been divided into 17 provinces and 112 *civitates*, or municipal districts. But years before the conquests of Clovis the prefects (or provincial governors) had vanished, and the demarcations of the provinces had been wiped out. The minute division of Gaul, which German scholars attribute to the Merovingians under such names as Gau and Hundertschaft, derives no support from the Chronicles of the sixth century, and rests for the most part on *a priori* argument or hypothesis. The one administrative division which the Franks of Clovis took over from the Empire was the *civitas* ; and the cities of the Merovingian times are generally the old Gallic cities of the Imperial period, such as Meaux, Tours, Cahors, Limoges. So absolutely does the *civitas* predominate for administrative purposes that, when a king acquires or surrenders territory, it is nearly always described as so many *civitates* (as when Guntram says to his treacherous enemies that they wished to expel him from his realm and " divide his cities " among them). The Gallo-Roman *civitas* always embraced a considerable extent of country surrounding the city, nor did the Franks separate the town from its rural territory. The *pagus* or canton was not a creation of the Franks ; it was a Gallo-Roman term. But the word *pagus* does not designate an official division either in the Imperial or the Merovingian times. The word occurs frequently in the works of Gregory, and a scrutiny of passages shows that he uses it in two senses : sometimes it means the whole territory of a city, and is almost synonymous with *civitas* ; sometimes it is only a small district, an old Gallic canton. The wider sense is the legal or official one ; the other is the popular. The *pagenses* are the inhabitants of the *civitas* and its territory is under the sway of the count.

The office of *comes* under the Frank kings was not of Teutonic origin. It is a title and dignity familiar in the Imperial period. Under the later Emperors there are *comites* holding the highest dignities at court, members of the Imperial consistory, governors of provinces, such as Egypt, Belgium, or Lyons. Before the Frank conquest, in the days of Sidonius and Salvianus, there were *comites* or *judices* for the government of civic communities. The tradition of the office was maintained by the German kings in Italy, Burgundy, and Northern Gaul and Aquitaine. The Burgundian Law bears the signatures of thirty-one counts. There are many legal documents addressed to *comites* by Cassiodorus, the minister of the Ostrogoth, Theodoric. There is an interesting case in which we can see a Roman count of the Empire continuing in office for many years under the kings of Burgundy. Gregory, an ancestor of the Bishop of Tours, before entering Holy Orders, had been for forty years the Count of Autun, from the year 465, in the nominal reign of Libius Severus, till two years before the victory of Clovis at Vouglé.

The *comes* was, from his very name, a companion of the King, a courtier and counsellor. He might be long resident at court, giving his advice on judicial decisions or edicts; he might hold some definite court office, as *comes stabuli* or *comes palatii*; but he was most commonly sent to represent the King's authority in the administration of a *civitas*.

The count was the delegate of the King, appointed and removable at the King's sole pleasure. Yet the most absolute power is generally subject to some limitations in practice. The King sometimes deferred to the wishes of the people or the bishop in his choice of a count, and an unpopular official might forfeit his place. An edict of Chlothar II. lays down the principle that the count should be a native of the district to which he is appointed, and should have property in it which might furnish security for pure administration. The native princes of the Bretons from the days of Clovis had the title and rank of count. Here and there there are traces of a tendency for the office to continue in the possession of a great family. Thus Palladius of Javols obtained the succession to his father, as Mummolus supplanted his father in the countship of Auxerre. Hortensius, of a high senatorial family in Auvergne, was count of that district in the reign of Theuderic, and his grandson Salustius was installed in the same office thirty years afterwards by the usurper Chramnus. In the same way Nantinus succeeded his uncle Maracharius as Count of Angoulême in 580. But these are exceptional cases of families of commanding social position in their district.

The King was not restrained in his choice for the office either by rank or race. Even under the early Merovingians there are more counts with Roman than with Frank names in the history of Gregory of Tours, and in his native Auvergne, a Sallustius, or a Hortensius, represents some of the greatest Roman families of the province. The Ripuarian Code suggests that a *puer regis*, *i.e.* a freedman, might be elevated to the rank of count, and, in the romantic career of

Leudastes, we see that a slave-cook, who had been branded as a runaway, might, by dexterity and boldness, raise himself to be Count of Tours. The appointment was made according to a fixed formula, the terms of which may still be read. The count is to have under his command Franks, Burgundians, or Romans. His first duty is to maintain unalterable fidelity to the King. He is to govern men in the right way according to law and custom, defending the orphan and widow, and crushing with severity all robbers and evildoers, to the end that the subjects may live in happiness and peace under his rule. He has in person to convey each year the proceeds of all the taxes in his jurisdiction to the Royal Treasury. At the mandate of the King, the count has to call out for service the fighting men of his district, and often to command them on the field. He is bound to visit the abode of any notorious thief or brigand, and at once place him under arrest. As *judex*, a name which he constantly bears, he is enjoined to observe, in all his decisions, the laws and ancient customs of the realm, and stern penalties are denounced against a corrupt or unjust judge. In his judicial capacity, as in all other respects, as has been said, the *comes* is the representative of the King and wields his powers vicariously. But, like his master's, the powers of the *comes* are very vague and undefined, often leaving room for arbitrary and oppressive action ; especially, his power of summary proceedings against supposed criminals, however much needed in that age, was apt to be exercised with a vigour which degenerated into ferocity. But the intention of the monarch, as expressed in his commission, is that the count's administration of justice, while stern to crime, should be just and guided by the general interest. And we may fairly gather from the authorities that on the whole the intention was fulfilled, yet here and there we have glimpses of wild excesses of authority.

It is, however, probable that the greater number of *comites* obeyed their instructions, and faithfully, if sometimes roughly, performed their prescribed duties. Their most important duty was to make the circuit of their districts and hold judicial courts. In these progresses the procedure of the count seems to have been modelled on the *conventus* of the Roman provincial governor, and on the courts of the *principes* in the Germany of Tacitus. The count's court or *mallus* was held in some public place, perhaps in the open air, never in his own lodgings, and it was open to all. In holding a *mallus* the count would be surrounded by the leading men of the place. Out of this concourse the judge would select a number of persons, lay or clerical, to assist him. The bishop would often take his place on the bench. These assessors of the count resemble the council of great folk who sat with the King in his court of judgement. The *rachimburgi*, according to the Salic Law, are to interrogate witnesses and weigh the evidence; but they are never treated as sole judges. The *mallus* would be no court without the presiding count or his vicar. The proceedings always assume his presence. He alone announces the decision of the court. It has indeed been maintained that he only formally announced the decision of the *rachimburgi*, and acted as their mouthpiece. But that would be a strange position for one who wielded the authority of the King in all matters of provincial administration; and it is a conclusion which is not borne out by the documents, which never separate the count from the *rachimburgi*, but treat them as forming one tribunal. Some authorities would seem to represent the count as the sole judge, giving his decision unchecked. Probably there were many variations in practice. There can be little doubt that a strong and arbitrary judge might often impose his will on a fluctuating and temporary body, called into existence for the occasion by his choice, here to-day and gone to-morrow. On the other hand, we may as readily imagine that a body of men of high position, and well acquainted with the locality and its legal traditions, might be able to impress their opinion with force on a count new to his office or without any legal training. The amount of judicial business in a count's territory must have often been overwhelming—crimes of every kind and degree, disputes about status and property and wills. No one man, especially if he were only a plain soldier or country gentleman, could possibly unaided cope with such a mass of business. And the count had many other duties, financial and military, which might require him to be absent for a time from his district; his place on the bench would then be taken by a *vicarius*, or, in some cases, the *rachimburgi* might sit alone; just as the nominal decisions of the King were often delivered by his council in his absence. Moreover, there are indications that the court of the count was not the only court for provincial administration. The judicial power possessed under the Empire by municipal *curiae* and their magistrates seems to have lingered here and there. At Bourges judicial sentence was pronounced by the leading citizens in a case described in the *Gloria Martyrum*. In other cases the bishop, supported by laymen of rank, may adjudicate. Peter, a brother of Gregory, under a charge of murdering a priest named Silvester, was tried and acquitted by such a tribunal. A similar court, composed of bishops and *viri magnifici*, tried the action of a Count Eulalius against his wife, Tetradia. It is a lurid picture of the morals of that age in its higher ranks. Eulalius, a monster of shameless vice, and a parricide, was deserted by his outraged wife, who placed herself under the protection of the Duke Desiderius, one of the great soldiers and most commanding personalities of that time, and became his wife. In her flight Tetradia had taken with her all the movable property of the house, the restoration of which was claimed by Eulalius. In a blood feud between the families of Sicharius and Austregesilus, which developed almost into a civil war, the bishop, supported by the count, summons the parties to meet with the object of making a peaceful settlement. There is no question here of formal legal procedure. The bishop, surrounded by leading citizens, does not pronounce any formal judgement, but makes an appeal to the disputants to close the quarrel on equitable terms.

Friction and collision between the count and the bishop of a municipal district were only to be expected, and they seem to have been frequent. The count and the bishop often belonged, as in Auvergne, to leading families of the province, who were jealous of one another, and may have had long-standing feuds. The counts wielded great and arbitrary powers in the name of the King. The bishop, who had perhaps held the office of count himself, possessed an even wider and more august authority, both temporal and spiritual. His office had been a powerful one under the later Empire ; it had grown in strength during the social confusion of the invasions, and in the collapse of the Imperial administration. The bishop had not only the mystic, sacramental gifts conferred by Orders, he was also chosen by the people and confirmed in his office by the approval of the prince. He was often a great personage at court, and held a high place in royal councils. He was also, by the steady flow of gifts and bequests (*ob remedium animae*), becoming probably the largest landholder of the province. Above all, in any quarrel, he could cut a man off from that sacramental grace which was of supreme importance in the eyes of the most depraved and lawless spirits of that age. Combining thus the power of a spiritual autocrat with that of a magistrate and *grand seigneur*, the bishop, if he was ambitious and self-assertive, must have been often a rather uncomfortable neighbour for the count. On the other hand, the count not unfrequently provoked and challenged the bishop or strained his powers to retaliate. A long list of such painful collisions might be drawn up from our authorities. Count Hortensius of Auvergne had, in an arbitrary way, imprisoned a relative of the Bishop Quintianus. That dignitary promptly retaliated by a solemn public curse, in the best ecclesiastical style, on all the house of Hortensius, and all his seed for ever. Nicetius, Bishop of Lyons, had a hot conflict with the Count Armentarius as to the limits of their jurisdiction, in which saintly arrogance is as manifest as the truculence of the count. In one of the many changes of sovereignty at this time, Limoges passed from Guntram to Chilperic, who immediately appointed new counts in the territory he had acquired. The new Count of Limoges was one Nonnichius, who was very zealous for his royal patron. It is probable that at a time when a district might change masters every few months, and when political treachery was in the air, the censorship of correspondence was very necessary. At any rate, by order of Count Nonnichius, two couriers, bearing letters which purported to come from Charterius, Bishop of Périgord, were seized. The letters contained very gross attacks on Chilperic, in which the bishop tells his correspondent that, in passing from the sway of Guntram to that of Chilperic, he felt like exchanging Heaven for Hell. Chilperic, as he sometimes did, displayed remarkable patience when the bishop came to court to make his defence, and apparently accepted the explanation that the latter was the forgery of a deacon who was plotting to drive the bishop from his see.

There is one more conflict between bishop and count which Gregory narrates with special care and minuteness in order to impress the lesson that God always avenges any injury to His priests. The modern reader will find a different interest in the tale. Nantinus, Count of Angoulême, was carried off by the

plague in that fatal year which desolated the households of
Chilperic and Guntram. But Gregory treats the count's death
as a special judgement for his despoiling estates of the Church.
The uncle of Nantinus, one Maracharius, had in his youth been
Count of Angoulême, had then taken Holy Orders, and been
elected bishop. He had been a vigilant administrator, building
churches and adding to the wealth of his see. In the seventh
year of his episcopate he was poisoned at a meal, apparently by
the arts of a priest who succeeded him, but who himself died
within a year, and was followed by Heraclius, a priest of
Bordeaux. Nantinus, the nephew of Bishop Maracharius, secured
his appointment as count, with the express object of avenging
his uncle's murder. He charged the new bishop with admitting
to his favour and intimacy the priests who were stained with the
blood of Maracharius, and he proceeded by violence to appropriate
the estates which Maracharius had bequeathed to the Church.
The struggle went on with varying fortunes. Nantinus was excommunicated, and again and again restored to communion,
sometimes by means of bribes and flattery. This sombre and
squalid episode in the history of mediaeval religion was fitly
closed by the Plague.

The most striking example of the trouble which an unscrupulous count might inflict on the bishop is to be found in
the history of Leudastes, Count of Tours. Gregory has described
the career of his arch-enemy and determined persecutor with all
the vividness of first-hand knowledge, and certainly with no
inclination to be gentle to him. After an adventurous escape
from servile grade in the royal kitchen, promoted by the lavish
favour of Queen Marcovefa to lucrative offices in her household,
Leudastes found himself rich enough to purchase by bribery the
Countship of the Stables from Charibert, and in a short time,
" for the sins of the people ", rose to the great office of Count of
Tours. In this high dignity the vanity and vicious instincts of
the *parvenu* at once asserted themselves. No woman was safe
from his libertine insults ; no fortune could escape his rapacity.
Dissension and false charges were propagated in order that the
judge might make a profit out of his corrupt decisions. But
such a career, in the rapid vicissitudes of the time, was apt to be
cut short. In the year 567 Charibert, the royal patron of
Leudastes, died, and, in the partition of his realm among his

sons, the city of Tours fell to the lot of Sigibert. Leudastes
had to fly, leaving all his treasures as a spoil to the Austrasians,
and he found an asylum at the court of Chilperic, where, for seven
years, he enjoyed the hospitality of the King. In the year 574
the army of Chilperic under his son Theudebert, after committing
frightful ravages along the Loire, entered the city of Tours, and
annexed its territory to the Neustrian realm. Two years before
the invasion Gregory had, by the will of Sigibert, been installed
in the see of S. Martin. Theudebert, on his entry into Tours,
presented to the bishop and the citizens their former count
Leudastes as one eminently fitted to hold the office again. The
bishop, who was an aristocrat as well as a pious churchman,
probably from the first felt a repugnance for this low-born
adventurer of evil life. But the conquests of Theudebert might
be precarious, and the possibility of Tours once more coming
under the sway of Sigibert made Leudastes for a time strangely
moderate and even submissive. He knew the social and moral
power of the see of S. Martin, and the influence of Gregory at
the court of Austrasia. Again and again, before the altar, he
solemnly swore to be loyally obedient to the bishop in all private
or ecclesiastical concerns. The defeat of Theudebert at Angoulême, and the flight of Chilperic for refuge to the walls of Tournai,
restored Tours to the realm of Sigibert, and Leudastes was
permitted to retire quietly into exile. The assassination of
Sigibert, which speedily followed, at once restored Chilperic to
his old sway, and Leudastes to the governorship of Tours.
This time all disguises were thrown aside. The count, when he
had to visit the bishop's house, appeared in arms, with helmet,
corslet, and lance. When he sat on the bench, along with his
assessors, lay and clerical, like an earlier Judge Jeffreys, he
would break into a storm of abuse against a suitor pleading for
justice, and then heap insults on the people surrounding the
tribunal if they murmured sympathy with the victim. He would
have priests haled away, with manacles on their hands, and
Frank warriors cudgelled by his lictors. In the face of all this
brutal abuse of authority, the bishop maintained that calm air
of authority with which he always bore himself. It was a time
to try the most iron nerve. The shrine of S. Martin gave shelter
to the lawless and rebellious son of Chilperic roystering and
intriguing with the equally lawless Guntram Boso. Merovechus

had plundered the estate of Leudastes, and the count had waylaid the servants of the young prince, whose violence, he alleged, was connived at by the bishop. A Neustrian army was watching the shrine which sheltered the rebel prince, and was devastating the environs of the city. There were plots in the air which were magnified by rumour, and the centre of them seemed to be the great city on the Loire, the key to the conquest of the rich lands of Aquitaine on which Chilperic's heart was set. The count, in spite of renewed vows of fidelity to the bishop, became more and more rapacious and violent, especially to Gregory's friends, and plundered without scruple the estates of the Church. The bishop, who had very decided views about the rights of the Church and her ministers, probably, in his quiet diplomatic way, conveyed to the court of Neustria the tale of these outrages. By whatever means the King heard of them, with a commendable decision he sent one of his courtiers, Ansovaldus, to check the dangerous violence of the Count Leudastes. Ansovaldus arrived on the festival of S. Martin. The brief chronicle merely tells that Leudastes was removed, and that the bishop and the citizens of Tours were allowed to elect some one to succeed him. Their choice fell on one Eunomius, who, if he had fallen on the sixth century B.C., would certainly have been treated by critical acumen as a mythical creation of etymology. Leudastes, in whose character avarice and arrogance seem to have had a larger place than policy, lost his head. He flew to the presence of Chilperic, and reproached him with throwing over the guardian of Tours for Neustria, at the beck of Gregory, who was watching for an opportunity of transferring it to the son of Sigibert. At the same time he meant to deal a blow at his former patroness, Fredegundis, and he told the King that Gregory had circulated a tale of the Queen's adultery with Bertram, Bishop of Bordeaux. In spite of all rumours about Fredegundis, Chilperic was a devoted husband, and it is refreshing to hear that he pommelled and kicked the count, and then ordered him to prison.

Our present object is to illustrate the conflicts between bishop and count which were often seen in that age, and we cannot, in this chapter, thread all the maze of intrigue woven around Gregory. It was a daring plot, characterised by the mingled craft and heady recklessness which the leading men of the

Merovingian age so often display. Fredegundis and Gregory
were to be ruined together by the rumour of imputations on her
virtue circulated by the bishop. Clovis, the son of Queen
Audovera, was to be raised to the throne, and Leudastes to
become duke, and his fellow conspirator, the deacon Riculfus,
was to have his reward in the see of Tours. What strikes us
most is the sacrosanct power of the episcopate, which even the
most lawless in that time feared openly to violate. Gregory's
danger for the moment was serious, and he felt this himself.
But the danger was from subtle ruses, which were really a confession of inferior strength. Troops were sent to watch the gates
of Tours. Suggestions through seeming friends were made to the
bishop that he should withdraw, with the treasure of the Church,
to the seclusion of his native Auvergne. Finally, in order to
ensure his appearance, to explain the charges against him,
Chilperic summoned all the bishops of Neustria to meet in synod
at Soissons. Then popular feeling ran so high in favour of
Gregory that the King thought it expedient to transfer the synod
to the more secluded royal domain of Berny. A carpenter at
Soissons had fearlessly maintained the innocence and sanctity of
the bishop. The populace at Berny, who were probably dependents on the royal estate, broke out in an equally frank way
against any insult to a priest of God. Chilperic, who was a
sagacious man, unless when he was under the immediate influence
of women, surprised the court of bishops by his patience and
moderation in the face of charges which assailed the honour of
the Queen, and which might veil a conspiracy against himself.
He proclaimed his readiness to hear witnesses or to accept the
attestation of the bishop, as the court should decide. Leudastes
was absent. Riculfus, the sub-deacon, offered his testimony,
but, by the law of the Church, a deacon could not be heard
against a bishop. The court allowed the inculpated prelate to
resort to a form of compurgation which accorded better with old
Teutonic custom than with the canons of the Church. At three
solemn masses, on three altars, Gregory swore his innocence of
all the charges against him. This oath was accepted as con-
clusive testimony, and the august court seemed at first to
threaten both Leudastes, the false accuser of a bishop, and even
his majesty Chilperic with excommunication. The sentence fell
on Leudastes. As to Riculfus, the prayers of Gregory, whom

he had treacherously injured, rescued him from the sentence of death, but only for an ordeal worse than any death. The kindly bishop, it is plain, was profoundly moved by the tortures which Riculfus had to endure. " Nothing even of solid metal could bear the strokes of rod and lash which the wretch had to suffer for six hours, laid on, not by one or two, but by a crowd of flagellants." In the end of the brutal tragedy the whole plot was revealed. Leudastes, who had been in hiding, reappears again in the chronicle to display his old lawlessness, and, after some lawless adventures, to meet with a tragic end.

The count is the most interesting and important provincial governor in the Merovingian system. His functions are, in the main, civil and judicial, concerned with the regular life of the people. The duke is rather more a military officer, and is often appointed to deal with emergencies and special crises. Under the early Merovingians he retained the character which his office bore under the later Empire. But circumstances tended to convert him into a provincial governor with a wider area than that of the count. Officially he has higher rank, and a duke may control the districts of many counts. Under Euric in Auvergne, Victorius was duke over seven cities with their territories. The same thing is found in the sixth century. Nicetius, by lavish presents, obtained the dukedom of Auvergne, Rodez, and Usès. Ennodius was made Duke of Tours and Poitiers. Lupus was duke of the vast territory of Champagne, so vast that an ambitious noble once dreamt of making it a separate kingdom. Another duke had under his sway all the cities south of the Garonne.

Ducatus is the name of an office and not of a territory. It is not a geographical expression in the sixth century, just as *comitatus* is not a district governed by a count. The duke was not necessarily a provincial governor. Many dukes never left the precincts of the court. They are mentioned in many legal documents as assisting the King in judicial or administrative work. In provincial government, the duke's functions being primarily of a military character, he is charged with maintaining peace and security. He has to guard against invasion of the frontiers or to intercept the bearer of secret dispatches, as Leudegiselus and Ebracharius did for Guntram in the troubled years 586–89. Or he might have to reduce a province to order, as Nicetius, replacing the Count Eulalius, pacified the region of Auvergne at about the same time. His commission, being often for a specific purpose, was generally only temporary. But, while it lasted, the duke was supreme, and the count became his subordinate, without, however, losing the authority of his commission, especially in the judicial sphere. Royal edicts and dispatches are addressed to both the duke and count. But the uncertainty felt by modern inquirers as to their relative status probably represents an uncertain line of demarcation in their functions, and it is not surprising that jealousy and collision of authority should occur. Duke Ennodius, who had been sent to govern the territory of Tours and Poitiers in 587, was removed by Childebert II., at the instance of the counts of the two cities. Another duke, Wintrio, a commander in the expeditions of that period, was driven away by the people of Champagne, and his life was only saved by a rapid flight. It was probably conducive to quiet administration that the greater number of counts in this period seem to have had no ducal superior. The dukes, drawn from great families, and coming with higher rank than the count, and with the command of military force, often displayed overweening arrogance in their office. Duke Beppolenus may be taken as an example. He had been a favourite of Queen Fredegundis, and served as her referendary. But, finding that he was losing the consideration at her court which he thought was his due, he transferred his services and allegiance to Guntram, the King of Burgundy. Guntram sent him, with full powers, to govern the cities south of the Loire which belonged to his nephew Chlothar, but which Guntram wished to administer for himself. The people of Rennes refused to receive Beppolenus. Angers a short time before had rejected with contumely a Count Theodulfus commissioned by Guntram, but armed with a fresh mandate he had assumed the office. Angers was now to have an experience of ducal government. Beppolenus seems to have been a mere plunderer, without even the decent forms of gentlemanly brigandage. He burst into granaries and cellars and appropriated whatever pleased him. Many of the citizens, doubtless defending their property, were struck down and slaughtered. Determined to reduce Rennes under Guntram's sway, he established his son, probably as count. But in a short time the people fell upon him and he was slain, with many of the leading men about him. The end of Beppolenus was worthy of his career. In 590 King Guntram ordered him, with another duke, Ebracharius, to levy an army against the rebellious Bretons in the district of Rennes and Angers. The two leaders were fiercely jealous and along the march assailed one another with insults and curses. They were only harmonious in the havoc and slaughter which they inflicted on the peaceful districts through which they passed along the course of the Vilaine and the Oust. Fredegundis, who had now conceived a bitter hatred for Beppolenus, her former favourite, had arranged for a corps of Saxons from Bayeux to support the Breton army under Warochus. A treacherous priest offered himself as guide to Beppolenus and led him face to face in a waste of marshland with an immense array. His colleague Ebracharius held aloof. It must be said that Beppolenus was a gallant fighter. For three days, amid the marshes, into which he had been decoyed, he held his ground against the Bretons. But his men were, in the end, all slaughtered or drowned in the morass : he himself, wounded by a spear thrust, fought on until he was overwhelmed. It is not unpleasant to find that his treacherous colleague met with his deserts. Ebracharius was deceived by a feigned sub-mission of the Breton king, and his army was set upon and decimated on its retreat across the Vilaine. The survivors who returned to Burgundy reported that Ebracharius and the Count Wiliacharius had been bribed to allow the destruction of the army, and both had to fly from the royal presence.

Having thus reviewed in detail the Frank kingship and organisation in the sixth century as it was created by Clovis, we shall proceed to consider how this instrument was used by his sons and successors. It had fine possibilities. A despotism, military in its origin and confirmed by a remarkable series of military conquests, found ready to its hand a system evolved through long centuries by the organising genius of the Roman race. The conquerors entered into a fair inheritance, and were fortunate in finding as their new subjects the Gallo-Romans, whose temper appears to have been singularly adaptable and patient in their trials. Possibly from the loss of their former pride of race, possibly from a philosophic or a cynical tolerance, perhaps even from a sense of quiet superiority which could afford to wait until the needs of the victors should require the

co-operation of the vanquished, the Gallo-Romans as a whole
acquiesced in the new order which they might well have resented,
and even succeeded in moulding it to their own customs and
ideals to a degree which gives remarkable testimony to the
vitality of the old institutions.

But the fusion of two great races under an autocratic government failed to achieve what, under Clovis at least, it seemed to
promise. The vices inherent in the nature of the victorious
race, rapacity, feud, and cruelty, were scarcely mitigated by its
adoption of the spiritual suzerainty of the Church and its adapt-
ability to the old civilisation.   The old barbaric temper was continually breaking through the restraints of law and organised
authority, and the centralisation of the Franco-Roman system
which was its strength proved often to be a grave danger when
the power was in unworthy hands.

CHAPTER V

THE SONS OF CLOVIS

THIS period may be roughly taken to extend from the death of Clovis in 511 to the birth of our great chronicler about 544. For his information as to this period of a generation Gregory must have had to depend chiefly on oral tradition ; but it was tradition of the best and most vivid kind, derived from old members of his family and social circle, of which we can catch many echoes in his works ; and it is specially minute and vivid about the events which occurred in his native Auvergne, of whose passion for independence and sufferings from invasion, Gregory has left an unfading picture.

Clovis left four sons, Theuderic, Chlodomer, Childebert, and Chlothar. His dominions were divided among them according to the Frank law of inheritance, *aequa lance*, according to our chronicler. But it would be difficult to make this description fit the actual distribution of territory. The boundaries between the different Frank kingdoms must have been always rather vague and fluctuating. The Franks, comparatively few in number, were still a band of warriors, cantoned on the Rhine, the Meuse, the Seine, and the Loire. The eldest son, Theuderic, took as his share the widest territory, which included Frank Germany, or Ripuaria, east of the Rhine from Cologne to Basle, and the nearer Frank conquests westwards to the Meuse. In rich and fruitful Aquitaine, so long a bone of contention, Theuderic had the eastern side, including Auvergne and Limousin. To Chlothar fell the first settlements of the Salian tribe from the Scheldt to the Somme, along with part of the old domains of Syagrius in the valley of the Aisne. Childebert

155

succeeded to the region of the Seine as far as the frontiers of Armorican Brittany, with possessions in Western Aquitaine not accurately defined. Chlodomer became lord of the valley of the Loire, and part of Western Aquitaine about Toulouse and Bordeaux. It is clear that Theuderic and Chlothar had under their sway regions in which the Frank race were far more strong and numerous than those under Childebert and Chlodomer. The capitals of the four sons of Clovis were Metz for Theuderic, Soissons for Chlothar, Paris for the kingdom of Childebert, and Orleans for Chlodomer.

It is customary to speak of the sons of Clovis in a rhetorical tone of loathing and contempt, but a scrupulous historical criticism will give a more balanced verdict. That these kings were guilty of most flagitious crimes seems to be certain. But we have to remember that we are dealing with the first flush of conquest by a young barbarian race in the early sixth century. The Franks had still all the savage instincts of greed, cunning, and hard cruelty. They were full of the pride of race and the pride of conquest. They had no tempering restraints from a high moral tone around them, and, although nominally Christian, the Church had not been powerful enough to tame the elemental passions which, in every age, seem ready to break through the thin crust of conventional restraint. These first kings of France were not worse than their successors of the next generation : they were, on the whole, better, and they were certainly abler and inspired with wider ambitions. It is noteworthy that in forty years of this first generation of the Merovingians, no fewer than five great expeditions beyond Frank soil were undertaken, into Thuringia, Burgundy, Spain and Italy, with the object of extending Frank dominion. These great efforts not only implied a wide outlook on the Western world, but a great power of military organisation for the enrolment and equipment of large armies capable of meeting formidable enemies beyond the frontier, and at least some provision for their commissariat, although it must be admitted that the Merovingian armies too often lived on the plunder of the regions through which they had to pass, including even those of their own countrymen. But it may be doubted whether the discipline and organisation of these armies were not the work of Gallo-Romans like Mummolus, the great Burgundian general, inheriting the military tradition of the Empire. And the great armies must have been composed in large part of the old Gallo-Roman population, inspired with a new military spirit by the warrior instincts of the Franks.

The sons of Clovis inherited from their father the idea of a mission of conquest. His brilliant and rapid success must have fired the imagination of his sons who followed his campaigns. The Merovingian house was no longer the obscure head of a wandering, warlike tribe. It was linked by affinities with nearly all the new conquering races. The great Ostrogoth had married a sister of Clovis, and his daughters were wedded to Alaric, the Visigoth, and the Burgundian Sigismund. A niece of Theodoric was the wife of Hermenefrid, the King of Thuringia, and a sister of Theodoric was married to the Vandal Thrasamund. These relationships must have drawn the Merovingians into close relations with a wider circle of nations. But royal affinities have seldom prevented the collision of national ambitions, and the Merovingians were soon to be in conflict with most of the races we have mentioned. Theodoric the Great had, as we have seen, used his commanding influence to restrain and mitigate such rivalries, although he failed to save the Visigothic power in Aquitaine. But his power waned in his last years, and in 526 he died, and thus a great bar to Frank ambition was withdrawn.

There were three points to which Frank ambition might be directed. There was the great Thuringian realm on the Saal and upper Weser. There was the kingdom of Burgundy stretching along the Rhone and Saône nearly to the Alps ; and there were the Visigoths, who, even after the conquests of Clovis, still held a wealthy region in Septimania, on the frontiers of Spain, in league with their Ostrogothic kindred, who held the province from the maritime Alps to the mouth of the Rhone.

Theuderic had the hardest task. He was face to face with an array of powerful tribes beyond the Rhine, ready, like all German tribes for ages, to press on into the rich and tempting plains of Gaul, Thuringi, Saxons, Alemanni. And in 515 he had to face a piratical raid of the Danes under their king, Chlochilaichus, on the lower Rhine, who, after spoiling and devastating the country, were preparing to sail away with their spoils and captives ; but, at the last moment, Theudebert, the heir of Theuderic, appeared with a strong force, and in a naval battle crushed the Danes and slew their king. In 516 Theuderic, by promises of territory, was drawn into a war in Thuringia. Hermenefrid, one of three brother kings, had slain one of them, and called in the aid of the Frank to crush the third. The united armies were triumphant and Hermenefrid was left sole ruler. But he soon forgot his pledges to Theuderic to cede part of his territory, and he wantonly invaded some tribes under Theuderic's sway and inflicted exquisite tortures on young boys and girls. Theuderic felt a deep and dangerous anger at the perfidy, but deferred his revenge. At last, in 528, he resolved to crush the treacherous Thuringian. Calling in the aid of his brother Chlothar, he routed the Thuringi on the Unstrut with such slaughter that the stream was choked with corpses. Among the captives was the niece of Hermenefrid, Radegundis, destined to be the famous Abbess of Poitiers. It is character- istic of Merovingian faith and the moral tone of the time that Theuderic, during the campaign, made a stealthy attempt to kill his brother, who was rendering him devoted service.

Meanwhile, in the year 523, the sons of Clovis, urged on, it is said, by their mother, invaded Burgundy. It was under the rule of Sigismund, the son of Gundobad—who is a puzzling character, a model saint according to hagiography—who had founded the monastery of S. Maurice, but who had murdered Sigiric, his son by the daughter of the great Theodoric. The great Ostrogoth, to avenge his grandson, aided the Franks by invading Southern Burgundy. The monkish biographer says that a great number of Burgundians were in league with the invaders. Sigismund was not a man of war, but, with the aid of his more virile brother Godomar, he faced the Franks in battle. He was beaten and fled for refuge to S. Maurice, but was delivered by traitors into the hands of Chlodomer, and, with his wife and children, carried a prisoner to Orleans. But at the opening of a new campaign in 524, Chlodomer, in spite of the solemn warnings of the Abbot of S. Mesmin de Micy, put the whole family to death and threw them into a well at Coulmiers. The atrocity, according to the saint's prophecy, was soon to be avenged. Godomar soon regathered his forces and offered battle, in which Chlodomer was killed. The issue is variously given in the chronicles. But the Franks were probably thrown back for a time, and the final conquest of Burgundy was deferred for a few years. For the Frank kings were occupied for some time with other cares and

ambitions. They seem not even to have had time or force to
repel a dangerous advance of Theodoric, in which he annexed
part of Southern Burgundy, including Martigny and Geneva, and
then, traversing Septimania, invaded Frank territory in Southern
Aquitaine, in the districts of Rodez and the Cevennes. Childebert
and Chlothar were more bent on appropriating the fair domains
on the Loire and in Southern Aquitaine of their dead brother
Chlodomer than on more distant enterprises. His three infant
sons were living under the care of their grandmother Clothilde
till they could, according to Frank fashion, partition their father's
realm. That their uncles were resolved to prevent. They were
withdrawn from their grandmother's care, and the cruel choice
was proposed to her between their degradation to plebeian rank
and their death. She preferred to see them dead rather than
shorn of their locks and deprived of their regal rank. Two were
brutally slaughtered by the hands of Chlothar. The third was
rescued by some of the nobles, *viri fortes*, took the tonsure, and
lived to be the founder of the monastery of S. Cloud.

While Theuderic was engaged in his campaign in Thuringia
a not improbable rumour spread that he had been killed. This
had a disturbing effect in Auvergne and Eastern Aquitaine,
which had come under the sway of Theuderic. These regions,
with old memories of municipal independence and a high civilisation, did not take kindly to Merovingian rule. Auvergne in
particular was long a hotbed of revolt. And the pillage and
cruelties which they had suffered in the conquest by Theuderic
in 509 were still fresh in the memory of the people. Revolt
broke out under the first Frank governor, Basolus, and was
calmed by a policy of singular restraint and moderation. In
Auvergne, as in Aquitaine generally, the great Gallo-Roman
families still retained the power and prestige conferred by the
possession of vast estates, peopled and tilled by crowds of
obedient serfs who could easily be turned into a dangerous
militia. They had still some relics of their ancient municipal
constitutions, the enduring memory of high Imperial office, and
the fading tradition of the ancient culture. The clergy, who had
at first been the great pioneers of Frank conquest, so long as it
meant a campaign against the Visigothic heretics, had found that
the Franks could trample on Catholics as well as on Arians, and
were ready to join in asserting local liberties.

The uncertainty as to the fate of Theuderic in Thuringia aroused the always smouldering fires of sedition in Auvergne. A great noble named Arcadius, the grandson of Sidonius Apollinaris, put himself at the head of the movement. The partition of Frank Gaul among the descendants of Clovis, with uncertain and fluctuating boundaries, sometimes rendered the allegiance of their Leudes equally uncertain ; and the subjects of one Merovingian might easily transfer their allegiance to another. Childebert was lord of a district of Aquitaine bordering on Auvergne, and Arcadius, who had rendered him service, seized on the rumour of Theuderic's death to invite Childebert to annex Auvergne. Childebert had heard much of the beauty and fertility of the province, and eagerly responded to the call. The chronicle is curt and mysterious. A dense mist covered the country, probably embarrassing Childebert's movements, and when he came up to the walls he found all entrance barred against him. One of the gates was forced and Childebert entered the town, but only to hear soon that Theuderic was alive and had actually returned from Thuringia ; and Childebert thought it well to retreat, without getting a sight of the pleasant, rich fields of Limagne. Theuderic suppressed his anger at the betrayal of Arcadius for a time ; but a terrible reckoning awaited Auvergne.

Childebert found scope for his energy in another direction. The news came that his sister Chrodechildis, the wife of Amalaric, King of the Visigoths, had been debarred from the exercise of her religion with the foulest insults and cruelty. The great Theodoric, grandfather of Amalaric, was dead, and the Visigothic government had lost his powerful protection. Amalaric was defeated and slain, and Childebert returned with a great spoil of sacred vessels, studded with jewels, taken from the churches. The ill-fated Chrodechildis died on the way to Paris, and was laid beside her father Clovis in the Church of the Apostles.

Childebert on his return joined Chlothar in 532 in preparing for the conquest of Burgundy. It was to be a great and final effort, and in a short campaign Godomar was defeated and fled into Italy ; and Burgundy was finally absorbed in the empire of the Franks. The brothers had invited the aid of Theuderic in their campaign. For some reason he declined : with the strange freedom which the Frank Leudes in that age sometimes asserted, his Franks boldly threatened to leave him and follow the standards of his brothers. Probably they were thinking of the booty which generally rewarded a Frank invasion. And apparently Theuderic so understood their mutiny. He at once proposed to them a raid on Auvergne, where they should win a spoil of gold and silver, flocks and herds, and captives, as much as their hearts desired. The wealth of Auvergne was proverbial, and the Frank warriors were allured by the vision of such a conquest. Arcadius, who had conspired against Theuderic, and provoked vengeance, fled to Bourges in Childebert's territory. His mother and aunt, the daughters of Sidonius, were driven into exile at Cahors, with the loss of their property. The army of Theuderic burst on Auvergne, desolating all along their advance. Theuderic found the city closed against him and encamped in the suburbs. The siege did not prosper, whether from the strength of the walls or, as Gregory believed, from the prevailing prayers of the bishop Quintianus. The army decamped and spread over the country with a terror of devastation long remembered in Auvergne, and of which Gregory evidently heard many tales as a child from his elders or the priests of S. Julian's. Everywhere the rustic folk fled to strong places in the mountainous region. Others took refuge in shrines of saints, of which that of S. Julian at Brioude was the most famous and sacrosanct. But no holy place in the end was inviolable to a Frank army on the war-path. The gates of S. Julian's were closed, but an opening was found through a window, and the church was at once thrown open to the rapacious invaders. The scene must have been described to Gregory by some who had seen it. The church was crowded with people who had fled to it for sure protection, with all their movable property. The plunderers seized all and proceeded to divide the captives among them. But the King, on the news reaching him, punished some of the impious malefactors with death and restored the plundered treasures. For he had ordered that within a circuit of seven miles the precincts of S. Julian's should be inviolable. The Frank who threw open the doors was struck with lightning : and that legend, in such an age, was a surer defence than any royal order.

The people of Auvergne retired to natural fortresses in their mountains, which were famous in old Celtic times. The fortress of Lovolautrum, one of the most impregnable, besieged in vain, was betrayed by the servant of a priest, who received his proper

M

due by being slain before the altar. In the high region of the Cantal there was a fastness the fame of which is still preserved in the name of Mauriac and in the features of nature. It was fortified by natural walls of rock which enclosed a spacious plain watered by many streams. Within its safe enclosure crops could be sown and reaped to sustain the defenders against any siege however protracted. But by the folly of the garrison a party of their men was intercepted and only ransomed by the payment of a large sum. The Franks, however, did not enter the place.

These are mere fragments evidently of what was a tragic history. It was a second conquest of Auvergne. The hagiography of the two following centuries gives hints of the sufferings of Auvergne in that evil time. Numbers were carried away into slavery. And of those left behind, many were reduced to the most miserable poverty.

Theuderic appointed a certain Sigiwald, a relative of his own, to be Duke of Auvergne, and ordered him to settle there with all his household. Sigiwald was not a man to soften the memory of old wrongs. He was guilty of many atrocities, and the servants of such a master perpetrated every sort of fraud, violence, and homicide. No one, under such a tyranny, dared to breathe a whisper of discontent. In the end Theuderic, in the Merovingian fashion, put Sigiwald to the sword, and ordered his son Theudebert to kill Sigiwald's son. They were evidently becoming dangerous. The Counts of Auvergne at this time, who had the civil and criminal administration in their hands, were overbearing even to the clergy. They were of great Gallo-Roman houses, and the house of Hortensius for three generations wielded great power in Auvergne, but evidently an offensive power. Hortensius by violent assertion of authority had incurred the just indignation of Bishop Quintianus, who took a priestly revenge by cursing all the race of Hortensius, with the prayer that none of them might ever be raised to the episcopate. Evodius, the son of Hortensius, grossly insulted Bishop Gallus. Another count, Becco by name, had left an evil name for petty tyranny. He had lost a hawk, and falsely charged a servant of S. Julian's with stealing it, and was about to put the boy to a most cruel death. His fury was only abated by a large bribe from the chief priest of S. Julian's.

There was one class, apparently the most helpless of all, who had nothing to fear from Sigiwald and his train, but who rather were regarded with awe and reverence. The ascetic solitaries of Auvergne captivated the imagination of Gregory from his earliest youth, and he has, with an art to which the critics have never done justice, thrown around the Arvernian hermitage a haze of romance which a purer Latinity might have failed to conjure up. The arrogant Duke Sigiwald was forced to be polite and deferential to these aged holy men of prayer, some of whom had seen the invasion of Attila and the disappearance of the last Prefect of the Gauls. When Sigiwald was encamped at Artonne in the Puy-de-Dôme and asleep in his tent, he was awaked to meet the hermit Portianus, a man of incredible sanctity and severe self-mortification, who had hastened to intercede for the victims of the invasion. Sigiwald in Teutonic fashion offered the saint a hospitable cup. His refusal was followed by a startling miracle which caused the Frank to release his prisoners and mitigate his severities. The Franks were evidently enjoying all the sport which the land of hill and woodland offers abundantly, and the chase of the wild boar is a peculiarly German taste. The hermits were equally famous for their tenderness to wild creatures : and the boar hard pressed in the chase sometimes found a refuge in the hermit's garden.

The Ostrogoths, as we have seen, had occupied a region west of the Rhone, and in 533 Theuderic and Chlothar determined to expel them. They sent their sons Theudebert and Guntharius in command of the Frank armies. Guntharius, for some reason, went no farther than Rodez. Theudebert continued the campaign alone, captured all the places beyond the Rhone and part of Septimania, and was pushing his advance into Provence, but was foiled and thrown back from the walls of Arles. In one of the towns of Septimania he was captivated by the charms of a Roman matron, Deuteria, who made advances to him, and whom in the end he made his wife. Soon after those events Theuderic died in the twenty-third year of his reign. In the usual Merovingian fashion Childebert and Chlothar attempted to deprive the young heir of his succession and to divide the great Ripuarian realm. But Theudebert had already shown himself a man of war, and with the loyal support of his Leudes defeated the treacherous scheme.

Gregory regards Theudebert as a great king remarkable for

all good qualities. The virtues he enumerates are generally such as appeal to the Churchmen. Theudebert reverenced the priesthood, endowed churches, relieved the poor. At the cost of his own treasury he remitted all the tribute due by the churches of Auvergne. And indeed he seems to have had some qualities rare among the Merovingians. After Duke Sigiwald had been put to death by Theuderic, he ordered Theudebert to make away with his son Sigivald. But Theudebert connived at his flight, and on Theuderic's death welcomed him back and restored the confiscated property of the family. A Bishop of Verdun, who had been cruelly oppressed and impoverished by Theuderic, appealed to Theudebert to relieve the poverty of his townsmen. The King at once responded with a nominal loan of 7000 *aurei*, the repayment of which he refused. His most intimate advisers were two Gallo-Romans named Asteriolus and Secundinus, one of whom conducted the correspondence of Theudebert with the Eastern Empire. Another Gallo-Roman in his service, one Parthenius, had with his sanction imposed the land tax on the Frank population, and, after the King's death, was stoned to death by the infuriated populace. Theudebert had apparently great ambitions far beyond the range of the provincial Merovingians, whose constant aim seems to have been to deceive and despoil one another. Drawn into the great conflict in Italy between Goth and East Roman, if we may believe Agathias, he once dreamt of striking at Byzantium. He was the first barbarian king who replaced the head of the Emperor on his coins with his own head and the daring inscription *Dominus Theudebertus Augustus*—in which lurked the ambition of reviving an Empire of the West. The three Frank kings nominally engaged together in the great Italian campaigns of the next eight years. But it was the nephew, Theudebert, who took the leading part. He was far the ablest, with the widest and most commanding outlook. He had the largest proportion of the Frank population in his realm, and he could command the service of powerful and warlike tribes from beyond the Rhine. He must have had great powers of organisation to arm and equip such vast armies and carry them across the Alps. Yet with the gifts apparently of a highly civilised chief, he had still the primitive instincts of his race, greed and faithless cunning and ruthless contempt for human life. He would accept the bribes of the Emperor and the Ostrogoth, and then attack the one and the other impartially, perhaps with the hope or ambition of becoming master of Italy on the ruin of both.

Justinian, after the defeat of the Vandals, when he was about to attack the Ostrogoths, offered the Frank kings a large sum for their aid. They accepted the offer, but with peculiar Frank faith they were equally ready to be bribed by Witigis. Just before his death Theodatus had tried to purchase their support by the cession of all territory which the Ostrogoths had won to the west of the Alps. The agreement, interrupted by his death, was completed by Witigis, and the Franks thus came into possession of the fair region, so long coveted, from the Alps to the Rhone and from the Isère to the sea. In 538, 10,000 Burgundian troops appeared to aid the Goths in the capture of Milan. In 539, Theudebert threw himself into the great struggle between Witigis and Belisarius. At the head of 100,000 infantry and 300 knights he attacked Goths and Romans in turn, and swept along the valley of the Po with ruthless devastation. But his tumultuary army was more than decimated by hunger and foul disease, and Theudebert retired across the Alps with nothing to compensate him for his losses. And the losses among his warriors were so great that it is said that from this time Gallo-Romans were enrolled in the Frank armies.

Shortly before this campaign of Theudebert, the relations of the brothers were strangely confused by perfidy. Childebert, who had combined with Chlothar to seize the realm of Theudebert, now adopted an opposite policy. He was childless himself, and Chlothar had several sons who on his death would, in Frank fashion, parcel out his dominions. Perhaps in Theudebert Childebert recognised an ability and a character rare in his race. And he proposed to adopt him as his son and heir. The result of the union was what might have been expected. Uncle and nephew combined their forces in an attack on Chlothar. Chlothar fled into the forest of Arlanne on the Seine, and fortified himself behind a barrier of felled trees. But he was only saved by heavenly aid vouchsafed to the prayers of Clothilde at the shrine of S. Martin. A frightful tempest of hail and lightning overwhelmed the camp of Childebert and Theudebert, swept away their tents, and flung their men on the ground helpless and paralysed with terror, while the army of Chlothar felt nothing

of the storm.   The influence of the aged Queen was probably
as potent as the virtue of S. Martin.   And it is pleasant to think
that she who had vengefully instigated the invasion of Burgundy
should in her old age have made peace among her sons.   It was
the last public act of her life.   In a few years she was laid by
Childebert and Chlothar beside her husband in the Church of
the Apostles in Paris.

While Theudebert was fighting in Italy, his uncles, Childebert
and Chlothar, joined in another campaign against the Visigoths.
They advanced as far as the Ebro and laid siege to Saragossa,
but were heavily defeated by Theudigiselus in an engagement
before the walls, and had to retreat with no results of their
expedition.   Gregory, as is his wont, attributes the salvation of
the town to the tunic of S. Vincent borne round the walls by a
procession of women with dishevelled hair.

Theudebert died in 547, and his son, Theudebald, or rather the
great nobles of Austrasia, continued the Italian policy of Theudebert, in the end with disastrous results.   In 553 a Frank army
under the Dukes Buccelenus and Chlothar intervened in the
struggle between Totila and the Eastern Empire, and attacked
them both in Northern Italy.   These conflicts belong to Italian
history.   We are only concerned with the fate of the Frank
armies.   Plague and famine destroyed the army of Chlothar.
The forces of Buccelenus were wiped out by Narses in the great
battle of Casilinum.   Theudebald was a sad degenerate of
unbridled passions.   He luckily died in the seventh year of his
reign, leaving no heir.   His grand-uncle, Chlothar, disregarding
the equal rights of Childebert, appropriated his vast territory, and
his widow, Vuldetrada ; but the union was banned by the Church,
and Chlothar resigned the lady to one of his dukes Garivaldus.
Childebert had no heir, and it grew more and more certain that
if he died before Chlothar, Chlothar would for a time wield sole
power over all the Frank conquests.

But in his old age Chlothar found the succession to Theudebald
an anxious inheritance.   The Saxons had been tributary to
Austrasia, but soon after Theudebald's death they rebelled and
roused the Thuringians to their aid.   In 555 Chlothar devastated
Thuringia and inflicted a crushing defeat on the Saxons.   But
they were still unconquered, and Chlothar prepared for another
campaign in which the fortune of war decisively changed.   And

one great interest in its history is the bold and even mutinous
spirit which a Frank army could display to a Merovingian chief.
As the Frank army approached their bounds, the Saxons became
more and more alarmed, and sent three successive relays of
envoys by an ever-increasing offer of concessions to ward off the
attack—tribute, cattle, valuables, and half their lands. In
each case the King was for accepting the offer, his leaders for
contemptuously rejecting it. At last Chlothar, with a spirit
which we cannot but admire, warned his mutinous host that they
were going forward to their ruin : they might go, but he would
not lead them. Then a strange scene followed. The soldiers
rushed upon him, tore his tent in pieces, and with insults and
execrations threatened him with death. The King had to yield.
His army was defeated with enormous slaughter, and he had to
sue for a humiliating peace.

While Chlothar was engaged against the Saxons there
occurred an episode which sheds a strong light on the relations
of the Merovingian family and on the state of Auvergne and
Eastern Aquitaine, the government of which Chlothar had
usurped on the death of Theudebald. He had appointed his son
Chramnus as governor. The young prince soon became execrated
by the people. He lived in the society of young men of the
worst character, and insulted the women of the proudest
aristocracy in Gaul. The bishop in Auvergne was a more
prominent and powerful person than in any other part of Gaul.
And the last election to the episcopate of Clermont had divided
the people into two factions, one supporting the successful candidate, Cautinus, the other devoted to his rival, Cato. Cautinus
had been appointed autocratically to the see by Theudebald
without the consent of the clergy or the people. He was a man
of the worst character, a shameless drunkard, and so intensely
avaricious that when a priest refused to surrender the titles of
some land he coveted, he buried him alive. He was so cowardly
that he abandoned his flock on the approach of the plague.
Cato was a model priest, beloved by the people, although evidently a man of hard pride and self-assertion. It is to the credit
of the character of Chramnus, or perhaps of his worldly wisdom,
that he leagued himself with the party of Cato. On the other
hand he conceived a hatred of Firminus, the Count of Auvergne,
a member of a great family who had held the highest office under

the Empire.   Chramnus removed him from his office and
appointed a certain Salustius, son of Evodius, and grandson of
Count Hortensius, both of whom had insulted or opposed the
bishops of their day.

In his government of Auvergne, Chramnus had as his chief
supporters and allies men of Gallo-Roman race in Auvergne or
Aquitaine. Ascovindus, a great magnate of Auvergne and a man
of high character, strove to recall him from his dangerous courses.
But unfortunately he had another adviser of the opposite type,
Leo of Poitiers, of a nature, says Gregory, answering to his name,
most fierce and rapacious of men, who had a contempt for the
holy confessors, and paid for his impiety by a sad end.   Chlothar
had heard of his son's conduct in Auvergne and ordered him to
leave the province.   Chramnus obeyed, but only to make trouble
in Eastern Aquitaine.   His friend Leo drew him to Poitiers, from
which as centre he aspired to make himself lord of all Aquitaine,
which had fallen to the share of Theuderic ; and the temper of
Aquitaine might suggest good hopes of success.   For Aquitaine
was not fully subdued by Clovis.   Its Gallo-Roman population
under the Visigoths still cherished their traditions of old culture
and to some extent of municipal freedom.   They had a deep
hatred of the Franks, and were always ready, with their energy,
vivacity, and love of intrigue, to lend a hand in any venture that
appealed to imagination and old patriotism.

We can divine from a brief hint in Gregory that a party in
Poitiers were urging on Chramnus in a great conspiracy against
his father.   The obvious thing was to secure the aid of Childebert,
King of Paris, who had been defrauded of his share in the dominions of Theudebald.   A compact was arranged by secret envoys,
and Chramnus, in a visit to Paris, bound himself by solemn
oaths to be his father's determined foe.   Chramnus with his
Aquitanian supporters marched on Limoges to bring that region
under his power.   The news of the revolt must have reached
Chlothar on the Elbe while he was still grappling with the Saxons :
and he sent orders for his sons Charibert and Guntram to
advance against his rebellious son.   They sought him in Auvergne,
but not finding him there they moved westwards to the region
of the Black Mountains, and there sent an embassy to demand
the restoration of all his father's territory which he had annexed,
and, in case of refusal, to challenge him to combat.   The reply

was that he could not give up what he had won, but that he
hoped to keep it with his father's goodwill. All was prepared
for battle, when a tempest and violent thunderstorm broke with
such violence over the opposing armies that they fell back on
their camps without striking a blow. Chramnus through a secret
emissary spread the rumour that Chlothar had fallen in Saxony.
The army of Childebert's sons in hot haste retired to Burgundy.
Chramnus at once pressed on, besieged and captured Chalon-sur-
Saône, and marched on Dijon. That the fortunes of Chramnus
had become the object of intense interest is shown by Gregory's
description of the scene at mass in the great church of Dijon.
The *Biblicae sortes* had been long condemned by the Church as
a pagan practice. It appears that in that age there were three
lections in the Gallic service of the Mass, the first from the Prophets, the second from the Epistles, and the third from the
Gospels. Laying the three books on the altar, the officiating
priests offered a prayer that God would reveal the future of
Chramnus. The first words of each lection were to be taken as
a heaven-sent omen. All three seemed to bode nothing but evil
to the prince. The gospel was from that passage in S. Matthew
predicting the ruin of him *qui aedificavit domum suam super
arenam.* The dark augury seemed to have produced little effect.
Chramnus calmly received the communion from the hands of
Bishop Tetricus, and pressed on to Paris to confirm his pact
with his uncle Childebert. The darkest rumours were coming
from Saxony. The Saxons, encouraged by messages from
Childebert, actually invaded Austrasian territory (Francia) as
far as Deutz, near Cologne, and the rumour spread that Chlothar
had fallen. Childebert and Chramnus, bound together to divide
his realm, invaded the Champagne country around Rheims, and
wasted it with fire and sword. One cannot help often thinking,
in reading the cold, bald words of the chronicle, what the owners
of those vineyards and pleasant granges on the banks of the
Marne and the Aisne must have suffered in those senseless,
brutal wars of the Merovingian kings. Chramnus had meanwhile strengthened himself by marrying the daughter of a great
Aquitanian duke named Willacharius.

But the ambitious schemes of Chramnus were doomed. In
558 Childebert sickened and died. And Chlothar came back
from his desperate campaign. He at once took possession of

the realm of Childebert, and the government of the Frank conquests was now in a single hand.

Chlothar seems to have taken no vengeance for the Aquitanian rising—not even on Chramnus. But the young prince was incorrigible. History is silent about his fresh rebellion. We are only told that he took refuge among the Celts of Brittany, with their chief Chonober, who, after killing or imprisoning his brothers, had established himself in sole sway. For the Bretons alone in Gaul maintained their independence against the Franks. Chlothar, now deeply incensed, invaded Brittany. The Breton chief tried to prevent son and father meeting in unnatural conflict, and offered to bear the brunt alone. But, as Gregory says, Chramnus was doomed. The Bretons were routed and their chief was slain. Chramnus, flying along the coast to some boats he had ready, was captured, and by Chlothar's orders was burnt alive with his family in a peasant's cottage.

The fierce King died next year, the fifty-first of his reign, having been seized with fever after a day's hunting in the forest of Compiègne ; with arrogant words on his lips : " How great must be the King of Heaven who thus kills mighty kings ". There might seem to be small space for religion in a character like Chlothar's. But S. Martin had an infinite charity. Chlothar had restored his church when it had been burnt down by duke Willacharius. And in his last year the old King and cruel sinner visited the shrine to lament his sins and entreat the saint's intercession for him. It seems doubtful whether such religion, ancient or modern, is any check on sin. It certainly was a feeble restraint in the days of the Merovingians. And great churchmen like Gregory, who had witnessed the enormities of a highly placed criminal, will give him a parting benediction if he has paid conventional deference to their order, or endowed churches out of taxes wrung from the people, or in his last hours prostrated himself before the altar of a saint. Organised religion, thinking chiefly of its own power, has probably never so revealed its real spiritual impotence as in that age of loud religious claims and defiance of all moral restraints.

Chlothar, dying in 561, was buried with pompous honours in the church of S. Medard at Soissons. He left four sons with equal claims to succession. But Chilperic had the ambition to appropriate the sole monarchy of his father, and rushed to seize the royal treasure at Berny, with which he tried to bribe the great subjects of his brothers to desert them. They made a combined attack upon him, and proceeded to divide the kingdom among them in orderly fashion. Charibert, the eldest son, obtained the city and district of Paris, and all the lands from the Loire to the Pyrenees, including Tours, Poitiers, Bordeaux, and Toulouse. Guntram, with his capital at Orleans, received the kingdom of Burgundy. Sigibert reigned at Rheims over the lands along the Meuse and Rhine, and the German peoples who had been conquered as far as the Elbe, together with Auvergne and part of Provence. Chilperic at Soissons ruled the old Salian country from the Meuse to the Somme. Charibert died childless in 567, and his portion was parcelled out among his brothers. Generally it may be said that each took a portion adjoining his own domains. But Sigibert, in addition to Tours and Poitiers, received the city of Bordeaux, far separated from him. Paris, which was continually growing in importance, was neutralised. How the boundaries of these kingdoms were defined we do not know. They were probably always vague and arbitrary, constantly changing with fresh partition on the death of a king or the varying fortunes of endless wars. And Aquitaine particularly, whose rich cities were constantly treated as prizes of battle, was again and again divided among the combatants with hardly any regard to geographical considerations. The division of Northern Gaul into Austrasia and Neustria is not recognised by Gregory of Tours. He uses, indeed, the name Austrasia to describe the north-eastern kingdom of Sigibert. But the name Neustria does not occur in the pages of Gregory, although some trace of it has been found in a diploma of King Childebert of the year 558. But the sharp and definite distinction between Austrasia and Neustria belongs to the early years of the seventh century. It is commonly said that, from the first, the distinction and conflict between the two realms were the result of a different proportion between the two races, North-western Gaul having a preponderance of Gallo-Romans, while in Austrasia the Frank conquerors predominated, and were swelled by further incursions from beyond the Rhine. Gregory gives no indication of such racial difference in the time of Chilperic and Sigibert. The northern part of Chilperic's realm must have had a strong German population : and Gallo-Romans were probably far the

majority in the districts of Rheims, Toul, and Metz. On the
other hand, Chilperic showed a certain taste or fancy for Roman
fashions and culture, while Sigibert brought hordes of Teutons
from beyond the Rhine to overwhelm his brother in the campaign of 574. The problem could only be solved with any
certainty if we had trustworthy statistics as to the distribution
and relative numbers of the two races in the east and west. Too
dogmatic conclusions seem to be drawn from more or less
probable conjecture.

The long, bitter struggle between Austrasia and Neustria has
also been commonly attributed to the rival ambitions and fierce
hatred of two women who came on the scene five years after
the death of Chlothar, and who, to many, seem to be the pro-
tagonists. For the romantic historian their fortunes and their
crimes almost monopolise attention, and their weird attractive-
ness has perhaps disturbed his sane judgement as to the real
causes of the prolonged struggle. Yet the inclination of the
philosophic historian to seek for general and impersonal causes
in history and to throw into the shade the influence of strong
personality in moulding events, has led some to underrate the
power of Brunihildis and Fredegundis. The Merovingians of
the first generation, although they were gallant warriors, showed
an Oriental indulgence in their relations with women, often of
the lowest rank. Their father Clovis, the great Theodoric, the
Vandal, Burgundian, and Visigothic kings of that period had
the instinct or the policy to guard their dignity or strengthen
their position by alliances in their own rank. The brothers of
Sigibert kept harems and married their maidservants or daughters
of their shepherds and tradesmen. Sigibert had more prudent
and refined tastes, and in 566 he sent an embassy to solicit the
hand of Brunihildis, the daughter of Athanagild, King of the
Visigoths. This was probably a stroke of policy to put a stop
to the wasteful wars which in the previous thirty years drained
the strength of both races. The charm and talents of the
Visigothic princess were famous, and have been celebrated both
in prose and verse. Gregory, who knew her well, describes her
exquisite grace and beauty, her purity of character, her wisdom
in counsel, and her charm of conversation. Fortunatus, the
literary adventurer from Italy, who arrived shortly before the
marriage, was genuinely ravished by her charm, and makes

Venus the mouthpiece of his admiration. And indeed Brunihildis, in such an age, and such a circle, deserved all admiration. Of unspotted purity in an age of licence and prurient scandal, her union with Sigibert was one of true and faithful love on both sides. At the court of Toledo she had imbibed something of the lingering Roman culture, and an admiration for the monuments and relics of the civilising energy of Rome. It will later be seen that, in her long conflict for the rights of the crown against the Frank nobles of Austrasia, she relied on the support of the great chiefs of Gallo-Roman race. And in that fierce and complicated struggle, Brunihildis developed a political skill, backed by a native energy and courage, which gave her a foremost place among the statesmen of the time. For the present, it only remains to be said that, although bred in the bigoted Arianism of her race, she became a sincere and devoted Catholic, chiefly under the influence of her husband.

The marriage of Sigibert, so different from his brother's unions, brought him great prestige. And Chilperic, who was intensely ambitious, determined to follow his example. He had repudiated his lawful wife, Audovera, by whom he had three sons, and was living in shameless libertinism. He sued for the hand of Galswintha, the elder sister of Brunihildis, and for the time dismissed his favourite concubine, a maidservant bearing the ill-famed name of Fredegundis. The doomed Galswintha, with a great train, loaded with treasure, made progress through the cities of Aquitaine. Fortunatus had watched its passage through Poitiers, and he dedicated to Galswintha one of his most elaborate poems. He seems to foreshadow her early death in the profuse and extravagant lamentations of her mother and sisters on her departure from Toledo. But the politic and venal poet gives only a vague hint of the manner of her tragic end. In a short time Chilperic was tired of the gentle, and perhaps melancholy, young wife, and Fredegundis returned to rule him for the rest of his life with an absolute sway. Galswintha found herself insulted in her own palace, and begged to be sent back to her father, offering all her treasure to the covetous Merovingian. Such an appeal might have melted the hardest heart, and might have softened even Chilperic's, in one of his better moods. But behind and over Chilperic was now one absolutely cruel and merciless, who "heads the count" of women's crime.

Poor Galswintha was one day found suffocated in her bed : the King made a simulated mourning, and in a few days Fredegundis was Queen of Neustria.

With the murder of Galswintha began the blood-feud in which for forty years Brunihildis pursued her vengeance on Chilperic and Fredegundis, and the forces of the two realms slaughtered one another on many battlefields from the Somme to the Garonne. But before giving a sketch of these murderous and senseless wars, the complications of which it is difficult now to unravel, it is well perhaps to form a conception of the royal leaders.

Sigibert was in personal character far superior to his brothers. He was a faithful husband, perhaps too much under the influence of his brilliant queen. He was a gallant and capable warrior, perhaps too fond of war. He had to face, in two campaigns, a menacing invasion of Avars pressing on from the east. In 562, when only twenty-seven, he defeated them on the borders of Thuringia. In a fresh invasion in 566 he was defeated and made prisoner, but extricated himself by bribes and diplomacy and made a friendly treaty with the Avar king ; and the Avars remained quiet for thirty years. If his energies had been more occupied in extending his empire to the east instead of in fratricidal wars, his fate and that of Gaul might have been happier. But he was ambitious and as eager to extend his sway in Gaul as any Merovingian. In 566 he used the forces of Auvergne to wrest the city of Arles from Guntram, but was beaten and lost for a time his own city of Avignon. He prosecuted the vengeance for Galswintha's murder with a steady vindictiveness equal to that of his wife, and with as keen a desire for Aquitanian cities as Chilperic's. In the final struggle with his brother he called in a wild host of Germans from beyond the Rhine, who spread havoc in rich regions around Chartres and Paris. He exulted in the prospect of uniting Neustria and Austrasia under his sole rule : and when setting out to annihilate his brother at Tournai, rejected the peaceful counsels and the solemn prediction of Bishop Germanus. But the Nemesis of victorious pride and ambition was at hand. At Vitry, near Arras, just as Sigibert was being raised on the shield in old Frank fashion, amid the applauding cries of the warriors of both realms, all his dreams were darkened by the hands of two

assassins who struck him down in the moment of triumph. He
was fighting against one of the worst of kings. But Sigibert,
in spite of some private virtues, remains in history a true
Merovingian.

The character of Chilperic evidently attracted the curious
observation of Gregory, who met him often and knew him well,
and the bishop has drawn it in minute detail. It is a puzzling
character full of contradictions. In many features Chilperic is
a true son of his race, greedy, faithless, sensual, and ruthless in
war. He swelled his treasury by rigorous taxation, confiscation
of estates by perversion of justice, above all by plundering the
Church, of whose ever-growing wealth he was outspokenly
jealous. He would declare null bequests to religious foundations.
He sold the succession to episcopal sees, disregarding the claims
of the clergy and appointing laymen who could pay his price.
His continual wars with his brothers to appropriate the cities of
Aquitaine were prosecuted by his sons with atrocious pillage and
slaughter, which did not spare even priests and abbots. The
threat that " any one who disobeyed his edict should have his
eyes put out " may be apocryphal ; but it is true to the character of the man. Gregory describes him in a phrase perhaps
too often quoted as " the Nero and Herod of his time ".

Yet Chilperic had ideas beyond the range of his family and
of his time. He gave, in certain cases, the right of succession to
landed property to a woman, in opposition to the prescriptions
of the Salic Law. He added four letters to the alphabet, and
ordered that the innovation should be observed in the teaching
of the schools and in the reproduction of MSS. He had an
admiration for the literature and civic culture of Rome. He
composed six books of poems on the model of Sedulius, full of
metrical faults, but celebrated by Fortunatus, whose quantities
are also far from faultless. He tried to revive the games of the
circus at Soissons and Paris. Stranger still is it that this severe
critic and robber of the Church took an interest in theology.
In theology, as we constantly see, the central object of interest
was then the doctrine of the Trinity, and for microscopic differences on that mysterious dogma, inaccessible to the reason, men
and races were ready to hate and fight one another, and condemn
one another to eternal torment. It was a bold thing, even for
a French king, to venture into that cruel arena, in which the

religion of Jesus in history is seen at its worst. Chilperic boldly revived the theory of Sabellius, by which the distinction of the Three Persons becomes a mere trinity of names and abstract conceptions, existing only in the mind of the thinker. He wrote a treatise on the subject, and debated it with Gregory with a curious subtlety and knowledge of ancient controversy. The debate, of course, ended in silencing the King. His taste for theological debate is seen also in an almost comical scene in which he attempted to convert Priscus, a Jew of Paris. Priscus was a goldsmith who catered for Chilperic's artistic tastes and had come to the villa of Nogent on business. Gregory was on a visit to the King and heard the curious debate, which he has fully reported. The Jew, who had boldly assailed the Gospel narratives of the Incarnation, Virgin birth, and Passion of the Redeemer, was overwhelmed with a shower of texts from the Old Testament which, according to old-fashioned criticism, foreshadowed these mysterious events. But the Hebrew remained obdurate, even though the King's arguments were reinforced by the bishop. But one cannot help being struck with the patience and good humour of the King. And, in spite of Gregory's bad opinion of Chilperic, his description of his parting with the King gives a very different impression. Chilperic would not set out for Paris without the bishop's benediction, and, before he mounted his horse, the pair, having washed their hands, celebrated a kind of Communion with bread and wine. Nor is this the only case in which Chilperic showed reverence for episcopal dignity. Some letters from a Bishop of Périgueux had been intercepted which were insulting to Chilperic. The King summoned the bishop and made a careful inquiry into the authorship, which was finally, but doubtfully, traced to a deacon notoriously hostile to the bishop. The King dismissed them both with a wish for their reconciliation, and begged the bishop for his benediction. It is difficult to reconcile this and other instances of Chilperic's scrupulous reverence for bishops with Gregory's final judgement of him—*Sacerdotes Domini assidue blasphemabat.* The probability is that Gregory, with his inordinate faith in his own order, resented the King's rather bitter sneers against the pride and luxury and greed of Churchmen which had too often a foundation in fact.

If Gregory seems unduly severe to Chilperic, he is probably

,too indulgent to Guntram. In spite of glaring vice, perfidy, and savage cruelty, Guntram is always the "good King". He never fell into any heresy ; he bestowed rich endowments on the churches, he always paid due deference to holy priests. In ordering prayers and fasts to abate the ravages of a plague, Gregory recognises a kindred spirit, a priest as well as king. And we may be assured that Guntram was, in the eyes of the Church, a really religious man. He was canonised, although few now would speak of " Saint Guntram ", and he and his relics worked miracles in popular belief. Yet this religious man, as lauded by churchmen, was sensual, faithless, cowardly, and, in spite of a certain good nature, at times savagely cruel. The Church of the sixth century, speaking through the lips of Gregory, was ready to condone and obliterate almost any moral enormity in one who respected her priests or enriched her churches. And let us not be too sure, in our self-complacency, that in our modern Christendom there is not sometimes a similar laxity to ostentatious conformity masking a very low moral character.

Yet it is generally admitted, and was proclaimed by the popular voice of the time, that Guntram was a kindly, good-natured man, who might have been a really good man in a better age. He was generous to the poor, he had none of the cold hauteur of rank in social life, and would dine sometimes with the traders of Orleans. On the death of Chilperic he restored all that in his reign had been unjustly taken from religious foundations, and gave fresh validity to bequests to the Church which his brother had quashed, while at the same time he made lavish donations to the churches and the poor. Easy-going and self-indulgent as he was, on the appeal of Fredegundis he at once went to Paris and undertook the guardianship of the widowed queen and her little son, and showed himself a kindly, gallant gentleman. Yet his life was in danger, and he had to surround himself with an armed guard during his stay. So much did he feel his danger, that one Sunday when the deacon ordered silence after the gospel at Mass, Guntram rose and addressed the congregation, beseeching them to be faithful to the royal line who were their defenders, and to leave him safe to guard his young nephews, who were the hope of France.

This seems noble and patriotic. Yet in the confused politics of the time, Guntram's part is not guided by any principle.

N

He is essentially a pacificist. But he is constantly obliged to intervene in the wars between his brothers, and his object seems to have been to hold the balance between them, a policy which led him often to change sides with a startling rapidity and cheerful, shameless perfidy. After the murder of Galswintha, he took part with Sigibert in his effort of revenge. Soon he formed a short-lived league with Chilperic. And so four or five times in these confused wars or alliances he changed sides as his timidity suggested. He declared for Chilperic when Sigibert's German hordes from beyond the Rhine were devastating the banks of the Marne, but on Sigibert's assassination at Vitry he protected his widow and infant son against Chilperic and the nobles of Austrasia. When the same fate overtook Chilperic himself, he gallantly gave his protection to his widow and infant heir. In dealing with such a puzzling, complex character, half-barbarian, half-Christian, cruel, yet with impulses of generous kindness, self-indulgent, yet with some instincts of public spirit, caring much for his own ease and pleasures, and yet evidently full of an anxious care for the future of his family and the Frank race, it behoves the historian to be more cautious and restrained than many have been in estimating Guntram's character. His atrocious cruelty and his voluptuousness are facile themes for rhetoric. But Guntram was no worse, probably somewhat better, than the standard of his age. His murder of the sons of Magnacharius for defaming his wife Austrichildis, and of her two doctors at her dying request, his cruel torture of the envoys of the pretender Gundobald, his punishment by crucifixion and stoning of one of his forest keepers who had killed a wild bull in his preserves in the Vosges—all these things shock us in a nominally Christian king, but they only show the ever resurgent savagery of the Teutonic nature, which was constantly breaking out in the age of the Merovingians. Gregory in his judgements may seem to be too much inclined to forgive great crimes in obedient sons of the Church. Yet his charity may also spring from a priest's experience of the strange contradictions in human character, and his wish to imitate the Infinite mercy. Only thus can we understand how a saintly bishop could claim a man like Guntram as one of the devoted sons of the Church. It must also be added that in all ages of the Catholic Church observance of the prescribed forms of devotion covers a multitude of sins.

In 567, after the stealthy murder of Galswintha, Chilperic openly married his imperious mistress Fredegundis, who henceforth became a wild dæmonic force in Frank politics. And she was pitted against a woman as strong and ruthless. Brunihildis had the old instinct of race to avenge her sister's murder, and inspired her husband to carry out her wishes. Guntram gave ready assistance, and the combined armies of Austrasia and Burgundy broke into the realm of Neustria. In the end the five cities in Aquitaine which had been the " morning gift " to poor Galswintha were made over as a *wehrgeld* to the avenging Brunihildis. But nothing could mitigate her stern hatred of her sister's murderers ; and nothing but passionate love for her children could ever soften the heart of Fredegundis in the deadly struggle with her rival. For more than thirty years the two fierce queens waged a truceless war with one another by stealthy intrigue or the dagger.

The murder of Galswintha, in a rare fit of moral indignation, united his brothers against Chilperic. Gregory is mysteriously silent on the details of what must have been a serious conflict. He merely tells us that they dethroned Chilperic. How he was restored so soon we are not told.

The death of Charibert in 567, after the arbitrary and shifting partition of Frank territory in the first generation, now rendered possible, and indeed demanded, that threefold division of Northern and Eastern Gaul which corresponded to actual facts of population and geographical features, Neustria, Austrasia, and Burgundy. The south of Gaul, Aquitaine, and Provence, was parcelled out in arbitrary fashion among the three northern kingdoms. Thus Avignon fell to Sigibert, Arles to Guntram. Sigibert was lord of Auvergne, Tours, and Poitiers ; Chilperic of Limoges, Bordeaux, and the banks of the Garonne ; Guntram could claim the distant territories of Agen, Saintes, Angoulême, and Périgueux. It has always puzzled the present writer how across alien territory and at long distances Chilperic could have effective rule in Limoges or Bordeaux, or Guntram at Agen and Périgueux ; or how Sigibert carried on war or the peaceful administration of Provence through the realms of Guntram. Certainly the chronicles give no clue to the problem. Ancient Aquitaine had been, even before the Roman conquest, broken up by constant divisions, often severed by zealous enmities ; and these sometimes reappeared in the sixth century in fierce hostilities between rival municipalities. Moreover, the régime of the Church had created a system of ecclesiastical provinces, generally corresponding to the *civitates* of the Empire. Into these rivalries and sharp divisions the Frank partitions introduced a fresh element of confusion and quarrel. And neighbouring bishops, who should have been bound in Christian amity to one another, might find themselves severed by the deadly enmities of the three northern kingdoms. Thus the fate of what might have been the happiest region in Europe, and which probably was so in the reign of Hadrian, was in perpetual peril from the savagery and perfidy of the Frank kings. Tours belonged to Austrasia, but was seized by Chilperic on the assassination of Sigibert; Avignon, in the domain of Sigibert, was occupied by Guntram (563). In 583 a furious conflict was waged for the city of Bourges between the armies of Guntram and Chilperic, in which the country was wasted with fire and slaughter never known before. But ten years before the deadly struggle for the cities of Aquitaine had begun to rage between Sigibert and Chilperic, Chilperic commissioned his son Clovis to invade the lands of Tours and Poitiers, which had been assigned to Sigibert. Guntram took part with Sigibert, and sent the patrician Mummolus, already famous for his repeated victories over the Lombards, in command of a Burgundian army to check the advance of Clovis beyond the Loire. The unconquerable patrician defeated Clovis in Touraine and compelled him to seek refuge in Bordeaux, one of Chilperic's cities. But sheltering there in apparent security, Clovis was suddenly attacked by Sigulfus, an officer of Sigibert, who probably was in command in some of the scattered possessions of Austrasia in Poitou or Albigeois. The prince was hotly pursued to the north, and returned to his father by a detour by way of Angers. At this point Guntram intervened as peacemaker, and convened a synod of all his bishops at Paris, to compose the feud of the two brothers. The bishops could not even obtain a hearing, and the war, so terrible for Aquitaine, broke out again in the following year (574). About the same time S. Germanus of Paris addressed a letter to Brunihildis urging her to exert her influence with Sigibert for peace. In that letter we can discern the feeling of religious observers about the desolating and demoralising struggle. Greed, ambition, and the insanity of strife made the bishop despair of the Divine mercy to France.

Sigibert cannot be absolved from the guilt of aggression in the beginning of his reign. But in 574 Chilperic was once more the aggressor. His designs on the fair regions along the Loire had been foiled by the genius of Mummolus. His son Clovis had been driven into ignominious flight from Bordeaux. The savage lurking in him was thoroughly aroused. Why these peaceful towns should be raided by the Franks of Neustria in an insane conflict between two brothers goaded on by their wives is a question which could only be answered by the Providence which ordained or permitted it. Chilperic in furious rage let loose his tumultuary armies on the cities beyond the Loire, under the command of Theudebert, his eldest son. It is characteristic of Merovingian faith that this Theudebert had, in the campaign of 564, been taken prisoner by Sigibert, generously treated, and restored to his father, after taking a solemn oath not to act against Sigibert again. That oath, needless to say, was now forgotten by Chilperic and Theudebert. The young prince, slaughtering and to slaughter, swept across the lands of Poitiers, Tours, and the cities on the Loire, routed with enormous carnage the Poitevins under the Duke Gundobad, ravaged with fire most of the territory of Tours, and spread the same desolation in the more southern towns, as far as Limoges and Cahors. The churches were burnt down, the priests dragged from the altar and massacred ; monks driven from their cloisters, and nuns insulted and outraged. According to Gregory, who had the year before been consecrated Bishop of Tours, the Church had to mourn a persecution worse than that of Diocletian. In the first conquests of Clovis there had been nothing to match the atrocities of his great-grandson, perpetrated on a peaceful population who had never since the conquest provoked such treatment. Meantime, Guntram and Sigibert were equally unable to stem the tide of the Neustrian invasion of Aquitaine. Mummolus was engaged with a vast horde of Saxons threatening Provence, Sigibert could not send Frank troops across Burgundian and Neustrian territory to repel Theudebert. His only general in that region was the Sigulfus who had chased Clovis from Bordeaux, and who seems to be the same as the Sigulfus who, a little later, aspired to be king of that region. Unable to meet the armies of Chilperic in

Aquitaine, Sigibert determined to strike at the heart of Neustria. He summoned to his standards the tribes who owned his sway beyond the Rhine. Chilperic secured the precarious aid of Guntram against their common peril. The league did not last long. For Sigibert, with threats too much for the nerves of Guntram, obtained leave to pass the upper Seine in Burgundian lands. Chilperic had to fall back to Chartres, and now, deserted by Guntram and face to face with a horde of German tribes, he made offers of a peace by which he was to restore Sigibert's possessions in Aquitaine on condition that Sigibert's German auxiliaries were withdrawn. The condition was not an easy one to fulfil. They had come in the hope of plunder. They had spread havoc in the fields and villages around Paris, and were furious at any attempt to check their ravages. It was only by the courage of Sigibert riding among them, sometimes by persuasion, sometimes by stern punishment, that they were finally restrained and ordered back across the Rhine. That was probably the most honourable day in Sigibert's life. The peace was signalised by three miracles before the shrine of S. Martin. But it was short and illusory. Guntram once again changed sides, and Chilperic, with fire and sword, advanced to Rheims. Sigibert roused all his strength to strike a final blow. He ordered two dukes to crush Theudebert in Aquitaine. Theudebert, with scanty forces, was easily defeated and fell in the battle. His corpse, outraged and despoiled, was, by the pious hands of a certain Arnulfus, arrayed in the vesture becoming a Merovingian and interred at Angoulême. Meanwhile the tribes from beyond the Rhine had been rapidly recalled, and Sigibert with a great army marched on Paris and secured all the towns along the Seine and as far as Rouen. Then a thing happened, dismissed by the chronicler in a brief sentence, but which is full of meaning to the modern inquirer. Sigibert wished to grant the cities he had conquered along the Seine to his German auxiliaries from beyond the Rhine; in fact, to sanction another German conquest of North-western Gaul. This might have been the prelude and precedent for other Teutonic invasions. Whatever Sigibert's inclinations may have been, his own Austrasian *leudes* forbade it. They were not going to place their estates at the mercy of a fresh horde of Teutonic invaders. The curt sentence of Gregory, " *A suis prohibitus est* ", is a forecast of the decline of Merovingian power which was to reach its final ebb in a century and a half. The same omen is seen in the offer of the *leudes* of Chilperic to abandon him and accept Sigibert as ruler of the western realm. He had now the fair prospect of uniting the two kingdoms under himself. Chilperic in terror had, with his wife and children, screened himself behind the walls of Tournai, one of the earliest conquests of the Salian Franks. Sigibert, apparently sure of Neustrian loyalty and of the sole sovereignty of the two kingdoms, pressed on to the siege of Tournai. His triumph seemed assured. Nemesis of old classic legend came in, as so often in later history, to spoil all plans, confound human ambitions, and overshadow the fairest hopes. S. Germanus made himself the voice of Nemesis by an ominous saying from Holy Writ. But the warning was not heeded. At Vitry, between Arras and Douai, it was arranged that Sigibert should be elected and proclaimed King of Neustria, according to old Germanic usage. Raised on the shield, he was uproariously saluted by the Neustrian armies. And at the very moment of his apparent triumph he was suddenly stabbed in both sides by two young servants, with poisoned daggers. The assassins were emissaries of Fredegundis. The cheering crowd had at once vanished, and Sigibert's body lay neglected and unburied till Chilperic, who had at once left Tournai and was hastening to Paris, stopped to give his brother decent burial. The murder took place eighteen days after the equally tragic death of Theudebert at Angoulême.

Brunihildis, with her children, had accompanied her husband to Paris in his triumphant march on Tournai. Her little son Childebert, the heir to the throne of Sigibert, in order to escape the deadly clutches of Chilperic, was skilfully and secretly carried away to Austrasia by the Duke Gundobad, and at once proclaimed King with the loyal support of the *leudes*. Brunihildis was relegated to Rouen, under the guardianship of the bishop Praetextatus, a trust for which he had to pay heavily in years of exile and care, which form one of the most interesting and instructive episodes of the Merovingian age.

The news of the triumphant advance of Sigibert in Neustria had probably soon spread through Aquitaine, and led to the easy defeat of Theudebert by Guntram Boso, and the failure of Chilperic's designs for the time. But Chilperic was no sooner restored to safety and power than the passion awoke again to

extend his power in Aquitaine, without a thought of the desolation
and carnage which these repeated invasions, inspired only by
cupidity and reckless ambition, inflicted on inoffensive populations. Merovech, his youngest son fit for war, was ordered to
march with an army on Poitiers. He stopped at Tours for the
Easter festivals, which his forces celebrated by devastating the
country. Before he started on his campaign he had probably
seen at Paris the widowed Brunihildis and conceived a lawless
passion for her. Under pretence of visiting his mother, Audovera,
one of the repudiated wives of Chilperic, he left his army and
hurried back to Rouen, where the Austrasian queen was living in
so-called exile. The wooing of nephew and aunt seems to have
been brief. Whether it was a union inspired by impetuous
passion or by some political designs of Brunihildis against her
hated rival Fredegundis, there is no hint in our authorities. At
any rate the marriage, although disastrous to Merovech, had no
effect on the course of events. The King would have gladly
broken a union which was a violation of religious law. But the
pair, who had fled to a neighbouring shrine of S. Martin, were
drawn forth by a pledge of safety, and with most affectionate
greetings were welcomed at a banquet by this strange King.
Brunihildis was allowed to return to Austrasia, but her husband
was retained at Soissons. And then a suspicious thing occurred.
An army from Champagne suddenly moved on Soissons. Fredegundis and her infant son had to fly, and the enemy apparently
captured the city. Chilperic, with an army, soon came up to
repel the invaders, who were routed with the loss of many of
their best troops. Chilperic believed that the attack on Soissons
was a treacherous plot of Merovech's, and he was punished by
the loss of his arms and liberty for a time, and then tonsured
and relegated to the monastery of S. Calais. Many things in
the career of the young prince indicate that he had designs on
his father's throne. Brunihildis most probably had a part in
them. The great *leudes* of Austrasia, Ursio and Egidius, during
the infancy and long minority of Childebert, were bent on
aggrandising themselves at the expense of the Austrasian crown.
The bitterest enmity between the Queen and these ambitious
nobles was growing, and was destined to have serious political
results. The great Queen, although she fought a long battle for
her children against this faction, may at one time have dreamt of

uniting Neustria and Austrasia under Merovech as they had been
for a moment under Sigibert, and the consolidation of the Merovingian power would have defeated the ambition of the Austrasian
nobles, who distrusted and hated her union with Merovech.
Fredegundis, far abler than Chilperic, penetrated from the first
the schemes of Merovech. When the young prince had taken
shelter at Tours, she inspired the most consummate traitor in
that faithless time, Guntram Boso, to entrap him. She followed
him up with deadly hatred, till at last, close beset, he ordered his
faithful Gailen to release him by the poniard. With the same
unslackening malice she pursued for years the bishop Praetextatus,
who had married Merovech and Brunihildis at Rouen, and who
was evidently privy to Merovech's treason. Merovech, from
what we see of his character and career, hardly seems to have
possessed the solid power to carry through a dangerous plan of
treason. Yet, with the genius of Brunihildis behind him, it may
at one time not have seemed to be hopeless.

The years between the murder of Sigibert in 575 and the
murder of Chilperic in 584 are bewildering in complications
of intrigues and policy. The ambition or greed of Chilperic to
extend his power in Aquitaine is unsleeping. The great men of
Austrasia saw and seized the chance offered by the long minority
of the infant King Childebert II. to aggrandise the power of
their class against that of the Crown. The widowed queen was
equally determined to defend the Crown. Her foes were powerful
and unscrupulous : Egidius, the Bishop of Rheims, a man of
immense ambition and faithless intrigue ; Guntram Boso, a man
who took an oath only to break it, and prostituted great talent
to treacherous ambition ; Ursio, Rauchingus, and Bertefredus,
coldly and recklessly cruel even beyond the depravity of that
cruel age. In the face of so powerful and unscrupulous a faction,
Brunihildis had recourse to Guntram to defend her son's rights.
The Burgundian king was glad to have the support of Austrasia
in warding off Chilperic's determined onslaught in Aquitaine,
where Mummolus, in fierce and bloody battles, was fighting with
some success against the Duke Desiderius in the south to save
the towns of Guntram, while in the north Chilperic had annexed
Tours, Poitiers, and Limoges, and remained in possession of them
till 581. One cannot help admiring his concentration and energy
in the conflict of those years. In 578 he was engaged in a serious

struggle on the Vilaine with Warochus, the Breton chief—a struggle in which Chilperic had to call up levies from Tours, Poitiers, Bayeux, and Le Mans, and even the *juniores ecclesiae*. These wars must have strained the resources of his treasury, for in 579 he imposed new taxes of such weight that many migrated into other territory and fierce revolts broke out. At Limoges the populace were so infuriated that they threatened the life of Marcus, the royal referendary, and seized and burnt the rolls of taxpayers. In the following year (580) Gaul was overwhelmed by a series of calamities enough to unnerve the firmest hearts. The forces of Nature seem to have conspired to match the fury and malignity of man. Incessant rains swelled the great rivers Rhone and Saône and partly overthrew the walls of Lyons. In the south of Aquitaine the earth was so convulsed that the walls of great cities collapsed amid universal terror. Even the Pyrenees were so shaken that great boulders were detached and spread havoc below. But the worst calamity was the great plague, which did not spare the palace. Chilperic himself fell ill, and two of his sons died of it. The affliction moved even Fredegundis to momentary penitence, and inspired Chilperic with a rare generosity to the poor and the Church. And the curious thing is that this man, who is regarded by churchmen as an enemy of the Church, had so often to take a part in ecclesiastical councils affecting the fate of great churchmen, and that in those meetings he seems to have behaved with fairness and courtesy and even reverence for episcopal dignity. It was at this very time, too, that he wished to impose on the Gallic church his Sabellian views of the Trinity ; and in this very year Gregory of Tours, while he was assailed by the intrigues and violence of the Count Leudastes, calmly held debate with the Spanish envoy Agilanes on the doctrine of the Trinity. These men of the sixth century, it has often seemed to us, were far less disturbed by the great calamities, wars, and political intrigues of their time than we feel in imagination after fifteen centuries.

Brunihildis also found or created for herself a party among the Austrasian nobles headed by Gogo and Lupus, men of character and high achievements. As the party of Egidius and Ursio leaned to the side of Neustria and Chilperic, the party of Brunihildis and Lupus appealed to the support of Guntram and Burgundy, which beyond the other Frank kingdoms retained the powerful impress of the Empire. Thus the struggle became one between Burgundy and Neustria, Guntram and Chilperic, the young Childebert of Austrasia being a pawn in the game. And the boy became more valuable in the struggle, as Guntram was childless, and Chilperic had lost his sons, and the kingdom was left heirless till, after his death, Chlothar was born. Thus Childebert, probably at the time quite unconscious of his possible destiny, might once have succeeded to the whole Frank Empire, and his great nobles have risen to even greater power. But in the ceaseless struggle he was helplessly transferred to the Neustrian or Burgundian side according to the momentary ascendancy of Egidius or Brunihildis and her party. At least three times he was adopted by Guntram and made his heir, with old Teutonic ceremonial, and at intervals he was proclaimed the heir of Chilperic. And all the while there was a fierce strife going on in Austrasia between the two aristocratic factions.

The quarrel began in Marseilles. At the death of Sigibert Guntram had annexed the half of that municipal region which belonged to his brother, and appointed a Burgundian, Dynamius, as prefect. The bishop Theodorus, who had the support of the people, stood for the interests of Austrasia ; the prefect, strange to say, had the support of the clergy. The feud was bitter and envenomed to such an extent that the bishop was for a time imprisoned by the clerical party, who were determined to drive him from his see. Their violence was extraordinary. They actually invaded the clergy houses, seized the holy vessels of the sanctuary, and plundered the property of the see. To such extremes of sacrilegious frenzy, in an age when even the sputum of a hermit was venerable, did the political feuds of the age carry men devoted to religion. Even a local feud so violent soon disturbed the relations between Burgundy and Austrasia. The Austrasian nobles seized the opportunity to break with Guntram, who was the great obstacle to their ambition in their conflict with the crown of Austrasia and Brunihildis. Guntram had adopted Childebert because there was no heir to Burgundy. The plague, and the deadly arts of Fredegundis by which the young Clovis had perished, had left for the time the realm of Neustria also without a successor to the throne. In 581 the grandees of Austrasia, headed by the bishop Egidius, went on a deputation to Chilperic to propose an alliance of Neustria and

Austrasia against Guntram. Chilperic accepted the alliance and promised to make Childebert his heir, but characteristically refused to abate a jot of his claims in Aquitaine. The noble faction determined to master the government of Austrasia and to overthrow the royalist party and Brunihildis. The chief of that party was Lupus, the Duke of Champagne, who was lauded by Fortunatus, with apparently unusual sincerity, as a wise, laborious statesman, capable of expounding his policy, and a warrior who had crushed the Saxon and Danish raiders on the rivers of the north. Ursio and Bertefredus made war on Lupus ; Brunihildis, who intervened to stop the combat, was grossly insulted by Ursio, who told her to retire or she would be trampled down by their horses; and he warned her that her reign was over and that her son reigned only under their protection. Bruni-hildis succeeded in staying the combat, but Lupus, plundered of all, had to seek a refuge in Burgundy. Here is a strange and ominous note in the history of the Merovingian kings, an omen of the end. But the great lords of Austrasia, under a weak boy king, for the present miscalculated their power. They had against them Brunihildis, a woman of dæmonic force and ambition, and with far greater statesman's craft than theirs, and there was the dim mass of the common folk, with whom Bishop Egidius and his great lords found little favour. They dreaded this aristocratic tyranny, against which Brunihildis and the monarchy seemed the only barrier. Chilperic, relying on his league with Austrasia, had opened a great campaign against the cities of Aquitaine and in Burgundy. A fierce attack was made on Bourges, with tremendous slaughter and savage desolation of that pleasant land. But Guntram, coming up in great force, surprised the Neustrian army, and inflicted losses so heavy that on the morrow Chilperic had to make peace and fall back on Paris, evacuating the country he had overrun. By some mysterious influence, his Austrasian allies had failed to give him active support. That secret influence almost certainly was the work of Brunihildis and her party working for Guntram against the alliance with Chilperic. The common soldiers rose up against the great lords and officers who had sold the Austrasian realm to the Neustrian king. They even burst into Childe-bert's tent in pursuit of the traitors, who fled or hid themselves. The arch traitor Egidius escaped with difficulty on his horse through a furious crowd, who would have stoned him to death. The party of Brunihildis triumphed, broke the alliance with Chilperic, and Burgundy and Austrasia were once more leagued to recapture the cities of Aquitaine from Chilperic.

Chilperic, dismayed at the failure of his combinations and the defeat of his Austrasian partisans, sent orders to his commanders to look to the fortifications of their towns, and defend themselves to the uttermost. He himself retired to the fortress of Cambrai. But his enemies, strangely, did not follow up their advantage. The young Childebert instead, tempted by a subsidy from the Emperor Maurice, descended on Italy to attack the Lombards, but on a mock submission, backed by a heavy bribe, he returned to Gaul. His uncle Guntram apparently remained inactive. Chilperic, relieved of anxiety, returned to Paris, to prepare for the splendid journey of his daughter Rigunthis, who was betrothed to Richaredus, the Visigothic king. There is a pathetic contrast between the lavish waste and magnificence of this display and the dangers and misery of the time. It is a startling proof of the power and arrogance of the Merovingian house. Fifty cars followed the princess, loaded with gold, silver, jewels, costly raiment, the so-called " gifts " of the Franks. She was escorted by 4000 men-at-arms, led by great nobles and courtiers, Waddo, Bobo, Domigisilus, Ansovaldus. A crowd of serfs were torn from their families, amid tears and desperate grief, to swell the retinue on its ill-omened march. The men of higher order, who were forced to join it, obeyed with slight hope of ever returning. They made their wills, or left their lands to the Church, being certain that once on Spanish soil they would never return. The princess set out with evil omens. Soon the expedition began to melt away. A splendid cavalry corps deserted one night to Childebert. Numbers of others glided off with their spoil. No regular provision had been made for the commissariat of the cavalcade. They lived, as Merovingian armies so often did, on the country or the towns they passed through. Every house or cottage was plundered. Vineyards were swept clean, and the trees stubbed to the ground. The chronicler, whose descriptive power is striking, confesses that he feels helpless to describe the ruin and misery caused by this wedding procession, and falls back on a famous passage in Joel (i. 4) to express his feelings.

Suddenly an event occurred which confused all the diplomacy and intrigues of the time. Returning from the chase on his estate of Chelles, near Paris, in the dusk, Chilperic, as he dismounted from his horse, was stabbed by an unknown hand. Conjecture as to the real author of the deed was rife. Some accused Brunihildis and her party ; others the great lords of Austrasia, now deep in the conspiracy of Gundobald. Others attributed the crime to her, who was capable of every crime, to Fredegundis, whose intrigue with a Neustrian noble had become known to her husband. His character has been blasted by Gregory of Tours with all the venom of priestly hatred. And his verdict has been accepted and intensified by some modern historians, with perhaps a too credulous criticism, who forget that sweeping epithets are not criticism, and not history. Chilperic was certainly far from being a model character ; what Merovingian was or could be ? He was cruel, ruthless, and lustful, like all his race. Like them he devastated whole regions, inflicted appalling tortures on any who disobeyed his commands, broke wills, and confiscated estates. But it is a little suspicious that these charges are mingled with sneers at the ludicrous prosody of his imitations of Sedulius, and resentment at his constant jeers and slanders against the Church and the bishops. He often said stinging things about their growing wealth and power at the expense of the State. But they stung because they were true. A churchman, especially in an age when the episcopate claimed an unchallenged power backed by Divine sanctions, is hardly to be trusted in his judgement of one who dared to criticise the Church.

Chilperic left a son of only four months. With him and such treasure as she could carry away, the widow sought the protection of the bishop in the cathedral of Paris. Her position was dangerous. The great lords of Neustria might desert her. Childebert had arrived at Meaux ready to assume the tutelage of the infant prince. Fredegundis at once sent urgent messages to Guntram to beg him to come and assume the regency of his brother's realm. The good-natured King came with a sufficient force, and was at once welcomed and recognised by the Neustrian leaders as the proper guardian of the young Chlothar. This must have been disquieting to both of the parties in Austrasia, that of Egidius and that of Brunihildis. Neustria and Burgundy were for the

time united, and the great men of Neustria swore allegiance
at once to the infant Chlothar and his guardian of Burgundy.
Childebert, evidently under the influence of his mother, asserted
the royal power and his territorial claims as the successor of
Sigibert and Charibert. Embassies were despatched to Paris to
demand the restitution of those parts of Aquitaine which Chilperic
had occupied, the third part of Paris conceded to Sigibert in the
pact of 567, and the surrender of Fredegundis, the double-dyed
murderess, and above all the deadly and pitiless foe of Brunihildis.
Guntram repelled those demands with indignant scorn. He
would yield nothing to the false intriguers who had made a secret
pact with Chilperic to deprive him of his throne and possessions
and made his nephew an enemy. All former treaties had been
invalidated by their treachery and the disregard of them shown
by Sigibert and Chilperic. He would at once bring under his
sway all the realm of Charibert with all his treasures. All that
Chilperic had taken from Austrasia in Aquitaine he would keep.
Fredegundis was inviolate under his protection. In this defiant
attitude towards Childebert, Guntram strove to fortify his position in Neustria. He restored their possessions to many despoiled
in Chilperic's reign. He confirmed bequests to the Church which
that King had alienated, and gave lavish alms to the poor. Yet
he felt constantly in danger, and never went abroad without an
armed escort. Probably his refusal to surrender Fredegundis to
the hate of Brunihildis inspired a fear of what that redoubtable
woman might do. At any rate, one Sunday in the middle of the
Mass, when the deacon had proclaimed silence, the King made
an appeal to the people to be loyal to him and not to kill him
as they had his brothers, but to leave him even for three years
to guard his nephews, the last of the kingly race, who were their
sole defenders. This is a curious plea for a race who by their
internecine wars might seem to have brought ruin to whole
regions of France. Yet the people fervently responded by prayers
for the King's safety.

Meantime, the armies of Childebert and Guntram descended
on northern Aquitaine, Guntram to reclaim the cities which had
been seized by Chilperic, Childebert to keep them under Neustrian
sway. The great towns of Tours, Poitiers, Bourges, and Limoges
were the hapless gages in this great strife. There was dreadful
slaughter, and the men of Tours watched the fires from their

walls, which even threatened shrines hallowed by relics of S. Martin.

Before or during these hostilities (for the chronicle leaves this doubtful) a promised conference (*placitum*) was held between the statesmen of Neustria and Guntram. The chief point in dispute was the possession of those cities in Aquitaine, once belonging to Sigibert, which Chilperic had occupied and which Guntram refused to give up. The Austrasian deputation embraced Egidius, Guntram Boso, Sigoaldus, and other Austrasian chiefs. They repeated the demand for restitution of Childebert's cities and the surrender of Fredegundis. Both were haughtily refused, and recriminations of a singular rudeness and ferocity passed between the deputation and the King. The meeting took place in 584, the year in which the pretender Gundobald was solemnly proclaimed King at Briva, and rumours of the event had reached Paris. When the versatile intriguer, Guntram Boso, deeply involved, as will soon appear, in the Gundobaldian conspiracy, ventured to address Guntram, the King roughly assailed him as a traitor who two years before had brought a certain Ballomer (so Gundobald was called), a fellow of the lowest origin, into Gaul as a rival to his throne. Guntram Boso, true to his reckless, daring character, offered a decision of the charge by single combat. The meeting broke up with sneers and threats against Guntram, who retaliated by ordering his men to cover the envoys with the offal and filth of the streets.

This mention of the pretender Gundobald naturally leads us to give some account of that strange conspiracy which in those years convulsed southern Aquitaine, was fostered by a powerful party in Austrasia, and seemed for a time to threaten the thrones of Neustria and Burgundy. It was a much more serious movement than some modern historians have recognised, for it was a deeply-laid scheme of an aristocratic party to overthrow the old Merovingians.

About the year 558 a woman presented herself before King Childebert with a boy who was, she alleged, a son of Chlothar, but whom Chlothar disowned. The boy had been carefully educated, and wore the flowing hair of the Merovingians. The childless Childebert was ready to adopt him, but on the demand of Chlothar resigned his charge. Chlothar once more denied that the boy was his, and had his hair shorn off. Chlothar died

in 561, and the youth was adopted by his son Charibert of Paris.
Then, by whatever claim, Sigibert of Austrasia claimed him and
sent him in exile to Cologne. For some years he was in poverty
and supported himself by painting frescoes for household decoration, a trade which was later cast in his teeth as a pretender to
royal rank. He then migrated to Italy and succeeded in attracting the interest of Narses, then at the height of his triumphs.
Probably the apparently obscure adventurer came with hints and
rumours of his high birth. He was well received, married, and
settled in family life. We next hear of him at Constantinople,
probably commended to the Emperor as a man who might be
useful in the West. There can be no doubt that the Emperor
Maurice so regarded him and lavishly supplied him with money
when Gundobald started on his adventurous enterprise in Gaul.

The Merovingian kings enjoyed all the freedom and variety
of the East in their conjugal relations. In their harems legitimacy
might often be doubtful, and it is quite possible that Gundobald
was really a brother of Sigibert, Guntram, and Chilperic. At any
rate he was well known in Gaul, through many a rumour passing
from the Eastern capital, as a reputed Merovingian who had the
attraction of mystery, and who had been able to secure the
countenance and support of the Eastern powers. Austrasia, as
we have seen, since the death of Sigibert was torn between two
factions, one leaning to an alliance with Burgundy, the other
eager for the support of Chilperic. And Neustria and Burgundy
were engaged in deadly combat in Aquitaine, in which they contended for the help of the Eastern kingdom. The rival parties
in Austrasia of Egidius and Brunihildis were often in fierce
conflict, the one for aristocratic, the other for the kingly power.
But at times they could forget their differences and work for a
common end. One section might regard Guntram as the enemy,
the other the King of Neustria. But in the end they combined
against both. If they could set up another Merovingian as sole
Frank monarch, the Frank aristocracy might, through the king
who would owe his place to them, wield an enormous and un-
challengeable power. Such seems the most probable explanation
of a tangled problem. Although Brunihildis had been a resolute
opponent of Egidius, Ursio, and their party, there are some clear
indications that she was a party to the Gundobaldian conspiracy.
Certainly King Guntram when he warned Childebert against his

mother suspected her of being involved in it. And when she
sent some artistic presents to Gundobald's sons in Spain, it was
suspected that she wished to have one of them for her husband.
In that age of desperate hatreds and fickle loyalty, the queen
mother of Austrasia would probably have slight scruples as to
the means of maintaining a precarious place. She was surrounded
by men who changed sides and broke solemn engagements with
a calm cynicism which perplexes and astounds the modern
inquirer. The parties were playing a game for high stakes
which might have shaken principles stronger than any of that
age.

Probably about 579 or 580, one of the Austrasian nobles,
Guntram Boso, appears at Constantinople on a mission to
Gundobald. The emissary was a typical German noble of the
time, brave, proverbially faithless, who took an oath meaning to
break it if it suited his plans. He must have been as adroit and
able as he was ambitious. He had in 575 commanded the troops
of Sigibert against Chilperic's son Theudebert in Aquitaine, and
was reputed to have slain that young prince. He was in the
plot to raise Merovech to the throne of Neustria, and yet inveigled him away from the sanctuary of Tours to have him slain
by bravoes of Chilperic. Such was the man to whose guidance
Gundobald committed himself. He was told that the Merovingian
line was dying out and near extinction, and that his claims as a
true-born son of Chlothar would be strongly supported in Aquitaine
and by the Austrasian nobles, who had committed themselves in
a formal council. The pretender received large supplies of money
from the Emperor, who thought he might obtain powerful Frank
support in Italy. Gundobald landed at Marseilles, where he was
received by the bishop Theodorus, an adherent of the Austrasian
interest and wielding a great popular influence. Thence Gundobald was taken to Avignon, which was in Childebert's domains,
and now occupied with a strong force by Mummolus, a Burgundian patrician and the great general of the age. Why
Mummolus gave up such a great position to take part with an
adventurer from the East is one of the mysteries of that puzzling
time. Perhaps his prestige had made him " suspect " in Burgundy. Perhaps, misled by reports as to the chances of the
pretender, he may have thought that his great renown as a
general would give him a commanding place in the campaign

which must now open between the forces of Gundobald and
Guntram. If Gundobald won by the strategy of Mummolus,
which had won so often before, the victorious general would
certainly be the foremost person under the new monarchy.
Suddenly the scene changes. Without a word of comment
from the chronicler, we are told that Guntram seized and threw
into prison the bishop Theodorus as the man who had brought
in a foreigner to bring the Frank realms under the sway of the
Empire. At the same time Gundobald was allowed to retire to
an island off the coast. What determined Boso to reverse his
whole policy is left unexplained. Boso was notorious, as we
have seen, for his treachery. It was a second nature to him.
He may have heard that Guntram, who in 581 had ordered all
the roads to the south to be closed, was now informed of the
plot and prepared, or the sight of the treasure which the pretender brought from the East may have so dazzled an avaricious
soul that for the moment he lost sight of the policy in which he
was a prime mover. These German nobles, especially of the
north-east, were still semi-barbarians, with untamed, impetuous
instincts of greed or cruelty. And towards the end of his career
Boso was charged with plundering a tomb on consecrated ground
and robbing the royal treasury. Such a man was capable of
anything. He divided his spoil with a duke of Guntram, and
took his way to Auvergne, of which he had been appointed
governor. The bishops Theodorus and Epiphanius, then flying
from the Lombards, were charged with complicity in the plot
and imprisoned. Theodorus could plead that he only obeyed
the orders, which he produced, of the council of Childebert.
King Guntram is said to have acquitted them, yet strangely
they were still retained in captivity. Boso visited the court of
Childebert, but on his return to Auvergne, through Burgundy,
was seized by officers of Guntram and brought before the King,
who was now fully informed of the danger from the conspiracy.
Boso threw the whole blame on Guntram's patrician Mummolus,
but only escaped by offering his son as a hostage until he should
bring that great officer a prisoner. His terms were granted, and
he set out with an Arvernian force to assail the great general
in his well-fortified position at Avignon, where he defended himself
with all the skill and resource to be expected of so great a captain.
The action of Boso aroused the anger of Childebert and his nobles.

They had already a general on the spot who had been engaged
in defending Austrasian interests in Marseilles. Gundulfus,
ordered with his forces to Avignon, succeeded in raising the
siege and setting Mummolus free for further efforts in Gundobald's
cause.

It is well to remind ourselves that while these things are
passing in the south, the Austrasian party are forming a compact
with Chilperic for an attack on Burgundy, and that Chilperic is
bent on the conquest of northern Aquitaine and an invasion of
Burgundy. In a combined attack, from north and south, the
lands around Bourges were desolated with a ferocity which even
Merovingian armies had never equalled : houses, vineyards,
even churches, were wiped out. But Chilperic's generals had
not the support from Childebert which they expected, and a
popular movement had overwhelmed the party of Egidius,
broken the league with Chilperic, and brought Austrasia into
league with Guntram ; and one great purpose of the alliance
was to recapture the towns of Aquitaine which the undeviating
policy of Chilperic had been to annex. Meanwhile Rigunthis and
her vanishing train were approaching Toulouse with a treasure
tempting to lawless eyes. And a great event in the north, the
assassination of the most ambitious of the Merovingians, altered
the whole balance of power by calling Guntram to the guardianship of Fredegundis and the young Chlothar, with the united
force of Neustria and Burgundy. The war between Austrasia and
Burgundy for the unfortunate cities in northern Aquitaine broke
out again, Tours and Poitiers and Limoges declaring for Childebert, Bourges for Guntram. But leaving this confused struggle,
let us once more turn our eyes to the Gundobaldians in the south.

The cities of Aquitaine, partitioned among the kingdoms of
the north, the continual prey of those jealous and rapacious
kings, annexed and lost, and again reconquered with frightful
slaughter and devastation, might well pray for some respite and
deliverance. They were still rich and strong in the yet lingering
tradition of Roman culture. Why should they not assert themselves under new leaders against the barbarism of the north ?
Two such leaders, both of Gallo-Roman stock, now offered
themselves, the duke Desiderius and the patrician Mummolus.
The one had for some years been the great general of Chilperic ;
the other of Guntram. Six years before, they had met in a

desperate battle near Limoges, in which Desiderius had fled before
the great strategist who had again and again thrown back the
Lombards across the Alps. In two campaigns Desiderius had
won for Chilperic the Aquitanian cities from the Loire to the
Pyrenees, from the ocean to Cevennes, and had become Duke of
Toulouse, wielding an immense influence in the south by his
great possessions at Alby and his military renown. Mummolus
had a great respect for the man whom he had once defeated.
The death of Chilperic, which had deranged all policies and made
Guntram for the time master of Neustria, left Desiderius a free-
lance. Desiderius and Mummolus had for some time an understanding with one another, and communication was easy between
Alby, the seat of Desiderius, and Avignon, where Mummolus
was now with Gundobald awaiting events. On the news of
Chilperic's death reaching Desiderius, he at once with a picked
force marched on Toulouse, seized all the treasure of the wretched
Rigunthis, and placed her under close guard. Some of her
retinue (*e.g.* Waddo) joined him in declaring for the pretender.
He and his two Gallo-Roman generals leaving Avignon marched
on Briva, a small place, but centrally situated for operations
on the great cities of southern Aquitaine. There, in December
584, Gundobald was crowned and proclaimed according to the
Frank usage. But the ceremony was darkened by strange
prodigies and evil omens which in a short time were to be sadly
fulfilled.

While the generals of Gundobald were preparing to seize the
Aquitanian towns for the new monarchy, Guntram's general,
the duke Gararic, was sent to occupy the northern towns in
Guntram's name, and in these very days, as news of the rising
became more and more distinct, as we have seen, the Austrasian
embassy to Guntram, which included Guntram Boso, was
fiercely reproached with their perfidy by the King and driven
from his presence. But they had spoken with an insolence
which they would hardly have assumed if the news of Gundobald's rising had not seemed to threaten the power of Guntram.
And in Southern Gaul the prospects of the pretender may well
for the time have appeared far from hopeless. The cities of
Aquitaine, as we have said, must have been sick and weary of
being bandied about among the Frank kings in the fluctuations
of incessant wars. The death of Chilperic, their worst oppressor,

seemed to offer a hope of relief. The new Merovingian, who
would owe his success to their support, might be a less cruel
master than the northern kings who crushed them in successive
invasions. And Gundobald's two renowned generals were true
Gallo-Romans who might naturally be sympathetic to the still
strong Gallo-Roman tradition and culture of Aquitaine. Their
policy was clear. All towns which belonged to Austrasia were
asked to take the oath of allegiance to Childebert. Those which
acknowledged the sway of Neustria or Burgundy were obliged
to swear fealty to Gundobald. He was the chosen champion of
the Austrasian nobles, and after crushing Guntram, he was to
be the ruler of Austrasia and Burgundy. When Aquitaine had
been gained for Gundobald, the Gundobaldian generals intended
to cross the Loire and establish the new monarchy on the Seine.

North of the Dordogne they had little difficulty. The bishops,
who then wielded the greatest municipal authority, generally
led their flocks to accept the pretender. Only one town, in
which the bishop was an obstinate adherent of Guntram, had to
be carried by force. Only two great cities in the south might
offer serious opposition, Toulouse and Bordeaux. Although
Desiderius was Duke of Toulouse, the bishop Magnulfus, who
was approached by the envoys of Gundobald, had recent memories
of what he and his city had suffered from a pretender named
Sigulfus, and he warned his people against this unknown
assailant of the thrones of Guntram and Childebert. His people
were prepared to resist, but the sight of Gundobald's army led
to immediate surrender. It is curious that at a banquet given
by Gundobald, the bishop who had opposed his admission was a
guest, and dared to insult his host, an imprudence for which he
suffered heavily—by exile and loss of his office. The bishops
were then the great potentates in city life, and Gundobald
exercised his new royal power in degrading or appointing them.
The remote town of Dax, at the foot of the Pyrenees, which had
belonged to Chilperic, received a new bishop in one Faustianus.
The notorious Sagittarius, a dissolute warrior priest, succeeded
Magnulfus in the great see of Toulouse.

The meeting at which the Austrasian nobles, including
Guntram Boso, had insulted the King of Burgundy, must have
aroused his suspicions as well as his anger. Mere rumour and
suspicion were soon translated into certainty. He learnt that

Poitiers and other cities of his had declared for Gundobald. Secret despatches from him had been seized which revealed the serious character of the rising. The two parties in Austrasia, now that Guntram was master of Neustria, seeing that Austrasia was isolated, found it necessary to combine their strength. Guntram Boso, the prime mover in the Gundobaldian conspiracy, had re-established himself. Egidius and Brunihildis were now united for the pretender who threatened Neustria and Burgundy. Guntram saw his danger and met it with vigour. Great levies were ordered in Burgundy and reinforced from the towns on their march to lay siege to Poitiers. Instead of advancing at once to meet Guntram's army, the Gundobaldian chiefs sent two envoys with wands, consecrated after the Frank fashion to make them sacrosanct.

Guntram was now thoroughly alarmed, and seeing the greatness of the crisis he rose to meet it. The envoys of Gundobald were at once, in defiance of all usage, imprisoned and questioned. They told the King that Gundobald claimed Merovingian descent and his due share of the kingdom, that he was coming with an army to assert his rights, and had the support of the most powerful men south of the Dordogne. Under severe torture they made further revelations. Gundobald had been invited to Gaul by all the great nobles of Austrasia and was in possession of the treasure of Rigunthis. It was clear that Guntram's policy towards Childebert must be altered. Childebert must be detached from the Austrasian party who were accomplices of the pretender, and Guntram summoned his nephew to a conference. Childebert came attended only by some of his courtiers, and heard with his own ears what the envoys had already disclosed. With all solemn form Guntram proclaimed Childebert his son and heir to all his dominions, and meanwhile restored all those cities of Aquitaine claimed by Austrasia. In a secret interview the young prince was told of those courtiers whom he should trust, and warned against the traitors, especially the arch-plotter Egidius, and his mother Brunihildis, who was now suspected of secret correspondence with Gundobald. The Austrasians were then addressed by Guntram, who presented to them their young king as already of full age, and demanded of them a cessation of all disloyal intrigues and absolute obedience to their sovereign. The ceremonial ended with three days of feasting.

This reconciliation of Austrasia and Burgundy had momentous effects in the south. The great captains of Gundobald instead of marching on the Loire began evidently to waver and hang back. They must have distrusted their military strength to face the armies of the two kingdoms. Desiderius, the Duke of Toulouse, a great strategist who had immense influence in the south, abandoned Gundobald, and probably took with him many who had followed his lead. The loss was disastrous both morally and materially. Mummolus could not venture to advance to meet Guntram's army. His only course was to retire to some strong fortress where the besiegers would be far from their base, and where in a long siege he might await some turn of events in Austrasia. Convenae, a strong place at the foot of the Pyrenees, near the source of the Garonne, was chosen as a refuge by the Gundobaldian leaders. Its foundation dates from the time of Pompey. At the close of the war with Sertorius it was peopled by a crowd of brigands and free-lances on the Spanish frontier, generally of the old Iberian race and in close sympathy with the people of southern Aquitaine. Lugdunum Convenarum was admirably placed for obstinate defence. It was built on an isolated height with strong walls and bastions, and at the foot of the hill was a perennial and capacious spring from which by a secret tunnel the defenders could draw their supplies of water unseen and unobstructed. And there were magazines of food supplies for a long siege. The mass of the citizens useless in defence were expelled and scattered over the country. Guntram's army had met difficulties on its march in crossing the Garonne or in an impious sack of the church of S. Vincent, which had been terribly avenged. Encamped around the walls, in country utterly desolated, they began to hold interesting conversations over the walls and even with Gundobald himself. Gregory, from the minuteness of detail, must have had the tale of the siege from some one actually present. But imagination has evidently decorated the narrative with too vivid colours. It is incredible that the soldiers of Mummolus should have appealed to the Gundobaldians with such effusive rhetoric, or that Gundobald should have minutely recited the story of his coming to Gaul with such pathetic force. Meantime all the engines and siege appliances known to the time were shaking the walls, and boulders and flaming casks were descending on the besieging forces. At last the besiegers determined to apply more subtle and effectual forces. The public men of that time, however able and distinguished, were often sadly wanting in loyalty and steady principle, and this is as true of Gallo-Romans as of Franks. The last melancholy scenes at Convenae in 585 offer a spectacle of shameless perfidy on both sides. Mummolus is tempted to desert Gundobald by false promises of safety for himself. He in turn deludes the wretched Gundobald into surrender by similar falsehoods. Mummolus, seeing he was betrayed, arrayed himself in full armour and only fell after a long conflict single-handed, which was worthy of the greatest warrior of the age. Gundobald, who now realised the treachery which had always surrounded him, after a pathetic appeal to Heaven to avenge, was slain by the hand of Boso—the man who had tempted him to his doom. His body, dragged round the camp with the foulest insults and outrages, was left unburied. The Gundobaldian leaders had meanwhile plundered the city and carried off even the sacred vessels from the churches. And the Burgundian army, bursting in, slaughtered the remnant of the population to a man, not sparing even the priests at the altars. The town was levelled to the ground, and the site remained lonely and desolate for 500 years. Of the Gundobaldian chiefs who escaped the slaughter, Desiderius, commanding great influence and resources, retired with his household to a fortified place. Waddo, the major-domo of Rigunthis, found a refuge under the protection of Brunihildis. The bishops, who had lent their great authority to the pretender's cause, had reason to dread the anger of Guntram. But he had a wholesome respect for the Church, and he referred their pleas for grace to a council assembled at Mâcon in that year. The council were true to their order. Only one bishop was lightly punished, and they even obtained for Desiderius the pardon of the King. The treasure which Gundobald had brought with him, much of which was deposited at Avignon, came into Guntram's hands. Part of it he gave to Childebert : his own share was, in accordance with his policy, given to the poor and to the Church.

We have dwelt at what may seem to some a disproportionate length on this episode in Merovingian history. That will not be the opinion of those who have studied the authorities. For it may be asked why did Gregory give such a carefully minute account of a movement which was a disastrous failure. He has evidently collected the facts or rumours with the utmost care. Part of his narrative, after the manner of greater historians, may be coloured by imagination and dramatic rhetoric. But who can read it without feeling that the facts generally have been gathered from the actors or witnesses of the drama ? Whether the chronicler realised the full meaning of the rising is doubtful, although he definitely traces it to the rebellious nobles of Austrasia. Modern critics are agreed that Gundobald was really a son of Chlothar, as he always claimed to be. But a careful education and intercourse with leading men in Italy and the East had given him greater culture and a softer and weaker character than belonged to the Merovingians generally. With the unscrupulous, daring energy of Chilperic, backed by the strategic skill of the two greatest soldiers of the age, we can imagine Gundobald anticipating the advance of Guntram and striking at Paris. Yet it is probable that Mummolus felt that the hasty levies of troops in Aquitaine were hardly fit to face the combined armies of Neustria and Burgundy, hardened in many campaigns.

Many ambitious or patriotic dreams were dissipated when Gundobald fell. He had strong support, especially from the Austrasian nobles and Brunihildis, and for a time from Childebert. The movement was aimed against Neustria and Burgundy, and especially to wipe out Guntram, and to establish with Merovingian prestige a monarchy of Gaul controlled by the great Frank nobles and supported by the Eastern Empire. There can be little doubt that the masses in Aquitaine, and the majority of the bishops, supported a rising which offered some hope of relief from the endless incursions of Merovingian hordes.

The failure of the Gundobaldian rising, organised by the nobles, gave a momentary appearance of strength to royalty. The death of Wandelen, the guardian of Childebert, gave Brunihildis the control of her son. Although she was for a time strangely leagued with the aristocratic party in support of Gundobald, they justly dreaded her boundless ambition, and in one year's time the nobles of Neustria and Austrasia were deep in a fresh plot to limit the kingly power. Childebert and Guntram were to be dethroned or killed, and in the name of Childebert's two sons, yet mere boys, the infamous Rauchingus was to rule in one kingdom, Ursio and Berthefredus in the other. Rauchingus indeed, claiming Merovingian descent, aimed at being king himself. Childebert, informed by his uncle of the plot, resolved to strike suddenly. Rauchingus was invited to Metz and was cut down mercilessly. Ursio and Berthefredus, already marching on Metz, on the news of their fellow-plotter's fate, threw themselves into a fortress in the Woevre. The danger was so serious that the kings resolved to unite their strength and counsels to meet it. A meeting was arranged, with Brunihildis present, at a little town called Andelot, between Langres and Toul. It took place on November 28, 587. On the famous pact of Andelot a mass of erudite a priori theory has been piled to support foregone conclusions. It is not a pact between the kings and their nobles, forced and imposed by the latter. The only parties to it are Kings Guntram and Childebert. Its object is to establish and maintain complete harmony and concord between them and their realms. They agree on the distribution of the possessions of Charibert and the cities which were the dower of Galswintha, so long in dispute. They agree, without reference to any other power, that the survivor of the two shall be the heir of both kingdoms.

The most important article related to the rebellious lords (or *leudes*), who in the feuds of the preceding years had changed from one side to the other. They were reciprocally to be restored to their original allegiances, and henceforth each king pledged himself not to receive or to attract the lieges of the other. Any donations to individuals or to churches which had been confiscated or recalled were now to be maintained or restored on both sides. This provision was merely intended to rectify acts of injustice committed in the tumult of civil war. It has not the wide significance attributed to it by some modern juristic theorists as intended to convert benefices into permanent donations. The treaty of Andelot is simply an effort to compose the differences between the two monarchs, and to remedy some of the wrongs caused by the late wars, and to prevent their recurrence.

The doom of Guntram Boso and some other leaders of the conspiracy against royalty soon followed. Boso had long been hated by Brunihildis for gross aspersions on her character. He had been convicted of sacrilege and peculation, and had placed himself under the protection of Agericus, Bishop of Verdun, entreating his intervention with Childebert, whom the bishop had taken from the font. The culprit was by Childebert reserved for the judgement of Guntram. That judgement was stern and instant. Boso took refuge in the lodging of Magneric, Bishop of Trèves. But the fury of Guntram would recognise no such protection for his great enemy. The house was set on fire ; the bishop was saved by his clergy. But Boso, attempting to fight his way, was transfixed with a shower of lances.

The rebels Ursio and Berthefredus had, with their households and armed retainers, fortified themselves in a church on the top of a hill which was a natural fortress. Childebert's army had to set fire to the building, and Ursio, facing the besiegers single-handed, dealt slaughter to all till a wound laid him low. Thus perished the worst enemy of Brunihildis, who had once threatened to trample her under his horse's feet. His comrade Berthefredus had for the moment escaped by galloping to the shelter of the church of Verdun. But no fear of sacrilege could protect him, and the sacred place was polluted with his blood. Only one of the band who had in 581 menaced the crown of Austrasia and carried on treacherous intrigues with Chilperic, now remained unpunished, the powerful Bishop of Rheims. His guilt was notorious ; but by bribes and humble adulation he managed to defer his fate. But in 589 another conspirator under torture revealed the fact that Egidius was a partner with Rauchingus and Ursio in a plot to murder Childebert. He was brought in 590 before a council of bishops at Metz. The fullest documentary proof was given of his manifold and deadly treachery. Death would have been the penalty for such guilt in a layman, aggravated in Egidius by patent falsehood, which in the end he confessed. But his brethren, after a respite of three days, in the hope of some pretext for saving him, were constrained to degrade him from his order and send him into easy exile at Strasburg ! Thus did the supposed guardians of morality deal with a man of the most corrupt character, the lover of the infamous Fredegundis, who had received her from her husband to convulse two kingdoms with the slaughter of thousands, who had been privy to a plot against his sovereign's life, who had acquired great estates by forged charters, who had first denied these charges and then freely confessed them, and especially to whose plots were due some of those deadly wars in which whole regions had been depopulated ! Evidently there was a different moral law for priest and unregenerate layman, if a scoundrel guilty of such enormities could for years hold a princely see, transmit the apostolic grace to many hands, and amid the lamentations of his episcopal judges, have to retire to a pleasant town in the Rhineland !

Brunihildis was really behind Childebert inspiring the ruthless energy with which these great traitors were finally crushed. But there was still treason lurking in the palace and bent on her destruction. This time the culprits were officers or servants of the court, Sunnegisilus, a Count of the Stables, and Gallomagnus, the Referendary, with a nurse of the royal children. Childebert was to banish his mother and take another wife. If he refused he was to be killed and his sons raised to the throne under the tutelage of the plotters. They were punished by degradation or banishment along with confiscation, in the end by extreme torture. The terror which such vengeance inspired in the Austrasian *leudes* was profound. Many felt themselves suspected and went into voluntary exile. Some of the greatest dukes lost their rank, and successors were appointed. Brunihildis, in her long struggle against the *leudes* of Austrasia, might seem to have won for the cause of kingship. The arrogant Teuton lords of the north-east who, with vast estates and armed dependents, wished to assert their power against the Crown, had found in this able and ruthless woman a redoubtable foe. Her power, however, exposed her and her son to perhaps more dangerous attacks from her great rival in Neustria. Fredegundis was an expert in the arts of assassination, and at least twice in those years her emissaries had attempted the lives of Brunihildis and Childebert.

The long ascendancy of Guntram over his nephews Childebert and Chlothar had brought nine years of comparative peace between the three Merovingian realms. But both Guntram and Childebert employed or diverted their forces in many expeditions against the Visigoths and the Lombards. In 585 and in 589 the Burgundian armies were fighting the Arian Richaredus in Septimania with fluctuating successes, and Septimania remained in possession of the Visigoths. Between 568 and 575 the Lombards had five times crossed the Alps in great strength, and three times had been thrown back by the armies of Burgundy under

Mummolus. The only result had been to extend the Burgundian frontier over the Alps. Henceforth Gaul was not much troubled by the Lombards. But the Emperor Maurice was bent on driving them out of Italy, and appealed to Childebert to come to his aid. The appeal was backed by a large subsidy. In 584 Childebert crossed the Alps, and drove the Lombards from the valley of the Po, but was bribed by them to retire. He returned again and again : in 585, after the collapse of the Gundobaldian rising; in 588, after the pact of Andelot; and finally in 590, when pestilence and famine compelled him to withdraw his dwindling forces from the walls of Verona.

The details of these ambitious but barren expeditions have little interest, even if we could be sure of the facts. But some conclusions clearly emerge on a general survey. Guntram and Childebert when they died had added nothing to the Merovingian Empire. They had failed against the Visigoths and the Lombards. They had not even subdued the stubborn Bretons. What was the cause of the failure ? They could raise immense armies on the Seine, the Rhone, and in Aquitaine, which included far more of the Gallo-Romans than of Franks. These armies went out with an imposing array of dukes and counts at their head. We hear of twenty dukes in command of one of these hordes. But hordes they were, not disciplined armies, in our modern sense, and their commanders seem to have been wanting either in the commanding power or the will to direct and restrain them. We know little of the organisation of these armies ; but it is probable that the levies hastily gathered at the command of the King had little of military training, and knew nothing of their officers. Their officers had probably as little military training as their men, and, from what we have gathered as to the upper classes from which the officers were drawn, they were often morally of a low type, sordidly ambitious, with no high public spirit to restrain innate cruelty and greed. They knew none of the restraints from high pride of social caste or stern official control which make the British officer a model of justice and generous feeling.

To illustrate these remarks we may take two expeditions of Guntram when at the height of his power and prestige. In 586 he ordered a great army to be levied for the conquest of the Visigoths in Septimania. Their objectives were Nîmes and Carcassone. All the tribes on Saône, Rhone, and Seine were

mustered, and the Aquitanian cities of Bourges, Saintes, Périgueux, Angoulême, and their neighbours poured forth for the
attack on Carcassone. The armies began their operations by
wholesale slaughter, plunder, and devastation in their own
country, even robbing the churches and murdering the priests
at their holy offices. Around Nîmes they burnt all the houses
and crops, and stubbed up the vines and olives. On the strong
places well provisioned they made no impression. Their only
prize was a solitary castle which was surrendered on sworn conditions which were instantly violated. The great army melted
away, and in their retreat perpetrated crimes which were long
remembered. But they paid heavily for them. In their retreat
they were decimated by hunger and hardship, drowned in the
rivers, slaughtered in feuds among themselves. The King's anger
was thoroughly aroused, and the generals took sanctuary in the
church of S. Symphorian. On a guarantee of personal safety
they presented themselves before Guntram and a court of bishops
and grandees to answer for their conduct. They were addressed
in a piece of rhetoric—of which probably Gregory was proud—
with the true sacerdotal ring. The armies of Burgundy are
brought low and disgraced because they have desolated the
churches of God, slain His priests, and profaned the relics of
saints and martyrs. Therefore it is that their swords are blunted
and their shields do not cover them in battle. There is no word
of the fate of thousands of peasants wantonly butchered at their
firesides or left to starve on their devastated farms. The reply
of the generals to the King's reproaches and threats casts a lurid
light on the social disorganisation of the age. They could only
plead that they were helpless in the face of the self-will and
contempt for all authority which now prevailed among the
people. Every one does what he pleases, with no respect or fear
for count, duke, or the King himself.

The magnificent army, marshalled under twenty dukes, which
Childebert despatched in 590 against the Lombards, displayed
the same disorganisation, with disastrous results. The troops
from Champagne began their campaign by spreading wholesale
havoc and slaughter in Metz, the capital of their King. They
were led by Audovaldus and Wintrio, two of the foremost men in
Austrasia. Their achievements in Lombardy amounted to the
capture of five castles. They lived by plundering the peaceful

population. And when, crippled by hunger and dysentery, they retired across the Alps, they had to sell their arms and clothes for food. It is clear that these Merovingian armies had neither discipline nor a commissariat. And probably one great cause of their want of discipline was their want of regular supplies. The most pathetic thing in those days is that great masses of peaceful peasants could be ordered by the King on distant expeditions, under corrupt and incompetent officers, with no proper training or discipline, no commissariat, no medical protection against the awful diseases then prevalent. For in the years following 585 the tale of drought, famine, and pestilence constantly meets our eyes. Multitudes were sustaining what was left of strength on wild weeds and seeds, turning any rubbish into an appearance of bread and dying swollen with the noxious food, or emaciated with utter want. And, as we have seen, the plague from the East, entering by southern ports, spread from Marseilles through the cities of Provence to Lyons, Metz, and Paris, carrying off whole households and princes of the royal house. And amid these horrors, armies were sent out for visionary conquests to return famine-wasted and diseased and decimated. And the perennial feuds between kings and nobles ran their troubled course to a goal which was already in sight to watchful eyes.

With the death of Gregory of Tours in 594 we have reached the term of the period covered by this book. And within a very few years of the bishop's death three of the principal actors on the stage passed away. King Guntram died in 596 ; Childebert in 596; and Queen Fredegundis in the following year. Her great rival Brunihildis had for twenty years been engaged in deadly strife with her son's rebellious and treacherous nobles to uphold kingship against the ambitions of oligarchy. She was a great and, as the times demanded, a ruthless statesman. With the fall of Egidius her triumph might have seemed secure, and with the death of Guntram her son became monarch of four-fifths of the Frank dominions. Brunihildis determined to wipe out Neustria and its boy king. But near Soissons Childebert's army suffered a strange defeat, and his death followed soon after. It was a great blow to kingship and the policy of Brunihildis. Childebert's long minority gave the great *leudes* of Austrasia a chance which they eagerly seized and opened a deadly struggle of twenty years. Childebert, dying at twenty-six, left two young boys to succeed

him in Burgundy and Austrasia, and their grandmother (now
more than fifty) had to maintain another desperate conflict of
nearly twenty years with her rebellious nobles and the power of
Neustria, which ended with her ghastly death inflicted by the son
of Fredegundis (in 613). Fredegundis had one apparent triumph
before she died in 597. Immediately after Childebert's death she
hurled the forces of Neustria against the army of his youthful
sons and defeated it with great slaughter. In the following year
Brunihildis is once more fighting the nobles of Austrasia, and
their chief, the Duke Wintrio, was slain by her arts or orders.
That was her last autocratic act in Austrasia. In 595, by
a combination of her enemies she was driven to take refuge
with her grandson Theuderic in Burgundy. In the following
year Theudebert and Theuderic resolved to avenge the defeat of
596 and recover the great territory which Chlothar had annexed.
The Neustrian forces were cut to pieces at Dormeille, and Neustria
was reduced to twelve cantons between the Seine, the Oise, and
the sea. But instead of combining to wipe out the kingdom of the
West with its memories of power and ascendancy, the hereditary
curse of the Merovingian race once more drove them into
fratricidal war. And the impelling force was Brunihildis' burning
desire to avenge her exile on the Austrasian nobles and crush the
boaster Theudebert, bringing the two kingdoms under Theuderic
and herself. She revived the power of the Gallo-Romans in
Burgundy, which had been shaken by the defection of the great
patrician Mummolus ; a Teutonic patrician was deposed or
killed, and a Roman, Protadius, became mayor of the palace in
place of a Burgundian. But Protadius, though able and vigorous,
soon made himself hated by his fiscal exactions and his insolence
to the Burgundian nobles. Thus Theuderic entered on the war
with very doubtful support from his vassals ; and when the
battle was about to open, mutiny broke out in the army of
Burgundy. Protadius was slain by a ferocious crowd, and the
young king was forced to make peace with his brother. But
the old queen never recognised defeat. A German patrician,
who had joined in the murder of Protadius, was put to death by
her orders and a Roman with a Teutonic name took his place.
At the same time another Gallo-Roman, of the true old type,
became mayor of the palace. Even the arid chronicle gives a
refreshing picture of a public man in these times of brutal

P

treachery. Claudius was a wise, patient, and energetic man, a
polished man of letters, very honest and loyal, but too gentle
and conciliatory for the manners of that age. The suicidal strife
of the Merovingians went on deepening in senseless atrocity.
How far it was urged on by the animosities or ambition of Brunihildis, how far by the clash of Teutonic and Roman sentiment
in the two kingdoms, is a matter of conjecture now. The
seizure of Alsace by Theudebert reopened the conflict. At the
battle of Toul the Austrasians were utterly routed and their king
was pursued to the Rhine. He summoned to his aid his German
subjects beyond the river, and a bloody battle was fought at
Tolbiacum, in which Theudebert was captured, relegated for a time
to the cloister, and in 612 put to death. The triumph of Brunihildis and royalty against the Teutonic lords of the north-east
seemed to be final and complete, and Theuderic for the time was
master of the greater part of Frank Gaul.

Theuderic and his ministers were preparing for a conflict with
Chlothar II., which was probably designed to wipe out that
remnant of Neustria which was still left. But while his army
was mustering he died of dysentery at the age of twenty-six. The
old queen was once more left to maintain the dynasty, with four
young princes all under eleven to protect. By old Frank custom
the four youths would have divided the realms of Theuderic.
But Brunihildis, with her ambitions for royalty and her Roman
Imperial sentiment, determined to have only the eldest, Sigibert,
the namesake of her husband, proclaimed king. This great
woman statesman, in the face of the Teutonic lords of the north-
east, was bent on establishing an Imperial power in Gaul of
the Roman type ; of course she was fighting for her own power,
but through that for the race to which she was allied. Using
her power in Burgundy, she raised two of her supporters to the
two great offices, the patriciate and mayoralty of the palace
(Warnacharius and Aletheus). But the Austrasians, resenting the
preponderance of Burgundy under the old queen, once more
roused themselves against the royal power. And they were
organised under two personages who were destined to make
history, Arnulfus and Pippin the Elder. They were both sprung
from old Austrasian houses, and both had held high office. Once
more, like Egidius and his party, they offered the crown of
Austrasia to the King of Neustria, still smarting under the defeat

of Dornieille. The designs of Austrasia were seconded by
treason which was spreading in Burgundy. For the charm and
dæmonic power of Brunihildis were waning with advancing age.
When Chlothar advanced to the Rhine, she, like her husband,
forty years before, summoned her German vassals to her aid,
but the levy was betrayed by the treacherous leaders who went
to summon them. When the Burgundian army advanced to
meet the Neustrians on the Aisne, it was under generals who
were sold to Chlothar. Brunihildis had probably secret knowledge of the treachery by which she was surrounded, for she had
given, some time before, instructions for the assassination of
Warnacharius, the mayor of the palace. But that high officer,
along with the patrician Aletheus, was at the head of the army
of Burgundy. The disloyal conspiracy must have been widespread, for before the armies engaged, the Burgundian troops
calmly fell back and marched homewards. The army of
Chlothar, apparently in no hot pursuit, captured three of the
princes on the Saône. The fourth escaped to Arles. Two of
them were put to death. But Meroveus, the third, was, by a
superstition of the time, spared, because Chlothar had raised him
from the font. Brunihildis was reserved for more exquisite
punishment. She had, according to Chlothar's reckoning, caused
the death of ten Frank princes, enumerated by the chronicler.
For three days she was subjected to ingenious tortures. Then
she was paraded, in such a condition as we may imagine, on a
camel before the whole army, and then, with her fainting limbs
fastened to a wild horse, torn in pieces. Brunihildis had, in the
fierce conflicts of that age, not spared her foes. But she did not,
at her worst, deserve such an end.

With the death of Brunihildis properly ends that portion of
Merovingian history which this chapter is intended to cover.
But as it marks a great crisis and turning-point in the history of
the dynasty, the nature of the change must be briefly indicated.

The murder of the three sons and heirs of Theuderic left to
Chlothar II. apparently the sole sovereignty of the three Frank
realms. They were now united under a single prince, as they
had been only once before for a brief space under Chlothar I.
The dreams and ambitions of Brunihildis might seem to have
been fulfilled in the man by whose commands she was done to
death. But the appearance was brief and illusory. The union

of the three kingdoms was a mere figment. Burgundy and Austrasia were each under the rule of a mayor of the palace. Warnacharius, the Mayor of Burgundy, the head of the rising German power in that kingdom, had betrayed Brunihildis, and now got his reward. He demanded and received a promise on oath that he should hold his office for life. Mayors with similar authority were appointed for Austrasia and Neustria. In the next year a great council of seventy-nine bishops was convoked, which extended the powers and immunities of the Church, and limited the royal powers of taxation and general administration. The power of the crown was steadily waning before the growing powers of the nobles and the mayors of the palace. Monarchy is sustained greatly by hereditary sentiment and imagination. Its hold in the imagination was never more clearly seen than during the century and a half in which an effete race maintained a mere shadow of authority.

BOOK II

THE SOCIAL ASPECT

CHAPTER I

In a previous chapter some account has been given of the great official class who carried on the administration of the Frank kings after the collapse of the Imperial system. These men were of various race and social grade. There was no preference for Frank above Roman for employment by the State, and a man of the lowest origin, even one with the brand of a fugitive slave, might rise to the highest place at court and in provincial government. Autocracy is often, from self-interest, more in sympathy with the plebeian than with the born aristocrat. In this chapter we propose to inquire into the origin, composition, and character of the highest social class under the early Merovingian kings. Had the Franks in the early sixth century an aristocracy of birth, tracing its origin to old German houses? Or, if this should appear to be a false assumption, how was the highest social class in the sixth century composed? What was its origin, and what was its general tone and character? The answer to this second question is specially important, because the chronicles of the period tell us far more of the men of commanding position in society than of the dim, common mass of humanity whose lot it has been in all ages to labour and to suffer whatever fate or political masters may impose.

Some light may perhaps be thrown on the fate of the old Frank aristocracy of birth by the policy of Clovis to the chiefs of his race on his return from his conquest of southern Gaul. As a wary, prudent statesman he was mild and tolerant to his Gallo-Roman subjects. He was equally ruthless to fellow chiefs and Frank nobles who might by race or rank challenge and

endanger his supremacy. When Clovis returned to Paris from
his southern campaign he still found himself not the sole master
of Gaul. Great chiefs of the Frank race still maintained their
authority at Cologne, Cambrai, and Le Mans. Sometimes they
had joined Clovis in his wars ; sometimes they had played a waiting game. They were probably as ambitious and treacherous
as he was, but without his commanding personality. Sigibert
of Cologne, the " Lame ", as he was called, had been crippled
by a wound in the battle of Tolbiacum. On a hint from Clovis,
his son sent a band to assassinate the old king one day when he
was asleep in his tent in the Buconian forest. The patricide was
soon avenged. The treacherous son offered Clovis a share of
his father's treasures, and Clovis sent officers, ostensibly to bring
back the gift, but with a much more deadly purpose. While
the son was bending over a chest of gold coin, his head was cleft
by a battle-axe from behind, and the warriors of Sigibert soon
afterwards raised Clovis on the shield. Chararic, whose tribe
were settled along the channel, along with his son was defeated
in battle and made prisoner ; their locks were shorn, and they
were relegated to Holy Orders. But on hearing of some ominous
words which had dropped from them, Clovis ordered them at
once to be beheaded, and their tribe and treasure passed under
his power. The same fate awaited Ragnachar, the debauched
and effeminate Frank chief of Cambrai, whose foul excesses had
alienated his followers. Clovis, with frugal treachery, sent the
leading men of the tribe some gifts of trappings with the show
of gold but only brass beneath, and then marched on Cambrai.
Ragnachar's warriors of course soon gave way, and brought
their chief in bonds into the presence of the conqueror, who,
after upbraiding his kinsman for the dishonour done to their
line by suffering himself to be taken alive, struck him down with
his own hand. When the vassals of Ragnachar, who had received
brass for gold as the price of their treachery, complained of
the inadequate reward, they were told they were lucky to get
off with their lives for betraying a Merovingian. The episcopal
chronicler, so far from seeing anything in all this to condemn,
sums up the tale of treacherous cruelty with the words : " God
daily subdued his enemies under his hand, and increased his
dominion ; since the king walked with an upright heart before
Him, and did what was pleasing in His eyes ". This approval

of savage deeds by a great churchman certainly gives a shock to modern minds. But it is tolerably certain that Clovis would have boldly justified his treatment of his kinsman, who would have used the same means to seize his place, and he might have even appealed to the God who was the God of Joshua and Jael and David.

In the slaughter of the Frank chiefs many others fell, any one, in fact, who was likely to challenge the title of Clovis. Clovis was mild and considerate to his Roman subjects, but ruthless to his Frank rivals and any possible pretenders to the throne. The cynical lament he made, that he was left alone among strangers, shows how determined he was that the new monarchy should stand out as the sole political power in Gaul, the heir of the omnipotent Roman Emperor and his Prefect, and, like them, unchecked and unchallenged by popular or aristocratic rivalry. His dynasty was destined, within a century from his death, to be undermined by a new aristocracy which it created, or which was evolved by the social and official conditions of the age. But the old Teutonic noble class had almost vanished when Clovis had established his power. The only remnant of the German *noblesse* was left among tribes such as the Saxon, Bavarian, and Thuringian, who had not strayed far from their original seats. Those who had, after long wars and wanderings, occupied provinces of the Empire, had, both in kingship and in the status of the noble caste, suffered profound changes. The descendants of the old German families must have been sadly thinned by incessant wars, hardship, and disease. The position of any who had survived was immensely altered when the king, who was once chosen from a great clan, and subject to constant checks and control from chiefs as high-born as himself, along with the assembly of armed warriors, had become the lord of a great territory, issuing his orders from his capital at Metz or Soissons, or from one of his many *villae* on the Meuse, the Marne, or the Seine. He had indeed a council of elders and officials, to advise or suggest decisions. The emperors, at the very height of a supreme autocracy, prepared their " divine " utterances with the guidance of trained lawyers and men who had gone through all the discipline of official life. But an official and military hierarchy is something very different from an ancient hereditary aristocracy whose title runs back beyond the memory of man.

Clovis and his sons and grandsons surrounded themselves
with skilled officials and soldiers ; but there is no trace in
code or chronicle of an ancient Frank *noblesse* in the sixth
century.

There are probably few purely antiquarian questions which
have been handled in a less dry light than that of the aristocracy
of the Franks in the century following the conquests of Clovis.
The enthusiastic admiration of German scholars for their early
institutions, and the passions of the French Revolution, have
combined to imagine a noble hereditary class among the Franks,
of which the authorities for the sixth century give no hint. In
the Salic Code there is no trace of a hereditary nobility. The
broad distinction in that Code is between the free and those
living in some form of servitude. It is true that the *wehrgeld*,
that is, the sum which expresses the value attached to a man's
life, for a free Frank is 200 *solidi*, while for a man *in truste
dominica* it is 600. But the distinction is not one between
commoner and noble. The man *in truste dominica*, who is also
called *antrustio*, was one who had sworn fealty to the king,
and who thereby enjoyed the king's special protection. He was a
dependent of the king, not an independent member of a hereditary order. His position was due, not to birth or wealth, but to
the king's will and choice, which might be revoked. And the
antrustio might belong to any social rank, even to that of the
serf or freedman ; he might be, and often was, of Gallo-Roman
birth. His *wehrgeld* varied according to his origin, but, as
antrustio, it was triple the amount at which his life was assessed
before he came under the royal faith.

The *antrustiones* of the Frank kings were the only privileged
class in the realm, and they were not a noble caste. They are
each created by the king by a mutual oath of fealty and protection. Teutonic patriotism feels bound to find in the *antrustiones* lineal successors of the *principes* of Tacitus and the old
German nobles with their *comitatus*. The theory is founded on
a single formula of Marculf of the following century. There
the new *antrustio* is required to present himself before the king
with his *arimannia*, *i.e.* his train of vassals. This would certainly
have been impossible for some of the *antrustiones* we meet with
in the chronicles, who were drawn from various social grades,
even the lowest. Moreover, the formula of Marculf stands

solitary in the records of the period, and the term *arimannia*
occurs only in this single instance in Frank history. However
tempting to that curious blend of erudition with lawless hypothesis which so often characterises the German critics, the sanest
even among the Germans recognise that this formula is but a frail
support on which to hang the theory that the *comitatus* of the
Germany of Tacitus still survived under the Merovingians.
In other German codes it is clear, from the different rates of
wehrgeld, that the nobles by birth and the king's companions
are distinct classes. The Salian Code knows nothing of a
hereditary nobility. The only class distinguished by a higher
composition for murder is that of the *antrustiones*, and the
antrustio owed his position solely to the will of the king. No
doubt men of old family, both Teuton and Roman, were drawn
into the ranks of the *antrustiones*. But they had no independent
rank outside the class, and they found themselves side by side
with men who had no social distinction except the confidence of
the sovereign. There is no trace among the Franks in the sixth
century of an independent aristocracy, as among the Visigoths
and Lombards, who hardly yielded to the king in pride of
birth, and some of whom might even challenge his supremacy.
For three generations the Frank kings built up their autocracy
unchallenged. Their danger was from real or pretended members
of their own house. When Clovis, in 510, had ruthlessly swept
away all possible rivals of his own race, he plainly had no fear
of any disloyal ambition among a Frank aristocracy. Having
killed off his royal kinsmen, he was not likely to spare any
Frank noble whose prestige was dangerous. Hence Gregory of
Tours seems to find no grade between the kings and the mass
of the people. And this must have been the feeling of the
Merovingians themselves. Thus Childebert I., fearing that
Clothilde might try to raise the orphaned sons of his brother
Chlodomer to royal power, asks his brother Chlothar to consider
whether they should be put to death, or shorn of the long hair
of their race and " sunk among the plebeian crowd ".

But we should be careful to separate legal and constitutional
ideas from the more fluctuating, but none the less real, distinctions of social convention. When ancient rank has disappeared
or is no longer recognised, wealth and office, even in democratic
societies, are always creating a new aristocracy, with claims as

self-assertive as the old. Even the most powerful and jealous
despotism cannot maintain a dead level of society. So long
as men are free to assert their ability in public service and to
accumulate wealth, so long must a differentiation of social grades
continue, and the strongest and cleverest will rise. And the
Merovingians rather encouraged the formation of a new aristocracy founded on the possession of riches and office, which in all
ages has been, according to Aristotle's dictum, the source and
stay of an aristocratic class. The old Gallo-Roman population
included a large number of senatorial families, with landed
property, whose ancestors had held municipal, and sometimes
Imperial, offices, and who still retained high respect and position
from birth and wealth, and were welcomed at the Frank courts
as *convivae* of the king, or elected, with the king's sanction, to
episcopal sees. Gregory is never weary of recording the senatorial descent of many of his brother bishops. In the long list
of his predecessors in the see of Tours, one after another is marked
out by the distinction of his origin from Roman families of the
noble class. And the poet Venantius Fortunatus is perhaps even
more fond of glorifying the family of his clerical friends and
patrons. Roman names also abound among the counts and
dukes and other dignified officials : Lupus and Desiderius,
Jovinus and Albinus, Firminus and Hortensius, Paeonius and
Palladius. Under a son of Clovis, two men of Roman descent,
Secundinus and Asteriolus, rose to high rank and favour, and
one of them was sent on an embassy to the eastern Emperor.
Under the same prince, in the realm of Austrasia, where the
Teutonic spirit was always strongest, a Roman named Parthenius
attained the highest official position, in spite of what would appear
to have been a detestable character. He was a glutton of the
Vitellian type. He had killed his innocent wife and one of his
friends on a baseless suspicion, and men said that their shades
haunted him in his dreams. In administration he could be
as arrogant as if he had belonged to the conquering race. In
fact, he used his power as provincial governor to bring Frank
proprietors under taxation from which it was alleged they had
been hitherto free. On his master Theudebert's death they
determined to have their revenge. Parthenius put himself under
the protection of two bishops, who carried him for refuge to the
church of Trèves, and hid him in a chest under a pile of sacred

vestments. The angry mob burst in, ransacked every corner, and at last discovered his hiding-place. With his arms pinioned, and overwhelmed with the foulest insults, the Roman oppressor of the Franks was stoned to death.

In Burgundy, after it had passed under Frank rule, men of Roman race were raised to the highest official rank, even to the Patriciate, a dignity inherited from the Empire, which the Burgundian kings had worn with pride. King Guntram elevated Celsus to the office, a Roman who combined, as we are told, the muscle of the warrior with a pompous eloquence and, what was more valuable to Guntram, the skill of a trained jurist. This great officer abused his power to plunder the estates of the Church, but his son, dying childless, restored the sacrilegious gains. Celsus was succeeded by another Roman, named Amatus, who fell in desperate battle with the Lombards in their first incursion into Gaul. The next holder of the Patriciate of Burgundy was the Gallo-Roman Mummolus, the most skilful and famous general of that age. His father was Paeonius, Count of Auxerre, who sent his son with gifts to procure the continuance of his office. The youth, who with supreme ability combined a faithless craft which never deserted him down to his tragic end, supplanted his father, and soon rose to the patriciate. It was a time of peril and anxiety on the south-eastern frontier. Five times between 568 and 575 the Lombards, or their Saxon allies, poured across the Alps spreading havoc to the Rhone. And thrice they were outmanœuvred by the Burgundian general and driven back to Italy. He commanded for Guntram in the campaign against the generals of Chilperic, and was the leading spirit in the serious rising to place the pretender Gundobald on the throne. But besides such men of commanding power there were undoubtedly Romans of low character, as in the days of Sidonius, who crept into office by flattery, corruption, and treachery. Yet, although the Frank kings might be cajoled by flattery, and even accept bribes for high office, they needed the trained skill and ability of the old régime to carry on the administration. And in many depart-ments of government the Romans had a monopoly of experience and training.

But the official aristocracy, from the first, not only included men of the conquered race, designated by ability or social rank; it was also open to men of the meanest origin. As in the Germany of Tacitus, " *in gentibus quae regnantur liberti super ingenuos et super nobiles ascendunt*". Autocrats in ancient or modern times have often welcomed the service of low-born talent, and in Gregory of Tours there are at least two striking examples of such an elevation. Andarchius was the slave of a Roman senator, probably in Auvergne. His cleverness commended him to the indulgence of his master, and the young slave received a good education and became an adept in Virgil and the mysteries of the Theodosian Code, with a tincture of mathematics—a range of culture probably far beyond that of the greatest Frank at court. But Andarchius began to look down on his illiterate master, and attached himself to the train of the great Duke Lupus. Lupus was a magnate of Austrasia who bore a leading part in the struggle between Brunihildis, during her son's minority, and the ambitious clique under Bishop Egidius. His character has been depicted by the poet Fortunatus in one of his best pieces. Lupus was a Roman statesman, wise, capable, and laborious, with great equipoise of judgement and rare powers of expressing his views so as to carry conviction. He was also a gallant soldier who had crushed the Danes. It was when he was sent on a mission to Marseilles that Andarchius entered his service. On the duke's return to Metz he secured for Andarchius a place at Sigibert's court, and he was employed on many missions, civil and military. In the end the old slave attained the title of *Honoratus*, which, as under the Empire, was a high reward of distinguished official service. Finally he found himself in his old district of Auvergne. But greed and social ambition led him to his doom. He wished to ally himself in marriage with a great person of that proud district, who haughtily repelled him. But Andarchius, who had acquired the arts of palace intrigue, by craft and chicanery secured a mandate from Sigibert which gave him a hold on the property of his reluctant father-in-law if he refused his bride. Andarchius, with combined insolence and cunning, seized one of the country seats of Ursus, chastised the menials who disobeyed his commands, and, after a drinking bout, lay down for a siesta. The insulted Ursus soon appeared upon the scene, with all his serfs, blocked the doors of the mansion to prevent escape, and piling all round the sheaves from the harvest fields, burnt Andarchius alive. It was a defiance of royal authority, but Ursus saved his life by taking refuge in the neighbouring church of S. Julian, and saved his estates by some welcome presents to the king.

An even stranger career is that of Leudastes, the Count of Tours, and the great enemy of Bishop Gregory. The future count was the son of one Leucadius who tended the vineyards in the Île de Rhé, which were part of an estate of Charibert. The young serf was taken for service in the royal kitchen ; but an affection of the eyes made the work irksome and he was transferred to the royal bakery. He was probably always an unwilling servant, and always chafed under the yoke, although with careful cunning he veiled his discontent. Three times he tried to escape from the hateful bondage, and at last he was brought back and branded with the loss of an ear. The brand might seem to have doomed him for ever to the lot from which he strove to escape. But a spirit so bold was not easily daunted. Charibert, like most of the early Merovingians, was very oriental in his ideas of marriage. Among the various rivals to Queen Ingoberg who caught his vagrant fancy were two daughters of a wool-comber, Marcovefa and Merofledis. Leudastes attracted the notice of Marcovefa and was speedily installed as keeper of her horses, but he did not rest till he had attained a title of high consideration under the last Empress of the West, that of *comes stabuli*, which put him on a level with the highest Frank courtiers. But the vanity and arrogance of the *parvenu* could never be hidden. The pampered favourite of the royal concubine used his opportunities to enrich himself by plunder and peculation. On Marcovefa's death he purchased from Charibert the continuance of his office, and soon afterwards was appointed Count of Tours. Men of an origin like Leudastes thus probably often rose to the rank of *antrustio*.

But besides the official aristocracy created by the king's will and dependent on his favour, there was a much wider class which may rightly be called aristocratic, with indefinite but powerful claims to social rank and exercising a corresponding influence. For social and political influence in every community is to a great extent independent of legal and constitutional prescription. This new aristocracy was composed of both Frank and Gallo-Roman elements. We have seen how great Roman families rose in the official hierarchy. But a far larger number,

living undisturbed on their ancestral estates, still enjoyed the
wealth and social consideration of generations before the conquest. The descendants of Sidonius still kept their old place in
Auvergne, and used it to intrigue for a bishopric, and even to
organise revolt against a son of Clovis. The Bishop of Langres,
an ancestor of Gregory of Tours, had held high office before the
fall of the Empire, and for forty years was a count under the
Burgundian kings. The Frank kings had after the conquest
come into possession of great estates which were previously
public land in the hands of the prefect. It appears from many
passages in the history of Gregory that these lands were used
by the kings to reward their zealous officers, or to attach men to
their service. The grant may have been made for a term of years,
or for life, with succession to the eldest son. But the grants were
not held on the feudal tenure of military service. That is an
institution of a later date. There is no trace of such a tenure in
Gregory, or in the codes, nor does the word *beneficium*, in its
legal sense, occur once in Gregory's pages.

The famous document called the Pact of Andelot, which is
given verbally in full by Gregory in his History, is the best
authority on this subject. It is a solemn covenant made in 587
between Kings Guntram and Childebert, along with Queen
Brunihildis, in the presence of the bishops and magnates of their
realms, with the object of arranging all causes of quarrel among
them and securing permanent amity and peace. One of the
most important articles of this covenant relates to the donations
which the kings had made to laymen or to the Church. In the
previous wars among the Frank kings, many of those grants had
been revoked or cancelled for disloyalty to an old sovereign or
hostility to a new conqueror. The sovereigns pledged themselves
to reinstate all those whose property had been thus confiscated,
and to secure them in possession for the future. The best opinion
finds in this no change from royal donations in perpetuity to
feudal tenure. That change had yet to come. The kings at
Andelot were only occupied with an effort to restore secure
enjoyment of property conferred by the Crown which had been
disturbed by civil war, frequent changes of frontier, and as
frequent changes of allegiance. A good many cases of this sort
can be discovered in the pages of Gregory of Tours. Godinus
transferred his allegiance, in a fierce struggle, from Sigibert to

Chilperic, and was enriched by Chilperic with lavish gifts of royal estates in the region of Soissons. When Godinus took a leading part in 575 in the Austrasian invasion of Chilperic's realm, and he was defeated, the estates with which Chilperic had endowed him were forfeited and went to enrich the church of S. Medard. In the same years Siggo, a referendary of Sigibert, had, like Godinus, been tempted to transfer his allegiance to Chilperic, and had received a similar reward. When he once more changed sides in that fluctuating conflict, and betook himself to the court of Sigibert's son, the fiscal lands at Soissons which Chilperic had granted him were resumed and passed to Ansoaldus, a Frank of noble birth, one of Chilperic's most faithful supporters, who, along with Waddo and Domigiselus, had been appointed to conduct the Princess Rigunthis on her journey to Spain. In the year 584 a conspiracy at the court of Childebert II. was discovered by his Queen. It was organised by the nurse of the royal children to procure the death of the Queen and Brunihildis with the object of gaining an ascendancy over Childebert through another union. Two great officials, Sunnegiselus the Marshal, and Gallomagnus the Chancellor, were involved in the plot. The guilty nurse was cruelly tortured, branded on the face with hot iron, and condemned to the task of grinding corn for the household. The two great officials were sent into exile for a time, with the loss of all estates which they had received from the King, retaining only their personal or inherited property (*proprium*). The same fate befell Guntram Boso when his career was closed by the decision of a *placitum* of Childebert in 585. In those years of treacherous intrigue, Boso was the most desperate and faithless plotter, often apparently from the mere love of it. He had received gifts of property in Auvergne from the fisc. On his condemnation and flight these grants were resumed. In the next chapter of this record we read that on the death of one Wandelinus, who had been guardian (*nutritor*) of Chilperic, the Crown lands which he had enjoyed reverted to the treasury ; and in another case, when the Duke Bodegiselus died, his gifts from the Crown passed without diminution to his sons.

Thus although in the sixth century there was no hereditary noble order, there was a numerous upper class made up of various elements and various races. Antrustions and courtiers, high officials, along with the possessors of landed wealth, more or less

Q

ancient, Roman or Frank, were all forming a new aristocracy. It was not yet an exclusive order, fenced and limited by constitutional rule. It was not hereditary, unless where wealth was transmitted. It rested partly on the foundation of royal choice and favour, partly on the social prestige which the long possession of wealth must always confer.

The new aristocracy had in its ranks families of ancient birth and the social standing which is always the appanage of great estates. But there is a striking passage in Gregory which shows that men of obscure birth might be raised by royal will, and the wealth it could bestow, to the highest social rank. In the year 585, Fredegundis sent two priests armed with poisoned daggers, who, in the guise of beggars, were ordered to assassinate King Childebert and procure the downfall, or the death, of his mother Brunihildis. When the priestly emissaries showed some nervous hesitation to undertake such a task, they were told that if they died in carrying out their mission, the Queen would enrich their relatives, and raise them to the foremost rank in the kingdom. And to this stimulating promise the weird woman added the gift of a medicated potion with which they were to fortify their nerves on the morning of their dangerous enterprise. It is to be observed that Fredegundis does not offer to elevate the relatives (*parentes*) of the two assassins to offices at court, or to the rank of "Antrustion". She promises such a lavish reward of riches as will raise them to the highest noble rank. The term "nobiles", used by the Queen, is a vague one, and used with some latitude in the literature of the time. It is seldom applied to men of Frank race in Gregory. He more frequently applies it to Romans of the upper class, especially of the clerical order, where it is the equivalent of *senatorius*. In the Lives of the Saints the monkish biographer constantly begins by saying that his subject was "*nobilis genere, sed nobilior fide*". This does not mean any long line of ancestors with a hereditary position. It means that the saint belonged to a good, respectable family, with no taint of servitude or plebeian birth, and with some family estate. The upper class of that time are described by many titles of rather vague, fluctuating meaning, and this variety tends to support the view that the class was not defined or circumscribed.

The great variety of titles given to the upper class in the chronicles of the period confirms the view that it was a class not definitely circumscribed. In some cases the title seems to mark a distinction of rank, in others it leaves it vague. In royal edicts, the title *Optimates* designates great officers of the palace. The same is the case with the titles of *Proceres, Majores, Seniores.* When Bishop Theodorus wishes to clear himself of treason, he alleges that he had only obeyed the instructions of King Childebert and his *Seniores.* On the other hand, the men who were plundered by Bishop Cautinus are called *Majores.* The *Franci utiliores,* whom Chilperic attached to his side after the death of his father, when he seized the treasures of Berny, are men of leading position and influence. The *viri fortes,* who saved Chlodovald, the son of Chlodomer, from the fate of his brothers, must have been Frank warriors of the same rank. So the *viri fortiores* of Soissons and Meaux ask King Childebert for one of his sons to rule over them. The *priores,* who made oath along with Fredegundis that the infant Chlothar was a legitimate son of Chilperic, consisted of three bishops and 300 *viri optimi.* On the other hand, *meliores natu,* who were torn from their homes to attend the Princess Rigunthis on her way to Spain, seem from the context to be middling proprietors, as opposed to the serfs or *liti* who were drawn from the royal estates. The word *senior* is particularly fluctuating. It is applied even to the King. It may also be used to describe the assessors, lay or clerical, who sat in judgement with the court. And these local dignitaries, who were probably landowners of the district, with a sprinkling of minor officials, are sometimes dignified by the title of *viri magnifici.*

The term *Leudes,* about which there has been much controversy, is also one of a fluctuating sense. It certainly does not designate an aristocratic class. In the Burgundian Law the *leudes* rank below the *optimates* and *mediocres* in the scale of *wehrgeld* as *minores personae.* In the Chronicle of Fredegarius they embrace the highest class and the poor. The term is never used absolutely to describe a single independent class. The *leudis* is always the *leudis* of somebody : the *leudis* implies a master, as when Clovis, after bribing the *leudes* of Ragnachar with pretended gold, contemptuously told them that they had been well served for betraying their master. The word might seem to be almost one of contempt in the mouth of Guntram when he doubted for a moment the legitimacy of the infant

orphan of Chilperic, and said it was probably the son of one of
his *leudes*. And the kings invariably speak of "our *leudes*".
Occasionally the *leudes* may be a powerful class, as when, on the
death of his father Theuderic, his heir Theudebert was defended
by his *leudes* against the usurpation of his rights by Childebert
and Chlothar. But the word cannot be confined to any higher
order of vassals or immediate dependents of the King : it
embraces all subjects of every social grade, and merely describes
their duty and allegiance to a sovereign master.

These many titles, so variously applied by the great chronicler
of the period, surely show that the upper class in Merovingian
Gaul was not a close, hereditary caste, fenced off from the mass
of freemen by strict legal or constitutional lines, but a class of
mixed elements, which was created by social causes, and whose
power, continually growing, rested on a social movement which
was independent of the will of kings.

That independence was first asserted in Austrasia, which was
in immediate contact with Germany, and where the great Frank
families were most numerous. On the murder of Sigibert in
575, a great struggle began between Brunihildis and a faction of
the Austrasian nobles during the minority of her infant son, a
struggle in which she was destined to be engaged till her tragic
end in 614. In the long minority of the boy King, she had to
face an opposition including Egidius, the Bishop of Rheims,
Guntram Boso, and Ursio, men bent on wielding a vicarious
power during the minority of Childebert. They tried to fortify
their power by an understanding with Chilperic in order to
dethrone Guntram of Burgundy, who favoured the Roman party
and Brunihildis. Their most formidable opponent was the Gallo-
Roman Lupus, Duke of Champagne, and the leader of the party
which supported the power of Brunihildis and the alliance with
Burgundy. In the year 581 the parties came to open battle.
The Austrasian nobles, led by Ursio and Berthefredus, levied an
armed force against Lupus. Brunihildis, in man's armour,
appeared in their midst, beseeching them not to prosecute the
ruinous strife. Ursio addressed her in very unceremonious
fashion, a style which he would probably not have dared to
assume to a born daughter of France. " Woman," he said,
" withdraw ; your son's royalty is not yours ; it is now safe
under our protection. If you do not withdraw you will be

THE ARISTOCRACY

trodden under the hoofs of our horses." The combat, however, was stayed, but the estates of Lupus were given up to plunder, and Lupus had to fly for refuge to the court of Guntram. During the minority of Childebert, Brunihildis was waging a long war with the Frank grandees of Austrasia, who were in secret communication with the Neustrian government, and aided by the fiendish plots of Fredegundis to humble her hated rival. The pacific Guntram died in 593, and his nephew Childebert, to whom he left his realm of Burgundy, three years afterwards. The long minority of Childebert's sons gave a final shock to royal power in Austrasia. Brunihildis struggled hard against the ambitious nobles who were fighting for their own hand, and intriguing with Fredegundis. Fredegundis's death in 597 did little to weaken the opposition now led by Wintrio, Duke of Champagne. But Wintrio, at the instigation of the old regent Brunihildis, was put to death in 598. That was a final effort of Brunihildis to maintain her hold on the Austrasian realm of her grandson Theudebert. The nobles rose up against her and the great Queen had to fly, and was only saved by a poor wayfarer who guided her to the seat of Theuderic in Burgundy, and who, according to a doubtful tradition, was rewarded by the bishopric of Auxerre.

But in Burgundy the old Queen found herself engaged in the same struggle with the German magnates as in Austrasia. Guntram, it is true, following the example of the old Burgundian kings, had sought the support of great Roman families, especially in the high office of patrician. But the rebellion of the Roman Mummolus for the time turned the scale in favour of the Germans, some of whom held high office under her grandson Theuderic when Brunihildis arrived; Colenus and Aegyla held the patriciate, and Bertoaldus was Mayor of the Palace in those years from 599 to 603, and all were Franks. In the same years Theudebert and Theuderic, on the death of Fredegundis, combined their forces for an invasion of Neustria. In a great battle at Dormeille on the Ouaine, the army of Chlothar was cut to pieces, and the King had to accept terms which involved the partition of the greater part of Neustria, and left the King only twelve cantons between the Seine, the Oise, and the ocean. Brunihildis must have felt this victory as a victory for her hated Austrasian foes over herself, and she burned to avenge herself for her exile and degradation. Colenus, the Frank patrician, disappears soon after her

arrival in Burgundy. She directly procured the death of the
Frank Aegyla, who succeeded him, and annexed his estates.
Bertoaldus, of course a German, then held the office of *major
domus*, which had by then become the most powerful in the
realm, and the old Queen's aim was to displace him. A Gallo-
Roman named Protadius was by her intrigues raised to the
patriciate, to further her designs. He was a fit instrument, able,
calculating, and subtle, but equally ruthless to enrich the treasury
and himself by despoiling the wealthy class, and to humiliate
the men of noble rank. Such a temper suited well the settled
policy of Brunihildis. Bertoaldus, whom she wished to get rid
of, was sent with a feeble escort on a hopeless mission to levy
the imposts on the Neustrian territory which had just been
acquired by Theuderic. He was met by the armed forces of
Chlothar II., who recovered some of his losses. Bertoaldus
courted death in one of three battles, since, as the Chronicler
tells us, he saw that Protadius (and Brunihildis) had resolved to
deprive him of his office, to which Protadius succeeded. And
now the Queen saw her chance of having her revenge on the
Austrasian nobles—the policy which she pursued relentlessly till
her end. With bitter sneers at Theudebert's base birth, with the
help of Protadius, she goaded Theuderic on to declare war. But
Protadius by his harsh administration had made bitter enemies
in Burgundy, and they firmly opposed the policy of Brunihildis.
When their efforts failed, the mutineers surrounded the tent in
which Protadius was playing at dice and slew him. Within a
few months two great Frank nobles were made to feel the vengeance of Brunihildis. Uncelenus, who had borne a treacherous
part in the murder, was mutilated, stripped of all his possessions,
and driven into exile. Vulfus, the other, was by orders slain in
his country seat, and his patriciate was given to a man of Gallo-
Roman birth. A few years passed in which the Queen was
engaged in other feuds, especially with the great monk Columbanus. But in the year 610 war was reopened suddenly by
Austrasia. Theuderic, having secured the neutrality of Chlothar,
with a great army overwhelmed Theudebert at Toul and pursued
him to Cologne. With the aid of levies from beyond the Rhine,
Theudebert renewed the struggle at Tolbiacum, and was once more
beaten in a scene of slaughter such as the monkish chronicler
evidently finds it hard to describe. Theudebert was captured,

stripped of all royal insignia, tonsured, and relegated to a monastery, only to be speedily murdered by his brother's command. Within five months the murderer died of dysentery at Metz, and Brunihildis in old age was left for the third time to guard the rights of an infant.

It was for the moment a great triumph. Austrasia had been beaten in two great battles with enormous loss. Neustria had been previously reduced to a narrow strip of territory. There might seem to have been a rare chance of uniting Burgundy and Austrasia, embracing far the largest Frank dominions under a single ruler, the heir of Childebert, and, by the added prestige of royalty, shattering the unruly ambitions of the great nobles of Austrasia. Such, we may conclude, even from the curt narrative of Fredegarius, was the aim of Brunihildis. Theuderic had left four sons, of whom the eldest was only twelve. According to Frank tradition, each of them was King, and had a claim to his share of territory. But we are briefly told that Brunihildis determined to make Sigibert, the eldest, sole monarch of the two realms, with a Gallo-Roman, Aletheus, as patrician. A German, Warnachar, was at the time *major domus*, and probably not very loyal to Brunihildis and her young ward. And she had determined enemies among the nobles of Austrasia, who resolved to save themselves from the imperious sway of the old regent who had always been their most formidable foe in their efforts against the Crown in Austrasia. Two great Franks led the attack. Arnulfus of high descent, with some literary culture, which afterwards raised him to the see of Metz, had by commanding ability gained the highest place. The origin of Pippin, his ally, is rather obscure, but he was the son of a high official in Austrasia, and at this time had a commanding influence. These men combined to offer the throne of Austrasia to Chlothar II., and probably Warnachar, the *major domus* of Sigibert, with many other Burgundian nobles, was privy to the overture. They were all inspired with fear of the ambition of Brunihildis, and she with advancing years (sixty-six) was losing the magnetism and fascinating charm which had made her such a vivid force for fifty years.

Chlothar, having parried with a vague reply an appeal of the Queen to withdraw from the realms of Theuderic's sons, advanced to the banks of the Rhine near Coblentz. Brunihildis was then at Worms, and, having little confidence in Austrasia, she despatched the youthful Sigibert with Warnachar and one Alboenus to summon a force from Thuringia and other regions beyond the Rhine to meet the army of Neustria. The Queen probably knew of the treacherous designs of Warnachar, and in the true Merovingian style she sent Alboenus with secret instructions to procure the death of the *major domus*. The plot failed owing to the finding of the torn letter of the Queen by one of Warnachar's slaves.

The *major domus* immediately took steps to frustrate the levy of trans-Rhenane forces, and came home to organise a vast conspiracy of nobles and bishops for the destruction of Brunihildis, the murder of all the seed of Theuderic, and the annexation of Burgundy to the realm of Chlothar. But Brunihildis, deprived of her great hope of German support, with all the splendid courage which makes her one of the foremost figures of the age, sent Sigibert at the head of a Burgundian army, with Aletheus the patrician and the Dukes Rocco and Sigoaldus, to meet the Neustrian army on the Aisne. But treachery had done its work effectually. Before swords were crossed, the Burgundian troops calmly retired without any hot pursuit, and Chlothar advanced by slow marches to the Saône. Of the three sons of Theuderic who were captured, one, called after the founder of the race, was saved by the always potent fact that Chlothar had been his godfather. The others were put to death. Brunihildis was reserved for a more exquisite agony. For three days she had to endure tortures over which the chronicler throws a veil. On the fourth, she was borne round the camp on a camel, then, fastened by her hair and arm and foot to the tail of a wild horse, she was torn limb from limb. In this ghastly scene of savage vengeance, the curse of the Merovingians, long haunting them, reached its predestined goal. With the death of Brunihildis, the old autocracy of the Merovingian race vanished for ever.

The career of Brunihildis was one long struggle against the plots of the German nobles in Austrasia and Burgundy. The death of Sigibert and the long minority of his successors, through three generations, gave aristocratic ambition a tempting chance. And for nearly forty years the daughter of Athanagild, the Goth, fought and intrigued, with more than masculine force, for the power of Frank royalty. It is hard to associate such a career with the picture of the young princess fresh from her Spanish home which is sketched with evident sincerity by Gregory, who knew her and her husband well. She was the choice bride of one of the few Merovingians who had the ideal of pure wedlock. She was, says the ascetic bishop, who was also a keen man of the world, as virtuous as she was beautiful, sage in counsel, and gracious and charming in intercourse—a striking contrast to the meretricious allurements of the low-born concubines of Charibert and Chilperic. In an age in which gross indulgence and vagrant intrigue in the royal caste were treated rather lightly, even by great churchmen, she and her gallant husband seemed to have escaped the breath of scandal. If Brunihildis's private character had not been beyond reproach, we may be sure that her bitter enemies in Austrasia and in the court of Fredegundis would not have spared her. The fierce Duke who threatened to trample her under his horse's hoofs, the son of Fredegundis who charged her with causing the deaths of ten Frank princes, and scattered her limbs among the rocks and woods of the Jura, did not dare to assail her virtue. That she was fierce and revengeful, that she could give blow for blow, that she could meet guile with guile, is only to say that she was a true daughter of her age, and knew the arts which alone could guard her and her young charges against the intrigues of Egidius, Ursio, and Warnachar, or the poisoned daggers of Fredegundis. Nothing but high courage and ability could have prolonged the authority of the Austrasian crown in the troubled years which followed the death of Sigibert. In the effective government of a great territory, and in the choice of great officers to carry it on, she must have done an immense work of administration of which the records of that age, more occupied with crimes and tragedies, have hidden all the minute details. That she was striving to arrest a great social and political movement which was destined to triumph not long after her death in the decrepitude of the Merovingian dynasty, and the rise to commanding power of the Mayors of the Palace, does not really discredit her statesmanship, even although she failed. Brilliant failures in history are probably as common as brilliant successes. She fought, no doubt, with family feeling, for her sons, grandsons, and great-grandsons. But so powerful a nature rose above mere personal attachments. In the wild conflicts of the time she felt that the Merovingian autocracy was better than a chaos created by the lawless ambition of great Austrasian nobles. She, a daughter of the Goths, became the zealous champion of old Roman ideas and order, and drew her support from great Gallo-Roman houses in Burgundy. She had, like all the greatest Germans of that time, a reverence for what Rome had done for the world. She cared for the maintenance of Roman roads and monuments. As a pious daughter of the Church she gave endowments to churches, hospitals, and nunneries. She obtained from Pope Gregory the Great a charter for her foundation at Autun. And the Pontiff's commendation of her statesmanship, justice, and devotion to religion need not be taken as calculated flattery to power. It is true that ecclesiastics of those times used a peculiarly unctuous adulation, both of their own ascetic class and of the worldly great, which often, and naturally, arouses some suspicion. And they were often too ready to close their eyes to faults, and even crimes, in men who had served the temporal interests of the Church. Yet it is possible that the charitable view of a character which, with many of the faults of that age, yet fought for order and spiritual ideals against wild selfish force, may be more historical and just than a sterner judgement based on the moral standards of a later and less tried age. Family affection, along with fierce hatred of a fiendish rival continually plotting against her, personal ambition indistinguishable from a consciousness of daemonic force, combined with resolve to hold society together in the face of wild forces of disruption—all these feelings probably met in the character of Brunihildis. It may seem an enigma to those who come to its interpretation with unsympathetic formulae. Yet it may be read, with a not uncritical charity, as it was probably read by Gregory the Great, in the light of the strange complexity of human nature.

CHAPTER II

THE LIFE OF THE COMMON PEOPLE IN THE MEROVINGIAN AGE

THE historian is generally occupied far more with great events and imposing characters than with the quiet, dim life which flows on in silent, monotonous toil beneath the glare and tumult of great tragedies or triumphs. It is natural that it should be so. The reader of history generally looks for the sensational and spectacular effects ; he thinks nothing of what is passing in the shade. And the historian has, from the nature of his sources, far more material for what is grand and striking in his tale than for the fate of those who labour and suffer silently, and whose rare moments of pleasure, making life tolerable, are only known to themselves. The common people of the Merovingian times were of small account in the eyes of the kings and their great officers and nobles. The fragmentary chronicles of the time are chiefly concerned with nobles and kings. Yet, carefully examined, they yield now and then some glimpses of the life of the common mass, its tragedies, its grinding poverty and diseases, its perils by road and river, its trading life in country towns. The most penetrating imagination, with the fullest learning, could never wake to life that dim, sunken mass who dragged out their lives in servitude and indigence, with no hope, and probably no desire, of any change. Yet an observant eye may catch here and there glimpses of their condition in the history of Gregory of Tours or in the Lives of the Saints. And it is the purpose of this chapter to glean what we can from these sources, and to present it to the reader.

Our first authority, who, from his style and quality, cannot

be disregarded, is Venantius Fortunatus, although he saw more
of the upper classes than of the crowd. But his poems are too
rare and precious a message from a dim generation to be
neglected. He came to Gaul about 565 to pay a vow at the
tomb of S. Martin at Tours for the cure of a disease of his eyes.
Of Fortunatus we shall speak more particularly in another
chapter. It is enough here to say that, with all the literary
vices of the decadence, he yet possesses a vivacity of talent,
a copious power of pictorial description, and even some
elegance, which, in the growing darkness, gave him a certain
distinction and fascination. His is almost the last gleam of the
old Augustan culture. The admiration for literary skill and
finesse had not quite died out, and the very consciousness of
their barbarous style which is so pathetically expressed by
Gregory and many biographers of the Saints, shows that there
was still a lingering love of the magic of the great masters. He
travelled far and wide in Gaul, and the wandering poet was
everywhere received with open arms, at the courts of Sigibert
and Chilperic, by bishops, dukes, and grand seigneurs, both
Frank and Roman. With special warmth he was welcomed at
the convent which Queen Radegund had founded at Poitiers ;
but the tale of that religious romance must be reserved for
another place.

Fortunatus repaid the hospitality lavished on him in many
elegiac pieces in which he recalls the pleasure of his visits, the
charms of rural scenes, the stately dignity of the many churches
or country seats which his patrons had erected, or the many
perils and adventures of his wanderings. What strikes one most
in reading these poems is the idyllic tranquillity which seems to
reign everywhere in these meadows and vineyards along the
Garonne, the Loire, and the Moselle. Yet in those very years
there were fierce irruptions of the Huns, repelled by Sigibert in
several campaigns ; there was desolating civil war between
Sigibert and Chilperic ; the great plague was reviving again and
again with appalling virulence, and men's imaginations were
disordered by strange convulsions of nature and stranger prodigies.
In the verses of Fortunatus there is no hint of all this calamity
and terror. The scenery of the Garonne and the Moselle is as
quiet and smiling as it is in the poems of Ausonius. There are
verdant meadows gemmed with flowers sloping down to the

river. There is the wealth of yellow cornfields rippling under the passing breeze, and vineyards on the terraced banks. Sometimes the torrent, flushed with sudden rains, is sweeping crops and herds from the field, and the traveller in his leaky skiff is drenched and tossed on his course to Trèves. Or again, the river bed is hardened under the torrid heat, and the fish are gasping in the mud; while " the sun with fiery ploughshare cleaves furrows in the glebe ". The traces of ancient civilisation are everywhere. The smoke of villas rises among their pine-woods and olives. Here and there, as a century before, the great lords are restoring their country seats with new baths, stately porticoes, and fountains spreading their coolness. In the ever-dangerous region of the Moselle, the castle of Nicetius is rising with its thirty bastions and its ballista, amid orchards and vineyards and meadows. Felix, the cultivated aristocratic Bishop of Nantes, has just built a new basilica with lofty dome, and frescoes "with breathing colours ", and accomplished a great feat of engineering in diverting the course of a river, which Fortunatus celebrates with all that wearisome iteration of idea under elaborately varied phrase which is the characteristic of the decadence.

The poet in his travels made the acquaintance of almost all the great personages of the time in Gaul, and he recalls their hospitable treatment in a frankly sensual tone. But he has an eye also, amid all his flattery, for the strong, public-spirited men who, in a world of fierce, selfish impulse, rapacity, and violence, kept alive a tradition of justice and order. Two of these stand out upon the page, Gogo and Lupus, Duke of Champagne. Lupus was a famous warrior who had shattered the Saxons on the Lahn ; he was also an able and just administrator. Gogo was a man of rank and character who had been chosen by Sigibert to escort his young bride, Brunihildis, from the Spanish court. He was a man of varied accomplishments, an orator, and a learned jurist. But he was above all a typical country gentleman, with the taste for sport and rural life which has characterised his class in all ages. We find him relieving public cares by salmon-fishing on the Rhine, or in hunting the stag and boar in the glades of the Vosges or the Ardennes, or watching the labours of his husbandmen. This picture of scenery and social life in the reign of Sigibert is disfigured by tasteless love of mere verbal effort, exaggeration, and insincerity. Yet through all the cloud of phrase-making we have a vivid picture of the fields and country life of Gaul in the age of the Merovingians.

It may seem strange that a foreign traveller could make his way in the sixth century with ease from Toulouse to Metz and Trèves. But we must remember that the great Roman roads in Gaul were still open. They continue to be mentioned in legal documents of the seventh century. In the year 589 the *evectio publica* for messengers of the King is still an established institution. Of course that privilege was reserved, as it was under the Empire, for functionaries of the State journeying on public business. But the records of the time leave the impression that travelling, at least for the well-to-do, was easy and expeditious. We are told that provincial bishops took only three days to assemble at Clermont for the funeral of Bishop Gallus in 554 ; and this time included the journey of the messengers sent to summon them. Five days were allowed for his brother prelates to attend the funeral of Bishop Gregory at Dijon. The journeys of the missionary saints, of the pilgrims to the shrines of S. Martin and S. Julian, of the envoys to the Roman see, seem all to have been accomplished easily and safely. Gregory of Tours made many journeys to visit his mother in the south of Burgundy, or to attend the kings at Coblentz, Metz, Soissons, or Paris. Even in winter, after heavy rains or in snow or frost, although Fortunatus may complain of their condition, the great roads seem not to have been often impassable. Of course great preparations had to be made for the journey of a man of rank, wagons to carry baggage and provisions, with horses for his servants. The train of a princess on her way to the Visigothic court in Spain would seem to have been like an army on the march. The private traveller might, like Sidonius, take tents to pitch at nightfall, or he might find hospitable reception at a monastery or some presbytery or bishop's house. We have a picture of one party of the time at first encamped under a starry sky, and then suddenly overwhelmed by a crashing thunderstorm which destroyed a neighbouring shrine of idols and set the woods on fire. And such parties, even when the master was a saintly bishop of Trèves, would sometimes turn their horses for the night into a neighbouring cornfield. Inns and lodgings were to be found in the large towns, such as Paris, Orleans, and Tours, and occasionally in country towns like Brivate, the seat of a much-frequented shrine of S. Julian. We hear of King Guntram once visiting Bishop Gregory at his lodgings in Orleans in 585, drinking wine with him, and giving him an invitation to dinner as he departed. One would like to know how the genial King himself was lodged in his progress from Nevers to Paris. Wherever it was possible, journeys seem to have been made by water. Fortunatus was in this way able to visit his great friends along the Garonne and the Moselle, though now and then there was a difficulty in obtaining a boat. Before his day, S. Geneviève had made long river journeys on the Seine and on the Loire from Orleans to Tours. Gregory once, returning from dinner with King Childebert at Coblentz and going on board his barge at the dead of night, was nearly swamped by a rush of uninvited passengers, and only saved by the relics of S. Martin. The Abbess Agnes of Poitiers used to tell a tale of a similar miracle of river travel. A salt merchant had gone on board his boat, moored at the bridge at Metz, and, after commending his company to the protection of S. Martin, lay down to sleep. In the morning the party woke to find themselves lying at the quays of Trèves, their boat having, during the night, threaded the rocky channel in safety. In the same way Bishop Apollinaris was borne asleep from Valence to Avignon through all the dangers of the impetuous Rhone. The mention of the perils of voyaging by river, not only from obstructions of rock and fallen trees, but from storms and waves, seems rather surprising. But the boats were probably small and of light draught so as to run up shallow tributaries which would, in our time, hardly be recognised as navigable. Yet, in spite of this danger and discomfort, the sick and crippled were often taken by river down the Loire, for their vigils and healing at the shrine of S. Martin. Ferries of course were common in the absence of bridges, and the unpermitted use of ferry-boats is punished in the Salic and Burgundian Laws. There is a pleasant tale which Bishop Gregory gives us of a ferryman on the Loire, equally charming for its realism and its miracle. The bishop, on a journey from Baugy, came to the river bank, and on his way across asked the ferryman about a place where he might fish. The man, probably wishing to humour the good bishop, told him how once the invocation of S. Martin had brought him a lucky catch. At Epiphany he found he had no wine in his cellar, and as he left his house he breathed a prayer to the saint to send him some wine wherewith to cheer him at the festival. Presently he heard a traveller from the other bank calling him to put him across. While he was toiling against the current a great fish leaped into the boat, the sale of which supplied him with ample means of festivity ! The bishop solemnly attests the truth of this story, and rejoices in such a repetition of the miracle of Cana.

The perils and discomforts of travelling, even for the great, were many and serious. Not to speak of sudden storm, flood, and icy or miry roads, there was the danger from brigands or armed enemies. Although, when marauding armies were not in the field, the country districts seem to have been, on the whole, secure and peaceful, still, in the absence of a regular police, travelling parties were liable to be stopped by highwaymen or by overbearing officials on their rounds with armed retainers. The lonely roads, often passing through the dense forests which then overspread great tracts of Burgundy and central Gaul, offered many chances to desperate marauders. When Gregory once made a journey to visit his mother on her estate in Burgundy, and was passing through a wood near the Rhone, he was suddenly surrounded by a party of brigands who threatened his life. As usual, the magic of S. Martin came to his aid ; the bandits took to flight, and could not be tempted even by charitable entreaty to share the food and drink which Gregory offered them. Probably the appearance of the retainers with whom he always travelled, seconded the terrors of the saint. In the Life of S. Gertrude we read of robbers carrying off a boy to sell him into slavery, and foiled in their attempt by his invocation of the saint. And men of high rank, with no temptation from poverty, sometimes "took to the road" as we used to say. The sons of a high official named Waddo ranged over the lands of Poitiers, attacking travelling merchants and even royal officers by night. When the count of the district strove to repress their outrages, they had the effrontery to appeal to the King, whom they vainly tried to bribe with a present of jewelled arms.

There are many indications that the households of the wealthy and official class then generally carried arms, and that men of rank, both Frank and Roman, travelled with an armed escort.

One scene sketched by Gregory is probably typical of many such encounters. When Guntram Boso, after his period of retreat at the shrine of S. Martin, was escorting his daughters on the way from Poitiers, he was met by the Duke Dragolenus. Both parties were armed. But Boso sent a friend forward with pacific proposals and an offer to let the Duke have his will of his treasures, if he would leave the way open for his daughters to reach their destination. Dragolenus met the proposal of Boso with jeering insult. He pointed to a rope at his saddle bow by which many a one had been dragged to the royal presence, and, lance in rest, he set spurs to his horse. His lance was shivered against Boso's armour, and his sword dropped to the ground. Calling S. Martin to his aid, Boso hurled Dragolenus from his horse with a thrust full in the jaws, and one of Boso's men drove a spear into his side.

Whether Gregory in his many journeys travelled with armed followers does not appear. The Bishop of Tours was in all probability sufficiently guarded from violence by the universal awe felt in those days for the sanctity of his office. But in that time of epidemic disease and ignorance of the laws of health, he or some of his attendants were constantly falling ill by the way, and as constantly restored by never-failing miracle. Ten years before his consecration as bishop, Gregory was seized with an alarming fever, and, in almost the last stage of exhaustion, insisted on journeying from Auvergne to Tours to try the virtue of S. Martin's tomb. With the fever still upon him, he attended the midnight service, and returned to his lodging to sleep. His faith or his constitution, or both together, prevailed, and he awoke to find himself in his usual health. On another journey two of his grooms, who were so weakened by dysentery that they could not sit on their horses, were cured by a draught of water mingled with some dust from the sacred tomb. Bad water or sleeping in damp and unhealthy quarters in that unsanitary age were evidently far greater dangers than assaults of robbers and desperadoes.

We do not hear of travellers coming across the Merovingian armies, which in the days of Gregory were so often carrying rapine and death all over Gaul. But here and there it becomes evident that for military reasons free communication between the realms of the Frank kings was interrupted or made difficult.

R

Roads and bridges were sometimes blocked by armed guards. Thus in 582, the kingdoms of Burgundy and Neustria being at war, Chilperic ordered a guard to be set at the bridge over the Orge, which separated the two realms. Similarly, in the struggle for the possession of Marseilles in 581 between Austrasia and Burgundy, Guntram gave orders that all the roads through Burgundy should be closed. The result was that the Duke Gundulfus, who was despatched to Marseilles by Childebert II. of Austrasia, was compelled to make a long detour by Tours through Aquitaine. On the failure of negotiations between Richaredus of Spain and Guntram in 587, the Visigothic king forbade any one from Burgundy to approach the cities of Septimania. Such an embargo must have cut off for the time all the inland towns from the coast of the Mediterranean, from the Rhone to the Pyrenees. Freedom of communication between Austrasia and Burgundy had been guaranteed by the Pact of Andelot in 587. Yet two years later, on a rumour that Brunihildis was opening communications with the sons of the pretender Gundobald, we find that King Guntram ordered all the roads through Burgundy to be closely watched. No one was allowed to pass, and baggage, clothes, and even shoes were searched for secret despatches.

Yet, in spite of all these obstacles and dangers, there was more active inland trade than the condition of the country might lead us to expect. It is true that the large villae, with their serfs and coloni cultivating a wide area, and manufacturing for themselves all articles needed in daily life, were comparatively self-sufficing communities, so far as the more important necessaries of life were concerned. But generally the luxuries and ornaments of life had to be drawn from the Eastern world and the seats of ancient civilisation, and distributed along the trade routes of Gaul. Such luxuries came, for the most part, to the ports of Marseilles and Bordeaux—oil, Syrian and Italian wines, silk, Egyptian herbs, and papyrus ; and they were forwarded by river or road. We read of fairs and markets in country towns, and business houses carrying on a prosperous trade at Orleans, Nantes, Trèves, and Paris, and even in secluded Auvergne. There are dealers in salt at Trèves, wine merchants at Orleans, jewellers and goldsmiths at Paris. And these traders were often organised, as, for instance, at Verdun, where, through the influence of the Bishop Desideratus, they obtained a loan of 7000 gold pieces from King Theudebert, which, we are told, raised them from poverty to a modest wealth. The merchants of Nantes owed much to the energy and skill of Bishop Felix in increasing the capacity of their port, which had probably an active trade with the British Isles and Spain.

Overland trade in Gaul must have yielded a considerable revenue to the Frank kings, as it did in the time of the Empire ; and it seems probable that the Imperial system of tolls and customs was generally continued after the Frank conquest. Under the Empire Gaul had been enclosed by a net of custom-houses on every side—on the Channel ports and the Rhine, at the foot of the Alps and Pyrenees, and great southern ports such as Arles and Marseilles. There were also octroi levies at the gates of important towns, and at ferries and bridges, a large proportion of which in the fourth century was handed over to the Imperial government. The amount so levied was $2\frac{1}{2}$ per cent on the value of merchandise in transit, with exemption for articles for personal use or farming purposes. There are a good many signs that this organisation was maintained under the Merovingians. The *teloneum* and *telonarii* of the Theodosian Code reappear in Frank edicts of the sixth and seventh centuries. In the Acts of the Council of Mâcon, in 581, a Jew is forbidden to hold the office of *telonarius*. In 562 King Chilperic conferred on the Bishop of Tournai all dues and customs along the Scheldt, whether on goods borne by the river or passing over the bridges. In 614 Chlothar II. was obliged, by complaints of oppressive exactions, to restore the scale of dues established in the reigns of Guntram, Sigibert, and Chilperic. King Dagobert in 629, when he established a regular market at S. Denis, suspended for two years all previous dues on merchandise leviable at the port of Rouen or on the Seine. The same monarch, among his munificent grants to the Abbey of S. Denis, made over to it a charge on the customs of Marseilles, and exemption at Valence and Lyons for six wagons of the house annually on the great route from the Mediterranean. In the year 681 all carts of the abbey were relieved of all such charges in Neustria, Austrasia, and Burgundy. It is clear from these facts that in the sixth and seventh centuries there was an active inland traffic in Gaul from the Mediterranean to the Seine, the Scheldt, and the Channel.

The persons engaged in this trade were generally Syrians and Jews. When King Guntram in 585 passed through Orleans on his way to Paris, on the feast of S. Martin, he was welcomed by a great crowd, among which were Jews and traders from the East, who escorted him through the town with banners and ensigns, singing his praises. There were Syrian merchants at Bordeaux when the pretender Gundobald had occupied it. One of them, a man of great wealth, bearing the classical name of Euphronius, had been tonsured by Bishop Bertram with the object of annexing his property. But the Syrian was said to possess an even more valued treasure in the sacred hand of S. Sergius which he had enshrined in his oratory, and which the pretender coveted as a sure guarantee of the victory of his cause. How and with what effort a single precious bone was secured is a curious tale of those strange times. More than a century before, in the reign of the Visigothic Theodoric I., in that same region, a trader " from the parts of the East " enjoyed close intimacy with S. Bibianus, the Bishop of Saintes, and carried his fame, now to us very dim, and some precious relics back to his Eastern home. There is a still more curious tale of the mingling of worldly greed and ecclesiastical zeal in those traders from the East. In 591 Ragnimodus, the successor of S. Germanus in the see of Paris, died. His brother Faramodus was a candidate for the succession. But a Syrian merchant, bearing the good ecclesiastical name of Eusebius, by lavish bribes obtained his election to the office. He also probably obtained a business return on the transaction, for we are told that he banished all the staff of his predecessor, and installed in the offices surrounding him men of his own race.

The Jews seem to have been numerous and widely scattered in the realms of the Merovingians, on the Riviera, at Arles, Marseilles, and Bordeaux, in Auvergne, Bourges, Orleans, and Paris. They were engaged in their hereditary and congenial trade of money-lending, or as goldsmiths and jewellers. Sometimes they are found practising as oculists or physicians. Their numbers and organisation often made them a serious power in the events of the time. In the siege of Arles in 507, in spite of some treachery in their ranks, they gave powerful support to the Visigoths against the Franks, and although they had joined in tumultuous attacks on S. Caesarius, in the end they took part with effusive grief in his obsequies. We hear of Jews owning vessels which sailed between Nice and Marseilles. At Bourges Jews were converted by a sermon of S. Germanus at the consecration of Bishop Felix. In the same city Leonastes, the archdeacon, having been partially cured of a cataract by the virtue of S. Martin, called in a Hebrew oculist to complete the miraculous work of the saint, and was signally punished for daring to invoke human skill to supplement spiritual healing. On the other hand, a Jew, who was probably a physician, at Bordeaux incurred a similar fate for a sceptical sneer at the medical power of S. Martin. Priscus, who figures prominently in the pages of Gregory, was a wealthy goldsmith at Paris in the reign of Chilperic, who seems to have been on the same terms with Priscus as James I. was with Geordie Heriot in Scott's novel *The Fortunes of Nigel.* The King plumed himself on his artistic taste, which was probably on the same level as his literary talent, and the Jew supplied him with many articles of vertu, such as that golden bowl studded with jewels which the King displayed with childish vanity to Bishop Gregory, and which was thought to rival the ornate art of Byzantium. It is needless to say that these rich Jews were the great bankers and money-lenders of the time. And there were many openings for their calling. In the collection of the revenue, the count who was governor of a district was responsible for the amount of its taxes to the central treasury. If his subordinate officers had failed to collect them in time, the count, in order to satisfy the immediate claims of the government, might have to obtain an advance on interest ; and the Jews were generally at hand to give convenient, but expensive, aid. In one case a certain Eunomius, Count of Tours, and his lieutenant Injuriosus, had obtained such financial support from a Jew named Armentarius, whose firm included another Jew and two Christians. All four were assassinated by the high officers to escape the repayment of the loan, and their bodies thrown into a well. From the days of Sidonius the Jews seem to have settled in considerable numbers in Auvergne. They were for a time well treated, and lived on good terms even with the bishops. Bishop Cautinus, who was far from being the most reputable of his order, was in the closest relations with them, not, as Gregory says, to secure their salvation but for the purchase of foreign luxuries, in which traffic, after the manner of their race, they were not the losers. In the corrupt and eager rivalry for the succession to Cautinus in the see, Eufrasius, a man of old Gallo-Roman family, employed the Jews to provide him with costly gifts to gain the patronage of the court. In the unscrupulous struggle for the sacred office in Auvergne, the Hebrews must have had a cynical satisfaction in holding the golden key to it, and may well have secretly despised the race which scorned, anathematised, and used them.

The records of the Church councils of that century throw some light on the strength and importance of the Jewish community in Gaul. By the Acts of a council held in Auvergne, in the generation when they were lending money to bishops to buy the luxuries of Marseilles or to bribe a courtier of Theudebert, Jews were debarred from intermarriage with Christians by sentence of spiritual outlawry on any priest who united them, and the kings were forbidden to appoint a Jew to govern a Christian province or to collect the taxes of it. For four days at Easter no Jew was permitted to be seen in the company of Christians. No Christian layman might sit at meals with a Hebrew, or share his hospitality. We can give our sympathy more freely to the enactments which forbade Christians to be sold in slavery to Jew masters, and which released, on payment of their price, the slaves of Jews who had taken asylum in a church. These enactments are forcibly repeated in many councils, and their vigour and iteration show how socially strong and how numerous the Hebrew race must have been in the Gaul of that century. Yet the assembled churchmen (so full of orthodox hatred of the accursed race) were individually often more gentle and charitable than their creed. For a bishop was a great civil as well as an ecclesiastical administrator ; and social ties and the necessary compromises of civil life often moderated the ferocity of ecclesiastical hatred. Churchmen, and even kings, made strenuous efforts for the conversion of Jews by friendly appeals to reason. But when milder evangelical methods failed, even saintly and kindly men did not hesitate to resort to force. The Jews always remained, in the eyes of a great bishop like S. Germanus or of a kindly monarch like Guntram, as they did in the eyes of Romans like Tacitus, " a detestable race, hateful to gods and men ".

Avitus, Bishop of Auvergne from 571 to 594, was, unlike some of his predecessors in the see, a man of piety and high character, universally respected alike by the people and the court of Sigibert. He passionately desired to draw the Jews into his fold, and used often to admonish them of their errors and their obstinacy. A single convert at first was the sole reward of his efforts, and he, on the occasion of his baptism, was foully insulted by one of his race. The people were with difficulty restrained by their bishop from stoning the offender to death. But on Ascension Day, 575, while the bishop was passing in procession to the basilica, the pent-up rage of the crowd broke forth, and the Jewish synagogue was levelled to the ground. Avitus probably disapproved of such violence, but he seized the occasion to press on the Jews his claim to be their pastor, and gave them the choice to accept the faith of Christ or to depart from Auvergne. For three days the Jews brooded over the awful alternative proposed to them, and then a great number sent a message professing their willingness to be baptized. It was the eve of Pentecost, and, after vigils, the bishop went to the baptistery in a white-robed procession, with flashing torches, and there baptized the kneeling throng and anointed them with the holy oil. The crowd of the faithful rejoiced as at a second descent of the Holy Ghost. It was said that five hundred Jews came to the font. But probably a larger number left their homes in Auvergne and retired to Marseilles.

Five or six years after the scene we have described, another effort was made for the conversion of the Jews of Paris by that strangest of all the Merovingians, King Chilperic. In spite of all aberrations of conduct or faith, he remained a loyal son of the Church, and eager to bring the blinded Hebrews, who were so useful to him, into the fold. The King was, in the year 581, at his villa at Nogent, where the Bishop of Tours had visited him, and was about to take his leave, as the court was on the point of removing to Paris. Priscus, the Parisian jeweller, who probably had been exhibiting some of his wares, was also there and about to depart. As the King was mounting his horse, he drew Priscus to him, and grasping his locks, begged Gregory to lay his hand on them in benediction. The Jew boldly declined the favour, and then began a curious biblical altercation, of the comic character of which Gregory seems perfectly unconscious. The King and the Jew rained on one another texts from the

Old Testament, to prove or to disprove the Divinity of Christ. At last Chilperic was silenced by the question, " Could God be born of a woman, subject to stripes, and condemned to death ? " and the bishop came to his aid with a repertory of texts such as those with which he once overwhelmed an Arian visitor from Spain. Needless to say that Priscus remained unshaken ; the King craved the episcopal blessing, and after eating bread and drinking wine with the bishop, mounted his horse and headed the cavalcade on the road to Paris.

This scene must have deeply impressed Chilperic with the obstinacy of Hebrew fanaticism, and during his sojourn at Paris he issued a peremptory order that all Jews should at once be baptized, under the penalty of having their eyes torn out if they refused. Yet, with that strange mixture of ferocity and geniality which characterised him, he actually assisted at the rite, and stood as spiritual father for some of the Jews at the font. The conformity was very perfunctory, and the supposed converts still clung in secret to their ancestral observances. Priscus, probably presuming on his position, remained openly obdurate, and was thrown into prison. But the cunning Hebrew knew well the power of money and the avarice of a Merovingian. By means of lavish presents and the plea that he must attend the marriage of his son at Marseilles, with a promise to conform to the King's will, he obtained his release. The proud Jew never dreamt of keeping his promise, and a quarrel broke out between him and a certain Phatir, one of the renegades who had apostatised at Chilperic's command. Phatir resolved to kill his more steadfast brother Hebrew. As Priscus was taking his way to join in the Hebrew rites in some secret conventicle, he was waylaid and assassinated by Phatir. The murderer and his accomplices took refuge in a neighbouring church of S. Julian, to escape the rage of the crowd, with whom Priscus probably was popular. After some confused and bloody scenes, Phatir managed to escape to Burgundy, but only to perish in the end at the hands of the kinsmen of his victim. The fate of a shadowy figure at the end of the sixth century may seem hardly worthy of such notice. Yet as a picture of Paris in that age it perhaps teaches more than any formal disquisition.

The student of society in that dim age would give much for a vivid picture of common rural life, or of the streets of a country town, even if the picture were as mannered and conventional as that which Sidonius and Fortunatus have left us of châteaux and bishops' palaces. As it is, we can only gather and piece together as best we can some slight and scattered glimpses vouchsafed to us by writers who were far more interested in miracles and prodigies than in prosaic facts of the life of their time. Indeed the bit of realistic incident which interests us most, is for them only the setting for a tale of supernatural wonder. And, after all, until the age of steam, the life of the country-side probably went on with unchanging monotony for many ages. The round of rural labour, of tillage and harvest, following the circle of the seasons, can never, in its sober colouring, offer much to strike the eye. The travelling merchant, or the duke marching with his men-at-arms on the great road, would see little as they passed of the peasant life buried in the woods of Champagne or the Ardennes, or secluded in the solitudes of a great estate in Aquitaine. But, even after fifteen hundred years, one may still faintly catch its quiet charm in Gregory or Fredegarius, or the Lives of the Saints. We may see the harvest field in Auvergne thronged with reapers in the hot noontide, who are supplied with beer by angelic hands ; or another field near Rheims, where men were ploughing, and as a stranger passed along the road bearing relics to a new chapel of S. Julian, one of their number was purged of a tormenting spirit who could not endure the mystery of sanctity. Or we may see S. Rémi making the round of one of the estates of his see, and cheering the harvesters with drink, and going on to visit the house of his cousin for dinner, where he replenished the exhausted cellar with good wine by a miracle hardly worthy of a saintly character. Or we hear a tale of fiscal oppression on other lands of the see. A poor tenant whose farm lay close to a royal estate had no rest from the exactions and plunder of the *Fiscalini*, and all his appeals to secular authorities for redress were in vain. At last he took bread and flesh and wine, with a candle in his hand, and reverently approached a chapel of S. Rémi. There he fed bountifully the crowd of the poor who in those days were generally gathered around such shrines, set an offering on the altar-tomb, and implored the saint for his aid and protection. Returning with some of the sacred dust, he scattered the trespassers on his fields in wild confusion. So a swineherd on a royal manor once lawlessly drove his hogs into a forest of the church of Rheims, and met a wolf among the underwood ; and as he charged down upon it, his horse shied, and his brains were dashed out against a tree.

It is somewhat amusing that the ecclesiastical crime of Sabbath-breaking provides some of the freshest pictures of country life. The superstition of the Hebrew Sabbath had not a firmer hold on the Scotland of the seventeenth century than it had on the Merovingian age. But while in Scotland the offender was only liable to the rebuke and penance inflicted by a Kirk-Session, in the Gaul of the sixth century he had to suffer the Divine judgement on life or limb or reason. There is hardly an act or incident in the round of rural life, grinding corn or baking, making hay or combing the hair on the Sabbath, which in the book of the *Miracles of S. Martin* is not visited with swift and dire retribution, often ludicrously disproportionate to the supposed sin. Indeed one hesitates whether to laugh or grieve at such perversion and abuse of the spirit of religion, darkening human life by the terrors of an antiquated code which had been abrogated in the walk through the corn-fields on a famous Sabbath in Galilee. It is fair to say that the intolerant superstition on the subject had outrun the saner judgement of the councils of the Church. The espionage and malignant gossip which the observance of the Sabbath must have fostered finds a melancholy record in many a tale of vindictive miracle. The Sabbath was in Jewish fashion reckoned from sunset to sunset. And thus a poor woman who had impiously baked bread on the eve of the Sabbath was punished by paralysis ! Even the most urgent work was forbidden on the Hebrew day of rest. Leodulfus of Bourges had cut and saved his hay, and then, fearing a change in the weather, he yoked his oxen on a Sabbath morning and began to cart it in, when a burning pain in his foot warned him to make a pause. After attending Mass he impiously renewed his labour, and was stricken with blindness for a year. The most ordinary and even necessary rural tasks, such as stopping a gap or mending a fence to keep out stray cattle, were visited by the immediate judgement of God. We can see indeed that there were some sceptics on the subject even in those days. We can only wonder that there were not more.

Many another pleasanter glimpse of country life comes to us

by chance from chronicle or saint's Life. There is the boy with clappers to scare away birds from a vineyard ; the woman who has to carry water for a whole mile to the villa, and at the well has the privilege of watering S. Martin's ass ; or the steward riding home drunk, flung over a precipice, and caught in the tree-tops. There is the woodman rising before dawn, getting a wallet of food from his wife which receives the blessing of a priest, crossing a tottering bridge with his wagon amid the cries of evil spirits of the torrent, who are hypnotised by the blessed bread. Or we meet the swineherds whose hogs had laid bare a quarry of lime which was destined to bind together the walls of the new church of S. Denis, or the lumberers felling timber for the roof on a hot summer day. These things may seem small to the serious historian. Yet it is these small things which tell us far more of the average lives of men than the subtleties of diplomacy or the thunder of battle.

We have seen in the Salic and Burgundian Laws that the granges of that day had fenced and well-tended gardens, and orchards which had to be protected against robbers and intruders. And in Gregory's visits to the haunts of the hermits of Auvergne we have a sight of charming gardens, stocked with potherbs and fruit-bearing trees, like that pleasance under whose whispering boughs the old monk Martius had sat for three generations. As in the Italy of Virgil's time, bee-keeping was an important part of rural economy in the Gaul of the Merovingians. We read of one citizen of Auch who had many hives, and in order to recover a swarm that had wandered, made a vow to devote all its wax to light the church of S. Martin if the saint helped him in his quest. On a rumour of invasion he buried 200 lb. of wax, and a deacon of Gregory's unearthed it with the never-failing accompaniment of miracle. The value of bees in that time is attested by the frequent mention of the theft of hives both in the codes and in the tales of miracle. There is a pretty tale of the poor sisters of a convent at Amiens who eked out their subsistence by keeping a few hives of bees. One night three of them were stolen, but in the morning the impious robber was found lying dead in the boat to which he had carried his spoil.

The wars and calamities of that time do not seem to have much interrupted the sports of the Frank kings and nobles. Hunting is the natural amusement of a warlike race, and long before the Franks had become masters of the Ardennes and the Vosges, rights of the chase were strictly protected in the Salic Law. In the early years of the sixth century, on the monastic lands of Arles, Gothic huntsmen on the track of the boar used to disturb the peaceful industry of the brothers. Auvergne was a paradise for the lovers of the chase, and we can still hear the sounds of it ringing in some of the pious legends of the district. One of its first Frank governors, the Duke Sigiwald, and his train used to range through its woods and mountain solitudes with their hounds, disturbing the quietude of many a hermitage. Sometimes the boar, hard pressed, would seek a refuge in the hermit's cell or in some little chapel among the woods. Or a servant of the monastery at Brioude who had found a missing hawk would have to be redeemed from the ferocity of a Frank lord by a heavy payment from the monastic treasury. When Merovech, the rebellious son of Chilperic, was in hiding in the basilica of Tours, the reckless youth was once tempted by a treacherous friend to go out for a day's hawking, from which by a happy chance he returned safely to his asylum. His father Chilperic was devoted to the chase. It was at a hunting seat on the Marne, as he alighted from his horse in the dusk of an autumn evening, that an unknown hand drove a dagger into his side. His brother Childebert once pursued a wild bull of famous size and ferocity up to the gates of the monastery of S. Calais (Carileffus), where the pious and sagacious beast sheltered itself under the protection of the saint. But King Guntram of Burgundy was the mightiest hunter of his race. That most singular and interesting of the Merovingians, with all his faults and vices, had a certain engaging *bonhomie* which made him popular. He was a genial country gentleman who was probably happiest when he was following the wild boar in the forests of the Vosges. And he was a stern keeper of his forests and of everything connected with the chase. If his hunting-horn disappeared, the negligent huntsman would be sent to prison. Three years before his death, the King, on a hunting expedition in the Vosges, once came upon the remains of a wild bull. The ranger of the forest, when asked for an explanation, accused Chundo, the chamberlain, of this breach of forest laws. When the chamberlain maintained his innocence, the King ordered the inquiry to take the form of judicial combat. Chundo proposed his nephew as his champion against the ranger of the forest. Both combatants fell, but the result was taken to prove the chamberlain's guilt. Before he could reach an asylum in the neighbouring church of Chalon, he was seized by Guntram's orders and stoned to death. A generation after the death of Guntram, the hunting tastes of the Frank kings were associated with pleasanter and holier scenes. Chlothar II., the son of Chilperic, had incurred the censure of his people by excessive devotion to sport. His son Dagobert had some of his father's taste for it, and in his early youth was once following the deer in the neighbourhood of a little hamlet with a neglected chapel, which had more than a century before been built by S. Geneviève. It enshrined the remains of S. Denis and two brother martyrs who had won their crown in the time of Domitian. The hounds of Dagobert, in hot pursuit, drove the deer up the village street, and it sought a refuge in the church. Years afterwards Dagobert found the same shelter from his father's anger, and had a vision of the three martyrs as he slept, which enjoined him to bring their remains from the obscurity where they lay, and to erect a worthier shrine in their honour. The command was piously fulfilled. The remains of S. Denis and his brethren were enshrined under a jewelled cross in a stately fane, and the church was endowed for ever with the customs of Marseilles and the rents of many manorial estates. There Dagobert himself was interred beside the altar, and there many of his successors reposed for ages till the rage of revolution left only *simulacra* of the glory of the kings of France. It is not often that a sportsman is also the founder of a historic church, and the biographer of Dagobert, in summing up his character, says, half apologetically, that with all his devotion to the Church and care for the poor, the King still kept some of the faults of his youth and remained a mighty hunter.

But the tranquil life of the country-side was in that age often darkened and disturbed by the calamities inflicted by civil war, fires, famine, and disease. The fierce feuds of the descendants of Clovis often desolated some of the fairest regions of France. A Theudebert or Chlothar at the head of a tumultuary host, controlled by no regular discipline and supporting itself by plunder, might, for no reason known to the country folk, burst on the corn-lands and vineyards of Rheims or Tours or Angoulême,

burning and slaying without mercy. Or a count, on the pretence
of collecting the taxes, might on a smaller scale desolate many
homes. But plague and famine were sometimes more terrible
and unnerving than any ravages. After all, a Merovingian army
could only desolate a narrow track on its march. Murrain and
famine could levy their toll on the remotest homesteads of a
wide district. Cattle plague was extremely virulent on the
lands around Tours, and farmers used to take the oil from the
lamps of the church to rub it as a charm on the heads and backs
of their cattle. A similar plague raged among the horses on
S. Martin's estates at Bordeaux, and was only stayed by a vow
of one-tenth of their number which were branded with the sign
of the saint. In times when inland transport was difficult,
famine was always a possible danger. It threatened great
estates in Gregory's time, as it had been dreaded in the days of
Ausonius. In the reign of the Burgundian Chilperic II. the people
in the Jura had only fifteen days' supply of corn for three
months remaining till the harvest. The monks of Condatisco were
compelled by sheer want to appeal to the King for aid. In the
year 585, probably as a consequence of the ravages and confusion of the Gundobaldian war, a severe scarcity prevailed over
a great part of Gaul. People were reduced to the most unwholesome substitutes for food. Roots, grape-stones, fern seeds, and
nuts were pounded up and mixed with a small modicum of
flour for bread. Multitudes died of sheer starvation. Merchants,
as in our own day, drew a cruel spoil from the public
necessities. Numbers of the very poor surrendered themselves
to slavery to obtain a dole of food.

The poverty of that age seems to have been appalling. The
most lavish rhetoric could hardly exaggerate the pinching want
which afflicted an immense mass of the population. It meets
our eyes on nearly every page of the saints' Lives, and in the
Acts of the councils of the Church. Incessant wars, devastating
vast regions, must have often reduced to beggary the humbler
country folk, or thrown them into captivity. There was hardly
any organised industry except agriculture, and that was concentrated on great villae with their coloni and serfs. Our great
towns indeed have their sombre and menacing crowd of the
unemployed. But modern cities provide in their factories and
warerooms a livelihood for the far larger crowd of a growing

population, who can no longer find subsistence in rural labour. And legislative effort or private munificence never fail to respond to the call of charity. But the Frank government had no machinery, even if it had had the will, to meet the calls of pauperism, unless some charitable monarch, *pro remedio animae*, assigned a villa or created a foundation for purposes of charitable relief. And private charity had not far to look for objects of its bounty. Helpless indigence was on every side calling for relief. Poor paralytics, who out of their little property had one ox left, would be drawn along the roads of Touraine asking for alms. Beggar caravans moved about the country, sometimes carrying with them a crippled or monstrous child to evoke greater pity. Or professional beggars went their rounds, armed perhaps with a letter of recommendation from a bishop. The cloisters of S. Julian at Brioude were thronged on days of high festival by the blind, the lame, the paralysed, not only to obtain healing but to beg for alms. Similar scenes might be witnessed every day in the courts of S. Martin at Tours. Every much frequented shrine was probably surrounded by a crowd of mendicants depending on casual charity. And attached to the greater churches there was, as we shall see in another chapter, an organised body of dependents. They were formally enrolled and received regular doles from the corporate revenues, and even lived together in a hospice provided for them. Special endowments were sometimes left for their " refreshment ", as in the will of S. Rémi or the foundation deeds of S. Denis by King Dagobert. And in some places the alms of the faithful were collected and distributed by persons appointed for the purpose. There were also hospices (Xenodochia) for sick and distressed foreigners, such as that established at Lyons by the piety of Childebert I. and his Queen Ultrogotho, and specially guarded against spoliation by the Council of Orleans in 549. And, as in the Theodosian Code, it was ordered by the same council that the archdeacon, or other leading churchman, should visit the jails on the Lord's Day, and see that the prisoners were supplied with necessaries. The councils also urge on the faithful the duty of devoting one-tenth of their possessions to charitable works, " if they wish for the remission of their sins and to be received into Abraham's bosom ". It is also laid down as a binding duty of each civic community to feed its own poor, and to rescue them

from a life of vagrancy. Bishops are charged to provide the
lepers of their dioceses with food and raiment, that they may not
be forced to wander abroad and spread the taint of their disease.
Agricola, a pious and ascetic Bishop of Chalon-sur-Saône, who
had built many churches, also erected a hospital for lepers outside his episcopal city. Another bishop, at the beginning of the
seventh century, S. Arnulfus, was famous for his charity, especially to those stricken with loathsome disease.

One is tempted to linger for a moment on a life which has
a charm of spiritual romance. Born in the highest rank, and
admitted in early youth to high place at the court of Theudebert
and Chlothar II., Arnulfus cherished an ascetic piety amid all
the temptations of pleasure and ambition, and was called by the
popular voice to the see of Metz. Troops of the poor gathered
round him, and men from foreign lands always found in him a
willing host and protector. He parted with his wealth, and even
with royal presents, to succour them. But the passion for the
solitary life of prayer was strong within him, and again and
again he was only chained to his office by the threats or entreaties of the King. At last his own will prevailed, and he went
forth to his chosen solitude amid the tears and laments of
orphans and widows, of the lame and the blind and the leper,
whom he had provided for and comforted. Even in his woodland
retreat he did not relax his care of these tortured outcasts,
tending and bathing them, and cooking their food. He was laid
to rest in the church of Metz, and we shall not too harshly
judge the tales of the virtue issuing from his tomb. The overwhelming misery of the time called forth an extraordinary
passion of pity. In spite of the grossness and cruel selfishness
in high places, many of the most delicately nurtured and well
endowed were ready to obey the command to " sell all that
they had " for the poor and afflicted, and to minister to the
diseased in the most loathsome offices. Queen Radegund, when
she forsook the palace of Chlothar for the convent at Poitiers,
would on Sundays gather in the filthy and diseased, cleanse them
with her own hands in a luxurious bath, apply unguents to their
festering sores, revive them with delicate meats, and give them
fresh garments for their foul rags. Chlothilde, the wife of Clovis,
expended her wealth on similar deeds of mercy, while she herself
wore the coarsest fabrics and, in her later days, lived on hermit's

fare of bread and herbs. Such overflowing pity and self-sacrifice for the weak and miserable would excite boundless admiration if the theology of that time would allow us to give vent to our feelings. But with that baleful tendency which theology, as opposed to real religion, has always shown to distort and degrade the divinest instincts in the interest of dogma, those deeds of love and pity were described or recommended as "*opes promissae*", a treasure laid up in the other world, a kind of spiritual insurance against the terrors of the Great Judgement. Of a surety, the motives of men's best deeds are often mixed. Yet we would fain believe that a theology of spiritual selfishness does not hold the key to the secret of those rare godlike natures who from age to age redeem our poor average humanity from dull mediocrity. For the great mass, however, loaded with sin, yet firmly believing in all they were told of endless bliss or torment in the world to come, the principle of *date et dabitur* was an easy solution of moral questionings.

If one may believe the records of that time, disease of every kind was more rife than even in the noisome and neglected slums of some of our great industrial cities. It is probable that in both towns and country places the laws of health as to food and air and water were then unknown or defied. It is also probable, from the prevalence of certain maladies believed to be specially hereditary, that disease was often due to constant inbreeding. It is curious to notice how often the acts of Councils in that century prohibit the marriage of near relations. These incestuous unions, as they were called, were heavily punished ; yet the constant iteration of ecclesiastical censure plainly shows that it was as constantly set at naught. A little imagination may help us to realise the cause of this. The rural population was generally grouped in little communities gathered round the great house or villa, like the manorial communities in mediaeval England. They were often isolated by great stretches of trackless moor and forest, and distance, combined with the necessity of daily toil, probably made intercourse with any but immediate neighbours difficult and infrequent. Thus nuptial choice was very restricted; a young man, with no other chance of marriage, might cast his eyes on his cousin, his sister-in-law, or even his aunt or widowed stepmother, and persuade an ignorant rural priest, in defiance of the canons, to unite them with the blessings

s

of the Church. Thus any morbid taint which, physicians tell us, is often neutralised by the blood of a healthy stock, would be rendered more virulent and break out in protean forms. At the same time it is to be remembered that most of the records from which our information is drawn, are tales of miraculous cure to glorify the virtues of a saint, and the tale of miracle is generally a tale of disease. Faith in supernatural cure was universal ; every afflicted sufferer sought the shrines from which it flowed ; the cases were elaborated by superstitious fancy and were the staple of gossip in the country-side, in the bishop's house after dinner, or in the hall of the monastery. Then collected and put in writing by an enthusiastic brother, they give the modern reader the impression of an extraordinary prevalence of disease.

It would be an endless and fruitless task to enumerate the cases which have been collected by Gregory in his four books on the miracles of S. Martin. The courts of S. Martin's great church, crowded day and night with people suffering from every kind of disease, must have been really a great hospital for faith-healing. The bishop, with such scenes constantly before his eyes, and receiving constant reports from his deacons and vergers of marvellous cures, acquired an almost medical interest in the history and symptoms of disease, and his descriptions of them often strike one as singularly minute and faithful. Neuralgia, gout, fever of many kinds, renal disease and dysentery, apoplexy and paralysis, smallpox, epilepsy, and sudden insanity—a ghastly company were there gathered to await the healing virtue of the saint's tomb. Gregory had finished 59 sections of his second book when his own case provided him with a painful subject. He was seized evidently with the most acute neuralgia in eyes and temples, which he describes very vividly. It seems to have lasted for many days, in spite of frequent touches of the sacred pall, and to have been aggravated by a faithless thought of seeking ordinary medical aid. Gout appears to have been common. Dysentery and fever of all kinds, of course, as we should expect, were extremely common. But far the most frequent afflictions are blindness and paralysis, which were often supposed to come suddenly as the penalty for sin or impiety. Fortunately the palsy frequently yielded to the influence of faith and long devotion. The horrors of smallpox were only too

well known, and are depicted by Gregory with painful vividness.
Many poor wretches were said to have been suddenly deprived
of sense and reason either by the shock of a ghostly apparition,
or of the dreaded " noonday daemon ", or by the more intelligible
cause of vicious excess. We hear also of renal disease, cured or
relieved by a seven days' fast before the altar, of dropsy and
stone, yielding to a saint's touch. Probably the most common,
and certainly the most distressing, malady of all was epilepsy,
the symptoms of which cannot be mistaken in Gregory. That
saddest of all human ills—the parent of so many others, moral
or physical—seems to furnish the most probable explanation of
endless cases of demoniac possession, which exercised the powers
of the saints. The demon was often a very real physical one,
born of morbid nerves and perverted moral sense, along with a
weird and almost preternatural acuteness of perception, amount-
ing almost to telepathy—especially a thrilling sense of terror
at the approach of purity and holiness. The awful secret
must be left to the modern scientific successors of S. Julian or
S. Martin, who devote themselves with pious skill to the care of
the energumens of our own time.

But these manifold diseases seemed to fade before the terrors
of the bubonic plague, which swept over Gaul and Italy at short
intervals for fifty-two years. Its symptoms would seem to
resemble those of the pestilence described by Thucydides, and,
like it, it took its rise on the banks of the Nile, spread over Syria,
Persia, and India, then passed from Constantinople to the ports
of North Africa, and thence to Spain, Italy, and Gaul. Again
and again Gregory pauses in his Chronicle to describe the recurring onslaughts of the pestilence. It profoundly affected the
imaginations of men, and many tales were afloat in Gregory's
youth of the signs which heralded or accompanied its onsets.
For sixty days a sullen roar had been heard under a hill which
overhangs the Rhone. Then the mountain mass broke away,
bearing churches and farmsteads along with it, dammed up the
current for a while, till it burst the barrier, and swept down
with desolating force to the walls of Geneva. The rustics of
Auvergne in those days of terror saw three or four suns in the
heavens. A comet blazed across the sky like a fiery sword. On
a day of festival, at the early service, a lark flew into the cathedral
and extinguished all the lights. A few years later strange

sounds ran through all the country-side of Tours, and weird flashes shot across the heavens towards the east. Bordeaux was shaken by an earthquake of such violence that many fled to other cities. The shock extended far into Spain, and from the sides of the Pyrenees great boulders descended on the flocks and villages below. Orleans was desolated by a fire which destroyed all the wealth of the community.

The plague broke out at Arles when Gregory was an infant, and his uncle, Bishop Gallus, was said to have warded it off from Auvergne by reviving the Rogations, with a procession to Brioude, in obedience to an angelic vision. But, a few years afterwards, in the episcopacy of Cautinus, the full force of the visitation was felt in Auvergne. The people fell in legions after two or three days' sickness; the supply of coffins failed, and the corpses were huddled into trenches in a confused mass. There was the same mortality at Bourges and Lyons, Chalon-sur-Saône, and Dijon. On one Sunday 300 corpses were counted on the pavement of S. Peter's in Auvergne. Bishop Cautinus, after flying from place to place to escape the contagion, died like one of the crowd. The good priest Cato, after burying countless dead victims, and saying masses for their souls, died worthily at his post. Gregory, then a young man of thirty, sought the guardianship of S. Julian at Brioude. One of his servants, for whom his fellows had called in the aid of charms and amulets in heathen fashion, perished miserably. Another recovered from the same malady by drinking a potion of the sacred dust.

Six years afterwards the pestilence was raging at Tours and in Burgundy; the sons of King Guntram died of it. In 580 a fell disease, apparently of the type of smallpox, raged over the whole country, and was particularly fatal among children. Two sons of Chilperic fell victims to it. In 584 we hear of its ravages in Spain and Narbonne. The population of Albi was almost wiped out. Soon afterwards a cargo boat from a Spanish port brought fresh contagion in its hold to the quays of Marseilles. One household of eight persons was in a few hours left without a living soul. Thence it spread through Provence, and up the Rhone to Lyons and Metz. Gregory had met near Rheims a traveller from Poitiers who had caught the fatal taint. King Guntram provided for the medical care of sufferers, and while ordering the observance of the Rogations, wisely warned people to eat only wheaten bread, and drink only pure water. In these tales of pestilence, when imagination was on fire, the horrors were probably magnified. There is always a tendency to exaggerate public calamities. Even in our own day, with all the checks from rapid publicity, accurate statistics, and a more sceptical and positive habit of thought, we see the press raising by vivid description mere passing incidents of human life to the measure of desperate catastrophes. The recuperative powers of Nature and of man are so exuberant that they seem able to recover from almost any strain, however exhausting. The devastation of Gaul and Italy by war and pestilence in those years, which might seem likely to reduce prosperous regions to barren wilderness, was rapidly repaired, as the exuberant growths of spring speedily cover up the decay of winter.

To cope with the endless and malignant maladies of the time there would seem to have been an adequate supply of physicians and surgeons even in country districts. In this, the most important of all the professions, the traditions of Roman civilisation were probably maintained unbroken by the invaders. From the time of Clovis to Theuderic II. a line of court physicians can be traced who, although they were sometimes of servile origin, were held in high consideration, and amassed fortunes on the scale of the Stertinii of Naples under the Early Empire. Some of them bore good Roman names, and even the medical title of archiater, which is familiar to the student of the Theodosian Code. Whatever may have been the skill of the doctors in the Merovingian times, they must have had some difficulty in maintaining their position against the marvellous and ever ready healing virtues of the saints, when an educated man like the Bishop of Tours tells us again and again that the supernatural cure is far more to be trusted than any cure by human skill. And indeed medical skill, even apart from such spiritual rivalry, seems to have been often distrusted by the patient. Austrechildis, the fierce queen of Guntram of Burgundy, when she was dying of the plague, attributed her death to the potions of her doctors, and bound her husband by an oath to kill them over her grave. In a terrible outbreak of smallpox at Tours, Gregory alleges that the doctors could do nothing without aid from the blessed tomb.

The bungling operations of oculists for cataract are described contemptuously in the story of a deacon whose sight was for the time restored by long prayer and fasting. The many specialists at Bourges had failed to cure Leonastes the archdeacon, of the same disease. He fasted and prayed for two or three months before the altar of S. Martin and his sight was beginning to return. But, wishing to hasten the process by temporal aid, in an evil hour, he consulted a Jewish oculist, who treated him with cupping. This failure of faith, or change of treatment, was too severely punished by life-long blindness. Tranquillinus, the court physician of Clovis, was baffled in his treatment of a lingering fever which prostrated the great Frank chief for two years. At last he advised that more potent aid should be sought by summoning the Abbot Severinus from his remote monastery of S. Maurice in the Jura. The abbot took leave of his brethren, never to return, and set out on his long journey. He wrapped the suffering king in his chasuble, and the fever left him. But even the most religious sometimes did not neglect the ordinary medical treatment of disease. S. Caesarius had poor health during his monastic life in Lérins, and the abbot sent him to consult the famous doctors of Arles, who inherited the Greek science lingering in that region. That great prelate showed his charity and broad-mindedness in nothing more than in his care for the sick. He founded a hospital with ample endowments, full equipment, and a staff of physicians. One of them, Helpidius, who combined deacon's orders with medical rank, was known in the circle of Cassiodorus as well as at Arles.

The church of a healing saint in the time of the Merovingians might seem to reproduce something of the tone and spirit of a temple of Æsculapius in the reign of the Antonines, except that there is a more orderly calm and more faith in science at Epidaurus than at Tours. The old paganism was still lingering in many places in Gaul. It is well known that the fiercest efforts of the Christian Empire long failed to abolish the performance of heathen rites in country places. They survived the Western Empire for generations, and popular devotion was only slowly weaned from the cult of heathen gods and demons by the cult of saints and martyrs. The councils of the sixth and seventh centuries are still compelled to launch their anathemas against the lingering reverence for stones and trees and fountains, and the practice of the people going out from the mass to offer meat

to idols. The procession of Magna Mater in her car, with
music and dancing in the old fashion among the fields and
vineyards of Autun in the fourth century was abolished by the
zeal of Bishop Simplicius. Gregory the Great found it necessary
to use stern measures to suppress the pagan worship which still
survived in sequestered places in Sicily, Sardinia, and Corsica.
The settlement of Germans in north-east Gaul gave new life to
paganism. In the sixth century the worship of an old Celtic
deity, identified in popular syncretism with Diana, still attracted
crowds of devotees in the region of Trèves. Bishop Gallus,
while still in deacon's orders, destroyed by fire a heathen temple
near Cologne, and hardly escaped the hands of the enraged
rustics who frequented it. At Javols there was a holy lake
where the country people used to come in their waggons to
feast for three days, and make offerings of linen cloth, fleeces,
and images of cheese and wax. At Brivate the sacred herds of
S. Julian are surely descendants of the oxen of the sun. In the
generation before, S. Caesarius had unsparingly denounced the
cult of spirits of the woods and waters, and the more deadly
arts of heathen sorcery.

We have hitherto in this chapter been chiefly occupied with
the country life of Gaul in the century following the fall of
the Empire. The very faintness and dimness of it, relieved
only by momentary flashes on some scene in the woods or a
village street, are tantalising yet pleasant to the historic imagination. For the life in the towns, strange to say, the materials are
even more scanty. From the Breviarium of Alaric it is clear
that in Aquitaine the municipal system of the Empire was still
to a great extent maintained. We find the *curia* and the
duumviri and the *defensores*. But instead of the provincial
magistrates of Imperial times, we find the *Comites*, with extensive
powers in jurisdiction, taxation, and military levies, as we have
seen. But, in matters affecting private life, such as wills,
tutelage, etc., the curia and its officers possessed a wide jurisdiction. And the curia has become more democratic since the
fall of the Imperial system. Its officers no longer wield the
personal authority conceded to the Roman magistrate ; they
now act as delegates of the curial body. In case of an alleged
crime, the accused is tried by five persons of his own class
designated by lot. The curia under the later Empire became

almost an *ergastulum* of slaves of the Imperial treasury, liable
personally for the taxes of the district. The liabilities were so
serious that men would fly to any refuge in order to escape
from them. In the sixth century, on the contrary, there are
indications that men of old senatorial family were proud to
belong to the local senate, whose functions had ceased to involve
ruinous obligations, and indeed conferred some power and dignity
under the new régime. The curia became in one sense more
democratic, more representative of the whole urban life. Its
numbers were no longer limited : the property qualification was
abolished. On the other hand, it included all men of high rank
and importance, and it decorated its magistrates with pompous
titles of the Empire. Simple decurions are styled *clarissimi*.
The curia of Vienne is *sacer senatus* : the town of Angers has its
magister militum.

Gallo-Roman society, in the wreck of provincial government,
as it had existed under the Empire, seemed to gather up and
concentrate what remained of its social life in its great urban
centres. It is clear that the cities of Provence and Aquitaine
were strongly fortified, and had little to fear except from treachery
within their walls. In the desolating invasion of Guntram's
army in 586 they were amply provisioned against a siege, and
the tumultuary army spent its force in burning the crops and
stubbing out the olive trees and vines. When the pretender
Gundobald fell back on the fortress of Convenae in the Pyrenees,
it seemed prepared to resist any assault. Built on an isolated
hill, it had a tunnel to the foot of it by which the garrison
obtained an unfailing supply of water, while the magazines were
well stocked with provisions. Gregory gives a most careful
description of the fortifications of Dijon, the town which was
the favourite seat of his ancestor, Bishop Gregory of Langres.
It was strongly fortified with walls fifteen feet in thickness and
thirty feet high, pierced like old Roman camps by four gates.
This fortress, erected by the Emperor Aurelian, towered over a
plain of marvellous fertility, and its vineyards on the western
slopes yielded a liquor which surpassed the most famous vintages
of Italy or the East. Two streams running beneath the walls
gave an unfailing supply of water. This minute and enthusiastic
description of an ancient town—linking the Empire with the
early Middle Ages, is the tribute of the Bishop of Tours to an

ancestor who, as noble and bishop, had seen the reign of the Emperor Valentinian III., and the accession of a grandson of Clovis. The Gallic towns had not only to withstand the attacks of Frank armies, but they sometimes levied war on one another. And some cities in Aquitaine were able to put considerable armies in the field. Thus, in 584, the forces of Blois and Orleans made a combined attack on Chateaudun, plundered and burnt the homesteads of the district, and carried off the flocks and movable property from the fields. The raid was retaliated with equal fierceness and awful devastation. In the disastrous conflicts of 584 the cities of Tours and Poitiers wished to be included in the realm of Childebert of Austrasia. But the city of Bourges, which seems to have been able to send as many as 15,000 fighting men into the field, mustered its forces in the cause of Guntram. There appears to have been a bitter and lasting feud between Tours and Bourges, and the army of Bourges burst into the lands of their enemies, burning and devastating, and not even sparing the churches. The ravages were so appalling that the authorities of Tours sent envoys to buy off the attack by submission to the King of Burgundy. These civic armies along the Loire must have been composed chiefly of Gallo-Romans whose ancestors a hundred years before, in the face of the invasion, had left their defence to captains like Aetius, in command of German mercenaries, including the Franks who were now masters of Gaul.

The great towns, and especially Paris, have their broad squares lined with shops and booths. One small place at the foot of the Pyrenees is said to have been crowded with shops, all belonging to one merchant. We are permitted to witness some striking scenes in the streets of Paris in the reign of Chilperic and Fredegundis. In the year 583, the Count Leudastes, having incurred the enmity of Fredegundis, presented himself in Paris, and flung himself at her feet in church while Mass was being celebrated. She repelled him with tears and curses. When the service was over, although he might have known that his doom was sealed, with incredible levity he strolled along the shops and booths, turning over curious wares, pricing silver plate, and noting articles for purchase. Suddenly the queen's servants burst upon him, and, although he defended himself, he received

deadly wounds in the head ; and, in crossing a bridge over the
Seine, his leg was broken by slipping between the planks. By a
special order to the doctors his life was cruelly prolonged for
the most hideous torture that could be devised.

Sometimes the scenes are more gay and pleasant. We may
be sure there was many a brilliant procession, such as that
which escorted Guntram through the streets of Orleans in 585,
with ensigns and banners, and singing hymns in Latin or Syriac.
Or a Merovingian queen might be seen riding in gorgeous attire
to Mass, with a train of courtiers. But we cannot help feeling
that the squalor and filth and prevailing poverty must have
thrown a deep shadow over the gleams of an occasional tawdry
splendour. City life was exposed to many dangers which are
now warded off or greatly mitigated. The absence of sanitary
precautions made the ever-recurring plagues of the sixth century
a constant terror even to the Court. Three young princes died
within a few months, victims probably of the foul exhalations
of the Seine. Fires also seem to have been common. The
buildings of the time were for the most part of wood—light,
frail structures which were easily inflammable, and which must
have speedily succumbed to fire. In the large towns, the
monasteries, and country houses, fires were frequent and often
disastrous. Any organisation for extinguishing them by human
skill was apparently unknown, but as the outbreak was so often
due to the devices of the Evil One, so it was constantly checked
by the prayer or virtue of some saintly person. By such means
S. Caesarius had once the glory of saving the city of Bordeaux
from the flames during his exile there. At another time the
convent which he had founded on the outskirts of Arles was
threatened with total destruction, and the nuns were panic-
stricken, when S. Caesarius averted the danger by appearing
suddenly. The convent of Nivelles, where a sudden conflagration had driven the nuns from the building, was saved by the
apparition of S. Gertrude, waving her veil over the flames. The
monastery of S. Claude, which was constructed entirely of wood,
was burnt down in a single night, the only thing saved being a
cruse of S. Martin's oil which a priest kept hanging at the head
of his couch. We hear of great fires in those years at Poitiers.
Bordeaux, Clermont, and in the palace at Metz. In the Life of
S. Leobinus we see the houses built close to one of the bridges of

Paris all ablaze, and the inhabitants vainly striving to quench the flames with the water from the Seine.   An even more vivid scene is sketched by Gregory in the year 586, evidently drawn from the description of one present at the fire.   A wise woman had for some time warned the Parisians to fly from the city ; they only mocked her as a vain sorceress, or one deluded by the "noonday demon" ("*daemon meridianus*") ; but she told them that she had seen a vision of one coming from the church of S. Vincent, taper in hand, and setting fire one after another to the merchants' houses.   On the third night after this prophecy, at dusk, a citizen whose house was next to one of the city gates, went to his store-room for oil, and left a lamp burning beside a cask.   It caught fire, the house was soon in a blaze, and the neighbouring buildings were speedily caught by the flames.   Fanned by a high wind which was blowing at the time, the conflagration swept across the city to the opposite gate, where an oratory had been built to S. Martin, on the spot where he had once healed a leper.   A citizen had replaced the rude wooden shrine by a more imposing building, and now, trusting either to its solid structure, or, as Gregory thought, to the power of S. Martin, the founder betook himself to its shelter with all his valuables.   The flames drew near, and soon the chapel oratory was apparently buried in sheets of fire and falling ashes.   The excited people called to its inmates to escape from destruction.   But the women calmly looked from the windows which the fire could not enter, and the oratory and surrounding houses and all the churches escaped by a marvel.   Thirty years before, in 558, the city of Tours was destroyed by fire, and all its churches were left in ruins.

To some critical readers, the facts of common life collected in this chapter will seem trivial and even worthless.   They will not be regarded as history at all.   The period is certainly not a very interesting one when compared with great ages of political reconstruction or artistic effort, affecting the whole future of European civilisation.   Yet in that period so undistinguished by great characters and momentous events, one may be pardoned for thinking that the social condition of the masses is more important and interesting than the bewildering and aimless feuds and campaigns of the Merovingian kings.

CHAPTER III

MORALS

It is a precarious task to estimate with any accuracy the general moral tone of any time, even the nearest to ourselves. There is no uniformity in the moral condition of any age which justifies the sweeping dogmatic generalisations which are so often delivered, not only by the half educated gossip but by highly trained historians. There are always the widest differences, both in external fortune and moral tone, among various social grades, which render any moral estimate of the combined aggregate precarious or futile. If this be true of any contemporary society how much truer must it be of a society separated from us, not only by many centuries, but by immense historic convulsions and changes of ethical sentiment. Moreover, the records of such a distant period are often fragmentary, imperfect, even contradictory. And the chronicler who, in all good faith, has tried to transmit to posterity a picture of his time, may have unconsciously yielded to the partialities or prejudices of his class. Moreover, the social outlook of every observer is necessarily limited, especially in ages when information is chiefly oral, and often accidental, the offspring of gossip, and not drawn from written records. And in every age the vices of society attract more attention than its quiet virtues ; and the audacity of crime and self-indulgence, from the very fact of their being startling exceptions to general conformity to moral rule, is apt to throw into the shade the more orderly life of the mass of men who, in every age, are saved from temptation to excess by the sobriety of family life and the call of industry.

The chroniclers of the sixth century were churchmen at a

time when the ascetic ideal was at its height. They judged their age, if sometimes with a curious indulgence to the great, yet by a standard which might bear hard on modern times.

Gregory of Tours, although the comparison is too flattering, may be called the Herodotus of the Middle Ages, and has many of the faults, and some of the merits, of his great predecessor. They are both raconteurs and fond of a lively tale. They are both, though in different degrees, credulous and not very careful in weighing the value of evidence for facts which they record. Gregory, like Herodotus, must have taken enormous pains in collecting evidence from all quarters, the gossip of court circles at Metz, or Soissons, or Paris, the tales of miracle or crime which beguiled the dullness of the monastery or the bishop's hall in the evening hours, the talk of Spanish or Italian envoys and travellers passing through Tours on their way to the North. The gathering of bishops at the councils must, from the record of their acts, have furnished Gregory with many facts about the life of the people all over Gaul. His ancestral connexion with the higher Gallo-Roman society, and many great ecclesiastics in Auvergne and Burgundy, is the undoubted source of minute and invaluable pictures of social life, of crime and tragedy ; and he has undoubtedly preserved for us facts and social traditions for which we cannot be too grateful. Yet, just as Herodotus often moulded his narrative under the influence of a religious theory of the government of the world and of human destiny, so the Bishop of Tours could not escape from the overmastering spirit of his caste and time. He lent an indulgent credence to the gossip about wondrous cures and signs and prodigies which poured in upon him from the vergers and minor clergy of S. Julian's and S. Martin's, or from the hermitages in the woods of the Jura or Auvergne. His motto in such divine things was " Beati qui non viderunt et crediderunt ". That is his simple canon in dealing with the mysterious and supernatural. Occasionally, where the Church and the world of the unseen were not concerned, Gregory could be calm and impartial according to his lights, even critical. But his overpowering belief in the imperial authority of the Church, and in the sacrosanct mission of her ministers, seems often to deflect his judgement from the line of impartial criticism. He can veil or condone the gravest faults or vices in a staunch champion of the Church. He could be stern to any one who invaded her rights, or showed less than due respect to her mysterious powers. In his carefully drawn character of Chilperic, one can see the vengeance of the Church damning to infamy the man who dared to denounce the pride, and luxury, and vanity of the higher clergy, and the greed of the Church in sweeping bequests into her coffers. He is sent down to posterity as luxurious, lewd, and cruel, but the charges are suspiciously connected with others of having defamed the priests of God, and invalidated wills in favour of the Church. Yet it is fair to say that Gregory often lays bare the crimes and self-indulgence of the ordinary clergy in a fashion which excites at once astonishment at his candour and respect for his honesty. As to ordinary lay society, outside the circle of strictly pious and ascetic people, Gregory is evidently a pessimist. The tale of the doom which in a vision he once saw overhanging the house of the Merovingians, the vivid report of the rapine, outrage, and defiance of all moral order which the dukes of Guntram's army made to the king after their campaign in the south, reveal the bishop's anxiety as to the moral condition of his time. It is only relieved for him by the many saintly lives he has chronicled of those who forsook all for Christ. Yet, in spite of the saintly vision, Gregory is keenly alive to the sin and tragedy and shame of his time—the tale of lawless love and shattered nuptial happiness, the shameless perfidy and defiance of God in the broken oath, the recurring violence of the unending blood feud, the bloody raid on the lonely country house, the stealthy onset with poisoned daggers by bravoes primed for their task with a witch's potion. These things, and many others like them, struck the imagination of the bishop, and he determined to preserve the picture for coming ages.

In his vivid Life of S. Patroclus of Colombier, to which reference has been made in a previous chapter, Gregory sketches the pessimist or ascetic view of a world lying in wickedness, as the saint saw it in his vision from the pillar. A similar attitude is that of the Bishop Nicetius in another tale.

On a Sunday in the year 534 the young Theudebert, who had just succeeded his father Theuderic, came to attend Mass in the cathedral of Trèves with a train of courtiers, some of whom had been debarred from communion for their evil lives. Bishop Nicetius was present, who had been a stern abbot and was a fearless preacher, never mincing his words in the presence of any one, however powerful. He had been esteemed and honoured by Theuderic, although the bishop had often publicly rebuked him for his vices. He did not hesitate once to excommunicate a band of courtiers who turned their horses loose in the cornfield of a poor farmer. On this occasion, after the Gospel, he announced that the Mass would not be celebrated, unless all excommunicated persons would retire. When the king remonstrated with him, a youth possessed by a demon broke out with a loud voice, and denounced Theudebert as an adulterer. The king, whose nerves were shaken, demanded the expulsion of such a dangerously outspoken person, and the bishop replied that the murderers, the adulterers, and incestuous persons in the king's train must first withdraw from the Holy Mysteries, and the king at last ordered them to do so. Again and again in those days the great bishop denounced from the pulpit the enormities of the time, and actually debarred King Chlothar from communion. His brother prelates, who, like many ecclesiastics in every age, regarded cautious opportunism as a duty to the interests of the Church, could not approve of such imprudent frankness, and Nicetius, left alone, had to go into exile till the accession of the generous Sigibert.

That voice from the altar of Trèves, there can be no doubt, was the voice of a great body of sober opinion, which condemned such scandalous lives as sincerely as Patroclus and Nicetius. The simple rustics, who flocked around a holy anchoret in the wilderness, attracted by his sanctity, we may be sure looked with little indulgence on the wild excesses of those of higher station. And even Gregory and the authors of the Lives of the Saints reveal a different tone prevailing among large numbers of the upper class themselves. There is the same contrast in the fifth century. Salvian, preaching from the text that the Roman world had perished through its vices, describes the life of Aquitaine as one of universal and shameless sensuality. Sidonius Apollinaris about the same time has left a picture of his class, devoted to a decadent literary ideal, but to all appearance generally free from gross vice. And here and there he shows us a great house whose master knows how to reconcile stately fortune with the quietism of a secluded spiritual life, such as S. Jerome had fostered in senatorial houses on the Esquiline before he retired to Bethlehem. There can be no doubt that, from the days of S. Martin a new spiritual ideal had cast its spell on many families of the higher class, and the movement had received a great impetus towards the end of the fifth century. Traditions of dim, saintly lives still floated over tombs buried in the woods of Auvergne in the youth of Gregory. This tradition of unworldly sanctity failed not in the sixth century. The Lives of the Saints are constantly disfigured by an unctuous and conventional tone. And yet, here and there, and not infrequently, they give us naturally and unconsciously the traits of a class obscure from their very virtues. These Lives in fact are invaluable to the student of secular society. For they offer us glimpses, here and there, of the life of a class on quiet estates in Burgundy or Touraine or Aquitaine, which stand out in startling contrast with the greed and luxury, the audacious violence or cynical perfidy of kings and courtiers which shock us in the pages of Gregory. The saints and bishops are often sprung from old senatorial or well-to-do families, living on some rural estate whose vineyards and cornlands are cultivated by serfs or freedmen. The tone of the household is as a rule devoutly Christian with a tendency to ascetic quietism. There is an oratory or private chapel where the chatelaine will spend hours of devotion, often far into the night. Her son is carefully trained from infancy in the Scriptures and in habits of devotion. He is sent to the neighbouring school, where he is imbued with the fast-fading tradition of Gallo-Roman culture. His father or grandfather may have been count of the district, and have been a courtier for a time, and the family may have wished the boy to follow a similar career, for, in such circles, public ambition was not at all incompatible with deep spirituality. The boy would be commended by powerful patronage to the Palatine service at Metz or Soissons, and for a few years he would have a training in official and courtly arts. So Aridius, the famous saint and abbot of Limoges, the friend of Gregory and Fortunatus, had risen to high favour and influence at the court of Theudebert. When the young courtier returned to his home, old family tradition would require that the hope of the house should marry and prolong its dignity. But to the grief of many a pious mother in that age, the young man, in spite of courtly training and aristocratic associations, had often caught a mysterious passion for secluded sanctity which rejected with scorn the counsels of affectionate worldliness. And one day he would disappear to bury himself in some secret glade in the forests of the Jura or Le Perche. Sometimes, even after he had received Holy Orders, he might for a time live on the paternal estate, working his lands with the serfs, and training their children to read and sing the Psalms. In the end he might found a religious house, and some of his pupils would take monastic vows. And often his mother, who had lost husband and son, with perhaps as pure a devotion, in her old age, would carry on the management of the estate, and tend her olives and vines to provide a revenue for the new foundation of her son. It is this class, with the proud and wholesome tradition of Roman family life, now warmed and inspired by Christian ideals, who were the salt of Gallo-Roman society, and saved it from ruin.

But the chronicles of the time offer to our eyes generally a very different picture, which confirms the pessimism of Patroclus from his pillar, or the sermons of Nicetius. It has been thought by some that these charges are directed against the conquering Franks. The question of the relative guilt of Frank and Gallo-Roman for the moral declension of the time is complicated and difficult. Gregory seldom gives any express indication of the nationality of the great actors or great criminals on his scene, and we have often to fall back on the evidence of the name. It is unlikely that Gallo-Romans of any rank assumed Frank names, although one or two instances occur where they did. On the other hand, we know that, in some cases, although probably not many, Franks adopted a name of Roman form. One of the best known instances is that of the Frank Claudius who was sent by Guntram to lure Eberulfus from asylum at Tours. In a list of those who appear in Gregory's pages as guilty of heinous deeds, it is calculated that the Roman names are about equal to the German. There is no proof that the Frank nobles were more demoralised than the corresponding class in Gallo-Roman society. In the higher ranks, a period of great change and convulsion had left its mark on both : both Frank and Roman character have been altered for the worse in opposite directions. The Frank warrior, in the three generations following the conquest, has lost some of his military virtue, and grown more cruel and faithless, and fonder of gold and luxury. On the

T

other hand, the Gallo-Roman of the highest rank, drawn into the circle of the court from early youth, or associating with Frank neighbours in the country, has lost something of the mild, peaceful culture of his ancestors, and become more ready for adventure, more fierce and daring. The change in the Frank character, which for centuries had been affected by such various influences, was probably more profound and complete. Long wanderings between the Euxine and the Channel, mercenary service in the Roman armies, in which their chiefs often rose to high command, and, in the end, the excitement of becoming masters of the fairest regions of the west, must have blurred or effaced many of the lines of old German character as it was known to Caesar and Tacitus. The Gallo-Roman character had come under influences equally powerful. After generations of the " Roman peace " it must have been rudely shaken by the sweep of great Hun and Vandal and Gothic invasions, by the failure of Imperial force and administration, by dreams of national independence. The unmilitary spirit of the Gallo-Roman population in the fifth century has been perhaps exaggerated. The defence of the capital of Auvergne in a prolonged siege by a mere handful under Ecdicius against the army of the Visigoths was a striking feat of stubborn gallantry. Thirty years later the flower of the Arvernian nobles under a son of Sidonius fell fighting for Alaric the Visigoth at the battle of Vouglé. Romans in increasing numbers, as the century went on, must have swelled the Frank armies in their great expeditions. There must have been thousands of the Gallo-Romans in the great host which invaded Italy under Theudebert in 539, and, in the army of Guntram which swept over Septimania forty years later, when Mummolus, a great Roman commander, defeated the invading Lombards at Embrun, his Burgundian troops were probably in great part of Roman race, with two Roman bishops fighting at their head.

Thinking only of describing the actual life of his time without analysis or attempted theory, Gregory has left unanswered a number of other questions which excite the curiosity of the modern inquirer. What were the relative numbers of the invaders and of the native race in different parts of Gaul ? What was the relative force in moulding the composite character of the future, of new military strength and spirit, and of social culture and organisation which was the heritage from the Empire ? How far did the conquerors yield to the charm of a civilisation higher than their own ? How far did the conquered submit to the prestige of victory ? How far did Frank and Gallo-Romans melt into one another and coalesce through intermarriage and social intercourse ? It is small blame to the Bishop of Tours that, with his limited training and his anecdotic habit of mind, he never thought of problems which are the most difficult even for men disciplined in historical research. Questions of the influence of race and its permanence admit only the most precarious answer. Climate and tradition and the *genius loci* have a marvellous power of maintaining old types in spite of all mixture of races. The Greeks of the time of Tacitus were a *colluvies nationum* ; they are still more so, after successive invasions, in the present day. Yet the modern Athenian still thinks of himself as inheriting the blood and traditions of the contemporaries of Themistocles and Pericles. The French of our time, at least before the late war, were regarded as reproducing the traits of character by which the Gallic race are described by Roman historians of the early Empire. The companions of Strongbow or the troopers of Cromwell who settled on Irish soil were the ancestors of men who have shown themselves the purest specimens of old Irish character in all its faults and virtues. How can any man, with any scientific assurance, apportion the share in forming the great modern French nation of to-day among its many constituent elements—Iberian, Celtic, Roman, and Teuton ?

Just as Gregory seldom marks distinctions of race, so he never expressly distinguishes, as to tone or preponderance of race, one division of Gaul from another. Yet from early times Iberian, Celtic, and Belgic divisions had been recognised by Roman observers. A generation before the birth of our historian the Visigoths were in occupation from the Loire to the Pyrenees ; the Burgundians along the Rhone and Saône in Provence ; the Franks had overrun the greater part of Celtic Gaul north of the Loire and of Belgic Gaul. Clovis and his sons had, shortly before the birth of Gregory, overrun Aquitaine and Burgundy, and in the partition of the realm of the Merovingians it was divided into the kingdoms of Neustria, Austrasia, and Burgundy. There must have been great differences among these regions in the relative proportion of the two races and in moral tone, which a modern historian would have attempted to seize and to account for. But such questions did not attract the eye of Gregory. Had he been a modern historian, he would have told us of the penetration of Roman language and culture in the north-west. We should have heard of the decided proponderance of the German element on the north-east along the lower Rhine, the Meuse, Moselle, and the Scheldt, where the people had always had Teutonic affinities, and where successive waves of German invaders, including the Salian Franks, had been settled for generations. We should have heard of the extent to which Franks in the sixth century had found a home in Burgundy, in the mountains of Auvergne, and the wealthy plains of Aquitaine.

We hear again and again how the cities of Aquitaine were the splendid prize for which the three rival Frank kingdoms contended with tremendous effort and the most ruthless destruction of life and wealth. From other sources we learn that these regions still retained the deep impress of Roman civilisation. There, in many localities, the municipal system of the Imperial times still to some extent maintained itself; the *curia* still exercised some of its old powers, and attracted to its membership men of the old Gallo-Roman families; and the Aquitanian towns would gladly have been relieved of the yoke of the Merovingians who treated the region as their prey. It seems probable that to the south of the Loire the Franks were only sparsely settled.

At the same time some writers have allowed themselves to be carried too far by the theory that the towns of the south had hardly any Frank inhabitants. Gregory indeed, as we have seen, gives few indications as to difference of race. And yet, even from Gregory, we can see that a certain number of rich and powerful Franks had found their way even to the foot of the Pyrenees. Thus when Chramnus had been sent by his father Chlothar to govern Auvergne, and was entering on a career of reckless and disloyal ambition, we are told that an Arvernian citizen of high position, bearing the German name Ascovindus, strove energetically to restrain him in his evil courses. So Gregory, on his way to the Austrasian court, once met a citizen of Poitiers, named Wiliulfus, who was seized with dysentery in the neighbourhood of Rheims. When the pretender Gundobald, along with the army of Mummolus, was besieged in the Pyrenean stronghold of Convenae, he maintained his troops by means of the resources and stores of one Chariulfus, a Frank merchant of great wealth and influence in the place.

It appears, then, that Gregory treats Gaul from the moral point of view as a whole. The two races are hardly ever distinguished, still less contrasted. Nor is there any indication that regions with such various history, and people with various elements, had, to his eye, developed special and peculiar moral characteristics, except, perhaps, in the intrigues and fierce self-assertion of Austrasian nobles in the long minority of Childebert II. and his sons, when they challenged and harassed Brunihildis as the guardian of the rights of royalty. The conquerors and the conquered from the time of Clovis are not seen in any fierce rivalry or racial discord ; on the contrary, they are tending to coalesce. Already in the days of Sidonius, Romans of rank, like a Syagrius, had mastered the speech of their German neighbours or " guests ", although the Bishop of Auvergne betrays a fastidious scorn for the coarse manners of the barbarians of six feet, who grease their hair and talk with such strident voices. On the other hand, the Visigothic King Theodoric II., in the dignity and refinement of his court and personal bearing, shows the enduring influence of Roman culture. The Roman gentlemen of the sixth century might perhaps still find the Frank tone and manners jarring somewhat on their taste, but the difference of language was rapidly vanishing.

The conquerors found themselves obliged to learn the language of the conquered population. In the fifth century Latin had become the language of public documents and administration at the Visigothic and Burgundian courts. Euric employed a Latin secretary. Gundobad of Burgundy, who had lived long under Ricimer at Rome, must certainly have spoken Latin. Theodoric II., the great King of the Visigoths, we are told, was a lover of Virgil. It is equally certain that the early Frank kings, employing Romans in administration, and surrounded by Romans of high rank, must soon have adopted Latin as the language of the court. Chilperic paraded his love of Roman culture, added letters to the alphabet, and wrote feeble imitations of Sedulius. The Frank nobles of course followed the example of the court. In an epitaph on a Frank lady of Paris, Fortunatus celebrates

her as the mild daughter of a fierce stock, who, in spite of her
barbarian origin, was Roman in tone and culture.   In the
greater part of Gaul in the fifth century, even many of the
common people must have known Latin or they could not have
followed addresses from the pulpit, such as that which Sidonius
delivered at an episcopal election to a congregation at Bourges.
In the sixth century the mass of the Franks would be compelled by the necessities of business and social life to adopt the
language of a population which immensely outnumbered them.
The tendency would be made imperative by the use of Latin in
all public documents, in the services of the Church and addresses
from the pulpit, and in the judicial proceedings before the court
in every provincial town.

Intermarriage between the two races had at one time been
forbidden both by the Roman and the German codes.   Yet the
example of the Frank chief Bauto, who was the father of the
Empress Eudoxia, must have helped to break down the social
barriers which parted Frank and Roman at the altar.   It is
hard to believe that the son of a great Roman house who had
risen to high favour at the court of Soissons or Metz would
not often win the hand of a Frank girl.   Love and romance, all
the world over, are more powerful than any barriers of caste
and race.

Thus although the social scene in the sixth century may
seem at times confused, its apparently discordant elements are
blending into a sort of unity.   Men of mark and promise, of both
races, are meeting at court and combining in service and counsel.
The meaner sort are mingling in the markets, the law courts,
and the churches, or fighting and plundering side by side in Italy
or Aquitaine.   If Franks often held the great dukedoms, Gallo-
Romans generally held the more important office of the great
bishoprics.   The conflict is not one of race but of ideals, a
contrast which is often seen in the same family.   Worldly
ambition, greed, violence, and vice are seen side by side with
humble piety, with mystical devotion, or an almost inhuman
asceticism.   The ideals of the Church are seen in continual
conflict with vices which never die out, and all the wild disorders
generated in an age of conquest and change.   And in reading
the frequent tales of lawless love, of perfidy, deceit, or violence,
we should remember the hidden life of old Roman gravity and

sobriety, or the painful striving for the citizenship of another
world.

Yet the moral picture of the Merovingian age is often truly
appalling. The crimes and excesses we shall have to notice
must have been to some extent stimulated by the evil example
of the sons and grandsons of Clovis. It is not necessary to
accept without reserve all the tales of depravity which cast a
deep shadow on the Merovingian race. The sons of the conqueror who had in twenty years brought under his sway some of
the richest regions of the west, and who wielded autocratic and
unlimited power, were exposed to temptations that would have
tried the most disciplined virtue. Their lives were certainly far
from immaculate ; but malignant gossip may have exaggerated
their corruption. They were at any rate not weak and effeminate.
They were engaged in constant wars in the heart of Germany,
in Burgundy, Aquitaine, Italy, and Spain, and, like their father,
fought at the head of tumultuary armies who were not easy to
control. Theuderic I., from his capital at Rheims, had to guard
the eastern frontier, and fought in two great campaigns against
the Thuringi, in battles so fierce that it is said the rivers were
choked with corpses. His brother Chlothar shared the labour
and peril of the second campaign. Chlodomer of Orleans fell in
the thick of battle with the Burgundians. Between 531 and
534 there were four great expeditions led by the Frank kings.
In the first, King Childebert attacked the Visigoths in Septimania, led a Frank force for the first time across the Pyrenees,
and carried his ravages up to the walls of Barcelona. Whatever
their vices may have been, men who could control vast armies,
and who personally led their troops in march and battle from
the Thuringian forests to the heart of Spain, cannot have been
mere degenerates and voluptuaries. And there is in some cases
a conflict of evidence as to their character. Venantius Fortunatus
was, it is true, a literary adventurer, who in his tours throughout
Gaul probably repaid hospitable reception with the flattery of
the most polished verse which a decadent tradition could still
yield. Yet even a literary adventurer, for his own sake, cannot
venture to be absolutely untrue to fact. Fortunatus wrote for
the eyes of men who were shrewd men of the world and knew
the secrets of court life. Yet in several cases he does not hesitate
to attribute great virtues and fine qualities to princes whom

Gregory has condemned to infamy. In Gregory, King Charibert is one of the most abandoned of his line, lewd of life, insulting his queen by amours with slave girls, adding a nun to his harem, defying priests and bishops, and laying violent hands on the estates of the Church. In one of his most elaborate poems, Fortunatus depicts him as a model of all royal virtue, a mild and equitable ruler, dispensing justice with an even hand, surpassing even Romans in command of Roman eloquence. So the courtly poet celebrates Childebert as a Melchisedek, both king and priest, who adorned a church at Paris with marble columns and gold and gems. He once gave 6000 *solidi* to S. Germanus for the poor. He was the friend of great saints famous in their day, Paternus and Leobinus, and visited an old bishop of Lyons on his deathbed, the succession to whom the king promised to Bishop Nicetius on the ground of his charity and virtue. In the second generation Chilperic and, stranger still, Queen Fredegundis, are endowed by the poet with every virtue. The king is a great warrior, dreaded by Goth and Dane and Saxon, and a judge of unswerving equity. His literary taste and skill are equal to his prowess. And Fredegundis, who shares the tasks of government, is sage and statesmanlike in counsel, and lavish in her munificence. It is possible that Chilperic's appreciation of the literary talent of Fortunatus may account for some of this eulogy. In 580 the royal pair were terribly stricken by the loss of their two sons, who died of that awful distemper which raged intermittently for sixty years in Gaul. And the three poems in which Fortunatus strives to console the parents, though loaded with the pedantry of the time, may well be the expression of a genuine sympathy for what was felt to be a great tragedy, a blow which moved even the fierce queen to momentary softness and repentance. In his treatment of Sigibert and Brunihildis, Fortunatus is less at variance with the chronicler. Sigibert was undoubtedly one of the best and greatest of his race. He had borne a great part in campaigns against the Huns in 562, and in the fierce struggle with Chilperic in 574 he had gathered to his standard a host of Germans from beyond the Rhine, whose fierce love of plunder he controlled with a fearless dignity. The apparent purity of his married life offers a rare contrast to the flagrant libertinism of his house.

It is perhaps too daring to suggest a doubt or qualification of the sweeping judgement universally passed by historians on Clovis and his race. A person like Fortunatus, vain, needy, and self-indulgent, it may be said, cannot outweigh the testimony of the grave Bishop of Tours who knew court life so well. Yet even from Gregory we have shown that the early Merovingians had some of the military virtue of their race. And even Gregory softens occasionally his picture of some of them by amiable and estimable traits. Guntram of Burgundy, along with some of the perfidy and cruel vindictiveness of his race and time, sometimes displays a generosity, justice, and bonhomie which made him decidedly popular. Theudebert, the grandson of Clovis, had his life been prolonged, would probably have been the greatest and best of the Merovingians. He seems to have been for those times singularly pure in his private life. Churchmen applauded his religious reverence and his generous benefactions to the Church and the poor. Surrounded by Roman advisers, he strove to equalise the condition of the two races when his minister Palladius was instructed to impose the tribute on Frank estates. Even in the picture of Chilperic, " the Herod and Nero " of the age, Gregory frankly reveals that, in his frequent visits to the court on trying occasions, Chilperic behaved to him with a courtesy, patience, and fairness which leave the impression that that very eccentric king had in his grain frustrated possibilities of a nobler life. There are one or two other considerations which would suggest that even under the worst kings the tone of the court cannot have been hopelessly corrupt. In a number of cases we find that a religious youth, " commended " to the royal service by aristocratic patronage, after some years returned to his home to devote himself to the severest religious life in a monastery or a hermitage. And some of the most devoted and pious bishops were elected to their sees by royal mandate, and were respected visitors at court.

The faithlessness attributed to the Franks in ancient writers reached its height in the relations of the Frank kings even with their nearest kin. Clovis by treachery and ruthlessness had swept from his path rivals probably equally treacherous at Cologne and Cambrai. His sons and grandsons, in insidious attacks on one another and shameless perfidy, almost improved on his example. When Chlodomer of Orleans fell in the last battle against the Burgundians, in 524, his infant sons were left

under the care of their grandmother Chlothilde at Paris. Their
uncles determined to divide the realm of Chlodomer between
them, and sent a crafty message to the old queen asking that
the boys might be entrusted to them to be raised to their father's
throne. When the young princes were in their uncles' power,
another messenger was dispatched with scissors and a naked
sword, to signify that the queen was to choose whether the boys
should be shorn of the long hair of their race and sink into the
common crowd, or should be put to death. The proud, angry
queen replied that if they were to lose their princely rank she
would rather see them dead. Chlothar at once drove his dagger
into his elder nephew. The younger flung himself at the feet of
Childebert and begged piteously to be spared. Childebert, the
more emotional or less cruel of the two, with tears in his eyes,
offered any price to save the poor child's life, but was fiercely
threatened if he continued to shield the boy, and Chlothar
completed the slaughter.

A few years before, Chlothar himself had almost lost his life
through the treachery of his brother Theuderic, who had summoned him to his aid in a great campaign of vengeance against
the Thuringian kings. It was the war in which Radegund, the
daughter of King Bertharius, was taken captive in the sack of
the capital, to become the unwilling wife of Chlothar. Theuderic
invited his brother to a conference in his quarters, in which he
had secreted some armed men behind a screen. The screen,
being too short, revealed the feet of the assassins, and Chlothar
called up his own armed escort. Theuderic knew well that his
wary brother had discerned his nefarious design, and strove to
propitiate him by the gift of a great dish of silver which Chlothar,
with many thanks, calmly carried back to his quarters. Then,
repenting of his needless generosity, Theuderic sent Theudebert,
his son, to ask that the gift might be returned ! To this strange
race crime and perfidy were the most natural things in the world,
and their mean avidity seems to have been equal to their
treachery. Brothers as they were, proud of their blood and race,
they appear to have regarded sworn alliances as only made for
convenience and to be broken at pleasure. They were like wild
animals, watching one another in mutual fear, and always ready
to spring. Among a race so faithless, to anticipate perfidy was
often the only means of safety.

The crimes of the second generation make perhaps even a darker tale than those of the first. Or it may be that the tale is fuller and more glaring, since it comes from a contemporary. Women appear more often on the scene, fierce, jealous, and coldly cruel, some stronger and abler than the men. Tacitus tells us that the ancient Germans " were almost the only barbarians contented with one wife, the only exceptions being a few of high rank whose alliance was courted for social reasons ". But nearly all the early Merovingians kept a harem on an almost Oriental scale. There was a sultana of high and legitimate rank, another of rank less high, and then a crowd of servile concubines. The corruption which inevitably followed can easily be traced by any careful student of the Chronicles. The honourable wife was sometimes disowned and relegated to obscurity to make way for a clever and more alluring mistress. Boy princes in the third generation became fathers at fourteen or fifteen years of age by slave girls. Chlothar had seven sons and one daughter by three different wives. One of those wives, Ingundis, the daughter of a serf on the royal estates, was the mother of the four kings who succeeded Chlothar in the partition of his monarchy. Ingundis, having social ambitions for her sister Aregundis, who possessed great attractions, once asked the king to find her a husband of rank and substance. He felt his amorous curiosity excited, and paid a visit to the *villa* where the fair Aregundis lived. The wooing was probably short, and Aregundis was added to the number of his lemans. The king, with grim humour, told her sister that he had found for Aregundis the husband of rank and substance she desired, in himself. The slave queen meekly replied that her lord might do what was pleasing to him.

The sons of Chlothar were as little fastidious about social distinctions as their father in selecting their numerous wives. Charibert, whose principal wife was the pious Ingoberga, the mother of the queen of Ethelbert of Kent, had in his harem two slave girls, the daughters of a woolworker, and another whose father was a shepherd. The king's vagrant amours incurred the sentence of excommunication from S. Germanus. Guntram of Burgundy, " the good king ", as Gregory calls him, seems to have been equally amorous, and equally indifferent to the social rank of the women who attracted him. One of his wives, Marcatrudis, the daughter of Magnacharius, a great noble, was believed from jealousy to have poisoned Gundobad, Guntram's eldest son by a slave concubine, and was banished from the palace. Queen Austrechildis, who succeeded her, was assailed with detestable calumnies by the brothers of Marcatrudis. They were promptly ordered to death by the exasperated king and their estates were confiscated. The lot of Guntram, like that of many of his house, in spite of power and wealth, was not a happy one. The lawless love and concubinage of the Frank kings no doubt were responsible for many of their tragic troubles. In these capricious unions the later Frank kings offer a striking contrast to the more prudent and statesmanlike alliances of Clovis and the great Ostrogoth Theodoric, and of the chiefs of other German tribes, Vandal, Visigoth, and Burgundian, whose marriages were often evidently dictated by motives of international policy. Sigibert was the only one of his family who followed this example. Disgusted, as we are told by Gregory, by the degrading liaisons of his brother, he sought an equal as his bride from the family of the Visigothic king Athanagild. Brunihildis is described as a princess of fascinating beauty and noble character, and, as she showed in a career of nearly fifty years, possessed of a masculine and practical ability, which made her a match for all the unscrupulous ambition and intrigue of that perilous time. She was welcomed in Austrasia with general joy and festivity. Yet the marriage of Sigibert and Brunihildis marked the opening of a period of deadly feuds and ghastly crime, the darkest episode even in the history of the Merovingians.

Chilperic, who had been led to repudiate his queen, Audovera, by the arts of his mistress, Fredegundis, had many wives or concubines. But the example of his brother Sigibert aroused his ambition to dignify his power by a higher alliance. He sought the hand of Brunihildis' elder sister, Galswintha, promising to repudiate all other connexions. The unfortunate princess was torn from her mother, to their mutual grief, and sent with an immense treasure and a splendid escort on her way to a fatal home. Fortunatus has left a picture of the sorrow and splendour of that procession which he saw passing through Poitiers in the year 567. But he gives no hint of the evil arts by which the young bride was soon to perish. The sensual king was for a brief space charmed by a new acquisition. But Fredegundis, who had recovered, or had never lost, her hold upon him, by insults and craft made her rival so miserable that the hapless princess begged to be allowed to return to her native country, and offered to leave all her treasure behind her. It is probable that Chilperic feared complications with Spain if he complied with her request. He took what he thought the more prudent way of having her secretly strangled in her bed. After a few days of affected mourning, Fredegundis was installed in the place which she held for thirty years. But the murder of Galswintha, as in tragic legend, was the *Até* which aroused a haunting vengeance, the primal curse which was the parent of offspring like itself.

In the long duel between the two queens, every stage is marked by blood. With Fredegundis the dagger or the poisoned cup are always the first and readiest means for her purposes.

That Fredegundis had great ability and a weird power of fascination we can infer, without the doubtful authority of Fortunatus. For eighteen years she seems to have been absolute mistress of the passions and the policy of Chilperic. Yet Egidius, the Bishop of Rheims, and Bertram of Bordeaux, were said to have been her lovers. And the murder of Chilperic was represented by popular rumour as suspiciously following on the discovery of a guilty intrigue with Landerich, the *major domus* of Neustria. Such scandals, however, especially in times of moral confusion, need only to be circulated to be believed. It is to be noted that some of these charges were connected with conspiracies to ruin Fredegundis and drive Chilperic from the throne. And in estimating her character, it is necessary to bear in mind the constant peril to which she and her husband were exposed, both from palace intrigues to change the succession and from Brunihildis, embittered and intensified by the passion to avenge the death of Galswintha, or by both interlacing and combined. This is not suggested in order to palliate the unparalleled enormities of treacherous cruelty of which Fredegundis was guilty, but to suggest an explanation of them.

When all allowance has been made for the temptations of new power and wealth operating on natures still untamed, and for dangers from greedy and jealous rivals, the tale of the Merovingians is in the main a ghastly record. And such defiance of moral restraints in the ruling house must, as at all times,

have tended to weaken the tradition of morality and religion
among their subjects, especially of the wealthy and powerful
order. The ordinary sensual vices are common to all ages, and
might seem to be ineradicable unless by a painfully slow elevation
of our mixed nature, corresponding in its slow, imperceptible
progress to dateless geologic changes which raised continents
from the depths of the sea. And it would probably be rash to
assume that those vices were more common and destructive in
the sixth than in the first or the fifteenth century. Still, the
pages of Gregory leave the impression that coarse sensuality and
drunkenness corrupted many lives in that age. Apart from a
morbid and hereditary nervous taint, drunkenness often springs
from the longing to escape, if for an hour, from the dullness
and monotony of life, whether in the workshop, the lonely
country house, or the monastic cell. If we find few traces of
this vice in the society of the last age of the Empire, this may
probably be due to the fact that the society of Symmachus and
Sidonius and Ausonius was eminently sociable, and knew how
to amuse its ample leisure. And if we hardly ever hear of a
Merovingian, among his other vices, being given to wine, he
may have been saved by perpetual change of scene to his endless
villae, the stress and excitement of war, and the distractions of
government and society. But the vintages of Champagne,
Burgundy, and Bordeaux were evidently too well appreciated in
those days, even by ascetics. Bishop Eonius (Eunius) who, while
celebrating Mass at Paris fell in a fit before the altar, was a confirmed drunkard and was often seen staggering as he walked. A
deacon of Châlons once came to S. Martin's at Tours to recover
his eyesight. The bishop interrogated him as to the cause of
his blindness, and drew from him the confession that seven months
before, on his way to church, he had met a friend with whom
he had spent the hour of matins in drinking, after a bad custom
of his district. Guntharius, the seventeenth Bishop of Tours, who
had been a prudent administrator as abbot of a neighbouring
monastery, after his elevation to the see, became so besotted
that he often failed to recognise his guests, or insulted them
with unseemly abuse. The two brother bishops Salonius and
Sagittarius, who fought under Mummolus against the Lombards
at the battle of Embrun, in addition to worse vices, used to
spend their nights drinking till the break of day, and were often

seen still over their cups as the morning service was beginning
in the neighbouring church. After these examples we are not
surprised to hear that the *cubicularius* Eberulfus, who had taken
sanctuary at Tours, profaned the precincts with drunken revels,
insulted the bishop before the saint's tomb, and almost beat
one of the priests to death because he delayed to bring him his
wine. Elsewhere we read of a citizen of Bayeux who, riding
home drunk in a storm, was thrown from his horse and, losing
his reason for a while, had to be closely confined. He was cured
by the virtues of S. Martin, and received the tonsure. But his
old vice with all its consequences returned upon him again and
again, and he died insane. We have another glimpse of the
interior of an ordinary household of Auvergne in the life of
S. Leobardus. Before he retired from the world, the saint, on
the death of his parents, went to visit his brother, and found him
so stupefied by wine that he could not recognise him and refused
to admit him. The experience probably ripened a natural
inclination in Leobardus for the monastic life.

The harem life of many of the kings, with no attempt to
disguise its shame, cannot have been favourable to pure morals
among their subjects. And we are often startled to see that the
lawless amours of royal people are treated by the clerical chronicler
in a cool matter-of-fact way, without any word of disapproval.
Nor does the Church, as a whole, seem to have exerted itself
with much vigour or sternness to check this degradation of
wedlock in high places. It is true that S. Germanus excommunicated Charibert for his union with Marcovefa, but the sentence
seems not to have been drawn forth by the king's promiscuous
concubinage, but on canonical grounds, by the fact that the
girl had already taken the veil and was the sister of one of
Charibert's many wives. But Gregory, in speaking of the
polygamous habits of Sigibert's brothers, seems to treat them as
socially rather than morally degrading. In the fourth generation
the sexual relations of the kings seem to have been as irregular
as in the first. Theuderic, the grandson of Brunihildis and
Sigibert, had sons born to him by concubines in his fifteenth,
sixteenth, and seventeenth years. But the boy king's irregularities were boldly denounced by S. Columbanus. It was believed
in monastic circles that Brunihildis encouraged her grandson in
his immoral connexions, lest a legitimate wife should deprive

her of her long ascendancy. When she brought the king's infant sons to the saint for his benediction, they were sternly repelled as children of the brothel. The saint rudely spurned the royal hospitality, shut the king from the gates of Luxeuil, and predicted the extinction of his race.

The system of domestic slavery was undoubtedly as corrupting in the Merovingian times as it was in the Aquitaine of Paulinus and Salvianus, or in the days of Horace or of Cato. The slave girl became the easy prey of a master's lusts. Hence the edicts of councils in the sixth century against the admission of *extraneae mulieres* to the clerical household, the constant iteration of which from year to year seems to show that they were too frequently ignored and required. Bertram, the great Bishop of Bordeaux, and Palladius, Bishop of Saintes, openly charged one another with licentiousness at the table of Guntram ; and Bertram was assailed by his brother-in-law as the lover of slave girls. Nor, from a good many indications, does it seem that the morality of some of the ordinary clergy was on a higher level. One tale, which Gregory relates with a candid minuteness, may have had many counterparts in that age. A certain clerk, notorious for his unclean life, came from Le Mans to Lisieux, then under Bishop Aetherius. He there seduced a lady of good family, and at length carried her off, disguised as a man, to another district. Her relatives pursued the guilty pair, put the clerk in bonds, and burnt the woman alive. Aetherius, who seems to have been a weak man, redeemed the seducer at a cost of 20 *aurei*, and placed him at the head of his diocesan school, with ample endowments and the support of his favour. Having made improper advances to the mother of one of his pupils, the man was once more in danger from indignant relatives, and was once more saved by the bishop and restored to his office. The ungrateful wretch now turned on his protector and, aided by the archdeacon, laid plots against the bishop's life, with the object of securing the succession to the episcopal see. Having failed in this, they assailed the bishop's character, and although he was over seventy and, according to ecclesiastical rule, always slept with attendant priests about him, they circulated the rumour that they had seen a woman leaving the old man's chamber. He was actually put in chains by these scoundrels, but managed to escape their clutches and made his way tò the presence of Guntram, who, with many grave faults, was kind, and meant to be just. The bishop was restored, amid the enthusiastic rejoicing of his flock. As to the fate of the infamous priest, history is silent.

Many similar tales of wild and lawless libertinism among the laity can be found in the pages of Gregory. We can only make a few selections to illustrate the dark side of the life of that time. The first casts a shadow over the fair fame of Theudebert I., one of the greatest and best of his race. When he had been sent by Clovis to reduce the south eastern provinces, and had carried his ravages up to the walls of Cabrières, he received a message from a Roman lady named Deuteria, the wife of a reputable citizen of those parts, inviting him to come and do what pleased him. He entered the town without violence or resistance, and was met by the fair and dignified Deuteria, who easily allowed herself along with her town to be subjugated by the conqueror. We know nothing of the fate of their union for years. But at length, when their daughter was growing to womanhood, Deuteria, fearing that the fair girl might attract Theudebert's fancy, put her in a litter to which wild oxen were yoked, and had her hurled from a bridge into the Meuse at Verdun. Theudebert had for seven years been honourably betrothed to Wisigardis, but the intrigue with Deuteria had prevented the prince from fulfilling his pledge. At length the Franks became indignant : Deuteria was abandoned, and Wisigardis, though only for a brief space, became Queen. And Theudebert is the man who, according to Gregory, endowed churches, relieved the poor with pious charity, and honoured the priesthood ! Verily the Church, in those times, was a merciful mother !

Deuteria was a Roman lady of position. And in another similar tale the erring wife is also Roman. The details must have come to the bishop directly, since the tragedy took place close to Tours. A citizen of Tours named Ambrose had a wife who carried on an adulterous connexion with one Vedastes Avus, a man stained with every vice and crime. Ambrose and his brother Lupus, on the eve of the latter's marriage, had gone to a country house at Chinon, where, after dining too well, they lay down together in a drunken sleep. The lady's lover, evidently at her instigation, stole in upon them as they slept and dealt

U

Ambrose a deadly wound. Lupus, covered with his brother's
blood, called loudly for help, and met with the same fate. Within
a few days the treacherous wife was married to her lover. There
is not a hint of any legal proceedings to avenge the crime. But
Vedastes got the reward of his evil deeds in a quarrel with
Childeric the Saxon, one of whose train pierced him with his
lance on the road to Poitiers.

A Burgundian, Duke Amalo, had an estate in the region of
the Jura. He had cast lawless eyes on a free maiden, probably
the daughter of one of his tenants, and, in the absence of his
wife, ordered her to be brought to him in the evening, when he
was heated with wine. The girl was dragged to his couch,
streaming with blood from the violence with which she was led
along by his servants, and was still further mangled by the
blows of the ruffian who vainly strove to overpower her resistance.
When he at last had sunk into a drunken stupor, the girl drew
the sword from beneath his head and, like another Judith, as
Gregory says exultingly, cleft his skull with a manly stroke.
With some lingering sense of honour, Amalo, as he breathed his
last, confessed his sin and ordered his servants to do no harm to
one who had so bravely guarded her purity. She escaped to
King Guntram at the neighbouring town of Chalon, who sternly
forbade the kin of the dead man to follow up their revenge.

Perhaps the most startling example of lawlessness in private
life is to be found in the career of Eulalius, a Roman Count of
Auvergne. The tale, which Gregory must have heard in his last
years, seems to reveal a sad decline from the moral tone of
Auvergne in the days of Sidonius. The mother of Eulalius was,
like Gregory's mother, a devout woman, who, when all the
household were asleep, would pass long hours in her oratory.
She had often upbraided her son for his wild life, and one morning she was found strangled on the spot where she had been
praying for him. Eulalius became the mark of universal suspicion. Bishop Cautinus refused him communion. But, at the
great feast of S. Julian at Brivate, Eulalius fell at the bishop's
feet, complaining that he had been condemned unheard. The
bishop confessed that he knew nothing but the prevalent rumour,
and allowed him to take the Holy Bread, leaving the judgement
to God and S. Julian. Whether this test was regarded by the
people as having cleared his reputation, the historian does not

say. It certainly did not improve his character. Coming to
his wife, Tetradia, from the embraces of slave concubines, he
would beat and insult her. Her jewels and trinkets were sold
to pay his growing debts. When Eulalius had once gone to the
court on official business, his nephew Virus, captured by his
aunt's charms or pitying her dishonour, determined to release
her from an intolerable position and marry her himself. He had
friendly relations with the great Duke Desiderius, and Tetradia,
with all the valuables which she could carry off, was placed
under his protection till her marriage with Virus could take
place. Eulalius when he returned was soon consoled for the loss
of his wife, but he determined to have vengeance on her seducer.
He overtook him in one of the deep gorges of Auvergne and
slew him. Duke Desiderius, who had lately lost his wife, immediately on the news reaching him that Virus had fallen, took
Tetradia to his home. Eulalius, whose love could never follow
the beaten path of virtue, carried off a nun from the convent
at Lyons and made her his wife. His concubines, jealous of this
new union, tried the effect of magic potions upon him, with
what success we are not told. But Eulalius appears to have
continued in his evil life.

The reckless impulse of sensuality, however, does not excite
so much surprise as the perfidy and unblushing perjury of that
age of religious awe. Perjury is common enough in some of our
own courts of law. But the perjurer now only fears prosecution
before an earthly judge with a possible temporal penalty. In
the sixth century men were taught that the false oath was constantly and immediately punished by God or His saints with the
most terrible bodily afflictions in this world, and would certainly
incur far more awful punishment in the life to come. Every
famous altar or martyr's shrine had its tales of supernatural
vengeance for the desecrated oath. They were attested by the
priests who had witnessed the miracle, even by great prelates
like Gregory. The saints, it is true, were often pitiful and
beneficent, healing disease, striking off the captive's chains, even
raising the dead to life. But, in every country-side, their vengeance for sin had often been manifested in inflicting blindness
or dumbness or paralysis, or even violent death. Men the most
depraved believed these things and trembled. And yet, from
the King on the throne to the meanest peasant, we find men

constantly braving all these terrors as they raised their hands
above the holy relics in an oath which they meant to violate.
The inference is, not that their faith was weak, but that greed,
ambition, hatred, or other selfish passion was stronger than
faith, and braved even the final sentence of exclusion from Divine
Grace.

Every famous shrine had its story of the fate of the perjurer.
Gregory himself had seen immediate punishment descending on
him. A man who had notoriously set fire to a neighbour's
house, in spite of the bishop's solemn warning, boldly approached
the shrine of S. Martin to clear himself. As he raised his hands,
in appeal to Almighty God and the power of S. Martin, the bishop
beheld him flung to the earth and enveloped in consuming fire
from heaven. The bishop had seen citizens of Tours, in the act
of making profane oath, similarly punished before the altar of
the Blessed Virgin and John the Baptist. Another perjurer's
tongue was paralysed, and his whole frame became as rigid as a
statue when he appealed to S. Marcellus of Chalon-sur-Saône.
At the feast of S. Eugenius at Albi, where itinerant traders laid out
their wares on booths, a girl secretly carried off some article which
had been shown her, and denied the fact. The trader demanded
an appeal to the judgement of the saint, and the girl's false voice
was choked as she began her oath, and she was left rigid before
the tomb. We have the tale of similar scenes of falsely repudiated debts before the shrine of S. Julian and many another
more obscure saint. In the reign of Theudebert I. a suit between
a certain priest and a Frank came before the King at Trèves.
The King, who was then visiting the shrines of the city for
purposes of devotion, ordered the priest, of whom he had no
good opinion, to establish his case by an oath on the tomb of
S. Maximin, who had entertained Athanasius in his exile. The
priest fell dead as he left the altar. An archdeacon, who was
charged with adultery by Bishop Nicetius, offered to swear his
innocence on the same altar, but, as he was descending to the
crypt, was seized with a fever and, on the point of death, made
confession of his guilt. The shrine of another Nicetius, the Bishop
of Lyons, was the scene of countless miracles, and a scrap of his
handwriting once convicted a heartless robber. The saintly
bishop had once given a wandering beggar a testimonial in his
own hand, commending him to the charity of the faithful, which,

after the bishop's death, had brought the poor man abundant alms. A Burgundian one day watched him entering a wood, beat him almost to death, and robbed him of six gold pieces and the more precious letter. The latter, however, the thief flung away, and the mendicant picked it up and went to make an appeal to Bishop Phronimius, who laid the case before the count. The culprit was seized, and of course denied all knowledge of the matter. But the bishop, producing the letter, ordered the accused to lay his hand on the sacred writing and swear that he was guiltless. The moment he did so, he fell on his back foaming at the mouth, and was taken up for dead. He recovered, however, confessed the crime, and made restitution. In the year 586 there was at Tours an officer in charge of the royal post named Pelagius. He had committed every kind of crime, waylaying people on the rivers or roads, plundering and even murdering his victims. He had a special hatred of the bishop, who strove to restrain his outrages, and the servants of S. Martin's had often been despoiled and almost beaten to death. At last he robbed a party carrying sacred vessels, and Gregory cut him off from communion. The culprit calmly appeared with twelve compurgators to clear himself by oath. Gregory refused at first to accept it, but at last, under pressure, he permitted the man to swear alone, and on the strength of that oath he was restored. In a few months, as he was preparing to reap a field which he had just annexed from a monastic estate, he was stricken with a fatal fever.

The matricularii of S. Martin's, who were supported by the church or the alms of the faithful, were accustomed, when absent from the church, to leave a deputy to receive and guard any donations made in their absence. On one occasion the deputy had received a small coin from a charitable worshipper, and then denied it with a solemn oath by the powers of the saint. The words had hardly passed his lips when he fell to the earth in a fit from which he never recovered. It would be tedious to go through the long list of perjuries committed by the kings and their great subjects in this age. It would seem that oaths were often taken only to deceive and to be broken. The most binding sworn obligations were constantly disowned and flung to the winds. The only excuse, if such it is, for all this faithlessness is that simple faith would have left a man defenceless in an often deadly struggle with faithless foes.

Mutual distrust and terror, as in the days of Thucydides, weak-ened all social bonds and scruples, and made men ready to risk even the anger of God. The Divine Judge and Avenger was more distant than the earthly revengeful foe.

In the year 532, Munderic, who claimed to be of royal descent, boldly demanded the allegiance of the people of Champagne, and numbers of the country people took the oath of fealty to him. Theuderic at first tried the effect of crafty diplomacy, but in the end was compelled to take the field against this bold pretender. Munderic threw himself, with a crowd of adherents, into the fort of Vitry. The siege went on for a week without success, for Munderic was evidently a brave and energetic leader. At last Theuderic despatched his henchman, Aregisilus, with instructions to entice the rebel from his stronghold by an oath of safe-conduct, and then to slay him. Munderic knew the value of a Merovingian's word, and had a foreboding of his own fate, but at last he yielded. The envoy, with hands laid on the altar, swore to protect him, and led him by the hand out of the castle gates. Immediately, on a prearranged signal, Theuderic's men rushed upon him. But before he fell he drove his lance through the perjurer's body, and then, drawing his sword, left a great heap of corpses around him.

Guntram Boso was one of the most powerful and perhaps the most unscrupulous noble of his time. He was fickle, yet on occasion bold to the extent of recklessness, a fond father and a faithless friend ; full of old-world superstitions, yet ready to insult the shrine of S. Martin, who had saved him from shipwreck on the Loire. He was the most rapacious in an age of ferocious greed ; he never took an oath to a friend without the intention of breaking it. The record of his perjuries has already appeared abundantly in these pages ; but the most astounding of his crimes remains to be told. A lady nearly related to Boso died and was interred in the church at Metz, with all her costly jewels and gold ornaments. A few days after the burial, the bishop and the duke, with a number of the leading people, went out of the city to celebrate the feast of S. Remedius. Guntram Boso seized the opportunity to secure so rare a spoil. He and his men barred the doors of the basilica, and proceeded to rifle the tomb of its contents. But the monks had observed them, and sent word to the bishop and the duke. Meanwhile the plunderers had mounted their horses and were preparing to escape with their booty, when something warned them of their danger, and they re-entered the church and laid their plunder on the altar, declaring that Boso had instigated the sacrilege. He was summoned before King Childebert and his accusers at one of his villas in the Ardennes, but failed to appear, and his ill-gotten wealth was added to the coffers of the State.

We conclude these illustrations of the daring perfidy of the time by a tale of perhaps the most cynical and cruel outrage chronicled by Gregory. Rauchingus, a Duke of Austrasia, was one of the richest and most powerful nobles of his time. His pride and vanity were only matched by his utter disregard of ordinary human feeling in trampling on all who were in his power. His ambition knew no bounds, and at the end of his career, along with the nobles of the young Chlothar II., son of Chilperic, he laid a plot to kill Childebert and rule over Champagne with Theudebert, the son of Childebert, as nominal sovereign. He used to torture the servants who waited at his table by holding flaming torches to their limbs, and gloat over their sufferings. Two of his young slaves had loved one another for two years, and sought the asylum of a church to protect them in their union. Rauchingus demanded that they should be given back to him. The priest, in obedience to the decisions of councils, replied that this could be done only after a pledge that their union should be respected, and that no corporal punishment should follow. After pondering for a moment Rauchingus replied that he willingly submitted to the condition, and then, laying his hands on the altar, he swore never to separate them, but that their union should be perpetual. The couple were restored to their master, who politely thanked the priest. When Rauchingus returned home he ordered the trunk of a tree to be hollowed out and sunk in a shallow grave, and the maiden and her lover were flung into it alive and buried. "Thus", said Rauchingus, "I have been true to my oath : they shall not be separated for ever." That such a monster should have held the highest social and official rank is a marvellous and damning fact.

In the class, both of Frank and Roman race, whose lives emerge in the light of history, character, in spite of all ghostly terror or more spiritual influences, seems to have been still untamed. Under a thin veneer of culture it retained much of

mere savage impulse, along with the simplicity and levity of the
savage. The sensual passions are strong in every age. But in
the age of the Merovingians the passion for wealth, combined
with the impulse to seize it by the most reckless and cynical
violence, displays a wild volcanic force which constantly
startles us. Clovis himself seduced the *leudes* of Ragnachar
by gifts of sham golden arms and ornaments, and it would
appear that the Franks, even of the highest rank, would stoop
to any mean art or resort to any act of violence to satisfy their
avarice. Kings and princes of the royal house, with immense
estates, and having the resources of great realms at their command, could often be as grasping as the neediest of their subjects.
Great nobles, of ample wealth, will plunder the province which
they administer, violently annex the villa of a neighbour or steal
his horses, or appropriate a farm dedicated to a saint. Great
bishops, by less violent means, are not less bent on adding to
the estates of their see. And the minor clergy will be sometimes
found appropriating funds dedicated to the poor by mean and
sacrilegious peculation. Gregory, who does not often moralise,
is struck by the *auri sacra fames* of his time. It was perhaps
not stronger than in our own time. But in those days it sated
itself by measures more open and violent than modern law and
sentiment will permit.

The illustrations of the prevailing avarice, especially in the
highest class, crowd upon one in bewildering variety from the
chronicles of the time. Charibert, for instance, coveted and
seized an estate with fine pasture for horses ; he established a
stud upon it, but, by some mysterious influence, to punish his
greed, his horses were seized with a frenzy, broke their bounds,
and in wild career scattered in all directions.

On his death Theudechildis, one of his numerous concubines,
the daughter of a shepherd, offered herself and her treasure to
Guntram of Burgundy. He promised the lady a hearty welcome
and greater honour than she had ever had from his brother.
But her wealth was her greatest attraction to Guntram. When
she arrived he coldly told her that her wealth would be more
properly in his hands than in the keeping of one who had been
only a concubine. She was stripped of nearly all she possessed,
and relegated to a convent at Arles.

The enormous wealth and waste of the Frank kings, and the

rapacity of the time, are probably seen in most concentrated form in the episode of the journey of the Princess Rigunthis to Spain in 584. She had been espoused to a Visigothic prince, and Chilperic, her father, determined to send her to Spain with a splendour of escort worthy of her future destiny, but with as little expense to himself as possible. Fifty carriages bore an immense treasure of bullion, jewels, and costly garments, which were chiefly the gift of Frank nobles. It was guarded by a train of 4000 men, dragged from their homes to which they never expected to return, amid tears and curses. Great Neustrian nobles, Bobo, Domigiselus, Ansovaldus, and Waddo, were in command of the escort, but their control seems to have been very weak. From the very first, and all along the way, numbers deserted, carrying off any valuables which they could seize. Orders had been issued that none of the expenses of transport should be borne by the treasury of the King. Requisitions were therefore made on all the towns through which the procession passed. And in the country districts even the humble cottage was plundered ; whole herds of cattle were carried off, and vineyards were devastated. When they approached Toulouse, the great escort, which had started in such splendour, had become utterly demoralised, with ragged dress and gay accoutrements lost or tarnished. It was determined that they should pause in their journey to refit and prepare the cavalcade to appear with some show of dignity at the Visigothic court. Meanwhile all Southern Gaul was convulsed by the Gundobaldian rising, and tidings of the murder of Chilperic had just arrived. On hearing the news, Desiderius, a great duke of those regions, who was about to join in proclaiming the pretender Gundobald, gathered an armed force and hastened to Toulouse, seized the treasure of the Princess, and put her under some sort of restraint till his return. By this time her escort and their leaders seem to have dispersed, some of them to join the army of the pretender under Mummolus and Desiderius. When the rising had been crushed, Fredegundis sent Cuppa, the marshal of the court, to release the unfortunate Princess from her long and painful duress, and bring her home. But there was no love between mother and daughter. Rigunthis seems to have inherited her mother's character, fierce, cruel, and adulterous. She treated Fredegundis with hauteur and scorn for her humble birth. Sometimes the ladies came to blows. But

Fredegundis was a dangerous person to provoke, and she hit on a device to tempt the girl's hereditary greed and perhaps make away with her. She invited Rigunthis to come and inspect some of her dead father's wealth, and take from it what she pleased. They entered the treasure-chamber, and the Queen drew from a chest a dazzling store of gems and ornaments to show them to her daughter. At last, as if weary, she told the girl to plunge her own hand into the coffer and bring out what she could. Rigunthis bent over it, and the Queen dashed the lid upon her neck and pressed it hard till the girl was nearly suffocated and her eyes starting from her head. She was only rescued by her maid calling the other servants to the rescue.

The tale of Rigunthis casts a lurid flash on that accursed house which was suffered by a mysterious Providence to riot, with hardly a momentary scruple, in the wealth drawn from the toil and misery of a suffering people, lavish for their selfish pleasures, mean and niggardly for the public weal, ever keen to scent any chance of gain. In the very year of this display and waste we are told that famine prevailed all over Gaul, which was probably to a great extent due to devastations of the Merovingian armies. The misery of thousands is condensed in the chronicle into a few matter-of-fact sentences. Crowds of people were living on all sorts of unnatural food, roots and weeds and herbs, and dying swollen and distempered, or of mere hunger.

And yet no stern moralist points the contrast between the dissolute luxury of the court and the miseries of the common people. No sense of responsibility for their subjects' welfare seems to have stirred in the minds of the new rulers of Europe.

The kings seem often to have accepted gifts from candidates for high office. The infamous Leudastes, after amassing a fortune in the service of Marcovefa, spent a part of it in purchasing a high place from Charibert, and amply reimbursed himself by a long career of shameless rapacity. Paeonius sent his son Mummolus with gifts to obtain his continuance in office as Count of Auxerre, and his son, by precocious diplomacy, used the occasion to supplant his father. Charegisilus, the chamberlain of Sigibert, who fell by his master's side at Vitry, had risen by adulation, and was an expert in annexing other men's estates and breaking their wills. Nicetius, who had been supplanted in the countship of Auvergne, obtained a dukedom from Childebert by immense gifts to the royal treasury. All this sounds very corrupt. But we should remember that the King's purse was liable for all the expense of government. There can be no doubt that the man who bought a court office from a Frank king expected to get some return in solid cash. And, in the loose organisation of those realms, peculation, or the undisguised plunder of the provincial population by their governor, was evidently not uncommon. It is hardly necessary to adduce instances in support of a commonplace. Marcus, the referendary of Chilperic, whose collection of the new taxes of 579 caused numbers to leave their homes, and aroused fierce revolt at Limoges, is said to have accumulated a vast fortune by his exactions. Stricken with disease, he took the vow of penitence and the tonsure, just in time to make his peace. A striking and illuminating case is that of Cuppa, who had been Master of the Stables at the court of Chilperic and high in Fredegundis's favour. In what capacity we know not, he burst into the lands of Tours like a foreign invader, and carried off cattle and anything he could seize. The population rose *en masse*, slew some of his retainers, and sent others in chains to be judged by King Childebert. They revealed that the raid had been organised by the stealthy help of the governor of the district. He was brought before the King in bonds, but he managed by bribing Flavianus, a powerful domestic, to return safely to his home, and probably to the office he had abused.

Some of the leading Romans who rose to the highest office in Burgundy and Austrasia seem to have been very corrupt. Celsus, who was created patrician by Guntram on his accession, was a man of great legal learning and readiness in applying it. But his avarice was unbounded ; and he signalised his tenure of office by appropriating many estates of the Church. Forty years later we read of a certain Protadius, who became *major domus* of Theuderic by the influence of Brunihildis and was a clever and energetic man, but he used his enormous fiscal powers to enrich himself and to cripple and humiliate the great nobles whom he made his deadly enemies.

Neither military discipline nor religious awe could put a check on the sacrilegious cupidity of Frank armies on a campaign. The forces of Theuderic in his invasion of Auvergne in 525 broke open the doors of S. Julian's and seized the sacred vessels and the funds which were devoted to the poor. In 576 the army of Chilperic spread havoc through the territory of Tours, and did not spare even the lands dedicated to S. Martin, in revenge for the shelter which had been granted to Chilperic's rebellious son Merovech. Two years before, Chilperic's son Theudebert had ravaged without mercy vast regions south of the Loire (Limoges and Cahors), burning the churches, slaughtering the priests, and carrying off the vessels from the altar. In the same fashion, when Guntram sent an expedition to crush the pretender Gundobald at the foot of the Pyrenees in 585, the soldiers began by attacking the church of S. Vincent at Agen, in which the people had placed all their valuables for fancied security. They set fire to the doors which they could not burst open, and swept off everything of value, including the most sacred vessels. But the climax of inhuman cruelty and impious greed was reached by the Burgundian army which swept down on Septimania in the year 585. Its outrages so shocked King Guntram that he demanded an account of the matter from his generals on their return, in a speech probably composed for him by Gregory. "Our ancestors", said the King, "won their triumphs by putting their trust in God, honouring saints and martyrs, and paying reverence to His priests. But we now have no fear of God before our eyes ; we plunder things dedicated to His glory, we slay His ministers, and treat with ridicule and outrage the relics of the holy martyrs. Therefore it is that our hands are weak, our swords have lost their edge, our shields do not protect us." The pious King seems to have paid but slight heed to the crimes, quite as flagitious and spreading far wider misery, by which his army left a trail of ruin behind it. Along the Saône and Rhone homesteads were given to the flames, their inmates were massacred, crops and cattle swept off by the savage marauders, up to the walls of Nîmes. And all these barbarities were inflicted on Guntram's own peaceful subjects. His army, composed of levies from Bourges, Saintes, Périgueux, and Angoulême, wrought like havoc on their march to Carcassonne. The cities of Provence, however, were strongly fortified and provisioned against a siege, so that the fury of the invaders had to expend itself in burning the crops and cutting down the vines and olive trees. In one case a fortress capitulated on a solemn oath guaranteeing the safety and property of the defenders. The Duke Nicetius of Auvergne immediately gave the place up to plunder and enslaved those whom he had deceived.   Yet he and his brother dukes, when they were called to account by Guntram, in a tone of indignant pessimism, laid all the blame on the universal lawlessness and contempt for authority which prevailed in their armies.   It may well be doubted whether these great officers, who fawned on Guntram with pious phrases, were so innocent of the outrages of their troops as they pretended to be.   We shall see that in their private quarrels they could be as fierce and rapacious and cruel as the plebeian crowd who swelled the Merovingian armies.

Duke Beppolenus, having lost favour with the Queen, transferred his allegiance in 586 from Fredegundis to Guntram, and was appointed to govern the district of Rennes and Angers. Rennes refused to receive him, and at Angers he at once began a career of outrage.   He broke into private houses, carried off their corn and wine and family treasures, and grossly maltreated, or even murdered, the owners.   Duke Waddo had been appointed *major domus* of the Princess Rigunthis in that ill-omened journey to Spain which ended at Toulouse in the turmoil of the Gundobaldian rising.   He there joined the ranks of the pretender, deserted him in the stress of the siege of Convenae, and attached himself to Brunihildis.   He was a cynically selfish person, and also fiercely overbearing and passionate.   Beretrudis, a great Frank dame, the widow of Duke Launebodis, who built the church of S. Saturninus at Toulouse, bequeathing some of her estates to the Church, left a daughter as heiress to the rest. Her son-in-law had stolen some horses from the stud of Waddo, and Waddo determined to have restitution and revenge.   Beretrudis's daughter had inherited an estate near Poitiers on which Waddo set his eyes.   He sent orders to the bailiff to prepare everything for his reception, down to the sweeping of the floors and the upholstering of the chairs.   The bailiff, faithful to his mistress, resolved to resist the usurpation with all the force at his command.   The wife of Waddo besought him not to risk his life on such a venture, and their son, who seconded his mother's prayers, narrowly escaped death from his father's battle-axe. Waddo arrived at the villa, sharply rebuked the steward for disobeying his commands, and killed him with a blow of his dagger.   The steward's son drove his lance through the duke's body, and he fell under a shower of stones from the menials of the household. He was borne back to his home to die.

The repetition of such atrocities is apt to become tedious from their very number. Yet perhaps the reader who wishes to have a complete picture of the time will bear with a few more tales, in some of which even churchmen show themselves as violent and unscrupulous as the worldly class.

Lupentius, abbot of Gabalis, had been charged by Innocent, the count of the district, with having spoken disloyally of Queen Brunihildis. He was summoned to the royal tribunal and found guiltless. On his homeward way the abbot was seized by orders of the count, and carried off to the villa of Ponthion on the Marne, severely handled, and then released. When he reached the Aisne, and had pitched his tent for the night, his enemy once more appeared, this time more determined on his destruction. His head was struck off and, along with his corpse, was sunk with stones in the river. Both head and body, with the kindly aid of an eagle, were recovered from the flood and laid in a tomb, from which a miraculous light and virtues of healing power ever after issued.

The murder of the deacon Peter, the brother of Gregory, is a vivid illustration of the dangers of the time, from which even the clergy were not safe. In the old age of Tetricus, Bishop of Langres, the deacon Lampadius abused his position to appropriate church lands and to defraud the poor of the funds allocated to their relief. Peter exerted his influence to have Lampadius removed from his office, and therefore incurred his deadly hatred. On the death of Tetricus, Peter procured the election to the see of a relative of his family named Sylvester. But the new bishop died in a fit of epilepsy before his consecration. Lampadius then conspired with the son of Sylvester to circulate a report that Peter had compassed the death of the bishop by secret arts. From this charge Peter cleared himself by an oath before a court of leading laymen and priests, which was held by Bishop Nicetius at Lyons. Two years after this trial, the son of Sylvester overtook Peter on the highway and slew him by a thrust of his lance. As he wandered from place to place to avoid the consequences of his crime, he murdered another man, whose relatives gave chase and hacked him in pieces.

As we have had occasion to record, even the holiest and

most venerated churches were sometimes turned into scenes of
fierce strife and bloodshed. In the year 580, when the plague
was raging in Paris, the altar of S. Dionysius was profaned by a
murderous conflict in which the highest officials and courtiers of
Chilperic bore a part. A great lady, having forsaken her husband
for an adulterous union, his relatives appealed to her father,
threatening her with death if her reputation were not cleared.
The father agreed to take a solemn oath that she was innocent.
A day for the ceremony was appointed, and a great company
assembled in the church of S. Dionysius. There, with hands
extended over the altar and its relics, the father swore that his
daughter was stainless. The injured husband's party proclaimed
that the oath was false, and an angry altercation arose in which
swords were drawn. A fierce conflict raged before the very altar,
the holy place streamed with blood, and the wounded lay in
piles on the altar steps. An interdict was laid on the church in
which such heinous sacrilege had been perpetrated, until the
case should come before the King. Chilperic remitted it to the
bishop, who, on due composition for the offence, with that
strange mercy of the Church, received the culprits back into
communion! As for the unfortunate woman, before she
came up for judgement she had ended her life by her own
hand.

This lawless violence of great officers, combined with desecration of sacred things, was witnessed in the town of Marseilles in
the year 573. The servants of Vigilius, the archdeacon, had
stolen seventy casks of oil which had just arrived in the port.
The owner of the cargo tracked the thieves to the house of the
archdeacon, but he promptly denied that any of his people could
have been guilty of such a crime. Thereupon the merchant
brought the case before Albinus, the newly appointed governor
of Provence, and boldly charged Vigilius with being privy to the
theft. It was the feast of Christmas, and the archdeacon in his
vestments was about to conduct the bishop to the altar, when
the governor sprang from his seat, violently assaulted Vigilius,
and ordered him to prison. The bishop, the leading citizens,
and the general congregation begged Albinus to accept sureties
and permit the archdeacon to join in the service of the solemn
season. But the governor was obdurate, and, undeterred by all
appeals to sacrosanct dignity, mulcted Vigilius in 4000 *solidi*.

The case, however, was brought before King Sigibert by a rival and enemy of Albinus whom he had displaced, and Albinus was compelled to atone for his violence by a composition of fourfold the amount of the fine.

The district of Tours witnessed many scenes of rapine and violence during the episcopate of Gregory, but assuredly few more startling to the modern reader than the blood-feud between the families of Sicharius and Austrigiselus. They were of high rank, the one probably Gallo-Roman, the other belonging to the Frank race. While the feast of Christmas was being celebrated at Manthelan, a village between Tours and Poitiers, in the year 584, the priest sent his servant to invite some of those assembled to drink wine with him. One of the invited guests, for some reason unexplained, struck the boy dead with his sword. Sicharius, who was on intimate terms with the clergyman, at once returned to the church and presbytery with an armed band to await the expected onset of Austrigiselus, who was probably an enemy of the priest, and had prompted the deed. Austrigiselus soon appeared with armed attendants ; a sharp conflict took place, and Sicharius, rescued by the clergy, took flight to his estate in the country, leaving his wounded servants with some valuables in charge of the priest. Austrigiselus thereupon made a raid on the presbytery, killed the wounded slaves, and carried off the property of Sicharius. A scandal so grave must have shocked the community. " A court of the citizens " assembled, which was probably, but not certainly, the curia of the Roman times, with the Defensor, and other leading men, and Austrigiselus was pronounced liable to punishment in the criminal court according to law (*censura legalis*). Sicharius, when he heard of the violent deed of his enemy, disregarded the decision of the court, and, heated with wine, impulsively took the matter into his own hands. Along with a confederate, and attended by armed men, he burst on the house where Austrigiselus with his son and brother were sleeping, killed them with all their slaves, and seized their cattle and other property. Gregory now thought it was time to intervene in what threatened to become a kind of civil war. Along with the count, he invited the contending parties to appear before him, appealed to them in the name of divine charity to be reconciled and arrange their feud by pecuniary composition, and added that, if the guilty party were unable to pay the stipulated satisfaction, the treasury of the Church would come to his aid.

The offer of composition was spurned by Chramnesind, son of one of the slain men. The assembly broke up, and Sicharius set out from Tours to lay the case before the King. But on his way he turned aside to visit his wife on his estate near Poitiers. There, as he was punishing an idle slave with the rod, the serf plucked the sword from his master's belt and dealt him an apparently deadly blow. The slave was seized at once, cruelly beaten, and, after losing his hands and feet, was hurried to the gibbet. A rumour soon spread to Tours that Sicharius had been killed. Chramnesind mustered his relatives and retainers and hurried to the scene. They gave the houses of Sicharius and all the crops on the estate to the flames, put the serfs to death, and swept off the herds and all the rural wealth which could be carried away. The Count of Tours now summoned the parties to his court, and by an illegal decision, according to Gregory, ordered Chramnesind to lose half of the composition, which by his lawless violence he had rejected. The other half was paid by Sicharius with the aid of the proffered wealth of the Church. After the havoc wrought on his estate Sicharius was probably not in a position to meet the demand himself. And, at the instance of the Church, both sides took a solemn oath never to revive the fatal feud.

For two years peace reigned between the two families. Sicharius and Chramnesind became apparently fast friends, constantly entertained one another, and sometimes even slept on the same couch. But the wild passion of revenge was only slumbering in the savage Frank. After one of their banquets, at which Sicharius, as usual, had taken too much wine, he told his boon companion that he owed him a great debt for having killed so many of his kindred, for the *wehrgeld* had raised him from beggary to riches. Chramnesind felt that the taunt must be paid for by blood. He at once extinguished the lights and cleft his enemy's skull with his poniard. The body was stripped and left impaled on a stockade, and the murderer at once hastened to the presence of Childebert to ask pardon for a deed which was justified, as he said, by duty to his kindred. But the great power at court was then the Queen mother, Brunihildis, and Sicharius had placed himself under her patronage. The final result was that

x

Chramnesind's estates were confiscated, and, after a short interval, restored by some mysterious influence, along with a royal letter relieving him of all further danger.

This painful narrative is given here because it throws a searching light on some darker aspects of the time. The chief actors are evidently men of high social condition, with manors and serfs and armed retainers. Yet Austrigiselus and his son are still untamed barbarians, caring nothing for forms of law and the solemn award of judges, and keen to exact vengeance for any wrong done to men of their blood. On the other hand, the Roman, when his estates have been ravaged, is not slower to avenge himself by slaughter and plunder. The Church, when it benevolently intervenes, is treated with scant respect, and seems to have little power to allay the blood-feud which, as Gregory says, was threatening to develop into a civil war at Tours. Even the justice of the King is perplexed and paralysed by secret influence and intrigue.

When we cast our eyes back on the sketch of morals which we have drawn from the chronicles, it would seem to be an unmitigated tale of passion and evil deeds—lust, greed, official oppression and arrogance, extracting wealth from the suffering masses to be spent in selfish waste, blood-thirst, as in pre-Christian ages. Yet the study of them is necessary for a full and truthful picture of that age. It would seem that the upper class, at least, constantly wore arms, ready for any encounter, and that they went abroad with an armed retinue, equally prepared for defence or for attack. And this appears to be true both of Romans and of Franks. The picture, which may be drawn from the letters of Sidonius, of the rather monotonous tranquillity of sequestered estates in Auvergne, or on the Moselle and Garonne, where the days passed without a thought of danger, or even any incident to ruffle the calm current of aristocratic life, is no longer true of Gaul in the days of the Merovingians. The convulsions of two or three generations have done their work. The "Roman peace", which gave the world almost unexampled calm and prosperity, has vanished. As in our own days, passion and greed and bold disregard of moral tradition have followed great wars and triumphs of military strength. It is the most pathetic lesson of history that the labours and happiness of peaceful development are so often wiped out by the upburst of elemental passions

which have only slumbered. The long tranquillity of the Roman
sway ended in the violence and darkness of the Middle Age.
The golden age of Victoria issued in social hysteria, the carnage
of a world-wide conflict, the greed of the profiteer, and the
destructive fury of anarchism.

CHAPTER IV

GREGORY OF TOURS AND HIS CIRCLE IN AUVERGNE

OUR knowledge of the social history of Gaul for 150 years, extending from the reign of Valentinian III. to the close of the sixth century, is mainly derived from two writers, Sidonius Apollinaris and Gregory of Tours. They were both Gallo-Roman aristocrats of Auvergne, and both rose to the episcopate. The interval between the death of Sidonius and the birth of Gregory was one of about two generations (479 to 539) ; but the interval for the younger writer was really much shorter than it seems to us. It was bridged by a lively and continuous tradition running in his own family, or gathered from long-lived contemporaries of Sidonius, who had perhaps known him and had seen, like him, the fall of the Western Empire and the triumph of the Visigothic power. Only twenty-five years before Gregory's birth, a son of Sidonius, who had fought for Alaric at Vouglé, was for a few months Bishop of Auvergne. Little more than ten years before the birth of Gregory, Arcadius, a grandson of Sidonius, had roused Auvergne to revolt against Theuderic. His daughter was the wife of Leontius of Bordeaux, who is commemorated in the verses of Fortunatus. Any observant reader of Gregory's most fascinating work, the *Vitae Patrum*, will notice the several links which connect his boyhood with the reign and conquests of Clovis, and the establishment of the Frank power in Auvergne. His father, Florentius, must have seen the first Frank bands bursting into their quiet valleys in 511. His uncle Gallus must have passed on to him tales he had heard from Quintianus, his predecessor in the diocese, who had been a bishop in Aquitaine in 506, and must have seen the fall of the

Empire. His great-grandfather, Gregory of Langres, who lived till the year of his birth and died at over ninety years of age, was a contemporary of Sidonius Apollinaris. Gregory himself or his father had visited nonagenarian anchorets in the dells of Auvergne whose birth was even earlier than the battle of the Catalaunian plains.

The materials for a life of Gregory must be chiefly drawn from scattered references to himself or his family in his own works. There is indeed a formal Life extant which some MSS. attribute to the Abbot Odo, probably the head of the monastery of Clugny in the tenth century. But the writer tells us that, although he had a mass of tradition about Gregory at his command, he had not used it, apparently because it was too full of the miraculous. Odo has chiefly drawn his narrative from the bishop's own works. Any additions seem to be of little value.

Georgius Florentius, called Gregory on his consecration, sprang from an aristocratic stock, both by his father's and his mother's side. His family belonged to that senatorial class who had, under the Imperial régime, won their status either by holding high office or by the favour of the Emperor. It retained its estates and its old consequence, apparently but little changed, under the new barbarian powers who had settled in Gaul. The paternal grandfather of Gregory was a senator named Georgius, who married Leucadia, a lady descended from Vettius Epagathus, a famous martyr of Lyons. There were two sons of this union, the elder, Gallus, who was Bishop of Auvergne from 546 to 554, and Florentius, the father of our Gregory. His mother was Armentaria, a granddaughter of Gregory, Bishop of Langres from 506 to 539, and niece of Tetricus, who succeeded him. On her mother's side she had two distinguished uncles, Nicetius, the Bishop of Lyons, and the Duke Gundulf. It was an episcopal house if ever there was one. With a certain pride Gregory tells us that, in the long line of his predecessors in the see of Tours, all except five belonged to his family.

The precise date of Gregory's birth is somewhat uncertain. He tells us that he entered on his episcopate 172 years after the death of S. Martin, and in the twelfth year of the reign of King Sigibert. The reckoning from S. Martin involves some difficulties, and we must fall back on the second date. Sigibert came to the throne, on the death of Chlothar, in December 561.

It follows that Gregory's elevation to the episcopate took place in 573. This is the one point of certainty from which to reckon. According to Odo, Gregory was thirty years of age when he was called to the see of Tours, and this would place his birth in 543. But Gregory tells us that his mother visited him a few months after his consecration at Tours, to seek the saint's virtue in relieving her of a painful ailment from which she had suffered for the thirty-four years since the birth of her son. Evidently this would require us to put his birth in the year 539, and that is, according to the best criticism, the true date. As for the year of his death, Abbot Odo states that he died in the twenty-first year of his episcopate—that is, in 594, the year following the death of King Guntram, the last surviving grandson of Clovis, and four years after the accession of Gregory's great namesake to the papal see.

The oldest member of Gregory's family known to us is his great-grandfather, Gregory, Bishop of Langres from 506 to 539. He was born about the year of Attila's invasion, and probably close to the scene of the great battle of 451. His career is one of the most interesting links between the society of the sixth century and the last generation of the Empire of the West. He was a younger contemporary of Sidonius Apollinaris, and saw the three great German powers steadily driving out the last officer of the Imperial administration in Gaul. He witnessed in his early youth the advance of the Burgundians to their seats on the Rhone and Saône, and that of the Franks to the Loire. He was over thirty when Clovis returned from the victory of Tolbiacum and was baptized at Rheims. He lived to see Burgundy annexed to the Frank Empire, a grandson of Clovis ruling at Metz, and, in a series of ephemeral victories over the armies of Belisarius, sweeping down to the Sicilian Straits. His experience must have been far more rich and varied than that of Sidonius, and yet not the faintest record of it has come down to us. We can only be assured that, like other great Gallo-Romans in the period of the invasions, he had a placid, prosperous life, undisturbed in the old possessions of his family, and rising to high office both in Church and State.

Gregory of Langres sprang from one of the noblest families of Eastern Gaul, with estates at Dijon and Autun. He was, for those days, well trained in letters, and at a singularly early age was made Count of Autun in the last years of the Western Empire, and continued in the office under the new Burgundian power. He held the office for forty years. On the death of his wife, Armentaria, he forsook the world and adopted a life of severe, if disguised, asceticism. He ate the coarsest food, and, while his guests were drinking wine, he would have water served to him disguised in a coloured glass. From him sprang a family of bishops. His son Tetricus succeeded him in the see of Langres ; two of his grandsons, Eufronius and Gregory, became bishops of Tours. He is the finest example of the easy way in which a great aristocrat of that age, often holding high secular office, passed into the prince bishop, beginning as a shy ascetic in worldly life, like the Vettius of Sidonius' letters, and yet never forgetting his hereditary rank, under the spiritual discipline of the Church. Like many others of his class he was called to the episcopate by popular voice. His home seems to have been at Dijon, where our Gregory's mother often stayed with her grandfather, and heard the tales which have come down to us in her son's charming, if very unclassical, pages. We have a picture of the camp of Dijon as it was in the bishop's days, which his descendant has sketched with unusual care. It was a fortress surrounded by strong walls 30 feet in height, with four gates, facing the four quarters of the compass, and thirty-three bastions in the entire circuit. Two rivers, which abounded in fish, either surrounded the town or intersected it from north to south. It probably offered a secure refuge to the Gallo-Romans when Huns, Burgundians, and Sueves were sweeping across the Rhine in the infancy of Gregory of Langres. The charm and fertility of the neighbouring district were then as attractive as they are now. All around spread fertile cornlands which called for light labour from the husbandmen, and the vineyards on the neighbouring hills could challenge the most famous vintages of classical lands or of the East. There Gregory of Langres had lived on his lands when he was Count of Autun, and there probably he continued to keep the same state as bishop of the diocese. But he had the peculiar marks of that ascetic sanctity which was the overmastering power of that age. And tales of wonder soon began to gather around him even in his lifetime. At the dead of night he would steal unseen into the baptistery which adjoined his house, for solitary devotion. And a choir of angelic voices had been

heard to join with him in chanting the psalms. He humbly
disclaimed the possession of miraculous powers, but when poor
creatures supposed to be possessed with demons were brought,
he would, with holy sign and prayer, strive to calm their agonies.
But no disclaimer could weaken the general faith in his healing
virtue. His granddaughter was relieved of a lingering fever by
merely resting a while upon his couch. Long after his death,
the manacles used to fall from the hands of prisoners as they
passed his tomb. When his son Tetricus had his father's remains
removed for burial in a new chapel, the face of the saint was seen
for a moment, as all believed, fresh and unchanged, as though
he were only sleeping.

The only tale of the bishop's life which brings it into the
field of ordinary mundane interest is that of the escape of his
grandson Attalus from captivity among the Germans in the
region of Trèves. The boy was given as a hostage in the settlement of the fierce feud between Theuderic and Childebert in
533. On rumours of fresh troubles or treachery, he, along with
others, was sold into slavery, and became the serf of a great
Frank landholder on the Meuse. The tale, which caught the
vigilant eye of Gibbon, gives us a rare glimpse of life on one of
the Frank estates in the north-east, thirty years after the conquest.
It is evidently a sumptuous establishment. The master of the
domain is a genial hospitable Frank, who gathers in his neighbours
and kinsmen for a good dinner on Sundays; who is not at all a
harsh or suspicious master; and who, although he sleeps with his
spear and shield beside his pillow, was easily cajoled and imposed
upon. But he had all the Frank greed and love of money; and
when the bishop sent an envoy to redeem his grandson, the
Frank requested a generous ransom. A young cook of the bishop,
named Leo, volunteered to manage the boy's escape. Leo offered
himself for sale into the German's service as a first-rate cook.
Once installed, he sent up dinners which called forth the praise
of the guests, and he became a prime favourite of his master.
After a year of cautious preparation, he took advantage of a
night of boisterous festivity, stole the arms of the Frank lord,
and, along with Attalus, fled on the best horses from the stable.
The tale of their flight across the Meuse, of their hiding from
close pursuit in the scrub and forest for three days, and their
finally finding a sanctuary, as the bell was ringing for matins, in

the presbytery at Rheims, is one of those flashes on real life which show us more that is interesting than heaps of dry disquisitions. The tale is so minute and circumstantial that we may well believe that it came to the historian direct from the lips of his cousin Attalus or his mother, Armentaria, in his early boyhood.

Gregory's uncle Gallus, who died in 554, when Gregory was about fifteen, had become his guardian on the early death of his father, Florentius. Gregory has repaid his uncle's care by a memoir which shows an affectionate reverence for his memory. Like so many others of his class, Gallus was possessed by the ascetic ideal in his early youth. Succeeding to high position and great possessions in Auvergne, he rejected an alliance with the daughter of another noble house and retired to the monastery of Cronona, with his father's reluctant consent. The reports of his self-discipline and devotion, and a voice of rare sweetness, attracted the notice of Quintianus, then Bishop of Clermont, who drew him from monastic life into his immediate circle. Gallus, like everybody else in Auvergne, had been despoiled and almost ruined in Theuderic's invasion of the district. But Theuderic, a true son of that age of strangely blended contrasts, if he was a cruel conqueror, was a good churchman, and, on favourable rumour, he summoned the accomplished high-born young deacon, along with other Arvernian clerics, to his court. Gallus rose to high favour with Theuderic and his Queen. In our own time we have sometimes seen clerical ambition coupled with the purest piety. And the noble of the sixth century often retained the instincts of his order under the garb of renunciation. Gallus followed the court on its progresses, and once joined it in a journey to Cologne. In that region bordering on Germany there were very many traces of old pagan worship which were still openly practised by the country people. Somewhere near Cologne, Gallus found a heathen shrine still frequented for the cure of disease, and also for gluttonous feasting. With one companion he set fire to the temple, and was with difficulty saved from the vengeance of the outraged people. He seems to have returned to Auvergne about the time when Bishop Quintianus died. The see of Clermont was in that age the object of pious ambition, or sometimes of very worldly and unscrupulous intrigue. The diocese was torn by cabals and eager canvassing to secure such a high place. Confident in his merit, or in his rank and the favour of the court, Gallus calmly announced that he should be the bishop, and was assailed with scurrilous abuse, and even with blows, by one of the clergy. He returned to court to find that the clergy of Trèves were clamouring to have him as successor to Bishop Aprunculus, who had just died. Theuderic informed them that he had another place for Gallus. But simony was then becoming rampant, and a clerical deputation from Auvergne arrived at court, prepared to bid high for the man of their choice. It is a case in which we can see a real value in royal consent to an episcopal election. Theuderic stood firm, rejected the corrupt proposals made to him, and gave immediate orders for the consecration of Gallus as chief pastor of his native diocese. When he was installed, he had to endure insolence, and even physical violence, from priests and great nobles. But the serene self-control of the great churchman, combined very probably with the cold hauteur of the noble, triumphed over all these petty insults, and Gallus became the stay and comforter of his people in evil days. In his episcopate, which lasted from 527 to 554, Auvergne suffered many calamities. It was devastated by fires and earthquakes, and in 546 it was threatened by the bubonic plague, which for fifty years was destined to be the recurring terror of the cities of Gaul. In answer to the bishop's prayers, a white-robed angel, appearing in a vision, promised that his people should be spared, but dimly foreshadowed his own death in eight years. The Rogations, which two generations before had been employed to soothe the people of Auvergne in the war with Euric, were now revived by Gallus with similar effect. Great processions set out to march to S. Julian's, and the promise of safety was fulfilled. When eight years had passed, Bishop Gallus was taken with a wasting fever, and he knew that his end was come. He gave the sacrament to his people for the last time, and on Sunday, as matins were being sung in the neighbouring church, he chanted the Fiftieth Psalm and passed away. His body lay for three days in the church, continually surrounded by the mourning people. It is hard to believe that Gregory, then a boy of fifteen, was not an eye-witness of the bishop's obsequies, which he describes with the minute faithfulness of a wistful affection. The memory of Gallus was an amulet to Gregory, and he has repaid the debt he owed to his second father.

There is another of Gregory's family who helped to form his character, and to whose career and many miracles he has given a large space. Nicetius, the uncle of Armentaria, was born on an estate in Burgundy about 513. In that year the devout character of his father, Florentinus, had led to his election as Bishop of Geneva, the royal consent had been given, and he was only prevented from entering on office by the entreaties of his wife, who told him prophetically that she bore under her bosom a future bishop. The child of such hopes fulfilled the prophecy. From early youth he was trained in sacred studies, and on his father's death he lived with his mother as head of the household, labouring with his hands beside his serfs even after receiving priest's orders, and teaching the slave children to read and chant the psalms.

His ascetic virtue and charity attracted the notice of his relative, Sacerdos, the Bishop of Lyons. That prelate, on a visit to Paris, was seized with fatal sickness, and on his death-bed was kindly visited by King Childebert. The dying man, as a last request, begged of the King to allow Nicetius to succeed him; and Nicetius was duly elected to the see with the suffrages of both King and people in 551. Gregory had been often with Nicetius, both as a child and after he had taken holy orders, and he was strangely fascinated by the bishop's character. Nicetius was an ascetic of the severest type, stern to himself and not gentle to others, offering a bold front to the secular powers and mercilessly punishing the vices of the clergy. He was also a diligent administrator ; he built or restored churches, and skilfully cultivated the farms and vineyards of the see. That his strong character made a deep impression on his contemporaries is clear from the number of stupendous miracles which are attributed to him. Yet one cannot help feeling, in reading his life, that the conventional ecclesiastical virtues which moved the admiration of the pious Gregory are not such as would attract our reverence. Nor was his character universally admired even in his own time. Rightly or wrongly, he left behind many fierce enemies and detractors, in whose eyes he seemed anything but a saint. When his will was read out in the forum, and it was found that the bishop had bequeathed nothing to the church where his remains were to repose, the disappointed priest exclaimed that Nicetius had only confirmed the impression of his character which men had generally formed of him in his lifetime.

Gregory in his Life of Nicetius has surpassed even his usual exuberance in the record of his miracles. It is a perfect mine of the miraculous, sometimes passing into the ludicrous and grotesque. Nicetius was evidently a strong bishop, and a holy man according to the conventional standards. Yet it may be doubted whether he had the more gentle and gracious charms of sanctity which have made the lives of S. Francis and S. Theresa a precious possession of the Universal Church.

Another friend of Gregory and guardian of his youth who demands notice was a man of a higher type than Nicetius of Lyons. Avitus belonged to a high family in Auvergne, probably the same as that of the Avitus who rose to be Emperor for a brief space in 455. Avitus, the friend of Gregory, had a long life from 511 to 594, and was elected to the see of Clermont only two years before Gregory's elevation to the see of Tours, and by the same friendly support of Sigibert. But he was thirty years older than Gregory, and on the death of Bishop Gallus he became his tutor in sacred learning and helped to mould his religious character. The interval of seventeen years between his episcopate and that of Gallus was a dark and disgraceful episode in the history of the Arvernian church. The succession was fiercely disputed, and with wavering fortunes for some time, between the supporters of the Archdeacon Cautinus and a presbyter named Cato. Cautinus finally managed to gain the support of King Theudebald, and became Bishop of Auvergne. But he disgraced his office by a career of self-indulgence ending in epilepsy, and by avarice and extortions from his clergy, enforced with incredible cruelty. Yet this sordid and abandoned creature maintained himself in his see for seventeen years. On the death of Cautinus the usual conflict broke out between the two opposing conceptions of the episcopate which we observe in some of the letters of Sidonius. To the ambitious son of an old senatorial house it offered a career of power and dignity hardly inferior to that of provincial governors in the great days of the Empire. To the pious recluse, whose ambition was sanctified by religious enthusiasm, it offered the chance of the highest service to men possible in those days. Some of the great families again and again in these years strove hard by worldly arts to

grasp such a prize.   On the death of Bishop Eufrasius in 515
the family of Apollinaris, a son of Sidonius, by bribes and
influence secured his succession for a few months, and, in the
face of great popular enthusiasm, postponed the succession of
Quintianus.   On the death of Cautinus a similar effort was made
by Eufrasius, belonging to the powerful family of Hortensius,
who had been a count of the district in the reign of Theuderic.
   But the bribes and lavish promises of Eufrasius failed to
secure their object.   Avitus, who was then archdeacon, had a
purity and elevation of character which, even in such an atmosphere of gross selfish ambition, was often a prevailing force.
He won the suffrages of the clergy and people, and then betook
himself to the court of Austrasia to submit himself for royal
approval.   The King, putting aside all sinister influences, gave
his assent at once, and, by a certain violation of the canons,
ordered that Avitus should be without delay consecrated in his
presence at Metz.   In justice, charity, and benevolence, as well
as in commanding influence, the new Bishop of Clermont did
credit to the judgement of Sigibert.   He was the stay of the
orphan and the widow, and gave shelter to wanderers from
foreign parts.   The Italian poet Fortunatus found in him a
generous patron.   In his reverence for ancient saints and relics,
and the anchorets who swarmed among the rocks of Auvergne,
Avitus was a true child of his age, and his influence undoubtedly
had a great effect in making Gregory its sympathetic chronicler.
He built a splendid chapel to receive worthily the remains of
S. Illidius, one of his precedessors in the fourth century.   An
oratory of delicate beauty, in honour of S. Antolianus, had been
erected with costly marbles by the wife and sister of Sidonius
fifty years before.   Gaps and chinks in the arches seemed to
threaten a total collapse of the building.   The bishop undertook
its restoration.   But Alchima and Placidina, in laying the
foundations of their chapel, had disturbed the bones of many
other saints and martyrs, and a vision of Antolianus himself predicted disaster to the restoration.   One day, when the workmen
had left the scaffolding for their mid-day meal, the whole structure
fell in and left apparently an immense ruin.   When the cloud of
dust had cleared away it was found, to the delight of the bishop,
not only that no one had been killed, but that, by the protecting
virtue of the saint, the altar with its marbles remained untouched

by the fall of the columns.   This is a glimpse of that restoration
of ancient shrines which was a marked feature of church life in
the sixth century, and in which Gregory himself bore a distinguished part.   Avitus was also a frequent visitor to those
secluded and romantic hermitages in Auvergne, where perhaps
for more than half a century the recluse had led a weird, half-
savage life, soothed by the perpetual charm of nature and
mother Earth, or driven alternately to ecstasy or frenzy by
angelic or infernal visions.   This life of spiritual defiance of the
world and all its lusts and ambitions and transient glories was
the ideal of Avitus and his kind in the sixth century, and became
the ideal of Gregory.   And to his enthusiastic and sympathetic
pictures of that lonely life we owe probably the most perfect
revelation of the religion of the early Middle Age.

These sketches of some of the older relatives of Gregory
seemed necessary to gain a conception of the influences which
formed his character, and the atmosphere in which he grew up.
It is perhaps necessary to review briefly the internal history of
Auvergne in the decade before his birth.   The stirring events of
that disastrous time must have left a deep mark on social life,
as they have on the hagiography of the sixth and seventh
centuries.   When Gregory was born, Auvergne had been for a
generation under Frank rule.   Theuderic, the eldest son of Clovis,
in 511 was detached from the main advance to annex Eastern
Aquitaine, Auvergne, and the valley of the Rhone, and, in the
partition of Gaul among the sons of Clovis, Auvergne fell to the
lot of Theuderic.   But the Arvernian people were never very
submissive to authority.   According to patriotic legend, the
sons of ancient Troy, the defenders of Gergovia against the greatest
of the Caesars, the race who had raised their compatriot Avitus
to the Imperial throne, had a peculiar pride and high spirit of
independence which was fostered by seclusion behind their
mountains.   And the fierceness of the first Frank invasion had
left bitter memories behind.   For two or three generations
Auvergne and Aquitaine had little love for the rule of the Franks.

The atrocities of the Frank armies were probably a disillusionment to men who were inclined to hail the accession of a new
Catholic power.   The commanding personality of Clovis was
soon withdrawn.   The jealousy and faithless feuds of his sons
gave an air of weakness to the Frank power in the eyes of a

population still proud of Roman tradition and Celtic nationality. In the early years of the sixth century the Franks seemed still little more than a band of invaders cantoned on the Meuse and the Seine and lower Rhine. South of the Loire they were settled in scanty numbers. The Frank conquest, as we have seen, had been heralded and prepared by the sympathy and active intrigues of the Catholic clergy, who groaned under Arian rule, and hailed with eagerness the conversion of the Franks and their great chief. But their first experience of the new champions of the Church was, to say the least, disquieting. The Frank conception of the Christian faith, however orthodox in theory, was rudimentary in practice. The army of a most Christian Merovingian would not only carry fire and sword into the secluded homes of peaceful fellow-Christians : they would, in spite of orders, rush headlong to the sack of a church or monastery, consecrated by the relics of S. Julian or S. Martin ; they would slaughter the priest at the altar, enslave the cowering congregation, and make a spoil of the rich vestments and jewelled crosses dedicated by ancient piety. The old Gallo-Roman nobles of the south were still very numerous, and still possessed broad domains peopled by armies of serfs and dependents who might easily develop into a formidable militia. Their towns, often surrounded by almost impregnable walls, still carried on something of their free municipal life, which was the glory of the Imperial period, and, as they showed again and again, they could put in the field thousands of armed citizens. The wonder is not that they occasionally rose in revolt, but that the revolts were not more frequent.

Ten years before the birth of Gregory, when Theuderic was engaged in a great war against the Thuringians, a rumour spread through Auvergne that the Austrasian king had fallen in battle. And a futile conspiracy to bring the province under the rule of Childebert was organised by Arcadius, a grandson of Sidonius Apollinaris. Childebert, who, in possession of the neighbouring parts of Aquitaine, with the avidity of his race, had gloated over the tales he had heard of the beauty and fertility of Limagne, appeared at once on the scene ; but the gates of Clermont were closed. Arcadius, however, by secret means obtained the King's admission ; but just as he entered there came the news that Theuderic was returned safe from Thuringia; and the treacherous Childebert quitted Auvergne as quickly as he had come. But for this

feeble and short-lived rebellion there came a terrible vengeance.
In 532, Chlothar and Childebert, instigated as was said by their
mother, meditated the annexation of Burgundy. Theuderic, who
had espoused a daughter of the Burgundian King Sigismund,
declined to join in the expedition. But his *leudes*, from whatever
cause, threatened to transfer their allegiance to his brothers if
he did not lead them to so fair a conquest. In order to appease
their greedy discontent he proposed to them another venture,
which should at once satisfy their passion for rapine and his
own settled purpose of revenge. He told them that if they
would follow him in an invasion of Auvergne they should have
gold and silver to their heart's content, cattle and raiment and
troops of slaves. The famous wealth of fair Limagne should be
at their mercy. Cruelly was the promise fulfilled. Gregory's
description of the punishment of Auvergne, which evidently
came to him from eye-witnesses, resembles the desolation of the
Palatinate by Louis XIV. or the devastation of the Carnatic by
Hyder Ali. The capital, indeed, was saved by the strength of
its walls, which fifty years before had kept the Visigothic army
long at bay, or, as Gregory preferred to believe, by the sanctity
and prayers of Bishop Quintianus. But on the country districts
the Frank army burst like a tempest. The peasants fled from
their farms, carrying their movable possessions to fastnesses
among the hills, or to what seemed the more impregnable security
of churches. Those who remained, rich and poor alike, lost
everything. Even the most venerated shrines failed to shelter
the fugitives. The most Christian Merovingians, whose crusade
against the Visigothic heretics had received the blessings of the
Church, were still half-pagan banditti, intoxicated with their
new wealth and the luxury of the fair lands they had won. The
basilica of S. Julian at Brioude in Auvergne, where the remains
of the martyr reposed, was the most sacred and frequented
church in those regions. Its miraculous cures were famous all
over Gaul. When the army of Theuderic appeared before it, the
church was crowded with refugees, kneeling around their little
household treasures. The savage invaders burst in upon them
and swept them all off into slavery, with the very priests at the
altar. It is to be feared that the victims would not find the same
comfort that Gregory does in the tale that the leaders in the
sacrilege, on their return, were seized by evil spirits and perished

miserably. Advancing up the valley of the Allier the invaders laid siege to the fortress of Lovolautrum, which, from the earliest times, had been deemed impregnable. The place only fell into the hands of Theuderic through the treachery of a priest's servant. The priest himself was slain at the altar, and probably the people were either enslaved or massacred. Turning to the west, and pressing through the mountains of Cantal, the Franks found themselves in front of Meroliac, which lay a few miles to the north east of the modern town of Mauriac. It was a singular natural fortress, formed by walls of rock a hundred feet high, which enclosed fields and gardens and vineyards with a never-failing supply of water. The imprudence of the defenders placed fifty of them at Theuderic's mercy, and they were obliged to purchase their safety by a ransom in gold. Theuderic had achieved his object by the temporary ruin of one of the richest districts in Gaul. The people were reduced to beggary or slavery. He left behind him to guard the province for Austrasia the Duke Sigiwald, whose acts of violence and robbery have left their mark on hagiography for generations. Of the administration of the Counts of Auvergne during these years, Evodius, Becco, Hortensius, only a few scattered traces remain. They were probably of Gallo-Roman race, but it may be doubted whether they were more equitable and sympathetic than the Frank duke had been. After such an experience, Auvergne seems to have subsided into a calm acquiescence in the sway of Austrasia. But the memories of that evil time, which came to Gregory from his mother, his uncle Gallus, and Quintianus, were evidently painful and vivid. And it is little wonder that thirty years afterwards, when the district had by the bounty of nature recovered from the violence of man, it was ready to support Chramnus the rebellious son of Chlothar.

Florentius and Armentaria, the parents of Gregory, were probably married in 534, about two years after the calamities we have described and about the year of Theuderic's death. Gregory's father died at an early age, and naturally his son has not much to tell us of him. The little he has to tell relates almost entirely to his father's ailments and his religious life, or what we should regard as his superstitions. Both Florentius and his wife were moulded on the spiritual type of their age, devoted to its ideals, completely mastered by its limitless faith

Y

in unseen powers. Of his father's worldly occupations or intellectual tastes we hear nothing. He must have superintended the work on his estates in Limagne. He probably had to make frequent journeys to other estates of his wife in Burgundy, with all the risk from brigands and fever which beset the traveller in those days. In his early youth he must have seen Theuderic's army ravaging Auvergne in the years of the conquest. But men of his class seem to have been little disturbed by wars and invasions which loom large in the chronicles. His life was probably of the calm, monotonous kind which his father Georgius had led in the days of Sidonius. But instead of composing fugitive verses, or third-rate imitations of Statius or Claudian, Florentius was reading the hours or visiting the patriarchs of the hermitage, or testing the virtue of some chapel of Illidius, Ferreolus, or S. Julian. The health of the upper class, from many indications, seems to have been in that age strangely precarious, perhaps an evil heritage from the age of indulgence described by Salvian. And Florentius would appear to have been a chronic invalid. In his eleventh year, as he told his son, he had been taken to be cured of a wasting fever by an anchoret named Martius, who died at the age of ninety in 525. He had founded a monastery in whose pleasant garden the old man used to sit and give his benediction to the crowds of the sick and possessed who came to him for relief. Florentius had all the abounding faith of that time in the virtue of relics. Soon after his marriage he begged a priest to give him some amulet to protect him against robbers and floods, or the more insidious assaults of passion. The sacred treasure was at his death passed on to his wife and son. Gregory, then a mere child, was once enabled by a dream to give his father relief from a torturing fit of gout by laying a cabbalistic name under his pillow, and, on the pattern of an ancient miracle, the boy assuaged another attack by the smoke of a fish's liver.

The shrine of S. Julian at Brioude was thirty or forty miles to the south of the capital of Auvergne. In the sixth century there were still traditions of heathen rites having been celebrated on the sacred spot. Its lands had been ravaged by the Burgundians in the fifth century; and in the first quarter of the sixth, as we have seen, it had been plundered and desecrated by Theuderic and his Duke Sigiwald. With the exception of S. Martin's at Tours, it was in those days probably the most attractive and

the most frequented centre of devotion.   Its festival, on the
28th of August, drew enormous crowds of votaries and invalids
from all parts of Gaul for the sake of its visions and mysterious
cures.   At this sacred season the inns and lodgings of the little
country town were crowded to overflowing, and in the press of
worshippers many were unable to find an entrance to the church.
The paralysed and epileptic, the blind and the deaf were laid in
the cloister that they might feel a far-off touch of the holy
martyr's hand.   Beggars along the cloisters imperiously claimed
their toll of alms.   It was a strange atmosphere which surrounded S. Julian's, genuine piety and crass superstition, the
clamorous claims of poverty easily passing into crime and thefts
from the very altar.   Florentius used to take his household to
Brioude for the holy season, which probably offered, beside the
comfort of devotion, some holiday amusements to relieve the
tedium of rustic life.   But the record of these holidays is often
darkened by some tale of sudden sickness among the household.
On one visit Gregory's elder brother Peter was taken with such
a violent fever that the boy's life was despaired of.   But after
lying for a night before the saint's tomb and drinking an un-
palatable potion compounded of the sacred dust, he was able
next day to take food and move about.   At the following festival
the young Gregory had sunstroke and a high fever.   He was
carried to the church of S. Ferreolus, about a mile from S.
Julian's, where the coolness and the secret virtues of the fountain
banished his pains.   The stories of Armentaria, Gregory's mother,
are of the same kind.   Soon after her husband's death, which
may have taken place in the first onset of the bubonic plague in
546, she probably went to live on the Burgundian estates of her
family.   Like her husband, she held intensely the prevailing
faith in relics, and treasured them in her oratory.   As a young
girl, she had found relief in a quartan fever from resting on the
couch of her grandfather, the sainted Bishop of Langres.   Some
of these potent treasures had once checked a fire in her house
which broke out when the household had retired to rest.   At
the feast of S. Polycarp she once is recorded to have seen the
Host escaping from the hands of an unchaste deacon, as he bore
it into church, and flying through the air to its place on the altar.
   To understand a character like that of Gregory of Tours,
and the whole drift and tone of his works, it is necessary to realise

the faith which enwrapped him in his infancy and inspired his whole life. The dim religious life of the early Middle Ages is severed from the modern mind by so wide a gulf, by such a revolution of beliefs, that the most cultivated sympathy can only hope to revive it in faint imagination. Its hard, firm, realistic faith in the wonders and terrors of an unseen world seems to evade the utmost effort to make it real to us. Its theory of life and rules of conduct put a strain on human nature from which modern easygoing self-indulgence recoils as impossible and repulsive. Chastity, humility, and charity were the cardinal virtues of the saintly life, as in theory they still are, but among the strictly religious of those days they were enforced and practised with a stern disregard of ordinary worldly considerations to us now almost inconceivable. " The way of transgressors is hard " : but in a different sense the path of the saint was harder. There could be no compromise with the world : no perfection without renunciation. In the momentous conflict with evil on which the fate of Eternity depends, Holy Church sustains the weakness of the combatant by her Sacramental Grace, only to be received through her appointed channels by believing her doctrine of things invisible. To question her authority or her message, to refuse obedience to her rules of conduct and observance, even the most apparently external and trivial, is sin so heinous that it may well be visited at once with physical punishment, sickness, or loss of bodily powers or of reason. To defy and disobey her ministers is the worst of crimes. Even kings must bend before an authority which is not of this world. For though the Church will consecrate their rightful claims, and render them their due, she is the guardian of a higher law and may, for the breach of it, exile the mightiest from God's Grace in this world and the next. Nor does she merely regulate her children's moral life ; she is their constant guardian against the ghostly powers of the unseen universe who swarm around the life of men, the demons who bring foul disease and tempt and waylay at every turn. Only the Christian warrior, armed with the panoply of the Church, can defy this terrible unseen host. It is the Church's high privilege to save men not only from the eternal doom, but from the torment inflicted by evil spirits in this present life. And against their arts she can summon the army of martyrs and holy ones departed, to whom is given, in virtue of their sanctity, to succour those who in faith invoke their help and mediation. And this is not mere spiritual help. The Divine Grace in its infinite compassion has rewarded their virtue by giving to their bones and dust, nay to shreds of their garments or of the pall upon their tombs, a strange efficacy to heal disease and drive away evil spirits, if the afflicted one use these sacred relics with unwavering faith. Human life being then such as it was, so full of violence with little regular restraint from law, so tainted with unchecked disease, so darkened by weird terror, it is little wonder that the magical and superstitious side of religion became the most powerful. It seemed to satisfy universal cravings. Its luxuriant growth was not kept down by any body of sceptical intelligence in the higher class.

European culture, which had been moulded by the penetrating intellectual influence of classical civilisation, had been long declining and was soon to reach its nadir. Such education as there was, was of a very rudimentary type, giving only a scrappy, imperfect knowledge of a few Roman poets, with only faint glimpses of Greek thought and science. Great nobles, and even men destined to high places in the Church, in the essentials of education, were hardly on the level of our humble villagers. Here and there we catch a trace of a rough common-sense scepticism about startling or ludicrous tales of supernatural wonders. But the whole drift of men's minds in every social grade was to submissive belief in any violation of the order of Nature as natural and expected, if it seemed to attest the power of holiness and was vouched for by the Church.

It was through this medium that Gregory saw both the secular and religious life of his time. His visions and early reverence for all holy places and memories marked him out in his parents' eyes as destined for the religious life. The tuition of his uncle Gallus, in whose care he was left after his father's death, was probably the best for Gregory's future career. It was at this period that Gregory, among his many illnesses, was seized with gastric fever. He was affectionately tended by his uncle and mother. But the case seemed desperate, when the boy himself, " by some divine suggestion ", bade them bear him to the tomb of S. Illidius. There with intense faith he vowed that if the saint restored him he would devote himself to the religious life. He received the tonsure and the diaconate. He became, in the words of Fortunatus, an *alumnus* of S. Julian, and probably spent much of his youth in attending the holy offices at the church of Brivate. Of his secular education he tells us little. At eight years of age he was learning the very rudiments. Whether he ever read deeply in the classical writers, as they were read a hundred years earlier in the schools of Auvergne and Bordeaux, may be doubted. Again and again, with modest humility, he laments his uncouth, rustic style, and regrets that he has had no tincture of the rhetorical skill which was imparted in the old schools of Gaul. It is true that here and there he shows a reminiscence of Virgil and Sallust, Prudentius, Orosius, and Eusebius. He makes occasional reference to the Elder Pliny and Aulus Gellius. In the preface to the *Gloria Martyrum*, he makes a rather cheap parade of the names in classical mythology, mostly drawn from Virgil. It has been suggested that these rather superficial traces of profane culture may have been the result of his intimacy with Fortunatus, who came to those regions in the early manhood of Gregory. In any case, his knowledge of the great classical writers was very slight and superficial, and no classical model has left any mark on his prose style. Under Archdeacon Avitus he was carefully trained in Holy Scripture and dogmatic lore, of which he sometimes makes a parade in tales of vivacious debate with Arians and Jews. At the same time he probably acquired the knowledge of the canons which was necessary in the government of such a diocese as Tours.

Thus his youth passed away attending the service of the altar at S. Julian's or S. Laurence's of Auvergne, visiting his grand-uncle Nicetius at Lyons, or his mother at Cavaillon, or making excursions with his elder friend Avitus to hermitages in Auvergne. He received deacon's orders at the regular time, and then came the event in his life which fixed for ever his devotion to S. Martin and determined his career. In 563, probably owing to habits of overstrained asceticism, his strength gave way and he fell into a serious illness. His thoughts had long been turned to the glories and virtues of the great saint of Tours, and he now resolved to try their efficacy by a visit to his tomb. On the way his attendants, struck by his alarming weakness, begged him to return to die at home in Auvergne. But his energy was invincible, he pressed on his journey, and his faith was rewarded by a complete cure. That he regarded this event as a turning-point in his life

seems to be shown by the formal fashion in which he notes that
it occurred in the 163rd year after the assumption of the holy
and blessed Bishop Martin, the holy Eufronius being in the
seventh year of his episcopate of Tours, and the most glorious
Sigibert in the second of his reign.

The year 563 was one long remembered for strange portents
and overwhelming calamities in Auvergne. The sun was surrounded with mysterious splendours which seemed to the rustics
as though the birth of other suns. In that year there was an
almost total eclipse, and a comet like a flashing sword blazed
across the heavens. A huge cliff fell with a prolonged roar into
the Rhone, damming up its waters, which at last, finding vent in
a raging torrent, swept down men and crops and cattle to the
walls of Geneva. At matins in the great church of Auvergne
a lark, darting through the aisles, extinguished all the lights.
The bubonic plague once more invaded the province and desolated Lyons, Bourges, Chalon, and Dijon ; and its ravages were
peculiarly swift and deadly. The sufferers died on the second
or third day after their first attack. The people, says Gregory,
fell in legions. Materials for coffins failed, the bodies were flung
in scores together into pits, and as many as three hundred
unburied corpses were counted on one Sunday on the floor of
S. Peter's Church. When many had fled from the pestilence, the
good priest Cato remained to bury the dead and administer the
last sacraments, but he, too, fell a victim at last. His rival, the
worldly and dissolute Bishop Cautinus, after skulking in various
places to escape the contagion, perished unregretted. Gregory
went to Brioude to place himself under the protection of
S. Julian. One of his servants caught the pestilence in an
aggravated form, and his fellow-servants called in a sorcerer of
the olden days, who applied his spells and incantations and
amulets, and Gregory attributed the boy's death to the use of
these pagan sorceries. Another servant who fell ill was saved
instantaneously by drinking a little of the dust from the martyr's
tomb in a cup of water. Gregory saw, in the contrast, the clearest
proof that the true refuge of any one who has been crossed in
baptism is in the help and protection of the saints.

Gregory himself, as we have seen, had personal experience of
this celestial guardianship. It followed him on the many journeys
which he took between Auvergne and Burgundy. Travelling in

those days was evidently full of danger or adventure, from the truculence of great nobles and their armed bands, or from parties of brigands who infested the woods, or oftener from the fevers and dysentery which were probably the result of bad water and unsanitary lodging. Once, on his way to visit his mother, his party was attacked by highwaymen. But the invocation of S. Martin at once drove them into such headlong flight that they would not wait for the refreshment which the good Gregory was ready to offer them. On another visit to his mother at Cavaillon, one of his servants, as so often happened, was seized with fever and dysentery. His master tells that having such risks in view, he always travelled with some dust from the holy tomb, and in this case it proved its efficacy. A fierce tempest which overtook him on his way back from Burgundy was dispelled by holding up the bag of relics which he always wore round his neck. He was devoted to the adoration of the Blessed Virgin at hours when others were asleep. And once, on a country estate in Auvergne, as he passed at midnight to the oratory for private prayer, he saw it lighted up with a strange splendour. The door opened of its own accord, and as he entered the radiance vanished, and in the darkness he was only conscious of the Virgin's power. In this round of devotion and growing faith in the unseen world, the years passed till his call came to the great See of Tours.

One hundred and seventy-two years from the passing of S. Martin, in the twelfth year of King Sigibert, Eufronius died in the seventeenth year of his episcopate. The biographer of the ninth century describes the enthusiastic election of Gregory by the assembled nobles, clergy, and people. He was well known at Tours from his devout visits to the shrine. In the long line of the Bishops of Tours, all but five had been members of his family. He possessed the rank, generosity, prudence, and spotless character which marked him out for high office in the Church. But his personal qualities were reinforced by powerful favour. Gregory was at court when the deputation carrying the *consensus* of the diocese arrived, and his modest refusal of the office was overpowered by the urgency of Sigibert and Queen Brunihildis. His ordination was hurried on to prevail over his modest reluctance, and he was consecrated by Egidius at Rheims within nineteen days from the death of his predecessor.

Gregory was the nineteenth in the long roll of Bishops of Tours, which he has drawn out in the last chapter of his History. The line ran back to a Bishop Gatian, whose tenure of office dates from the first year of the Emperor Decius, 249, at a time when the surrounding population were fanatically pagan, and, from fear of insult and violence, the Holy Mysteries had to be celebrated in caves and secret places. The third in the succession was S. Martin, the great object of Gregory's adoration, who extirpated the heathenism of the region and built many churches on old scenes of idol worship. In looking down the line of those who succeeded the great apostle of Gaul, one is struck by the number who were men of wealth and senatorial descent, like Gregory himself. The bishop's office gratified a curious mixture of worldly and spiritual ambition. And a sincerely devout and ascetic man like Gregory never forgot that he was an aristocrat, and never fails to record the high birth of priests and anchorets who had forsaken all for Christ. Along with the gentleness and humility inspired by a profoundly religious discipline, Gregory showed early a courage and steadfastness of character, combined with prudence and knowledge of men, which marked him out as a statesman capable of dealing with great emergencies. It was probably these qualities which led the Austrasian court to hurry on the election of a supporter to the See of Tours in a year of great trouble on the Loire.

Gregory was little over thirty when he suddenly found himself in charge of a diocese which from its position on the Loire was a storm centre in the long struggle between Neustria and Austrasia for the rich lands and cities of Aquitaine. In that tumultuous time the city of Tours often changed masters. In 567 it had fallen to the lot of Sigibert on the death of his brother Charibert. But the greed of Chilperic, which had displayed itself in a treacherous invasion of Sigibert's kingdom in 564, soon broke out again. It was rekindled by the blood feud between the two fierce queens springing out of the ghastly murder of Brunihildis' sister Galswintha through the jealousy of Fredegundis. The quarrel was for a time composed by the surrender to Brunihildis, on the judgement of Guntram, of the five cities in Aquitaine which Galswintha had received from Chilperic as her morning gift. But this was only a temporary lull. In place of these distant possessions in the south, Chilperic resolved to seize

Poitiers and Tours (belonging to Sigibert by compact), and
launched against them an army under the command of his son
Clovis, in the very year of Gregory's consecration as bishop.
Sigibert appealed to Guntram for aid in repelling such wanton
aggression, and the Burgundian king sent an army under
Mummolus, the greatest captain of the time. He had just
repelled an invasion of the Lombards at Embrun, and he had
equal success against the Neustrian forces. Clovis was utterly
defeated and fled to Bordeaux. The people of Poitiers were compelled to renew their oath of allegiance to Sigibert. Guntram
summoned a synod of his bishops at Paris to compose the strife
between Sigibert and Chilperic. The attempt failed. Chilperic
would listen to no mediation, and despatched another army under
his son Theudebert to recover Poitiers and Tours and the regions
beyond the Loire. Theudebert, when a prisoner of Sigibert, had
been generously treated by his uncle, and had taken an oath of
loyalty to him. But, with the characteristic faithlessness of his
race, he now plunged into the struggle with ferocious energy.
He defeated the Austrasian forces under Gundobald with
enormous slaughter and entered Poitiers in triumph. Then turning to the north he spread havoc along the Loire up to the walls
of Tours. The sight of their ravaged lands drove the citizens to
abandon their allegiance to Sigibert and to change masters, as
they had many times to do in the next few years. Theudebert
then pressed on to Limoges and Cahors, leaving a wilderness
behind him. The churches were burnt down and plundered, the
priests slain at the altar, virgins of the Church were insulted and
defiled. The Arian Visigoths had never been guilty of a tithe
of the sacrilege which was now wantonly perpetrated by the
Catholic Frank. And Gregory has to confess that the mourning
of the Church was more bitter than in Diocletian's persecution.

It was amid such scenes that the young bishop came from
the religious quiet of Auvergne to take up his heavy charge.
One would think on reviewing the history of Touraine, in those
years, that even the strongest nerves would have been shaken.
Yet Gregory seems to have preserved, through all the troubles
and vicissitudes of the time, an unruffled calm. This was partly
the result of rank and temperament, but still more of faith in
the grandeur and supernatural powers of the Church. And there
was hardly a pause in the strain which Tours and its bishop had

to endure during the deadly struggle of Neustria and Austrasia, and the repeated efforts of Chilperic to annex the cities south of the Loire. After Theudebert's victory at Poitiers it was within a year, along with the Aquitanian cities, restored to Sigibert on a great defeat of Theudebert at Angoulême. When Sigibert, apparently at the height of his hopes and fortunes in 575, was cut off amid a festive scene at Vitry by the deadly arts of Fredegundis, Tours once more came under the power of her husband. And during all these changes Gregory had to endure the insolence and cynical brutality, alternating with unscrupulous dissimulation, of Count Leudastes, who for fifteen years lost or resumed his office with each change of allegiance. The old slave cook, who had bought his office from Charibert in 565, lived to plague Gregory and his diocese till 583, when he met a cruel but deserved end. In that long career of wild ambition and reckless caprice Leudastes played many parts. Whenever he feared that the city might come under Austrasian rule he would pay court to Gregory and the magnates of the district. On the report of Sigibert's assassination all his inbred vices broke out, and he insulted and trampled on all ranks at Tours. Gregory had an aristocratic, as well as moral, scorn for this low-born and dissolute parvenu, and his calm hauteur probably irritated Leudastes more than open defiance. If he had to visit the bishop's house, he would appear fully armed with helmet, cuirass, and long lance. Then after insult and false insinuations, he would swear solemn friendship with his hand on S. Martin's pall. But the truce did not last long. He had himself been plundered by the lawless Merovech during his stay in Tours, and he recouped himself and gratified an insatiable rapacity by exactions levied on rich citizens. Nor did he spare the estates of the Church. During nearly three years of this official licence and tyranny, the bishop bore all these insults with a cautious and patient dignity. At last he struck silently. A quiet, mysterious deputation appeared before Chilperic to set forth the wrongs which the Church and people of Tours were suffering from his Count. In spite of all sinister influence, the King ordered Leudastes to be deprived of his office, and left to the bishop and the people to elect his successor. Their choice fell on one Eunomius. But Leudastes was not of a temper easily to accept defeat. He thought Queen Fredegundis, whose favour he had enjoyed, and

Bishop Gregory were the authors of his official degradation, and
he determined, by means of court intrigue and subtle slander,
to ruin both by a single stroke. Clovis, the son of Audovera,
Chilperic's banished wife, was hated and suspected by Fredegundis,
and apparently not without reason. The Queen's position was
at the time not quite secure, and Clovis had a party who set his
claims to the succession above the sons of Fredegundis. Leudastes
combined with an ambitious and unprincipled priest of Tours,
named Riculfus, to excite suspicion of Fredegundis's fidelity in the
mind of her uxorious husband and to have her children dis-
inherited, leaving Clovis heir to the throne. When that prince
came to power the conspirators were to have their reward : the
one was to become Bishop of Tours, the other a duke in the
highest rank next the throne. A humble sub-deacon, also
called Riculfus, was engaged, by the promise of the archdeaconry,
in the plot to entangle Gregory, and he strove to worm himself
into his confidence. Meanwhile Leudastes, in a private audience,
began to insinuate that Neustrian interests were not safe in the
hands of the bishop. Although Gregory was known to be a
supporter of Sigibert, he was rather a favourite of Chilperic, and
the King repelled the calumny with scorn. With imperturbable
assurance Leudastes went on to accuse Gregory of having said
that the Queen was the mistress of Bertram of Bordeaux. This
was too much for Chilperic, and he soundly thrashed and kicked
the informer. Not in the least disconcerted by his treatment,
Leudastes told the King that two friends of Gregory, Plato and
Gallienus, if put to the torture would, on the evidence of the
sub-deacon Riculfus, confirm all he had said. In accordance with
the deep-laid plot, Riculfus, pretending alarm for some rash words,
asked his bishop, in accordance with the canons, for leave to
retire into another diocese. It was a subtle device to cast suspicion on Gregory and to save himself from having his evidence
severely tested in the cruel fashion of those days. But the
historian of the Franks, who tells us all these intrigues, must
have had secret channels of information, and he was fully conscious of the perils amid which he lived. He told Riculfus that
he must bear the consequences of anything he had said, and
refused him permission to migrate. But Riculfus was soon
carried a prisoner to Soissons, and there deposed that in the
presence of Plato and Gallienus, the bishop had slandered the

Queen. Leudastes was then deputed to go to Tours and bring
up to court the two witnesses of the defamation. He arrived in
Easter week of 580. The priest Riculfus, confident in his destiny,
in a manner which seems extraordinary to us, strode about the
cloisters, and did not hesitate to heap the vulgarest and coarsest
insults on the great bishop. In particular, he sneered at his
Arvernian origin, which provoked Gregory to tell him that all
but five of the bishops of Tours had been members of his family.
Soon Leudastes came and carried off Plato and Gallienus in
chains, with dark hints of what awaited a greater criminal. For
once Gregory was forsaken by the proud calmness of spirit which
sustained him generally through the dangers of that evil time.
He retired to his oratory for prayer, and in an agony of doubt
as to the future, he allowed himself, in violation of the decision
of Councils at which he had himself assisted, to read his fate in
a chance verse of the Bible. He opened the Psalms, and his eye
first caught the words—*Eduxit eos in spe et non timuerunt : et
inimicos eorum operuit mare.* The omen was destined to be
fulfilled. Leudastes demanded the execution of his prisoners as
a final step to the ruin of Gregory. But both Fredegundis and
Chilperic had a prudent awe of the spiritual prestige of the
bishop, and they proceeded cautiously. A great duke with an
armed escort was sent to Tours on the pretence of guarding the
city against an imaginary attempt of Guntram to annex it.
Acquaintances of Gregory were bribed to suggest to him, with
feigned sympathy, that he should retire to the safe seclusion of
Auvergne. Alike by military menace and treacherous counsel
Gregory remained unmoved. As a last resort, an episcopal synod
was summoned for August 580, and Gregory appeared among
his brethren. Apparently the synod was at first intended to
meet at Soissons. But, as the common people showed a dangerous
attitude towards those who were assailing a bishop of such high
fame and dignity, the synod was ordered to assemble in a more
tranquil atmosphere, at the royal villa of Berny. There the
reverend fathers were saluted in a long poetic eulogy of Chilperic
by that venal flatterer Venantius Fortunatus. He was a decadent
alike in style and morals. His first thought was to secure safety
and patronage ; and with no other guiding principle, his perverted skill in manipulating words, above all his art of silence
and suppression where truth would have been inconvenient or

dangerous, he gained all that he cared for, ignorant applause and sensual ease. In this poem, while Chilperic is extolled for unfailing justice, gallantry, and culture, Fredegundis is a model of all the graces and virtues. But there is not a word of the serious business for which the Council had met. Above all, and worst of all, the shameless versifier has no word of sympathy for the great bishop who had befriended and sheltered him when he was an " esurient " adventurer.

Bertram of Bordeaux, the reputed lover of the Queen, presided at the synod, and began, in modern French style, by trying to get the accused bishop to incriminate himself. Gregory coolly replied that if others had spoken the calumnies against the Queen, he had never conceived the thought. But even at Berny there was an excited crowd who denounced the charge against a priest of God, and prayed God to succour His servant. Chilperic was shaken and subdued by the display of popular feeling, and calmly said he was ready to produce his witnesses, but if they preferred to leave the matter to the pledged faith of the bishop, he would willingly accept their decision. The evidence of Riculfus was at once put aside on the ground that a person of lower grade could not be heard against a bishop. Leudastes had prudently disappeared. There remained a ceremony of Christian compurgation which, although contrary to the canons, seems to have been demanded by the King. Gregory was obliged to say Mass at three altars, and after each celebration to take a solemn oath that he had never spoken the words against the Queen's honour. When the bishops returned from the oratory to announce that Gregory had proved his innocence at the altars, it now remained for them to cut off from communion the King himself and Bertram as false accusers of their brother bishop. Chilperic replied apologetically that he had only reported what he had heard from Leudastes. Leudastes had already fled. But he was pursued by that terrible curse which was the Church's most powerful arm—that he should be cut off from all communion with God or man in this life and the next, rejected of God and all His saints, accursed body and soul, in the house or in the field, and doomed to eternal fires. Such was the manner in which the mediaeval Church guarded the sacred person of a bishop. But in spite of all, Leudastes managed to escape secretly to Tours, and to carry off some of his ill-gathered

wealth to Bourges, where he had friends. But the people, with
the Count at their head, eager for such a spoil, stripped him of
his treasures, but failed to capture the culprit. With untamed
audacity he mustered a band at Tours, fell on those who despoiled him, and recovered some of his wealth. But the Duke
Berulfus determined to crush him. Leudastes, leaving his wealth
behind, took refuge in the church of S. Hilary at Poitiers. But
his old instincts were as powerful as ever. He used the basilica
as a base from which he issued forth to plunder the houses of the
citizens, and defiled the sacred precincts with his debaucheries.
As at S. Martin's of Tours, the authorities of S. Hilary's seem to
have been strangely tolerant of such excesses, or slow in repressing
them. It is to be feared that, in spite of the fame of S. Radegund,
the moral tone of her foundation was dangerously lax. But at
last she was aroused to expel the dissolute ruffian who was
polluting her precincts. Leudastes had to go, and for a time
found refuge among his friends at Bourges. In spite of all his
fearless audacity the end of his career was certain and near.
But here for the present we leave him.

Riculfus, the sub-deacon, the most treacherous accuser, was
condemned to death, but his life was spared at the prayer of
Gregory. He was only reserved, however, for tortures worse
than death. For six hours the miserable wretch was suspended
with pinioned arms from a tree. Then he was stretched on a
wooden horse, and lashed with thongs and clubs and rods by all
who could approach his mangled body. At last he revealed the
whole dark plot—the ruin of Fredegundis and her sons, the succession of Clovis, Riculfus to be Bishop of Tours, and a dukedom
for Leudastes.

When Gregory, released from his anxieties, returned to his
diocese, he found it in confusion. The news of the result of
Gregory's trial seems to have travelled slowly, and his fate
remained for some time uncertain. The interval of suspense
offered the presbyter Riculfus a chance of asserting himself.
By nature vain and presumptuous, Riculfus imagined that the
bishopric of Tours, which the conspirators had promised him,
was already in his grasp. He installed himself in the episcopal
palace and took an inventory of its valuables. As master of
the estates of the Church, he began to enrich the higher clergy
who supported him with gifts of vineyards or meadows. The

inferior order were beaten into submission with clubs and blows of his own hand, and insolently told to recognise their master— one who had purged the diocese of the breed of Auvergne. In the midst of such scenes Gregory suddenly arrived, and was joyfully welcomed by the people in general. Only the impudent usurper held sullenly aloof, and would not salute the bishop. He even in a fit of frenzy threatened him. Gregory, with the support of his suffragans, ordered the priest to be interned in a monastery, where he was strictly guarded. But one bishop of the province seems to have refused to support the dignity of his metropolitan ; and as his conduct throws a curious light on Gregory's life and the episcopal character, we may be permitted a short digression.

Felix, Bishop of Nantes, at the mouth of the Loire, was a man of the highest birth, descended from a Gallo-Roman noble family in Aquitaine. He is celebrated in the poems of Fortunatus not only for his ancient descent, but for his Roman culture, public spirit, and practical talent. Threatened by the encroach- ments of the Breton tribes, who were little under Merovingian control, he, without material force, protected his diocese by skilful diplomacy. He was also one of those bishops who thought themselves bound to execute great public works which no one else would undertake. In particular he conceived a plan of diverting the course of the Loire in order, as Fortunatus says, to recover marsh land for agriculture. It was probably in pursuit of this scheme that he proposed to annex an estate of the Church of Tours, which Gregory absolutely, and probably with some sternness, refused to part with. A bitter and envenomed quarrel arose between the two bishops which, as reported by Gregory, does little credit to them either as Christian priests or as gentle- men. Many letters seem to have passed between them in a style which one might describe as Billingsgate, if it had not been made more crushing and impressive by curses drawn from the Scriptures. Felix told Gregory that his brother had assassinated a bishop ; Gregory rather feebly retorted that if Felix were Bishop of Marseilles, the ships of that port, instead of oil, would only bring paper to supply the material for his slanderous letters ! This unedifying dispute was clearly a result of the secular and worldly character of the episcopate in the sixth century. Here were two men of high aristocratic origin placed in absolute

command of great estates of the Church. By a curious con-
tradiction in our very complex nature, they could combine an
ascetic spirituality with jealousy of one another's rank and an
arrogance of wealth, combined with an unchastened bitterness
of temper of which a worldly well-bred layman of our day would
be rather ashamed. It is needless to say that Riculfus found a
ready protector in Felix, who had taken a part against Gregory
in the trial at Berny. In violation of his duty to his metropolitan, Felix actually sent men to the monastic prison of Riculfus,
who by sworn falsehoods obtained his release, and the scoundrel
was received by the Bishop of Nantes with open arms.

This was the most dangerous passage in Gregory's life, as he
evidently felt himself. The one great danger of a bishop of
Tours in those days was the internecine feud between Neustria
and Austrasia, in which Tours was the most important strategic
position in the obstinate struggle for the towns of Aquitaine.
Its fame as the most sacred shrine and asylum in Gaul made the
position of its guardian bishop an anxious and uneasy one. It
was enough to disturb the calm of the most pious bishop to
have within his cloisters two such selfish and ruthless plotters as
Guntram Boso, the most faithless man in a faithless age, and
young Merovech, a son of Chilperic, who had married his aunt,
taken the tonsure, and attempted to seize his father's throne ;
and then been obliged to take refuge in S. Martin's. This royal
ruffian, with threats of violence, presented himself before Gregory
at the Mass and demanded the *eulogiae*, which Gregory, with
the consent of a brother bishop, reluctantly granted to him.
And at the same time he had to face a peremptory demand to
expel the apostate, or the whole region would be desolated.
But this was not the worst. Strange as it may seem, and almost
incredible, from his house, close to the great church, he must
have often heard refugees of rank revelling with their courtesans
and boon companions in the precincts of the most holy place in
Gaul, and apparently been unable to restrain their lewd frivolity.
It is not surprising that Gregory, after celebrating the nocturnal
vigils, when he lay down on his couch, saw, in a dream, an angel
flying through the air over the basilica, and proclaiming in a loud
voice " that God had stricken Chilperic and all his sons, and that
no one issuing from his loins should rule over his realm for ever
more ". The contrast between the power of the bishop who

z

held the keys of the unseen world and the enormities glaringly
perpetrated before his eyes strike one in this most honest
chronicle as quite extraordinary. Why, we may ask, whatever
their rank, was such licence of indulgence granted to Merovech
and Guntram, who owed their safety to the sanctity of S.
Martin's, and why were they allowed to abuse it ? Perhaps, if
we could interrogate the shade of Gregory, we might receive
some calm statesmanlike reasons for forbearance in a perilous
time. It is dangerous to dogmatise about anything in an age so
far and so dark as the sixth century.

The times were indeed gloomy. Within a few chapters of
the chronicle we have the record of such convulsions of nature
and ravages of pestilence as must have shaken the stoutest
hearts and awaked all the terrors of the unseen world. A deluge
of rain for twelve days swelled all the rivers to a height never
seen before, and swept away flocks and crops and houses, causing
the walls of Lyons to collapse. Terrible and ominous glares of
lightning were the prelude to an earthquake which shook down
the walls of Bordeaux, sent boulders down the Pyrenees and,
with a far - spreading roar, extended into Spain. Fires from
heaven burnt up the city of Orleans and the crops and villages
in quiet country places. And, to complete the horror, the plague
broke out again all over Gaul, sparing no age or rank. Gregory
speaks with extraordinary pathos of the little children whom
he had held in his arms at the font who were carried off by the
pestilence. It invaded even the palace ; Chilperic was seized,
and lost some of his children, so that even the cruel heart of
Fredegundis for once felt a movement of pity or alarm.

Yet in that very year the good Gregory evidently enjoyed a
brisk and lively debate on the doctrine of the Trinity with a
legate from the Visigothic court in Spain. The Arian heresy is
almost the only aberration from the Catholic faith which Gregory
mentions. And for Arianism he had, for so good and charitable
a man, a bitter hatred. To us now, accustomed to the elastic
theology of our pulpits, this may seem absurd and extraordinary.
But in those days theology and statecraft were closely inter-
locked. It was a question whether the future of Western Europe
should belong to the German conquerors who had accepted the
faith of Nicaea or to those who rejected it. And the Arian
Visigoths both in Gaul and Spain were fierce and cruel persecutors.

In Gaul, indeed, the Arian heresy had disappeared since the victories of Clovis, except in the south-eastern corner. But the Visigothic power was still fanatically Arian. And a Catholic could not forget that the German tribes generally who overthrew the Empire were of the Arian faith, and the Franks were the sole exception. Moreover, the conquering Arians had been, with the exception of the noble Theodoric (the Ostrogoth), fierce persecutors. Euric had closed the Catholic churches and kept bishoprics long vacant in Aquitaine and Auvergne. The Vandals had by ruthless persecution almost extinguished the orthodox in North Africa. In Spain the royal family in Gregory's time displayed the most ardent zeal for their creed, and severely punished any of their members who turned Catholic. When Brunihildis' daughter Ingundis was betrothed to her cousin Hermenegild, her grandmother Goiswinta tried the most ferocious means to force the girl to recant. She stood unshaken, and converted her husband. Then broke out a ferocious civil war between father and son, in which all ties of nature were flung to the winds, and Hermenegild, taken captive, died by his father's orders.

It has been observed by a German critic that Gregory, who seldom refers to events outside Gaul, has almost gone out of his way to record the Vandal persecutions in Africa and the Visigothic in Spain. And, for the religious feud in the Visigothic royal family, he is almost the sole authority. In the same spirit he has given an animated account of his debates on the Trinity with two Arian envoys to the court of Chilperic in those years, who called at Tours on their journey. Their mission was probably connected with the fate of Ingundis, the daughter of Brunihildis and wife of Hermenegild. The minute and rather egotistic care with which Gregory has inserted these controversies in his History is entirely consistent with the spirit of militant orthodoxy in which he prefaces that History with a creed as minute and rigorous as the Athanasian.

In the confusion following the death of Chilperic, and the civil war aroused in the south by the pretender Gundobald, with the support of powerful nobles, the bishop's life must have been anxious and troubled. For he was a statesman as well as a churchman, and he had to guard his diocese, which was, from its position, eagerly coveted by rival princes, and specially endangered by civil war. Hence we can see the necessity of the

many visits of Gregory in those years to the courts of Childebert
or Guntram. Thus in 585, when Guntram, on his way to be
present as godfather at the baptism of Chilperic's son at Paris,
visited Orleans, Gregory was there to meet him. He witnessed
the King's reception by cheering crowds of Syrians, Jews, and
Romans, and he applauds the King's firm refusal to restore the
Jewish synagogue which the Christians had destroyed. The King
was most deferential to the clergy present, made the round of
the chapels of the saints, and even visited Gregory in his lodging
in the abbot's house. The bishop, of course, received him with
respectful pleasure, begged him to receive the *eulogiae* of the
Blessed Martin, and in return was invited to the royal table.
But the pleasure of Guntram's hospitality must have been
rather spoilt by the presence of Bertram of Bordeaux and
Palladius of Saintes, who had borne a more than suspicious part
in the rising of Gundobald. Guntram was keenly excited about
a movement which seems to have been aimed chiefly against
himself, and which had secret support from some of the great
Austrasian nobles. To add to the King's anxieties, Gregory had
brought with him to his presence two great officers, the Count
Garacharius and the Duke Bladastis, who had been involved in
the Gundobaldian rising and had taken sanctuary in S. Martin's
at Tours. When Bertram was presented to Guntram the King
fiercely reproached him, as a scion of the Merovingian line,
for bringing this plague from abroad upon his own house. Palladius was bitterly upbraided with perfidy and perjury. Two
other episcopal conspirators were similarly addressed. Yet this
eccentric King, after receiving their blessing, sat down with them
at table, with a bright and genial face, as if no word of reproach
had escaped his lips. In the middle of the banquet some of
the young deacons, whose voices in the Mass had pleased him,
were asked to sing from the Psalter, and, as the dishes passed
round, Guntram told his guests that the splendid plate came
from the captured Gundobaldian treasure which had fallen into
the hands of the traitor Mummolus !

The strangest incident in this strange tale is that the King,
turning to those bishops who had been in league with his
enemy, begged them to pray for his nephew Childebert and
for the future of his house, which was threatened with extinction. And this, at the very time when Guntram had a feud

with Childebert for the possession of Marseilles, and when he believed that his life was threatened by the arts of Brunihildis. Truly, it would need a skilful psychology to read the character of a Merovingian. On the following Sunday Bishop Palladius had been imprudently chosen to celebrate Mass. At the first words of the service from the bishop's lips, Guntram rose excitedly to leave the church, although Palladius the day before had sat at table with him and given him his blessing. With some difficulty the King was mollified, the celebrant was recalled from the sacristy to which he had retreated in disgrace, and the service proceeded. But worse followed. At the banquet after Mass, Bertram and Palladius were once more invited guests, and, losing all restraint, began to assail one another furiously with charges of adultery and perjury.

Soon after, we find Gregory at the court of Childebert at Coblentz. There was a tension in the relations of Guntram and his nephew at this time in spite of the warm adoption of Childebert as his heir in the alarm of Gundobald's rising. There were intriguers trying to sow dissension between them, whom Gregory strove to counteract. A synod of bishops had been convened at Mâcon to deal with those southern prelates, Theodorus, Bertram, and others, who had more or less openly given countenance to the usurper. But, owing to the treatment of Childebert's supporter, Theodorus of Marseilles, the Austrasian bishops delayed their appearance. Meantime Gregory, who was evidently a peacemaker in that difficult time, was entertained at court. One night, after dinner, he came down to his barge to cross the Rhine to his lodging, when a rush of people, also wishing to cross, would have swamped his boat but for the ever-prevailing relics of S. Martin. On his homeward journey he visited places of sacred interest, and he specially mentions his stay at a monastery in that region, founded by a Lombard monk who was a devotee of Gregory's patron. Gregory was immensely edified by the monk's enthusiasm for S. Martin and his abundant tales of miracle. The monk had wandered through that same pagan region and, with Divine aid, destroyed the worship of Diana, along with many noxious relics of heathenism. And, as a signal display of Christian ardour, he had raised a pillar on which he had stood, with stiffened limbs and icicles hanging from his beard, through all the rigours of a winter in the Ardennes. It is consoling to hear that the good sense of the neighbouring bishops compelled the mad or ambitious ascetic to descend from his pillar and live more humbly with his brethren.

Shortly after this tour in the north-east, Gregory was called by the people and magnates of Poitiers to give his benediction at the burial of S. Radegund, the foundress of the convent. She died on the 13th of August in 587. Her own bishop was absent on a prolonged visitation, and Gregory had to perform the last rites, to him a congenial duty ; and he has described the scene very vividly, with a rather lavish display of the resources of a decadent rhetoric. Still, it is a sincere and enthusiastic effort to preserve for posterity a memorable scene in the Church life of his time, and he is a mean critic who will think of the style rather than of the intention of the gift. In spite of all the rhetoric and the rather effusive phrase of the church-man of every age, there can be no doubt that the bishop had a sincere reverence for Radegund, and was greatly moved, as under the guidance of the abbess he visited all the hallowed spots where Radegund had slept and prayed and read her sacred books and wept in penitence. It is strange that such a holy shade, who moved such reverential feeling, should not have left a purer and more enduring spell on the sacred house which she had founded. Within two years of her death, as we shall see, her foundation was convulsed and desecrated by the scandalous revolt of a band of nuns under the leadership of a daughter of Charibert and her cousin, a daughter of Chilperic.

In the midst of this distressing scandal, Gregory, as a trusted statesman, was summoned by Childebert to Metz. Cholera was then raging in the north-west, and, on his way, near Rheims, he had met a leading citizen of Poitiers who, with his son, was stricken with the disease. On Gregory's arrival he was ordered, along with Felix, to go on a mission to King Guntram at Chalon to effect a settlement of the many grave differences which then troubled the relations of the two kings. Guntram seems to have been in a dangerous temper on account of some suspicious and unfriendly acts of his nephew, and Gregory had to use all his art to explain them. It is from this interview that we derive that record of the famous pact of Andelot which, by the King's orders, was read aloud to the envoys of Childebert, and

which Gregory has preserved. It is not within our present scope
to go into the details of this instrument, or the debate which
followed. It happened to be Easter Day, and at the close they
all attended the Mass. The service was followed by a banquet
where, as Gregory tells us, the fare was as abundant as the talk
was gay and lively. Guntram had forgotten all his grievances
and was in his most genial mood, delighting the bishop with his
views on theology, church building, and provision for the poor,
and the rest of the company with lively jests. He sent them all
away loaded with presents and charmed with his warm and
gracious courtesy. And this same man was capable of the most
savage cruelty and subtle treachery ! It says much for the calm
wisdom and transparent sincerity which guarded Gregory in
such a time, perhaps even more surely than his trusted relics.

The year 589 must have been a busy year for Gregory.
Although, according to Odo, he seemed small and slight, he must
have had a fund of endurance to bear all the labours and anxieties
which his position imposed upon him. The scandal and chaos
in the convent at Poitiers still demanded vigilant attention. In
this year, too, died Ingoberga, the repudiated Queen of the libertine
Charibert, and mother of Bertha, the wife of our King Ethelbert
of Kent. She was devoted to charity and the religious life, and,
as she felt her end approaching, she sent for Gregory to help her
to make her peace. Gregory hastened to her side, and, along
with a notary, recorded her bequests to the shrine of S. Martin
at Tours. She appears to have been possessed of considerable
wealth. The Merovingians, amid all their gross infidelities, seem
to have felt bound in honour to make ample provision for the
women whose love they had forsaken. In the same year the
bishop had to protect his see from an unexpected invasion of
the tax-collectors of his sovereign Childebert. Two great officers,
the *major domus* and the count of the palace, came down to
levy the tribute (land tax) in accordance with old census registers
of the reign of Chlothar. But Gregory boldly maintained that
that King, from his awe of S. Martin, had ordered them to be
burnt, and that Charibert and Sigibert had successively recognised the immunity of S. Martin's domain. The present threatened levy was founded on a municipal copy of the old census
register, surreptitiously and treacherously supplied by private
citizens. We have seen that Gregory was a trusted and powerful

adviser of Childebert in critical times. And he seems easily to
have obtained from the King a confirmation of the long exemption
of Tours from fiscal exactions. It is certain that, in doing so, the
bishop was even more concerned for the glory of S. Martin than
for the pockets of his people.

It is difficult to give a vivid impression of Gregory's life,
with all its endless burdens and cares, without going into the
details of faded and trivial stories which would weary the reader.
Yet any one who wishes really to know that strange time must
brace himself to follow these obscure tracks and try in imagination to revive the facts. The tale of Ingitrudis and her daughter
Berthegundis will excite his curiosity and probably baffle it. We
can only give a glimpse of it. Ingitrudis, of the Merovingian
race, and like her race sensual and reckless, had founded a
convent, and ordered her daughter, a married woman, to leave
her husband and become abbess, probably to relieve herself of
the labour of administration. The daughter obeyed, and the
injured husband appealed to Gregory of Tours. The bishop
told her that the canons forbade a wife, under a threat of
excommunication, to forsake her husband. Still obdurate, with
all the family wealth, she in the end took refuge in the far from
reputable household of her brother Bertram of Bordeaux. Her
husband finally appealed to Guntram, who was related to
Ingitrudis, and he sternly ordered Bertram to restore the
woman to her husband. The bishop dismissed her from his own
house, but secretly ordered her to assume the religious garb and
take the vows of penitence at S. Martin's, where she once more
repelled her husband's attempts to recover her. On the death
of Bertram she seemed left alone in the world, and soon a
bitter conflict broke out between mother and daughter about
a division of the family property, which now included the estate
of Bertram. The matter was carried by Ingitrudis before the
King's council, and a certain allocation between her and her
daughter was made, but was rejected by the latter. In a short
time Ingitrudis fell ill, and appointed a grand-daughter to succeed
her as abbess, a choice which gave Gregory some trouble, as it
aroused discontent among the sisterhood. After the death of
the foundress, her daughter appealed to Childebert to give her
the government of the house. From some unknown cause, he
reversed his previous judgement and assigned to Berthegundis the

whole estate of the family and all that her mother had bequeathed
to the convent.   Armed with this document and attended by a
cohort of the worst criminals, Berthegundis stripped the house of
all its property, leaving only bare walls.

In 590 a deacon of Gregory's came back from Rome with
momentous tidings, perhaps the most important and interesting
passage in the History.   Gregory had sent him in the previous
year to bring back relics of the saints.   He brought back something far better, the description by an eye-witness of the election
of the greatest of the popes.   This great historic event was
strangely ushered in by the most appalling calamities of nature,
a terrific earthquake in Syria, portentous rains and floods in
Italy which swept away houses and men and cattle from the
countryside, undermined the walls of Verona, and overthrew
some of the most ancient buildings in Rome.   The bubonic
plague, which had at intervals swept across Europe during fifty
years, broke out again with extraordinary virulence in Italy.
The ghastly scenes in Rome, as they are described to us, recall
the terrors and horrors of the plague of Athens in the pages of
Thucydides, or the plague of London in the days of Milton and
Pepys.   The deacon of Tours had seen at a great intercessory
service of prayer, within the space of one hour, eighty men
falling and dying on the floor of the church.   Pope Pelagius was
among the victims of the pestilence, and the deacon saw the
enthusiastic election to the Papal chair of the shrinking and
reluctant Gregory.   In the interval between his election and
his confirmation by the Emperor, Gregory, striving in every
way to sustain his people in their agony, appealed to them in
a solemn address, which his namesake has preserved, by penitence
and contrition to turn away the wrath of God for their sins.
And he therefore enjoined them, abbots and monks and priests,
widows and laymen, women and children, to go forth from
seven churches singing a sevenfold litany and to meet at the
basilica of the Blessed Mother of God, there with prayers and
tears to obtain pardon for their sins.   This unique and precious
record also embalms our Gregory's admiration for the saintly
virtues, statesmanlike skill, self-abnegation, and lavish charity
which, along with all the culture of the time, made the great
pope one of the highest in the annals of the Catholic Church.
In Odo's life of Gregory of Tours we have a pleasant picture of

the meeting of the two Gregorys in Rome. Romantic history
has often strained fact and chronology to bring great historic
personages into intercourse. In this case criticism must reluctantly abandon the tradition followed by Odo. Gregory of Tours
died in 594, and brought up his history with various visits and
travels to 591. Had he gone to Rome to visit the pope, it must
have been in 592 or 593. He put the last touch to his History
in the twenty-first year of his episcopate, *i.e.* in the year of his
death. It is hardly conceivable that, with his reverence for
the great pope, he should not have left the faintest hint of such
a memorable experience as that of meeting him in Rome.

In the month of November 590 a council of all the bishops
of his realm was convoked at Metz by Childebert to try Egidius,
the Bishop of Rheims, for treasonable plots against Childebert
and Guntram. Egidius was convicted reluctantly by his
brothren, although the evidence was clear, and they gained
for him, instead of death, the milder sentence of deposition and
exile. Gregory does not say that he was present. But he
states that, in spite of the wintry weather, the bishops could not
disregard the King's command. And the minuteness with which
the proceedings are described leaves little doubt that he took
part in them. The description also of the intolerable cold,
the swollen rivers, and the roads broken up by torrents of rain
seems to come from a vivid and painful memory of a journey
from Tours to Metz. Probably more painful was the feeling
that Egidius had once been his friend and had consecrated him
seventeen years before in the Cathedral of Rheims. These
journeys, to a man slight and frail, and often laid low by illness,
must have been, in those days of difficult travelling and bad
lodging by the way, very trying and exhausting. Yet our
bishop never shrank from the toil where the interests of Church
or State were concerned. We hear of two more journeys to meet
the King before Gregory's death. In 591 he stayed some time
at court, and on his return visited the convent of Poitiers and
the neighbouring monastery of Ligugé, and was rewarded by
tales of miracle to his content and edification. He drew as
much enjoyment from these monastic tales as a modern does
from a round of theatres and picture galleries, and his rude art,
which is far too much despised, has given some of them a romantic
interest.

His immense range of work as pastor and statesman never extinguished his love for theological controversy, which, for him, was the only field of intellectual interest or dialectic. He evidently enjoyed his debates with Jews and Arians. He possessed, like the other churchmen of his time, a minute and literal knowledge of Holy Writ, and appeals to it as the final standard of belief with all the uncritical faith of later theologians. In almost his last year one of his priests came to him with grave doubts as to the possibility of a bodily resurrection, which Gregory gives in their hardest and most desolating form. We are startled that in such an age of rigorous faith a churchman should venture to unfold, and even sustain by argument, such daring scepticism. And we are still more astonished that the bishop meets it without surprise or anathema, in a series of arguments from Bible texts, more or less apposite. This debate, along with Chilperic's Sabellianism and strong hints of a scepticism as to miracle, lead one to suspect that even in that age of abandoned superstition and materialist religion there was still lingering in secret places that sincerity and freedom of intellect which alone make human progress possible.

There was sometimes also seen then a singular licence of irreligious imposture. Towards Gregory's last year, when probably his health and elasticity were failing, plague, famine, and earthquake, along with the arts of religious pretenders, appeared to him to be an ominous fulfilment of a heart-shaking prophecy in the Gospels : *Exsurgent pseudo-Christi et pseudo-prophetae.* Clad in beasts' skins and claiming miraculous and prophetic gifts, a strange enthusiast came travelling across France from Arles. In an age of such eager credulity, his bold claims to mysterious powers and foresight were eagerly admitted and welcomed. Knowing well the subtle power of woman in religion, he brought with him a " Sister " Mary, who shared his honours. Immense crowds, not only of rude rustics, but of priests and clerks, flocked around him, bringing their sick for his healing touch, and showering upon him lavish gifts. But Bishop Aurelius at Velay peremptorily crushed the impostor by the arm of flesh, which, in such a case, is often better and more relevant than argument or anathema. It was perhaps better that the mild and diplomatic Bishop of Tours was not troubled with the impostor. Instead, he had a visit from an Armenian bishop, Simon, who brought him tidings of the destruction of Antioch in an earthquake. He had been carried off a captive in a cruel and desolating invasion by the King of Persia, ransomed at a great price by a brother bishop, and now had made his way to Tours. His necessity was of course relieved by pious people, and he rewarded their charity by miraculous tales of the great ruin at Antioch, which Gregory reproduces with all the art he commands.

The present writer is inclined to think that Gregory is much more of a literary and historical artist than modern critics will allow. Much of that kind of art lies in arrangement and the proper placing of events, and the impression which such arrangement leaves on the reader's mind. Many unpleasant things, for example, are told of King Guntram in this History. But he had what was, in the eyes of our Gregory, the great saving virtue, reverence for religion and Holy Church, and his farewell is appropriate. In the year in which Fredegundis invited him to come to Paris and raise the infant Chlothar above the font at baptism, Guntram was near his end and tortured by gout. He was, moreover, rather viciously assailed by Childebert for proposing to do a favour to Neustria in violation of their compact. Guntram, firmly but with all kindness and courtesy, maintained his right and duty, as head of the house, to usher the infant prince into the grace of the Church. He commanded the Bishops of Autun, Lyons, and Chalon to attend him at the ceremony. It was performed with all proper state, and Guntram, as he held the child, solemnly prayed that he might be worthy of his race and name—a prayer, alas! which has a more doubtful burden to us than to Guntram.

Almost the last page of the History is darkened by a terrible visitation of the plague which had swept over Gaul at intervals for more than fifty years. It is melancholy that Gregory should attribute its ravages in Limoges to the wrath of God for Sabbathbreaking. But the district of Tours, which was free from such guilt, seemed to have suffered even more heavily. There had been a great drought which burnt up the crops and pasture. The pestilence spread even among the flocks and herds, and numbers of deer and other wild creatures were found dying in their retreats.

In spite of the sweeping ruin of this calamity, the pious

bishop believed that the Divine anger had been softened
by the prayers and fasting and almsgiving which no doubt
he ordered. The great ambition of Gregory's life was to glorify
the memory of the great saint, missionary, and bishop to whose
spiritual and supernatural care he owed so much. And so the
History fitly closes with a minute and invaluable record of the
eighteen bishops of Tours from Gatian in the reign of Decius
(249) to his own succession in 573. Gregory was, personally, far
from being a vain or arrogant man. But he had deeply ingrained
in his nature the Gallo-Roman faith in long descent and hereditary
culture, the not unwholesome belief that a long tradition of
dignity and public spirit furnishes a strong claim to high place
in Church or State. He also has the natural ambition of a man
who has borne a great part to survive the wreck of time. Leading an extremely busy life, beset by plots and dangers from
warring kings, he had found time to be a great church builder.
He had restored with added splendour the basilica in which
S. Martin and his successors had been consecrated, and in doing
so he had recovered hidden and forgotten relics which he restored
to their proper place for the adoration and healing of the people.
Many another church and oratory in his diocese he built and
consecrated with a precious store of wonder-working relics.

Gregory again and yet again laments his want of literary
culture and his "rustic style". He has evidently some ideal drawn
from faint glimpses of classic art, which he feels he can never
approach. Yet he has, and most justly, a determination that
his works shall survive, as a true picture of his time. He leaves
a full list of them, and in the most solemn tone of ecclesiastical
anathema he adjures his episcopal successors to preserve and
transmit them, absolutely untouched and unaltered. Gregory,
from his limited culture, is seldom recognised by pedantic scholars
as the commanding figure that he was. With all proper modesty
and religious humility he knew it. He saw more of the Merovingian world than any man of that time. He held the greatest
see and most sacred spot in Gaul, full of great memories, the
scene of continued miracles, thronged with princes and nobles,
flying from wrong or from justice, continually visited by great
envoys or curious travellers who claimed the hospitality of the
bishop. He was constantly engaged in diplomatic business at
the courts of rival and warring kings, privy to all their plots and

faithless designs, and striving to soften their enmities. He was himself the mark for deadly plots for his ruin. With proud reserve he tells us little of the toil and hardship and danger of his frequent journeys to court, and the strain which all this labour outside that of his proper office imposed upon him. When he was at home in his bishop's house, his quiet must have been often broken by the noise and scandal of outbreaks of violence and debauchery in the sacred precincts. His person was of course sacrosanct, but he was not exempt from the danger of fierce intrusion at the very altar. And his studies or private devotions were liable to be constantly disturbed by the vergers and attendants at the shrine rushing in to announce some fresh wondrous effluence from the holy place in miraculous release from disease or evil spirits. To him, however, these announcements were always welcome and always expected. He lived in an atmosphere of miracle at home or on the journey. And his works show that he was continually collecting and recording those tales to gratify and sustain the faith of coming ages. He felt no gulf between the natural and supernatural. So far from exciting any surprise or scepticism, the news of any strange or sudden cure or aversion of evil, at once fitted in to his theory of the government of the world. It confirmed faith in Divine omnipotence, and, above all, in the power of the saints. His great pleasure, amid the distractions of a bishop's life, was to keep a record of all such tales that reached him. He gathered them eagerly from any quarter, and scrupulously recorded them, with every minute and picturesque detail which, with his rude but deliberate art, he wished to transmit to posterity. The classical purist and literary critic may scorn such narratives. In doing so, he shows not only ingratitude, but a *borné* spirit. They are, to all genuine students of the early Middle Age and the history of religion, simply invaluable. Who, but the pedant, cares about the Latinity, if the Latin be true, sincere, and vivid ? And it is clear to any sympathetic student that Gregory gave enormous pains, with his limited command of approved literary style, to make these tales vivid, interesting, and picturesque, as well as spiritually edifying. He must be a very hidebound critic who cannot feel a charm and catch a glimpse of a vanished world in the books on the miracles of S. Martin. It has been said by a great modern historian that we can never recover the secret or revive the life and faith of the Middle Age : it is parted from us by an impassible gulf. And yet we think the nearest approach to that far-gone age might be made by a sympathetic study of Gregory's tales of miracle, so rich in human interest, so boundless in faith in Unseen Powers.

BOOK III

THE ECCLESIASTICAL ASPECT

CHAPTER I

MONACHISM

THE anchoretic type of renunciation long preceded the cœnobitic both in the East and West. It was an impulse which had been felt long before the coming of Christ, both in heathendom and in Judaism. In fact, its source and original home is the East, with its passivity and love of the dreamy contemplative life, and its Manichean contrast of flesh and spirit. *Beati mundo corde, ipsi Deum videbunt* was the inspiration of many an Indian sage centuries before the Divine words were spoken in Galilee. The Essenes and Therapeutae and Nazarites, in solitary or social asceticism, had anticipated the Christian ascetic movement by centuries. Neo-Platonist reverie and renunciation far surpassed in intensity and delicate refinement the rude, cruel self-torture of the solitaries of the Thebaid or of the Jura and Le Perche. One of the most startling things in the history of the human spirit is the contrast, perpetually emerging, between the conventional life of the senses and the loftier ideal of the spirit. The reconciliation of a life in the world with a life detached and unworldly is only possible to a small number of naturally saintly souls, endowed with a rare fineness and delicacy of spirit, a balance of self-control, a sweetness of the blood which transforms the grossness and commonness of life by the magic of idealism. But salvation to spirits as pure, but less strong, is only possible, generally, by violent revolt, which may not always spring from a religious impulse. Lucian is the type of the spirit emancipated from all metaphysical or anthropomorphic dreams. Yet no monk of the third or fourth century had such a withering contempt for the average worldly life, pursuing phantoms of pleasure and ambition for a brief space, and then vanishing into the grey light of the land where all things are forgotten. The elegant sophist and littérateur had in him the making of the Cynic friars. The Neo-Pythagorean discipline, exemplified in Apollonius of Tyana, the rule of life prescribed for Isiac priests, the dreams of mystical detachment preached by Platonists from Maximus Tyrius to Macrobius, all show an ascetic movement in paganism long before the triumph of the Church.

It does not fall within the scope of this book to trace the growth of Christian asceticism from Paul and S. Antony and Pachomius to S. Basil, whose rule did for the East what the rule of S. Benedict did for the West. Nor can we do more than allude to the impetuous yet regulating force given to the movement by great churchmen : S. Jerome, S. Ambrose, and S. Augustine. The solitary austerities of the Eastern deserts, the dreams of lonely perfection, so often crossed by visions from the pit, and passing into mere lunacy, were gradually tempered and restrained to an ordered life of labour and prayer in cœnobite societies. The passion for solitary prayer and contemplation, along with maceration of the body, characterised the ascetic movement in the East. But there arose many imitators in the West of the austerities of Syria and the Thebaid in the first half of the sixth century, and perhaps even earlier. It was a kind of contagion from the Eastern deserts, borne by many a pious pilgrim from Gaul, who visited a laura on the Nile or a hermitage in the Cyrenaica on his way to the holy places. The example of the East was followed by many in the West in the most revolting excesses of self-torture, which are too painful to describe, too degrading to the earthly tabernacle of the spirit. An Arvernian anchoret walled himself up for years so as never to be seen by men. Another loaded himself with chains in a similar prison, festering with sores and crawling with vermin ; another would burden his shoulders with a huge stone day and night. And yet another, who told his tale of self-torture to Gregory of Tours, had long stood on a pillar through frosts and torrid heat, before admiring, almost worshipping, crowds. But such a spirit of insane renunciation could not long fascinate or be approved by the practical temper of the West. Ecclesiastical statesmen, more or less gently, reproved and remonstrated with those who so desecrated the human body, and who might mingle a craving for admiration with a genuine spirit of penitence and an ideal of sanctity. And the popular sentiment supported episcopal authority in condemning such austerities. In the days of S. Jerome the mob of Rome had poured their contempt on the monks at the funeral of Blaesilla, a great Roman lady, who was believed to have died of her austerities. And about the same time the pagan poet, Rutilius Namatianus, vented his scorn on the self-torturing fanatics who then swarmed in the islands of the Tyrrhenian seas. Hardly less severe on the excesses and vices of monasticism was the judgement of S. Jerome, who himself gave such a stimulus to the passion for retreat.

The excesses of anchoret austerity, however, continued far into the sixth century, and many are described with admiration by Gregory of Tours. But long before his day, and long before the Benedictine rule had begun to mould the monasticism of the Western world, great houses for united religious life had been founded in Gaul. S. Martin had created the foundations of Ligugé at Poitiers and Marmoutier at Tours, and 2000 monks had attended his obsequies. A religious house, bearing his name, was built by S. Germanus of Auxerre. Honoratus founded the great house of the isle of Lérins, amid sands and scattered pine trees, stunted and twisted by the sea blasts, which became a famous school of theology, sometimes with a tinge of heresy. It gave some distinguished prelates to Southern Gaul in the fifth century : Caesarius and Hilary of Arles, Lupus of Troyes, Eucherius of Lyons. Above all, it was the home of S. Vincent, who, although perhaps out of sympathy with Augustinian theology, first formulated the great motto of the Western Church—*Quod semper, quod ubique, quod ab omnibus*—the words which, by a strange recurring spell, drew her greatest son in the last century from the bosom of the English Church. There also Salvianus took refuge from the wild confusion on the Rhine to compose his treatise on the government of God. About the same time John Cassian founded the monastery of S. Victor at Marseilles. He had been a monk at Bethlehem, and had studied the spirit of Egyptian monachism in the Thebaid for his work on the cœnobite life, which had a powerful influence on all founders of religious orders from Benedict to Loyola. Towards the middle of the fifth century Romanus and Lupicinus founded three monasteries in that region of primeval forest to the north of Lake Leman, and bordering on the lands of the Alemanni.

The Lives of the Fathers of the Jura in Gregory shed a light on the impulses which drove men to the cloister in that age, and also on the early decay of the religious life in Gaul. The confusions of the last years of the Western Empire, the inner collapse of Roman society, and the penetration of the German tribes, had profoundly shaken the routine and security of old social life ; and, as always in such revolutions, their effect was most disastrous in the lower ranks of society. There was a portentous increase of poverty, and, just as in the Cynic movement of the second century, broken men, labourers, and artisans, without any real call to the religious life, sought a refuge from the hardships of a precarious existence. The idle poor were probably as trouble-some to an abbot of these days as the pampered descendant of a great house. It is clear, from the experience of Romanus, that, among the crowds who flocked to the monastery in the Jura, there were many with as little inclination for labour as for prayer. In the early days of monasticism in Gaul discipline seems to have been unstable, dependent largely on the personality of the superior. If industry for a while won abundance from a virgin soil, men rioted in unaccustomed luxury. If hard seasons brought stinted fare they murmured and rebelled, and many even fled back to the world which they ought never to have left. Even in Lérins when S. Caesarius, as cellarer, strove to introduce a severer régime (in 489) the monks rose up against his rule and procured his removal from his office.

The motive of the monastic life, in its purer and better form, was (originally) the desire to escape from the vanities and tempta-tions of a world corrupt, fleeting, and, as men believed, verging to its close ; and to prepare the soul, by abstinence and contem-plation, for the life to come. But, with elements of a lofty spirituality, it was an ideal often vitiated by crude materialist conceptions both of the rewards of holiness and of the doom awaiting the impenitent. It has often been condemned as a cowardly retreat from social duty, a spiritual egotism seeking only a reward in the coming life, as solid and material as earthly prosperity or the favour of an earthly king. And it is hard to absolve some of the early recluses from this charge, either in East or West. Religion was in fact to many very materialist and anthropomorphic, a mere sort of barter, as Plato would have said, of one pleasure for another, of the fleeting for the lasting. On the other hand, we should remember the condition of society from which the recluse wished to escape. If he was of royal or noble blood, he knew the ghastly secrets of great houses ; he had from his early youth been, perhaps, seduced by all the allurements of rank and luxury; he had seen men coarsened and hardened by indulgence and cruelty, profaning holy relics or the very Body of the Redeemer by perjury at the altar, ready to break any oath or tie of nearest kindred for a selfish object, now cringing in abject superstition, now wallowing in vice. Was salvation possible in such a world as that ? On the other hand, the man of the meaner lot had felt the weight of despotism under a king or some great proprietor. He had had his humble cottage burnt or violated in a military raid ; he had had his humble suit repelled by an unjust judge ; he saw no escape from the dull servitude of a hopeless life except one. But there was an intermediate class—the youth of families secure in the possession of estates and social dignity, and often surrounded by an atmosphere of devotion ; and it is more difficult to account for their retirement from the world. Many of them, living in the placid refinement of a great house, or entering on a promising career of ambition at court, seem to have been overtaken by a strange weary scepticism about the value of it all, a sense, little known in our time, of the vanity of this transient life and of the intense reality of the world to come. Words of the Divine Founder literally construed, the magical power of examples of detachment and devotion, the dream of anticipating faintly, by continual prayer and praise, the sinless beatitude of the eternal world—all this mystic piety, fortified by messages from the unseen world in dream and miracle, drew many a high-born youth with bright prospects of happy marriage and social rank, to forsake it all for the hermitage. This pathetic tale constantly recurs in the Lives of the Saints. The parents are generally virtuous and devout people. But their son's renunciation often fell on them as a shock and heavy trial. For to that Gallo-Roman aristocracy, with its mingled Celtic and Roman traditions, the continuity of the family in its old dignity and permanence was a thing to be guarded jealously. Yet the devout mother may have been herself responsible for the desertion of family ideals by the son whom she had trained in her own religious life. And thus many a pious dame of the sixth century, who had still a clinging pride of worldly rank, must have felt herself tortured by contending feelings when her first-born, the object of many dreams and many prayers, buried the hopes of his family in a hermit's solitude. There is many a half-hidden tragedy of this kind in the Lives of the Saints.

From the days of Abraham, the hermit from the East in the time of Sidonius Apollinaris, who founded a monastery in Auvergne, the little monastic society gathered spontaneously, as it were, around the cell of an anchoret. He had fled from the world, or even sometimes from ecclesiastical life, to work out his salvation more surely and more undisturbed in the forest recesses of Le Perche, the Jura, or Auvergne. It is singular how soon and widely the fame of his austerities, his visions, his more than earthly powers, spread among the country folk. They flocked around his retreat to catch a sight of this marvel of the powers of holiness. They also came with a blind instinct that such spiritual strength must be an all-powerful ally against the arts of the Evil One and his unseen hosts, to whom they attributed the many plagues of their afflicted lives. The man who, from his sanctity and nearness to God, could give comfort and relief from the worst curses of humanity, became to their eyes semi-divine. What wonder, also, that some among them, feeling the need of guidance and leadership in a lawless world, should gather round such an one and choose him as their spiritual ruler to save them from the world or from themselves? And thus the solitary hut in the forest grew into a monastic house, with the hermit as its first abbot. Gregory records many such foundations. In some of them we seek in vain to discover from what sources the society was permanently maintained. In some, such as Condatisco in the Jura, it was, at any rate at first, supported by the manual labour of the brothers who felled the woods and planted corn and vines in the clearings which they made, and built a mill on the neighbouring stream. But we are not told by what right or concession they occupied the ground. And yet it would appear from the Burgundian Code that even wild woodland was private property in the region where the Fathers of the Jura seem to have settled freely. A similar obscurity surrounds the foundation of Loches on the Anger by

Ursus, with Leobatius as its first abbot, in the reign of the Visigothic Alaric. The abbot and his brethren were " to earn their bread in the sweat of their brow." *Qui non laboret nec manducet* was to be the motto of the house. With great labour a mill had been erected on the banks of the river, with a dam and millrace to turn the wheel. And the reply of Leobatius to the Gothic noble who demanded possession of it shows clearly that the monks had no resources save what their labour could procure. There is no more idyllic picture in the tales of Gregory than the life of the Abbot Martius who founded a monastery in Auvergne. From his early youth he had led a life of austerity and devotion to all good works. But, to make his detachment from the world more complete, he cut out with his own hands a rocky cell for himself in the side of a mountain, and there, on his couch of stone, he had often angelic visions. He was also endowed with powers of miraculous healing, and men flocked to have the blessing of his touch, among them Gregory's father, Florentius, who, in his twelfth year, was relieved of a fever by the saint. His crowd of admirers finally compelled Martius to leave his mountain cave and form them into a society. He was a man evidently of great charm of character, in Gregory's striking phrase, " fenced round by an armour of sweetness." He had, as a young man, seen the Hun invasion thrown back at Chalon ; he had seen, in middle life, the last prefect of the Gauls, and in his ninetieth year he saw Auvergne invaded by the Frank Theuderic. Yet, in spite of all these troubles, in his old age he had surrounded his monastery with fertile gardens and orchards, with a pleasant prospect, where he used to sit under the whispering boughs. Yet, if we may judge from the record of Gregory, the only wealth of the pleasant monastery of Martius lay in abstinence and labour.

One of the most famous of hermit founders in the sixth century was Patroclus. He was born of humble parentage and kept sheep in his boyhood, until one day, stung by an insult, he forsook his flock and sought such education as the neighbouring school provided. His keenness of intellect soon marked him out among his fellows, and through the patronage of a powerful courtier he was taken into the service of King Childebert I., where he became universally popular. On his father's death he returned to his home, and his mother naturally desired

him to marry and give her the consolation of a daughter. But
Patroclus, when he turned his back on a career of ambition,
had evidently felt that strange spell which in that age so often
drew men irresistibly to the life of renunciation : " he would
not want any earthly bride ". He was tonsured and ordained
by the Bishop of Bourges, and devoted himself to the ascetic
life with a fervour so unregulated as to incur a severe rebuke
from his archdeacon. With a consuming " thirst for the wilderness ", he built himself an oratory at Néris ; yet strangely began
to train boys of the neighbourhood in what passed then for
good letters. It is clear that the saint was sometimes distracted
and wavering between opposite ideals. His miraculous power
made him a public character ; and he was tempted by the Evil
One to return to the world. He tried the auspices in a common
fashion of the day, by writings placed on the altar, and after
long fasting and prayer, the answer came that he should " hasten
to the desert ", hold fast to the solitary life. After founding a
convent near his oratory, with only an axe and a mattock on
his shoulder, he buried himself in the forest that lay between
the Char and the Allier. Once more ambition, or the Evil One,
tempted him to forsake his hermit's life and go back to the world.
But, like Lucian's Charon, he was taken by a spectral guide to
the top of a high pillar and bidden to look down upon the scene
of fraud and violence and lust which lay there below. And the
angelic visitant admonished him to think no more of the world,
lest he should perish with it. His purpose was now fixed for
ever, and on returning to his cell he found a Divine gift and
memento, in a tile stamped with the Cross. He founded the
great abbey of Colombier, appointed its first abbot, and retired
to solitude for the rest of his life. But the remains of the recluse
were fiercely contended for, and the blind and the possessed long
came for cure to his tomb.

We have said that in many cases of these hermit foundations
there is a curious silence as to the source from which the monastery
drew its support. In some we can see that, at least at the
beginning, the brethren maintained themselves by hard physical
labour, clearing the forests, growing corn, and planting vineyards.
But the reverence for the ascetic life, and the belief that by
lavish gifts sin could be wiped out and happiness purchased
in the world to come, if they did not create, fortified and enriched

many a religious house, so that, in the fifteenth century, the orders which were vowed to poverty had become the largest landholders in Europe. We may give some examples of this perilous endowment from the records of our period.

One of the most romantic tales of a monastic founder is that of Bracchio. He was a German in the train of a great noble, Sigivaldus, who in the early years of the sixth century was a powerful official in Auvergne. In a hunt in the Arvernian forests a huge boar, pressed hard by a crowd of hunters, took refuge in the cell of S. Aemilianus, a hermit, who had made there his home, and who, like others of his brotherhood, had a strange sympathy with all wild creatures. The young Bracchio followed hard, and was embraced and welcomed by the hermit, while the furious beast stood gazing quietly. A like change was wrought on the young hunter by the old man's discourse on the pride of life and the eternal reward of renunciation. Bracchio could not leave his lord's service, but he was drawn to the life of prayer, and, painfully conscious of his ignorance, which made him unfit for even the lowest ecclesiastical rank, began to learn the rudiments of letters from passing strangers. When his lord died, he hastened to join Aemilianus in his retreat. After a few years the old man died and a monastery grew up around them. The tale is provokingly condensed. But the hermit left Bracchio his successor, and a grant of lands from Ranichild, the daughter of Sigivaldus, his old master, secured the future of the monastery at Menat. Two other monasteries he established at Tours, where once, in devotion before the shrine of S. Martin, he had a glorious vision, which was vouchsafed to none of the bystanders. His last years were passed in his monastery in Auvergne, and he was buried in a pleasant spot near the old oratory which had seen his conversion.

The endowment of Bracchio's monastery dates from the middle of the sixth century. But from the conversion of Clovis and his Franks there are traditions of great possessions granted to the Church. It is true that our authorities in the Lives of SS. Rémi, Leonard, and Carileffus are not free from suspicion as to their date. And the recurrence of a similar tale in all of them may weaken confidence in their historic truth. But the monastic movement undoubtedly gained fresh strength and momentum in the early years of the Frank monarchy. New converts, men of war and gross pleasure as they were, the early Merovingians, hardly weaned from their old paganism, found a congenial atmosphere in the superstition that surrounded the monastic anchoret. Miraculous power was the part of Christian belief which they could most easily understand and assimilate, and which aroused a wholesome fear. Rude and violent as they were, they may have had an awe and wonder at the austerity and resignation of all the delights of life by some of the great churchmen and the pious exiles of the wilderness. Clovis signalised his conversion by grants of land in many parts of France, as far as Metz, to the churches of Rheims, Laon, and Soissons. S. Rémi, at the entreaty of the pious queen of Clovis, received as much land as he could go round and mark off during the King's midday sleep, and apparently he was not always welcomed by the tenants. Chlodoald, the grandson of Clovis, bequeathed estates to the church in the Ardennes and Bourges, and richly endowed a monastery at Nogent. Chlothilde created splendid foundations out of her boundless wealth at Tours, Andelys, Laon, and Rheims, almost rivalling the munificent gifts with which in the following century her descendant glorified the shrine of S. Denis. Even the sporting expeditions of the kings turned out fortunate sometimes for the church. S. Leonard, of noble stock, claiming even to be connected with Clovis, had been raised from the font in the arms of S. Rémi, and from early years had an ambition to follow in his fotsteps. He rejected all offers of court dignity, and buried himself in the forest of Pauvain, near to Limoges. It happened that this was a favourite hunting-ground of the royal family. Thus the saint became known to Clovis, who made a liberal grant of forest lands to him, and there S. Leonard built a monastery and an oratory to the Mother of God on a hill overhanging the river Vienne. The saints felt always a liberal compassion for prisoners and captives, even for those condemned for crime ; and Leonard gathered in a motley company : brigands whom he enticed from rapine to honest labour, along with men of his own rank and stock, who may have been quite as predatory, but who sold their lands to join the brotherhood. In another romantic life, probably of the ninth century, which may perhaps have been written to establish a monastic title, under all the realistic invention, there may be a grain of truth. It is the life of S. Carileffus, the founder of the monastery of S. Calais (Anninsola) in the reign of Childebert. Born of pious parents in Auvergne, the saint was early seized with the passion for the holy life and set out to find a home in the forest of Perticus. Thence, with two companions, he passed into the Cenomannic country to seek a less disturbed solitude. In a wilderness of brushwood and impenetrable forest, amid some overgrown ruins of a former age, they made themselves a rude cabin roofed with boughs. It is well known that the hermits of the forests in Gaul or in the Thebaid in their loneliness established a strange intercourse with the wild creatures who surrounded them. Human gentleness cast a spell on wild animal impulses. The forest surrounding the cell was then infested by a wild bull of marvellous size and fierceness. But the creature, under the spell of S. Carileffus, became mild, and each day came to him to be stroked and petted. King Childebert, hearing of the famous bull on a hunting expedition, determined to capture it, and in a hot chase, at last found it sheltering behind the saint. After a violent scene the fierce King in the end was subdued by the sweetness of the saint, and also by draughts of some good wine which the saint could offer. And the King made him a grant of lands from the fiscal estates to found a monastery, as much as the saint could ride round in one day upon his ass. Chilperic I. seems to have been the only one of his race who grudged those lavish endowments to the Church. He viewed with distrust its growing power, and bitterly complained that the treasury was impoverished by endless donations to religious purposes. Yet even he, in the terrors of the plague and overwhelming family affliction, in the end became a liberal benefactor of the churches and the poor.

In monastic records of the sixth century we hear little of the constitution of the monasteries, the relation of the abbot to his monks, or of any rule under which the society was governed. In monastic societies there would appear to have been great spontaneity and comparative independence, till the general adoption of the rule of S. Benedict in the middle of the seventh century. The monastery was a little realm by itself, and any rule which it took for guidance was a matter of choice with the founder or first abbot. Basil, Cassian, Caesarius of Arles, were all drawn upon for various monastic rules. Sometimes the Eastern spirit and discipline, connected with the names of

Pachomius or Macarius, furnished suggestions. In other cases, the discipline of a society depended on the character and powers of government of the superior. It is little wonder that, under such indefinite control, there should be frequent signs of instability and a lapse from high ideals. The monasteries of the Jura were early in their history infected with the taint of luxury, ambition, and insubordination. The monastery of S. Aemilianus in Auvergne had lost its fervour and discipline under a negligent abbot, and had to be brought under sterner rule by the severity of S. Patroclus. Even Lérins had declined from its early sanctity, and resisted the effort of S. Caesarius to elevate its tone and habit of life. From the Acts of Councils in the sixth century, it is clear that there was a serious laxity in morals and administration in the monastic life, such as had aroused the anger of S. Jerome a century before. There was murmuring, idleness, and discontent, even defiance of authority. Monks wandered abroad and formed illicit connexions. They created scandal by their relations with nuns. They were detected in vulgar thefts. Their avarice was sometimes exposed by the discovery of secret hoards of wealth at their death. Among the solitaries of the Thebaid, ambition and craving for worldly position, envy, backbiting, and evil speaking were too common, as might be looked for in little societies shut off from the wider and humaner interests of the world, and where people see too much of one another. Even abbots were prone to lax morality. They sometimes alienated monastic property without leave ; they received women in their chambers ; they even contracted clandestine marriage. They made excursions far from their monastery, in which they were too often likely to forget the strictness of their vows.

But the censure of these faults by the bishops in Council show, from their decisiveness and severity, that monasteries were coming under episcopal control.

Already in 451 the Council of Chalcedon had ordered that no one should found a monastery without leave from his bishop. The same rule was laid down by the Council of Agde in 506. The subordination of abbots and monks to episcopal authority is asserted in sweeping terms in 511 by the Council of Orleans. The abbot is bound to obey the bishop in all things and is liable to his censure ; he is required to meet the bishop once a year at any place which the bishop might appoint. On the other hand, monks are bound, under severe penalties, to yield absolute obedience to their abbot. They may not leave their monastery to found a cell without the bishop's or the abbot's permission. If they wander away from their house to lead a vagabond life, they may be apprehended by the abbot, with the bishop's help, and treated as fugitive slaves. In 533 it is enacted that an abbot who despises the command of the bishop is to be deprived of communion for a time.

When we remember the classes from which in that age monastic societies were often drawn, and the haphazard, unregulated mode of their formation, there is nothing surprising in these unpleasant revelations. High birth indeed, and such culture as it conferred, as we shall see in the tragic and scandalous history of S. Radegund's convent, gave no security for an orderly life of devotion. But the sunken, obscure classes, can be as self-indulgent and rebellious, as little responsive to a severe religious ideal, as those who have been cradled in luxury and self-will. The first founders, ascetics themselves, with the boundless charity of their Master, welcomed to their fold the repentant sinner, the jail-bird, the renegade slave, all in fact who flocked around their cell and marvelled at their miracles. For the saints had a singular indulgence for men whom the civil magistrate had condemned. Many of their most admired miracles were performed to release these victims of civil justice. There can be little doubt that a new monastery of the fifth or sixth century was a momentary haven of refuge for many who had no real call to the religious life. Moreover, it does not appear that a searching novitiate, to test the endurance of the would-be spiritual athlete, had yet been imposed by any general rule. That was one of the great gifts of S. Benedict to Western monasticism.

But the weakness of early monastic discipline in an age of social disorder, following on the collapse of a great imperial system, should not make us unjust to the services of the monastic system to the future of Europe. Moral disorder is at all times apt to strike the eye more than the quiet life of virtue and self-sacrifice. And men are generally more ready to censure than to praise. We may be tolerably sure that, for one or two recreant monks who disgraced their profession, there were scores striving to live up to their spiritual calling. Labour and prayer and unworldliness were an ideal which, however often forgotten, was generally a high example and inspiration for many ages of turbulent history. Catholic writers, such as Montalembert, may have spoken in too rapturous tones of the triumphs of monastic sanctity. They have sometimes allowed their own ideal to colour the actual facts. Yet cool inquirers of another faith, or of no faith, Maitland and Guizot, even Voltaire, Gibbon, J. S. Mill, and Renan, have candidly and even warmly recognised the services of the monks, especially under Benedictine rule, to European civilisation. In a turbulent and chaotic time they gave an example of an ordered life, of obedience to chiefs elected by themselves, of industry for the common good, of a calm dignity of moral force which could guard itself against the violence of kings and feudal lords. Above all, the institution bridged the gulf between the ancient and the modern world, and saved from the wreck of a classical civilisation some of its more precious treasures. It is difficult to imagine what form modern civilisation would have taken, or how long its development might have been delayed, if ancient literature and the fading tradition of its culture had perished utterly. In the very years when S. Benedict was elaborating his discipline another side of the monastic ideal was being revealed on the shores of Calabria by Cassiodorus. After long serving faithfully the Ostrogothic government, in the failure of all his secular hopes he retired from the world to his ancestral estate overhanging the sea, where he built a monastery with fish-ponds and orchards and fair gardens, everything to make the ascetic life bright and happy. But he had the higher aim to make it cultivate and to provide a shelter in that barbarous time for the treasures of ancient learning which were in danger of perishing. A library of great range was being continually replenished by skilled copyists, under the direction of Cassiodorus himself. He has had too slight a place assigned him in the work of moulding the ideal of monasticism in Italy. Yet he must share with S. Jerome and the learned monks of Lérins and Bangor the credit of making the monastery a centre of enlightenment as well as of moral discipline.

The original conception of the monastic life was one of absolute detachment from the outside world, a state of spiritual exaltation and absorption in things Divine. It was, and remained

for ages, the highest ideal of Christian perfection. The priesthood, however venerable from its service at the altar, was necessarily drawn into closer relations with secular life, and might
offer temptations to a worldly ambition. Hence for a long time
the monks were laymen, perfectly distinct and remote from
the clergy. To the most enthusiastic among them the simple
life of renunciation seemed to confer a higher spiritual rank
than even the priesthood. And the desire to take Orders, which
often appeared in their lower ranks, was treated as a dangerous
ambition, and denounced by Cassian as a temptation of the
Devil. " It is," says Cassian, " an old opinion of the Fathers
that a monk must, at any cost, avoid bishops and women. For
both bishops and women, once you are entangled with them,
do not leave the monk to the peace of his cell, and to fix his gaze
on the contemplation of heavenly things." The first houses
founded by an inspired enthusiast with no ecclesiastical authority,
and at first subject as a body to no control, merely sought a life
of prayer, contemplation, and self-denial. They had often no
ordained priest in their ranks. They were merely a more fervent
body of lay people, devoted entirely to religion, but they were
subject to ecclesiastical authority in just the same way as other
lay people. Their abbot was elected by the monks, and under
no control save such as their opinion might exercise. They had
in early days no church within their walls. They therefore
attended Mass in some neighbouring church. But as this was
manifestly undesirable, it became necessary (where all were
unordained) to call in a secular priest to celebrate. But his
introduction gave rise to many difficulties which troubled the
bishops. Sometimes he would claim a share of the offerings
made to the monastery, or he might claim to administer the sacraments to a congregation from outside the walls, thus turning
the chapel into a parish church. In the end, Gregory the Great
found it expedient to permit the ordination of persons within
the walls to celebrate Mass. But he held still that the monastic
life was one quite distinct from the clerical, and he made the
severance as deep as possible in the interest of the higher religious
status of the monk. A monk resident in the house could not
serve a cure outside, nor could he leave his cell without permission from the abbot or the bishop. If, with consent, he obtained
a cure outside, he lost all rights and status in his monastery.

2 B

But the clergy, having once gained a footing in the monastery, became a menace to its independence, and to the peculiar monastic ideal. We have seen that very early there were contending ideals and ambitions, and the ambition for Holy Orders was often a form of worldliness masking itself under high spiritual claims. Many of the best abbots, including S. Benedict himself, mistrusted the priestly pride in mysterious sacramental powers which was incompatible with monastic humility and obedience. And as the monks threw off their lay character and sought for ordination, they inevitably fell more and more under the growing power of the episcopate.

The glimpses of monastic life of the fourth and fifth centuries in the Lives of Saints and the Acts of Councils, however interesting they may be, are generally faint and broken, and leave much to the imagination. But there is one picture of it which is invaluable for fullness and vividness of detail as to the constitution and daily life of a conventual society and its relation to the bishops. Unfortunately it shows in a lurid light how rapidly and scandalously conventual life might fall away from the ideals of a founder of the severest ascetic type, and how readily it might, from the character and associations of its members, reproduce all the licence and turbulence of the secular life of the time. The Convent of the Holy Cross at Poitiers was founded and endowed by S. Radegund in the boyhood of Gregory of Tours, and he was called in to celebrate her obsequies in 587. By a fortunate fate she did not live to see the collapse of discipline, the wild insurgent recklessness, the shameless defiance of all decent instincts, which gave a shock to the religious mind of Gaul, and needed all the power of kings and bishops to quell them. We are permitted to see something of the inner life of the convent in the not altogether edifying revelations of the poems of Fortunatus. In no other picture of the time do we see so clearly how easily a too rigorous asceticism, bursting its fetters, may abandon itself to all the caprices of self-will and even the orgies of sensuality; yet in no other contemporary description can the faults and virtues, the details and the atmosphere, of monasticism in the sixth century be so clearly discerned. We need not therefore apologise for according to the Convent of the Holy Cross a fuller treatment than even its historical or religious importance would appear to justify.

The early girlhood of S. Radegund, a princess of the Thuringian house, was cast on years of fierce warfare in the heart of Germany. One of her ancestors had given an asylum to Childeric when he was banished for a time by the Franks. And the Thuringian queen who eloped with Childeric was popularly believed to have been the mother of Clovis. It fell to Theuderic to bear the brunt of those struggles which Clovis and his sons had to wage with the German tribes beyond the Rhine. The three brother kings who divided Thuringia, like the Merovingian kings in Gaul, were fiercely jealous of one another and eager for sole power. The father of Radegund, Bertharius, had been treacherously slain by his brother Hermenefred, and he, goaded on by his ambitious wife, resolved to crush his brother Baderic, with the aid of Theuderic, which he secured by promises of territorial compensation. Baderic was overwhelmed, but Hermenefred promptly repudiated his compact. The Austrasian Franks had many long-standing grievances against Thuringia. Hostages had been put to death with every ingenuity of barbarism. The Teutonic capacity for calculating, cold-blooded atrocity of outrage was exercised with special gusto on women. Theuderic was fiercely roused, and appealed to his Franks for vengeance upon the faithless Hermenefred. With his brother Chlothar he invaded Thuringia, but the resistance was stubborn, and the Frank armies met with heavy losses. At last the Thuringians were decisively defeated on the Unstrudt, which was choked with corpses. As his share of the booty the victor received the orphan daughter of Bertharius. She was only a child of eight, but her girlish beauty attracted the king's eye, and she was at once marked out to be one of his wives. The poor child was carried away to Gaul, with poignant memories of the wild scenes of storm and havoc in which her house went down, and little thought of her future destiny. Her lord and master immured the girl in one of his *villae* on the Somme, near St. Quentin. Under what influences she fell in those years we can only conjecture. We are only told that the king desired her to be trained in letters and the arts proper to her sex. The Merovingians, amid all their lust and violence, were devoted sons of the Church. And Radegund probably had tutors and spiritual directors who prepared her for a far different destiny than that of a queen of Chlothar. She was trained in the fading literature of her time, in the Fathers and the Lives of the Martyrs, and that inner life of religion which more and more recoiled from the life of indulgence and convention. The ascetic impulse in those days was " as a wind blowing where it listeth ", and it evidently came early to Radegund. When she emerged from the *villa* at St. Quentin she was hardly a promising bride for a Merovingian king ; she was already prepared to be a bride of Christ. She made an attempt to escape from a union which she loathed, but was captured and wedded to Chlothar at Soissons in 538. But she was not the bride whom he had promised to himself. Her habits were those of the most rigorous ascetic. She would eat nothing but bread and herbs. She had made herself a hospital nurse, and tended the most loathsome cases of disease. Such tastes in a great princess must have seemed to be a defiance of all accepted conventions of rank and etiquette. And her cold austerity must have sorely tried the small patience of a self-indulgent, self-willed Merovingian. Chlothar found that he had married a nun. Radegund's frigid, ascetic piety might have exasperated even a more self-governed temper. But the Frank kings were generally indulgent, and even chivalrous, to the women whom they loved. Like all martial races they yielded readily to female charm and influence. Chlothar was a valiant and strenuous warrior. In five campaigns he had fought the powerful confederacy of the Saxons and Thuringians. He had crushed the power of Burgundy and led a French army up to the walls of Saragossa. For a time he was left the sole monarch of the realms of the Merovingians. It is difficult not to admire so much buoyant energy. But it was combined in him with unbridled sensuality, and a temper of fiendish cruelty. His harem was on the scale of Baghdad or Constantinople. He murdered with his own hand the two orphan sons of his brother Chlodomer. He ordered his rebel son with his wife and children to be burnt alive. It is not strange that Radegund should shrink from such a lover ; the wonder is that such a fierce sensualist should have borne for some years such an ethereal and reluctant wife as Radegund.

The crisis came when Radegund's young brother, who had grown up at court, was put to death by her husband. This decided the queen. Under the pretext of seeking spiritual con- solation, and apparently with no opposition from Chlothar, she betook herself to Bishop Medard (at Noyons), a man of famous sanctity and miraculous power, over whose remains Chlothar afterwards built the great church of Soissons. She found the holy man at the altar, and besought him to consecrate her to the Lord. The bishop not unnaturally hesitated to tamper with the indissoluble bond which had been sanctified by the Church. And the Frank warriors who formed the queen's escort fiercely forbade him to sever a Frank queen from her husband. In the mêléc that followed, Radegund retired, put on the dress of the convent, presented herself once more before the bishop, and adjured him solemnly not to delay her consecration, "or the Great Shepherd would one day require of him the soul of one of His sheep". Medard put aside his fears and, laying his hands on the suppliant's head, devoted her to the religious life. She put off all her costly jewels and ornaments and laid them on the altar, along with innumerable articles of female dress which might seem to the profane to have come from the list of a fashionable modiste of modern Paris. Having visited many centres of miracle and sanctity, she set out for the country of the Loire and descended the river from Orleans to the tomb of S. Martin, where her extravagant display of devotion must have surprised even the most experienced acolyte of that focus of superstition. The king had assigned to her a *villa* in the neighbourhood of Poitiers, and she found her way to the shrine of S. Hilary, near the spot where she was to end her life. Her austerities were redoubled as the news reached her of her husband's natural indignation and desire to reclaim a wife for whom, in spite of all his faults, he probably felt a real affection and respect. Along with his son Sigibert and Germanus, Bishop of Paris, he arrived at Tours on the pretext of devotion, but really to recover his queen. But the fiercest of the Merovingians now discovered that he had to deal, not only with a will stronger than his own, but with the secret, all-pervading power of the Church. A letter from Radegund obtained the intercession of S. Germanus, and prostrate before S. Martin's altar the king penitently gave up his journey to Poitiers. He resigned his love for the little maid whom he had rescued from the house of Thuringia, a love which may have been the one pure spot in a tainted life. By his authority, and with the ample wealth placed at her disposal, Radegund was left free to accomplish her desire of founding a convent at Poitiers. Pientius the bishop and the Duke Austrapius lent their aid in the building. It was organised on the same rule which Caesaria, sister of the great bishop of Arles, had adopted for her foundation. And it is interesting to note that Caesaria, in sending a copy of her Rule to Radegund, very strongly warns her against the danger of overstrained asceticism. The convent was erected close to the city walls, with ample gardens, luxurious baths, and the conveniences for a pleasant life, all in striking contrast to the personal austerities of the foundress. It had towers and bulwarks from which, forty years afterwards, the sisters looked down from their windows on the procession which conducted S. Radegund to the tomb. On the day when she entered her convent, never to go forth till her burial, we are told, there was general joy and festivity in Poitiers. The streets and squares, and even the roofs of the houses, were crowded with spectators. The spectacle of a queen of France burying herself as a simple sister in the house which she had founded created a great sensation. She set the fashion. This was to be no plebeian society. Two hundred sisters professed to devote themselves to the life of prayer and renunciation on that day, along with Queen Radegund. But they were chiefly drawn from great aristocratic houses of the old régime, with a sprinkling of Frank ladies of the blood royal. How far the convent gained from its exclusive and aristocratic character, its history will reveal.

The power of the bishop was steadily growing in the sixth century. The Council of Epaon in 517 had enacted that no new monastery should be founded without episcopal sanction, and by the Acts of the Council of Arles (554) all monasteries were placed under the jurisdiction of the bishop in whose diocese they lay, and he was empowered to control the discipline of all congregations of women. When Radegund established her convent at Poitiers, she formally dedicated to its support all the wealth with which her husband had endowed her. The nuns also, by legal instrument, made over all their property to the foundation. Agnes, whom she had trained from early youth, was installed as the first abbess, and Radegund, to the eye of the world, never took any position higher than that of an ordinary sister. However she might demean herself, by voluntary humility, to menial and even disgusting drudgery, she could not put off her rank as a princess of Thuringia and Queen of France. And her rank was reinforced by the ascendancy derived from culture and a severity of life which, even in that time, was almost unparalleled. When her arrangements were complete, she addressed a letter to the bishops which is of great interest. It recites the facts of the foundation and endowment, announces the election of the first Abbess Agnes, and the confirmation by the most excellent princes, Charibert, Guntram, Chilperic, and Sigibert, signed with their own hands, of her grants to the convent. But she evidently, from her experience of the violence of that wild time, has fears that her young foundation may be assailed by great potentates ; its property may be alienated, its rule relaxed, its abbess may be displaced. And she invokes the protection of the chiefs of the Church by the most solemn appeals to the judgement of God, the Blessed Mary and Saints Hilary and Martin, if earthly power fails, to restrain the sacrilegious robber and intruder. At the same time she calls on the kingly house to which she had been affianced, along with the bishops, to guard her foundation from all change, molestation or loss. She prays that her body may be laid in the basilica of the Mother of God which she is building, and that this supplication of hers may be preserved for ever in the archives of the Church.

To this letter the bishops, including Eufronius of Tours, S. Germanus of Paris, and Praetextatus of Rouen, sent a rescript which is also preserved. They found that women from their dioceses had joined the congregation at Poitiers, and, as their pastors, they solemnly prohibit any one who has entered the convent of her own free will from ever quitting it on any pretext. More especially, any nun who is seduced into marriage is to be trodden under foot as the vilest of her kind ; and she and " the foul adulterer " to whom she is united are to be cut off from communion, anathematised, and handed over to the Divine vengeance.

The convent, as we have seen, was placed under the rule of S. Caesaria of Arles. The time not given to the exercises of religion was occupied with sewing, spinning, embroidery, and copying MSS. But, as in the monastery of Cassiodorus, which was founded about the same time, humane letters were not neglected, and the first two morning hours were devoted to study, and during meals and hours of labour some book was read aloud by one of the sisters. Radegund herself was a diligent student, often prolonging her reading far into the night. And while sacred literature was being read in the cloister or refectory, she aroused the listeners by questions as to the meaning of what they heard, or she explained it to them for the benefit of their souls. The books in vogue were probably lives of holy persons, such as then were eagerly sought for, tales of miracles, and manuals of devotion. Her two biographers have gone beyond even the usual licence of hagiography in the minuteness of their pictures of her inhuman and degrading austerities. From her consecration by S. Medard till her last sickness, nothing to please the palate, nothing but coarsest bread, vegetables, and water, passed her lips. Haircloth and the hardest bed which ingenuity could devise made the night sufficiently torturing and appeasing to a cruel God. The meanest, most disgusting offices, such as no modern pen would venture to describe, were performed by a queen of France. It is hard to be patient towards this horrible travesty of religion and degradation of the human form which, according to all Christian belief, was consecrated by the Incarnation. It is probable that in the enumeration of these self-inflicted tortures, down to the last repulsive detail, the writer was drawing on a morbid imagination to do the more honour to his subject. It is enough to say that on certain days Radegund received a crowd of the poor and diseased, washed them from head to foot in the bath, tended their sores and ulcers, and even joyfully clasped a leprous woman in her embrace ! Then, putting fresh clothing on them, she them gave a meal of such delicacies as she never tasted herself, attended them like another Martha, and then left them to enjoy themselves, often, apparently, in rather roystering fashion. This curious indulgence of an ascetic for more sensual natures seems to have characterised Radegund in all her conventual discipline. The fasts of the Church were indeed strictly observed. But at other times very generous concessions were made to weak human nature. It was a society which had many members accustomed to the licence and luxury of great houses, and very probably these noble and royal ladies needed to be humoured. Spacious baths of the old Roman fashion were provided. Games of chance were not forbidden. Great churchmen, and even lay guests of distinction, were regaled at well-cooked feasts. S. Radegund would seem to have felt that her own rule of life, the path to perfection, was only for an elect few. For common human nature, while obedient to the rules of the Church, she seems to have had a charitable indulgence which a modern puritan would have found it hard to feel. Her imprudent hospitality to the wandering littérateur and *bon vivant*, Venantius Fortunatus, and her indulgence to her sisterhood, if they do not cast a cloud on her fair fame, yet, when we read of the dissolution of discipline and the scandalous orgies which followed her death, may suggest a doubt whether Radegund's wisdom was equal to her piety.

About ten years after the foundation of the Convent of the Holy Cross, Venantius Fortunatus arrived in Poitiers. Fortunatus, to whom we have already briefly alluded in a previous chapter, is a solitary and singular figure in an age when the light of ancient culture was dying rapidly away and the finer spirits were retiring from a world of brute force which seemed to them verging to its close, and the only literature was the record of sanctity and miracle. He is almost the last link between the classical and the mediaeval world. Born in the district of Tarvisium, in North-Eastern Italy, about 535, he received the usual tincture of old and now fading rhetorical training at the school of Ravenna, and gained academic fame by his poetic facility. A disease of the eyes led him to seek the aid of S. Martin at his neighbouring shrine. Fortunatus was cured of his malady, and resolved to visit the tomb of the saint at Tours. It is just possible that the condition of Italy at the time may have had something to do with his plans. For thirty or forty years Italy had been desolated by continual wars, and the Lombards under Alboin were about to descend from the Julian Alps on the native district of Fortunatus. The cloisters of S. Martin's at Tours or the court of Sigibert may well have seemed to a timid man of letters a welcome retreat from the storm which was about to break on the valley of the Po. He crossed the Alps about 564 and, in spite of occasional longings, was never destined to see Italy again. Tours was the goal of his journey, then under the episcopal rule of Gregory, who became his generous and sympathetic friend. But he visited every part of Gaul, from the foot of the Pyrenees to the court of Sigibert at Metz. He was everywhere received with open arms by bishops and abbots and great dukes, many of whom are mere shades to us now, and who live only in his verses. The interesting thing in the history of Gallic society in that age is that an unknown wandering scholar was welcomed by these people as he would have been a hundred years before by Sidonius at Avitacum. The old culture was not altogether dead. But Fortunatus had other qualities which commended him, besides literary dexterity. He was frankly a *bon vivant*; he enjoyed a good dinner and the elegant comfort of a great house, and he repays hospitality with his complimentary verses, which must have been appreciated at least by his hosts. Even if not one of them could write a verse with the purity of the ancient style, they must have felt the charm which lingered even in the faint echoes of it. And Fortunatus, in spite of his faults, must have had some personal attraction which attached so many people to an unknown stranger. He was quick, clever, accomplished, with the immense, if often tasteless, facility which the Roman schools could impart, even in their decadence. He had probably the genial superficial sympathy which is a pleasant counterfeit of friendship. Above all, he could flatter, as cultivated men had been accustomed to do for generations, as they flattered in the circle of Symmachus and Sidonius. Along with all the social and literary conventionality of that decadent age, he seems to have been pious in a way, although he was certainly not ascetic. If he had not had some religious feeling, he could hardly have been at home with Gregory of Tours. He could not have found favour with such a devotee as S. Radegund if they had not had some common ground of religious life. He regaled his patron Gregory with tales of S. Martin's miracles in Italy, and chronicled in prose and verse the many miracles of S. Medard. He is full of the religious ideals and the religious materialism of his time. His episcopal friends are lauded for feeding the hungry and clothing the naked, and thus "sending their wealth on before". Another side of his character is shown when, in return for a present of apples from Gregory, the poet promises him the fruits of Paradise. In his religious poetry he displays all that starched and monotonous conventionality which wearies one so often in the Lives of the Saints. In a consolation to Chilperic and Fredegundis on the death of their children there are some really touching lines, but the poet might have spared the afflicted pair the needless illustration of inevitable doom by an arid list of Biblical worthies, patriarchs, kings, prophets, and apostles, ranging from Abel to S. Peter, who could not escape the last enemy. And yet, in the tender lines on the death of the infant prince Dagobert, who had just been baptized, Fortunatus evidently feels the pathos of the hope of a great line extinguished so early. Yet his eulogies are often probably purchased and insincere. Fredegundis is not only in his pages, what she undoubtedly was, endowed with intellect, charm, and statesmanlike capacity ; but she is a model of virtue. In the poem on Galswintha there is not a hint that the poor Spanish princess, torn from her home to be the bride of Chilperic, had been done to death by the fiendish queen who succeeded her. Probably the poet needed all his suppleness and dexterity to keep a safe course through all the cross currents of the fierce feuds of the sons of Chlothar.

Yet Fortunatus strove and managed to please them all. The eulogist of Chilperic and Fredegundis had on his arrival in Gaul celebrated in pseudo-pagan style the nuptials of Sigibert, and, in Christian style, the reception of his bride into the Catholic Church. His honesty was not tried in doing honour to the valorous king who had to guard the Rhine, or to the fascinating princess, as able as she was ruthless and unscrupulous, who for forty years held her own against the designs of Fredegundis and the intrigues of the nobles of Austrasia. The poem which does least credit to the loyalty of Fortunatus to his friends is that which he addressed to Chilperic on the eve of the Council of Berny. Gregory of Tours, who had been a generous friend of Fortunatus, was being put on his trial ; his rank and his very life were probably at stake. Yet in a long poem, full of adulation of Chilperic and his terrible queen, there is not the faintest allusion to the great bishop who had befriended him, and whose character and position were assailed by an infamous conspiracy. Yet, notwithstanding all faults and even vices of conventionality, servility, and selfish cowardice, Fortunatus had the grace to know a fine character when he saw it. And it is never hard to see when he is sincere in his judgements of character. For example, his poems in honour of Lupus, Duke of Champagne, bear the stamp of genuine admiration and devotion for one of the finest characters of the time, equally renowned in war and in council, and the gallant and chivalrous champion of Brunihildis and her infant son against the traitorous attempts of the Austrasian nobles and bishops. And that he could appreciate a good woman is seen in his picture of Palatina, the wife of a great noble, Bodigisilus, a woman of radiant charm, whose sweet wisdom and gentle modesty were an even greater power than her beauty.

But it must be admitted that Fortunatus was hardly an estimable character ; and it is startling to find that such a man should have been the trusted friend and adviser of Radegund for twenty years, and even occasionally an inmate of her convent. When he came to Poitiers (in 567) he was not yet in Holy Orders, and, in spite of his ecclesiastical friendships and unctuous style, he was a thorough man of the world, of the type of Ausonius, a hundred years before. He must have had some power of attracting and attaching people to him which could hardly have been wholly due to accomplishments and literary facility which were rare in that age. He is a true child of the decadence, full of a depraved literary ideal to which sonorous, conventional phrase took the place of sincerity of thought and feeling. He was also a needy adventurer in a time of great convulsions, violence, and perfidy, when even the powerful and high-born found it difficult to guard their heads. His only armour was his keen wit and supple dexterity, with probably a certain personal charm. He rose in the end to be Bishop of Poitiers, and therefore his religious character must have satisfied his contemporaries. But the religion of that time was generally so materialist and mechanical that strict observance and conformity gave little assurance of those inner qualities of the heart which we are accustomed to associate with religious profession. Such are the contradictions and inconsistencies of human nature, that Fortunatus may have been a better man than he appears to us. Yet we cannot resist the feeling that it was an evil day for Radegund's convent when he entered its walls.

Fortunatus was accepted and installed as an adviser and protector of the convent, and was in the closest relations of confidence with Radegund and the Abbess Agnes. He possessed undoubtedly some qualities and advantages which enabled him to serve them. He had cultivated the favour of the Merovingians by unstinted flattery. He knew all the great churchmen and high officials, and formed an intimate friendship with

many of them. The convent from its position was exposed
to many dangers in the constant wars between Neustria and
Austrasia. Poitiers and Tours had changed masters several times,
and monastic estates might be annexed by the unscrupulous
arts or violence of great potentates professing a formal devotion
to the Church. The letter of S. Radegund addressed to the
bishops on the foundation of her convent shows by its iteration
and emphasis how real she felt the danger of spoliation and
intrusion to be. It might come from the bishop of the place
or from the power of princes or great nobles ; it might take the
form of appropriating monastic property or violating the rule
and constitution which the foundress had established, or foment-
ing breaches of vows and discipline. Against all such assaults
or machinations Radegund most solemnly appeals to the bishops
to defend the convent by all the terrors of ecclesiastical authority.
And, in the end, she orders the bishop to invoke the power of
the Catholic king to vindicate the Order established by her will.
Signs are not wanting that even in the lifetime of Radegund all
did not go well with the convent, and there was a strange friction
with the bishop Maroveus. When in the reign of Chlothar the
convent was founded, the bishop of Poitiers was Pientius, between
whom and Radegund there were cordial relations. Pientius
died in 564, and when he was succeeded in the see by Maroveus,
there soon appeared signs of a mysterious change. The new
bishop displayed, almost ostentatiously, complete indifference to
the interests and the fortunes of the convent, and he maintained
this attitude to the very end of Radegund's life. The causes of
it are left unexplained by Gregory, although he has stated the
facts with great frankness and minuteness. But it is to be
observed that Maroveus was, almost certainly, a Frank of the
higher class, and that he took a prominent part in the political
feuds and diplomacy of the time. He found Fortunatus in the
closest relations with Radegund in the first years of his episcopate,
and Fortunatus was an Italian, a man of culture and supple tact,
who had a powerful influence with King Sigibert. It is possible
that Radegund and her Italian confidant may have offended a
bishop jealous of his powers. It is also possible that the tone
of the convent, in spite of Radegund's sanctity, may have excited
the suspicion of a bishop who was also a man of the world.
The cold attitude of Maroveus displayed itself on two great

occasions when the presence and countenance of the bishop might have seemed obligatory. S. Radegund, from her enthusiastic piety, was eager to acquire any relics of sanctity. She had heard a rumour of the remains of the martyr Mammes lying at Jerusalem, and despatched Reovalis, a leading physician at the time who afterwards became a priest, to beg for a share in the sacred treasure from the Patriarch. That dignitary, with a great concourse of the faithful, approached the martyr's tomb and gently touched his hand, with the reward of a finger which the Patriarch transmitted to Radegund. The priceless relic was welcomed at Poitiers with solemn joy and vigils and fasting. But to all appearance the bishop bore no part in the ceremonial. Another case is even more startling. Fired by the example of the Empress Helena two centuries and a half before, Radegund conceived a longing to have a portion of the True Cross, as the most precious of all sacred things. With the sanction and diplomatic aid of King Sigibert, she despatched a mission to the Eastern emperor to gain the object of her longings. The emperor gratified them, and added to the boon a copy of the Gospels bound with gold and gems. When the priceless relic arrived at Poitiers, Radegund begged her bishop to place it in the church with the solemn forms usual on such occasions. Strange to say, Maroveus refused, took horse at once, and retired to one of his country estates. Distressed by this behaviour, she appealed to Sigibert to command another prelate to perform the ceremony. Eufronius of Tours was commissioned by the king to do so. He came with his cathedral clergy, and in solemn pomp the priceless treasure was safely deposited in the sanctuary of Holy Cross. After an ineffectual attempt to regain the favour of her bishop, Radegund placed her convent under the direct protection of the king. The quarrel with the bishop became more and more embittered during the remaining years of Radegund's life. It must have been very deep and inveterate, for it even survived her death.

Apart from this quarrel, the calm monotony of monastic life seems to have been little disturbed by events in the outer world. Fortunatus would appear to turn his eyes away from the wars and tumults which must have convulsed the region of the Loire. During the twenty years of his friendship with Radegund there were only a few brief intervals of peace between the Merovingian

kings. The plague was decimating the population in rapidly
succeeding onslaughts. The Lombards, descending from the
Alps, were driven back from Provence by the power of Burgundy
and the strategy of Mummolus. The brother kings were constantly engaged in internecine struggles, interrupted now and
then by faithless negotiations and precarious truce. The news
of many a raid or feud must have come to the convent in those
unquiet years. And in the Life of Radegund we are told that
she was sorely troubled by the sanguinary conflict between her
husband's sons. She wrote to them often entreating them to
cease from their feuds, and her prayers went up continually
for the peace of her distracted country. Yet in the verses of
Fortunatus we hear nothing of politics or war. Now and then
we can see him on a journey, amid furious gales and icy cold,
on the rivers of the north. But the everyday life of Radegund,
Agnes, the young abbess, and their rather self-indulgent chaplain
and adviser, seems to have been as little troubled, as frivolous,
and as formal, as that of the country houses of Auvergne on the
eve of the Visigothic invasion. It is a singular alliance of professed asceticism with all the vanities of a decadent culture.

The relations of Radegund, the Abbess Agnes, and Fortunatus
offer a curious problem which has suggested various interpreta-
tions. Severe historians like Guizot and Thierry have refused
to find any food for scandal or suspicion, even in expressions
which might seem to be too warm for merely spiritual sympathy.
Radegund was at least ten years older than the poet, and must
have been nearly fifty when Fortunatus came to Poitiers. He
always addresses her as " Mother ". And her extreme asceticism,
with which the poet once or twice finds fault, along with her
stately rank, would seem to guard sufficiently her fair fame.
Agnes the abbess, and the spiritual daughter of Radegund, was
of course much younger, and appears to have possessed a dangerous charm. Certainly some of the verses which Fortunatus
addresses to her have the warmth of the love poems of Tibullus.
And the verses in which the poet solemnly protests that their
love was pure seems to hint that malignant gossip had been at
work. Far be it from us to lift the veil which hangs over this
possible romance of conventual life in the sixth century. There
is a pathos in it which must always repel any rude hand. It is
probable that the warm imagination of a son of Italy, whose

fancy had been nurtured on ancient lyrical models, may have cast the glow of an earthly passion over feelings which were really innocent or held in severe restraint. But common religious emotion between the sexes has sometimes had a perilous tendency, and a more chivalrous nature than that of Fortunatus would have shrunk from leaving to posterity verses which might cast even a shade of suspicion on one who was dedicated to a more spiritual love.

The truth is that, whatever his religious character may have been, Fortunatus was, by his own confession, a rather coarse, self-indulgent person, without much self-respect. He almost rioted in the luxury with which the kindness of the two ladies of the convent surrounded him. Women, even of the most religious life, personally may have a strange indulgence for the sensual weaknesses of men, and will even cater for them. Radegund and Agnes soon discovered that their guest was inordinately fond of the pleasures of the table, and the kitchen of the convent seems to have been capable of gratifying the taste even of a *bon vivant*. Dishes of meat and vegetables, dressed with rich sauces, eggs, milk, butter, and fine fruit, from the farms of the convent, were sent to the lodgings of Fortunatus, and acknowledged with keen appreciation. Wine also was not stinted, and the poet, apparently without a blush, pens some of his epigrams in a maudlin state as he confesses, with a trembling hand. Yet this unconcealed self-indulgence apparently gave no shock to the taste or principles of his ascetic patronesses. There may have been redeeming qualities in the man which made them forget or forgive his grossness. Or his skill, in those days, in turning phrases which fed their vanity, threw a veil over his faults of character. Apparently, in defiance of the rules of Councils, the two ladies even entertained him at sumptuous repasts within their walls, when the table was loaded with dishes of silver and crystal, and decorated with roses. How Radegund, whose austerities are painted with a too vivid detail by her biographers, can have reconciled herself to such scenes, must be left to a subtle psychology. Probably the table talk of the accomplished man of the world was bright and interesting, a pleasant relief from the deadly dullness of mechanical devotion and the gossip of the cloister. Sometimes it might take a graver and more melancholy cast, when the daughter of Thuringia

would talk of the wild scenes of slaughter and havoc in which
her ancestral towers were given to the flames by the prince to
whom she was reluctantly wedded. In some of the poet's verses
we seem to hear the echo of these mournful memories of her
youth. Radegund's was probably a very mixed character. The
fierce self-will of her ancestors was softened, but not extinguished,
by her Roman culture and discipline. The tone of her letter
of foundation to the bishops, amid its intensity of devotion,
betrays the autocratic instincts of the daughter of kings. It is
possible that here we may find the secret of that constant friction
with Bishop Maroveus which went on all through her life, and
his repeated refusal to give her convent his protection, and to
take his proper part at high religious functions. We may more
than suspect also that the discipline of the house may have
excited uneasiness in the bishop who was its guardian.

A few years before the death of Radegund an incident occurred,
which is told by Gregory with somewhat suspicious reserve, but
which he seems to regard as an ominous precursor of the sad
scandals which we shall have to describe. A nun of severe life
escaped over the walls and took refuge in the shrine of S. Hilary,
which was close at hand. She spread the gravest charges against
the abbess, which, Gregory alleges, he had ascertained to be false.
The abbess at that time must have been Agnes. The accusations
were probably false ; but there must have been something wrong
with a society of high-born and profoundly devout women
when such charges were lightly made against those devoted to
stainless purity. The sister was forcibly drawn up over the
walls by ropes, made a humble confession of her sin against
God and the Lady Radegund, and begged to be left in solitary
penitence. Her repentance must have been of a strange kind.
For at no distant date we read of her breaking out of her cell,
with similar charges against the successor of Agnes, and joining
in the wild revolt which was led by Chrodieldis.

The death of S. Radegund took place on the 13th of August
587, in the sixty-sixth year of her age. The description of her
obsequies has been preserved for us with obvious care by Gregory.
He tells us that, on a message from the convent, he went to
Poitiers. He found her bier surrounded by the sisters, 200 in
number, bewailing the loss of their spiritual mother in the words
and tone so often recurring on the death of a saint. He gazed

2 c

for a moment on that face of marvellous beauty, which had charmed the brutal Chlothar, fifty years before, and which was now glorified by death. Maroveus, the bishop of the diocese, was at a distance engaged on a visitation. The Bishop of Tours was in a serious difficulty. Was the saintly woman to be buried without the last rites, or were they to be deferred until her bishop's return ? The abbess gave an answer which implied that they could not await Maroveus ; and all the leading citizens at once called on Gregory to consecrate the tomb, and trust to his brother prelate's charity to condone the intrusion upon his province. Gregory consented at last ; the procession moved away beneath the walls to the Chapel of S. Hilary, which Radegund had long before designated as her last resting-place. The chanting was choked with sobs, and overpowered by the wailing of the nuns along the walls. It may be suspected that Maroveus was voluntarily absent, and that the abbess did not much regret it.

Radegund was fortunate in the time of her death. She escaped the scandal and horror of a wild outbreak among the sisterhood, which seemed to undo all her work and to give the lie to her hopes. It was inspired and led by two sisters of the highest social rank, Chrodieldis, a daughter of Charibert, and Basina, her cousin, the daughter of Audovera, the repudiated wife of King Chilperic. The story of this scandalous disorder, which taxed all the efforts of the bishops and the governments of Austrasia and Burgundy, for nearly two years, to quell, would be almost incredible if it did not come to us from Gregory, who had a personal knowledge of all the details. He regarded it, after his fashion, as due to the arts of the Evil One, plotting to undo the holy work of S. Radegund ; and he narrates it with the minutest care, and clearly with no desire to conceal the facts. It is a startling revelation of the wild insurgent forces which the Church in that age had to control and tame. It also illustrates the relation of monastic houses to the bishops and the Crown.

In the first days of the year 589, a band of forty nuns, led by Chrodieldis, appeared at Tours, and sought an audience of the bishop. They had walked all the way from Poitiers along roads flooded by incessant rains, and were exhausted with fatigue and want of food. They came to claim the bishop's protection and hospitality, while their leader repaired to the court of her relations in Burgundy, to seek redress for their wrongs. Chrodieldis charged

the abbess, Leubovera, with grave offences, and indignantly
complained that, under her rule, the daughters of Frank kings
had been humiliated and degraded to the level of the lowest-born.
Gregory, who was above all a gentleman, received his tumultuous
visitors with fatherly kindliness, and invited the ladies to go
with him and lay their case before Maroveus, their bishop. The
imperious Chrodieldis replied that they would go to the King.
Gregory then, with the calm dignity of a father in God, warned
them of the awful severance from communion which the bishops
had threatened against such offenders against discipline in their
letter to S. Radegund when she founded the convent. But
nothing could shake the determination of Chrodieldis and her
company. They would not go to Maroveus; for the state of
the convent was chiefly due to his neglect of his duties. He had
haughtily refused to consecrate the holy relics, and the fragment
of the Cross which had been brought from the East; and he
had left Eufronius of Tours to perform the rite. He had compelled Radegund, after many entreaties, to place her house
under the guardianship of the King, who desired that it should
be under the spiritual care of the bishop. To the King they
would go. Gregory chided the self-willed princess for rejecting
his sober advice, but begged her, at least, to defer her journey
to the court till the milder spring weather had set in. Chrodieldis
would yield to no persuasion, and, committing her company to
the care of Basina, she set out for the court of King Guntram.
That genial prince received her with all honour, and ordered
an episcopal visitation of the convent to investigate the charges
against its government. But, before the princess had returned
to Tours, their new freedom and licence had played havoc among
her sisters whom she had left behind. Tours was the most sacred
shrine in Gaul, haunted by mysteries of the power of sanctity;
yet, from many tales, it is clear that its moral atmosphere was
far from pure, and that crass superstition often gave a shelter
to grossness and licence. The holy town of S. Martin, where
so many miracles were enacted, was also infested by bands of
bravoes and desperadoes, who were ready for any adventure or
any excess. Many of the nuns, in spite of their boasted birth,
had formed disreputable *liaisons*; some of them had married
in due form. Meanwhile the expected bishops did not come,
and the rebel nuns, gathering around them a gang of brigands,

murderers, men stained with every crime, fortified themselves under the walls of S. Hilary's, as if for warlike defence, and declared that they would not return to their convent until the hated abbess was expelled. When the bishops did arrive, including Maroveus, the bishop of the diocese, they at first remonstrated with the mutinous sisters and urged them to return to the convent. But, as they remained obdurate, the bishops proceeded to cut them off from communion. The granddaughter of Clovis rose to the occasion. Her crowd of mercenaries broke into the sacred conclave, and used the most brutal violence ; bishops and attendant clergy soon lay prostrate and wounded on the pavement ; others fled in all directions. One deacon of Autun only escaped by swimming his horse across the swollen Clain. Chrodieldis sent out emissaries to seize the monastic estates, and threatened, when she re-entered the convent, to fling the abbess from the walls. Any servant of the monastery whom she could seize was compelled by blows and violence to execute her orders.

The bishops reported their decision to the episcopal commissioners appointed by Guntram. They professed to agree with the sentence of excommunication which had been pronounced. But in unctuous tone they recommended a gentler handling of the matter, so that, by prayer and exhortation, " the wandering sheep might be brought back to the fold ". Maroveus himself, who had joined in the original sentence, began to waver under the scurrilities with which he was assailed. He begged his brethren to withdraw the anathema and permit him to give an audience to the offenders. But this was naturally refused. In the meantime King Childebert was appealed to both by the abbess and the rebels, and he sent a priest named Theutharius to compose the quarrel. But the nuns, when summoned to an audience, refused to appear before even the royal commissioner, till the ban of excommunication upon them was removed. The bishops, however, were inexorable. A severe winter had set in, and a scarcity of fuel added to the hardship among these wild women who had abandoned the comforts of the convent. They began to melt away. Some returned to their homes, others to their original convents, from which they had been drawn by the fame or charm of Radegund. A few, probably of the more desperate or less reputable, remained under their audacious leaders, Chrodieldis and Basina, surrounded by their ruffianly bodyguard.

At last Chrodieldis ordered a band of cut-throats and criminals, of every age, to storm the convent and drag the abbess forth. The abbess was a martyr to gout, and, as the noise of the assault reached her, she ordered her attendants to lay her in the oratory before the casket which contained the fragment of the Holy Cross. The bands of Chrodieldis with lighted torches ranged everywhere, and at last burst into the chapel. One of them was about to pierce the abbess with his sword, when he himself was cut down by one of his companions, who may have felt some compunction at such a crime in such a place. The incident gave Justina (a niece of Gregory), who was prioress, time to extinguish the lights and hide the abbess under the altar cloth. But Justina's loyalty nearly cost her her own life. Dashing on in the darkness, the invaders laid rude hands on Justina, whom they took for the abbess, and dragged her, with torn robes and dishevelled hair, to the Church of S. Hilary, where they kept her in confinement. The bishop tried to release her by threatening to deprive the city of the sacraments at Eastertide, which was approaching. But it was only through the timely arrival of Flavian, a high official of the court, that the tumult was composed. Meanwhile, the arrogance of Chrodieldis was growing day by day, so that even her cousin Basina deserted her. Her armed retainers waged open war with those of the abbess, and before the tomb of S. Radegund, and the casket of the Holy Cross, murders were perpetrated every day. The kings of Austrasia and Burgundy then appointed a commission of bishops to deal with the scandal, by canonical rule. But they declined to interfere till the insurrection had been quelled by the civil power. A certain Count Macco was then ordered to use force, if necessary, and he only overpowered the defiant resistance of Chrodieldis's bands by vigorous military measures. The ruffians who survived the struggle were put to all the tortures of rack and mutilation. Chrodieldis screened herself under the protection of the Cross, threatening that, if violence were done to her, the daughter and the cousin of kings would one day have her revenge.

The bishops at last met to deliberate on the feuds that had almost brought the convent to ruin. They heard evidence on all the accusations which Chrodieldis and her party made against

the abbess and her government of the house ; and then drew
up judgement to be submitted to the kings. It is a valuable,
but most melancholy document. The gravest charge against
the abbess, of adultery with a man concealed in woman's dress,
is dismissed in spite of some suspicious circumstances. The
complaint of the sisters that they were starved and miserably
clad was answered by pointing to the general scarcity of the time,
and the well-stocked wardrobes of the convent. But it was not
denied that men were freely permitted to use the baths, that
games of hazard were played, that plays of a distinctly satyric
type were produced, and that laymen were entertained within
the walls. The abbess could only plead that these violations of
decency, or of canonical rule, had the sanction of S. Radegund
in her time. She admitted that her niece had been openly
formally betrothed, in the presence of high dignitaries, within
the convent walls, and that part of her bridal dress had been
cut from a rich pall which had been offered for the altar. It
does not surprise one to hear that, in a religious house conducted
with such extraordinary laxity, some of the nuns were found
to be pregnant. And it says much for, at least, the charity of
the bishops, that the abbess was absolved with a significant
warning to be more circumspect for the future.

But the offences of the rebellious sisters admitted of no
palliation. They had broken away from their convent, in
violation of their vows, and treated with contempt the monitions
of the bishop. They had outraged with violence and contumely
the prelates assembled in the Chapel of S. Hilary, and spilt the
blood of the attendant deacons. They had offered defiance to
the King in the person of his envoy Theutharius. Then the
monastery had been invaded and plundered, the loyal nuns had
been beaten and wounded in the very chapel ; the abbess had
been dragged away to confinement with every circumstance of
outrage and insult. They had employed a body of armed
ruffians against an officer acting under royal command, and at
least one murder had been perpetrated before the altar. They
had abstracted, and refused to restore, the royal charters securing
possession of the monastic estates. It is little wonder that the
bishops cut them off from communion till they purged their
offences, and advised the King to prevent their return to the
house which they had disgraced and desecrated. Even then,

with an energy worthy of a better cause, they refused to give up the struggle. Disregarding the judgement of the bishops, they appeared in person before King Childebert, making fresh charges against the abbess of adulterous connexion with persons who were in secret communication with Fredegundis, Childebert's arch-enemy. It was a time of political danger and suspicion. The inculpated persons were brought before the King, but the charges were dismissed. This was Chrodieldis's last throw.

At this time a dangerous conspiracy had been unearthed for the assassination of Childebert, in which Egidius, Bishop of Rheims, was involved, with some of the highest nobles. And an episcopal synod was summoned for the trial of Egidius for treason at Verdun. Finally, amid the rigours of a winter of extraordinary severity, the prelates were ordered to assemble at Metz. We are not here concerned with the fate of the intriguing bishop. But before the synod closed, they found themselves unexpectedly confronted with other business. Basina and Chrodieldis presented themselves before the bishops, begging to be relieved from the sentence of excommunication. The former, who was always the milder and less hardened, penitently promised not to repeat her offences, and to live in charity with the abbess. Chrodieldis protested that she would never return to conventual obedience while the Abbess Leubovera held her place. Yet, by the entreaty of their kinsman, Childebert, both women were restored to communion, and ordered to return to Poitiers. Basina dutifully went back to the convent. Chrodieldis, true to her character, remained obdurate, and received from her long-suffering cousin an estate in Touraine. It had belonged to Waddo, who had held high office at court, but had joined in the rising of the pretender Gundobald. He and his sons were of the true type of the lawless baron of the Middle Ages, seizing estates, plundering peaceful traders, at last defying royal officers, ending their lawless career by death or banishment. The lawless Chrodieldis was a proper successor to their lands. The veil has dropped upon her later years.

This episode is not presented to the reader as a fair or typical specimen of monastic life in the sixth century. So far from that, we believe that the moral condition of the convent of the Holy Cross was quite abnormal, and that from obvious causes. The foundress was a Queen of France, herself of rigorous personal sanctity, but also one who had an indulgence for the frailties of human nature, especially in those of her own rank, which was dangerous to conventual discipline in a lawless age. By rank and family connexions, Radegund gathered about her a body of women who, by breeding and early associations, were ill fitted for the rule of obedience by which alone such communities can be held together. Above all, she had among them a daughter of Chlothar, who if she had been a man might have outdone the fiercest and most self-willed princes of her house. The second cause of the catastrophe was the choice of Agnes as head of the society, and the presence of the self-indulgent Fortunatus as their companion and adviser. When Agnes mysteriously disappeared, she was followed by the Abbess Leubovera, whose suspicious laxity, both in her own life and in her government, had much to do in preparing the *émeute* of Chrodieldis and Basina. The poems of Fortunatus leave on us the impression that Agnes was too weak a woman to preside over the life of an ascetic society, and that the poet was not likely to strengthen her. Two widely different ideals met at the sumptuous feasts with which the ladies regaled their favourite. There was the old semi-pagan humanism to which the world of sense and conventionality had all the charm it had for the circle of Ausonius ; and there was the ideal of superhuman sanctity to which S. Radegund dedicated her own life. With the suppleness and elasticity of the true literary temper, Fortunatus could write a questionable epigram, and then with perfect sincerity prostrate himself before a vision of holiness. Yet we must admit that such a combination is a dangerous one : the Heavenly love too easily catches some stains of earth. We cannot help feeling that it would have been well for Radegund and her foundation if she had never known Fortunatus ; it would probably have been better for Agnes. Fortune and the world are always too kind to men like Fortunatus, as they are too harsh to weak women. Within a few years the poet became Bishop of Poitiers; and probably died in the odour of conventional sanctity. There is a pathetic silence as to the end of Agnes.

The relation of religious houses to the bishops and the King in the sixth century was still fluctuating and uncertain. It is true that, as we shall see in another chapter, the power of the bishop was steadily growing, and that the Councils of the sixth century gave him large powers over the foundation of monasteries, and their government and discipline. The episcopal power is recognised by the State, but is unable to deal with such atrocious defiance of conventual discipline as that which disgraced the foundation of S. Radegund. The bishops were face to face with the pride and lawless arrogance of women, who, when their passions are aroused, are often more lawless and reckless than men, and women who rated themselves far higher as of royal kindred than as virgins of Christ. It is to the honour of Gregory and his episcopal colleagues that they did not yield to these arrogant pretensions. It was left for a Merovingian king to condone the insults, not only to the Church, but to his own chosen envoys, and to endow the chief rebel with an estate in Touraine.

From such tumultuous scenes we cannot expect to draw much clear and definite information as to the relations of the monastic houses to the bishop and the royal power. The monasteries at first established spontaneously and without definite authority, and composed of laymen grouping themselves together for a higher religious life, enjoyed great independence. The power and authority of the bishop over them was no greater or more special than over the moral and spiritual life of the mass of the Christian people. But the necessities of religious life and the introduction of ordained priests into their ranks brought them more and more into contact with the bishops and secular clergy. And their growing spiritual influence and prestige, combined with their ambition, naturally called for more spiritual control. The independence which the monks enjoyed had produced many irregularities, which from the beginning of the fifth century the Councils in Gaul set themselves to correct. From the year 511 no one is to be permitted to found a monastery or an oratory without his bishop's consent. Monks are forbidden to leave their house to engage in worldly or ecclesiastical business outside its walls. None but priests of mature age and proved character are to say mass in nunneries. The discipline of all religious houses is to be under the inspection and control of the bishop. The abbots are under his spiritual power. Yet, however elaborate the regulations, it seems certain that they were often more honoured in the breach than in the observance. The religious houses grew steadily in power and in independence, even while the formal bonds uniting them to the Church seemed to be drawn more tightly. Their rapidly growing wealth, the favour of princes which they so often enjoyed, together with a steady internal development, the fruit of what was after all the greatest religious movement of the age, were combining to raise these great foundations to the eminence which they enjoyed in later centuries. They lost, it is true, the shadow of independence, but gained the substance of power and influence.

CHAPTER II

SAINTS AND MIRACLES

THE modern reader of Gregory of Tours is naturally inclined to discredit him as a historian on the ground of the space which he gives to the supernatural and the saintly persons who possessed the power of wielding or counteracting the forces of Nature. Yet, had he not done so, he would have done violence to his own deepest beliefs, and he would have given a maimed and misleading picture of his age. From ancestry and temperament, Gregory was deeply persuaded of the omnipresence and continual activity of spiritual powers. A fixed, irreversible order of Nature was a conception absolutely unknown to him. When there might be a question as to the natural or a miraculous cause of some event, his inclination, from pious instinct, was to prefer the miracle. And in this theory of the government of the world, he is merely a representative of the almost universal conviction or sentiment of his age. The mass of men were still pagan in the sense that they still believed that a multitude of unseen powers were working under all the phenomena of life and nature, that demons floated round the life of men, and that a man of rare sanctity could in life, or from his tomb, work wonders as marvellous as his sanctity. To that universal belief Gregory has given the fullest expression in all his works. In his *History*, he delights to record how a divinely sent stag revealed to the army of Clovis a ford across the swollen Vienne, how a great general once made a search for a martyr's bones as a sure guarantee of victory. And his other works are almost exclusively devoted to the record of the marvels of saintly lives. His great predecessor in the see of Tours has naturally a foremost place.

Gregory's devotion to S. Martin knew no bounds. In his first
mention of the saint he celebrates him " as the man by whom
Gaul was irradiated with the beams of a new light, who by many
wonderful works had made known Christ as very God among
the peoples, and conquered the unbelief of the heathen ". And
Gregory has a mission, conveyed to him in a dream, to tell of
all the miracles daily wrought at S. Martin's tomb, how the
lame are made to walk, the blind to see, demons are put to
flight, and all manner of disease is healed. This grateful task
was performed in a work divided into four books, with 207
chapters, each on some miracle of the saint. In another book
we have a collection of the miracles of the Blessed Martyrs,
which are contrasted with the figments of Greek and Latin
legend, the flight of Saturn, the adulteries of Jupiter, the rape
of Proserpine, the terrors of the Eumenides. Of course S. Julian,
the great saint of Auvergne, at whose shrine Gregory and his
family had so often worshipped, must have his chronicle of
wonders wrought at his tomb at Brioude, some of them witnessed
by Gregory himself. Another work, containing 112 chapters, is
consecrated to the Glory of the Blessed Confessors, and intended
to rescue their great deeds and virtues from the oblivion which
was beginning to cover them.

Gregory was the precursor of a great effort of systematic
hagiography, which extended roughly from the sixth to the
tenth century. In that period of four centuries these records
multiplied with the most extraordinary fecundity, and were
redacted and expanded with fresh touches by pious ingenuity.
They were practically the only literature of that dull dark time.
The Bollandists have rescued an immense number from the
oblivion into which they were falling even in Gregory's life. The
Collection was begun in 1643, and continued down to 1794,
when its placid course was interrupted by the Revolution.
M. Guizot has been at the trouble to reckon that the 53 volumes
of the Collection, which were completed at that date, contained
about 25,000 lives. The work, begun again in 1837, is not
yet complete. Any one with historical imagination and a
desire to know really the history of human thought must be
grateful to the pious hands which have saved such a record
from oblivion. M. Renan, with his idealist sympathy for all
great spiritual movements, has said that the possession of these

volumes would turn a prison cell into a paradise. Certainly Gregory's legends are pleasanter and more instructive reading than his secular history. They are the revelation of another world than that which meets us in the curt, bald chronicle of the violence, intrigue, and brutal egotism of that evil time. They also reveal a world of imagination and fervent belief which no modern man can ever fully enter into, even with the most insinuating power of imaginative sympathy. It is intensely interesting, even fascinating. But the interest is that of the remote observer, studying with cold scrutiny a puzzling phase in the development of the human spirit.

Between us and the early Middle Ages there is a gulf which the most supple and agile imagination can hardly hope to pass. He who has pondered most deeply over the popular faith of that time will feel most deeply how impossible it is to pierce its secret. The chasm that severs us from that vanished world is not to be measured by centuries ; it is the severance made by a great intellectual and spiritual revolution. The Western world was, in the sixth century, nominally Christian, but it was still pagan to the core. The doctrines of the Creeds recited in the churches were overshadowed by a popular religion with a vast anthropomorphic mythology, created by the fanciful devotion of the crowd, but gradually accepted and sanctioned by the authority of the Church. This popular tradition, not yet formally recognised by Councils, had been canvassed and formulated by great doctors of the Church, and took final shape and symmetry in the theology of Gregory the Great, who forms the link between the dogmatic system of the Fathers and mediaeval scholasticism. A vast, all-embracing theory of the Universe and the life of man, with materials from Hebrew scripture, classical paganism, or Magian and Gnostic speculation, far more than the simple Evangel, dominated men's minds for a thousand years ; it inspired the visions of the celestial or infernal worlds in Dante and Milton. The creeds of the Church formed but a small part of the religion of the people and the clergy in the age of Gregory of Tours.

Gregory the Great recognised two sources of religious belief, Holy Scripture and Tradition. Tradition is a very convenient and elastic term. It might embrace deductions of the Fathers from Apostolic teaching, or elaboration and amplification of it : or it might mean the growing belief and devotional sentiment of the body of the faithful, gravitating towards dogmatic certainty. All this mass of floating learned opinion or pious craving for extended range of devotion, the Catholic Church, with that deep knowledge of the human soul which is her special gift, skilfully absorbed into her dogmatic system, and used to strengthen her influence. In leaving her pagan bondage she never hesitated " to spoil the Egyptians ". The simple gospel was early overlaid and sophisticated by the forms and traditions of subtle Greek and Oriental speculation. The early simplicity of the Supper of the Lord and the love feasts of the infant Church were transmuted and glorified to the imagination by a symbolism of gorgeous rite which might be traced, in part, to the Hall of Initiation at Eleusis or the Caves of Mithras. The process went on because the craving for continuity in religious faith is so ineradicable. Classical and Teuton pagans, the army of Constantine or the army of Clovis, the dilettante student trained in the schools of Bordeaux, or the Druid converted by a miracle of S. Martin, could not shake off in an hour the ingrained religious feelings of a thousand years.

Thus the conversion of Europe to Christ was for a long time very superficial, as the great Frank chief showed when, on hearing the tale of the Crucifixion, he fiercely vowed that if he and his Franks had been there, they would have avenged it. And the Christ whom he professed to accept was only another Odin who had helped him in the stress of the fight at Tolbiacum. The old pagan spirit was not dead ; it died hard. The profound anthropomorphism of the human spirit, in its effort to realise the spiritual world, almost renewed its youth and creative energy in spiritual regions below the Supreme Godhead. All the region beneath that was humanised and materialised. All the phenomena of Nature were permeated and inspired by wills and forces of the human type. As in Greek mythology, the line between Divine and human faded and tended to vanish, or rather, the mortal and the human encroached upon the unseen and Divine. Just as in the Antonine Age, the old classical divinities, or the purer and loftier conceptions of Deity afloat in the Platonic schools, receded behind a host of genii and demons, born of anthropomorphic fancy, so the sublime Persons of the Trinity seemed to exert less power over the lives of men than the hierarchy of angels and infernal spirits, along with the ever multiplying army of martyrs and saints, whom the devotee summoned to his defence and support. The Eucharistic devotion kept up the memory of the Great Sacrifice ; yet it tended to become a spectacle and sacred drama of Divine suffering ; and the Second Person of the Trinity, who had descended into material form, seemed to withdraw more and more into transcendental distances for the mass of men. Yet no sympathetic reader of the Lives of the Saints, amid all the tales of trivial miracle and old-world superstition, will fail now and then to recognise the tones of a pure and simple piety, redolent of Galilee, which must be true and precious for all ages. The closing scene in the life of the Abbot Aredius, when, on the approach of death, he gathered his monks around him, and begged of them, if they really loved him, to love the commands of Christ, makes one almost forget the rather crude imitations of Gospel miracles with which his biography is decorated or disfigured by the inventive fancy of those who tried to honour his memory. And, in his last prayer to the Redeemer—" let Thy hand guide me to a place of refreshment and consolation "—there is a tone, tender and spiritual, which must appeal to all ages of the Christian Church. But above and beneath this simple piety, imagination and ambitious speculation had framed a vast hierarchy of Being embracing the Universe, and filling, with its various grades of dignity and function, the immense interval between the Supreme and Infinite and His worshippers below. Vaguely shadowed forth in the Old Testament or in S. Paul or the Apocalypse, it was elaborated out of Talmudic, Magian, or Gnostic materials, into a vast symmetrical scheme by Augustine, the pseudo-Dionysius, and Gregory the Great. It was embodied in the theology of the Church, accepted as a firm basis for scholastic reasoning, and in coarse, broad outline, implicitly believed by the masses. At once mystical, and yet mapped out in clear-cut symmetry, it was peculiarly fitted to capture the mind of the Middle Age. Yet, in its motive and spirit, it is simply another effort, like that of Gnostic or Neo-Platonic fancy, to span the infinite gulf between the human and the Divine. And, as in every Apocalypse, of Plato, Plutarch, or S. John, the weakness of reason is forced to picture the supermundane sphere in material images and the glowing colours of sense, in human or animal forms, subtle fire and vivid movement, priestly vesture or spears and axes of the warrior, various colours of radiant gems, and the music of heavenly choirs in the angelic worship of another world.

A mathematical symmetry reigns through the Universe : in a system of triads, there is an exact correspondence between the celestial hierarchy and the hierarchy of the Church below, in the number of the sacraments and the grades of worshippers. The Godhead of the Three in One is withdrawn to an infinite distance, beyond range of human thought or speech. Around this mystery of Godhead are marshalled, as it were in concentric circles, or in a series of descending triads, the angelic host, three divisions of three orders, in various degrees of proximity to the Supreme. In comparison with man, angels are incorporeal spirits, possessing immeasurable knowledge, but in their three great orders there are wide differences of character and function. The Seraphim stand nearest to God, engaged continually in passionate adoration, and never quit His presence on any lower ministry. The lower orders of angels have to deal with the lot of man ; they are ministers in the government of the world, or in guarding its several peoples, or in helping individual men, or in conveying to them monitions of the will of God, by voices from heaven, such as those heard by Adam in the garden, or by Moses from the burning bush, or by the Virgin mother at the Conception.

The number of the angels is practically infinite. It is true that it was diminished by the loss of those spirits who fell from heaven through pride. But the gaps then made in the angelic ranks will, in the procession of ages, be filled up by the redeemed from the ranks of men. Meantime, the triple orders of the celestial hierarchy have their counterpart in the triple sacerdotal orders upon earth : the Church above and the Church below are marshalled in corresponding symmetry ; and the law of supermundane triads has also its antitype in the three Sacraments of Baptism, Eucharist, and Holy Chrism, and in the triple ranks of the devout, Baptized, Communicants, and monks. Thus the Church below is, to the mediaeval mind, an image of the great Church worshipping in the immediate presence of the Triune ; and the splendour thrown around the altar, the many coloured marbles and flashing gems, the lights and clouds of incense, are only faint symbols of the unimaginable glory of the courts above.

The Christian was believed to be surrounded and guarded

by angelic ministers, and yet their presence is only dimly felt
and seldom recorded.   It is probably an ominous sign of the
moral condition of that age that immensely greater heed is paid
to the evil spirits who swarmed around the life of man, even
of the meanest and most insignificant.   There were two creations
in God's image, the angelic and the human, but both were cast
down by pride.   The fall of the angels was deeper, more irredeem-
able, than the fall of Adam's race, because the angels were not
encumbered by infirmities of the flesh, and, as their nature was
loftier far and purer, so their degradation was the deeper and
more hopeless, since it was self-chosen.   But they retain their
original knowledge, ubiquity, and power, only henceforth to
tempt, seduce, and corrupt the bodies and souls of men.   Their
awful prince, once the nearest to the Eternal Throne, cast down
by pride and envy of the Supreme, is the great example of the
saying, *corruptio optimi pessima*.   Abandoned to his evil nature,
he has gained a freedom which is the truest servitude, blinded,
unrepentant, unpardonable.   Yet has he retained for the time
the great powers of his order, restrained, indeed, by the goodness
of God, but permitted to tempt to sin, to waylay, and inflict
physical evils, and only resisted by Divine grace, or the help
of angel and saint.   At the end, his powers will be for a time
let loose, and his miracles and glory will sometimes deceive even
the elect.   The Church for a time will lose its power in presence
of Antichrist ; prophecy and holy doctrine will be hidden, the
grace of wondrous works will be withdrawn, and the power of
the Evil One will seem for a while to triumph.   Yet only for a
while ; for he will be suddenly struck down by the coming of
the Great Judge, and before the eyes of saints and angels he
will be hurled to eternal torment without hope of pardon.

The august lord of the fallen angels became in popular fancy
a very different personage from the ideal Satan, as he is glorified
by the genius and sympathy of Milton.   He has, in truth, become
rather vulgar.   The lofty fallen Archangel in the *Dialogues* of
Gregory the Great, which did so much to create the Devil of the
Middle Ages, is no longer a weird, mysterious power of the
unseen world, but ludicrously commonplace, appearing in all
sorts of vulgar disguise, attempting to affright rustic imagination, and playing mischievous pranks.   He is a dangerous, but
not omnipotent, fiend, yet easily discomfited by the holy sign

or a dash of holy water. He may appear as a black boy or an ill-omened bird. He may create the terrors of a haunted house by the sounds of a menagerie, or he will hold his infernal court in a ruined shrine of Apollo on the Appian Way, and question his fiendish emissaries as to the mischiefs they have done. And the physical characteristics with which he was endowed by popular imagination correspond to his vulgar, repulsive, or ludicrous qualities. It was comparatively late that he is allowed to appear in human form. He is generally seen in a grotesque or hideous combination of the most disgusting animal forms, howling, screaming, grovelling, and leaving behind a stench as he vanishes. His demon subjects display all his malevolence and ludicrous vulgarity. All human sin and misery, the great convulsions and calamities of nature, are traced to their evil arts, making sport of the lives and souls of men, or terrifying in more cruel caprice. They are specially the cause of all physical pain, insanity, and disease, in which a devilish agent is at once assumed as a matter of course. It was a devil, according to Gregory of Tours, who once at Limoges raised a sudden gust of wind which, with a poisonous cloud of dust and offal, blinded a little child playing on its mother's lap. It was a demon which one day at Angers suddenly smote a man with the contortions of paralysis. Before the high altar at Tours, at the conclusion of the Mass, another evil spirit, with loud imprecations on the power of S. Martin, quitted the body of its victim, as the foam and blood spouted from his mouth. One of the sisters once saw thousands of demons hovering over S. Radegund's convent. Another, according to Gregory the Great, once swallowed a devil which was perching on a lettuce ! And a demon is said to have stripped a priest of his stockings for having lightly used the word " devil ". But such touches of the ludicrous seldom relieve the dark monotony of this picture of superstition. In the baleful arts of witchcraft and sorcery it prolonged its reign even beyond the Middle Ages. Women inspired by evil spirits with dark prediction, or secret powers of malison, were at once employed and execrated by persons in high places. A woman of Verdun long plied a profitable trade for her master by detecting hidden thefts. The bishop expelled the unclean spirit by exorcism. The witches of Paris in 584 were tortured by Fredegundis on the suspicion that they had aided in an intrigue to get rid of a young prince.

The demons' most maleficent power, that which plays the largest part in this tale of superstition, was in the field of demoniacal " possession ". It is one side of the universal belief that the human spirit was in communication with the surrounding world of spirits, both for good and evil. Strange efforts of genius, dreams, and visions came by revelation beyond known powers of Nature. Madness or momentary frenzy sprang from the visitation of some spirit outside the human personality. Everything out of the ordinary course, and not easily explicable, was referred to unseen powers, baleful or benevolent. The mysterious and supernatural cause was the more probable and the more readily accepted. The only question was whether the author was God or an infernal spirit. The nervous and convulsive maladies lent themselves always readily to superstitious theory and cure. Nervous maladies were protean in their symptoms, obscure in their causes, and often baffling to medical skill. Hereditary taint, vicious indulgence, morbid imagination—all these may have been the parents of those shocking disorders which the devotee of the age of Gregory of Tours not unnaturally attributed to some evil spirit. Epilepsy, hysteria, melancholia, all the noisome brood born of a disordered and depraved nervous system, in their violent physical effects, and still more in their frequent perversion of reason and natural instincts, or in the explosiveness of passion, may well have seemed to an unscientific age to be a mysterious visitation of unseen powers. And the maladies were sometimes rendered more virulent by the unnatural conditions of cloistered life, by solitude, religious excitement, or overstrained asceticism. The universal conviction that any abnormal mental state in which perverted sense or violent animal impulse overcame the control of the reason, was caused by the indwelling of a demon, put a ban on scientific treatment, and deepened the mystery and the horror. Surrounded by such an atmosphere, the malady of the sufferer was intensified by disordered imagination. The morbid fancy which could in a night call forth stigmata on the breast of a man, could easily conjure up a malevolent spirit haunting one's dreams and catch demonic voices of mockery or obscene temptation. And dreams, the ever fruitful source of superstitious terror, would only confirm the faith in demonic visitations.

The repulsive symptoms of epilepsy are unmistakable in many of these tales of possession. One of them, particularly, is very instructive. Landulfus, a citizen of Vienne, was long afflicted with this disease, and, believing himself to be assailed by the arch-enemy, used to fall to the ground, with bloody froth spouting from his lips, and then lie for a time, as if dead. The fame of S. Martin's healing power came to his ears, and he betook himself to his tomb, full of faith. But the boldness of the demon only became more defiant. Close to the shrine the poor wretch might sometimes obtain a respite. But when he came forth, the evil spirits were again awaiting their prey, and returned to the attack with the clash of unseen arms. If the sufferer threw himself to the ground, a crowd of frogs swarmed over his body, and he would hear jeering voices telling him that since he was their bond-slave S. Martin could give no help. Only the sign of the Cross put the foul crew to flight. Then the enemy resorted to stratagem. He came in the guise of an ancient man, professing to be S. Martin, and bidding the afflicted one to adore him. The votary replied, " If thou be S. Martin, make the holy sign over me and I will believe ". At the mere mention of the Cross the devil vanished in smoke. At last, as Landulfus stood one day in a sort of stupor before the saint's image, the whole basilica shone with a strange splendour, and the saint told him his prayers had been heard, and that he would be healed of his infirmity. His health returned, but he began to take wine to excess, and became paralysed on one side. Then he took the tonsure, devoted himself to the ascetic life, and once more was restored to soundness by the powers of the saint, or by healthy regimen. No comment on such a story is needed either by the pathologist or the student of religion. The tale of Landulfus may serve as the type of scores of other such stories. There is a strange uniformity in them which sometimes leads one to suspect a pious adherence to conventional models approved by faith. The demonology of that age may seem to the modern mind now grotesque and absurd, now pestilent and degrading—a *damnosa hereditas* from paganism. And it brought with it an obscene train of sorcery and witchcraft, spells and charms, which were denounced in Roman and Barbarian Codes, and anathematised by Popes and Councils, yet which persisted with a singular vitality. The prohibitions were very illogical in men who often firmly believed in diabolic powers themselves. And the savage punishments dealt out for so many ages to those who were suspected of wielding them, degraded humanity at once by giving a sanction to superstitious credulity, and by the cruelties with which imposture was repressed.

It is refreshing to turn from these repulsive scenes to another field where sanctity and charity were clothed by the poetic imagination of the people with a strange charm, and beneficial powers drawn from the unseen world. To cope with the host of evil spirits who infested the life of man, besides the angelic ministers before the Throne, another class of guardians was demanded by the religious imagination. In the Lives of the Saints angels play only a small part. They are too ethereal in their nature and their origin, too remote from the life of humanity, to satisfy the needs which the deeply rooted anthropomorphism made so imperious. The saints who had won a glorious place by lofty virtues or a martyr's death, having worn the human form, were still in sympathy with their brethren on earth, and their prayers and intercession were powerful with God. The glorious polity of the City of God united in one communion those still militant in the flesh with those who had won the crown. At every Eucharistic sacrifice the closeness of the union was realised. Probably many of the early converts vividly remembered that their pagan ancestors had paid annual rites at an altar to great spirits who had won the admiration of their fellows by heroic deeds, patriotic devotion, or even by the glory of surpassing physical beauty. And from Hesiod to Plutarch, men's minds had been accustomed to the thought of human nobleness passing into the rank of heroes or daemons, possessed of unearthly powers and knowledge, yet with a fellow feeling for that human nature which they still shared.

From the Nicene Age, with some differences of opinion, the Church had sought the patronage and advocacy of departed saints and martyrs. In the age of S. Augustine and Paulinus of Nola rustic pagans had been weaned from their old gods by means of a new mythology. Gregory the Great treats the cult of the saints as an established doctrine and practice, and powerfully justifies it, by argument and illustration, while he strives to guard it against abuse either by the tendency of anthropomorphic worship, or by a materialist selfishness, seeking to make the saints ministers to mere worldly desires. How the holy ones departed could be present to hear the prayers of widely scattered worshippers, what was the secret of their apparent omniscience, were questions variously answered by the doctors of the Church. Augustine was confessedly puzzled by the problem. The great Pope gave perhaps the most satisfying answer to the faithful soul : in the brightness of the beatific vision, seeing God face to face, the saints see also all things in the world of men. But he nowhere, according to his most recent exponent, teaches that invocation is obligatory on Christians, or essential to salvation. His contemporary and namesake, the Bishop of Tours, goes much further, both in his explicit teaching and in the voluminous records which he compiled of the efficacy of saintly virtue. After a singularly trivial anecdote telling how a holy priest of Poitiers banished a troublesome fly from his wine-cup by the sign of the Cross, he gives his theory of the cult of the saints. They have triumphed by the aid of God. Therefore we are bound to seek their powerful help and patronage to gain by their intercession what our own merits could never obtain. But again, Gregory says : " Since we behold wondrous miracles issuing from the tombs of the Blessed ones, we are admonished to pay them all due reverence, from whom we cease not to ask the cure of our diseases ; by their prayers we doubt not to win remission of our sins ; and not only that, but salvation from the torments of Hell ". And at the end of the Second Book of the *Miracles of S. Martin*, he prays to the saint and confessor to grant him forgiveness, purge away his errors, cleanse his heart and mind from the ghastly leprosy of voluptuousness, and from all concupiscent desires, and, at the Great Judgement, when on the left hand of the Judge his sentence is pronounced, he begs S. Martin to cover him with his holy pall, while angels say, " This is he for whom Martin pleads ".

Critics as far removed from mediaeval faith as Renan and Guizot have warmly recognised the charm of the Lives of the Saints and their importance both for the study of religion and of the society of the time. To say that they take the place of the forsaken gods and daemons of the later Empire, that they are created and divinised by a materialist imagination to fill the void between man and the remote Supreme, that tales of miracles wrought by them came to satisfy the craving for an immediate, personal government of the world in an age when the conception of the iron regularity of natural law was still unborn—all this is true, but it is only half the truth. The saintly legend had deeper roots in the spiritual nature of mankind. The age of the Merovingians, although the picture of it is sometimes painted in too sombre colours, was undoubtedly, at least in the higher ranks, an age of grossness, cupidity, and violence. Oppression and the cruel caprice of arbitrary power were rampant. The passion for wealth and the contempt for the rights of the weak in gratifying it, might in a few days change a smiling countryside into a desert of smoking ruins. There was a brutal insensibility which never felt a quiver at the sight of torture and suffering. And in the ordinary life of man, as in the course of government, there seemed no chance of improvement, no glimmering hope of a better time. But the moral and spiritual instincts of humanity have a strange vitality : the better nature in individuals and in masses dies hard. The flight of many from the world to the hermitage created a host of spiritual heroes in whom the masses saw their faint ideals of goodness marvellously realised. The strange energy of renunciation, the violent rebound from the lusts of the flesh and the pride of life, seemed to be a moral miracle, as startling as any physical wonder could be. In this dedicated life, free from the vulgarity of worldliness, fearless yet humble, strong yet tender to all things weak, with a sublime contempt for objects of common desire, the people saw the revival of slumbering ideals, almost dead, the appearance of a strange new power in the face of brutal force, the revenge of the weak upon the mighty. This especially caught the popular imagination when a person born to proud place, such as S. Clothilde, S. Radegund, or S. Bathilde, turned their backs on state and luxury, lavished their wealth in alms to the poor or houses for the service of God, submitted to the sternest rule of conventual life, tended those who were sick of the most loathsome disease, or sold the very vessels from the altar to minister to want or redeem the captive. Tales of the marvellous sanctity and self-denial of a solitary who had sought a retreat in the Jura or Auvergne or the forests of Champagne spread with strange speed among the country folk. They came in crowds to visit his cell, bringing offerings of food and wine, and laying their sick before him for his healing word.

When the saint drew near to death, he was surrounded by a throng of those for whom he had had pity, lamenting the departure of their father and protector, and asking, rather too often in stereotyped phrase, "why he was leaving them orphans ". He passed away amid love and wonder and regret and highly wrought feeling, in which, as through a luminous haze, his figure rose to unearthly stature ; his tomb became a sacred spot from which his spirit continued the ministry of his earthly life. This enchanted world of powerful sanctity was the refuge of man's pious imagination from the misery and monotonous dullness of that evil time.

The tales of such lives form the peculiar literature of the sixth and the following centuries. Classical literature was long dead : even the memory of the great models was growing ever fainter and rarer ; there was hardly a gleam of classical grace and finish left in prose or verse. History remained in the mere ghosts of arid chronicle. The Lives of the Saints became the real literature of the time, whether aesthetic or religious. For priests and people, they took the place of history, theology, and poetry. The authors constantly beg their readers to forgive their unlettered style and utter want of literary art. Again and again Gregory of Tours laments that he has no rhetorical training, and that the reader will find even simple grammatical faults in his rustic style. Yet these writers, with only a barbarous, decadent Latin at their command, absolutely destitute of skill in arrangement, or delicacy and purity of expression, have the charm and merit of sincerity and directness of vision. The narrative, though often bald, monotonous, or confused, has also at times a singular vividness, born of intense feeling, and the wish to give honest expression to the thought. The writers know exactly what their readers want, and some of them can tell a tale well. The age was one not only without literature proper but without public interests of a secular kind. Ordinary life was monotonous and insipid, relieved only by gossip about raids of Merovingian armies, the atrocities of a Governor, or some tragedy of domestic life on a lonely estate. The real mystery and charm of romance hung about the hermit in the forest, or the stately bishop living in the great world, yet far removed from it in spiritual detachment, or the royal lady or high officer of the court, who forsook its splendour and luxury for stinted fare and solitude. The reader, indeed, will often be shocked and disgusted by austerities and self-inflicted torture which seem to violate all instincts of self-respect. On the other hand, he will meet with the tenderest, most delicate sympathy, rare in such an age, for all the misery inflicted by high-handed oppression, for the cruelties of war, for poverty or loathsome disease. Moral force is asserting itself fearlessly and, at times, triumphantly against overbearing physical force, whether of the crowd or of the great. Pity, gentleness, and tenderness of heart, compassion for all weak things, are revealing their strange power against brutal arrogance and selfishness. The reader may at first be repelled by the barbarous style of such narratives, the monotonous catalogue of virtues and miracles, the conventional tone of religious sentiment for purposes of edification. But in many of these tales he will discover a picturesqueness, and even a romantic charm, which was perhaps as enthralling to a company of monks as the tales of the *Arabian Nights* to a circle of eager listeners at Cairo or Baghdad in the twelfth century. Ignatius Loyola, who was a gay cavalier before he was a soldier of God, found his favourite reading in the Lives of the Saints, and in *Amadis of Gaul*. Gregory of Tours might seem to have little aesthetic feeling, and he certainly never thought himself a literary artist. Yet, in his books on Miracles, and the *Lives of the Fathers*, he has left us many vivid pictures of natural scenes and common life which linger in the memory. We see the crowds of votaries thronging to a festival at S. Julian's of Brivate, with a due proportion of beggars, horse thieves, and charlatans, or the impotent and epileptic hurrying by river or road to swell the crowd in the courts of S. Martin's. Or we are taken to the hermit's cave in the gloom of primeval forest, infested by brigands and wild beasts ; or the little garden of another is suddenly visited by a roaming hunter, or a Frank cavalier with his yelping pack. Or we catch the lights and visions which hovered at dead of night over long hidden and forgotten tombs of holy virgins and martyrs. Scenes like these formed the poetry of the age. And it is hard to believe that Gregory, in some of these sketches, was not conscious of the romantic charm which they would have for future ages.

In the earliest times, there were immense tracts of Gaul covered with primeval forest. In the four or five centuries of

Roman occupation, the ancient wilds had been largely reclaimed by careful culture ; and Roman *villae*, with their corn lands and vineyards and meadows, spread everywhere. But in the years of barbarian invasion, there is reason to believe that new growths of brush and woodland had encroached on the area of cultivation. In what is now the garden of France, Roman camp towns like Magdunum became buried in woods, where some wandering pious exile from the world found his way to a retreat among thickets and underwood. A hermit in the forest of Le Perche, in the district of Chartres, had felled trees which forty men could hardly move. The forests of the Jura offered a great attraction to those eager refugees from the world. And in the romance of the *Fathers of the Jura*, we can see the founders of two famous monasteries making clearings in forests of immemorial age. Deserts of thorns and brambles meet us constantly in these Lives. The names of many famous abbeys embalm the fact that they grew up around a hermitage in the woods. The life of the solitary, even when he had made his home in some cave perched high on a steep cliff, or built a hut among the deep copse-wood, was apparently not long concealed and undisturbed. Brigands often infested the region, or curious rustic folk came to spy upon the sequestered life of the anchoret. The hunting party of some Frank noble following the wild bull or the boar would suddenly burst in upon the hermit's retreat, which he had fondly thought inviolable. Here was an immense and tempting field for the story-teller with an eye for adventure and peril in scenes of gloom and mystery and loneliness where men see visions and dream dreams.

S. Sequanus, in search of a spot where he might found a monastery, was told of a remote place near the sources of the Seine. But the relative to whom the estate belonged warned him of the savage character of the natives. In popular rumour they were said to feast on man's flesh and blood, and no one could safely enter their country without an armed escort. The saint with his peaceful company found himself in a deep forest the recesses of which were seldom penetrated. The band forced their way along difficult and narrow tracks, often choked with brambles or darkened by the deep shade of interlacing boughs ; and at last came to a gloomy cavern which was said to be a hold of robbers and unclean spirits. After a prayer for blessing and protection, the saint there laid the foundations of his cell. The wild inhabitants of the forest soon came around it, and were so touched by the sight of strange courage and gentleness that they not only left S. Sequanus unharmed, but even became his helpers. The den of robbers and demons became an abode of peace.

But the woods screened other scenes of a gentler and more romantic kind. Many a tomb of saint or martyr had been forgotten in the vicissitudes of generations of strife and confusion, and many a roofless oratory had been long buried in the copse and brushwood. On the outskirts of the district of Tours, there was a low hill, covered with an impenetrable screen of bramble and wild vines. A rumour had spread that there lay the remains of two holy virgins ; and on nights of high festival, gleams of a mysterious light had been seen by the eyes of the pious watchers amid the brushwood. At last, one of the bolder spirits had the courage to approach the spot, and, amid the darkness, saw a candle flashing with extraordinary brilliance. One of the rustics, to whom the tale was told, had a vision of the holy maids with a warning to build them a shelter from the storms which they could no longer endure. He forgot the message from the other world, but soon had another warning, in which awful faces threatened him with death within a year if he did not obey. He at once went with his axe, stubbed up the underwood, and laid bare the tombs, on which there lay great drops of wax exhaling a fragrant odour. Then he yoked his oxen and loaded his wagon with stones and built a chapel on the holy ground. The aged Eufronius, Gregory's immediate predecessor in the see of Tours, was asked to consecrate the new shrine, but pleaded in excuse his advanced years and the wintry weather which made the roads impassable. But he, too, had his vision of the neglected virgins, who visited him with sad faces and tearful entreaty. It is needless to say that the storm at once died away as he set out to perform the rite, and he was rewarded by a sight of the virgins, who revealed to him their forgotten names (Maura and Britta).

In the Church of Venerandus in Auvergne there were many ancient tombs of Parian marble. The vaulted roof had been long neglected, and finally fell in upon a sarcophagus, shattering the lid into fragments. A fair girlish form was revealed, with long flowing hair, and showing no traces of decay. She seemed to be asleep rather than dead. Her name and family were never known. Her body had lain exposed for nearly a year, when the widow of the count of the district, who had lost her sight in a long illness, saw a vision which bade her lay a slab upon the coffin and her sight should be restored. As the lid closed upon the coffin her eyes were opened. Another legend of two lovers had so captivated Gregory that he gives it twice at length. A married pair had lived together in virgin purity and were buried in the same church. Their tombs, originally placed at opposite sides of the church, one morning were found lying side by side, and there they lie together for ever. Nor should we pass over the pretty legend of Hilarius of Dijon. His life and that of his household were a model of sanctity and purity. He had himself interred in a great tomb of Parian marble, which was also to be the resting-place of his wife. When his tomb was opened to receive her, the husband's arm was seen raised to clasp his wife in an eternal embrace. In Dijon also dwelt Gregory, the Bishop of Langres. His house adjoined the baptistery in which were the remains of many saints, and at dead of night he used to leave his bed and pass into the choir, the door being opened by an unseen hand. Once a deacon followed the old man and saw him enter the church. There was a long silence, and then for three hours he heard the chanting of many voices and knew that the saintly bishop was among his celestial peers.

At a town not far from Dijon there was a similar legend afloat. In the cemetery of Autun there lay the bodies of many of the faithful of old days. Close to the graveyard was the Church of S. Stephen, from which sounds of sweet psalmody used often to be heard at the dead of night. Two citizens of Autun, who were making the round of the sacred places for devotion, one night entered the church with the thought that the monks were at Vigils. As they rose from their knees, in a suffused radiance issuing from no visible source, they could see a choir of singers, none of whom they knew. One of the ghostly choir approached them, chided them for breaking in on their secret devotions, and threatened them with death if they did not at once depart. One of them obeyed and went away. The other, who lingered on the spot, died in a few days.

One cannot read these tales without a feeling that the writer, to whom we owe deep gratitude, was not only an enthusiastic believer in the Divine world ; he was also striving, in the shackles of his barbarous Latin, to be a romantic artist. One might, in a daring mood, call him a poet, in the sense that he tries to lift his reader above the level of vulgar commonplace, into a region vibrating with strange forces, and lighted with colours that never were on land or sea. He is also an artist because he constantly turns narrative into vivacious and dramatic dialogue. The demon, as he is driven from the poor wretch whom he has tortured and defiled, takes his revenge in rhetorical objurgations on the superior power he feels creeping over him from S. Julian or S. Martin. Or long buried and forgotten virgins of the Church upbraid a rustic trampling on their neglected grove, or appeal to a bishop to say his words of blessing on the oratory which at last gives them eternal repose.

It is not within the scope of this book to investigate the psychology which lies behind the Lives of the Saints. That great problem has long exercised the acumen and learning of a host of critics, more or less sympathetic with the faiths of the past. Critical science can easily reduce the vision of the Middle Age to calculated imposture or to the more fantastic dreams of spiritual hysteria, or to ignorant credulity, eager to accept any report from the unseen world, and decorate and enlarge what it has heard. It is more than doubtful whether an age trained to believe only in the teaching of the laboratory and the microscope could ever recover the secret of legends which defy all laws of nature. In the atmosphere in which these records or imaginings of saintly lives were evolved, science in one sense was unknown. The conception of rigid, uniform natural law, of blind forces moving on pitilessly, with no apparent regard for the individual fortunes of man, would have been treated not only as inconceivable, but as impious. There was no hard and fast line between the natural and the supernatural. Or rather, the supernatural, the miraculous, the immediate action of spiritual powers on this lower world, seemed far more probable and credible than the operation of mere physical causes. If a man ill of a nervous disease, after visiting a physician and then a saint's tomb, was cured, the cure was attributed rather to the virtues of the saint than to the skill of the physician. And a sufferer's faithless trust in the mundane method might be punished by the recurrence of the disease.   A sudden storm which separates two armies about to engage is a miraculous answer to Clothilde's prayer.   If the gibbet on which a penitent thief hung is blown down in the night, the occurrence is traced to a mysterious cause.

Miracle was always expected, and therefore it constantly occurred.   The Evil One and his legions are ever around us with unearthly powers and cunning.   They must be encountered by the directly exerted power of God or by the " virtues " of His saints, whose sanctity makes them powerful at His Throne. In the gloom of an age depressed by physical calamity, the violence of the mighty, and still more by the terrors of superstition, men craved to have guardianship of celestial champions, without whose personal sympathy they would have felt themselves helpless and forlorn.   Such a habit of mind is not to be explained in mere terms of negation.   It is not to be traced merely to ignorance of the laws of nature and of the unerring uniformity of physical causation.   We have seen that, although the modern scientific spirit was yet unborn, there was plenty of scepticism about so-called miracles in the days of S. Martin and in the days of his successor Gregory.   Men who conduct their daily lives on the unconscious assumption that to-morrow will be as yesterday, that like causes will produce like effects, that " seed time and harvest will not cease ", can never be, after all, utterly destitute of the conception of order in nature.   But in an age which combined the capacity for intense faith with the most materialist conceptions of the Divine government, the idea of uniform order in nature is overlaid and obscured.   In such an age the wish for supernatural interference with it becomes father to the thought.   Any startling, unexpected occurrence often becomes to the heated imagination a miraculous event, and even the simplest natural events, if they have a striking effect on human fortune, may be transmuted into miracle.   It is well known that, without any conscious dishonesty, the observer of any incident in human life or nature is apt to see more or less than what actually occurs.   No two witnesses will ever give identical accounts of the same facts.   In the report of the facts, especially if they are such as to arouse the imagination or the passions, they are sure to be altered or coloured.   Even in our own day, what a different air can be given to the same political facts in our daily press by writers opposed in their political or religious views ! What different conceptions of a battle may be drawn from the sympathisers with the contending armies, even when they are competent military observers ! But strong religious feeling of the purest kind is often apparently the most indifferent to truth of fact. The truths which nourish it far transcend in importance the trivial incidents of daily life ; they are nearer and more vivid. Their eternal verity and momentous importance throw everything else into the shade, and may discredit even the evidence of the senses. Or the evidence of the senses will be interpreted in the light of enthusiastic faith. No hard and fast line seemed to separate the mediaeval saints from the saints of the Apostolic age, either in lofty purity or in strange, secret command over powers of darkness and forces of nature. The age of miracle did not close with the last of the band to whom such wondrous powers were imparted by their Lord. Such powers, it was believed, are in every age at the command of the elect few who have trodden underfoot the world, the flesh, and the Devil. The miracle of a lifelong renunciation and superhuman purity made all other miracles easily credible : nay, they were expected and demanded by unquestioning faith. Souls so fed by secret springs of grace must surely, it was thought, be endued with might to counter infernal arts, to heal the sick, and even to bring the dead back to life, much more to perform the many rather trivial wonders attributed to them. The humility of the saint might sometimes disown the wondrous deeds claimed by the multitude at his hands. But no one believed him, and he was forced, against his will, to yield to the craving for miracle. But he was probably himself as devout a believer in supernatural powers, for good or evil, as any of the eager crowd who thronged around his cell. Long, lonely vigils in the depths of a haunted wood, an imagination inflamed by legends of saintly triumph over the hosts of Hell, nerves unstrung by abstinence and self-torture—all this prepared a man to hear strange voices and to see strange visions of fiendish malice or angelic succour. He told the tale of his terrors and of his ghostly succour with the most perfect faith in his experience, and the tale was received and welcomed by hearers who only heard what they expected and welcomed. The doubts of a chance sceptic were not founded on any rational criticism, and they were drowned and overwhelmed by the enthusiastic credulity of the many who expected wonders, and were overjoyed when the wonders came. Men of evil lives, who had a wholesome terror of the Judgement to come, trembled and believed, although many of them did not obey. Thus the saint himself and his votaries, whether devout like him or selfishly worldly, were all united in believing in these supernatural powers.

No modern man, perhaps hardly even the most devout Catholic of the present day, can ever put himself in the attitude of that submissive yet creative faith. Many Christians of the sixth century, Roman and Teutonic, were still impregnated with the instincts of the old pagan spirit. There was little difference apparently between the man in Homer's time, who believed that Artemis had sent a stag across his path, and the fishermen of Naples who would scourge their patron saint for sending them a bad haul of fish. And yet he would show himself a dull, unsympathetic student of religion who failed to see a higher element in the mythopoeic faculty of the Christian. Criticism in the modern sense was still unborn, and even the rigorous feeling for truth, the resolve only to believe what was credibly attested, was generally wanting in men of the holiest character. But the character and religious faith which lay behind the miracles of the Middle Age were often of a different order from the credulity of paganism. Behind and above all questions of fact or authorship rose the overshadowing mass of the Catholic faith, essential to the salvation of the individual soul. There was a vast spiritual theory of the Universe accepted by the Church which surrounded man's life with graded hosts of spirits, good or evil, engaged in perpetual conflict. There was the miracle of sanctity wrought by Divine Grace in some rare souls. In the presence of this great mass of spiritual truth, about which there could be no question, all criticism of tales which seemed to confirm or harmonise with them became trifling, and might even become dangerous. It is the inner spiritual truth, not the mere external fact, which is important to the religious mind. Granted that a saint may not actually have done such and such a work or actually spoken the words attributed to him, as a great modern theologian has said, they are such as you might expect from him : they are true in idea, if not in fact. Nothing was more certain than that there were elect souls, raised far above their fellows by detached spirituality, living near to God and powerful with

Him by their prayers. If miracle is possible, since miracle is a corollary from the personal government of a benevolent Deity, what more natural than that He should send succour and healing through those who have fought the good fight victoriously?

The growth of sacred legend, in such an atmosphere as that of the sixth century, founded on an original basis of lofty and pure character, absolute renunciation, and lavish works of charity, was the most natural thing in the world. It sprang from one of the finest human instincts to idealise qualities which rise above the vulgar, commonplace level, and which respond to cravings so often overlaid and obscured by the hard coarseness of common life. Even in our time there is a readiness to believe and circulate and decorate stories equally fictitious, about men who, by native force and high service, have risen above the bourgeois level. There is also a less laudable tendency to accept and propagate, with fertile imagination, any vagrant rumour of sensual weakness, or innocent eccentricity, in men who are bearing a great part in great affairs, and to reduce them to a level at which we are not humbled by a greatness that we cannot understand. The classical and middle ages made saints or heroes of their rare characters ; we seem sometimes to take a pleasure in picturing ours as dwarfs or debauchees.

The rude, humble folk who created the legends of the saints were, luckily for humanity, of a higher strain. The saint in that dark time of grossness and violence, was the one hope of men who had only faint and far-distant glimpses of a better world. When he died, after many years of self-discipline, prayer, and pitiful charity out of his scanty stores, he left a memory and influence which, in many cases, many ages have not dimmed. Pious people in France are probably still invoking the aid of saintly men and women who lived in the days of Clovis or Chilperic. Crowds of poor, ignorant folk in those days flocked around the grave of their holy benefactor, who had fed them, when he could, out of his poverty, and prayed for them effectually, and consoled their misery. The power and virtue of such souls did not cease at death ; they lived and were powerful in the world beyond. Men felt that their friend was now praying for them powerfully in the presence of God, and such help must surely prevail over disease, and death itself, and the infernal arts of the Evil One. The holy man had not left them orphans;

2 E

he was still with them, and, having felt for all their griefs here
below, he would and could surely send them help from on high.

It is by the help of some such reflections that we should
approach the legends of the sixth century. They are not mere
myths, in the sense that they have a germ of fact to start with,
although it may in its course receive many additions and much
embroidery from imagination. The great age of hagiography is
that from the sixth to the tenth century. It is a period usually
depicted as the darkest in European history. And it certainly
was an age, from its whole system of faith, utterly destitute of
any canons of evidence or of capacity for scientific criticism.
There is an interesting passage in Gregory's *Lives of the Fathers*
in which he assails a class who deride the tales of miracle, whether
supported by written evidence or tradition, or even attested by
an actual eye-witness. They are all summarily refuted by the
Gospel saying : *Beati qui non viderunt et crediderunt.* Gregory's
own principles of evidence are of the most liberal and elastic
sort. Written narrative and tradition, with no investigation
of their sources, are to be treated with as great respect as the
evidence of one's senses. They are to be accepted without
question, in the face of any doubt which should impeach the
goodness or power of God and his angelic or saintly ministers.
The miraculous is quite as much to be looked for as the natural
occurrence. The bishop of Tours, like John Wesley, affirms that
he had himself seen many wonderful cures of disease ; he had
himself been able to work them by means of relics. He had
heard of many more from monks and bishops, and from the
vergers and acolytes of the Cathedral of Tours, who constantly
brought him reports of the wonders wrought before the saint's
tomb. He questioned his informant as to the facts ; but it is
noteworthy that the names of those relieved by supernatural
grace are seldom given, and the bishop relies implicitly on the
good faith of his staff. By an eccentric logic, a man who wrought
miracles himself is, on that account, treated as the unassailable
witness to the truth of another miracle. By a similar process
miracle is the proof of possessing the orthodox faith, and none
but the orthodox believer can work a miracle.

The truth is that the Catholic of those days needed no
miracles to strengthen his faith, although miracles might be used
to crush a heterodox opponent. And he needed no evidence for

miracle except the bare assertion of the witness or the subject
of it, or a written record even of unknown authorship, which
became at once to him a sacred scroll. When a deacon of Autun,
afflicted with blindness, approached the tomb of S. Nicetius to
share in its famous " virtues ", one of the clergy came up holding
a roll which recited the wonders that the saint had wrought.
He handed this to the blind man to confirm his faith in the
efficacy of the saint. The deacon laid the volume on eyes which
were unable to read the record and immediately their sight
returned !

Such records rapidly grew and multiplied, written and
accepted with the same implicit faith. The germ might be the
bald record of a saint's death in the sacred calendar. Or it
might be a few memorial words, like those on the slab buried
in the woods on the Seine, which marked the resting-place of
the holy virgin Crescentia. This would soon develop into a
brief biography by some friend or disciple, which, along with
some solid fact and real traits of character, combined an effort
of enthusiastic, excited imagination to give unearthly lustre to
the simplest occurrences. The monastic biographers are humble
about their culture, and constantly plead indulgence for their
rude style. Yet they often show a ludicrous literary ambition, an
impotent wish to excite the admiration of their even more unlettered brethren, as the life of S. Bathilde or S. Geneviève was
read out in the refectory. It was an innocent vanity. And
the glory of his subject would inspire an enthusiast to rise to
the level of its wonder and dignity. Just as in schools of the
Empire, a rhetor's class was trained to dilate on the feelings of
Dido as she watched the departure of Aeneas, or those of Menelaus
as he gazed on Troy in flames, so in the monastic school, the
young clerk was exercised in decorating and expanding the
memorials of the saints. Unchecked by any weak doubts about
the sources of his story, full of faith in the secret powers of a
holy life, what appealed to his imagination, or might serve for
edification, or filled in to completeness the picture he had formed
of his subject, became as certain and credible as if he had seen
it all with his own eyes. And although he knew little of books,
venerable rolls in the library, the consentient voice of tradition,
the analogies in other Lives, and stories of Holy Writ, helped to
strengthen his faith and to assist and swell his narrative. So

holy a man, he said to himself, must have done such things ;
others like him have done them ; therefore he did them all and
probably more : such was the pious syllogism. There was no
boundary line for the biographer between history and sacred
fiction. Thus, memories of Bible story, or of other Lives of
holy men, were, half unconsciously, woven into the tale, which
grew under the hand of the rude literary artist. He was composing a sacred romance to satisfy his own starved fancy, and
that of the brothers who awaited his recital. And, as in all
hieratic art, there was a tone of conventional uniformity and
monotony. The same saintly virtues, the same miraculous
works, the same efforts to deepen faith and renunciation, meet us
everywhere. Any variation from the accepted type would have
startled and shocked the reader or hearer in that age. Moreover, the original Life often obtained a rapid circulation in regions
far from the early home of the saint. The life of S. Martin by
Sulpicius Severus, within two or three years, was widely read
in Italy, Illyria, Egypt, and Cyrenaica. The tale of a holy life,
which had a fascination for the feelings and imaginations of men,
would certainly gain in bulk and variety in its travels ; and,
when it came back to its birthplace, it would bring many a
fresh grace of novelties and unconscious accretions, the source
of which would be unquestioned, if they were edifying and
gratifying to faith. Who shall say that the poor illiterate monk,
striving to glorify his patron saint, for the strengthening of others,
and for his own support in the terrors of the unseen world and
the agony of temptation, was a mere paltry deceiver when he
drew a picture which, to the cold modern critic, unconscious of
any spiritual struggles, perfectly satisfied with this world as it is,
will seem a lawless romance rather than a true biography ?

Yet these records, accepted with such simple faith, were, in
respect of their authenticity, of very various, and often doubtful,
value. Some are authentic historical sources, such as the *Life
of S. Caesarius*, which was composed by two contemporaries and
intimates of the great bishop of Arles. The Lives of S. Germanus,
of the Abbot Aredius, of S. Bathildis, S. Gertrude, S. Medardus,
and others, seem to have been composed by writers who
had probably first-hand information. But the Lives of many
saints of the sixth century, Clothilde, and her grandson,
Chlodovald, Lupus, Sigismund, Rémi, and others of less note,

e.g. Bibianus, the Patres Jurenses, Eptadius, Eparchius, and Carileffus, are, according to the latest criticism, by monkish authors of the eighth or even of the tenth century. To the critical eye, they betray their later origin by anachronisms, or by their style and grammar. They are indeed sometimes, like Hincmar's *Life of S. Rémi*, founded on an earlier life, perhaps by a contemporary of the saint. But the writer, whose hand convicts him of being of the Carolingian age, will often pretend that he personally knew the subject of his memoir and had actually seen his miracles.

The biographer of the *Patres Jurenses* professes to have talked with the Abbot Eugendus, who lived in the sixth century, and yet, from his use of some ecclesiastical terms and his picture of the monastic life and organisation, it seems certain that he belonged to a far later generation than that which saw the settlement of the Burgundians at Geneva. Other Lives, like those of Eptadius and Eparchius, betray the same anachronisms. The biographer of the former professes to be his contemporary and to have seen some of his miracles ; and yet he draws on Fredegarius and the life of Epiphanius by Ennodius for part of his narrative. The life of Eparchius, which also professes to be by one who knew him, is even more suspicious. The tale of one miracle is evidently copied from Gregory of Tours, with minute additions of detail, and the barbarisms of style belong to the ninth century. Other lives, it is to be feared, were composed to make good the title of a monastery to its lands. Such is the life of Carileffus. The bishops of Le Mans in the ninth century, coveting the fair lands of Anninsola, afterwards named S. Calais, strove to bring the monastery under their power. The monks, wishing to maintain their independence, determined to support their rights by a life of S. Carileffus, their founder in the sixth century. We have seen how the saint aroused King Childebert's wrath by interfering with his pleasure in the chase, and how the repentant king gave him, for the foundation of a monastery, a tract as large as he could ride round on his ass in one day. The writer of his life was a foreign monk, who had found a refuge in the house of S. Calais probably early in the ninth century. He protests that he will avoid all fiction, and only tell what he has collected from ancient rolls, or from the traditions of the district. But he has evidently used the life of S. Avitus,

which was composed in the early ninth century, to expand his
own rather barren record.

The *Life of S. Rémi* is a good example of the growth of hagiography from the sixth to the ninth century. The life of the
great bishop of Rheims extended from 437 to 533, through a
period of the most momentous changes in history. The story
goes that, in the time of Gregory of Tours, there was in existence
a biography of S. Rémi of an elaborate character, with abundance
of curious and valuable facts, which Gregory may have used
for his narrative of the early conquests of the Franks. Egidius,
bishop of Rheims, of evil fame, both as an intriguer against
Brunihildis, and one of the lovers of Fredegundis, begged the
wandering literary adventurer, Venantius Fortunatus, to compose a popular abstract of this life. It was widely read and
circulated, and threw the original into the shade. In the confusion of the reign of Charles Martel, the Cathedral of Rheims
suffered heavily; the archives were neglected, and many priceless MSS. were scattered ; and, in particular, the solitary original
life of S. Rémi remained only in a few leaves, stained and mouldering. Hincmar, the occupant of the see in the eighth century,
professes to have heard from his elders that they had seen a
book on the "virtues" of the saint, of immense bulk and written
in an archaic hand. He set to work to restore the life, partly
from the scattered and mutilated leaves which he had found,
partly from historical works of an earlier age. And he claims
credit for having left his sources unaltered in their style.

The most recent critics have dealt hardly with the life of
his great predecessor by Hincmar. Hincmar, who was beyond
doubt a great figure in the events of his time, was also a man
of great ambition. He was in the thick of the theological
controversies of the time on Predestination and Free Will. He
was also involved in a struggle with several Popes, especially
with Nicholas I. He claimed powers for the see of Rheims
which the Holy See would not recognise, but which Hincmar per-
tinaciously asserted. A perhaps unduly dogmatic criticism sees
in the life of S. Rémi a document founded on mere falsehood, to
glorify the power and authority of the great prelate who received
Clovis and his warriors at the font of Rheims, and to magnify
the importance of the see. To investigate the truth of these
charges does not fall within the scope of this work. The

imputation of bad faith and deliberate deception seems to be pressed unduly, and with an animus which, on so remote and shadowy a subject, seems rather ludicrous. Perhaps a sounder criticism is that Hincmar's life of S. Rémi is portentously long and dull. Immensely interesting facts are buried and lost amid long hortatory passages, which form the bulk of the memoir. Either the vanity of the preacher or the impotent wish to edify, has, on a great theme, sacrificed the charm that might have been thrown around it.

But although we may not always be able to accept the results of destructive criticism of hagiography, there can be no doubt that many influences were at work to propagate mere fiction as genuine record. The art of printing which fixes for ever the utterance of an author in its original form has lessened the chance of forgery or interpolation, such as, in those ages, were perpetrated without scruple or check. MSS. could easily be effaced or altered. Texts were few and tended to disappear, and the difficulty of comparing them, even if the wish and skill had been available, was great. The recasting of ancient Lives in different style, with additions from local tradition or mere pious fancy, was a favourite occupation in the monastery. William of Malmesbury tells us of a monk of Canterbury who busied himself with sending out fresh editions of Lives that had been lost or which were written in formless style. Each religious order, diocese, or town had its sacred patron, and it was a point of honour that his fame should not grow less. It is significant that the narrative became generally more circumstantial the farther it was removed from the scene and time of the original life.

Such pious frauds, reprobated even by worldly morality, were lightly and, almost unconsciously, perpetrated in an age far more concerned with faith in the power of holiness and the mission of Holy Church than with historical truth. Even our own great John Henry Newman could excuse them if they were true in idea and consonant with the Faith. Literary morality was not very scrupulous either in classical times or in the early ages of the Church. The Athenian government of the fourth century B.C. had to adopt legislative measures to preserve the text of the three great masters of Attic tragedy from contamination. The Platonic school did not scruple to foist on their great master treatises which he would have disowned. A crowd of apocryphal gospels and epistles long perplexed the criticism of the Early Church. The Sibylline forgeries of the Antonine age are quoted by the great Apologists against unbelievers as of equal value with the Prophets of Israel. Dionysius the Areopagite, a contemporary of S. Paul, became the reputed author of works which were composed not earlier than the sixth century, and which, in spite of their doubtful origin, did more even than the Apocalypse to mould the celestial mythology of the Middle Ages, and even that of the Puritans. It is well known that in the first three centuries there were afloat a host of apocryphal gospels and epistles, passing under great Apostolic names, and embodying the doctrine of some of the warring sects and heresies of the time.

The most learned and philosophical scholars have held the most opposite views as to the cult of the saints in the early Middle Ages. Men widely severed in religious belief, such as Guizot and Renan, regard it as the one refuge of idealism from the grossness and dull suffering of the time. Historians, as far apart as Dean Milman and Fustel de Coulanges, treat it as a revived paganism under altered forms, coarse and mechanical in its conception of devotion, a reproduction of the old Roman theory of a barter between the worshipper and his God or saint. Probably both views have some truth. No candid student can fail to see that reliance on the intercession of the saints and the Virgin Mother was often combined with a lofty spiritual life. In the effort of the human spirit to find avenues to the remote Supreme and Infinite, through many ages in heathendom and Christendom, the pious imagination has sought many mediators in a celestial hierarchy, linking the human and the Divine ; and, if the adoration of saints had its lower side, it also consecrated high and rare examples of spiritual refinement, detachment, self-abnegation and also of boundless charity and pity for the victims of oppression, desire, and want. If it gave its heroes superhuman rank and powers, it also held up before a gross age an ideal of those qualities which have moulded modern civilisation. Severe purity, charity to the poor and afflicted, at the cost of immense self-sacrifice, were an influence and a pattern which the world then needed, and the need for which has not ceased.

At the same time a scrupulous historical conscience cannot ignore the grave perversions and aberrations of the popular religion which are depicted with the fullest sympathy by great churchmen like Gregory of Tours. To any one with reverence for a historic faith, it is painful to dwell on what seems a degradation of the religious sentiment. Yet the revelation is necessary for any penetrating conception of the moral condition of that time. A coarse materialism ran through the whole fabric of religion. The future life was imaged in the strongest, coarsest colours of the senses. To secure its bliss or to escape its eternal torments became the deepest concern of man here below. But that could only be done by the effectual aid of the Church, through its sacramental acts and the prayers and intercessions of its saints. To be cut off from the Church was therefore the most awful fate that could befall a man, a fate dreaded by the most hardened sinner, who would give up anything to be reconciled with her, except his sins. And the Church, never unmerciful to human nature, was ready to be reconciled by penitence and, above all, by lavish donations. The amount of such gifts in the sixth and seventh centuries, known to us by documents still extant, is stupendous. And the motive, often boldly and expressly avowed, is to save the soul from punishment, or purchase happiness in the next world. Such donations to religion are often styled in monkish narrative, " opes praemissae ", a loan or investment with an eternal return. The Church preached with unction from such texts as " date et dabitur ", " terrena pro caelestibus ". The motto " paupertas januam reserat caeli " may mean boundless wealth to a monastery or the Church of a great saint. The saint, who in his lifetime lived on beggars' fare, might, a few years after his death, become the celestial owner of many manors all over Gaul, granted to secure his intercession. In making such lavish benefactions the donor felt perfectly assured that he was covering a multitude of sins. Thus the saintly Clothilde exhorted her husband, who had certainly many sins to cover, if he wished to extend his earthly realm, and reign with Christ in heaven, to found in Paris a church in honour of the prince of the Apostles. Thus Dagobert built a gorgeous church to S. Denis, and endowed it with manors in many provinces, hoping the prayers of the saint would wipe out many stains upon his life, which the charity of his biographer attributes to the weight of imperial cares and the allurements of youthful temptation.

The sympathy of the Church above for the Church militant below may be, for the believer, a fascinating and sustaining doctrine. But the excesses into which it was carried by popular imagination in the early Middle Ages are often shocking or ludicrous. One may respect the faith in saintly guardianship for holy ends. But it is a different thing to believe that the saint would stoop from his high place to satisfy the most selfish and trivial desires, and that, if he refused to do so, he might be upbraided, or even threatened, as a faithless friend. It is not astonishing in such an age that sensualists and men stained with every crime should try to gain ghostly aid for their designs, as they often did not hesitate to perjure themselves with a hand laid on the altar. But it is astounding that men imbued with the higher teaching of the Church, like Gregory of Tours, should chronicle the tales of vulgar magic that meet us in his writings. Some of them also show a very coarse and even pagan conception of the condition and tastes of the departed, which borders on the ludicrous and profane.

A noble citizen of Tours, dying childless, left the Church his heir. His widow attended regularly, for a year, the masses offered for his repose, and always provided a sextarius of the famous wine of Gaza for the oblation. But, as her attendance became less regular, the subdeacon, who seems to have been a toper, substituted for the famous vintage a common wine of the harshest and roughest flavour. It pleased God, says the narrator, to reveal the fraud. The departed husband appeared to his wife and complained that all his labour in this world had been in vain, since in the oblation he found only a taste of vinegar! The lady went to the next mass and drank of the sacred cup ; the draught was so acid that she thought her teeth would fall out. The deacon was severely rated by the angry wife and amended his service for the future. When departed spirits have such a taste for good wine, it is little wonder that the faithful on earth should have liquor supplied to them by unseen hands. At the Church of S. Julian in Auvergne relics were once to be placed under the altar on a certain day. The good people were invited to keep vigil during the night preceding the great event, and a monk in charge of them made the watch as pleasant as possible by serving out wine liberally from the monastic cellar. When the midnight service was over, he invited them to another refection. As he re-entered the cellar to fetch fresh wine, he found the vessel, which had been half emptied by rather liberal draughts upon it, discharging a river of wine which rushed towards the door. Apparently the liberality of the exuberant cask was fully tested, but it bore the strain, and was still brimming in the morning.

There is no more gracious figure in hagiography than S. Geneviève, who braved all the perils of that stormy time to redeem the captive or bring food to a famishing town. Once she was engaged in preparation for the building of her shrine of S. Denis, and lime and stone and wood were being got together. One day, when the woodmen and carpenters were shaping logs and piling them on waggons in a forest glade, the presbyter who was in charge of the work told the saint that the workmen's cask was exhausted, and he must go to the town for fresh supplies. She had the vessel brought to her, and then, kneeling with streaming tears, she prayed, and made the sign of the Cross. The vessel was filled to overflowing, and the workmen had an unfailing supply till their task was finished.

Here we have divine power exercised to further a great religious foundation. But the saints often employed their extraordinary gifts for mere private gratification. S. Rémi was once visiting the estates of his see in the Ardennes, and, on his way, cheerily addressed a crowd of harvesters. In the neighbourhood he had a female cousin who sent him an invitation to spend the night at her country house. While he was engaged in religious conversation with his hostess, her steward, like the similar official in *The Bride of Lammermoor*, came to whisper to his mistress that, owing to sales, the cellar was exhausted, and only a miserable supply of wine remained in one cask. The saint noticed her confusion and consoled her with promise of unearthly help. Meantime S. Rémi made the round of the gardens and offices, and came to the cellar. He questioned the shamefaced butler as to his stock of wine. Then, ordering him to stand apart, he went behind the cask where a few drops only remained, made the sign of the Cross, and knelt long in prayer. Immediately the vessel overflowed and flooded all the pavement. The saint enjoined the cellarer to tell the wonder to no one, a command which was, of course, disobeyed. The conclusion of the tale is instructive. When the lady of the manor learnt, as she soon did, how she had been supplied with wine, she recognised that her invitation to S. Rémi had been divinely inspired. And with all scrupulous legal forms, she provided that the Church of Rheims should be heir to her estate.

The saints were naturally jealous and potent guardians of the possessions with which their votaries endowed their shrines, and surrounded them with a ghostly police. Noble and official brigands were always ready to annex a fair manor by force or chicanery. But the plunderer of high or low estate had as firm a belief as the priest that the saint could terribly punish any offence against him. The chance of robbing a rich church was tempting, but the danger, recognised by all, was also great. Thus, any story of baffled cupidity was readily accepted as a proof of the saintly power. Men heard how a tax-gatherer, who had seized some of S. Julian's sheep on summer pasture, had died in a torturing fever; how a thief, having carried off a jewelled cross from the altar, had fallen asleep in a corner of the church and been surprised by the vergers; how the Frank count, Sigivald, had been stricken with sudden disease after he had appropriated a villa dedicated to the saint. On another occasion, a visitor to the Church of S. Julian turned his horse out to pasture and spent the night in devotion. When he returned at dawn his horse was gone and could nowhere be found. The man returned to the church, and told the saint, rather irreverently, that he had done nothing to deserve such a loss, and imperiously demanded that the horse should be restored. The saint seems to have pardoned the irreverent tone, and, when the man left the church, his horse was found standing outside, having been recovered at the very moment of the prayer. Irreverence sometimes went even further. A coarse rustic scepticism, in spite of all spiritual terror, sometimes broke out against the apotheosis of an ordinary man. And even the true believer in saintly efficacy could not forget that the saint had once lived the common life of his kind, although his virtue may have won him extraordinary powers in the other world. A Spanish ambassador to the court of Childebert was once entertained by Gregory at the bishop's house at Tours. They found a link of sympathy in a common devotion to S. Martin.

The envoy's grandfather had built a church in honour of the saint, where he and his wife daily implored his protection. A child who was born to them sickened and died in three months, and the agonised mother laid it before the altar, reminding the saint, whose relics lay below, of the many miracles which he had wrought, and imploring him to bring the little one back to life, in recognition of its parents' faith. The prayer ended curiously: " If thou wilt not do this thing, we shall not bend our heads at this shrine, nor kindle lamps for thee, nor make any offering in thine honour." The saint apparently did not resent the menacing tone of the prayer, and, on the following morning, the child was found restored to life. Sometimes, however, the saint inflicted physical punishment on any one who cast a slur upon his fame. Nicetius, bishop of Lyons, the grand-uncle of Gregory, along with the severe virtue which led to his popular canonisation, seems to have been a man of a hard imperious temper, which did not desert him in the shades. When his will was opened it was found that he had left nothing to the Church in which he was buried. The priest of the Church, not unnaturally, used some strong words about this parsimonious neglect. On the very next night, he had a vision of Nicetius, along with two other bishops, who appeared in shining raiment. Nicetius explained to his brethren that this was the man who had reproached him with avarice, forgetting that he had bequeathed something more precious than gold, even his own sacred dust. Thereupon Nicetius applied his fists so vigorously to the priest's throat that he awoke with swollen jaws and hardly able to swallow.

Nicetius regarded his mouldering remains as a more precious possession than any worldly estate for the Church. And so the Church treated the relics of the saints. A church could not be consecrated unless the remains of some holy person were placed beneath the altar. The saint was seldom long enshrined till strange virtue began to spread its influence from the tomb. Poor nervous subjects, victims of vice, or tainted with hereditary poison in vein and nerve, came to the altar tomb to seek relief by prayer or reverie or vague, eager craving. The nervous system of man is a strange, unfathomable deep. It may be the source of unutterable torture, passing into wild vicious insanity. It may also be the spring of a comfort and gladness, which may,

not without a show of reason, be taken for the touch of an unearthly hand. Who can tell what wonders might be wrought
on rude, simple imaginations, saturated with the superstition
of many ages, exalted and overstrained by vigils of passionate
hope and devotion, amid the gloom or splendour of a sanctuary
haunted by traditions of saintly power ? Now and then, a
poor epileptic or half-paralysed sufferer would feel the calming
effect of the scene, and some strength of former days at last
faintly coming back. The horrors of an evil past would seem
to melt away in a soothing vision of a happy future. The cure,
though not complete, would awaken old hope and energy, which
have always great curative power. The growing legend of such
marvels soon spread through the countryside. Thenceforth the
saint's tomb began to draw crowds of people, sick of all manner
of diseases, coming to it with a faith which may have been
sometimes rewarded. And it is not improbable that, in the
panics of the great plague which raged over Gaul at intervals
for more than sixty years, the efficacy of these powerful shrines
may have diffused a hope and confidence which acted like a
charm on contagious fears.

It is not unnatural that pious gratitude should treasure any
memorial of such beneficent powers. The instinct on which
the cult of relics rests is one of the deepest in human nature,
the wish for a token to recall a beloved or venerated presence.
Such a wish, in the sphere of religion, in the love and reverence
for Divine and holy persons, becomes even more urgent and
imperious. And, at a certain stage, the use of relics might be
plausibly defended as a means of preserving religious associations
or strengthening their hold. But, from the fourth century, the
instinct of love and devotion had begun to develop into a superstition which was destined to keep its hold for twelve hundred
years or longer. In the days of Augustine there was a trade
in " the limbs of martyrs ". The Theodosian Code had prohibited the exhuming of their bodies for sale. In the sixth
century the value attached to relics grew apace. They were
collected, with great trouble and expense, from all quarters,
and by any means, sometimes even by theft.

Those relics were often of the most trivial kind. Anything
whatever which was associated or in contact with a saint's tomb,
from which powerful virtue had issued, was prized and sought

for eagerly. It might be some threads from the pall, or dust, or oil from the lamps in the sanctuary. And it is noteworthy that these sacred treasures were accepted without the slightest inquiry or doubt of their genuineness. They were constantly worn on the person to ward off disease or the perils of a journey. They seem to have been a regular part of the dress in Gregory's family. The bishop never was without such protection, like his father before him. That worthy man in a perilous time, going on a journey, once asked his priest for some relics of many saints which he possessed, and whose names he hardly knew. A few grains of holy ashes in a golden case, he used to tell his son, had carried him safe through endless dangers from floods and robbers and bands on the warpath. With such faith in any relic of a holy life, men went to endless pains and expense to seek for such treasures, even in distant lands, for altars in Gaul. Young deacons were sent to secure relics of the Apostles. S. Radegund sent a mission through all the East to acquire such memorials of sanctity. Among others, she had the good fortune to secure a portion of the True Cross which had been discovered 250 years before by Queen Helena at Jerusalem. The treasure was enshrined in a coffer of silver in her convent at Poitiers, where Gregory, with his own eyes, had seen the oil in the lamp before the altar, fed by no human hand, yet perpetually over-flowing. Another envoy was despatched to beg the Patriarch of Jerusalem for a memorial of S. Mammes Caesariensis. The patriarch with solemn forms, and, surrounded by a great con-course, approached the tomb and begged the saint to let his power be known among the nations by granting Radegund's prayer. A finger was softly detached from the skeleton hand, and sent to Poitiers, where, for a whole week, with fasts and vigils, the thanks of the congregation were offered up for such a priceless gift. And even worldly powers felt the value of relics as strongly as the monastic recluse. In the great conflict in Aquitaine, between the forces of Guntram and the pretender Gundobald, the opposing armies did not scruple to violate churches and despoil them. Yet these very men set an immense value on an apocryphal relic of an Oriental saint, a joint of one of his fingers, which was treasured in the oratory of a Syrian trader of Bordeaux. In those years the city of Saragossa, besieged by King Childebert in 542, was saved by a tunic of

S. Vincent which was carried round the town in a procession of
the people fasting and clothed in sackcloth. Relics, being
necessary for the consecration of a Church, were often sought
from other shrines which were rich in those treasures ; and they
sometimes caused the most startling effects as they passed
along the countryside.

Once a priest, bearing relics from Auvergne for a new Church
of S. Julian at Rheims, was passing an estate where numbers
of men were ploughing. One of them at once fell into convulsions
and loudly called on his comrades to leave their teams and
pay honour to the saint. The evil spirit within him was awed
by the approach of the martyr's power, and the poor wretch,
with loud cries, flung himself on the road before the relics. His
diabolical tormentor was cast out in a rush of blood, by a touch
of the sacred casket.

It is little wonder that the possession of such treasures of
supernatural power should be an object of envy, sometimes
fiercely contended for. Sometimes relics were appropriated by
arts bordering on theft. The scene at the tomb of S. Nicetius
was certainly often repeated. It was reported to Gregory by
one of his deacons on his way back from Rome with relics. As
he prayed before the tomb, it was surrounded by a swarming
crowd eager for any memorial of the holy man. Wax from the
candles, threads from the pall, even a pinch of dust from the
altar, were all carried off in triumph. An even more curious tale is
told of the strife for relics of S. Lupicinus of Lempdes in Auvergne.
This man had immured himself in an ancient ruin and, cut off
from even the sight of man, receiving poor doles of bread and
water through an aperture in the wall, dragged out his life in
indescribable torture, self-inflicted. When his end came the
people fought for fragments of his dress, and even for particles
of the bloody sputum which, in his last agony, he had cast upon
the wall! A great lady of Trezelle in Auvergne, who had
ministered to his wants, wished to carry the body to her own
village. The inhabitants of Lempdes energetically resisted her
claim, saying that by race and family he belonged to them.
They took the remains and were about to lay him in his native
soil, when the lady appeared with her retainers, put the villagers
to flight, and bore off the body to Trezelle, in a solemn procession.
The men of Lempdes penitently recognised the will of God and

joined in escorting the saint to his last home, where he continued
to assert his power by many miracles.

In a town of Savoy, at the foot of the Pennine Alps, a pious
woman had long coveted some relic of John the Baptist of
Maurienne, and she made a vow not to depart until she obtained
a fragment of his body. The people of the place resisted her
entreaties ; but, for two long years, she persevered in constant
devotion before the altar. In the opening of the third year,
exhausted by vigils and fasting, she suddenly beheld over the
altar a thumb shining with wonderful radiance. She rose from
the pavement and received the Divine gift in a golden casket.
Three bishops, probably hearing of the marvel, arrived soon
afterwards to obtain a share in the treasure. Night after night
they continued in prayer, having spread a cloth to catch any
effluence from the sacred apparition. At last they were rewarded
with three drops of blood. The cloth on which it fell was divided
and received with enthusiasm by their people. But the relics
of S. John of Maurienne sometimes aroused less pious reverence
and became the object of very worldly ambition and greed.
Maurienne at that time belonged to the diocese of Turin, and
the Archdeacon of Turin represented to his bishop that the
relics should not belong to a meaner church, and he set out to
claim or appropriate them, with the bishop's leave. He kept
vigils before the altar, and put out his hand to seize the casket.
But, in the very act, he was struck senseless, and died on the
third day. The treasure of Maurienne was thenceforth safe.
Yet pious theft of this kind was sometimes condoned by the
saint and the relic worked as efficaciously as if it had been honestly
acquired. A devout worshipper at S. Martin's had long wished
to abstract secretly some slight pledge of his power. Finding
this impossible during public worship, he stole into the church
at night, and cut away a small part of the bell rope by which
the people were called to service. Gregory adds that this simple
relic brought healing to many through faith in Martin, and he
seems not to condemn the theft. Indeed, he had himself been
guilty of the same thing. Once attending a festival at S. Julian's
he plucked off some threads from the pall, and took them as a
safeguard for his journey to Tours. On his arrival, the monks,
who had just built a basilica in S. Julian's honour, begged the
precious relic for their new altar.

2 F

Gregory and all his family for generations were the slaves of this superstition. They treasured relics of the most trivial kind and used them constantly as magical charms to cure disease, to extinguish a fire, to ward off attacks of robbers, to escape from a sinking boat. It would be difficult to distinguish this degraded miracle under Christian forms from the pagan arts of magic and sorcery. Both pagan and Christian were equally devoid of the conception of universal law in nature, and equally ready to ascribe events and phenomena to personal agency of good or evil spirits. In the controversy between Origen and Celsus neither of them denied supernatural wonders on the side of his opponent. But the pagan miracle to Origen is the work of a demon : to Celsus, the Christian miracle is wrought by magic. Celsus might, had he lived in the sixth century, have found confirmation of his view when the youthful Gregory, warned by a vision, placed a scroll inscribed with the words "Navae Jesus" under his father's pillow to cure a fit of gout, or shook a bag of sacred dust over a servant sick of fever. The man who regarded the ancient magic as damnable and would have condemned the poor sorcerer to the stake, to all outward appearance was practising the same arts himself. The Councils, it is true, put their ban on augury, the casting of lots, sorcery and witchcraft. Yet these Fathers in God returned to their cathedrals to sanction, or tacitly permit, essentially similar arts. There was, of course, a saving element in ecclesiastical miracles which, to the higher minds, marked them off from heathen superstition. They were ultimately traced to the enduring powers of a holy life. Yet the materialism of pagan superstition still lurked under Christian forms. Nominal Christians valued these occult powers as a means of warding off the ills of human life or of gaining some selfish, or even criminal, end. King Chilperic had made a solemn compact, ratified by oath, with his brother that neither should enter the city of Paris without the other's leave. In a short time he determined to violate the pact, and thought to save himself from the consequences of such perfidy by having the relics of many saints borne before him as he entered the city. He believed that the saints would condone a perjury. There is a still more startling instance, in which heathen superstition is combined with a trembling belief in S. Martin's power, and at the same time in his readiness to wink at perjury. It would be hard to find in the lurid annals of superstition more shocking scenes than those witnessed in the basilica of Tours when Eberulfus, a great officer, had sought its protection from the vengeance of King Guntram for the murder of Chilperic. During his stay there, the wildest riot and confusion reigned in the courts of S. Martin's. The guards who were set to watch Eberulfus plundered the neighbourhood, and carried off the cattle on S. Martin's lands. Eberulfus, who appears to have been constantly drunk, brutally assaulted the attendant priests, and even assailed the bishop at vespers with foul abuse. Meanwhile Guntram had despatched a certain Claudius to lure Eberulfus from his retreat, and either kill him or bring him back a prisoner. On his way to Tours, Claudius visited Queen Fredegundis, who bore a bitter hatred to Eberulfus, and received from her large gifts and larger promises if he delivered him up for vengeance, or slaughtered him in the very sanctuary. In spite of his Roman name, Claudius appears to have been a Frank, and, as he went on his way to Tours, after the custom of his race, he consulted the auspices. At the same time he questioned people whether S. Martin's power would be manifested on a man who broke a solemn oath. Convinced that he could not capture Eberulfus without forswearing himself, he took that oath by all that was sacred in the Church at Tours, fully determined, on the first chance, to break it. Eberulfus' suspicions were disarmed ; they sat together at a feast, and in the midst of flowing hospitality, having got rid of the servants of his victim, Claudius raised his hand to deal the murderous blow. But even then he felt an awe of S. Martin and prayed to him to bring him safe to his home. The cloisters and precincts of the shrine became the scene of a fierce struggle in which blood flowed freely. Gregory adds that vengeance fell on those who were guilty of the defilement. Both Eberulfus and Claudius died pierced with wounds. To call all this heathenism is too flattering. It would be hard to find an instance of a heathen temple desecrated with such cynical crime.

The deeply rooted pagan instincts even in pious Christians often reveal themselves in tales of that dark time. Old heathen arts of divination and witchcraft were anathematised by Councils. Yet they were still practised and encouraged by Christian support. A witch at Verdun made a revenue for her masters. The witches

of Paris suffered awful torture for having caused the death of
a young prince by their incantations. A pythoness at Tours
predicted a bishopric for Guntram Boso who was a slave of
sorcerers and magic arts, and who never took an oath without
breaking it. She also, consulted by King Guntram, had foretold
the day and hour of Charibert's death. Even in Gregory's
family, when a servant fell ill at Brivate, a sorcerer had been
called in to use his charms and incantations.

The trial of the Sortes, *i.e.* an attempt to discover the future
by a random opening of the Sacred Books, like the Sortes Virgi-
lianae, was condemned by severe Churchmen. Yet at least three
times in the record of Gregory we find the omen from the sacred
text sought by professing Christians. In the church of Dijon
in 556 the books of the Prophets, Apostles, and Evangelists were
laid on the altar for this test, with a prayer that the Lord would
thus reveal what was in store for the rebellious son of Chlothar I.
The casual verses, which were read at the Mass, all appeared full
of dark omen for the prince. From a similar trial of Holy Writ
in the interests of lawless ambition, at the altar of Tours, Psalter
and Gospel gave back to the rebel Merovech an equally gloomy
answer. It is noteworthy that Merovech had previously consulted a pythoness. The bishop of Tours expresses no disapproval of this heathenish profanation of the altar. Indeed,
there is clear proof that he resorted to the same methods of
divination himself. At a serious crisis of his fate, when he was
threatened with ruin by a conspiracy of the Count Leudastes and
two of his own clergy, in gloom and disquiet, he entered his
oratory, and opened the Psalter if perchance he might light
on some verse of hope and consolation : the verse which
first caught his eye was—*Eduxit eos in spe et non timuerunt :
et inimicos eorum operuit mare* (Ps. lxxvii. 53). Within a short
time Leudastes and his comrades narrowly escaped drowning on
the Loire.

At a time when even in Christian households the old world
charms were still in vogue, we need not wonder that impostors
sprang up who exploited rustic superstition with wonders of the
old type. Towards the end of Gregory's life a certain Desiderius
appeared at Tours, claiming immense miraculous gifts derived
from frequent mystic intercourse with SS. Peter and Paul. But,
according to Gregory, his arts were necromantic, inspired by

demons. He was, as it turned out, a gross sensualist, who traded on the fears or hopes of an ignorant people. In the territory of the great Saint, he boasted that he was a greater S. Martin. The people in crowds brought their sick and palsied to him for healing, and the unfortunate patients had to submit to a treatment which seems to have been far more physical than spiritual. The reluctant muscles were stretched and torn almost as if they were on the rack of the Merovingians, and many died in the violent process of cure. It is pleasant to hear that Gregory seized the rascal and banished him from Tours. Another " seducer " appeared in the realm of the bishop of Tours about the same time. He came from Spain, with relics of SS. Vincentius and Felix, clothed in white tunic of Egyptian fashion, with vases of miraculous oil depending from a cross. He arrived when the bishop was at dinner, and called for a procession to do honour to the holy things. Gregory was grand seigneur as well as bishop, and, with official dignity, he told the stranger that his relics could rest in a holy place till the morning, when they would then be fitly welcomed. At the earliest dawn, the adventurer appeared, burst into Gregory's chamber, and, with vulgar arrogance, declared that he would report the neglect to Chilperic. He made his way into the chapel, and, with coarse vulgar accent, which offended the ears of the aristocratic bishop, actually performed some kind of service. Thence he made his way to Paris, and, with a crowd of ignorant devotees, made the round of the holy places. Ragnemodus, the bishop, sent his archdeacon to ask him to place his relics in the church and join in the festival of the Ascension. The bishop was met with curses and insults, and at once ordered the fellow to prison, where all his store of strange samples, teeth of the mole, bones of mice, and the fat of bears, was exposed. The disgusting apparatus of a mongrel superstition was, by the wholesome orders of the imperious bishop, flung into the Seine, and the wretched impostor was ordered to depart from Paris. He appeared once more, however, and was cast again into prison. Yet, with an energy worthy of a better cause, he broke his bonds, and was found in the basilica of S. Julian, where Gregory saw him lying in a drunken sleep, at the midnight service. Reeking with the odours of debauch, he was seized by four of the clergy and flung into a corner of the church, which had to be cleansed before the service could proceed. On the next day he was found to be an escaped serf of the bishop of Begorra from the glades of the Pyrenees.

In that age all seemed lawless in nature, as all was lawless and cruel in the life of man. The calamity of the time, whether from the crimes and ferocity of the great, or the cataclysms of nature, disordered imaginations which were already open to any marvel from the unseen universe. Suffering from the recurring invasions of pestilence, from as constant invasions of tumultuary armies of jealous princes, drained and terrorised by the oppression of dukes and provincial governors, to the afflicted people the more startling phenomena of nature became unearthly signs or omens. Even to the educated it does not seem to have occurred that a God who permitted such tragedies of guilt and suffering would hardly trouble Himself to announce their approach. Gregory's History is as full of signs and startling convulsions of nature as the early annals of Rome, and they are very much of the same kind. And they are generally inserted artistically near the record of some great crime or calamity. In a year of the great plague there is a huge landslip which dammed the course of the Rhone and flooded the country down to the walls of Geneva : four suns appeared in the heavens, and a comet blazed like a flaming sword. Another year of pestilence was marked by an eclipse, a violent earthquake, and torrential rains. The year of the wild disorders in Radegund's convent at Poitiers saw floods which broke the banks of all the rivers, and the milder signs of trees blossoming and bearing fruit on the verge of winter. The Northern Lights were a frequent cause of wonder and terror. And the lightning in crashing thunderstorms, twisting itself into coils of serpents falling from the clouds, appeared to Gregory to forbode the death of kings or the ruin of the realm.

It would be profane and futile to treat with superior scorn a stage in the spiritual evolution of our ancestors. It little becomes us who have lived through an age enslaved, until recent years, to the dominant materialism of nineteenth century science, to cavil at the credulity of those who, amid a profound darkness and in an atmosphere charged with fear, ignorant of any save a few scattered links in the chain of physical causation, ascribed to the high and beneficent agencies of Deity and sanctity powers without whose aid the human heart might well have quailed in despair.

CHAPTER III

THE organisation of the Church under the bishops is dealt with in another chapter. In this chapter we shall attempt to form some conception of the routine of religious life, the sacred buildings and services, and the crowds who frequented thém, with many incidents of rude invasion and desecration of the sacred precincts. Something must also be said of the moral character of the ordinary clergy of that age. If too great prominence and importance may seem to be given to this side of life, it is well to remember that not only are our chief sources of information, for this age, ecclesiastical, but that the Church of a district was then a centre of activity and interest such as we can now hardly imagine. If religion had no very potent influence on conduct, the theory of religion and the vast spiritual power of the Church profoundly affected the imagination of men even when their conduct was little in keeping with their beliefs. And the miraculous virtue which issued from the relics under the altar, magnified by popular rumour and legend, had a magnetic power on the popular imagination. Nor were lower influences wanting to swell the effect. A growing list of benefactors lavished their wealth on sacred buildings and services and provision for the clergy and the poor. The church was probably the only building in many a district with any dignity or merit of artistic effect. Marbles and jewels, frescoes and tapestry adorned the walls and the altar. Great attention was paid to music and chanting. Stately processions were marshalled on high festivals, with banners and lights and incense. To people sunk in dull and sordid poverty, unrelieved by temporal hopes and pleasures, the service in a great church must have seemed to open vistas into another world.

Whatever effect the Frank conquest may have had on the general economic fortunes of Gaul, there can be no question that the wealth of the Church had grown rapidly in the two or three generations from the death of Clovis. Without doubt, pure religion and benevolence inspired many of the donors and benefactors of that time. But the dominant conception of the relation of this short life to the eternal life to come furnished the most powerful motive for such beneficence. To purchase "remissio peccatorum" and a "merces futura" was the confessed inspiration of many a bequest by pious or by guilty souls. Charters of donations and many a passage in Gregory of Tours, Fortunatus, and the Lives of the Saints record this motive of pious gifts. The Frank kings and queens, Clovis and Childebert I., Guntram, Clothilde, Bathilde, and Dagobert, endowed many shrines of saints with wide domains all over Gaul. Nor were the bishops less generous. They were often men of old and wealthy families, and they controlled, subject to certain rules, the revenues of their sees, one quarter of which was assigned for the maintenance of their rank. Their paternal fortune before their elevation was left at their own disposal. But all acquired during their tenure of the see, on their death, became the property of their church, and in many cases their patrimony was bequeathed to it also. Gregory has left the record of such benefactions by former occupants of the see of Tours.

The testaments of S. Rémi, S. Caesarius, Bertram of Le Mans, and many another prelate bequeathed countless manors all over Gaul to churches and religious foundations in which they had a special interest. It is little wonder that, in elections to a bishopric, the wealthy candidate had often a great advantage. The good people saw the prospect of a generous addition to the treasury of their church. These ecclesiastical wills leave on our minds a striking impression of the wealth of the great landholders from among whom the bishops were often taken, and of the churches or monasteries who became their heirs. Such churches as those of S. Denys and Le Mans, S. Julian's of Auvergne, and S. Martin's of Tours, must, as time went on, have become possessors of estates that might surpass the measure of the largest lay fortunes. There was probably some justification for the complaint of Chilperic I., that in his day the public treasury was impoverished and all wealth had passed into the hands of the Church.

The right of the Church to receive bequests or donations, which had been secured to her by Roman Law, was guarded by the Barbarian Codes and the Constitutions of the Frank kings. The grants were made not to the Universal Church, but to particular local churches or religious houses. The legal owner was the bishop or abbot, who administered the corporate property through his agents, received the revenues, and authorised all legal acts which were necessary to defend or transfer the title. But the bishops' power over the estate was limited by several Acts of Councils. The progressive increase of the wealth of the Church was their great motive, excused or dignified in their eyes by the interests of religion. At the council of Carthage in 398, and at Agde in 506, the *Acta* prohibited the alienation of church lands, except in cases of proved necessity, and of such necessity the judgement of three co-provincial bishops was required. Thus, as bequests poured in, the landed wealth of an ecclesiastical corporation was constantly growing, with no danger of ever being diminished unless by forcible seizure or revolution. That outrages on corporate property were not infrequent is too evident both from the Chronicles and Conciliar Acts. Towards the end of Gregory's life (586) a royal officer in the district of Tours was guilty of a long series of violent crimes. He treated with contempt all the expostulations of the bishop, and actually, among other acts of violence and rapacity, plundered and killed a party of the servants of the Church, for which he was punished with excommunication. Gregory was a mild man and relieved the culprit of the sentence on his taking an oath of innocence, which was certainly a perjury. Within four months he had appropriated some lands belonging to a religious house. This time the punishment came direct from God. The offender had no sooner begun to reap the crop on the misappropriated lands, than he was seized with a fever, of which he died in three days. In another case, property was extorted from the bishop of Saintes by the threats of Antestius, an officer of King Guntram. The bishop had been spending Lent on an island, and was returning to his church for the Easter festival. He was stopped by Antestius, who

would not let him enter the church till he had formally transferred the coveted property. Similar attempts were made on
estates dedicated to S. Julian in Auvergne. Sigivaldus, the
governor of the district in Theuderic's reign, tried by fraudulent
arts to annex some lands which had been given to the Church
by Tetradius, bishop of Bourges. In this case also, a fever was
the penalty from which the avaricious Sigivaldus only escaped
by abandoning his prey. Eberulfus, the chamberlain of Guntram,
and the probable assassin of Chilperic, among his countless crimes,
had seized a villa of the Church and pillaged its accumulated
stores. One Pastor, whose lands adjoined those of S. Julian,
cast a covetous eye on some farms of *coloni* on the estates of the
saint. A deputation of the clergy was sent to expostulate with
him and met with an armed force. But the violator, who had
dared to take part in the annual festival in August, was struck
by lightning as he sat at a banquet. Eparchius, the son of a
man of rank, had built a religious house on the Charente. The
fame of his sanctity and miracles attracted the generosity of
the pious, and one, Walderic, had left an estate in honour of
the saintly recluse. Another great lord of the district, named
Chrotharius, laid hands on it, and, although when stricken with
disease he would have restored it, the Divine vengeance was
implacable.

The Acts of Councils, by their threats and warnings, reveal
the prevalence of the same profane avidity. A council of bishops
met at Tours in 567, the year of the death of Charibert and of
the fateful and ill-starred marriage of Chilperic and Galswintha.
The venerable men were evidently dismayed by the wild licence
of the time and the omens of yet coming calamities, and they
have left a severe enactment against those who presumed to
invade the domains of the Church. The violator is to be three
times admonished by the injured clergy to make restitution,
and if, on a third warning, he remains obdurate, they are all,
of every degree, to assemble, and, since the Church has no other
arms, they are, trusting to the help of Christ, to pronounce his
excommunication, reciting that awful Psalm, the cviii., probably
the most desolating anathema ever uttered. We may imagine
the effect of a choir at Rheims or Tours chanting, with all the
fury and the conscious power of a Church which held the keys
of Hell, the words, " Fiant filii orphani et uxor ejus vidua ;

deleatur nomen ejus et dispereat de terra memoria eorum : qui insurgunt in me confundantur ".

The Churches and monastic foundations in the Merovingian realms, with a few privileged exceptions, had to pay their share of the taxes. Their rapidly growing wealth attracted the eyes of more than one of the Frank kings, and in 544 Chlothar I. ordered that all the Churches should pay one-third of their revenues to the public treasury. This would have meant to the Churches of Paris, Le Mans, and Cahors the surrender of the whole income of many of their estates. The bishops reluctantly assented to the indiction, with the single exception of Injuriosus of Tours, who told the king that, if he filled his coffers with money which was dedicated to the poor, God would take his kingdom from him. The king, like many others of his day, dreaded the power of S. Martin quite as much as the power of God, and for a long time, not only the Church, but the whole district, was exempted from taxation. In 589 King Childebert's officers set out to make fresh census-lists for revenue purposes, and, in due course, they arrived at Tours. Gregory, the bishop, pointed out that for three reigns Tours had known nothing of taxation. No claim for taxes had been heard of in the fourteen years since Childebert came to the throne. That monarch, on an appeal to him personally, renewed the exemption granted by his predecessors. In 534 the same indulgence had been granted to the Churches of Auvergne by Theudebert, who is eulogised by Gregory for his reverence for the priesthood, his munificence to the Church, and his bounty to the poor. In return for these immunities the Church conferred corresponding benefits. Perhaps the one bright moment for the peasant amid days of toil was the hour in church, with stately processions in varicoloured vestments, advancing to the sound of rhythmic chants, through aisles hung with rich tapestries and decorated with brilliant frescoes and marbles, to the sanctuary gleaming with the radiance of jewels on the Cross. Fortunatus expended his decadent art in celebrating the splendour of many of the new churches and baptisteries which were being dedicated during his travels through Gaul, and he tells us—" Ad nova templa avide concurrunt undique plebes ". And we may easily imagine the charm of the basilica at Bordeaux, erected by Leontius with arches shining with silver and gold, and vivid frescoes, or of the service in the great church of Paris in the days of S. Germanus, when it rang with angelic music. Many of the churches in the fifth century were unpretending structures of wood. But before the close of that century a great movement for church building and restoration had set in, and Sidonius Apollinaris has celebrated in verse the architectural efforts of his brother bishops. In the sixth century, notwithstanding the invasion, the movement advanced even more rapidly, and the great bishops must have spent vast sums in building from the growing wealth of the Church.

It is not easy from our authorities to frame a full and accurate picture of the aspect and arrangement of these buildings. Minute details familiar to the chronicler are taken for granted and slurred over. Yet we may recover a few glimpses of them.

The architecture of these basilicas was probably, as to the exterior, simple and even bald. The interior was " *triformis* ", a nave (*capsum*), with two aisles, divided by lines of pillars, a semicircular apse, and sometimes a transept. There were various chambers or chapels attached to the main building, and, surrounding the greater churches, there must have been other buildings within the sacred precincts, the *domus ecclesiae* where the clergy lived, the Matricula, or hostel for the poor, who were inscribed on the roll, and drew regular alms, and the rooms for the vergers and keepers of the church. At S. Martin's and other churches, where the right of asylum was recognised, it seems that there were lodgings close to the church for the refugees who had claimed the protection of the saint. The dimensions of two great basilicae are given by Gregory in his second book. Briccius, the immediate successor of S. Martin in the see of Tours, had built a small chapel over the saint's remains. In 461, Perpetuus, feeling that this humble chapel was unworthy of the miraculous virtue of the saint, determined to erect a more stately structure, which was celebrated in verse by the facile pen of Sidonius. Thither, not without a miracle, the sacred remains were translated by a concourse of bishops, abbots, and the minor clergy, and deposited in a vault whose walls were of bronze and silver and gold. The basilica was not indeed of the vast dimensions of some of our cathedrals of the twelfth century. But it must have been an imposing structure. It was in length 160 feet, 60 in breadth, and rose 45 feet to the vault. It had, in all, 52 windows, 120 columns, and 8 doorways. About the same time,

Namatius, the eighth bishop of Auvergne, built at his own cost a great church close to the walls. Its proportions were very similar to those of S. Martin's at Tours. But it was rather loftier, and, having two transepts of elegant architecture, it was in the form of a cross.

The clergy of a great church met at meals at the *mensa canonica* (and were expected to do so). Once when a brother, named Patroclus, who was inflamed by an ideal of extreme asceticism, kept away from the common table, he was sternly rebuked by the Archdeacon, and the choice was given him to leave the society or to live on equal terms with his brethren. One cannot help applauding the genial Archdeacon who rebuked him. And, in spite of the ascetic spirit of the times, many a pleasant dinner was given in the church house after Mass, or on great festivals of the Church, where there was no stint of food or wines. The good Gregory often sat at the head of such banquets, and we have no doubt that he never relaxed his dignity as a gentleman and prince of the Church, or impaired the sanctity of the great office for which he had so much reverence. There are tales in Gregory of some drunken priests and bishops. But they are few, and they are a proof rather of the honesty of the historian than of the demoralisation of the clerical order.

The *Cursus Divinus* and the observation of the Hours were strictly observed. A bishop staying in Paris would rise to take part in midnight services. There were at least two celebrations of the Mass, one regularly at nine o'clock, and food or drink were forbidden till after the Holy Mysteries. Great attention was paid to singing and chanting. A good voice and a musical taste might make the fortune of a young ecclesiastic, as an uncultivated tone might make him ridiculous. The regular attendance of the faithful was imperiously enforced, and they were expected to take their part in the service. The practice of withdrawing before it was concluded was denounced and roughly repressed by S. Caesarius at Arles. Great stress was laid on preaching by that illustrious bishop, and the pulpit of those days did not spare the faults of the audience, even of the higher rank, and denounced the flagrant vices of the court circle, in the very presence of the king. This plain speaking sometimes led to scenes, even in the most solemn ceremonial, which are truly astonishing, as in the case recorded in the last chapter of King Theudebert at Trèves.

An equally strange scene took place in Paris, fifty years later, after the death of Chilperic. King Guntram had come from Burgundy to protect Fredegundis and her infant son. The family curse which haunted the Merovingian house had made their palaces reek of blood. Guntram, the most kindly and genial of his race, was showing his best qualities. He was correcting many of the injustices inflicted by Chilperic, and restoring endowments which he had declared invalid, and yet he felt himself in continual danger from assassination, and went even to church with an armed guard. On one Sunday, after the deacon had demanded silence for the performance of the Holy Mysteries, the king turned to the congregation and made an appeal which, strange as it may seem, has an air of solemn sincerity. " I adjure you ", he said, " men and women who are here, to keep an inviolate loyalty to me, and not to slay me as you have slain my brothers. Leave me, even for three years, to guard and nurture my nephews, who are my adopted sons, lest haply, which may Eternal God avert, when I fall, you may perish with these infants, when there is none of our race strong enough to defend you ". No Merovingian ever spoke more worthily. In a far from blameless man, often fiercely cruel and self-indulgent, there lingered a deep sense of the duty of his house to his people. It is not strange that the people responded with fervent prayers for the prince.

It is not easy, from our authorities, to frame a full and accurate picture of the churches where these scenes occurred. Minute details, familiar to the chronicler and the men of his time, are taken for granted, and omitted. But, in addition to the great churches, chapels or oratories at this time were being built by landed proprietors on their estates, to provide for the spiritual needs of their households and dependants. From the early part of the sixth century, the Councils began to take these chapels under their surveillance. The lord was required to provide a permanent endowment, and provision was made for a regular service of clergy, chosen by the lord, generally from among the people of his estate, but subject to the assent and spiritual control of the bishop. The services at the oratory were for ordinary and regular devotion. For the great festivals, as in the time of Ausonius, the population of a rural estate were required to resort to the mother church in the neighbouring

town. As the modern French village is the descendant of the
group of dwellings around the great house of the ancient Gallo-
Roman villa, so an immense proportion of the parish churches
of France spring from these ancient oratories. Many of these
are mentioned by Gregory, and chiefly for the wonders wrought
by relics with which a chapel was always consecrated. Sometimes, in obedience to a vision, it was built over the unsheltered
remains of a forgotten saint. Or the oratory may be 'a chamber
consecrated in a great house adjoining the hall. Or a building,
used for secular purposes, might be set apart for prayer. We
have the description of one such ceremony at Tours. When
Gregory came to the see, he determined to consecrate a chamber
in the bishop's house which Eufronius, his predecessor, had used
as a store-room. The ceremonial was on the scale of the dedication of a great Church. After night-long vigils in the neighbouring basilica, a new altar was consecrated, and the relics of four
saints, including S. Martin, were brought, with due pomp and
form, to be deposited beneath it. A procession of priests and
choristers, in white robes, along with the magnates of Tours,
and a crowd of the common people, bore the sacred remains to
their resting-place. Suddenly, as they entered the doorway
of the chapel, it was flooded with an awful radiance which dazzled
and affrighted all. They were reassured when told by the bishop
that it was the power of S. Martin which had manifested itself,
and all joined in singing the verse—*Benedictus qui venit in nomine
Domini; Deus Dominus, et illuxit nobis.*

We can still see glimpses of the material preparations for the
building of some of the churches. The ecclesiastical estates
supplied the stone and lime and wood, and, apart from more
artistic labour, the Church had at her command an army of
serfs for the meaner tasks. But skill and art must have been
called in to design and decorate those piles which lasted for so
many generations, and dazzled the worshippers of the time by
their splendour. The Church on earth must be adorned with
all that was most beautiful and precious among the possessions
of man as a tribute to God and His saints, and to lift the soul in
imagination to the ineffable glory of the courts above. An age
of general luxury and artistic taste in private life can hardly
conceive what the gorgeous interior of a great church meant
to the simple folk of that rude age. Their lives were generally

passed in dull toil and squalid poverty. Religion, whatever their practice might be, was their supreme interest; the life eternal the great reality. The Catholic Church with that consideration and indulgence for common human nature, which has been one great source of her power, strove to satisfy at once the senses and the demands of faith. The churches were erected not only for the honour of God, but for the solace and delight of men, to instruct and impress them by pictured history or symbol, to gratify their senses, or to inspire solemn awe of the great mystery which links this life with that which is to come. Nothing is clearer in our authorities than that the churches of that time were gorgeously and sumptuously decorated, and that lights and music, and the ordered pomp of ceremony, were used to the full to make the House of God a real joy to His worshipper.

Probably most of the art of those days was spent on the decoration of the churches. The walls were often covered with frescoes, recalling scenes in the life of Christ and the saints. S. Paulinus had used this art on the walls of his churches at Nola, to wean a semi-pagan population from their attachments to their old gods. Gregory the Great, in rebuking an iconoclast, inculcated the doctrine that sacred paintings might be used to instruct the ignorant, in the way best fitted to their minds, without encouraging idolatrous adoration. The walls of Gallic churches were then warm with colour. Gundobald, the pretender from Constantinople, who for a time shook the throne of the Merovingians, had in early life earned a living by painting sacred frescoes. The wife of Namatius, who erected the Church of S. Stephen in the suburbs of Auvergne, wished to make it bright with colour and sacred legend. When far advanced in age, dressed in black, she would sit in the new basilica, with a volume of saintly lives in her lap, and suggest to the artist the subjects which she wished to be figured on the walls. Other decorations were rather for richness and splendour than edification. Gorgeous tapestry, with threads of gold, was hung around the altar, and on the surrounding walls of the sanctuary. Rich veils were often drawn across the chancel, and curtains hung over the great doors. The palls which covered the tombs of famous saints were costly and magnificent. Silver often shone from the pillars and the roof, as in the Church of S. Caesarius at Arles, or the basilica of S. Bibianus at Bordeaux. Jewelled crosses stood over the altar, and the holy vessels were often of great value. Some idea of the cost of these things may be formed from the will of the Abbot Aredius of Limoges. He was the heir to a large estate and devoted his fortune to founding the monastery of S. Hyrieix, Haute Vienne, and to the building of churches. In his will he leaves a catalogue of sacred furniture and vessels which he bequeathed, giving the cost of each article. The total value of his donations runs up to more than 1400 *solidi*, which would probably be equivalent to £6000 or £7000 of our money. Two silver cups cost 300 *solidi*, a silver paten, 72. One co-opertorium, all of silk, was valued at 300. The curtains of the doors cost about 3 *solidi* each. The pall covering an altar of S. Hilary, interwoven with gold thread, and sprinkled with pearls, was valued at 30 *solidi*. A crown and cross in the chapel of the saint, which was silver gilt and studded with gems, was reckoned to be worth 100 *solidi*.

Thus the movable wealth of an important church was often very great for those days. It was carefully guarded by sacristans and vergers who slept in the precincts of the building, and who appear often to have made their rounds in the middle of the night. The precaution was greatly needed. For the festivals drew together immense crowds, some of whom came for more practical purposes than devotion, and the jewelled crosses and vessels were sorely tempting to the eyes of greed and poverty. Once at a festival, after evening service, a thief concealed himself in a dark corner of a basilica, and when all was quiet, scaled the chancel rails, pulled down a richly-jewelled cross above the altar, and then, sweeping the tapestry from the walls, to conceal his spoil, after vainly trying to find an exit, threw himself down to sleep. At midnight the keepers of the church, as they made their rounds, with torches, caught the flash of a single gem on the stolen cross, and pounced on the culprit who at once confessed his crime. Strange to say, nothing is said of his punishment. Such an offence might seem to call for or excuse a miracle.

To the superstition of the age every altar tomb which held the remains of a saintly person became immediately a perennial source of unearthly power, before which the most hardened criminal trembled to take the oath that might draw down the doom of perjury, or where the victim of palsy or epilepsy might hope to obtain relief. The shrine of the great Apostle of Gaul at

2 G

Tours had a peculiar fame for miraculous cures, not only from the virtue of the great saint, but also from the devotion to his memory of his successor, who has so vividly and faithfully pictured for posterity the superstitions and religious longings of his time. It may be said with safety that the religious life of that age found its most characteristic expression in the courts of S. Martin at Tours. Gregory, in his four books devoted to the wonder-working power of the saint, has collected 207 cases of miraculous cure. He records with pride that in one year, 589, three blind persons, five possessed with demons, or more probably epileptic, and twelve stricken with paralysis, had been relieved of their tormenting afflictions. At a single great festival, four were cured of blindness, two of paralysis, and two of demoniac possession. This catalogue of miracles, to a modern mind, is a melancholy revelation of abject superstition and of various and prevalent disease. And from the medical point of view, the sadness is deepened by the thought that, through all these years, the plague was desolating Gaul at brief intervals. It is singular that the power of the saint seems not to have checked or mitigated the pestilence from the East. All the while, the services of the Church were going on in untroubled order by day and night. Processions were passing to and fro, through the streets, between the Cathedral and the basilica of S. Martin. Yet, when we read the books on his miracles, the church would appear to be a hospital crowded in all its courts and purlieus with people suffering from every kind of loathsome or painful malady. If his healing power was the glory of S. Martin, it must have laid a heavy burden on his priests and servants. But they all, down to the humblest verger, implicitly believed in his mysterious efficacy. There were, indeed, sceptics and scoffers in that time, as in the days of S. Martin himself, who profanely jeered at these tales of wonder, and asked how could one, long since turned to dust, have power to raise the dead to life, and restore sight to the blind. But the mass of men and women felt no such questionings. They came to be healed with the great secret of faith-healing, an unwavering confidence in the efficacy of faith and unseen powers.

It is difficult to imagine how the Church received all those who claimed the good offices of the saint. They seem to have lain in the court, or before the altar, for days, for months, even for years, many of them no doubt supported by the alms of the faithful. One paralytic woman had remained for eight years in the precincts. We hear of others in constant prayer before the sacred tomb, for two or three months, before the relief came. Three days, by a suspicious iteration, was often the time in which the light dawned on the darkened eye, or when the rigid and distorted limbs recovered their suppleness. In a moment, the patient would rise from his place and walk to the altar to receive the Eucharist. But the cases which must have most seriously disturbed the calm of the sanctuary were those supposed to be under demoniacal possession, which even Gregory tells us was diagnosed by the most skilled physicians as epilepsy, or " falling sickness ", as the rustics called it (*cadivum*). Whatever the cause may have been, close intermarriage, or vice, or heredity, there can be no doubt that nervous disease of the most repulsive type was then terribly prevalent. The miserable victim, thrown into convulsions, and foaming at the mouth, believed himself the prey of the Evil One, and beset with demons. In the sanctuary he might have momentary relief, but, if he left the church, he was immediately surrounded by the din of infernal arms. If he threw himself on the ground, he was covered with swarms of frogs. Strange voices came to his ear, ridiculing the power of S. Martin. The Devil appeared even in the form of the saint, and asked the sufferer to adore him, but vanished when he was asked to make the sign of the Cross. Sometimes these afflicted creatures would break in on the sacred service with wild ill-omened cries.

Once when Gregory was invited to dedicate some relics of S. Julian in a new basilica of S. Martin, while the service was proceeding, an energumen, clapping his hands, with blood streaming from his mouth, demanded why S. Martin was calling in S. Julian's aid to heighten his tortures. It is to be feared, however, that these wild, probably inarticulate, cries may have been interpreted by the priests who heard them as an unwilling flattery of their patron.

These churches were not only spiritual hospitals : they were also almshouses on a great scale. Whatever the economist may think of it, it is one of the great glories of the Mediaeval Church that it took upon itself the burden of the poor, in an age when poverty was general. The Church had great possessions ; but a large proportion of its revenues was systematically devoted to charity. Acts of Councils, as well as tradition, required that one quarter of the Episcopal revenues should be allotted to the relief of indigence, and official beneficence was lavishly supplemented by private charity in bequests and donations. The command in the Gospel was often literally interpreted and obeyed by new converts to the religious life. Thus many of the great shrines, especially on days of high festival, were surrounded by crowds of poor people importuning the faithful for alms. Of the poor dependant on a great Church, Gregory distinguishes two classes, the *matricularii* and *pauperes*. The former were an organised body, duly registered, supported by regular rations, and living in a hospice attached to the Church. The saint was said to feed them. The beneficence of the Church was often supplemented by gifts or bequests, or by occasional feasts provided by private persons, or by the alms collected at the church door by a responsible officer, which formed a common stock. The unenrolled mendicants were freely allowed to solicit alms in the porticos of the church, probably awaiting their chance of being placed on the official register. The country places also swarmed with beggars who were sometimes armed with a letter from a bishop or other holy man, commending them to the charity of good Christians. The enrolled beadsmen of the Church were generally exempted from military conscription, but, with rude weapons, they sometimes defended the basilica against violence, as in the sanguinary conflict between Eberulfus and Claudius which raged in the cloister of S. Martin in 585.

These sanguinary feuds arose from the right of asylum which was an inheritance of the Church from paganism, and which had been guarded and delimited by Roman law as it was by Gregory the Great. From the early days of Athens the fugitive had found protection in a holy place. The mercy of the early Church reserved for the fugitive slave and the criminal a similar asylum, and the Church of the Middle Ages displayed an extraordinary clemency or pity for criminals condemned under forms of law, and no miracle is more common than the release of crowds of such malefactors. We may feel a hesitating wonder at this exertion of ecclesiastical or supernatural power to defeat the decisions of civil justice. And it seems to be one of the instances in which spiritual ideals conflicted with the demands of civil order. Yet we must remind ourselves that it was an age of cynical violence and injustice, even under the forms of law, and that the Church was true to the spirit of her Founder in being tender to the sinner in the hope of his repentance. And courage was needed to do so. No bishop could expect anything but trouble and danger from offering shelter to the outraged slave of a cruel aristocrat or the man flying from the vengeance of a Charibert or a Chilperic. Moreover the refugee was often a man of ferocious passions and dissolute life, who polluted the sacred precincts with bloodshed or scandalous excesses, who might even offer insult to the bishop himself in the very sanctuary. And the protection of a worthless man involved in some traitorous intrigue might bring a Merovingian army to ravage the lands of the see and block the doors of the basilica.

There are few passages in Gregory which throw a more vivid light on the social and religious life of his time than those describing the flight of desperate people to the shelter of the Church. It was perhaps the most vivid thing in his own experience at Tours and gives the most vivid conception of a curious side of Church life. For, indeed, the scenes in the sacred courts of S. Martin, about the year 576, beggar all description—the combination of abject superstition with shameless licence, of a desire to share in the privileges of religion with a readiness to defy all laws, human or Divine. Merovech, the son of Chilperic, who was in command of an army to recover the towns of Aquitaine, deserted his task and betook himself to Rouen, where Brunihildis, after her husband's assassination, was residing. There can be little doubt that the young prince had traitorous designs against his father, and whether from love or policy, he persuaded Bishop Praetextatus to violate the canons by marrying him to his aunt. The pair took refuge in a Church of S. Martin at Rouen from the justifiable anger of Chilperic. Their asylum was respected and they were allowed to come out on a sworn assurance of safety. But their union was short-lived. Brunihildis escaped to join her infant son in Austrasia. Merovech was shorn of his long hair and consigned to the cloister. But the young Merovingian had friends and faithful retainers who delivered him from jailers and brought him safely to the asylum of Tours. It was the hour of High Mass in the Cathedral when the fugitive entered the open doors. The deacons were distributing the *pain bénit* to those who had not approached the altar, when they saw a hooded and suspicious figure and passed him by. The fierce young prince was enraged, and, pressing through the crowded church, demanded of the bishop why the *eulogiae* were denied to him. It is more than probable that Gregory, having been often at the Neustrian court, recognised the son of Chilperic, who had been guilty of the double offence of incest and apostasy ; and he and his brother bishop, Ragnemod of Paris, at first refused to break canonical rules. But, when the prince threatened to enforce his claim by the sword, the mild bishop, under protest, gave way, and Merovech received the " blessed bread ", and, with his attendants, was lodged in the precincts of the church. Following the precedent of Roman law, a deacon was despatched to Soissons to announce that the son of Chilperic had sought the protection of S. Martin. Suspicion of treason was in the air, and not without good cause, and the envoys were treated as spies, stripped of all their belongings and hurried into an exile from which they only returned after seven months. A despatch was sent to the bishop ordering him to expel the apostate Merovingian, with the threat that Chilperic would ravage the environs of Tours with fire and sword.

Guntram Boso was a typical aristocrat of the time. Faithless and rapacious, he never took an oath of fidelity without intending to break it, if he found it to his interest to do so. Pursued by the vengeance of Fredegundis, he had found a refuge at the Church of S. Martin, and, in spite of his isolation, he somehow kept himself informed as to the movements of the time. In particular, he speedily heard of the adventures of Merovech and he probably understood his ambitious designs. It was Guntram Boso who drew the young prince to Tours, in the hope that, together, they might escape to the court of Austrasia. Merovech on his side, alarmed by the determination of his father to seize him, was equally eager to join Brunihildis and prosecute his designs. He would spend a night of vigil before the saint's tomb, on which he laid precious gifts, and beg S. Martin to succour him and grant him the kingly power he longed for. Guntram, a Frank, was probably far more pagan than Christian. The prayers of such a character before the altar were probably infrequent. But he sought less Christian sources of comfort and revelation. He sent a henchman to consult a wise woman who, from the days of Charibert, had been famous for Pythonic skill in divination. The designs of Merovech and Guntram are revealed in the oracular answer. Chilperic was to die within a year, and Merovech was to become sole monarch. As for Guntram Boso, he was destined to be duke for five years, and, in the sixth, he was to reach the loftier rank of bishop of a city not obscurely hinted at, the city of S. Martin. It was the summit, in those days, of aristocratic ambition to be chosen to rule a diocese ; and the vain, excitable, and half-pagan Frank could not refrain from communicating the revelation of his coming fortune to the bishop whom he was to succeed. Gregory only laughed at the vain prophecy and the man who could accept a promise from the Devil. Lying on his bed after midnight service, Gregory had another revelation of a surer kind. He dreamed that he saw an angel flying through the air who, as he passed over the basilica, cried with a loud voice : " Alas, God hath stricken Chilperic and all his house, nor shall any one sprung from his loins ever possess his kingdom for ever more."

The apparently monotonous life of the refugees in S. Martin's was broken by various incidents, rumours of danger, their own ambitious plots, and the feasting and revelry which was strangely tolerated in the sacred courts. The priests of the basilica probably supplied the wants of the poorer fugitives from justice. Those of higher degree brought their train with them, who lived in the neighbourhood of the Church, and catered for all the pleasures of their masters. The cloisters were often full of these attendants, and women of the town ; and the noise of revelry often rose above the chanting in the choir. It is a curious thing that the bishop once, at least, dined with Merovech, and had to listen to coarse jests and sneers against the character of Fredegundis and Chilperic. Gregory was a saintly churchman, but he was also a cool-headed man of the world, with the dignity of a great office and the social traditions of a great family. He could calmly maintain the dignity of the Church, and yet pay due respect to the great race of Clovis. At this banquet Merovech, with that strange conflict of passion and ideals which so constantly meets us in men of his time, asked the bishop for some sacred word for the edification of his soul. With all his characteristic fearlessness, the bishop turned to the book of Proverbs and read the ominous lines, *Oculum qui adversus aspexerit patrem, effodiant eum corvi de convallibus.*

Meanwhile Fredegundis, who, with a far more statesmanlike mind than her husband, realised the danger from the wild ambition of Merovech, anticipated by deadly plots the more open military measures of Chilperic. The Count of Tours at this time was Leudastes, who, by his unscrupulous character, was a fitting instrument in the hands of the Queen to crush the prince whom she at once hated and feared. Attempts to entice him from his hiding failed ; but a party of Merovech's retainers were waylaid and massacred. It so happened that Marileifus, the chief physician of Chilperic, was passing through Tours on his way back from the court to his home at Poitiers. Merovech resolved to have vengeance for the murder of his men on the medical attendant of Fredegundis. He gave orders that he should be seized and plundered of the treasure which he had with him. Marileifus was stripped of all his wealth and would have lost his life if he had not managed to escape from the assassins to the shelter of the Church, which thus strangely protected at the same time the would-be murderer and his victim.

Fredegundis's hatreds never slept, and she now enlisted in her service an agent more dangerous and subtle than the violent Leudastes. Guntram Boso, for the moment the trusted friend of Merovech in their common asylum, had commended himself to the Queen by having, according to sinister rumour, been privy to the death of her stepson Theudebert on the field of Angoulême. A secret emissary secured the treacherous service of the duke by the promise of high reward. He never more enjoyed himself than in betraying a friend. Assuming that Fredegundis had made all arrangements outside the precincts of the Church to waylay the unsuspecting prince, Boso proposed to him in a genial way that they should break the deadly monotony of their confinement by riding out for a day's hawking in the country. To the astonishment of Boso, they returned without untoward incident. Something had gone wrong with the plans of Fredegundis, or the passion for sport, which was ingrained in all the Merovingians, would have cost Merovech his life.

Meanwhile Chilperic wished to lay hands on the reputed murderer of his son, Theudebert, and yet felt an awe of S. Martin who shielded him. The King had his forces ready, but he determined to write a letter to the saint in his celestial abode, asking whether he might lawfully, that is, without danger to his august person, drag the fugitive from his hiding. A deacon laid the King's letter on the tomb, along with a blank sheet, to receive the saint's reply. The deacon watched for three days beside the altar, but no answer came. The King then resorted to more mundane diplomacy. If Boso could not be punished, at least he could be used as a tool to prevent Merovech, the traitorous son, rejoining his aunt-wife Brunihildis, and organising an attack on the throne of his father. He therefore exacted from Guntram a solemn oath that he would not allow Merovech to make his escape to the court of Austrasia without informing Chilperic. Guntram Boso, who never hesitated at a perjury, with his hand on the sacred pall, swore what the King's envoy dictated, with the cool intention of doing the opposite. The treasures of Marileifus, the court physician, had provided ample funds for their plans of escape. Crowds of bravoes and military adventurers swarmed around the basilica, ready for any dangerous or criminal service. Even the awe of S. Martin might not long afford protection to the murderer of a son of Chilperic, and another son who was deep in an intrigue to dethrone his father. A force of five or six hundred armed men were soon ready to escort Guntram and Merovech to the court of Austrasia. But Merovech seems not to have had the cool daring of his companion. The " wise woman " had promised him the throne. But he mistrusted the pagan prediction and he resorted to a form of Christian divination not less superstitious, which was condemned by the canons and Fathers of the Church. He resolved to try the "Sortes Biblicae ". Laying the Psalter, the book of Kings, and the Gospel on the tomb, the prince watched for a whole night, and prayed the saint to vouchsafe some sign that his ambition would succeed. Three days he spent in fasting and prayer, and then opened the sacred rolls to read his destiny. It was a gloomy and sinister answer which he received alike from Psalm, Chronicle, and Gospel. The burden was summed up in the ominous words, *ideo tradidit vos Dominus Deus vester in manibus inimicorum vestrorum.* Merovech was overwhelmed by the awful words, and knelt long in tears before the altar. But his more energetic and daring comrade hurried him away on the road to Luxerre with their formidable escort. The young Merovingian soon after met his predicted doom. Hunted from one refuge to another and at last beset on all sides, he died voluntarily by the sword of a faithful squire to save himself from a more cruel end.

Meanwhile Chilperic had gone as near to violating S. Martin's as a very hair-splitting conscience, or rather a fear of temporal punishment at the saint's hands, would allow him. His generals ravaged the lands of S. Martin's, and deprived the poor in the hostels of the Church of their subsistence. When a rumour spread that the hunted Merovech might attempt to regain his asylum, Chilperic ordered all the doors of the basilica to be blocked by his armed men, leaving only one for the priests entering to perform the sacred offices. These incidents, which we have recorded at some length, may serve as sufficient illustration of the attitude of the bolder and more lawless spirits of the time even to the power and protection of the Church.

In some cases a formal compliance with the rules of asylum was boldly put aside and open violence was used. Thus in the evil days when Chramnus was playing the tyrant in Auvergne, the Count Firminus, whom he had deposed, fled to the church with his mother-in-law for safety. Emissaries of Chramnus were sent to expel them, if necessary, by force. They engaged the refugees in conversation, walking up and down the aisles, and at last, having gradually drawn them to the open doors, they seized them and flung them forth. So the wife of Duke Ragnovaldus, who had been defeated by the generals of Chilperic in the contest with Guntram for the cities of Aquitaine, was dragged without scruple from the church of S. Caprasius of Agen. The mission of Claudius in 584 to kill or drag away in chains Eberulfus, the supposed murderer of Chilperic, is the most astounding revelation of the small respect which a materialist and selfish superstition may feel for the real sanctities of religion, and of the scenes of ferocity and slaughter which might be enacted in a holy place. It is true that the emissary of the Burgundian king was warned, in executing his task, not to profane the shrine by violence. But he deceived his victim by a solemn perjury, he allured him to his fate by the semblance of convivial fellowship, and had him struck down in the sacred courts by his following. Claudius himself soon atoned for his sacrilege by a ghastly death in the abbot's cell, to which he himself had fled for refuge. The retainers of Eberulfus and the beadsmen of S. Martin avenged, with their clubs and daggers, the indignity to the Church and the murder of their master.

Such records of bold crime and sacrilege might seem incredible if they did not come to us from a great Churchman, who had the fullest knowledge of the facts, and the strongest motives for suppressing them, and they suggest some obvious reflections. There was then a great and often effectual reverence for a Church consecrated by saintly memories. It was in theory an inviolable refuge. Yet, although open force might not be attempted, the safety of the fugitives was constantly threatened by subtle plots to entice them from their asylum, while the environs and lands of the church might be desolated by an invading army and its doors blockaded. The saint's ghostly power undoubtedly is a thing to be reckoned with, but the saint might apparently be cajoled or importuned into a betrayal of his clients. Moreover, there may be scenes of revelry and debauch, and even bloodshed, which seem strange in a home of sanctity. It was a great thing, indeed, that an immense spiritual force like that of S. Martin should be able to check, in some measure, the violence and selfish rapacity of the time. And yet we cannot help feeling that saintly ideals have been lowered by a materialist superstition which injured profoundly both morality and the higher religious life. But we must not expect humanity to progress too rapidly. Men only advance by slow and hesitating steps. We always carry a heavy load from the past which, if it maintains a bond of piety, often causes us to halt on the way towards the distant goal.

With regard to the whole moral tone and practice of the Church, in that age, there is a danger of adopting too sweeping and precarious conclusions. A very able historian of the time of Gregory the Great has sketched with ample knowledge the moral character of the Italian bishops and clergy under that illustrious Pontiff. The facts which he has accumulated give a lurid picture of clerical vice, malversation, and neglect of duty. But he wisely says " We must take care not to exaggerate the corruption ". With less judgement and self-restraint he observes that the record " cannot for a moment be compared with the flagrant crimes which are attributed to the French clergy of this period " ; and he gives parallel lists of clerical offences in France and Italy. Yet any one who carefully compares them will hardly come to the conclusion that the Gallic clergy were worse than their contemporary brethren in Italy. And it may well be doubted whether the social convulsions through which Italy had passed in the hundred years before Gregory the Great had not relaxed the discipline of the Church quite as much as the rule of the early Merovingians had done in Gaul.

The moral tone of the Gallic clergy of the sixth century is to be judged chiefly from the works of Gregory of Tours and the Acts of Councils. The business of a Council, so far as discipline was concerned, was not to record facts, but to prohibit, under ecclesiastical penalties, offences against morals or clerical order. But the prohibition is really a record. If a vice or offence is frequently denounced, we may fairly conclude that it not unfrequently occurred. As might be expected, the sexual relations of the clergy occupy a large place in Acts of Councils. Between 538 and 583 there are at least ten enactments forbidding all ranks of the clergy to have any intimate relations with women outside the circle of their nearest relatives. No woman is to enter the apartments of a bishop without the presence of two priests or deacons, and he is to be constantly attended by two of his clergy, both by night and day, who are to be the guardians or the witnesses of his blameless life. Married men of rank often took Holy Orders ; but, from the hour of ordination, they were required, under heavy penalties, to live apart from their wives and treat them as sisters : marriage after ordination is absolutely prohibited. Proved adultery among the higher clergy was punished by removal from office and perpetual seclusion in a monastery. The dangers of clerical life, in remote parishes, from ordinary attendants or from widows and virgins who had taken vows of sanctity, are guarded against with significant emphasis. No woman is ever to enter the walls of a religious house of men, and none but priests of tried character and advanced years are to be admitted to convents of women. Negligent or indulgent bishops who winked at any breaches of these rules are warned of the consequences. It is interesting to reflect that prelates of dubious character were probably present when the warning was enacted and afterwards signed the proceedings, men like Bertram of Bordeaux or Egidius of Rheims. Finally, monks and clerks were forbidden to go on vagrant excursions beyond their district. A bishop of Paris

once excommunicated a deacon who had innocently lingered
too long in the society of his early friend, the Bishop of Angers.
These efforts to restrain all sensual or romantic passion in the
priesthood, while they may cover over many a sin and tragedy,
reveal also the resolve of religious society to keep itself pure
and free from suspicion, according to the standards of the time.
That the effort may have often failed is only too probable from
the constant iteration of warnings. Yet a church cannot have
been so absolutely corrupt as Mr. Dudden represents it, which,
year after year, holds up this severe ideal to its priests. The
candour of the prelates in the Acts of Councils shows that it was
an ideal not seldom violated. But it is not true to say that
" the clergy high and low were as brutal and degraded as the
abandoned kings and nobles among whom they lived ". It is
indeed a gross libel on a great number of moral or even holy
men, if we may judge from our authorities. In the works of
Gregory and in the Lives of the Saints we are made acquainted
with a great number of bishops and abbots, and the great majority
of them are men of high character and even of saintly life. Among
the eighteen of his predecessors in the see of Tours, whose career
Gregory has sketched, only two, Briccius and Guntharius, were
men of even suspected morals. The rest were apparently men
of unspotted character, and lavished their wealth on the building
of churches and in charity to the poor. In the diocese of Auvergne,
which assuredly in those days was not a model of the ecclesiastical
life, we can only recall one bishop, Cautinus, whose morals were
openly assailed. The others of that period, Eufrasius, Quintianus,
Gallus, and Avitus, were men of stainless life, and some of them
even models of ascetic piety. In other sees we may refer
to Caesarius of Arles, Germanus of Paris, Nicetius of Lyons,
Leobinus of Chartres, Medardus of Noyon, and Paternus of
Avranche, who were famous ascetics before they were called to
the chief pastorate. To condemn the bishops of Gaul in the
sixth century to infamy in the sweeping fashion we have referred
to is not only historically inaccurate, but it tends to obscure the
great public services which bishops, possibly some of them not of
immaculate life, rendered to a disorganised society. They were
the only popular leaders and defenders of the oppressed : their
bounty was the only hope of the indigent. A class which could
show so many pious and holy men, which could fearlessly resist

overbearing kings and their often fiercer officials, which generally used its dignity and resources for beneficent purposes, should
not be branded as worthless and depraved, even if some of its
members, such as Egidius of Rheims and Bertram of Bordeaux,
may have been guilty of grave moral faults.

Yet it must be admitted that the clerical scandals revealed
by Gregory of Tours, and the suggestions of them in the Acts
of Councils, are not altogether pleasant reading. There can be
no doubt that some of the bishops and the lower clergy came to
their sacred office with but slight qualifications for it, either in
character or learning. Some of the bishops, it is true, who
sprang from territorial families, or who had borne high office
at the Court, proved themselves the most pious and blameless
of their order. But the power and wealth of a prelate in those
days were a great temptation to worldly or selfish and sensual
men. Many of the lower clergy, drawn from the serfs on great
estates, whether they were relegated to the solitude of a remote
parish, or rose to some office that promised a career of ambition,
often fell below even the standard of average lay morality. They
were, in many cases, rapacious, licentious, and violent. A man,
perhaps, of servile origin, ministering to a flock in some secluded
district, ignorant and undisciplined in character, and denied
the comfort and support of family ties, might easily slide into
vicious indulgence. He might count on the impunity of distance
to cover his violation of the canons : his untamed passions
might even lead him to defy or do violence to his bishop. These
things need not surprise us in an age of recent social convulsion,
followed by recurring civil wars which must have been as demoralising as they were desolating. The consolatory thing about
these scandals is that, in some cases, the moral sense of the
people took its revenge on the recreant priest in a very summary
and edifying fashion, without waiting for the more regular and
tardy methods of ecclesiastical discipline.

It is easy to make a catalogue of clerical crime and vice from
the pages of Gregory of Tours. Yet, when the note-taker has
done his best, the number of them, out of such a numerous body,
seems surprisingly small. It may be doubted if, from an equally
candid chronicle, a keen historical student might not find as
many in the Church of the eighteenth or nineteenth centuries.
Yet truth demands the statement of some unpleasant facts.

Drunken habits are found even among bishops. One prelate of Auvergne was so addicted to this vice that he had once to be carried away from a banquet by four men, and finally brought on epilepsy by his indulgence. Another, celebrating Mass in Paris, fell down before the altar, screaming in a loathsome convulsion, and had to be carried out of the church. A presbyter, named Eufrasius, of a good family in Auvergne, who tried to obtain the bishopric by simony, was apparently a charming man in society, but he delighted to send away his Frank guests drunk from his table, and his love affairs were notorious. A deacon of Paris deserted his diocese and attached himself too closely to the society of a genial bishop of Angers, who had built himself a chamber on the city walls, where he gave too pleasant dinners. As the company descended from this one evening with a linkboy in front, the deacon, very unsteady in his gait, struck the boy on the head, and, falling headlong, seized the bishop's girdle and would have dragged him down, had not the abbot caught his lordship and held him back. The dissolute deacon was killed by his fall. We hear of a deacon at Langres who made away with the alms for the poor in his charge. An archdeacon of Massilia connived at his servants plundering a merchant vessel of its cargo, and defended them from civil justice. It is evident that some of the clergy, eager for promotion, were disloyal to their bishop, organised cabals against him, sometimes grossly insulted him, and vilified his character. Gregory himself had to endure this treatment from some of his clergy involved in the plot of Leudastes to eject him from his see. The presbyter to whom the succession was promised, if the plot succeeded, insulted Gregory to his face in the choir of his cathedral, threatening to sweep the diocese clear of Arvernians. And, when Gregory was absent at Court, the arrogant priest installed himself in the church house, appropriated the sacred funds, and bribed the higher clergy to support him, with grants of vineyards and meadows, while he dealt out blows and insults to those of lower degree. Gregory bore all this with the calm dignity and gentle hauteur which distinguished him. He was absolved on his oath, and his accuser Riculfus, the deacon, was made to atone for his treachery by the most exquisite tortures which Fredegundis could devise, and which the bishop, who had pleaded for mercy to the culprit, affirms " nothing, even of metal, could endure." It is

evident, from the annals of Auvergne and Tours, that keen clerical
ambition, allured by the power and wealth of the episcopate,
was the most flagrant vice of the order, and that all the sacrosanct dignity of the bishop, guarded by the decrees of councils,
often failed to hold in check priests who had taken the vows of
obedience.   The Council of Auvergne in 535 might well warn the
clergy against allowing themselves to be drawn by powerful
nobles into rebellion against their bishops.   The vice of incontinence of course appears in these chronicles, but not perhaps so
frequently as we should expect.   As in Boccaccio, and our own
middle ages, a lowly abbot might by mean arts obtain stolen
intercourse with the wife of one of his tenants.   But in such cases
the lynch law enforced by the laity in those days might seem to
have been, on the whole, more salutary than the often singular
indulgence of the Church.   The fascinations and the substantial
power of the two great queens of that time seem to have laid
men often at their feet.   In their bold and criminal moves in the
deadly game which went on between Neustria and Austrasia,
they could command any service the most criminal and the
most desperate.   Fredegundis, at one stage of the duel, resolved
to procure the assassination of Childebert II., and the death or
capture of his mother Brunihildis.   She had daggers specially
made, with deep-sunk grooves, to contain a deadly poison, which
might render the stroke doubly sure.   She handed the weapons
to two clerks of her choice, with full instructions how to perform
their task, and lavish promises of reward for themselves, and of
high honours for their families, if they fell in their attempt.
When the clerical assassins showed some signs of nervousness, the
Queen inflamed their courage by a secret potion, and gave them
a flask of it to drink on the day when they were to deal the blow.
In her danger and humiliation after the murder of Chilperic,
Fredegundis had sent another clerical assassin to worm himself
into the good graces of Brunihildis, and, in some hour of careless
confidence, to strike her down.   But his disguise was pierced by
those keen eyes : under torture he confessed his mission and was
sent back to his mistress, who requited his *maladresse* by depriv-
ing him of hands and feet.   Nor can we forget that awful scene in
the Cathedral of Rouen when the aged bishop Praetextatus was
struck down at the Easter Mass.   When the old man rose with
a cry for help, and stretched out his hands, streaming with blood,

towards the altar, not one of the attendant clergy came to support him.

After scenes like these, other offences of the clergy denounced by the Councils seem almost trivial. They are forbidden to alienate or mortgage properties of the Church without leave from their diocesan. No cleric is to lend money on usury or to engage in trade. They were also denied the pleasures of coursing and hawking, which must have been very tempting to a vigorous priest whose parish lay in the forest regions of the Jura or Perthes. A sporting parson in the English Church has not always been the worst pastor of souls, and it may be doubted whether an occasional morning with hawk and hound might not have been a corrective to more serious faults. A taste for sport then cost a bishop three months' exclusion from communion, while a young deacon, by a kindly concession to the youthful weakness for sport, is let off with only one.

The conversion and victory of Clovis ensured the victory of the Catholic Church in the West. The Arian religion of the Teutonic invaders might, at one time, have seemed to ensure the triumph of the hated heresy. But the Church had a deeper and more potent inspiration, and a closer and more sympathetic hold on the religious instincts of the age, and military and political events furthered her triumph. The death of the great Theodoric, the most majestic example of the union of steadfast belief and generous tolerance, pathetically closed a heroic effort of reconciliation. The Burgundian and Visigothic powers, whether languidly or fiercely devoted to the Arian heresy, had been overthrown, and the Vandal power in Africa, which had almost wiped out the Catholic Church in that region by ferocious persecution, had been overwhelmed. These great events had dissipated for ever the fear or the hope that the creed of Arius would be the faith of Western Europe. But the Catholic leaders still retained a horror of the Arian heresy, and a suspicion of its tendency to undermine the dogma of the great Councils by a dangerous self-assertion of reason. The hatred and fear of Arianism in that age anticipated the dread of rationalism and modernism among ourselves, and the orthodox had some reason to fear it. The Arian powers had shown both in Gaul and Africa the fiercest intolerance. In Aquitaine, two generations before, the Visigothic king, Euric, had deprived dioceses of chief pastors, left churches desolate, and even put many priests to death. The Vandals in North Africa had tortured a Catholic people by almost unexampled cruelty and high-handed tyranny. As ruthless a spirit prevailed at this time among the Visigoths in Spain towards all who professed the Catholic faith. Goiswintha, the wife of King Leuvichild, surpassed even her husband in fanatical cruelty, and it was chiefly at her instigation that multitudes of Catholics had to endure hunger, torture, spoliation, and exile. The nemesis came in a deadly feud in the royal house which developed into a civil war. Ingundis, a daughter of Sigibert and Brunihildis, became the bride of Hermenigild, the son of Leuvichild. She was welcomed with effusion by the Queen, who at first, with bland enticement, tried to allure Ingundis to accept rebaptism by an Arian priest. When the princess firmly refused to disown her baptism into the Catholic Church, she was subjected to brutal torture and violence, and even flung into a pond to drown. Still the girl remained staunch, and actually, in the end, won her husband to her own faith. The result of Hermenigild's conversion was a fierce civil war, in which the forces of the Eastern Empire were called in. It is a repulsive subject which we may dismiss without further narrative. Even Gregory of Tours deplores that a son should raise his hand against a father, however depraved by heresy. It must be enough to say that, in the end, after many repulsive incidents of cruelty and treachery, Hermenigild was taken and put to death by his father's command. It is profoundly uninteresting to hear that Leuvichild may have closed his days in the Catholic Church. The Church might well repudiate such a convert, who could violate all ties of kin for a metaphysical dogma.

The hatred to the Arian sect burns in the pages of Gregory of Tours. Nothing could well be fiercer than the tone of that usually amiable bishop towards Arian doctrine. He prefixes to his History a technically minute profession of his faith in the doctrine of the Trinity. And, after his narrative of the career of Clovis, he draws the lesson that all prospers with those who confess the Trinity in Unity, while ruin and damnation are the portion of the heretics who deny it, from Arius, the impious founder of the sect, who is now in the fires of Hell, down to Alaric and the princes of Burgundy who, along with their kingdoms, have lost their souls. Envoys in those days were often passing between the Visigothic court in Spain and Neustria. In the year 580 Agila, an envoy of King Leuvichild, stopped at Tours on his way to the court of Chilperic. He seems to have called on the bishop, and, with doubtful courtesy and to us surprising zeal, immediately began to assail the Catholic dogma as to the Second Person of the Trinity. With manifest self-complaisance the good bishop has recorded the debate between them in which they bandied texts of Scripture in the facile style of such controversy. But Agila was evidently not one of those Arians who, in the present day, might easily pass for moderately orthodox. He is an easy-going agnostic who, in the spirit of the paganism of the Empire, sees good in all religions and no harm in bowing before the altars both of Jupiter and of Christ. This was more than Gregory could bear. He and his guest interchanged fierce recriminations in a scene where Gregory, for once, forgot that he was a Christian and a gentleman. Four years later, in 584, an ambassador named Oppila, on his way to ward off an invasion of Spain by Childebert, to avenge his sister's wrongs, arrived at Tours. It was the Easter festival, and Oppila was courteously received by the bishop, who asked him at once if he was of the Catholic faith. Oppila replied that he held what Catholics believed. He joined the procession to the church from the bishop's house. But he did not communicate. Nevertheless, in spite of grave suspicion, he was invited to the banquet which followed the service. Gregory then made inquiry about his faith, and asked him why he had not communicated. His answer is interesting. Oppila replied that he objected to the form of the " *Gloria Patri et Filio* ", the Arian form being " *Patri per Filium* ". This at once aroused all the ardour of Gregory's dialectic, and his unfortunate guest was bombarded with a mass of quotations from Holy Scripture, more or less irrelevant. But Oppila, like many other Arians of that day, was evidently separated from orthodox dogma by rather microscopic, metaphysical distinctions, born of the subtlety of the Eastern schools. It was a strange subject for dinner-table talk ; but Gregory thought he had won, and the disputants parted in peace, with the usual result of neither convincing the other.

The Catholic clergy had an even more potent force than reason and Scripture at their command to confound the impious heresy. If a faith could call down the wonder-working power of God it must be true. Miracle was in the air. Everybody, Catholic or Arian, believed in it. If their creed was true, why should not Arian priests work miracles as well as priests of the orthodox Church ? King Leuvichild thought so, and demanded of one of his bishops to show an equal power over nature to that of the Catholics. The unfortunate man, knowing well his impotence, resorted to deceit. He bribed a beggar to feign blindness and, with the sacred words and signs, pretended to restore his sight. But the punishment of the fraud was that the beggar really lost his sight. In this case the Divine justice seems to have been undiscriminating. In another curious case there was a striking confirmation of the Catholic dogma. An Arian priest and a Catholic deacon, weary of a fruitless debate on the mystery of the Trinity, agreed to decide the case in the old judicial fashion, by a trial by ordeal. A ring was thrown into a cauldron of boiling water, and whichever champion of his faith should have nerve and luck to draw the ring from the bottom, with flesh unharmed, his creed was to be victorious. It was a cruel test, and the deacon was naturally nervous. But an Italian who was present boldly faced the trial, and after nearly an hour's search in the torturing water, brought up the ring. The Arian who gallantly faced the inhuman test, drew out his arm with the flesh stripped off to the bone. It is singular and interesting to see that what we might think the rationalistic side in these unedifying controversies had as firm a belief in miracle as the Catholic.

With such religious hatred in the air, it is not surprising that the Councils should have exerted their powers to exasperate it. They forbade the Catholic clergy to meet heretics in social life. In a Council of 517 it was enacted that any clergyman of the higher grade who accepted hospitality from a heretic priest should forfeit the peace of the Church for one year. Junior ecclesiastics, for a similar offence, were to be punished with stripes. At the same time it appears that four years after the victory of Clovis on the plains of Poitiers, heretical clergy were seeking ordination for themselves and consecration for their churches. The Council at Orleans in that year provides for both cases, with easy clemency to the heretic. And a few years later (517) priests are enjoined by Catholic charity to give the last unction to dying heretics who ask for it. In 541 the

Council at Orleans ordains that those who, being baptized into
the Catholic Church, have, from the weakness of the flesh, fallen
into the snares of heresy, may be received back to communion
on confession of their error.   In these enactments we can see
that heresy is still vigorous in Gaul, and that the Church, conscious of her strength, is also conscious of danger.

The Jews, of course, were the worst of heretics ; they not
only denied the Son of God, but they were descended from His
murderers.   They were of alien race, maintaining with jealous
pride and exclusiveness their ancient religious customs and
traditions, which always formed a bar to social intercourse and
sympathy.   Yet they were widely diffused over almost all the
provinces of the old Empire, Asia Minor, Africa, Italy, Spain,
and Gaul, and wherever they went, with their genius for trade
and finance, they generally prospered.   Yet under the Imperial
law they lay under serious disabilities.   Heavily taxed, they
were shut out from all public office, civil or military.   They had
not the right of free testamentary bequest.   A Jew could not
marry a Christian woman or hold Christian slaves.   In an
émeute a Jew who did violence to a Christian might be burnt
alive.   The ferocious Arian legislation of the Visigoths went
even further than the Roman Code of Justinian.   And in the
Letters of Gregory the Great and the History of his namesake
of Tours there are examples of episcopal arrogance which bore
heavily on the Jews.   The bishops in Council revive all the
severity of the Roman Code.   It is enacted, for instance, that
no Jew could hold the office of governor or collector of taxes,
although a Hebrew capitalist might be called on to give those
officials financial assistance.   No Jew on any pretence of business
is permitted to have any private conversation with a virgin
devoted to God or to presume to linger in a nunnery.   Intermarriage between Christians and Jews is sternly forbidden.   A
Christian who accepts hospitality from a Jew may be deprived
of the holy rites for a year.   The legislation as to Christian slaves
of Jewish masters becomes more and more rigorous.   In 538
it is laid down that such slaves, if they take sanctuary, are not
to be restored without a sufficient ransom.   In 541 we find that
Christians in servitude to Jewish masters, if they object to
remain with them, may be liberated on payment of a fair price.
And in the same year any attempt on the part of the Jewish

master to proselytise a slave is punished by the loss of the slave; and the slave who has obtained manumission by conforming to Judaism is condemned to lose his new freedom. In the Acts of 583 we read that any Christian may redeem a Christian slave from a Jewish master. Gregory the Great protested to Brunihildis against the traffic in Christian slaves from Gaul. In the Council of 627–630 the sale of Christian slaves to Jewish masters is absolutely forbidden. It is enacted that any such contract will become void, and the vendor will forfeit communion. Lastly, during certain days at Easter, no Jew is to be seen mingling in the crowd of Christians in public places. Such enactments reveal the fears and bigotry of the clerical legislators. They also show the social importance of the Jews. To these legal hardships and insults inflicted on the Hebrew race must be added the danger from fitful and capricious outbreaks of popular hatred, or from episcopal arrogance. In Italy, Sicily, and Auvergne we read of their being turned out of their synagogues, or of the synagogue being burnt to the ground. Or a crowd of Jews might be driven by sheer force to the baptismal font.

Yet there were some things which rendered the fate of the Jews in Gaul more tolerable than it might at first sight seem to be. Some of the great bishops and statesmen did not view the race with the same fear and abhorrence as that felt by the masses. The great Theodoric, when the synagogue at Ravenna was burnt down by Christians, ordered it to be restored at the cost of Christians, and he had the violators flogged through the streets. Gregory the Great, while he sternly checked the innate tendency of the Jew to encroach if he gets the chance, protected them in their strict legal rights, deprecated and discouraged violent methods, and urged his suffragans to try the effect of charity and mild persuasion. In Gaul, in spite of occasional outbursts of hatred, the Jews for long periods seem to have been left undisturbed ; and they were evidently prosperous in the great towns where they settled. The perennial vigour and obstinacy of their race and their age-long aptitude for trade and finance, necessarily made them a powerful and essential element in a poor and disorganised society. They were ship-owners with peculiar facilities for communication in the Levant and the remoter East, through the freemasonry of their race. They had the command of capital when capital was scarce, and could provide an advance to a royal tax-gatherer on the revenues of his district, or they would make a loan to an ambitious priest who wished to obtain the succession to a diocese by presents at the court of Austrasia. They were the purveyors of jewels or articles of virtu to the court and fashionable world of Paris. Or a Jewish oculist might be called in by an archdeacon of Bourges to operate for cataract. Or a Hebrew trader, travelling to the north, might be entrusted with confidential letters of a bishop of Auvergne in dangerous times.

Yet it is clear that the Jews were often on good terms with bishops, even when the bishops denounced their blindness and tried to bring them to the font. When Gallus, the Bishop of Auvergne, was being carried, with great pomp and universal mourning, to his tomb in the basilica of S. Laurence, the Jews joined the procession with lighted torches, and shared in the general grief. His successor, Avitus, used to preach to them and exhort them to behold the Son of God behind the veil of prophecy. The baptism of one Jew who yielded to the bishop's rhetoric unfortunately ended in a riot and the destruction of the local synagogue. The bishop made another more effectual appeal, coupled with what amounted to an order, that those who declined baptism should migrate to another district. At Pentecost, after vigils, in a procession of white-robed clergy with flashing torches, more than 500 Arvernian Jews yielded to the persuasive eloquence of Avitus and advanced to the font. The more obstinate or conscientious retired to Marseilles, where, no doubt, they found a welcome from many of their people, engaged in the trade of that busy port.

It is curious to find Chilperic who, in his amateur theology, had incurred the charge of Sabellian heresy, undertaking a mission for the conversion of the Jews of Paris. His own faith, it is to be feared, was theoretical rather than practical ; but he exerted his authority to bring the obstinate Hebrews into the Church by blandishments or by threats. Once, at his villa of Nogent, in the presence of the Bishop of Tours, he laid his hand in kindly way on the head of Priscus, a Jew merchant, who supplied the court with many articles of taste or luxury, and invited the bishop to do the same and secure his conversion. Priscus, however, firmly resisted, and the Jew and the King plunged into a long and curious debate on the common ground of the Old Testament, by which alone the King and the bishop undertook to overwhelm the Jew. It is the style of uncritical and unhistorical abuse of Hebrew Scripture to which later times have not been unaccustomed. The King, after a preliminary exhibition of his Biblical lore, handed over the task to Gregory, who evidently pleased himself immensely with his cannonade of texts from Psalm or Prophecy or even from Genesis. Priscus was unyielding, but at last became silent. The King, after receiving the bishop's blessing, mounted his horse to return to Paris. Shortly afterwards Chilperic, by a sudden impulse, gave orders for the baptism of many Jews at Paris, in the forcible fashion which Gregory the Great deprecated. Priscus, true to his ancestral faith, again refused to conform, and was thrown into prison ; but he secured his release by bribes and an evasive promise to obey the royal order. Soon afterwards, by the hand of a Jewish renegade named Phatir, he was struck down as he was stealing on the Sabbath to perform his Mosaic rites in a secluded conventicle of his religion.

The writings of Gregory and even the Lives of the Saints here and there reveal the fact that there were even in those days not a few rather cynical sceptics who had no sympathy with the eager faith in supernatural powers. What class they belonged to we are not told, except in the case of one daring Jew who, meeting a priest in Bordeaux when he was hastening to S. Martin's festival to obtain relief from a quartan fever, told him that the dead man, " who had mingled with the clay, had no succour for the living ". The miracles of Nicetius of Trèves seem to have particularly aroused this rationalist criticism, and Gregory meets it with a systematic thoroughness which shows that he felt the seriousness of the attack. These people, he says, with their moral perversity will not credit the written record, the solemn testimony of eyewitnesses, even the plain evidence of their own senses. He had evidently met some of those sceptics who boldly challenged his narratives of miracle, and he replied to them, by a curious *petitio principii*, that Aredius, the saintly Abbot of Limoges, the friend and tutor of Nicetius, must be an unimpeachable authority for the miracles of Nicetius, since Aredius himself had the same power ! " If you distrust such an authority," says Gregory, " you distrust the goodness of God."

The clergy of the sixth century were but ill equipped for

controversy with heretics and unbelievers. Even Gregory the
Great, living at the centre of religion and culture, had little
learning, either secular or sacred. And his latest biographer gives
a lucid description of the conditions of culture at the time, which
limited the intellectual range even of so powerful a nature as
the great pontiff's. The last lights of secular culture had died
away with Boethius and Cassiodorus. The Church, amid the
wreck and chaos of the time, was the one support of the life
beyond the senses ; and the Church, in the passion and agony of
renunciation, had lost, in some cases often gladly, the taste for
the alluring charm of the literary art of the pagan ages. Jerome
and S. Augustine had resigned it with a lingering regret. But
even theological lore and subtlety were becoming far less attractive than the ascetic culture of the spirit, the subordination of
intellectual pride and worldly passion to a spiritual discipline
which was needed to enter by the narrow gate to eternal life.
The old metaphysical controversies were almost dead. The
great battles about the mystery of the Divine nature were over
in the East. Monophysitism, Manicheism, and Sabellianism
had hardly extended to the West, which had always less taste
for these abstract problems than the Orient. The semi-Pelagian
heresy, which had occupied some subtle minds at Lérins in the
fifth century, had been silenced by the Councils of Valence and
Orange, and only makes an appeal in the pulpit of Arles in the
days of S. Caesarius. One of the rare references to dogma in the
Acts of the Gallic Councils of the sixth century binds the clergy
to the decisions of Nicaea and Chalcedon. The great Pope and
the Church both in Italy and Gaul were far more occupied with
moral life, with organisation and discipline, than with niceties of
intellectual belief. The clergy of all grades, from their training
and associations, were not prepared to feel much speculative
interest in exploring the evidence for creeds formulated by
inspired Councils.

The higher clergy were often drawn from the aristocratic
or official classes. They were generally men of action rather
than students and thinkers. Nor was the education, which was
open even to the wealthy and aspiring, of a kind to produce
keen speculative minds. Even in the fifth century, before the
Imperial system had fallen, all the bent of school training was
towards a perverse, tactless rhetoric and an impotent effort

to imitate inimitable models. Early in the fifth century the knowledge of Greek was dying out, except perhaps in the district around the ancient colony of the Phocaeans and at Arles. Dialectic (Philosophy) had shrunk to a mere drill in formal logic, with anecdotic and frivolous reminiscences of the great Greek thinkers. In the sixth century, at least in Gaul, even this degenerate school tradition, which had moulded Sidonius and Ausonius, Prosper and Mamertus Claudianus, had been broken by the invasions and social disorganisation. It is true that schools of some sort, even in remote places, are mentioned in the Lives of the Saints. And some of the bishops maintained schools at the centre of their dioceses. The range of instruction varied greatly in different places according to circumstances and the aptitude of the teachers. Here and there the pupil may have gained a scrappy knowledge of Propertius, Sedulius, Orosius, and Eusebius, and some power of writing feeble imitative verse. In some rare cases the training may have embraced the Seven Liberal Arts of Capella with a tincture of Roman Law. But, by the regretful confessions of many writers of that day, education in general was very rudimentary, both as to the quality and body of the knowledge. A smattering of Virgil and Sallust, arithmetic, and some parts of Scripture learned by heart, would seem to have been all the education which some, even of the great churchmen, received. Yet there were some exceptions. King Guntram, in the face of bold simoniac bribes, to his credit once chose for the see of Bourges one Sulpicius, who was skilled in rhetoric and " second to none as a composer in verse ". Ferreolus, Bishop of Uzès, a descendant of the great noble Tonantius Ferreolus, composed some volumes of epistles modelled on Sidonius, his ancestor's friend. If there was little cultivation of rhetoric in the old classical fashion, some attention seems to have been paid to the style of sermons. Praetextatus, Bishop of Rouen, during his exile composed a collection of sacred orations which he read to a gathering of brother bishops. Some of his critics found them wanting in art, while others approved of them as conforming to the approved standards of such oratory. But the Church in Gaul was absolutely barren in anything deserving the name of theological literature. There were indeed some commentaries on books of Scripture, such as Gregory's lost exposition of the Psalms. But almost all the literary effort of the time expended itself on those Lives of the Saints which were the chief literary and spiritual food of the age. They were at once its romance and its manual of holy living and holy death. The young aspirant to the priesthood with a scanty knowledge of some fragments of great literature, got a verbal knowledge of Holy Scripture, the Liturgy, and the Canons of the Church, with a careful training in his clerical duties. He knew his Bible well and literally enough to face a heretic, in an altercation, with text for text. He could address his flock on Sundays in a Latin which would have shocked and amazed Cicero or Quintilian, or even Symmachus, but which, in its loosening structure and growing barbarism of vocabulary, was far better fitted to appeal to his rude audience than the chiselled and finished rhetoric of the great age.

Yet there is a feeling of pathos in reading the confessions of " rustic style ", along with the ambition of style which we meet in Gregory and the Lives of the Saints. They would write better if they could. They had caught faint glimpses of the literary charm and force of the great age. They try to give a borrowed distinction to their own style by snatches and reminiscences of a few of the canonised authors of the past. Even in the feeblest of the Lives there sometimes emerges a hopeless literary ambition amid a paralysing barbarism. As in the days of Sidonius, it seems to be a faint comfort in the sense of decadence to recite the mere names of men who were the glory of ancient letters, or of the great Fathers of the early Church : of Demosthenes, Cicero, or Virgil ; of S. Jerome, S. Augustine, or Basil. There must have been a lingering tradition of taste and learning in some of the Gallic schools, and here and there a literary descendant of one of the professors of Ausonius, a melancholy enthusiast amid the gathering darkness. His pupils might write halting verses, though there were few to know a halting verse when they met it. But master and pupil alike felt that the light was failing.

CHAPTER IV

THE BISHOPS

ANY survey of the Merovingian age must give a large place to the bishops. This is not merely because our chief authorities are ecclesiastical, inspired by a profound belief in the spiritual and temporal power and rights of the episcopal office. It is also because, from its source and character, amid the disruption of the Imperial system and the confusion of convulsive change, the episcopate, wielding all the powers and fascinations of the Church, became perhaps the most potent force in controlling and remoulding the society of the West. And the interest of this magical ascendancy lies in the fact that it was a moral and spiritual power ; it had at its command no physical and material forces to defend itself against violence and to make its words of counsel respected. The bishop, indeed, from the times of the Empire, had assured to him a great official position. Ecclesiastical demarcations followed, for the most part, the lines of old Roman administration. The bishop had his seat in some great civic centre, a *civitas*, with a wide extent of rural territory over which his rule extended. He had important civil and judicial functions assigned to him, to sit with the civil governor in court and advise or mitigate his decisions, to protect his flock from injustice and oppression, to guard the provision for the poor, to care for prisoners and captives. Thus, especially in wild, cruel times, the bishop tended to become not only a shepherd of souls but a protector of his people's temporal interests. In the tumult and confusion of the invasions the bishop often stepped into the place of the Imperial officer who had vanished. Sometimes he led and animated his people in defending themselves ; sometimes by intellectual ascendancy and trained diplomatic tact he softened the impact of barbarism, and even fascinated and mastered the barbarian chief. This influence was not seldom maintained when the victorious German had to face the unaccustomed task of organising and governing his conquests. He was under the awe and spell of Roman civilisation ; often with a touching deference and self-restraint he wished to save what he could out of the wreck of the Empire, and to use the old administrative skill of Romans. And among these, the most skilled and powerful were the bishops. They had a long tradition of service and command, of dignity and sacred duty. They were often men who added to personal sanctity and self-discipline the authority derived from noble ancestry and knowledge of the world. In the collapse of a great and ancient social order, the Church alone remained erect and confident in its sacred powers. The rude warrior chief found the bishop in possession. He met him generally with reverence, and used his authority to support and consolidate his own.

But we must never, in interpreting that age, forget that the episcopal power and influence ultimately spring from sources in the unseen world. The bishop, even to the pagan Frank when he first drew nigh to Rheims, was a mysterious sacrosanct person, possessing, according to floating rumour, strange wonder-working powers. To the instructed Christian he was literally a *Vir Apostolicus*, one who drew by direct transmission from the Great Founder those sacramental powers which, in the belief of that age and of many an age to come, far transcended any powers of this world. The deepest, most urgent interest of this brief life was to ensure the soul's safety from the terrors of the eternal world, and that could be done only through the sacraments and intercessions of the Church and the saints. The most terrible fate that could befall any man was to forfeit communion with that Divine society in whose hands lay the issues of life and death. The most criminal and abandoned sinner believed and trembled, even in the act of crime. He might be destitute even of a germ of conscience ; he might be without pity or natural remorse for the greatest enormities ; but he never ceased to cling to the Church and to believe in the necessity of her sacramental acts and prayers, and absolution, and in the efficacy of relics and miracles. The dread mysterious powers of the Church were concentrated in the hands of the bishop by direct succession from the Apostles, and by them transmitted and delegated to her priests. For a long time it was by his act alone that admission to the Church was conferred in baptism. The awful power of the priest in the holy mysteries came to him only through the bishop's hands at ordination. He alone could by his doom cut off the impenitent from the Church on earth and from all hope in the world to come.

Wielding such tremendous spiritual power, and having absolutely under his control a great spiritual army in the clergy, the bishop was bound to have a commanding place in secular affairs. He was also capable of impressing with a salutary fear and reverence the German converts to the Church. Even before their conversion the Frank chiefs lent an ear to the counsels of such a potentate as the Bishop of Rheims. When they became the loyal, if ignorant, sons and champions of the Church, its chief pastors gained a new and redoubtable influence over them. Their kings were often men of reckless character and dissolute lives, faithless and violent. Yet they had, as a rule, a wholesome dread of the awful penalties which the Church had ready in her armoury, and a shrewd eye for the blessing she could offer to their ambition. Nor was the courage wanting to assert the power of the Church over recreant kings and nobles. One bishop at High Mass, in the presence of the king, ordered a throng of debauched courtiers to leave the church, and he was obeyed. The same bishop more than once excommunicated the dangerous King Chlothar in spite of all his threats of vengeance. Sometimes a king bowed before the ecclesiastical dignity of bishops who were morally degraded, and who were even repudiated by popular feeling. Two bishops of infamous character had, after long impunity, been degraded from their office by sentence of an episcopal synod, but, on an appeal, they had been exculpated and restored by a singular papal clemency. Renewed scandals and ferocious violence aroused popular indignation to such heat that King Guntram was obliged to relegate the reprobate ecclesiastics to a monastery. Just at this time the King's son fell grievously ill, and the courtier friends of the two criminal bishops suggested that the imprisonment of the " holy " men might have drawn down the calamity ! Guntram, who knew their guilt, ordered their immediate release, and actually begged their prayers

for the safety of his children ! If such was the abject reverence
for the episcopal office, even when held by depraved and abandoned men, we can understand the influence which was wielded
by bishops such as SS. Rémi, Avitus, Nicetius, and by Gregory of
Tours, who, in addition to the supernatural claims of their office,
brought a record of spotless sanctity and a proved capacity for
governing men. The need of the age was for statesmanship; and
the Church often supplied the want. The bishop often had to
travel to court, and there he took his place as one of the advisers
of the king, in the great councils of the realm, by the side of the
highest secular officers and the nobles. With his inviolable
dignity he could oppose, or even rebuke, a Frank monarch with
a freedom and fearlessness which no secular courtier would have
dared to use. He sat beside the count as adviser or assessor in
provincial tribunals, and he often defended his flock against the
oppression of royal officers, and, although often assailed by secret
detraction and intrigue, he was hardly ever exposed to insult or
violence. Even when suspected of treason, he could only be
tried by an episcopal court. Bishops were even sometimes
called on to mediate between the kings in their almost incessant
wars, or to go on embassies to foreign powers. For such functions
they had peculiar qualifications. In the early times of the
Frank monarchy they were generally men of Gallo-Roman
stock, sprung from old senatorial families with a long tradition
of social dignity. As time went on, many of them, especially
those directly nominated by the king, had held office at court
as Domestic, Referendary, or Count, and had acquired a knowledge of administration and the habit of command. In his
official career the future bishop had formed many powerful
friendships, which would secure influence and support for the
interests of the Church. When we consider their combined temporal and spiritual power, we cannot wonder that the Frank
kings began to be jealous and suspicious of the domination of the
chiefs of the Church. Chilperic complained that the royal power
and the wealth of France were passing into the hands of the
Episcopate. The danger from it was clearly revealed by the
support given to the pretender Gundobald by Theodore of Marseilles and Bertram of Bordeaux, and the conspiracy against the
Austrasian court which was organised by Egidius of Rheims.
Policy or superstition indeed forbade the kings to court an open

conflict with the Church. They did not, like the Eastern emperors, meddle in theological controversy, if we exclude the blundering Sabellianism of Chilperic ; nor did they interfere in the internal government of the Church. The bishop in his diocese remained an absolute monarch. But in several important respects the Church lost some of the freedom it had enjoyed before the fall of the Empire. In the election of a bishop by the clergy and the people, in which the Roman state seldom interfered, the Frank kings, as we shall show, claimed to have a voice more or less decisive. So great and rich a prize was often directly awarded to one of their courtiers. The contest had varying issue. But in the end the Church in its Councils had to recognise the consent of the monarch as necessary for consecration by the metropolitan. It is also clear, from the records of Councils, that they could not be convoked without the king's consent, and that his approval was necessary to give effect to their decisions. Further, as the clergy were exempt from military service, no bishop could ordain a freeman without royal permission, with the result that the priesthood was largely recruited from the servile class.

But in the purely spiritual sphere the Gallic bishops of the sixth century were singularly free from external control. The see of S. Peter had sometimes asserted an authority in Gaul in the fourth and fifth centuries, although in the end of the fifth Popes Gelasius and Symmachus had found themselves paralysed by the invasions in deciding between Arles and Vienne for the primacy of Gaul. In the sixth century the Gallic Church was left free to organise itself, without any interference or dictation from Rome. The successive invasions of Italy, and the successive triumphs of Gothic, Eastern, and Lombard princes, while at times they might seem to leave the popes as the one representative of Roman power in Italy, crippled or suspended their efforts to maintain or extend their sway in the West. From the time of S. Caesarius of Arles to the accession of Gregory the Great there is hardly a sign of any recognition of the papal power in Gaul. In the history of Gregory of Tours there is only a single reference to any appeal of the Gallic clergy to Rome ; and it is one which is somewhat damaging to the authority of the Holy See. The two infamous brothers who held the sees of Embrun and Gap, tainted with every vice and absolutely shameless in their depravity, had been degraded from their office by a synod at Lyons, but were allowed by King Guntram to appeal to Rome. The Pope, John III., absolved them and ordered them to be restored to their dioceses. During all this century the bishops held their Councils subject only to the sanction of the Frank kings. In their proceedings there is no trace of any papal control, and indeed the papal scheme for the organisation of the Gallic Church is in one important point set aside or ignored. The Archbishop of Arles had by successive popes been constituted vicar of the apostolic see in the West. But only once, at the Council of Agde in 506, held under the authority of the Visigothic king Alaric II., did the Archbishop of Arles preside. At other later synods the presidents were the Archbishops of Lyons, Bourges, and Vienne. Thus the Gallic Church did not come under the sway of any patriarch or primate. The national churches of the East, of Egypt or Syria or Palestine, were organised under the rule of a patriarch. But in the nationalities of the West, the fluctuating conditions of their political life forbade the rise of a patriarchal government corresponding to those of Byzantium, Alexandria, Antioch, and Jerusalem. The old præ-fecture of the Gauls was partitioned among various Teutonic monarchies ; and Gaul itself, at first divided between Visigoth, Frank, and Burgundian, was, after the Frank conquest, split up by inheritance among the descendants of Clovis, with boundaries continually shifting and blurred. The Archbishop of Arles or Lyons, of Bourges or Vienne, might for the moment seem clothed with primatial dignity. But no enduring central Episcopate could under such conditions be established, and the policy of Rome did not view with favour such a concentration of ecclesi-astical power. Even the power of metropolitan bishops in Gaul was wavering and feeble. The organisation of the Gallic Church had followed the lines of demarcation in the Roman administra-tive system. And the prelate of the chief town of a province naturally acquired a predominant authority as metropolitan over the other provincial bishops. But the ecclesiastical im-portance of chief towns was liable to serious alteration in an age of wars and new conquests. The Archbishop of Arles could not hold metropolitan rank in Frank territory when Arles was governed by Theodoric the Goth. The metropolitan of Lyons might have bishops nominally under his sway who belonged to

the realm of the Visigoth or the Frank. Further, the metropolitan derived his consequence from the size and importance of
his city. But, owing to wars and invasions, the relative importance
of cities often greatly changed. A once rich and populous place,
deserving the name of metropolis, might become impoverished
and lose a large part of its population. Thus it came about, not
only that no great central episcopal power established itself in
Gaul, but that the authority even of the metropolitan bishops
was circumscribed, and is little heard of in the Acts of the
Councils of the sixth century. The Bishop of Rome did not
wish to see the rise of a spiritual power in the West which might
be a rival to Italian ambitions. The ordinary bishops, paying a
distant reverence to the Roman see, saw their wealth and diocesan
power growing steadily, with only an occasional check and limita-
tion from the Frank kings. And with the Frank kings they could
treat, at least, on equal terms. Each in his own sphere commanding supreme spiritual power, and called on to assist in the
civil government of his district as well as in the general councils
of the realm, the bishops were not inclined to defer to the fading
authority of an archbishop in a decaying provincial capital. In
this way, by gradual decline, the power of the metropolitans grew
less and less effective. They retained, indeed, a certain authority
in episcopal elections and in deciding disputes among the bishops
of their provinces. But from the sixth to the eighth century
even this authority steadily decayed, and in the early years of
the Carolingian dynasty it had almost vanished.

Thus the power of each bishop in his diocese was one almost
uncontrolled and despotic. It was most deeply rooted in his
absolute power over the clergy. He was the source from which
they drew their orders and sacramental powers. No man could
be ordained unless in the diocese of his birth, except perhaps
with the consent of his bishop. In dispensing the sacraments
the priest was merely the delegate of his superior. He was
supported from funds which were under the bishop's absolute
control, and dispensed at his pleasure. His whole life and
conduct were subject to episcopal discipline, with a certain
right of appeal to the episcopal synod. No priest could leave
the bounds of his diocese without his bishop's leave, nor be
admitted to office in another diocese without letters from his
bishop. He could not present himself before the king with

any petition, nor appear before a secular judge, without the express permission of his ecclesiastical superior. He was strictly forbidden to seek the patronage of the great to shield him in evasion of duty or in wrongful possession of the goods of the Church. Any conspiracy of rebellious clerks against their bishop is sternly repressed. The enactments against clerical incontinence, or even the temptations to it, against the bearing of arms, or hawking and hunting by the higher orders of the clergy, were salutary and necessary measures. But it is also clear that the ordinary priest is more and more treated as an *ascriptus glebae* (or *dioecesi*), which he often was literally by birth, with few personal rights. It is probable that this was often a benevolent despotism, softened by charity and the respect due to all who ministered at the altar or in the hour of death. But it was still a despotism.

But beside the various orders of those who took a part in Divine service, the lectors, exorcists, subdeacons, deacons, and presbyters, there was a great body attached to the Church who could claim the title of " clerici ". The greater churches were served by a numerous corps whose functions were more humble than the priestly, but who were protected and dignified by the clerical name, the acolytes, vergers, custodians of the holy things in the hours of darkness, those generally engaged in the more menial and mechanical offices. This class, enjoying to some extent the sacrosanct character of the higher clergy, were yet free from some of its restraints and obligations. They could marry, they could trade and lend at usury. They had been in Imperial times released from the dreaded burden of the Curia. Alike in the Imperial and the Merovingian times, such a position, however humble it might seem, was coveted for its safety and its immunities ; and both the emperors and the Frank kings, in the interest of the State, had to guard the entrance to it as offering a door of escape from public duty. But it must have been a numerous class, and they were almost absolutely under the bishop's power. He was their sole judge, and could correct and punish. Even their children were under his sole authority. He could strip them of their clerical privileges, while they could not renounce their duties. The *clerici* of a diocese, high and inferior, thus formed a great class over whom the bishop had almost boundless control, and which was a formidable bodyguard.

The redemption of captives, which so often shines out in the charitable works of saints and great churchmen, added large numbers to the army of the Church. Many of them were admitted to the priesthood or took monastic vows. And the increasing number of men in holy orders who were of servile origin, while it may have tended to lower the status of the priesthood, must have raised the power of the bishop. Moreover, the emancipation of serfs, which was recommended as a pious duty *pro remedio animae*, tended to the same end. The ceremony was performed with solemn forms, redolent of old Roman law, before the altar in the presence of the clergy. The archdeacon drew up the formal deed of manumission in which the master renounced his rights of patronage, which were transferred to the Church and the patron saint. The new freedman obtained the most powerful protection in that age, but he also became liable for dues and services, and he and his descendants became the subjects of the bishop. Thus the bishop had gathered into his hands a vast temporal power, in addition to his august spiritual authority as the channel of Divine grace from its source in the apostolic age. He dispensed at his will the stipends of his clergy, and held them in a dependence almost as complete as that of the serfs on his estates. He was the master of great territorial possessions, with thousands of obedient subjects. Around his great Church there was gathered a crowd of the poor who were fed by the wealth of the Church and who were ready to take up arms in its defence. He had a seat on the bench of justice beside the count or governor, and had a potent voice in suggesting and controlling their decisions. Or he travelled to court with a stately train, and there took his place in the great councils of the realm by the side of the highest ministers and nobles. He could oppose, and even rebuke, a king on occasion with a fearless freedom which no secular courtier would have dared to use. And although sometimes assailed by secret treachery and intrigue, he was hardly ever in danger of violence.

A position of such power and dignity was necessarily one of laborious and varied activity. The diary of a bishop like S. Germanus or Gregory of Tours would be a priceless possession. Baptisms, ordinations, daily services and preaching in the church, the consecration of new basilicas and oratories on distant estates, questions of finance or the protection of Church lands, were regular duties of daily routine of which the bishop could not relieve himself. There were many others less regular, but in their number and frequency putting a constant strain on his energy: journeys to the king's presence, or on embassies, attendance at Church Councils or at the obsequies of a brother prelate, the frequent reception and entertainment of passing travellers or envoys on their way from abroad, or the superintendence of some great engineering work called for by public demand or convenience. Above all, there was the vigilant care for the discipline of a great clerical army often scattered in remote rural parishes. The bishops made regular tours of visitation in their dioceses, and in those days of slow and difficult communications this must have been often an arduous task. In earlier times, when Christianity was spreading among the pagans in rural districts, there had been created an order of Chorepiscopi to perform some of, if not all, the bishop's functions in the country. In the sixth century those country bishops are seldom heard of. But the bishops had now the assistance of a functionary called archpresbyter, who at this time appears to have developed into the head or dean of a rural chapter. Thus we hear of a certain Munderic who, about the middle of the sixth century, was by Guntram's command ordained bishop on condition that he acted as archpresbyter of Tonnerre, with the right of succession to Tetricus of Langres. Intrigues against Guntram led to Munderic's expulsion from this office, and, after many vicissitudes, we find him installed again by Sigibert with jurisdiction over fifteen parishes at an obscure place called " Vicus Arisitensis ". The powers and functions of these " suffragans ", if we may call them so, seem to have varied, and they probably depended on the will of the bishop and the needs of the diocese. The functions of the archdeacon are better defined. The diaconate, from the apostolic age, was an office of power and dignity, with some limitations as to service at the altar. It was particularly charged with dispensing the sacred revenues to the poor, and the superintendence of the moral life and conversation of the faithful. In ancient patristic language, the deacon was to be " the bishop's eyes and ears and right hand and heart ". The archdeacon, whether originally chosen by the bishop from among the deacons or coming to his charge by seniority, gathered up all the powers and functions of the diaconate, and rose to still higher power. He was the chief guardian of the treasury of the Church and watched over the provision for the poor, orphans, and widows. He attended the bishop at the altar, ministered the sacred cup, and ordered the details of the holy offices. He had a share in conferring the minor orders and had powers of censure over the inferior clergy. Although in this century the archdeacon resided in the episcopal town, yet he had a general superintendence of the whole diocese, and could, by the bishop's order, inquire into the spiritual state of parishes and the condition of ecclesiastical buildings and finance. It is not surprising that, with the eyes of the diocese upon him, he should often have been marked out for the succession of the see, and sometimes, if ambitious and unscrupulous, that he should have troubled the bishop by factious intrigue.

The election to an office of such vast powers as the bishop's was a matter of great importance, and the share in it of the people, the clergy, the bishops, and finally the State, from early times varied greatly both in theory and practice. The one fixed principle as to the election of a bishop was that only a bishop could institute him and invest him with his sacred powers and commission. As to the share of the people in his choice, the language in which it is described from the earliest times is wavering and uncertain. Sometimes the community at large joins in the election ; sometimes it has only the power of rejecting an unworthy candidate ; sometimes the people are present to offer their judgement and testimony as to his fitness. The decisions of the Councils also leave the popular share in the election doubtful. But it seems to have been generally agreed among the Fathers of the fourth century that a bishop should not be forced on an unwilling people ; and the good sense which generally guided the Western Church frowned on any attempt to do so. Pope Leo I. (445) and the Emperor Valentinian III. rebuked the bishops of the provinces of Arles and Vienne for disregarding the wishes of the " people " as to their future pastor. But the word " people ", in records of these elections, is a vague term, and sometimes seems to embrace all classes—the clergy, the notables or *honorati*, the municipal *ordo*, and the plebeian class. If all these came to an election, it might be questioned whether any basilica of that time could hold them. And the

manner of voting also is a subject of doubt.   It could hardly be
by any written form.   It may have been by show of hands.
But more probably it was generally by acclamation or the
opposite.   All we can gather is that the metropolitan and his
co-provincial bishops were bound, in selecting and instituting
a new bishop, to do their best to interpret the prevailing feeling
of the Christian people about the merits of the candidates for
the office, and not to disregard it.   If the people were divided
in opposing factions, then the presiding bishops might and
did exercise their power to consecrate the man of their own
choice.

In the century preceding the Frank conquest, from various
causes, the power of the people in episcopal elections seems often
to have asserted its predominance.   On the fall of paganism the
Christian bishop succeeded to the dignity of the chief priest of
the Augustan cult in the municipal community, who had been
chosen by popular voice from among the great senatorial families.
The bishop, in the confusion of the times and the decay of the
old Imperial system, was obliged to assume many secular functions of municipal government, and the people naturally turned
their eyes to some member of the old territorial houses (with
hereditary power and dignity) as likely to be their safest leader.
In that way Sidonius Apollinaris, a literary *grand seigneur*, who
had borne a part in the great world of Rome, was called to the
bishopric of Auvergne during the Visigothic invasion.   The
popular power also gained for the time from the fact that the
Church in Gaul was long a missionary Church, and only became
fully organised in the sixth century.   S. Martin, for example,
was made Bishop of Tours by an extraordinary outburst of
popular enthusiasm, which completely overwhelmed the provincial bishops, who had a lofty contempt for the great saint
and missionary.   When Aeonius, Bishop of Arles, felt that his
end was near, he appealed to the clergy and citizens to elect
Caesarius as his successor, and his wishes were obeyed.   During
the years of the Visigothic settlement in Southern Gaul, on the
death of S. Martin, Briccius was raised to the see of Tours by
the unanimous voice of the people.   On a charge of immorality,
after some curious tests of his innocence had been applied,
Briccius was expelled by his flock with every mark of ignominy,
and one, Justinianus, was elected in his place.   Meanwhile

Briccius had gone to appeal to the Pope, confessing that his calamity was a punishment for reviling S. Martin as a madman. Justinianus, who had followed him to Rome to vindicate the decision of the people, died " by the judgement of God ". His successor Armentius, also elected by the people, also died on the return of the saintly Briccius with the absolution of the Pope. He came back to his see, apparently, with the consent of the people, and enjoyed, we should say undeservedly, " seven happy years ". Two things emerge from this apparently dull tale of unpunished hypocrisy : one is the absolute power of the people at the time in appointing and degrading a bishop ; and the other is the unscrupulous charity with which churchmen will sometimes screen offences which lay opinion condemns.

But, in other cases, the power of the people in elections was neutralised by dissension caused by the number of competing candidates. The prize was the greatest open to provincial ambition, and men of high birth and wealth did not hesitate to seek it by intrigue, seductive promises, and even by open bribery. The people broke into furious factions, each clamorously backing its favourite candidate. We have two invaluable pictures of such scenes from the pen of Sidonius Apollinaris at the elections to the vacant sees of Chalon and Bourges in 470 and 472. In the former case the metropolitan of Lyons and his co-provincials disregarded the three popular candidates, and boldly selected a man who was not a candidate at all. The people, rendered helpless by their divisions, in the end angrily acquiesced. In the other case, the election to the metropolitan see of Bourges, the competitors were so numerous, and rivalry and intrigue were so rampant, that in the end the people renounced their right to declare their choice, and, in the absence of the metropolitan, left the decision in the hands of the Bishop of Clermont. He took some time for reflection, and having convoked another assembly of the people he designated a layman named Simplicius, and justified his choice in a long oration. It is interesting to observe the qualities which marked out Simplicius for the sacred office. He was a man of high birth and riches ; he had shown practical talent as an administrator ; and he had a high moral and religious character, which apparently distinguished him from the competitors whom the Bishop of Clermont calmly ignored. In these instructive cases of episcopal election the rights of the people in theory are undisputed, and the task of selection for the see is only assumed or accepted by the presiding prelates because the electors were hopelessly paralysed by their dissensions.

But after the Frank conquest a new and powerful force appeared to assert itself in the choice of a bishop. It was not to be expected that the new monarchy founded on force would long abstain from interfering in the appointment of a dignitary with such high spiritual claims and such growing temporal power. The Frank kings, who seldom showed anything but respect for the princes of the Church, were bound to it by policy and by faith. The Church hailed them as, alone among the new royal Teutonic houses, its faithful sons and champions. And Clovis and his successors knew well the value of such a character. The early Merovingians had perhaps more statesmanship than the conventional estimate gives them credit for. They had a wholesome, if superstitious, dread of the power which could defy them and inflict upon them a doom more terrible than any that they themselves could impose. But they also recognised in the bishop a great popular leader, who had succeeded to much of the power of the old municipal authorities, and who, from rank and official prestige, might become a valuable agent and ally in civil administration. If the choice of such powerful functionaries were left entirely to the will of the people and the provincial bishops, the Church, through its great chiefs, might make itself a dangerous rival of the State. Clovis, even in his pagan days, was deferential to the bishops, and specially to S. Rémi. Yet there is extant a letter of S. Rémi which shows how early the young royal convert began to bend the bishops to his will. The Bishop of Rheims had been reproached by his colleagues for ordaining an unworthy priest named Claudius against the Canons. He replied that he had done so at the will of a man who was a great conqueror and ruler, and the defender of the Catholic faith. The letters of Clovis to the bishops and of the bishops to him show that both sides recognised one another's strength, and that both expected to profit by the alliance. But while paying profound deference to the Church, the Frank kings from the first determined to have a powerful voice in the selection of the bishops. And, without any overweening self-assertion, they easily found their opportunity in the dissension and corruption which frequently characterised an episcopal election.

The Acts of Councils, for at least the first half of the sixth century, give no hint of royal interference in episcopal elections. The Councils of 511 and 533 and 538 do not refer to it. Election by the clergy and the people, with the final seal of the metropolitan, seems to be the rule. It is only in the Council of 549 that the king is recognised as a partner in the election. And in 557 that recognition is roughly and peremptorily withdrawn ; the old rules of episcopal election are reaffirmed, and any candidate who presumes to usurp the dignity merely on the strength of a royal mandate is to be rejected by the provincial bishops. The details of episcopal elections in Gregory of Tours from 515 will show that the Acts of Councils are not to be treated as a final and exhaustive authority for the history of the Church in the choice of its chiefs. And the testimony of Gregory cannot be lightly set aside, because the earliest instances of royal interference in the election of bishops are from his own native district of Auvergne in the generation just before his birth. It is singular that the first case is one in which a descendant of Sidonius Apollinaris is concerned. Eufrasius, the twelfth bishop of Auvergne, died four years after the death of Clovis. The choice of the Arvernian people fell on Quintianus, who had fled from Rodez on a charge of disloyalty to the Visigoths. But the son of Sidonius, who had led the chivalry of Auvergne in the great battle of Vouglé, was a powerful candidate, and his wife and sister were eager in his cause. They appealed to Quintianus to forgo for a time his preferment, and Apollinaris, by lavish bribes, obtained the office from the King, and was accepted by the people of the diocese ; but he lived only four months, and Quintianus was ordained his successor by the command of Theuderic. Here, in the year 515, it is plain that the royal mandate, won by corrupt intrigue, overrides the choice of the people, and that the people submit to it without a murmur. In the case of Quintianus there is not a word of any second election by the people. They are simply convoked to witness his ordination by the order of Theuderic, and in presence of his commissioners. When the see of Trèves became vacant in 527, the King designated for the office the abbot Nicetius, who had often rebuked his vices. The people obediently assented, and

Theuderic issued the order for his institution. Here again we have the *congé d'élire* of our modern practice by which the appointment is really made by the Crown, and the assent of the nominal electors is tacitly assumed.

Gregory does not conceal the fact that simony was becoming rampant at this time. And certainly the elections to the see of Auvergne, for which he had peculiar means of information, give one no very high conception of the clerical character of that region. They also show that the power of the court in episcopal elections was irresistible. On the death of Bishop Quintianus there was great intrigue and agitation about the succession to the see. Gallus, the uncle of Gregory, who along with fervent piety was not without old family pride, announced that all this excitement was futile, and that he meant to be the bishop, a declaration for which he actually suffered violence from a priest. He took his way calmly to the court, and, in spite of the efforts and proffered bribes of the clergy, he was sent back with a royal order for his institution. But the ecclesiastical life and discipline of Auvergne must have been in a perilous condition when priests could boldly offer to purchase the apostolic office, and when the holder of it could be assailed with blows and insults. It seems as if an honest, if loose-living, king might be surer in his choice of a chief pastor than a mob of provincial priests, who were maddened by faction and jealousy, and had lost all sense of the grace of the Episcopate. And the choice of the King did fall on the right man. Gallus had been long known to Theuderic and his court, and, by his courage and devotion in the terrors of fire, earthquake, and pestilence, he amply justified the royal choice.

Twenty years later, when Gallus died, the appointment of his successor exhibits the same spirit of faction and the same recognition of the royal power. There were two aspirants to the sacred office—Cato, an aged and devoted priest, though inordinately vain of his services ; and Cautinus, the archdeacon, a man of doubtful character. The Austrasian king, Theudebald, was then a minor, and the provincial bishops, seeing that Cato had strong popular support, proposed to consecrate him at once, and, by influencing the King's council, to protect him from the consequences of the irregularity. Cato, however, whether from proud confidence in his merit, as Gregory says, or from caution, repelled the officious patronage of the bishops, and determined to win the bishopric in regular fashion (*canonice*). He was formally elected by people and clergy, and, without waiting for consecration, began to assume the airs of episcopal authority. In particular, he threatened to remove Cautinus, the archdeacon, and probably not without good grounds. But the archdeacon, who was evidently a shrewd man of the world, humbly begged to be allowed to do the bishop-designate a service by winning from the court the royal sanction for his consecration. The offer was contemptuously rejected. Cautinus, however, determined to go to court without leave, and for a different purpose than that which he professed. He departed by night, announced the vacancy of the see to the King's council, and secured the royal order for his own institution. In violation of the Canons, he was consecrated there and then in the church of Metz. The messengers sent by Cato to the court arrived too late. Cautinus, escorted by a train of clergy and court officials, was sent back to Auvergne, and, with strange inconsistency, was enthusiastically received by the clergy and people of the diocese. Here we see how royal power, even when the king is an infant, can enthrone a bishop in the face of a great body of popular opinion. Cato refused to recognise or submit to Cautinus as bishop; there was a standing feud between them, and the result was that the Arvernian clergy were divided into two camps, one devoted to the bishop and the other to his less fortunate rival.

In a short time the see of Tours became vacant, and Cato was designated by the people for the approval of Chlothar. The King issued his mandate, and the clergy, with the abbot at their head, hastened to "announce the royal will to Cato". But Cato had attached himself to Chramnus, the rebellious son of Chlothar, who was then supreme in Auvergne, and he had obtained from Chramnus a promise that, on his succession after Chlothar's death, Cautinus should be ejected from the bishopric of Auvergne and Cato should succeed him. Cato for some days deferred his answer to the deputation from Tours, doubtless weighing his chances of preferment. At last he mustered a crowd of the poor people, to whom he had lavishly ministered, and who clamorously entreated him not to forsake them. This is all attributed by Gregory to Cato's vanity. But a devoted priest, such as Cato evidently was, may well have wished to relieve the diocese of a bishop like Cautinus, who, according to Gregory, had drunk himself into epilepsy, and in order to secure a property left by S. Clothilde had buried alive a priest who refused to betray his trust. The deputation returned, and the people of Tours proposed one Eufronius, of Gregory's race, as bishop. Chlothar sharply answered that he had issued his mandate for the ordination of Cato, and demanded to know why his orders had been set at naught (*jussio spreta*). Just as the reason had been explained, that Cato himself had refused the see of Tours, Cato himself appeared at court and begged of the King that Cautinus might be ejected from the bishopric of Auvergne, and that he might be his successor. When this impudent request was treated with contempt, the vain priest actually begged for the see of Tours which he had just declined. It is needless to say that he was dismissed in confusion from the presence. Nothing can be clearer in all this rather tangled story than the practical supremacy of the king, when he chose to assert it, in episcopal elections. It is significant that it was in the following year, 557, that the Council of Paris enacted that the ancient system of canonical election must be observed, and that no bishop should be thrust on a diocese by the mere authority of the prince. Eufronius, the new bishop of Tours, by the choice of the people, was a member of that council.

An even more striking case of royal supremacy is that of Emerius of Saintes. All canonical rules had been disregarded at his election. He had been installed by the mere fiat of Chlothar, and he had never received the benediction of the metropolitan. On this ground, or more probably on others of a personal character not revealed, he was removed by Leontius of Bordeaux and his co-provincials, and a certain Heraclius, by the consent of the diocese, was chosen in his stead. By this time Charibert was on the throne of Neustria, and an envoy was sent to notify the proposed election for his sanction. The reply of the King is the most decided, and apparently undisputed, assertion of the royal power in the election of a bishop. By the King's order the wretched envoy was flung on a cart piled with thorns and was driven into exile, and Charibert fiercely demanded if it was thought that no son of Chlothar was left to uphold his acts. Emerius was reinstated by a commission appointed by the King, and Leontius for his part in the affair was mulcted in a sum of

1000 *aurei*. Gregory, in a curt comment, would seem to admit
that Charibert was rightfully vindicating an insult to the royal
authority.

Domnulus, the pious abbot of S. Laurence's at Paris, had
rendered much trusty service to Chlothar, and the King watched
for an opportunity of promoting him. The bishopric of Avignon
fell vacant, and Chlothar designated him for it. But Domnulus
begged that he might not be banished from the King's presence
to a society where his rude culture would be ill at ease among
a society of pedants and philosophers such as that of Provence.
The position would be one rather of humiliation than of honour.
Chlothar for the time yielded to his entreaties, but soon afterwards appointed him to the bishopric of Le Mans. There is
not a word of any popular election. After twenty years in that
office, in which Domnulus amply justified the royal choice by
his extraordinary devotion, the bishop, now enfeebled by disease,
begged that the abbot Theudulfus might be his successor.
Chilperic, who was then on the throne, at first agreed to gratify
the dying bishop's wishes. But, probably influenced by a court
intrigue, he changed his mind, and finally gave the office to his
major domus, Bodegisilus, a profligate man of the world, who
was tonsured and received all the orders within forty days.

The same royal control of episcopal elections, coupled with
open and audacious simony, meets us in the history of Burgundy.
In the year 584, the great see of Bourges being vacant, a crowd
of competitors strove to purchase the succession by offering bribes
to King Guntram. The King, in a virtuous mood, roughly
repelled them as guilty of the crime of Simon Magus, and gave
the dignity to one Sulpicius, a man of the foremost senatorial
rank, and second to none " in verse-writing and all rhetorical
art ". Yet this same prince only a few years before had been
guilty of the very crime which he now denounced. The see of
Uzès had been held by Ferreolus, a literary imitator of Sidonius,
and a descendant of the great prefect Tonantius Ferreolus, one
of Sidonius's dearest friends. There was a contest for the
vacant chair. At first a former governor of the province,
Jovinus, obtained the King's " precept " for the appointment.
But a deacon named Marcellus, belonging to one of the great
families, secured his ordination by the provincial bishops. He
was violently dispossessed by Jovinus, but in the end he " won

by bribery ". Gregory curtly records this without comment as a matter of course.

In the Lives of the Saints we find the same fluctuating and varying procedure at these elections as we have found in Gregory of Tours. Sometimes the king anticipates the popular choice; and again, he follows and confirms it. When the see of Chartres became vacant, we are told that " God inspired the heart of King Childebert " to decree the election of S. Leobinus. And the people at once, with one voice, proclaimed that the saint was the choice, not only of the King, but of God. In the following century the royal choice or command becomes even more frequent and imperative, although it often coincides with the voice of clergy and people, or sometimes composes the conflict between opposing factions. Thus Licinius, designated by the unanimous voice of the people and the nobles, became Bishop of Angers " by the command of the king ". The formula preserved by Marculf represents probably the ordinary recognised procedure in such cases. A consensus of the people is transmitted to the king humbly begging him to appoint a certain person distinguished by birth, culture, purity, and charity. In reply, the monarch, taking counsel with the great officials of the palace, and satisfied that the candidate possesses the proper qualities for the office, issues his precept for his ordination to the metropolitan and his suffragans. The *suggestio* of the people may be followed, but in the royal order it is never alluded to.

There is no sign that the Frank kings gave a preference to candidates of their own race. Their nominees, indeed, are oftener Gallo-Roman than Frank, even when they had to decide between competitors of the two races. The Roman was probably, by tradition and culture, better fitted for the pastorate, and the superiority was freely recognised by the conquerors. There is not a word in Gregory of Tours or Fortunatus to show that unfair preference was ever given to a Frank.

But, of course, the King had his personal preferences. Gregory, in his scathing character of Chilperic, says that, in his reign, few of the clergy were selected for the bishop's office. Although the Councils had placed their ban on the appointment of laymen to the high office without the interval prescribed by canonical rules, in the fifth and sixth centuries these rules seem to have been often neglected in indecent haste. To transfer a court marshal or the governor of a province to the spiritual charge of a diocese, without any preparatory discipline in his sacred duties, might seem both ludicrous and profane. Knowing what we do of the ordinary life of a duke or count or referendary, his sudden appearance as the spiritual governor of a diocese must have been, to say the least, often startling. Yet for the episcopate in those days, being quite as much a temporal as a spiritual office, long service at the court or in provincial government, on one side, may not have been an altogether bad preparation. The times were stormy; society was unsettled. The people had to be defended against the usurpations of great officials and great nobles with but scant respect for human rights, or any law human or Divine. A man who had himself borne a great part at court, or in the government of a province, might be the best defender of his people against official oppression. And there are signs in Gregory of Tours that, even in those evil days, there were men in the inner circle of the court who, according to the religious ideals of that age, were spotless and devout, and that even the most dissolute of the Merovingians could respect such a character. And thus, while some of the courtier bishops may have disgraced their office, there were others who reflected credit on the royal choice.

A long list might be drawn up of bishops who were translated from high civil or military office to the charge of a diocese, and probably our existing authorities may leave such a catalogue very incomplete. We find in it counts and dukes, and rectors of a province, referendaries, domestics, and mayors of the palace. As might be expected, they are of widely different character. The episcopate, with its vast temporal power, great possessions, and sacrosanct dignity, might not unnaturally attract both the most coarse and worldly ambition and the most refined and spiritual. Its commanding temporal power and wealth might seem to a referendary or governor of a province to offer even stronger attractions than the highest offices under the king. To some of the finer spirits, who had been caught by the ascetic enthusiasm of that age, it would promise a far more beneficent and majestic authority than any office which the Merovingians could confer. It was an age of the most violent moral contrasts, passionate ideals of passionless sanctity, and shameless cynicism of greed and sensual indulgence. The same contrasts may be expected and found in bishops taken from the official class. Probably the most favourable specimen was Gregory of Langres, the great-grandfather of Gregory of Tours. He came to the episcopal chair late in his long life, after forty years of office as Count of Autun. Of his official life we know nothing except perhaps that he was a severe judge. Yet few men of that time had lived through so many great events. Cradled in the tumult of Attila's invasion, he had seen the Imperial functionaries disappear, the Burgundians spreading along the Saône, and in his closing years the Frank conquest of Burgundy, and of the Visigoths in Aquitaine. Through all these momentous vicissitudes, with successive change of masters, the Count Gregory seems to have held his place undisturbed—whether by prestige of high family descent or by native tact, or by popular support, who can tell ? The baldest chronicle of such a career would throw an invaluable light on that obscure period of transition. That he had the support of the people among whom he so long acted as secular governor seems certain from his unanimous election to the see of Langres in 506, on the eve of the overthrow of the Visigothic power at Poitiers. Of his episcopate of more than thirty years we again know nothing, except that he was a model of ascetic sanctity, which probably kept him in calm seclusion from the wars and tumults raging around him.

Baudinus, sixteenth Bishop of Tours, had held the highest offices under Chlothar. He seems to have been an irreproachable bishop, distinguished by his lavish charities. Doubtless there were other courtly bishops with the same stainless record, who, with the instinct and habits of government, devoted themselves to spiritual duties with a loftier purpose when they received the apostolic commission. Of a number of these prelates drawn from official life Gregory tells us nothing either good or bad, but judging by his usual unsparing candour, we may interpret his silence as a favourable verdict.

But there are, unfortunately, many other cases of grievous scandal. Innocentius, Count of Javols, had accused the abbot Lupentius of having slandered Brunihildis. The abbot was summoned to court and was found innocent. On his way back he was waylaid and murdered in his tent on the Aisne, and his head was flung into the river. Yet Innocentius, his murderer,

2 K

by the favour of the Queen, was soon afterwards made Bishop of Rodez, and signalised his episcopate by violent litigation about Church lands with Ursicinus of Cahors. A character not more estimable is that of Bodegisilus, who, from being major-domo of Chlothar, was raised to the see of Le Mans. Bodegisilus received all the orders and was consecrated within forty days. From the first he was a monster of cruelty and shameless rapacity, a very wolf among his flock instead of a pastor of souls. He despoiled them openly, or by sinister influence on the judicial bench. He was guilty of brutal violence even with his own hands. He used authority to plunder even his nearest kindred. His wife was even worse, if that were possible. She tried to retain property which had been given to the Church and of which her husband was only a trustee. She inflicted obscene torture on men and women, the details of which Gregory hesitates to describe. It is difficult not to think that rumour about this depraved pair may have exaggerated their enormities. It is astounding that any population should have tolerated such a ruffian and his even more fiendish wife. Yet the monster died in his bed. It is consoling that even the aureole of the sacrosanct priesthood has not been able to save him from infamy.

The court of the Merovingians was hardly a nursery of priestly sanctity, although one here and there seems to have been able to keep unspotted an ascetic piety which generally came to him from a devout mother. But the choice of the clergy and people of a diocese was sometimes as fallible as the patronage of a king. It is painful, and not perhaps very profitable, to exhume these frailties from forgotten graves. Yet if we wish to have a true picture of the time, we need not shrink from the frankness of Gregory, with which, with all his reverence for his order, he revealed strange inconsistencies between practice and profession in the episcopate. Eunius, Bishop of Vannes, in a region then convulsed by rebellion and civil war, had gone as envoy for a rebel chief to Chilperic, who promptly ordered the bishop into exile. Recalled from exile, though not restored to his see, Eunius visited Paris. He had become a confirmed drunkard and was often seen reeling helplessly as he walked ; and once, while he was celebrating Mass, he fell down in a fit before the altar. Another bishop, Droctigisilus of Soissons, was so grossly self-indulgent that he lost his reason, and was not permitted to meet King Theudebert when he visited the town. In a curiously apologetic tone Gregory adds that, although he was gross in eating and drinking beyond the limits of clerical decency, " no one had ever made a charge of adultery against him " !

A court of forty-five bishops, at the instance of Fredegundis, was convoked in 577 in the Church of SS. Peter and Paul, which had been built by order of Clovis and where he and his queen were buried. The synod was summoned to try Bishop Praetextatus of Rouen on a charge of treason, and the president was Bertram, the Archbishop of Bordeaux. He was marked out for the position by illustrious, even royal, birth and rank, as well as by some brilliant personal qualities. He was by his mother's side closely related to Guntram of Burgundy, and both he and his mother showed the self-will and self-indulgence of the royal caste. Inheriting great riches, he maintained all the state of a high noble, and used to drive out in a carriage with four horses and an imposing retinue. Although Frank by race and temperament, Bertram affected the lingering elegance and polish of old Gallo-Roman society. Like his friend King Chilperic, he dabbled in Latin verse-writing, and was rallied by Fortunatus on his plagiarisms and halting prosody, although the inveterate parasite declares that Bertram is swept along by the tumultuous swell of verses which would have captured the applause of Roman critics. Bertram was in high favour with the court of Neustria, and according to rumour was in too high favour with its voluptuous queen. In Aquitaine he was entangled in the rising under Gundobald, and, along with the Austrasian party led by Aegidius, he lent his support to the movement, although he cautiously avoided taking part as metropolitan in the consecration of bishops designated by the pretender. In his household life he was notoriously licentious. If we may believe the scandalous gossip of the time, he kept a harem in his episcopal palace. With all the *bonhomie* and careless hauteur of the great aristocrat, he seems to have safely defied the censure of bourgeois morality, like some of the popes and cardinals of a later age. When the Gundobaldian rising was crushed, and the southern prelates who had borne a part in it came to make their peace with King Guntram, among them were Bertram of Bordeaux and Palladius of Saintes.

Gregory, who was staying at Orleans during the visit of Guntram, has left a lively narrative of the reception of the traitorous bishops by the King. Bertram was sarcastically thanked for his fidelity to his royal race. Palladius was severely charged with perjury and deception. Yet, such was the curious character of Guntram, or such the potent spell of sacerdotal dignity, that the bishops were not only safe but even treated with courtesy. The King accepted their benediction and invited them to his table. Guntram, however, was evidently dismayed and agitated by the perils which threatened his race, and appealed to the bishops for their prayers. But on the following Sunday at Mass, the passion which was always lurking under all his good nature broke out. Palladius, who had consecrated one of Gundobald's bishops, was the celebrant. The King rose in a fury, refusing to hear the sacred words from a perjured traitor, and was about to leave the church when he was surrounded by the other bishops, who protested that, having seen Palladius at the King's table, they believed him restored to favour. Palladius was recalled from the sacristy to which he had retired, and the service went on. Yet in spite of all, Palladius and Bertram were again invited to the King's table, and there, in the royal presence, they furiously assailed one another with charges of perjury, adultery, and fornication. During the same visit of the King to Orleans, Bertram had to face similar reproaches from the husband of his sister Berthegundis. Their mother, Ingitrudis, had induced her daughter to leave her husband and enter a convent, a life for which she was plainly unfitted. The desertion was condemned by Gregory as a violation of the Canons. In the end Berthegundis again left her husband, and with much treasure of her own and her husband's, took refuge with her brother at Bordeaux. The husband repeatedly begged the bishop to restore his wife, but, being always repulsed, he now appealed for redress to the King at Orleans, and accused Bertram of corrupting his sister's maids. Guntram fiercely ordered the bishop to restore Berthegundis to her husband, and Bertram obediently submitted, but, by secret messengers, told her to assume the conventual garb and retire to the convent of S. Martin. There we must leave her. Soon afterwards Bishop Bertram died. He was a great figure, with powerful influence on the politics of that tumultuous time. But it is to be feared that the blood of the Merovingians in his veins, and the wealth and worldly power of the episcopate, had left few traces of the Christian priest.

We have, for another purpose, referred to two rather disreputable bishops who had successfully appealed from the sentence of an episcopal synod to Rome. Salonius and Sagittarius were brothers who had received holy orders from Nicetius, Bishop of Lyons, and under him had been trained, it must be said, very ineffectually for the priesthood. Probably from birth and local influence, they rose together at an early age to the sees of Gap and Embrun.

Born probably at the foot of the Western Alps, which in the years of their youth had been crossed again and again by Frank or Lombard armies, they had drunk in the air of battle, and been trained to arms. They seem to have been untamed young aristocrats of the brutal type, who adopted the ecclesiastical profession merely for the chances of power and riches which it offered, and with no intention of accepting its peculiar restraints and obligations. They soon began to shock that not very squeamish age by their reckless enormities ; wholesale plunder of their people, adultery, violence, and murder were perpetrated by these Fathers in God with a brutal cynicism which might seem to verge on insanity. And, with hardly a brief return to decency, such was their career till its close. They actually sent an armed band to attack a brother bishop on the festival of his consecration. The ruffians stripped him of his robes, threatened his life, and slaughtered some of his attendants. They were tried and sentenced to be degraded by a synod which, strange to say, was presided over by Nicetius of Lyons, by whom they had been trained and consecrated. When on appeal they were absolved and restored by the Pope, they speedily broke out again in acts of violence which aroused the population and compelled the King once more to intervene. When they were summoned to the court for an investigation into the charges against them, one of them, Sagittarius, with extraordinary levity, ventured in conversation to attack the King's rather easy conjugal relations and to impeach the legitimacy of his children. This was too much even for Guntram, who was always inclined to be indulgent to the reprobate pair. They were at once deprived of their escort and all in their possession, relegated to a monastery " for penitence ", and placed under an armed guard to prevent any communication with the outer world. We have already described the fit of superstition in which the King ordered their release, and begged as they departed for their prayers for his children. These interesting brothers, on emerging from their cells, embraced one another and returned to their dioceses. For a time they seemed to be models of ascetic devotion. They kept the fasts and vigils, and were unfailing in the ritual duties of their order. But this interval of devotion was very brief. Religious restraints were soon flung off, and their feasts and drinking bouts were prolonged far into the night, so that when the clergy in the neighbouring church were performing the matin service, the bishops were still in the fever of debauch. As morning broke, along with their concubines and dissolute companions, they slept far into the day, and only rose to begin again the same round of self-indulgence.

Such instances of individual failure to rise to the high standards of the episcopal office as we have here described must not be taken as characteristic of ecclesiastical life in the Merovingian age. They are rather glaring exceptions to a general dignity and even eminence of virtue and ability, to which the strength and influence of the Episcopate is the best testimony. We may indeed venture to say that never in the long history of the Church of Rome did her bishops wield a greater power than in sixth-century Gaul. They were independent to a great degree of the central authority of the Papacy. They were men of rank and learning. The population of their dioceses looked up to them not only as the guardians of their spiritual welfare but as the protectors of their temporal interests. The boundaries of their provinces did not fluctuate as did the political frontiers of an age of struggle and conquest. They exercised some of the functions and retained some of the prestige of the vanished officialdom of the Empire. Even as regards the Frank monarchy they acted with independence and fearlessness, and were treated with respect and deference ; and in their dealings with its subordinate officials, and in particular with the counts, their authority is seen to be unquestionably superior, and they are seldom worsted when disagreement became acute even to the point of violence. They provided the one stable element in the changing society of the age. The continuity of the Roman system and the old traditions of administration and culture found in them almost their sole official

expression ; while the steady march of ecclesiastical polity continued uninterruptedly under their leadership. The state-craft
of the Roman Church, permeating and winning over the new
barbarian monarchy, worsting the Arian powers, conserving her
dogma, her authority, and her system, fortifying her power,
building up and extending the material symbols and revenues
which betokened in the temporal sphere her spiritual sway, has
seldom appeared to greater advantage than when she is seen
emerging triumphantly from the wreck of the old order to
dominate the new.

LIST OF THE PRINCIPAL ABBREVIATIONS
USED IN THE FOLLOWING NOTES

	ABBREVIATIONS
Agathias. Historici Graeci Minores, vol. ii. Ed. Dindorf	Agathias
Ammianus Marcellinus. Ed. Gardthausen. (Teubner, 1874.)	Amm. Marc.
Cassiodorus. Variae. Ed. Mommsen, M.G.H. Auct. Antiq. xii. (1894)	Cass. Var.
Chronica Minora. Ed. Mommsen, M.G.H. Auct. Antiq. xi. 2 (1894)	Chron. Min.
De Coulanges, Fustel. Histoire des institutions politiques de l'ancienne France . . .	
Vol. ii. L'Invasion germanique et la fin de l'Empire (5th ed. 1922)	De Coul. ii.
Vol. iii. La Monarchie franque (4th ed. 1922) .	De Coul. iii.
Vol. iv. L'Alleu et le domaine rural (3rd ed. 1922)	De Coul. iv.
Dill, Sir S. Roman Society from Nero to Marcus Aurelius (1904)	Dill i.
Roman Society in the Last Century of the Western Empire (2nd ed. 1910). (This work was first published in 1898.) . . .	Dill ii.
Dudden, Rev. F. Homes, B.D. Gregory the Great. 2 vols. 1905	Dudden
Ennodius. Opera. Ed. Vogel, M.G.H. Auct. Antiq. vii. (1885)	Ennod.
Fortunatus, Venantius. Opera. M.G.H. Auct. Antiq. iv. (Carmina, ed. Fr. Leo (1881); Opera pedestria, ed. B. Krusch, 1885) . .	Ven. Fort.
Fredegarius. Historia Francorum Epitomata. Ed. Migne, lxxi.; also M.G.H. R. Merov. ii. (1888) pp. 89 ff., ed. Krusch	Fred. iii.
Chronicon. Ed. Migne, vol. lxxi.; also M.G.H. R. Merov. ii. pp. 118 ff., ed. Krusch . .	Fred. iv.
Gesta Francorum, sive Liber Historiae Francorum. Ed. Krusch. M.G.H. R. Merov. ii. pp. 238-328	Hist. Franc.
Gibbon, E. Decline and Fall of the Roman Empire. Ed. Bury. Methuen. 7 vols. .	Gibbon
S. Gregory of Tours. Ed. Migne, lxxi.; also M.G.H. R. Merov. i.; Historia, ed. Arndt; Cetera Opera, ed. Krusch, 1885	G.T.

506 PRINCIPAL ABBREVIATIONS

ABBREVIATIONS

S. Gregory of Tours. Historia Francorum libri decem — G.T. Hist.
Miraculorum libri duo. i. De Gloria Beatorum
Martyrum . . . . — Glor. Martyr.
Miraculorum libri duo. ii. De Miraculis S.
Juliani . . . . — Mir. Jul.
Liber de Gloria Confessorum . . . . — Glor. Conf.
De Miraculis S. Martini libri quattuor . . — Mir. Mart.
Vitae Patrum . . . . — Vit. Patr.
Guizot, M. Histoire de la civilisation en France.
5th ed. (Paris, 1884.) . . . . . — Guizot
Hodgkin, T. Italy and her Invaders, vols. iii. and
iv. (Oxford, 1885.) . . . . . — Hodgkin
Isidorus Hispalis Episcopus. Ed. W. M. Lindsay.
(Oxford, 1911.) . . . . . . — Isid.
Jordanes. Getica. Ed. Mommsen, M.G.H. Auct.
Antiq. v. (1882) . . . . . . — Jord. Get.
John of Antioch. Fragmenta, apud Müller. F.H.G.
iv. pp. 535 ff. . . . . . . — Joh. Anti.
Lex Salica. Ed. Geffcken. (Leipzig, 1898.). . — L. Sal.
Lex Burgundionum. Ed. Bluhme (1863). M.G.H.
xiv. ; Leges (Pertz), vol. iii. pp. 407 ff. . . — L. Burg.
Lex Ripuaria. Ed. Sohm (1883). M.G.H. Leges
(Pertz), vol. v. p. 185 ff. . . . . — L. Rip.
Loebell. Gregor von Tours und seine Zeit.
(Leipzig, 1869.) . . . . . . — Löb.
Mansi, J. D. Sacrorum Conciliorum nova et amplis-
sima Collectio (1759 et seq.) . . . . — Mansi
Monod. Études critiques sur les sources de
l'époque mérovingienne. (Paris, 1872.) . . — Monod
Monumenta Germaniae Historica . . . — M.G.H.
Scriptores Rerum Merovingicarum . . — R. Merov.
Panegyrici Latini xii. Ed. Bährens. (Teubner,
1874.) . . . . — Panegyr.
Priscus, apud Müller. F.H.G. iv. pp. 69 ff. . — Prisc. frag.
Procopius of Caesarea. De Bello Gothico. Bonn
edition . . . . — Procop. Goth.
Prosper Tiro, Chronicon i. Ed. Mommsen,
M.G.H. ix. p. 341 ff. (1892) . . . . — Prosper
Salvianus. De Gubernatione Dei. Ed. Halm,
M.G.H. Auct. Antiq. i. (1877) . . . — Salvian. De Gub. Dei
Sidonius Apollinaris. Epp. et Carmina. Ed.
Luetjohann, M.G.H. Auct. Antiq. viii. (1887). — Sidon. Ep. Sidon. Carm.
Thierry, Aug. Récits des temps mérovingiens . — Thierry

The references to Gregory of Tours are to Migne, vol. lxxi., throughout.
The spelling of proper names is, in general, that of M.G.H.

NOTES AND REFERENCES

PAGE LINE
4 7 who clearly foresaw] Bell. Gall. i. 33. 4.
5 3 Ennodius, Vit. S. Epiphanii, p. 351 *sqq.* (ed. Hartel).
  17 G.T. Vit. Patr. vii. 1.
  33 Fred. iii. 2. Liber Hist. Franc. 1 *sqq.* : Historia Daretis Phrygii de
         orig. Franc. 1 *sqq.* (In M.G.H. R. Merov. ii.).
   5 prose and poetry] *e.g.* Lydus, Mag. iii. 56; Isid. ix. 2. 101; Sidon.
         Carm. xxiii. 245. Ven. Fort. vi. 2, 97.
  15 Gallienus] Aur. Vict. Caes. 33. 3 ; Panegyr. x. 17.
  21 Franks on the Euxine] Panegyr. v. 18 ; Zosimus i. 71. 2.
  37 Tac. Hist. iv. 12.
7 1 Bell. Gall. iv. 4.
   8 ferocity and faithlessness] Panegyr. iv. 18 ; vi. 4. Vopisc. Proc.
         13. 5.
  21 Amm. Marc. xvii. 8. 3.
  35 consulship] A.D. 377. A.D. 385 Bauto.
  40 Arbogastes] G.T. Hist. ii 9 [pp. 59, 60 in Migne].
8 2 Zosimus iv. 58. Gibbon iii. 182.
   9 Claudian, De laud. Stil. i. 220 *sqq.*
  16 G.T. Hist. ii. 9.
  21 Gaiso] Cod. Theod. vii. 18. 16 ; ix. 38. 11 ; cf. Cod. Just. iv. 61. 12.
  23 Aetius] Chron. Min. i. 472 ; Jord. Get. 34 (176) ; Sidon. Carm. v.
         212 *sqq.*
  28 G.T. Hist. ii. 9 sub init.
9 3 Sidon. Carm. v. 212 *sqq.*
  15 Prisc. frag. 16. (Müller, F.H.G.)
  25 Franks from beyond the Rhine] *i.e.* Ripuarian Franks. Jord
         Get. c. 36, § 192.
  27 Tonantius Ferreolus] Sidon. Ep. vii. 12. 3.
  33 Jord. Get. c. 41, § 217.
10 31 story in Fredegarius] Fred. iii. 11.
11 9 G.T. Hist. ii. 12.
  17 Maurice] This may, however, be a slip or confusion of Fredegarius
         for Marcianus (regn. 450-7).
  20 *e.g.* Löb. p. 432.
  24 scepticism] Bury ap. Gibbon, iv. 100.
12 14 Aegidius] G.T. Hist. ii. 11.
14 21 aid of S. Martin] G.T., S. Mart. i. 2.
  24 Prisc. Frag. 30 [F.H.G. p. 104].
  39 cf. Fred. iii. 11.
15 18 G.T. Hist. ii. 18.
  28 cf. Bury's note on Gibbon, iv. 49. He may be the great Odovacer.
  33 Jord. Get. 45, § 237.

16   16   forces of . . . decay]   Hodgkin, ii. 532-611.
17   10   Jord. Get. 33, § 168.
     18   Prosper, M.G.H. ix. p. 484.
     34   Cartagena]   Chron. Min. (M.G.H. x. 664 ; xi. 232).
     36   Basiliscus]   Procop. Bell. Vand. i. 6.
18   7   Ricimer]   Hodgkin, ii. 398 *sqq.*
19   9   Thierry, p. 98 *sqq.*
20   23   Jord. Get. 44, § 231.
21   2   Sidon. Ep. v. 6 and 7.
     16   Glycerius]   Jord. Get. 45, § 239 ; Joh. Anti. fragm. 209. 2 ; Müller, F.H.G.
     19   Sid. Ep. v. 6 and 7.   Or is he the Roman emperor Julius Nepos ? G.T. Hist. ii. 28.
     24   G.T. Hist. ii. 28.
     33   battles]   Hodgkin, iii. 20 *sqq.*
22   6   Jord. Get. 56, § 284.
     16   Sidon. Ep. v. 16. 2.
     28   Ennodius]   Vit. S. Epiphanii, p. 351 *sqq.*   Ed. Hartel.
     38   Sidon. Ep. vii. 7. 1.
23   33   Jord. Get. 47, § 244.
24   6   Arvandus]   Sidon. Ep. i. 7 ; Gibbon, iv. 39 ff.
     27   banishment of Sidonius]   Sidon. Ep. viii. 3 ; ix. 3.
     30   Victorius]   Sidon. Ep. vii. 17.
     35   Sidon. Ep. viii. 9. 21 ff.
25   6   a more prosaic chronicle]   Probably Jord. Get. 47 ; cp. Bury's Gibbon, iv. 100.
     9   formal cession]   Procop. Goth. i. 12.
27   14   M.G.H. R. Merov. iii. 204 *sqq.*
     35   quarry]   ibid. Vit. Gen. c. 18.
     39   prisoners]   ibid. c. 26.
28   1   ten years' siege]   ibid. c. 35.
     24   ibid. c. 50.
     26   tribune]   ibid. c. 36.
     27   Defensor]   ibid. c. 41.
29   6   ibid. c. 56 ; G.T. Hist. ii. 43.
     23   M.G.H. R. Merov. iii. 239 *sqq.*
     27   G.T. Hist. ii. 31.   Ven. Fort. Op. pedestr. pp. 64 ff. [The compilation is probably not the work of Venantius Fortunatus.]
30   9   dove]   Vit. S. Remig. c. 15, p. 297.
     15   G.T. Hist. ii. 9 fin.
     19   Principius]   Sidon. Ep. viii. 14 ; ix. 8.
     34   Vit. S. Remig. c. 3, p. 263.
     37   A.D. 459.   Cf. p. 14 above.
31   1   Vit. S. Remig. c. 11, p. 291.
     11   Sidon. Ep. ix. 7.
     18   sparrows]   Vit. S. Remig. c. 5, p. 266.
     23   maiden]   ibid. c. 9, p. 285.
32   14   ibid. c. 7, p. 274.
     36   ibid. c. 11, p. 292.
33   11   ibid. c. 17, p. 306 *sq.*
     24   M.G.H. R. Merov. iii. p. 336.
34   3   dogmatism]   ibid. p. 243.
     23   bubonic plague]   G.T. Hist. iv. 5 ; Glor. Conf. 78.
     31   M.G.H. R. Merov. iii. 92 ; Vit. S. Bibiani.
     35   remained a pagan]   Vit. S. Bib. c. 2.
35   6   taxation]   ibid. c. 4.
     21   Theodoric]   ibid. c. 6.

35	29	Sidon. Ep. i. 2 ; Gibbon, iv. p. 9.
	36	Sidon. Ep. viii. 6. 13.
	38	Vit. S. Bib. c. 8.
36	5	Ven. Fort. Carm. i. 12.
	8	R. Merov. iii. p. 125 *sqq.* " Vitae Patrum Jurensium."
	14	Sidon. Ep. iv. 25. 5.
37	10	R. Merov. iii. p. 149 ; Vit. S. Lupicini, c. 10.
		G.T. Vit. Patr. i. 5
	15	Sidon. Ep. v. 13 ; cf. ii. 1.
	35	jovial] Sidon. Carm. xii.
38	12	G.T. Vit. Patr. vii.
	37	Ven. Fort. Carm. iv. 2.
39	7	Mansi, ix. 21
41	23	Guizot, i. 245 *sqq.*
42	4	faithless] Procop. Goth. ii. 25. Ed. Bonn. Salvian. De Gub. Dei, vii. 64
	21	Amm. Marc. xvii. 8.
43	1	On this whole subject cf. De Coul. iii. pp. 304-506.
	16	Guizot, i. 259.
	22	Gesta Francorum] Or Liber Historiae Francorum. Ed. Krusch, R. Merov. ii. pp. 238-328 ; ch. 4, p. 244.
44	19	great authority] Sir Henry Maine, " Ancient Law," 1861 ed., p. 297.
46	6	eel nets] L. Sal. xxvii. 19.
	7	boats at the ferry] ibid. xxi.
	10	dogs or hawks] ibid. vi. vii.
	33	Guizot, i. 273 n.
47	2	bull of the royal herd] L. Sal. iii. § 5 add. iv.
	3	bees] ibid. viii.
	8	abduction of slaves] ibid. x.
	25	costs as much] ibid. xvi. 1 ; xlii. 5.
	28	antrustio . . . conviva] ibid. xli. 3 and 5.
	30	life of an ordinary Frank] ibid. xli. 1. Roman] ibid. xli. 6.
	37	600 *solidi*] ibid. xxiv. 6-7. De Coul. iii. p. 430.
48	8	to call a woman] ibid. xxx. 3 and 5.
	32	loss of an ear, etc.] See ibid. xxix. De Debilitatibus.
	35	G.T. Hist. viii. 21.
49	1	took down a poor victim] ibid. lxvii.
	5	jump on a horse] ibid. xxiii.
	36	Tac. Germ. 21.
	40	death] cf. De Coul. iii. 461 f.
50	10	de vita . . .] L. Sal. li. 2.
	20	G.T. Hist. x. 10.
	26	G.T. Mir. S. Mart. iii. 53.
	28	Becco] G.T. Mir. Iul. 16.
	36	De Coul. iii. 487
	40	ibid. 481 *sqq.*
51	27	Burgundian Law] ibid. 484 *sq.*
	31	Bavarian Code] ibid.
	36	ibid. 478.
52	5	See the Capitulary of Chilperic, M.G.H. cap. 1 (1), p. 4.
	11	noble of Auvergne] G.T. Hist. x. 8.
	14	ibid. ix. 19.
	22	Fredum] De Coul. iii. 403, 496 ; G.T. Mir. S. Mart. iv. 26.
	26	L. Sal. xliv.
	31	another chapter] ibid. lix.

52	39	Sala] Stubbs, " Constitutional History of England," i. 55.
	40	L. Rip. tit. 56, § 3.
53	6	symbolical form] L. Sal. lviii.
	14	four rods of poplar] ibid. lx.
	34	Leudes] See Bury's note on Gibbon, iv. 125.
54	5	*arimannia*] See n. on p. 218, 35 *infra.*
	7	grafio] L. Sal. li., liv.
	30	ibid. lvi.
	38	mallus] De Coul. iii. 309 *sqq.*
55	4	or his officer] ibid. 317.
	15	conventus] cf. Cic. Verr. ii. §§ 32-4 ; Hor. Sat. i. 7. 22.
	18	Tac. Germ. 11, 12.
	19	rachimburgi] cf. Stubbs, op. cit. i. p. 54 ; De Coul. iii. 314 *sq.*
	22	ibid. 360.
	32	heavy fine] L. Sal. lvii. 3.
56	2	ibid. l. 3.
	10	ibid. lvii.
	28	impossible to be present] ibid. l. 4.
	33	De Coul. iii. 317.
	40	L. Sal. l. 4
57	2	ibid. liv.
	7	L. Rip. tit. lix. See De Coul. iii. p. 420.
58	2	L. Sal. liii.
	29	a passage in the Salic law] ibid. xiv. 2.
	36	combined oath] ibid. xxxix. 2 ; xlii. 5 ; lviii.
59	11	De Coul. iii. 444.
	13	L. Sal. xiv. 2.
	27	in haraho] De Coul. iii. p. 432 *sqq.* Cf. Ducange, s. v. *arahum.*
60	19	lidus] L. Sal. xxvi. 1. Probably a *colonus adscriptus glebae* and a degree higher than the serf (*servus*).
	26	villas] On this see De Coul. iv. 1 ff.
61	12	Avitacum] Sidon. Ep. ii. 2. 3. Prusianum] ibid. ii. 9. 7.
	17	Curtis] G.T. Hist. x. 16 ; L. Sal. vi. 3 ; vii. 7. = class. Latin *cohors* (chors). *e.g.* Varro. R.R. 1. 13. 2 ; Cato, De agric. 39 ; Martial, xi. 52. 14.
	36	rubric of the emended law] L. Sal. Cap. ix. 9.
62	23	cf. Guizot, i. 297 *sqq.*
63	10	G.T. Hist. ii. 33 fin.
	32	crossed the Rhine] Fred. ii. 46.
	35	Aetius] Authorities in Clinton s. anno 438.
	37	G.T. Hist. ii. 9 fin.
64	12	Fred. iii. 17 ; G.T. Hist. ii. 28.
	29	G.T. Hist. ii. 34.
	33	aid of Clovis] G.T. Hist. ii. 32, 33 ; Chron. Min. i. 234.
65	1	G.T. Hist. ii. 33 fin.
	25	Leo] Sidon. Ep. iv. 22 and often.
	28	L. Burg. Praef.
66	12	Guizot, 1. 300
67	8	Burgundian neighbours] Dill, ii. p. 362.
	12	L. Burg. iv. and often.
	19	L. Burg. xxii.
	22	ibid. xxxviii. 7.
	23	intermeddle] ibid. lv.
	25	quarrelsome entry] ibid. xxv.
	27	ibid. ci.
68	9	ibid. liv.

PAGE LINE

68 16 L. Burg. lxxxiv. 2.
    18 another enactment] ibid. lxxxiv. 1.
    24 final term] ibid. lxxix.
    36 ibid. xxviii.
    39 ibid. xxxi.
69 6 ibid. l.
    13 ibid. l. 5.
    29 ibid. x.
    30 ibid. vi.
    37 ibid. lxiii., lxx.
70 2 ibid. xxvi.
    4 ibid. xxxiii.
    7 ibid. xxxv.
    13 ibid. xxi.
    28 ibid. xlix., lxxxix.
71 3 ibid. xxix.
    4 royal messengers] ibid. lxxvi.
    13 ibid. xlvii.
    34 ibid. v.
    36 woman's hair] ibid. xxxiii. Cf. xcii.
72 13 ibid. xii.
    15 slave . . . chastity] ibid. xxxv.
    19 ibid. xxxvi.
    20 ibid. lxviii.
    22 ibid. xxxiv.   Tac. Germ. 12 (for *ignavos et imbelles et corpore infames*). It was, however, a common way of executing women.
    29 right of daughter] ibid. xiv. 1.
    30 ibid. lxxiv.
    31 ibid. li.
    33 ibid. xiv. 5.
    35 ibid. xl.
    37 attestation] ibid. lx.
73 3 ibid. xlv.
    11 ibid. lxxx.
    19 In 502 the Church (or at all events a bishop) was against it : see Gibbon, iv. 128.
75 4 wolf] ibid. xlvi.
    5 vineyards] ibid. lxxxix., ciii., cvi.
    8 vagrant herds] ibid. xlix. Cf. lxxxix.
    13 ibid. xxxviii.
    16 meal] ibid. vi.
    17 boat] ibid. xciv.
    20 outlaws] ibid. xxix.
    21 fire] ibid. xli.
    22 steward] ibid. l.
    23 quarrel] ibid. xii., xlviii.
    28 present] ibid. praef. ii. § 4.
    39 ibid. cii.
77 4 G.T. Hist. ii. 12.
    13 Fred. iii. 12.
78 15 Aprunculus] G.T. Hist. ii. 23.
    18 Volusianus] G.T. Hist. ii. 26. Verus] ibid. ii. 26 ; x. 31, 8.
    31 Fred. iii. 15.
    36 Caesar's time] Bell. Gall. ii. 4, §§ 7-10.
79 3 Sidon. Ep. v. 5 ; cf. viii. 8.
    10 Gibbon, iv. 103.

PAGE LINE

79 13 G.T. Hist. ii. 27. Fred. iii. 15.

35 Paulinus, " Eucharisticos," line 575. Cf. Löb. p. 99.

80 6 G.T. Hist. ii. 27 ; Fred. iii. 16.

81 6 Löb. 102.

29 ibid. p. 106.

82 1 G.T. Hist. iii. 33.

5 Parthenius] ibid. iii. 36.

13 Celsus] G.T. Hist. iv. 24.

16 Amatus] ibid. iv. 42.

17 Mummolus] ibid.

21 ibid. ii. 27.

26 G.T. Glor. Martyr. 60.

34 Procop. Goth. 1. 12, p. 63, ed. Bonn ; Löb. 94.

83 1 Chilperic II.] Fred. iii. 17.

5 G.T. Hist. ii. 28.

22 ibid. ii. 23.

30 Fred. iii. 18. Cf. G.T. Hist. ii. 28.

84 15 ibid. iii. 19.

36 thirty years afterwards] G.T. Hist. iii. 6. See Hodgkin, iii. 360 f., 412, 415.

85 15 G.T. Hist. ii. 31.

86 4 barbaric way] cf. p. 32, l. 35.

13 G.T. Hist. ii. 29.

27 ibid.

87 7 ibid. ii. 30.

11 Rhaetia] Ennod. Panegyr. c. 15.

12 G.T. Hist. ii. 31.

34 Vit. Rem. 15 ; M.G.H. iii. 296 ff.

88 12 letter] Given in Mansi, viii. p. 193.

14 Avitus] Migne, lxxi. p. 1154.

89 10 G.T. Hist. iii. prol.

22 only 3000] So G.T. Hist. ii. 31. But see Fred. iii. 21.

26 G.T. Hist. viii. 15 ; Vit. Patr. vi. 2 ; ibid. xvii. 5.

39 Gibbon, iv. 107.

90 1 Fred. iii. 21.

23 ibid. 22.

29 G.T. Hist. ii. 32.

34 Fred. iii. 23.

91 8 G.T. Hist. ii. 32.

16 ibid. ii. 33.

92 6 Migne, lxxi. pp. 1154-6.

16 G.T. Hist. ii. 34.

29 Hodgkin, iii. 355 ff. ; Procop. Goth. i. 12, p. 65 (Bonn).

93 6 Cass. Var. ii. 27 fin.

34 Cass. Var. ii. 41.

37 Ennod. Panegyr. 15, p. 212. Ed. Vogel.

94 18 G.T. Hist. x. 31, § 7.

24 Breviarium Alarici] Teuffel-Schwabe, § 488. 2.

35 Quintianus] G.T. Hist. ii. 36 ; Vit. Patr. iv.

40 Verus] G.T. Hist. x. 31, § 8.

95 3 Galactorius] Acta Sanctorum, July [27], vol. vi. p. 434.

10 G.T. Hist. ii. 35.

27 warnings] Hodgkin, iii. 393 ff.

38 Hodgkin, iii. 396 f.

96 8 Vit. Remig. 19. M.G.H. iii. 311.

21 G.T. Hist. ii. 37 ; Psalm xviii. 39, 40.

NOTES AND REFERENCES 513

PAGE LINE
96 28 Fred. iii. 24 ; Procop. Goth. i. 12, p. 67. Bonn ed.
97 5 G.T. Hist. ii. 37.
 18 Carcassonne] Procop. B. Goth. i. 12, p. 67.
 28 Life of S. Caesarius] M.G.H. iii. 459; Vit. Caes. i. 5.
 38 ibid. 6.
98 5 ibid. 6.
 9 ibid. 8.
 13 ibid. 9. Cf. Ruricii Epist. i. 17, ii. 10.
 17 ibid. 10.
 25 ibid. 14.
 32 ibid. 18.
 35 ibid. 19.
 37 ibid. 20.
 39 ibid. 21.
99 6 ibid. 22.
 9 ibid. 26.
 12 ibid. 24.
 15 ibid. 28.
 34 ibid. 29.
100 8 ibid. 30.
 15 ibid. 31.
 32 Hodgkin, iii. 402.
101 1 Jord. Get. 58.
 3 Vit. Caes. 32.
 20 ibid. 36.
 31 ibid. 37.
 38 ibid. 38.
102 10 Hodgkin, iii. 404 ff. ; Gibbon, iv. 118.
 35 Gemellus] Cass. Var. iii. 16.
 36 provincials] ibid. 17, 42.
103 14 Cass. Var. iii. 16 fin.
 15 tribute of the fourth indiction] Cass. Var. iii. 32.
 17 stories of Massilia] ibid. iii. 41.
 21 great official] Marabadus. Ibid. iii. 34.
 23 ibid. iii. 38.
 32 Angoulême] Ecolisna. G.T. Hist. ii. 37 fin.
 34 Bordeaux and Saintonge] Hist. Franc. 17 ; R. Mer. ii. 270.
 39 See Mansi, Conc. viii. 356.
104 19 Epistle of Clovis to the Bishops. Migne, lxxi. p. 1158.
 29 G.T. Hist. ii. 38. Yet see Bury on Gibbon, iv. 119.
105 22 his successor] Briccius. G.T. Hist. x. 31. 4.
 23 Perpetuus. G.T. Hist. ii. 14 ; x. 31. 6 ; S. Mart. i. 6.
 29 largess] Hist. Franc. 17 fin.
108 5 Caesar, B.G. vi. 23.
 10 Batavi] Tac. Germ. 29.
 12 Chatti] ibid. 31.
 14 Bructeri]. ibid. 33.
 17 Marcomanni] ibid. 42.
 24 merchants] e.g. for amber. Ibid. 35 ; Pliny N.H. xxxvii. 45.
  See also Tac. Ann. ii. 62.
109 12 Maroboduus] Velleius Paterculus, ii. 108, 109; Tac. Ann. ii. 44-46,
  62-63.
 22 Hodgkin, iii. 264.
111 6 Löb. 176 n.
 15 Hodgkin, iii. 266.
112 24 G.T. Hist. v. 26 ; viii. 14.

2 L

112 25 fiscus] L. Sal. xliv. 10 ; lvi. 1[9].
    26 palatium] De Coul. iii. p. 128.
113 8 G.T. Hist. iii. 14 ; vii. 32.
    10 Pact of Andelot] A.D. 587. Given in full G.T. Hist. ix. 20.
    12 ibid. vii. 33.
    17 ibid. vii. 36. Bury, " Later Roman Empire ", ii. 61.
    21 G.T. Hist. vii. 8.
    23 Agathias, i. 3 and 4.
    25 females] De Coul. iii. p. 40 ; L. Sal. lix. 5.
    30 Sigibert] G.T. Hist. iv. 52 ; v. 1.
    33 installation] De Coul. iii. p. 54.
    37 ancient Germany] Tac. Hist. iv. 15.
    39 three instances] G.T. Hist. ii. 40 ; iv. 52 ; vii. 10.
114 6 Briva] Brives-la-Gaillarde (dép. Corrèze).
    23 figment] De Coul. ii. (L'Invasion germanique), pp. 531 ff.
    37 ibid. p. 543 ff.
    40 no trace] ibid. p. 536 ff.
116 8 populus . . . publicus] De Coul. iii. 133 ff.
    23 distinctly stated] L. Ripuar. praef.
    29 Löb. 167.
    39 G.T. Hist. ii. 34.
117 5 defender] G.T. Hist. vii. 8.
    9 L. Sal. xli.
    14 L. Sal. 1.
    18 Baddo] G.T. Hist. viii. 44 ; ix. 13.
    21 ibid. ix. 14.
    27 autocratic authority] Gibbon, iv. 122, with Bury's note.
118 23 G.T. Hist. ii. 37.
    31 put his army in motion] *Commovere exercitum, e.g.* G.T. Hist. ii. 37.
119 12 ibid. iv. 30.
    13 ibid. v. 27.
    15 De Coul. iii. p. 292.
    24 G.T. Hist. iv. 30 ; vi. 31.
    29 Fred. iv. 87.
    34 G.T. Hist. v. 27 ; vii. 42.
    40 patricians] Gibbon, iv. 139, and Bury's note.
120 16 G.T. Hist. iv. 14 ; iv. 29 ; iv. 42.
    17 De Coul. iii. p. 297.
    33 G.T. Hist. viii. 30.
121 12 plunder of Auvergne] Gibbon, iv. 135.
    14 G.T. Hist. iv. 14.
    37 ibid. vii. 8.
122 14 Arvandus] Gibbon, iv. 39 f.
    31 Ragnachar] G.T. Hist. ii. 42 ; Hist. Franc. 18 ; Löb. p. 177, quotes
        Acta Sanctorum Oct. i. 149.
123 5 G.T. Hist. ix. 36.
    17 ibid. iii. 14.
    39 ibid. iv. 16.
124 15 ibid. iv. 20.
    22 ibid. v. 2.
125 4 G.T. Hist. v. 19.
    20 Convenae] St. Bertrand de Comminges in Hautes Pyrenées.
    36 De Coul. iii. p. 251.
126 1 De Coul. iii. 253.
    7 ibid. 260 ; L. Burg. xxxviii. ; L. Ripuar. lxv. 3.
    10 ibid. 264-5.

PAGE LINE

126 16 Theodosian Code] lib. xii. tit. 1 De Decurionibus.
21 Council of Auvergne] Letter of bishops to Theudebert. Mansi,
Concil. viii. 804.
25 De Coul. iii. 266.
32 G.T. Hist. iv. 2.
37 ibid. v. 29.
38 Löb. p. 162.
127 5 G.T. Hist. ix. 30.
12 De Coul. iii. p. 271.
32 Vit. Arid. 24, Migne, lxxi. p. 1130.
34 G.T. Hist. v. 29.
128 5 ibid. v. 35.
19 De Coul. iii. p. 269.
20 forced to exempt] G.T. Hist. ix. 30.
35 Lob. p. 262.
129 9 G.T. Hist. iii. 25.
10 ibid. x. 7.
19 De Coul. iii. p. 272 f.
35 G.T. Hist. vii. 23.
130 26 De Coul. iii. 278-82.
28 G.T. Hist. iii. 36.
29 ibid. vii. 15.
33 G.T. Vit. Arid. 24.
131 15 *e.g.* G.T. Hist. iii. 30 ; vii. 21.
16 ibid. iii. 7.
18 ibid. iii. 18.
26 De Coul. iii. p. 321.
35 ibid. 325.
132 18 Becco] G.T. Mir. Iul. 16.
19 Leudastes] G.T. Mir. Mart. ii. 58.
25 in another] De Coul. iii. p. 320 ff.
29 At Vermandois] G.T. Glor. Martyr. i. 73.
133 12 De Coul. iii. 332.
13 G.T. Glor. Conf. 93.
19 sons of Magnacharius] G.T. Hist. v. 17.
21 Chundo] ibid. x. 10.
27 Three Franks] Rauchingus, Ursio, and Berthefredus. Ibid. ix. 9
and 12.
35 Sigibert] ibid. iv. 52.
134 7 Gailenus] G.T. Hist. v. 19 fin.
15 ibid. v. 40.
135 1 ibid. vi. 35.
14 Leudastes] ibid. vi. 32.
32 ibid. iv. 25 ; v. 17, 36.
136 7 De Coul. iii. p. 339.
22 G.T. Glor. Conf. 71 ; De Coul. iii. p. 344.
32 L. Sal. 18 ; G.T. Hist. x. 5.
36 ibid. v. 19 ; x. 19.
137 26 De Coul. iii. 135 ff.
138 30 Conda] Ven. Fort. Carm. vii. 16.
33 G.T. Glor. Conf. 41 ; Hist. vii. 23 ; x. 21 ; Löb. 142 n.
35 referendarius] De Coul. iii. p. 154.
40 G.T. Hist. v. 3.
139 1 ibid. v. 29.
4 De Coul. iii. 155 ff.
12 Löb. 141.

139 19 De Coul. iii. 158 f. ; G.T. Mir. Mart. i. 25.
    22 Sidonius] Ep. ii. 2 ; ii. 9.
    35 major domus] De Coul. iii. 166 f.
    38 three times] G.T. Hist. vi. 9 (Badegisilus); vi. 45; vii. 27 (Waddo); ix. 30 (Florentianus).
140 1 De Coul. iii. 170.
    9 ibid. 169.
    25 Löb. 140 n. 2.
    31 count] De Coul. iii. 196 ff. duke] ibid. 216 ff.
    36 comes palatii] See note on G.T. v. 19, p. 339. Ed. Migne.
        comes stabuli] De Coul. iii. 148.
    39 ibid. 184.
141 13 nearly always described] G.T. Hist. ix. 20 fin. ; vi. 12 ; vii. 6
    23 ibid. vi. 34.
    25 small district] cf. De Coul. iii. 187 ff. for instances ; *e.g.* G.T. Hist. vi. 12 Pagus Isiodorensis.
    27 ibid. vii. 47.
    29 comes] De Coul. iii. 197 f.
    34 Sidon. Ep. vii. 2 ; Salv. Gub. iii. 9.
142 5 G.T. Vit. Patr. vii.
    13 De Coul. iii. 211.
    16 Waitz, ii. 37 ; G.T. Hist. v. 48.
    22 ibid. iv. 4.
    24 Palladius] ibid. iv. 40.
    25 Mummolus] ibid. iv. 42.
    26 Hortensius] G.T. Vit. Patr. iv. 3.
    28 Salustius] G.T. Hist. iv. 13.
    30 Nantinus] ibid. v. 37.
    34 De Coul. iii. 208.
    39 L. Rip. 53.
143 1 G.T. Hist. v. 49.
    4 De Coul. iii. 212.
    12 G.T. Hist. vi. 19 ; vii. 12.
    36 De Coul. iii. 213.
    39 Tac. Germ. 12.
144 2 De Coul. iii. p. 350-78.
    7 rachimburgi] L. Sal. lvii.
    36 De Coul. iii. 220 ff. for examples.
145 4 G.T. Glor. Mart. 34.
    5 De Coul. iii. 385.
    6 Peter] G.T. Hist. v. 5.
    9 ibid. x. 8.
    17 ibid. vii. 47.
146 1 ob remedium animae] *e.g.* Mir. Jul. 14.
    14 curse] G.T. Hist. iv. 35 ; Vit. Patr. iv. 3.
    16 G.T. Vit. Patr. viii. 3.
    26 G.T. Hist. vi. 22.
147 1 G.T. Hist. v. 37.
    24 ibid. v. 48, 49, 50.
149 16 Ansovaldus] G.T. Hist. v. 48.
150 19 Berny] Brinnacum = Berny-Rivière in Dept. Aisne.
    23 Thierry, ii. 173.
    31 G.T. Hist. v. 50.
151 8 reappears] ibid. vi. 32.
    17 De Coul. iii. 217.
    21 G.T. Hist. ii. 20.

PAGE LINE

151 22 Nicetius] ibid. viii. 18.
24 Ennodius] ibid. viii. 26.
24 Lupus] ibid. vi. 4 ; ix. 14.
27 another] ibid. viii. 18.
29 ducatus] De Coul. iii. 218.
31 comitatus] ibid. 200.
37 G.T. Hist. viii. 30 ; ix. 28.
40 ibid. viii. 18.
152 6 Waitz, ii. 53.
11 Ennodius] G.T. Hist. ix. 7.
14 Wintrio] ibid. viii. 18.
21 Beppolenus] ibid. viii. 31.
36 ibid. viii. 42.
153 9 ibid. x. 9.
155 13 ibid. iii. 1.
157 10 see Hodgkin, iii. 354.
18 as we have seen] See p. 95.
23 Oman, " Dark Ages," 113.
35 Chlochilaichus] So Arndt and Migne, ap. G.T. Hist. iii. 3. Oman, loc. cit., has Chrocholaicus. Beowulf, who was his brother, calls him Hygelac.
158 1 war in Thuringia] G.T. Hist. iii. 4 and 7.
20 Sigismund] ibid. iii. 5 and 6. Cf. Procop. Bell. Goth. i. 12.
159 2 Advance of Theodoric] Hodgkin, iii. 414.
12 cruel choice] G.T. Hist. iii. 18.
27 in 509] See above, p. 97. T.G. Hist. ii. 37.
28 Basolus] See Fauriel, "Histoire de la Gaule méridionale sous la domination des conquérants germains," vol. ii. p. 111.
160 3 Arcadius] ibid. iii. 9.
17 was forced] G.T. says Arcadius " cut the bar ".
24 ibid. iii. 10.
34 conquest of Burgundy] ibid. iii. 11. Cf. Mir. Jul. 13.
161 9 ibid. iii. 12.
27 G.T. Mir. Jul. 13.
39 Lovolautrum] G.T. Hist. iii. 13. Near Clermont-Ferrand.
162 3 Mauriac] Meroliacensis castor [castrum]. Arndt says it is Chastel Marthac.
16 Sigiwald] G.T. Mir. Jul. 14. Cf. Hist. iii. 13, 16, 23.
28 Hortensius] G.T. Hist. iv. 35. Cf. Vit. Patr. 4 ; and above, p. 146, 14.
33 Evodius] G.T. Vit. Patr. vi. 4.
35 Becco] Mir. Jul. 16.
163 12 Portianus] G.T. Vit. Patr. v. 2.
21 boar] ibid. xii. 2.
25 Theudebert and Guntharius] G.T. Hist. iii. 21.
29 Provence] To Dehae = Dio [dept. Hérault].
34 ibid. iii. 23.
164 1 Good qualities] ibid. iii. 25.
8 Sigivald] ibid. iii. 23, 24.
10 Bishop of Verdun] ibid. iii. 34.
15 Asteriolus] ibid. iii. 33.
18 Parthenius] ibid. iii. 36.
24 Agathias] i. 4 init.
26 coins] cf. Procop. Goth. iii. 33, p. 417 ; and Hodgkin, iv. 612 n. A partial account of the relations of Theudebert with the East Romans in G.T. Hist. iii. 32.

165   8   Theodatus]   Procop. Bell. Goth. i. 13.
      14   Hodgkin, iii. 532-4.   Procop. Bell. Goth. ii. 12.
      15   ibid. iv. 348-54.
      31   G.T. Hist. iii. 24.
      33   ibid. iii. 28 ; Hist. Franc. c. 25.
166   5   ibid. iv. 1.
      9   ibid. iii. 29.
      16   ibid. iii. 36.
      19   Buccelenus]   ibid. iv. 9.   Cf. iii. 32.
      24   Oman, p. 119.
      25   Theudebald]   ibid. iv. 9.
      35   Saxons]   ibid. iv. 10 ; iv. 14.
167   17   to **170.** 16 an episode]   G.T. Hist. iv. 13 to 20.
170   18   ibid. iv. 21.
      24   restored his church]   ibid. iv. 20.
      37   ibid. iv. 21.
171   3   divide]   ibid. iv. 22.
      11   Oman, 160, 161.   Some reference to this division in the Pact of Andelot, G.T. Hist. ix. 20 init.
      12   Charibert died]   ibid. iv. 26.
      29   diploma of King Childebert]   Hallam, i. 119 n. (note viii. to ch. 1).
172   3   hordes of Teutons]   G.T. Hist. iv. 50.
      30   ibid. iv. 27.
173   1   Venus]   Ven. Fort. vi. 1. 99.
      20   Audovera]   G.T. Hist. iv. 28.
      22   Galswintha]   ibid. iv. 28 ; Ven. Fort. vi. 5.
      29   Ven. Fort. vi. 5, 125 ff.
      31   vague hint]   ibid. 252 f.
174   16   Avars]   G.T. Hist. iv. 23 and 29.   (He calls them Huns (Chuni) ; see note in Migne.)
      26   Arles]   ibid. iv. 30.
      31   host of Germans]   ibid. iv. 50.
      36   Germanus]   ibid. iv. 52.
      37   Vitry]   ibid. *villa cui nomen est Victoriacum.*
175   19   threat]   ibid. vi. 46.
      25   Salic law]   L. Sal. lix. 5.
      25   four letters]   G.T. Hist. v. 45.   Cf. Claudius in Tac. Ann. xi. 13.
      29   ibid. v. 45.   But see vi. 46.
      30   Fortunatus]   Ven. Fort. ix. 1. 99 ff.
      32   circus]   G.T. Hist. **v.** 18.
176   2   ibid. v. 45.
      9   Priscus]   ibid. vi. 5.
      27   bishop]   By name Charterius.   Ibid. vi. 22.
      35   *blasphemabat*]   ibid. vi. 46.
177   2   G.T. Hist. viii. 1.   Fredeg. iv. 1.
      8   See Migne's note, vol. lxxi. p. 615.
      22   poor] *e.g.* ibid. vii. 40.
      23   dine . . . with traders]   ibid. viii. 1.
      24   restored]   ibid. vii. 7.
      34   one Sunday]   ibid. vii. 8.
178   9   ibid. iv. 50.
      14   protection to his widow]   ibid. vii. 7.
      24   Magnacharius]   ibid. v. 17.
      25   doctors]   ibid. v. 36.   envoys]   ibid. vii. 32.
      27   forest keepers]   Chundo.   Ibid. x. 10.
179   2   married]   ibid. iv. 28.

PAGE LINE

179 8 five cities] Pact of Andelot, ibid. ix. 20, pp. 497-500, Migne.
 20 dethroned] ibid. iv. 28.
 25 division in 567] Oman, p. 161.
 40 severed by zealous enmities] Most of the Aquitanians were of Iberian type (Strabo, iii. 1. 6). But the Bituriges who lived about Bordeaux appear to have been a Celtic tribe : so it is not improbable that there were rivalries due to race.
180 13 seized by Chilperic] ibid. v. 1.
 14 occupied by Guntram] ibid. iv. 30.
 15 Bourges] ibid. vi. 31.
 17 ten years before] ibid. iv. 46.
 28 Sigulfus] ibid. iv. 48.
 37 letter to Brunihildis] Printed with the works of S. Germanus in Migne, lxxii. 77-80.
181 12 let loose] ibid. iv. 48.
 17 solemn oath] ibid. iv. 23.
 27 Gregory] ibid. iv. 48.
 35 Saxons] ibid. iv. 43.
 39 a little later] ibid. vii. 27.
182 2 tribes . . . beyond the Rhine] ibid. iv. 50. Cf. below, p. 211, 5.
 19 three miracles] ibid. iv. 50 fin. Mir. Mart. ii. 7.
 39 curt sentence] ibid. iv. 52.
183 13 saying from Holy Writ] Prov. xxvi. 27.
 26 Brunihildis] G.T. Hist. v. 1.
184 4 Merovech] ibid. v. 2.
 27 routed] ibid. v. 3.
 29 punished] ibid. v. 14.
185 4 ibid. v. 14.
 10 death of Merovech] ibid. v. 19, latter part.
 37 some success] ibid. v. 13.
186 1 Warochus] ibid. v. 27.
 8 Marcus] ibid. v. 29.
 10 series of calamities] ibid. v. 34.
 18 plague] ibid. v. 35.
 27 Sabellian views] ibid. v. 45.
 30 Agilanes] ibid. v. 44.
187 19 Dynamius] ibid. vi. 11. Cf. Ven. Fort. vi. 9 and 10.
 36 deadly arts] ibid. v. 40.
 39 Grandees of Austrasia] ibid. vi. 3.
188 6 Lupus] ibid. vi. 4.
 7 Fortunatus] Ven. Fort, vii. 7 to 9.
 26 campaign] G.T. Hist. vi. 12. Cf. vi. 31.
 31 make peace] ibid. vi. 31.
189 12 ibid. vi. 42.
 15 journey of Rigunthis] ibid. vi. 45.
190 3 death of Chilperic] ibid. vi. 46.
 29 with him] ibid. vii. 4 ff.
191 1 swore allegiance] ibid. vii. 7.
 5 embassies] ibid. vii. 7.
 26 one Sunday] ibid. vii. 8. Cf. above, p. 177, 34.
 39 great strife] ibid. vii. 12.
192 4 conference] ibid. vii. 14.
 27 strange conspiracy] A good account is in Bury's " Later Roman Empire ", ii. 161 ff.
 34 G.T. Hist. vi. 24.
193 4 painting frescoes] ibid. vii. 36.

PAGE LINE

193 40 warned Childebert] ibid. vii. 33.
194 2 presents] ibid. ix. 28, 32.
13 Guntram Boso] ibid. vi. 26.
17 commanded] ibid. iv. 51.
21 inveigled him away] ibid. v. 14.
195 6 seized] ibid. vi. 24.
12 treachery] cp. ibid. v. 14 *nulli amicorum sacramentum dedit quod non protinus omisisset.*
21 plundering a tomb] ibid. viii. 21.
23 divided his spoil] ibid. vi. 24 fin.
40 action of Boso] ibid. vi. 26.
196 11 desolated] ibid. vi. 31.
197 1 Desiderius] ibid. v. 13.
2 thrown back] ibid. iv. 42 f. Cf. Hodgkin, v. 217-23.
11 understanding] ibid. vi. 26 ; vii. 10.
15 marched on Toulouse] ibid. vii. 9.
20 Briva] vide note p. 114, l. 6.
22 crowned] ibid. vii. 10.
24 prodigies] ibid. vii. 11.
28 Gararic] ibid. vii. 13.
35 ibid. vii. 14.
198 8 oath of allegiance] ibid. vii. 26.
17 one town] Probably Périgueux ; cf. ibid. vii. 26 ; if so, the bishop was Carterius, ibid. vi. 22.
21 Magnulfus] ibid. vii. 27.
34 Faustianus] ibid. vii. 31.
35 Sagittarius] ibid. vii. 28.
199 12 two envoys] ibid. vii. 32.
32 secret interview] ibid. vii. 33.
200 5 Desiderius . . . abandoned] ibid. vii. 34.
13 Convenae] St. Bertrand de Comminges, 50 miles S.E. of Pau.
15 foundation] See note in Migne, lxxi. p. 438.
20 defence] For this siege see G.T. Hist. vii. 35-39.
201 23 Desiderius] ibid. vii. 43.
24 Waddo] Löb. p. 204.
29 Council at Mâcon] G.T. Hist. viii. 20.
30 one bishop] Ursicinus of Cahors.
31 for Desiderius] ibid. viii. 27.
32 treasure] ibid. vii. 40.
202 33 Wandelen] ibid. viii. 22.
38 fresh plot] ibid. ix. 9. Cf. Löb. p. 205.
203 7 fortress on the Woevre] Castrum Vabrense.
11 pact of Andelot] Given in full, G.T. Hist. ix. 20.
36 doom of Guntram Boso] ibid. ix. 10.
204 2 reserved] ibid. ix. 8.
9 Ursio and Berthefredus] ibid. ix. 12.
21 Bishop of Rheims] Egidius, ibid. x. 19. Cf. ix. 14.
205 11 Sunnegesilus] ibid. ix. 38. Cf. x. 19.
11 nurse] Called Septimina.
28 twice] ibid. viii. 29 ; x. 18.
39 five times] For details cf. Hodgkin, v. 215-23.
206 5 in 584] G.T. Hist. vi. 42.
8 again and again] Hodgkin, v. 258-74.
22 twenty dukes] G.T. Hist. x. 3 init.
37 in 586] ibid. viii. 30.
207 33 G.T. Hist. x. 3.

PAGE LINE

208 12   sustaining] ibid. vii. 45.
    35   near Soissons] At Trucia (Droisy). Cf. Hist. Franc. c. 36.
209 5   triumph] Fred. iv. 17. The battle appears to have been fought
               at Laffaux, near Laon.
    10   Wintrio] ibid. 18.
    12   refuge] ibid. 19.
    16   Dormeille] ibid. 20.
    27   Protadius] ibid. 27.
    35   patrician] Vulfus. Ibid. 29.
    37   Roman] Ricomer. Ibid. 29.
    40   refreshing picture] ibid. 28.
210 1   Claudius] ibid. 28.
     8   Theudebert] ibid. 37.
     9   Toul . . . Tolbiacum] ibid. 38.
    20   Death of Theuderic] ibid. 39.
    37   Arnulfus and Pippin] ibid. 40.
211 7   advanced] ibid. 42.
    12   Warnacharius] ibid. 41.
    21   death of Brunihildis] ibid. 42. The place is said to be *Rionava*
               vico super Vincenna fluvio.
    37   See above, p. 170, 2.
215 6   fugitive slave] *e.g.* Andarchius (G.T. Hist. iv. 47) and Leudastes
               (ibid. v. 49). See pp. 222, 223.
216 4   *e.g.* Ragnachar, ii. 42.
     7   Sigibert the lame] ibid. ii. 40.
    17   Chararic] ibid. ii. 41.
    23   Ragnachar] ibid. ii. 42.
    37   words] ibid. ii. 40 fin.
217 11   cynical lament] ibid. ii. 42 fin.
218 2   no trace] cf. De Coul. iii. pp. 76-87.
    35   formula of Marculf] i. 18 ; M.G.H. Leges v. p. 55, *una cum arma*
               sua. As has been shown by Zeumes, the editor, *arma* is the
               right reading, not *arimannia.* Indeed there is no MS. evidence
               for the latter word. Ducange (*s. v. Herimanni*) adopts *arimannia*
               and interprets as a military force : Bignon as simply *familia.*
219 5   *e.g.* Löb. 125.
     6   *comitatus*] Tac. Germ. 13, 14.
    24   G.T. Hist. ii. 42.
    35   plebeian crowd] ibid. iii. 18 *utrum incisa caesarie ut reliqua plebs*
               habeantur.
220 8   Aristotle's dictum] Probably Ar. Pol. vi. (iv.), c. 6, 1294 a 19 ff.
    17   predecessors] G.T. Hist. x. 31.
    25   Secundinus and Asteriolus] ibid. iii. 33.
    28   Parthenius] ibid. iii. 36.
221 9   Celsus] ibid. iv. 24 and 42 ; Paulus Diac. Hist. Lang. iii. 4.
    17   Mummolus] G.T. Hist. iv. 42 and index.
222 2   Tacitus] Tac. Germ. 25 fin.
     6   Andarchius] G.T. Hist. iv. 47.
    17   Fortunatus] Carm. vii. 7, 8, and 9.
223 4   Leudastes] G.T. Hist. v. 49.
    20   Marcovefa and Merofledis] ibid. iv. 26.
224 5   Bishop of Langres] G.T. Vit. Patr. 7.
    19   Pact of Andelot] G.T. Hist. ix. 20.
    39   Godinus] ibid. v. 3.
225 6   Siggo] ibid. v. 3.
    16   nurse] Called Septimina, ix. 38.

225   26   Guntram Boso]   ibid. ix. 10.

       33   Wandelinus]   ibid. viii. 22.

       35   Bodegiselus]   ibid.

226   9   passage in Gregory]   ibid. viii. 29.

       27   seldom applied]   Löb. 134 ; G.T. Hist. viii. 16.

       32   *nobilis genere*]   De Coul. iii. 85.

227   4   proceres, etc.]   ibid. 82 ff.

       5   Theodore]   G.T. Hist. vi. 24.

       8   Cautinus]   ibid. iv. 12.

       9   utiliores]   ibid. iv. 22.

      11   viri fortes]   ibid. iii. 18.

      14   viri fortiores]   ibid. ix. 36.   Cf. p. 123, 6, above.

      15   priores]   ibid. viii. 9.

      18   meliores natu]   ibid. vi. 45.

      22   seniores]   iv. 52 ; viii. 31.

      27   viri magnifici]   De Coul. iii. 76 ff. ;   Bury note on Gibbon, iv. 121.

      32   chronicle]   Fred. iv. 41, 85.

      39   Guntram]   G.T. Hist. viii. 9.

228   4   Theuderic]   ibid. iii. 23.

      34   Brunihildis . . . appeared]   ibid. vi. 4.

229   14   Wintrio]   Fred. iv. 18.

      19   poor wayfarer]   ibid. iv. 19.

      31   same years]   A.D. 600 according to Fred. iv. 20.

230   2   Aegyla]   Fred. iv. 21.

      11   Bertoaldus]   ibid. 25, 26.

      18   Protadius succeeded]   ibid. 27.

      27   two . . . nobles]   ibid. 28, 29.

      31   a man of Gallo-Roman birth]   Ricomeris.   Ibid. 29.

      33   Columbanus]   ibid. 36.   See also Stokes, " Ireland and the Celtic Church ", 137 ff.   Dudden, ii. 86-98.

      40   describe]   Fred. iv. 38.

231   18   determined to make Sigibert]   ibid. 39.

      34   ibid. 41.

      37   Chlothar]   ibid. 40.

232   16   sent Sigibert]   ibid. 42.

      40   picture of the young princess]   G.T. Hist. iv. 27.

234   4   Dudden, ii. 71.

236   1   Fortunatus]   A well-documented account of him in Teuffel-Schwabe, § 491, 4-11.   Best edition that of Fr. Leo in M.G.H. Auct. Antiq. iv.   His works also in Migne, lxxxviii.

      38   scenery]   *e.g.* Ven. Fort. Carm. x. 9.

237   1   ibid. i. 20.

      5   ibid. vii. 25 ; x. 9.

      7   the sun with fiery . . .]   ibid. i. 21, 14.

      11   restoring]   ibid. i. 18.

      13   castle of Nicetius]   iii. 12.

      15   Felix]   ibid. iii. 5 to 10 ; esp. 7. 35 (*fucis animantibus*) and 10. 5 ff. (*currere prisca facis flumina lege nova*).

      27   Gogo]   ibid. vii. 1-4.   Lupus]   ibid. vii. 7-9.

      31   to escort]   Fred. iii. 59.   Hist. Fr. 57.

238   6   Roman roads]   De Coul. iii. 254 ff., where much evidence is given.

      7   *evectio*]   G.T. Hist. ix. 9.

      15   funeral of Bishop Gallus]   G.T. Vit. Patr. vi. 7.

      18   funeral of Bishop Gregory]   ibid. vii. 3.

      26   not impassable]   G.T. Hist. x. 19.

          great preparations]   Glor. Conf. c. 18 and 19.

PAGE LINE

238 31 tents] G.T. Hist. vi. 37. Cf. Sidon. Ep. iv. 8. 2.
32 reception] Glor. Conf. 87.
33 one party] Vit. S. Ared. 29.
36 bp. of Trèves] Vit. Patr. xvii. 1.
39 inns and lodgings] *Metatus* often mentioned. Mir. Mart. i. 33 ; iv. 21.

239 1 Brivate] Mir. Jul. 24, 28.
2 visiting] G.T. Hist. viii. 2.
10 S. Geneviève] Vit. Genov. 39, 51 (Seine) ; 45 (Loire).
12 Gregory] G.T. Hist. viii. 14.
15 Agnes] Mir. Mart. iv. 29.
22 Apollinaris] Vit. Apoll. c. 7 (M.G.H. iii. p. 200).
30 taken by river] Mir. Mart. ii. 54 ; iv. 14.
31 forrios] of. L. Sal. xxi.
33 pleasant tale] Mir. Mart. ii. 16.

240 11 brigands] cf. above, p. 71.
20 Gregory] Mir. Mart. i. 36.
28 Life of S. Gertrude] De virtutibus S. Geretrudis, c. 8.
32 sons of Waddo] G.T. Hist. x. 21.

241 4 Dragolenus] ibid. v. 26.
21 falling ill] Mir. Mart. iii. 43. Cf. 60.
23 Gregory] ibid. i. 32, 33.
29 two of his grooms] Mir. Mart. iii. 43.

242 3 bridge over the Orge] G.T. Hist. vi. 19.
6 Guntram gave orders] ibid. vi. 11.
10 Richaredus] ibid. ix. 1.
18 roads through Burgundy] ibid. ix. 28.
23 inland trade] De Coul. iii. 256 ff, with many references—a valuable passage.
38 salt at Trèves] Mir. Mart. iv. 29. Wine merchants at Orleans] G.T. Hist. vii. 46.
40 Verdun] ibid. iii. 34.

243 4 Nantes] Ven. Fort. Vit. Germ. 47.
6 British Isles] There can be little doubt that in Vit. S. Columbani, c. 45, ed. Migne, Scottorum refers to the Irish. De Coul. iii. 258 is in error in supposing this passage to refer to Scotland.
14-40 octroi levies] cf. De Coul. iii. 248-53, which gives all the evidence.
23 Council of Mâcon] c. 13.

244 1 Syrians] De Coul. iii. 257.
4 traders from the East] G.T. Hist. viii. 1.
9 Euphronius] ibid. vii. 31, and note in Migne.
18 trader] Vit. S. Bibiani, c. 8 init.
22 Ragnimodus] G.T. Hist. x. 26.
34 money-lending] *e.g.* iv. 35 ; vii. 23.
goldsmiths] *e.g.* Priscus. Cp. below, p. 247, 33.
35 oculists and physicians] See note to p. 245 below, lines 4 and 10.
37 siege of Arles] See p. 99, above ; cf. Vit. Caesarii, i. 29.

245 2 owning vessels] G.T. Glor. Conf. 97.
3 S. Germanus] Ven. Fort. Vit. S. Germ. 62 (166).
4 Leonastes] G.T. Hist. v. 6.
10 sceptical sneer] Mir. Mart. iii. 50.
18 golden bowl] G.T. Hist. vi. 2.
29 Eunomius] ibid. vii. 23.
34 Sidonius] Ep. iii. 4 ; vi. 11 ; viii. 13. 3.
37 Cautinus] G.T. Hist. iv. 12 fin.

246 2 Eufrasius] ibid. iv. 35.

246   14   intermarriage]   Council of Orleans, 533, § 19 ; Mansi, viii. p. 838.

      17   Easter]   ibid. 538, § 30 = Mansi, ix. 19.

      21   enactments]   Council of Mâcon, 581, §§ 13-16 = Mansi, ix. pp. 934-35.

      38   Tacitus]   cf. Tac. Hist. v. 3, *invisum deis.*

      40   Avitus]   G.T. Hist. iv. 35 ; v. 11.

247   33   Priscus]   ibid. vi. 5.

248   16   spiritual father]   ibid. vi. 17.

      19   Priscus]   ibid.

249   21   beer]   Glor. Conf. c. 1.

      24   tormenting spirit]   Mir. Jul. 32.

      25   St. Rémi]   Vit. Remig. c. 7.

      30   poor tenant]   ibid. c. 26.

      40   swineherd]   ibid. c. 27.

250   23   Conc. Aur. 538, xxx. 1.

      27   poor woman]   G.T. Mir. Mart. iii. 31.   Cf. 56.

      29   Leodulfus]   ibid. iv. 45.

      36   stopping a gap]   ibid. ii. 13 ; iii. 29.

251   2   clappers]   ibid. ii. 26.

      3   carry water]   ibid. iv. 31.

      4   steward]   ibid. i. 20.

      6   woodman]   Glor. Conf. 31.

      10   swineherds]   Vit. S. Genovef. c. 18.

      21   gardens]   G.T. Vit. Patr. xiv. 2.

      24   bee-keeping]   Mir. Mart. iv. 15.

      34   convent at Amiens]   ibid. i. 17.

252   8   Sigiwald]   G.T. Vit. Patr. xii. 2.

      18   day's hawking]   G.T. Hist. v. 14 med.

      20   devoted to the chase]   ibid. vi. 46.

      23   wild bull]   Vit. Carileffi, cc. 6, 7.

      33   hunting-horn]   Glor. Conf. 88.

      37   Chundo]   G.T. Hist. x. 10.   Cf. De Coul. iii. 457 ; Löb. 34.

253   7   Chlothar II.]   Gesta Dagoberti, c. 1 fin. [M.G.H. ii. p. 401].

      9   Dagobert]   ibid. cc. 3, 4, 17, 18, 19 [ibid. p. 401 f., 406 f.].

254   7   cattle plague]   Mir. Mart. iii. 18.   Cf. Hist. x. 30.

      10   plague . . . among horses]   Mir. Mart. iii. 33.

      16   famine]   G.T. Hist. ii. 24.

      17   fifteen days' supply]   Vit. Lupicini, c. 3.

      18   monks of Condatisco]   G.T. Vit. Patr. i. 5.

      21   severe scarcity]   G.T. Hist. vii. 45.

255   9   paralytics]   Mir. Mart. ii. 47 and often.

      11   beggar caravans]   ibid. ii. 24.   Cf. iii. 16.

      13   professional beggars]   *e.g.* with letters from Bp. Nicetius, Vit. Patr. viii. 9.

      15   S. Julian]   Mir. Jul. c. 9.   Cf. c. 11.

      19   S. Martin]   *e.g.* Mir. Mart. i. 40 ; ii. 8, 14, and often.

      22   enrolled]   Mir. Mart. i. 31.   Called *matricularii*, G.T. Hist. vii. 29, and Migne's note. Vit. Arnulfi, c. 18 [M.G.H. ii. p. 439] ; De Coul. iii. 587.

      24   special endowments]   Vit. Remig. 32 [M.G.H. iii. p. 339] ; Gesta Dagoberti, c. 29 fin. [M.G.H. ii. p. 411].

      28   persons appointed]   Mir. Mart. i. 31.

      29   Xenodochia]   Council of Orleans, 549, § 15 (= Mansi, ix. 132), and often.

      33   Theodosian Code]   Cod. Th. c. 20.

       same council]   § 20 (= Mansi, ix. 134).

PAGE LINE

255　37　one-tenth]　Letter of bishops after Council of Tours, 567 (= Mansi, ix. 809).

　　　39　binding duty]　Conc. Tur. 567, § 5 (= Mansi, ix. 793).

256　2　lepers]　Council of Lyons, § 6 (= Mansi, ix. 943).

　　　4　Agricola]　Glor. Conf. 86 ; G.T. Hist. v. 46.

　　　7　Arnulfus]　Vit. Arnulfi in M.G.H. ii. 432 ff.

　　　14　poor]　ibid. c. 7.

　　　21　tears]　ibid. c. 18.

　　　24　did not relax]　ibid. c. 21.

　　　33　Radegund]　Vit. Radeg. i. 24 [M.G.H. ii. p. 372].

　　　38　Chlotilde]　Vit. Chlotildis, c. 11 [M.G.H. ii. p. 346].

257　11　theology]　De Coul. iii. 566.

　　　28　iteration]　*e.g.* Councils of Auvergne, 535, § 12 ; Orléans, 538, § 10; Tours, 567, § 21, and often.

258　25　For examples of these diseases in Mir. Mart. cf. fever (ii. 52 and often), renal disease (iii. 36), dysentery (i. 37 ; ii. 1), apoplexy (i. 22. Cf. Glor. Conf. 79), paralysis (ii. 7), smallpox (iii. 34 probably. Cf. Vit. Patr. 19. 2), epilepsy (ii. 18. Cf. Vit. Patr. viii. 8), insanity (i. 26).

　　　31　Gregory's neuralgia]　ibid. ii. 60.

　　　34　gout]　cf. Glor. Conf. 40.

259　4　noonday daemon]　*Meridiani daemonii incursum.* Mir. Mart. iv. 36, where see Migne's note. Cf. Hist. viii. 33.

　　　8　epilepsy]　Identified by Gregory. Mir. Mart. ii. 18.

　　　22　bubonic plague]　*Lues inguinaria,* often mentioned in G.T. Hist., and nearly always accompanied with such prodigies as are mentioned below, lines 32 ff. (from G.T. Hist. iv. 31). Cf. iv. 5 ; v. 35 ; vi. 14 ; ix. 22 ; x. 23. Also probably Mir. Mart. ii. 52. On the widespread extent of this plague see Bury's " Later Roman Empire ", i. 399-403.

　　　23　Thucydides]　ii. 47 ff.

260　1, 2, 6　Tours, Bordeaux, Orleans]　G.T. Hist. v. 34.

　　　9　warded it off]　ibid. iv. 5.

　　　13　Auvergne]　ibid. iv. 31.

　　　24　charms]　Mir. Jul. 45.

　　　28　sons of King Guntram]　G.T. Hist. v. 17.

　　　31　sons of Chilperic]　ibid. v. 35.

　　　32　Spain and Narbonne]　ibid. vi. 33.

　　　34　Marseilles]　ibid. ix. 21, 22.

　　　36　through Provence]　ibid. viii. 39 ; ix. 13.

　　　39　Guntram]　ibid. ix. 21.

261　23　Stertinii]　For the large sums made by these physicians cf. Pliny, H.N. xxix. §§ 7, 8.

　　　25　archiater]　G.T. Hist. v. 14; x. 15. Cf. Mir. Mart. ii. 1 ; Cod. Theod. xiii. 3.

　　　33　Austrechildis]　G.T. Hist. v. 36.

　　　37　smallpox at Tours]　Mir. Mart. ii. 51.

　　　40　oculists]　Mir. Mart. ii. 19.

262　3　Leonastes]　G.T. Hist. v. 6.

　　　13　Abbot Severinus]　Vit. Severin. c. i. [M.G.H. iii. p. 168].

　　　18　Caesarius]　Vit. Caesar. c. 7 fin. [M.G.H. iii. pp. 459 ff.].

　　　23　hospital]　ibid. c. 20.

　　　25　Helpidius]　ibid. c. 41. Letter to him from Theodoric the Great in Cass. Var. iv. 24.

　　　29　Temple of Aesculapius]　Dill i. pp. 462-63 ; Pater, " Marius the Epicurean ", Part i. c. 3.

PAGE LINE

262 32 old paganism] *e.g.* at Brivas, Mir. Jul. c. 5; at Argentomacus (Argenton), Vit. Arid. 28 (ed. Migne), 44 (ed. Krusch). Cp. Vit. Patr. vi. 2; xvii. 5; De Coul. iii. 508.

        37 Councils] *e.g.* Orleans, 533, § 20 [=Mansi, viii. p. 838]; C. Tur. 567, § 33.

263 1 Magna Mater] Glor. Conf. 77.

        4 Gregory the Great] cf. Dudden, " Gregory the Great ", ii. 147-52.

        9 Diana] G.T. Hist. viii. 15; Vit. Caes. ii. 18 [M.G.H. iii. 491, n. 2]. She seems to be in some way connected with the " noonday demon ", p. 267, 7, below. Cf. Migne's note to Mir. Mart. iv. 36, and Krusch's n. to Mir. Mart. iii. 9.

        10 Gallus] Vit. Patr. vi. 2.

        13 holy lake] Glor. Conf. c. 2.

        17 sacred herds] Mir. Jul. 31.

        18 oxen of the sun] Homer, Odyss. xii. 263-396.

        19 S. Caesarius] Vit. Caes. i. 55 [M.G.H. iii. p. 479], and Krusch's note.

        28 Breviarium Alarici] See Guizot, i. 320 ff., esp. 323.

        32 Comites] See above, p. 142 ff.

        40 curia] Dill ii., Book iii. c. 1.

264 6 local senate] cf. Avitus, Hom. de Rogationibus, p. 110, 26, ed. Peifer, quoted by Löb. p. 106. Cf. also De Coul. iii. 236.

        13 decurions] Also called *honorati* in Formulae Arvernenses, 1 b. See De Coul. iii. 236.

        21 Guntram's army] G.T. Hist. viii. 30.

        25 Convenae] G.T. Hist. vii. 34.

        30 Dijon] ibid. iii. 19.

265 8 Chateaudun] (*Dunum*) ibid. vii. 2.

        14 Bourges] ibid. vi. 31.

        28 one small place] Convenae. G. T. Hist. vii. 37.

        29 merchant] Chariulfus.

        31 scenes in the streets] ibid. vi. 32.

266 6 procession] ibid. viii. 1.

        16 three young princes] ibid. v. 35.

        26 prayer or virtue] *e.g.* Glor. Conf. 56.

        27 Bordeaux] Vit. Caes. i. 22.

        29 convent of Arles] ibid. ii. 26.

        32 convent of Nivelles] De virt. Geretrudis, c. 3 [M.G.H. ii. p. 466].

        35 monastery of S. Claude] Patr. Jur. iii. 18 [ibid. iii. p. 162].

        38 Poitiers] Mir. Mart. iv. 32.

        39 Bordeaux] ibid. iv. 47 ; Vit. Caes. i. 22.
Clermont] Vit. Patr. vi. 6.
Metz] Vit. Arnulfi, c. 20.

        40 Leobinus] Life by Ven. Fort. c. 19 [62-4].

267 3 scene] G.T. Hist. viii. 33.

        27 Tours] ibid. iv. 20.

269 25 religious theory] See Wells and How, Commentary on Herodotus, Introd. § 32, p. 43 ff.

        35 impartial] *e.g.* Mir. Mart. iii. 38.

        39 condone] *e.g.* Clovis, G.T. Hist. ii. 40 fin.

270 3 Chilperic] ibid. vi. 46.

        10 crimes of clergy] See Dudden, " Gregory the Great," ii. 54, and his instances quoted from G.T. Hist.

        15 vision] ibid. v. 14 med.

        17 dukes] ibid. viii. 30.

        31 Patroclus] Vit. Patr. ix. 2. We are reminded of Lucian's " Charon ", c. 5 *et seq.*

270 35 Nicetius] Of Trèves. Vit. Patr. xvii. 5.
271 17 King Chlothar] Vit. Patr. xvii. 2 fin.
    32 Salvian] Dill ii. 140 ff.
       Sidonius] ibid. 187 ff.
    40 Jerome] ibid. 124.
272 33 Aridius] G.T. Hist. x. 29 ; Vit. Arid. c. 3.
273 28 adopted a name] Löb. 58.
    29 Claudius] G.T. Hist. vii. 29.
274 21 Ecdicius] Sidon. Ep. iii. 3 (esp. § 7) ; cf. G.T. Hist. ii. 24.
    23 son of Sidonius] Apollinaris, ibid. ii. 37. He apparently escaped
       himself, as he appears to have been a bishop afterwards. Glor.
       Mart. 65. Cf. G.T. Hist. iii. 2 ; and below, p. 308, 15.
    27 great host] 100,000. Cf. Procop. B.G. ii. 25. p. 247 (ed. Bonn) ;
       Hodgkin, iv. 348.
    31 Embrun] G.T. Hist. iv. 42 ; Hodgkin, v. 219-23.
275 14 *colluvies nationum*] Tac. Ann. ii. 55.
    32 Roman observers] *e.g.* Strabo, iv. 1. 1. See, for others, Rice
       Holmes, " Caesar's Conquest of Gaul ", 288 ff.
276 37 Ascovindus] G.T. Hist. iv. 16.
    39 Wiliulfus] ibid. ix. 13.
277 3 Chariulfus] ibid. vii. 37 ; Löb. 81 n.
    15 tending to coalesce] See De Coul. ii. pp. 549 ff.
    17 Syagrius] Sidon. Ep. v. 5 and Dill ii. p. 376.
    18 Bishop of Auvergne] Sidon. Carm. xii. 6 *quod Burgundio
       cantat esculentus | infundens acido comam butyro.*
    21 Visigothic king] Sidon. Ep. i. 2.
    30 Latin secretary] Leo, see Sidon. Ep. viii. 3 and Dill ii. p. 368 f.
    31 Gundobad] See Gibbon iv. 45.
    37 Chilperic] G.T. Hist. v. 45.
    40 Fortunatus] Ven. Fort. Carm. iv. 26. 13 *sanguine nobilium
       generata Parisius urbe | Romana studio, barbara prole fuit. |
       ingenium mitem torva de gente trahebat. | vincere naturam gloria
       maior erat.*
278 5 Sidonius] Ep. vii. 9. 5 ff.
    14 intermarriage] See De Coul. ii. 548 ; and cf. his learned note on
       p. 399 ibid.
    16 Bauto] Friend of Symmachus [Symm. Ep. iv. 15, 16]. Cf. Dill ii.
       22 ; Gibbon iii. 222.
279 19 two great campaigns] p. 158, above.
    22 Chlodomer] p. 158, above.
    27 Barcelona] p. 166, above.
280 1 King Charibert] G.T. Hist. iv. 26 ; Mir. Mart. i. 29 ; Ven. Fort.
       vi. 2.
    9 Childebert] Ven. Fort. ii. 10. 21 | *Melchisedech noster merito rex
       atque sacerdos | complevit laicus religionis opus.*
    13 Paternus and Leobinus] Ven. Fort. wrote the lives of both these
       saints.
    16 Chilperic and Fredegundis] Ven. Fort. ix. 1, 2, 3.
    25 loss of two sons] G.T. Hist. v. 35.
    32 Sigibert and Brunihildis] Ven. Fort. vi. 1, 1a.
    35 fierce struggle] G.T. Hist. iv. 50.
281 15 religious reverence] ibid. iii. 25.
    31 royal mandate] *e.g.* Nicetius of Trèves, Vit. Patr. xvii. 1.
    39 Chlodomer . . . fell] G.T. Hist. iii. 6.
282 10 queen replied] ibid. iii. 18. Cf. p. 159, above.
    19 treachery] ibid. iii. 7.

PAGE LINE

283   5   Tacitus] Germ. 17 fin.

       18   Ingundis] G.T. Hist. iv. 3. Chilperic was the son of Aregundis. See Fred. iii. 46.

       35   two slave girls] Merofledis and Marcovefa. G.T. Hist. iv. 26.

       38   good king] ibid. iv. 25.

284   1   Marcatrudis] ibid. iv. 25.

       4   Austrechildis] ibid. iv. 25 ; v. 17 ; v. 36.

       20   Brunihildis] ibid. iv. 27.

       33   Galswintha] ibid. iv. 28.

       36   Fortunatus] Ven. Fort. vi. 5. 223.

285   19   Egidius] ibid. v. 19 fin.

       20   Bertram] ibid. vi. 50 med.

       24   Landerich] Hist. Franc. c. 35. Cf. Löb. 25 n.

286   25   G.T. Hist. v. 41.

       28   deacon of Châlons] Mir. Mart. iii. 38.

       33   Guntharius] G.T. Hist. x. 31, § 17 ; Gl. Conf. viii.

       37   Salonius and Sagittarius] G.T. Hist. iv. 43 ; v. 21.

287   3   Eberulfus] ibid. vii. 22.

       7   citizen of Bayeux] Mir. Mart. ii. 53.

       15   went to visit] Vit. Patr. xx. 1.

       26   S. Germanus] G.T. Hist. iv. 26.

       38   S. Columbanus] Fred. iv. 36.

288   10   councils] *e.g.* Orleans, 511, § 29 (=Mansi, viii. p. 356); Auvergne, 535, § 16 (=Mansi, viii. p. 861 f.).

       13   Bertram and Palladius] G.T. Hist. viii. 7.

       19   one tale] ibid. vi. 36.

289   12   Deuteria] ibid. iii. 22 to 26.

       27   endowed churches] ibid. iii. 25.

       34   Ambrose] ibid. vi. 13 ; vii. 3.

290   8   Amalo] ibid. ix. 27.

       25   Eulalius] ibid. x. 8.

292   9   a man] ibid. viii. 16.

       14   citizens of Tours] Glor. Mart. xx.

       16   another perjurer] ibid. liii.

       20   a girl] ibid. lviii.

       25   repudiated debts] Mir. Juliani, 19.

       27   priest] Glor. Conf. 93.

       32   archdeacon] ibid.

       37   handwriting] Vit. Patr. viii. 9 ; cf. p. 255, above, l. 13.

293   14   Pelagius] G.T. Hist. viii. 40.

       30   deputy] Mir. Mart. i. 31.

294   1   Thucydides] iii. 82 f.

       5   Munderic] G.T. Hist. iii. 14.

       33   church at Metz] ibid. viii. 21. For Boso's perjuries cf. ix. 10 fin.

295   10   Rauchingus] ibid. viii. 29 ; ix. 9 ; and especially v. 3.

296   6   Ragnachar] ibid. ii. 42.

       20   auri sacra fames] ibid. iv. 47 ; quoting Verg. Aen. iii. 56.

       26   Charibert] Mir. Mart. i. 29.

       31   Theudechildis] G.T. Hist. iv. 26.

297   2   journey of Rigunthis] ibid. vi. 45 ; vii. 9, 15.

       36   bring her home] ibid. vii. 39.

       39   treated Fredegundis] ibid. ix. 34.

298   30   Leudastes] ibid. v. 49.

       33   Paeonius] ibid. iv. 42.

       36   Charegesilus] ibid. iv. 52.

       39   Nicetius] ibid. viii. 18.

PAGE LINE
299 9 Marcus] ibid. v. 29. Cf. 35 ; vi. 28.
15 Cuppa] ibid. x. 5.
28 Celsus] ibid. iv. 24.
32 Protadius] Fred. iv. 24-27.
39 forces of Theuderic] G.T. Hist. iii. 12 ; Mir. Jul. 13.
300 1 in 576] ibid. v. 14.
5 two years before] ibid. iv. 48.
11 church of S. Vincent] ibid. vii. 35.
16 Burgundian army] ibid. viii. 30.
301 12 Beppolenus] ibid. viii. 42.
18 Waddo] ibid. vii. 27, 38.
24 Beretrudis] ibid. ix. 35.
26 Launebodis] Ven. Fort. ii. 8.
302 8 Lupentius] G.T. Hist. vi. 37.
21 deacon Peter] ibid. v. 5.
303 3 altar of S. Dionysius] ibid. v. 33.
25 Marseilles] ibid. iv. 44.
304 8 ⎫
to ⎬ Sicharius, Austrigiselus, and Chramnesind] ibid. vii. 47 ; ix. 19.
306 3 ⎭
308 14 son of Sidonius] His name was Apollinaris. G.T. Hist. iii. 2.
16 Arcadius] ibid. iii. 12.
18 Leontius] Ven. Fort. i. 14 to 16.
309 1 Gregory of Langres] Vit. Patr. vii.
4 nonogenarian anchorets] ibid. xiv. 3, 4.
9 formal Life] Migne, lxxi. 115-128.
29 Tetricus] Vit. Patr. vii. 4.
31 Duke Gundulf] G.T. Hist. vi. 11.
32 Gregory tells us] ibid. v. 50, near end.
36 entered on his episcopate] Mir. Mart. ii. 1.
310 8 thirty-four years] Mir. Mart. iii. 10. It must be noted, however,
that in the sentence *tempore quo transactis parturitionis doloribus
me edidit* (so given in Migne), *me* is not found in the MSS.
11 twenty-first] Odo, Vit. Greg. c. 26.
29 grandson of Clovis] Theudebert I. (533–548).
38 Gregory of Langres] Vit. Patr. vii.
311 9 Eufronius] G.T. Hist. x. 31, § 18.
13 Vettius] Sidon. Ep. iv. 9 ; Dill ii. p. 213.
19 camp of Dijon] G.T. Hist. iii. 19.
37 tales of wonder] Vit. Patr. vii. 2-4.
312 15 Attalus] G.T. Hist. iii. 15 ; Gibbon, iv. 136 f.
313 9 memoir] Vit. Patr. vi.
14 Cronona] Cournon in Puy-de-Dôme.
15 voice] Vit. Patr. vi. 2.
20 Theuderic] ibid. c. 2.
32 heathen shrine] ibid.
314 2-17 ibid. c. 3.
20-25 ibid. c. 6.
31-37 ibid. c. 7.
315 3 Nicetius] Of Lyons. Vit. Patr. viii. 1.
20 elected] ibid. 3.
23 bishop's character] ibid. 3. Cf. G.T. Hist. iv. 36.
37 will] Vit. Patr. viii. 5.
316 13 Avitus] G.T. Hist. iv. 35.
20 tutor] Vit. Patr. ii. introd.
25 Cautinus and Cato] G.T. Hist. iv. 7, 11.

2 M

PAGE LINE

316 28 disgraced his office] ibid. iv. 12.
    34 Letters of Sidonius] See Dill ii. p. 215 f.
317 1 Bishop Eufrasius] G.T. Hist. iii. 2.
    2 Apollinaris] ibid. iii. 2.
    6 Eufrasius] ibid. iv. 35.
      Hortensius] Vit. Patr. iv. 3.
    9 Avitus] G.T. Hist. iv. 35.
    21 Fortunatus] Carm. iii. 21, 22 (ed. Leo).
    27 S. Illidius] Vit. Patr. ii. 4.
    28 Antolianus] Glor. Mart. 65.
318 23 Theuderic] G.T. Hist. ii. 37.
319 13 fire and sword] Hist. iii. 12 ; Vit. Patr. v. 2 ; Glor. Mart. 52 ; Mir.
      Jul. 13. 23. This invasion took place in A.D. 525.
    32 Arcadius] G.T. Hist. iii. 9-12. Cf. p. 160, above.
320 6 threatened] ibid. iii. 12.
    21 Quintianus] Vit. Patr. iv. 2.
    31 basilica of S. Julian] Mir. Jul. 13.
    40 perished] G.T. Hist. iii. 12.
321 2 Lovolautrum] ibid. iii. 13.
    8 Meroliac] ibid.
    18 Sigiwald] Mir. Jul. 14.
    20 Evodius] Vit. Patr. vi. 4 ; Hist. iv. 13. He had two sons, Salustius
      and Eufrasius.
      Becco] Mir. Jul. 16.
    21 Hortensius] G.T. Hist. iv. 35 ; Vit. Patr. iv. 3.
    31 Chramnus] See p. 168 ff., above.
    37 father's ailments] *e.g.* Vit. Patr. xiv. 3. Cf. p. 322, 19, below.
322 30 cabbalistic name] Jesu Nave. Glor. Conf. 40.
    32 fish's liver] ibid.
    38 as we have seen] pp. 161, 23 ; 320, 36.
323 18 Peter] Mir. Jul. 24.
    23 young Gregory] ibid. 25.
    32 relief in a quartan fever] Vit. Patr. ii. 2 fin.
    37 Host escaping] Glor. Mart. 86.
325 23 scepticism] *e.g.* Glor. Conf. 81 ; Mir. Mart. i. 9 ; Vit. Patr. xvii. init.
    35 gastric fever] Vit. Patr. ii. 2.
    40 tonsure and diaconate] Probably about the year 563 (Monod. 29).
326 1 Fortunatus] Carm. v. 3. 11 *Martino proprium mittit Julianus
      alumnum.* Cf. Mir. Jul. 2.
    8 rustic style] Vit. Patr. ix. introd. ; ibid. ii. introd. ; Hist. prol.
      init. ; Mir. Jul. 4 ; Glor. Conf. praef.
    11 Virgil] *e.g.* Aen. i. 118 (Hist. iv. 30) ; Aen. iii. 56 (ibid. iv. 47).
      Sallust] *e.g.* Catil. 3, § 2 (ibid. iv. 13 ; vii. 1).
      Prudentius] Cathemerinon, vi. 133 (Glor. Mart. 106) ; Periste-
      phanon, i. 82 (ibid. 93) ; Apotheosis, 449 (ibid. 41).
      Orosius] Referred to or quoted Glor. Conf. 1 ; Hist. i. Prol. ; i. 6,
      37 ; ii. Prol. 9 ; Mir. Jul. 7.
    12 Eusebius] Rufinus's trans. of Hist. Eccl. vii. 14 (Glor. Mart. 21).
      Also referred to Vit. Patr. vi. 1 ; Hist. ix. 15 ; i. Prol. ; i. 34 ;
      ii. Prol.
      Pliny] His lost work *De arte grammatica* (Plin. H.N. Praef. § 28),
      Vit. Patr. prol.
    13 A. Gellius] ibid.
    21 Avitus] Vit. Patr. ii. introd.
    23 Arians and Jews] Hist. vi. 40 ; vi. 5.
    32 strength gave way] Mir. Mart. i. 32.

PAGE LINE

327   6   portents]   Hist. iv. 31.
     30   sorcerer]   Mir. Jul. 45.
328   6   highwayman]   Mir. Mart. i. 36.
     12   travelled with some dust]   Mir. Mart. iii. 60.
     13   tempest]   Glor. Mart. 84.   Cf. Mir. Mart. i. 34.
     19   lighted up]   Glor. Mart. 9 ; Odo's " Life ", c. x.
     27   biographer]   Odo, c. 11.
     31   all but five]   G.T. Hist. v. 50 sub fin.
329   1   long roll]   ibid. x. 31.
     27   struggle]   cf. p. 181, above, for all this paragraph.
331 11 ⎫
     to ⎬ Leudastes and his persecution of Gregory]   Hist. v. 48-50 ; vi. 32.
336 13 ⎭ See above, pp. 147-51.
331 38   Eunomius]   ibid. v. 48.
336 14   Felix]   Hist. v. 5 ; v. 50 ; Ven. Fort. Carm. iii. 4 to 10.
     25   recover marsh land]   Ven. Fort. iii. 10.
337 22   Merovech]   Hist. v. 14.
     32   an angel]   ibid.
338 12   convulsions of nature]   ibid. v. 34, 35.   See p. 186, above.
     30   lively debate]   ibid. v. 44.   Cf. vi. 40.
339 12   ardent zeal]   ibid. v. 39 ; vi. 18, 33, 40.
     19   by his father's orders]   ibid. viii. 28.
     20   German critic]   Löb. p. 285.
     26   Arian envoys]   G.T. Hist. v. 44 ; vi. 40.
     34   confusion]   ibid. vii. 13.
340   4 ⎫
     to ⎬ Gregory was there . . . perjury]   ibid. viii. 1-7.
341 14 ⎭
340 25   this plague]   Seemingly in reference to Gundobald : see Migne.
     38   pray for his nephew]   ibid. viii. 4.
341 16 ⎫
     to ⎬ Coblenz . . . brothers]   ibid. viii. 13-15.
342   3 ⎭
341 17   adoption]   ibid. vii. 33.
     19   intriguers]   ibid. viii. 13.
     24   Theodorus]   ibid. viii. 12.
342   6   S. Radegund]   ibid. ix. 2 ; Glor. Conf. 106.
     23   shall see]   p. 386 ff.   G.T. Hist. ix. 39 ff.
     29   to Metz]   ibid. x. 20 init.
          cholera]   The dysenteria so often mentioned.   For the incident see
          ibid. ix. 13.
343   3   Easter Day]   ibid. ix. 20 fin.
     16   small and slight]   Odo, Vit. Greg. c. 24 erat enim statura brevis.
     20   Ingoberga]   ibid. ix. 26.
     21   mother of Bertha]   ibid. iv. 26.
     31   tax-collectors]   ibid. ix. 30 ; De Coul. iii. 269 f.
344 11   Ingitrudis]   ibid. ix. 33 ; x. 12.
345   9   election of Gregory the Great]   ibid. x. 1.   For the plague and
          calamities cf. Dudden, i. 211-16, with all his references.
346   1   meeting of the two Gregorys]   Odo, c. 24.   See Dudden, i. 242 n.
          Cf. Löb. 12.
     13   to try Egidius]   G.T. Hist. x. 19.
     35   Ligugé]   Mir. Mart. iv. 30.
347   9   bodily resurrection]   G.T. Hist. x. 13.
     15   Chilperic's Sabellianism]   ibid. v. 45.
     25   ominous fulfilment]   ibid. x. 25.

347   26   *exsurgent*]   Mark, xiii. 22.
     28   strange enthusiast]   G.T. Hist. x. 25.
348   1   Simon]   ibid. x. 24.
     7   Antioch]   ibid.
     16   reverence for religion]   *e.g.* vi. 36 ; vii. 7.
         farewell]   ibid. x. 28.
     31   plague]   ibid. x. 30
349   6   record]   ibid. x. 31.
     17   restored]   ibid. ix. 31, § 19.
     21   church and oratory]   cf. Ven. Fort. Carm. ii. 3 ; Glor. Conf. 20 ; Hist. x. 31, § 19.
     24   rustic style]   cf. p. 326, 8, above.
     27   works shall survive]   G.T. Hist. x. 31, § 19.
355   11   Neo-Platonic reverie]   cf. Dean Inge, " The Philosophy of Plotinus ". ii. 165 ff.
     24   Lucian]   Dill i. 337 f.
356   4 f.   Apollonius of Tyana . . . Isiac priests . . . Maximus Tyrius] Dill ii. 106 ff.
     10   asceticism]   cf. Dom Cuthbert Butler, " Benedictine Monachism ", c. 2.
     24   Arvernian anchoret]   Perhaps Caluppas, Vit. Patr. xi. i.
     31   another . . . chains]   Perhaps Senoch of Tours, Vit. Patr. xv. 1, or Hospitius of Provence, G.T. Hist. vi. 6 init.
     32   huge stone]   Lupicinus, Vit. Patr. xiii. 1.
     35   pillar]   Ulfiliacus, G.T. Hist. viii. 15.
357   5   Blaesilla]   Hieron. Ep. 39, § 5.
     7   Rutilius Namatianus]   De reditu suo, i. 440 ff.
     10   S. Jerome]   *e.g.* Epp. 60, § 7 ; Dill ii. p. 133 f.
     17   S. Martin]   Mir. Mart. iv. 30.   Sulpicius Severus, Vit. Mart. c. 10.
     20   S. Germanus]   Glor. Conf. 41 and note, ap. Migne. Honoratus]   Hilarius, Sermo de vit. S. Honorati, cc. 3, 4 [Migne, l. 1257 ff.].
     24   prelates]   Dill ii. p. 215.
     31   Salvianus]   Dill ii. p. 137.
     34   John Cassian]   His works, Migne xlix.   His Rule appears to be taken from the fourth book, " De coenobiorum institutis ".
     39   Romanus . . . Lupicinus]   Vit. Patr. i.   Cf. above, p. 36 ff.
358   11   Cynic]   Dill i. 350 f.
     16   Romanus]   Vit. Romani, cc. 12, 13 [M.G.H. iii. p. 137].
     25   S. Caesarius]   Vit. Caesarii, c. 6 [ibid. iii. p. 459].
359   1   Plato]   Phaedo, 69 A.
     18   intermediate class]   *e.g.* Patroclus, Vit. Patr. ix. 1.
360   8   Abraham]   G.T. Hist. ii. 21 ; Vit. Patr. iii. ; Sidon. Ep. vii. 17.
     32   Condatisco]   Vit. Patr. i. 2.
     37   Burgundian code]   See above, p. 68, l. 36.
     40   Loches]   Vit. Patr. xviii. 1.
361   3   *Qui non laboret*]   cf. 2 Thess. 3. 10.   Vg. is *si quis non vult operari nec manducet.*
     4   mill]   Vit. Patr. xviii. 2.
     10   Martius]   Vit. Patr. xiv.
     17   Florentius]   ibid. xiv. 3.
     22   fenced round]   ibid. 2 *lorica dulcedinis esse vallatum.*
     33   Patroclus]   Vit. Patr. ix.   Cf. Hist. v. 10.
362   5   earthly bride]   ibid. i. *non conjungor mundanae conjugi.*
     8   thirst for the wilderness]   ibid. 2 *qui iam eremi sitiebat.*
     22   Lucian's Charon]   c. 6.

363   6   Bracchio]   Vit. Patr. xii.

     26   Menat]   Vit. Patr. xii. 3.

364   9   Clovis]   Vit. Remig. c. 17 [M.G.H. iii. p. 306].   On donations to the Church cf. De Coul. iii. 574 ff.

     12   S. Rémi]   See above, p. 33.

     15   Chlodoald]   G.T. Hist. iii. 18 ; Vit. Remig. 20 [M.G.H. iii. p. 313]. For Nogent see Hist. Franc. c. 24.

     17   Chlothilde]   Vit. Chlotild. c. 11-13 [M.G.H. ii. p. 347].   For Andelys cf. Bede H.E. iii. 8, where we learn that girls were sent there from Britain.

     21   her descendant]   Dagobert, Fred. iv. 79.

     22   S. Leonard]   Vit. S. Leonardi, c. 2 [M.G.H. iii. p. 396 ff.].

     32   prisoners]   *e.g.* ibid. i. c. 2 ; Vit. Rad. i. c. 11 [M.G.H. ii. p. 368] ; G.T. Mir. Mart. ii. 35 ; iv. 39 and often.

     40   S. Carileffus]   Vit. S. Carileffi, cc. 6-9 [M.G.H. iii. 389 ff.].

365   21   grant of lands]   ibid. c. 10.

     23   Chilperic I.]   G.T. Hist. vi. 46.

     29   liberal benefactor]   ibid. v. 35 fin.

366   7   S. Aemilianus]   Vit. Patr. xii.

     11   S. Caesarius]   See above, p. 98, 5.

     32   episcopal control]   cf. Dudden, ii. 79 f.

     33   Council of Chalcedon]   Guizot, pp. 430, 431.

     37   Council of Orleans]   Esp. § xix. (Mansi, viii. p. 354).

367   6   in 533]   Council of Orleans, § 21 (Mansi, viii. p. 838).

368   23   Cassiodorus]   For his later life see Hodgkin, iv. 383-96 ; and Dudden, ii. 169.

369   11   says Cassian]   De coenobiorum institutis, xi. 17 [Migne, xlix. 418].

     32   Gregory the Great]   Dudden, ii. 190 n., quotes Greg. Epp. ix. 18 ; xii. 15.

371   1   S. Radegund]   A.D. 519–587. Her life in prose by Ven. Fort. There are two other lives, the first (I.) almost a reproduction of Ven. Fort., the other (II.) by a contemporary nun of Poitiers, Bandonivia. [M.G.H. ii. 358-95.] For references to her in the poems of Fortunatus see Jacob's index in Krusch : ed. of the prose works [M.G.H. Auct. Antiquiss. iv. 2]. See also Thierry, p. 358 ff.

     3   one of her ancestors]   Bisinus, p. 10, l. 37, above.

     6   mother of Clovis]   Basina, G.T. Hist. ii. 12.

     12   Bertharius]   G.T. Hist. iii. 4. Ven. Fort. Vit. Rad. c. 2. Krusch ap. Ven. Fort. Vit. S. Rad. c. 2 reads *Bertechario.*

     25   defeated]   G.T. Hist. iii. 7.

372   18   he had married a nun]   Ven. Fort. Vit. Rad. c. 5 *de qua regi dicebatur habere se potius jugalem monacham quam reginam.*

     37   Radegund's young brother]   ibid. c. 12 ; and see note in Migne, lxxxv. p. 501. Cf. G.T. Hist. iii. 7.

373   10   before the bishop]   Vit. Rad. c. 12.

     16   articles of dress]   ibid. c. 14.

     28   along with his son]   Vit. Rad. II. 6 and 7 [M.G.H. ii. 382].

374   1   Pientius]   Vit. Rad. II. c. 5.

     3   Caesaria]   G.T. Hist. ix. 40, 42.

     6   warns her]   See the letters of S. Caesaria to S. Radegund, M.G.H. Epistolae Merovingici et Karolini aevi, i. 452.

     7   the convent]   For its luxury see G.T. Hist. x. 16. Cf. ix. 42.

     11   looked down]   Glor. Conf. 106.

     13   entered her convent]   Vit. Rad. I. c. 21.

     19   two hundred sisters]   Glor. Conf. 106.

PAGE LINE

374 26 power of the bishop] See De Coul. iii. 566 ff.
27 Council of Epaon] § 10 = Mansi, viii. 560.
29 Council of Arles] §§ 2 and 5 = ibid. ix. 702.
375 5 letter to the bishops] G.T. Hist. ix. 42.
25 rescript] ibid. ix. 39.
39 humane letters] Vit. Rad. II. 9 ; Acta SS. August. [13], vol. iii. p. 61.
376 2 diligent student] Ven. Fort. Carm. viii. 1. 53-60.
11 austerities] Vit. Rad. I. c. 17 ; Acta SS. August. [13], iii. 88-89.
38 baths] G.T. Hist. x. 16.
377 7 Fortunatus] See Jacob's index to the poems of Ven. Fort. in Krusch's ed. of the prose works, pp. 117-19. Cp. also above, p. 236.
20 Tarvisium] Ven. Fort. Vit. S. Martini, iv. 665.
22 rhetorical training] P. Diac. ii. 13.
38 every part of Gaul] Ven. Fort. Praef. § 4. He even went to Britain (Carm. iii. 26).
378 8 *bon vivant*] Ven. Fort. Carm. vi. 7 ; xi. 9, 10, 12 ff. ; vii. 14, 25 *lassavit dando, sed non ego lassor edendo.*
28 regaled his patron Gregory] See Mir. Mart. pref.
28 S. Medard] See Krusch, p. 67 ff.
33 sending their wealth on before] Ven. Fort. Carm. iv. 26. 73 *ut modo praemissas dives haberet opes.*
35 fruits of Paradise] ibid. v. 13. 6.
38 consolation] ibid. ix. 2 and 3.
379 4 tender lines] ibid. ix. 5.
10 poem on Galswintha] ibid. vi. 5.
18 pseudo-pagan style] ibid. vi. 1.
19 in Christian style] ibid. vi. 1a.
29 long poem] ibid. ix. 1.
37 Lupus] ibid. vii. 7, 8, and 9.
380 3 Palatina] ibid. vii. 6.
381 6 letter of S. Radegund] G.T. Hist. ix. 42.
40 attitude of Maroveus] ibid. ix. 40.
382 3 relics] Vit. Rad. II. 14.
13 another case] G.T. Hist. ix. 40.
383 14 journey] Ven. Fort. Carm. v. 11 ; xi. 25 and 26.
34 warmth of the love poems] *e.g.* ibid. viii. 9. 5-6 ; 10. 1-4 ; xi. 2. 5 ; xi. 16 and 17. Cf. xi. 6. 1-4.
384 17 pleasures of the table] cf. p. 378, l. 8, above.
40 more melancholy cast] Appendix Carminum " De excidio Thoringiae ", ed. Leo, p. 271.
385 16 an incident] G.T. Hist. ix. 40 fin.
36 obsequies] Glor. Conf. 106.
386 18 wild outbreak] G.T. Hist. ix. 39-43 ; x. 15-17, 20.
34 forty nuns] G.T. Hist. ix. 39.
387 35 bands of bravoes] ibid. ix. 40.
388 4 bishops did arrive] ibid. ix. 41.
24 Maroveus himself] ibid. ix. 43.
389 4 to storm the convent] ibid. x. 15.
13 Justina] cf. Ven. Fort. Carm. viii. 13 ; ix. 7. 81.
390 2 drew up judgement] G.T. Hist. x. 16.
391 3 appeared in person] ibid. x. 17.
9 dangerous conspiracy] ibid. x. 18.
12 trial of Egidius] ibid. x. 19.
17 Basina and Chrodieldis] ibid. x. 20.

392 34   bishop of Poitiers]   Paul.   Diac. Hist. Lang. ii. 13 ;   Vit. Rad. II.
             Praef.
393 30   from the year 511]   Council of Orleans.   Cf. p. 366, l. 37, above.
395 22   stag]   G.T. Hist. ii. 37.
     24   great general]   Mummolus : the bones were those of S. Sergius.
             G.T. Hist. vii. 31.
396   2   celebrates him]   ibid. i. 36.
      6   mission]   Pref. in Mir. Mart.
     13   contrasted]   Pref. in Glor. Martyr.
     29   the Bollandists]   See H. Delehaye, " History of the Bollandists ".
397 27   Gregory the Great]   On his theology see the able chapter in Dudden,
             ii. 296 ff.
398 22   fiercely vowed]   Fred. iii. 21.   Cf. above, p. 90, l. 1.
     37   host of genii and demons]   Dill i. p. 425 ff.
399 12   Aredius]   G.T. Vit. Ared. c. 33 [Migne, lxxi. p. 1138] *manus tua*
             perducat me in locum refrigerii et consolationis.
     29   Gregory the Great]   See Dudden, ii. 358-69.
     36   Plato]   Republic, x. 614 A-21 C.
     37   Plutarch]   De sera numinis vindicta, c. 22 ff. [563 B].   De genio
             Socratis, cc. 21, 22 [589 F ff.].
400   3 ff.]   This summary is based in the main on Dionysius Areopagitica's
             Caelestis hierarchia.
401 35   *Dialogues* of Gregory the Great]   Dudden, ii. 365 ff., esp. 368.
402 19   sudden gust]   Mir. Mart. iii. 16.
     22   at Angers]   ibid. iii. 27.
     24   at Tours]   Mir. Jul. c. 34.
     27   one of the sisters]   Vit. Rad. II. 18.
     29   according to Gregory the Great]   Dial. i. 4.
     31   of his stockings]   ibid. iii. 20.
     36   woman of Verdun]   G.T. Hist. vii. 44.   Cf. v. 14.
     39   witches of Paris]   ibid. vi. 35.
404   3   Landulfus]   Mir. Mart. ii. 18.
     37   sorcery and witchcraft]   See Mommsen, Strafrecht, 639 ff.   Maury,
             " La Magie et l'astrologie," pp. 151 ff.   For the Barbarian Codes
             see Ducange, s.v. maleficus, *e.g.* Lex Salica, 21.   Ripuaria, 82.
     39   Councils]   Auxerre, 578, § 4 [Mansi, ix. 912].   Narbonne, 589, § 14
             [ibid. ix. 1017].   Quoted by Dudden, ii. 111 n.
405 12   angels]   cf. Dudden, ii. 358-62.
     27   Hesiod to Plutarch]   Dill i. 427 ff.
     36   cult of the saints]   Dudden, ii. 369-73 ;   Delehaye, " Les origines du
             culte des martyrs," pp. 29 ff.
406   6   satisfying answer]   The passages in support of this view are given
             by Dudden, ii. 372, viz. Homil. in Evangelia, 40, § 8 [Migne, lxxvi.
             p. 1309];   Mor. xii. 21 [ibid. lxxv. p. 999];   Dial. iv. 33 [ibid.
             lxxvii. p. 575].
     16   theory of the cult]   Glor. Martyr. 107.   Cf. Mir. Juliani, 50.
     19   again Gregory says]   Mir. Mart. iv. prol.
407 30   S. Clothilde]   Vit. Chlotild. c. 11 [M.G.H. R. Merov. ii. p. 346].
             S. Radegund]   Vit. Rad. c. 13 [ibid. p. 369].
             S. Bathilde]   Vit. Bathild. c. 11 [ibid. p. 496].
408   4   leaving them orphans]   *e.g.* of S. Radegund = Glor. Conf. 106.
     22   no rhetorical training]   See p. 326, above.
409 18   Ignatius Loyola]   Ranke's " Hist. of the Popes ", i. 136 (ed. Bohn).
     26   crowds at Brivate]   *e.g.* Mir. Jul. 28.
410   7   Magdunum]   This seems to be Méhun, near Bourges.
     13   Fathers of the Jura]   *e.g.* Vit. S. Romani, c. 1 [M.G.H. iii. 132].

PAGE LINE

410 16   names of famous abbeys]   *e.g.* S. Germain des Prés.

     19   steep cliff]   S. Caluppa, Vit. Patr. xi. 1.

     22   hunting party]   cf. pp. 363, 365, above.

     29   S. Sequanus]   See Acta SS. Sept. [19], vol. vi. p. 38.

411 14   two holy virgins]   Glor. Conf. 18, with notes ap. Migne.

     37   Church of Venerandus]   ibid. 35.

412   7   two lovers]   ibid. 32.   Cf. G.T. Hist. i. 42 fin.   A similar story in Glor. Conf. 75.

     13   Hilarius of Dijon]   Glor. Conf. 42.

     18   Gregory of Langres]   Vit. Patr. vii. 2.

     29   Church of S. Stephen]   Glor. Conf. 73.

413 10   objurgations]   *e.g.* Mir. Mart. ii. 20, 37 ; Mir. Jul. 30.

     13   appeal to a bishop]   Glor. Conf. 18.

     38   attributed to . . . saint]   G.T. Hist. v. 6.   Cf. Mir. Mart. ii. 19, 60 ; iv. 1.

414   1   sudden storm]   G.T. Hist. iii. 28.

     19   scepticism]   *e.g.* Glor. Conf. 6 ; Virtut. S. Geretrudis, c. 11 [M.G.H. ii. p. 470].   Gregory was himself sometimes sceptical, Glor. Mart. 5.   Cf. 84.

416 36   modern theologian]   Cardinal Newman.   Cf. below, p. 423, l. 34.

418 12   interesting passage]   Vit. Patr. xvii. Pref., quoting S. John xx. 25, 29.

419   3   deacon of Autun]   Vit. Patr. viii. 12.

     16   Crescentia]   Glor. Conf. 105.

     28   rhetor's class]   cf. Mayor on Juvenal vii. 150 ff. ; Persius, iii. 45.

420 17   Sulpicius Severus]   Dial. i. c. 23.

421   2   latest criticism]   See Krusch's introductions to the several lives in M.G.H. Rer. Merov. ii. and iii.

     19   draws on Fredegarius]   Vit. Eptad. 6 with Fred. iii. 23 (cf. G.T. Hist. ii. 32).

     20   Ennodius]   Vit. Epiphan. § 136 ff. (ed. Vogel).   [M.G.H. Auct. Ant. vii. p. 101].

     23   one miracle]   cf. Vit. Eparchii, c. 10, with G.T. Glor. Conf. 101 [99, ed. Krusch].

     35   ride round]   Vit. Carileffi, c. 10 ; M.G.H. Rer. Merov. iii. 393.

422 27   Life of S. Rémi by Hincmar]   cf. Krusch ap. Ven. Fort. Opera 2, p. xxii, and M.G.H. iii. 239 ff.

423 37   Athenian government]   By the orator Lycurgus.   Cf. Plutarch, Vit. X. Oratorum, 841 f.

     40   Platonic school]   *e.g.* such treatises as Alcibiades II., Hipparchus, Epinomis, Minos.

424   2   apocryphal gospels]   See Dr. M. R. James, " Apocryphal New Testament ", Oxf. 1924.

     3   Sibylline forgeries]   See Rzach's article in Pauly-Wissowa, s.v. Sibyllinische Orakel, 2117 ff.

     5   Dionysius]   See Westcott, " Essays on the Religious Thought of the West ", p. 142 ff.

     20   Milman]   " Hist. of Latin Christianity ", Book XIV. c. 2.

     29   mediators]   cf. Dill i. p. 425 f.

425 14   to be cut off]   De Coul. iii. p. 567.

     24   opes praemissae]   Ven. Fort. Carm. iv. 26. 74.

     27   januam reserat caeli]   cf. Vit. Patr. xi. praef. *semper paupertas saeculi regiam reserat caeli* : for *regia* (*porta aedificii primaria*) see Ducange, s.v.

     34   Clothilde]   Vit. Chlotild. c. 8 [M.G.H. ii. 345].

425 37 Dagobert] Gesta Dagoberti, c. 17-20. Cf. c. 23 and 33 [ibid. ii.
406-7, 409, 413].
426 21 noble citizen] Glor. Conf. 65.
37 S. Julian] Mir. Jul. 35.
427 11 once] Vit. Genov. c. 21 [MGH. iii. p. 224].
24 S. Rémi] Vit. Remig. c. 7 [ibid. iii. p. 273].
428 17 S. Julian's sheep] Mir. Jul. 17.
18 how a thief] ibid. 20.
21 Sigivald] ibid. 14.
23 visitor] ibid. 21.
38 ambassador] Mir. Mart. iii. 8.
429 14 Nicetius] Vit. Patr. viii. 5.
430 32 trade in " the limbs of martyrs "] S. Augustin, De opere Mona-
chorum, c. 28 (Migne, xl. p. 575) alii membra martyrum, si
tamen martyrum venditant. Lucius, "Les origines du culte des
Saints," 246 ff.
33 Theodosian Code] ix. 17 (De sepulcris violatis), § 7.
431 6 regular part of the dress] Glor. Mart. 84. Cf. e.g. Hist. viii. 14.
17 S. Radegund] See p. 382, above.
22 oil] Glor. Martyr. 5.
25 S. Mammes] Vit. S. Radeg. ii. 14 (M.G.H. ii. p. 386). Krusch
denies that this Mammes was S. Mammes Caesariensis, refer-
ring to Tillemont, Mémoires, iv. 150.
39 Saragossa] G.T. Hist. iii. 29.
432 7 once a priest] Mir. Jul. 32.
19 S. Nicetius] Of Lyons. Vit. Patr. viii. 6.
26 S. Lupicinus] Vit. Patr. xiii. 1-3.
433 5 Maurienne] Glor. Martyr. 14.
32 bell-rope] Mir. Mart. i. 28.
35 himself guilty] Mir. Jul. 34.
434 3 cure disease] cf. e.g. Mir. Mart. ii. 1, iii. 1.
4 extinguish a fire, etc.] Glor. Martyr. 84.
5 sinking boat] G.T. Hist. viii. 14. Cf. Glor. Martyr. 83.
13 to Celsus] Orig. c. Cels. i. 6.
16 Nave Jesus] Glor. Conf. 40.
18 sacred dust] e.g. Mir. Jul. 45.
21 Councils] See above, p. 404, 7.
31 King Chilperic] G.T. Hist. vi. 27.
435 3 Eberulfus] ibid. vii. 22 and 29.
40 witch at Verdun] ibid. vii. 44.
witches of Paris] ibid. vi. 35.
436 2 pythoness at Tours] ibid. v. 14.
7 sorcerer] Mir. Jul. 45.
16 rebellious son of Chlothar I.] Chramnus, G.T. Hist. iv. 16.
20 Merovech] Hist. v. 14.
24 same methods] ibid. v. 50.
37 Desiderius] ibid. ix. 6.
438 18 year of great plague] ibid. iv. 31.
22 another year of pestilence] ibid. x. 23.
23 year of wild disorders] ibid. ix. 44.
27 Northern Lights] e.g. ibid. vi. 33 ; viii. 8 and 17 ; ix. 5.
29 coils of serpents] ibid. viii. 42 ; ix. 5.
440 13 charters of donations] Examples in De Coul. iii. p. 575 ff., with refs.
27 testaments] Testament of S. Rémi in Pardessus No. 118, and Vit.
Remig. c. 32 [M.G.H. iii. 336 ff.]. Testament of S. Caesarius in
Pardessus No. 129, that of Bertram ibid. No. 230.

441   1   Chilperic]   G.T. Hist. vi. 46.

     4   right . . . to receive bequests]   Cod. Justiniani, i. 2 (De sacro-sanctis ecclesiis) ; i. 13, 14.   For the barbarian codes and charters of kings see De Coul. iii. 574.

    15   council of Carthage in 398]   §§ 31, 32 [Mansi, iii. 953-54].

    16   council of Agde]   § 7 [Mansi, viii. 325].

    24   royal officer]   *Pelagius quidam*, G.T. Hist. viii. 40.

    37   Antestius]   ibid. viii. 43.

442   3   Sigivaldus]   ibid. iii. 16 ; Mir. Jul. 14.

     8   Eberulfus]   G.T. Hist. vii. 21, 22.

    11   Pastor]   Mir. Jul. 15.

    16   Eparchius]   G.T. Hist. vi. 18 (cf. Glor. Conf. 101).   Vita Eparchii, c. 16 [M.G.H. iii. 563].

    25   council of Tours in 567]   Second council, § 24 [Mansi, ix. 803 f.].

443   6   in 544]   G.T. Hist. iv. 2.

    17   in 589]   ibid. ix. 30.   Cf. De Coul. iii. 269 ff.

    24   in 534]   ibid. iii. 25.

    37   "ad nova templa "]   Ven. Fort. Carm. iii. 23. 17.

    39   Leontius]   A great church builder, *e.g.* Ven. Fort. Carm. i. 6, 8, 15, 16 ; iv. 10.

444   1   S. Germanus]   cf. Ven. Fort. c. ii. 9. 49, 50.

     3   wood]   *e.g.* Glor. Martyr. 52.   Cf. Hist. v. 2.

     5   Sidonius]   *e.g.* Ep. ii. 10. 4 ; iv. 18. 5.

    15   triformis]   cf. Vit. Caesarii, i. 57.   Dudden, i. 57.

    29   Perpetuus]   G.T. Hist. ii. 14, 16 (cf. iv. 20).   On this great building see the valuable remarks of Mr. O. M. Dalton in the introd. to his translation of Sid. Ep. p. ciii. f.

    32   pen of Sidonius]   Ep. iv. 18.

445   1   Namatius]   G.T. Hist. ii. 16.

     8   Patroclus]   Vit. Patr. ix. 1 fin.

    14   pleasant dinner]   *e.g.* Mir. Mart. iii. 8 ; Glor. Conf. 5 ; Hist. ix. 20 fin.

    20   drunken priests and bishops]   Salonius and Sagittarius (Hist. v. 21) Cautinus (ibid. iv. 12), Eonius (ibid. v. 41).

    26   nine o'clock]   Vit. Patr. viii. 11 fin.

    28   singing and chanting]   Glor. Conf. 47 (two choirs) ; Vit. Patr. vi. 2.   Cf. ibid. 5 ; Vit. Caesarii, i. 19 [M.G.H. iii. 463].

    31   expected to take part]   ibid. i. 19.

    32   withdrawing]   cp. the sermon of Caesarius ap. Migne, xxxix. 2077.   Council of Orleans, 511, § 26 (Mansi, viii. 355).

    35   stress on preaching]   Vit. Caes. i. 15, 18, 54, 55.

    40   Theudebert at Trèves]   Vit. Patr. xvii. 2.

446   2   King Guntram]   G.T. Hist. vii. 8.

    29   chapels or oratories]   For many examples see De Coul. iii. 518, 519 ; ii. 441, 442, and notes.

447   5   mentioned by Gregory]   Glor. Conf. 50 ; Mir. Jul. 47 ; Mir. Mart. iii. 8.

     8   forgotten saint]   *e.g.* Maura and Britta.   Glor. Conf. 18.   Some-times they were built over tombs.   Glor. Conf. 95, 99.

     8   chamber in a house]   Glor. Conf. 3, 8.

     9   building]   ibid. 20.

    25   benedictus qui venit]   Psalm 117 (118), 26.

448   18   S. Paulinus]   Carm. xxvii. 580-95 (ed. Hartel).

    20   Gregory the Great]   Dudden, ii. 74 ; 76 n. 1.   Many passages from G.T. there quoted.

    24   Gundobald]   G.T. Hist. vii. 36, *tune es pictor ille qui tempore Chlothacarii regis per oratoria parietes atque camaras charaxabas ?*

PAGE LINE
448 27 wife of Namatius] G.T. Hist. ii. 17.
34 tapestry, etc.] ibid. ii. 29 ; Glor. Conf. 55.
38 silver] Vit. Caes. i. 32 [M.G.H. iii. 469].
40 jewelled crosses] Mir. Jul. 20. Cf. Gesta Dagoberti, 20 [M.G.H. ii. 407].
449 2 Aredius of Limoges] His will in Migne, lxxi. 1143-50, esp. 1147.
24 thief] Mir. Jul. 20.
30 doom of perjury] De Coul. iii. 569 ff.
450 9 in one year (589)] Mir. Mart. iv. 6.
scoffers] ibid. iii. 50.
451 2 paralytic woman] Mir. Mart. iv. 6.
12 epilepsy] Mir. Mart. ii. 18.
18 in the sanctuary] ibid. ii. 18.
27 relics of S. Julian] Mir. Jul. 34.
452 10 matricularii] De Coul. iii. 587. See also n. on G.T. Hist. vii. 29 in Migne, lxxi. p. 434.
20 letter from a bishop] Vit. Patr. viii. 9.
25 sanguinary conflict] G.T. Hist. vii. 29.
30 fugitive] *e.g.* Cylon's confederates in 632 B.C. (Bury, "Hist. of Greece ", p. 179).
453 23 ⎫
to ⎬ Merovech] G.T. Hist. v. 14 ; cf. v. 1-2.
457 38 ⎭
455 39 oculum] Proverbs, 30. 17.
457 34 ideo tradidit] 1 Kings 9. 9. The quotation in G.T. Hist. v. 14 is not in the words of the Vulgate or LXX., though the sense is the same.
40 died voluntarily] G.T. Hist. v. 19 fin.
458 6 ravaged] ibid. v. 14 fin., 19.
19 Firminus] ibid. iv. 13.
24 wife of Duke Ragnovaldus] ibid. vi. 12.
27 mission of Claudius] ibid. vii. 29.
459 36 record] cf. Dudden, i. 385 ; cf. ii. 54 ff.
460 39 Bertram or Egidius] G.T. Hist. v. 50 ; ix. 14.
461 13 the clergy] Dudden, ii. 55.
21 Briccius and Guntharius] G.T. Hist. x. 31. 4 ; 31. 17.
26 Cautinus] ibid. iv. 12.
463 1 one prelate] Cautinus, G.T. Hist. iv. 12.
4 another] Eonius, ibid. v. 41.
7 Eufrasius] ibid. iv. 35.
10 a deacon] Theodulfus, ibid. x. 14.
12 genial bishop] Andoveus, ibid. x. 14.
19 deacon at Langres] Lampadius, ibid. v. 5.
20 archdeacon of Massilia] Vigilius, ibid. iv. 44.
23 some of the clergy] *e.g.* ibid. v. 37 ; vi. 11.
27 presbyter] Riculfus, ibid. v. 50.
464 1 annals] *e.g.* Vit. Patr. vi. 4.
6 Council of Auvergne in 535] Art. 4. Mansi, viii. 860.
11 lowly abbot] Dagulfus, G.T. Hist. viii. 19.
20 Fredegundis] ibid. viii. 29.
32 another clerical assassin] ibid. vii. 20.
37 awful scene] ibid. viii. 31.
465 6 lend money] Council of Orleans (538), art. 27 = Mansi, ix. 18.
7 coursing and hawking] Council of Epaon (517), art. 4 = Mansi, viii. 559.
40 Euric] G.T. Hist. ii. 25.

PAGE LINE
466   5   Goiswintha]   ibid. v. 39.
       27   Leuvichild]   ibid. viii. 46.
       35   he draws the lesson]   ibid. iii. 1.
467   2   Agila]   ibid. v. 44.
       17   Oppila]   ibid. vi. 40.
468   4   Leuvichild thought so]   Glor. Conf. 13.   Cf. Hist. ix. 15.
       11   another curious case]   Glor. Martyr. 81.
       29   in social life]   Council of Epaon (517), art. 15 = Mansi, viii. 561.
       37   Council at Orleans]   511, art. 10 = Mansi, viii. 353.
       39   priests are enjoined]   Council of Epaon (517), art. 16 = Mansi, viii.
             561.
469   1   Council at Orleans]   541, art. 8 = Mansi, ix. 114.
        7   Jews]   cf. Dudden, ii. 151.
       27   governor or collector of taxes]   Council of Mâcon (583), art. 13 =
             Mansi, ix. 934.
       30   private conversation]   ibid. art. 2.
       31   intermarriage]   Council of Orleans (533), art. 19 = Mansi, viii. 838.
       33   hospitality]   Council of Epaon (517), art. 15 = Mansi, viii. 561.
       36   sanctuary]   Council of Orleans (538), art. 13 = Mansi, ix. 15.
       39   fair price]   Council of Orleans (541), art. 30 = Mansi, ix. 118.
470   1   proselytise]   ibid. art. 31.
        2   manumission]   ibid. art. 31.
        4   redeem]   Council of Mâcon (583), art. 16 = Mansi, ix. 935.
        6   Christian slaves from Gaul]   cf. Gregory the Great's letter (ix. 213,
             215), quoted by Dudden, ii. 158.
        8   forbidden]   Council held by Sonnatius (*circ.* 630), art. 11 = Mansi,
             x. 596.
       10   Easter]   Council of Orleans (538), art. 30, and Council of Mâcon
             (583), art. 14 = Mansi, ix. 19 and ix. 934.
       24   Theodoric]   Dudden, ii. 152.
471   1   advance . . . loan]   G.T. Hist. vii. 23 ; iv. 12, 35.
        4   purveyors of jewels]   ibid. vi. 5.
        6   oculist]   ibid. v. 6.
        7   Hebrew trader]   Sidonius, Ep. iii. 4 ; iv. 5.
       12   Gallus]   Vit. Patr. vi. 7.
       18   baptism]   G.T. Hist. v. 11.
       24   500 Arvernian Jews]   ibid. v. 11.
       36   Priscus]   ibid. vi. 5.
472 10   Chilperic]   ibid. vi. 17.
       16   Phatir]   ibid. vi. 17.
       23   daring Jew]   Mir. Mart. iii. 50.
       27   Nicetius of Trèves]   Vit. Patr. xvii. introd.
473   1   Gregory the Great]   Dudden, ii. 288 f.
       25   S. Caesarius]   Vit. Caesarii, i. 60 (M.G.H. Script. Rer. Merov. iii.
             p. 481).
474 26   Sulpicius]   G.T. Hist. vi. 39.
       28   Ferreolus]   ibid. vi. 7.
       32   Praetextatus]   ibid. viii. 20.
475 16   rustic style]   *e.g.* Vit. Patr. ix. introd.
477   2   bishops]   cf. De Coul. iii. 566 ff., with his numerous references.
478 23   one bishop]   Nicetius of Trèves.   Vit. Patr. xvii. 2.
       30   two bishops]   Salonius and Sagittarius, Hist. v. 21.   Cp. note on
             p. 501, 5, below.
479 34   Chilperic]   ibid. vi. 46.
       37   Theodore . . . Bertram]   ibid. vi. 24 ; vii. 31.
       39   Egidius]   ibid. x. 19.

PAGE LINE

480 2 Sabellianism of Chilperic] ibid. v. 45.

36 One single reference] ibid. v. 21.   Briccius, fourth bishop of Tours after S. Martin, also appealed to the Pope, ibid. x. 31. 4.   Cf. below, p. 488, 1.

481 10 Council of Agde] 506 = Mansi, viii. 336 fin.

482 37 leave the bounds] Council of Epaon (517), art. 5 = Mansi, viii. 553 Cf. Sidon. Epist. ix. 10 ; and Mr. Dalton's note on vol. ii. p 241 of his translation of Sidonius.

483 19 clerici] De Coul. iii. 585.

36 children] Council of Orleans (511), art. 4 = Mansi, viii. 352.

484 1 redemption of captives] Council of Orleans (511), art. 5.

5 servile origin] De Coul. iii. 588 ff.

485 16 Chorepiscopi] ibid. 515 f.

20 archpresbyter] ibid. 515.

22 Munderic] G.T. Hist. v. 5.   .

32 archdeacon] De Coul. iii. 516. Cf. Ducange, s.v.

37 bishop's eyes] Constitut. Apost. ii. 44 ; iii. 19, 20 (quoted by Ducange, s.v. Archidiaconus) *ceterum sit Diaconus Episcopis aures et oculus et os, cor pariter et anima.*

486 16 election] De Coul. iii. 523 ff.

20 fixed principle] ibid. 544.

31 forced on an unwilling people] ibid. 529 f.

35 people] ibid. 543.

487 28 S. Martin] Sulpicius Severus. Vit. Mart. 9.

33 appealed to . . . citizens] Vita Caesar. i. 13 [M.G.H. iii. 461].

36 Briccius] G.T. Hist. ii. 1 ; cf. x. 31. 4.

488 20 two invaluable pictures] Sidon. Ep. iv. 25 ; vii. 9.

489 28 letter of S. Rémi] This letter and that of Clovis to the bishops (l. 34) are given in Migne, lxxi. 1157 f.

490 7 Council of 549] Held at Orleans, art. 10, *cum voluntate regis =* Mansi, ix. 131.

9 and in 557] Council of Paris [date uncertain, between 556 and 573], art. 8 = Mansi, ix. 746, *non principis imperio.*

21 Quintianus] G.T. Hist. iii. 2.

39 Nicetius] Vit. Patr. xvii. 1.

491 17 with a royal order] G.T. Hist. iv. 5, *rege opitulante* ; Vit. Patr. vi. 3.

33 Cato and Cautinus] G.T. Hist. iv. 6 and 7 ; De Coul. iii. 550.

492 26 see of Tours] G.T. Hist. iv. 11 and 12.

493 5 Eufronius] ibid. iv. 15.

19 Council of Paris] cf. note to p. 490, 9, above.

25 Emerius] G.T. Hist. iv. 26.

494 1 curt comment] ibid. iv. 26 *et sic principis est ultus iniuriam.*

4 Domnulus] ibid. vi. 9.

27 bribes to King Guntram] ibid. vi. 39.

33 Ferreolus] ibid. vi. 7.

495 6 see of Chartres] See Vit. Leobini, c. 44 [M.G.H. Auct. Ant. iv. 2, p. 77], *rex caeli . . . Childeberti cor ita . . . inflexit ut de beato Leobino monacho . . . eligendo regale daret decretum.*

14 Licinius] Vit. Licinii, c. 11, 12. AA.SS. February, ii. 679 (quoted by De Coulanges), *regis imperio subrogatus est Licinius ut praeesset ecclesiae Andegavensi.*

16 formula] See Marculf, quoted by De Coulanges, p. 555, n. 3.

26 gave a preference] De Coul. iii. 559.

35 character of Chilperic] G.T. Hist. vi. 46.

497 2 Gregory of Langres] Vit. Patr. vii.

PAGE LINE
497 25 Baudinus] G.T. Hist. iv. 3 and 4 ; x. 31. 16.
    36 Innocentius] ibid. vi. 37 and 38.
498 5 Bodegisilus] ibid. vi. 9 ; viii. 39.
    33 Eunius] ibid. v. 27, 30, and 41.
    40 Droctigisilus] (or Doctigisilus) ibid. ix. 37.
499 8 convoked in 577] ibid. v. 19. [It was in the Church of S. Peter
        in Paris, not in that of SS. Peter and Paul.]
    22 Fortunatus] Ven. Fort. iii. 17 and 18 (ed. Leo).
    27 too high favour] cf. G.T. Hist. v. 50.
    28 entangled] ibid. vii. 31.
500 2 lively narrative] ibid. viii. 1-7.
    26 Berthegundis] ibid. ix. 33.
501 5 Salonius and Sagittarius] ibid. iv. 43 ; v. 21 ; cf. vii. 37.

INDEX

Acts of Councils, marriage of near relations constantly prohibited by, 257 ; their evidence as to the moral tone of the clergy, 460 *sqq.*, 465 ; on the attitude of clergy towards heretics, 468 *sq.* ; enactments against Jews, 469 *sq.* ; creed formulated by, binding upon clergy, 473 ; and royal interference in election of bishops, 490, 493, 495

Aegidius, last defender of the Roman cause in Gaul, 10, 12, 18, 19, 20, 31, 78 ; elected ruler of Salian Franks, 11, 12, 13, 30 ; his successes against the Visigoths, 14, 35 ; Frank invasion and death of, 14, 15, 31, 32

Aetherius, Bishop of Lisieux, story of plot against, 288-9

Aetius, 18, 140 ; his resistance to Frank invasion, 8, 9, 36, 63, 265 ; murdered, 10

Africa, North, Vandal conquest of, 24 ; Arian persecutions in, *ib.*, 465, 466

Agnes, Abbess of Poitiers, 374, 375, 392 ; miracle recounted by, 239 ; her relations with Fortunatus, 380, 383, 384, 392

Alans, the, Franks defend Rome against, 5 ; Franks defeated by, 8

Alaric, 25, 77, 89, 98 ; surrenders Syagrius to Clovis, 79 ; his conciliatory policy to Roman and Catholic subjects, 94 ; the *Breviarium Alarici*, 94, 263 ; Theodoric's warning to, 95, 157 ; his conference with Clovis, 95 ; defeated and slain at Vouglé, 96 ; his relations with S. Caesarius, 98 *sq.*

Alemanni, the, Rhineland invaded by, 7, 8, 86 ; raids on the monasteries of Lake Leman by, 37 ; defeated by Clovis at Tolbiacum, 86 *sq.* ; Theodoric advises caution against, 93

Alsace seized by Theudebert, 210

Amalaric, King of the Visigoths, 102 ; defeated by Childebert, 160

Amalo, Duke, his end, 290

Anchorets (*see* Hermits) ; of Auvergne, 163, 309, 317, 318, 326, 432 *sq.* ; their practices Oriental in origin, 355, 356 ; excesses of their austerity, *ib.*, 357 ; development of monasteries round famous individuals, 360, 361, 362

Andarchius, the slave, career and murder of, 222

Andelot, the Pact of, 113, 203, 224, 342 *sq.*

Angels and demons in popular beliefs of the age, 400 *sq.*, 414

Antrustiones, high rank of, 53 *sq.*, 218, 219, 225 ; heavy money composition exacted for murder of, 57, 60, 117, 218, 219 ; serfs raised to rank of, 223

Apollinaris, Bishop, miracle performed for, 239 ; his bishopric obtained by bribery, 490

Aprunculus, Bishop, his plot to hand over Burgundy to the Franks, 78, 83

Aquitaine, Gallo-Roman aristocracy undisturbed in, 5, 25, 159, 168, 196, 198, 319 ; Vandal pressure on, 17, 23 ; Visigothic monarchy founded in, 18 ; Euric's Arian intolerance in, 25, 465 *sq.* ; the Church desires to see the Franks masters of, 64, 88, 94, 99, 159 ; Frank conquest of, 96 *sqq.*, 100 *sqq.*, 103, 104 ; risings against Frank monarchy in, 123 *sq.*, 125 ; partitions of, among Merovingian kings, 155 *sq.*, 159, 160, 171, 179 *sq.* ; Ostrogoths invade, 159, 163 ; conspiracy of Chramnus in, 167 *sqq.* ; constant warfare for the cities of, 179, 180, 181 *sq.*, 184, 185, 188, 189, 191 *sqq.*, 196, 197 *sq.*, 264, 265, 276, 329 *sq.*, 331 ; conspiracy of

Gundobald in, 192 *sqq*., 202 ; Gallo-Roman culture strong in, 196, 198, 276, 319 ; Imperial municipal system retained in, 263, 319 ; hostilities between cities of, 265 ; low morality of, 271 ; Frank population of, probably sparse, 276

Arcadius, revolt of, in Auvergne, 160, 161, 308, 319 *sq*.

Arianism, of Burgundian kings, 20, 83, 89, 90, 92, 94 ; Arian persecutions, 24, 93, 94, 465, 466 ; hatred between Catholics and Arians, 24, 25, 64, 78, 88, 89, 94, 105, 175 *sq*., 338 *sq*., 465 ; a league of Arian powers possibly contemplated by Theodoric, 92 *sq*. ; Jewish support of, 99 ; Arians less sacrilegious than Catholic Franks, 330 ; Gregory's detestation for, 338, 339

Aristocracy, Merovingian, 215 *sqq*. ; its ambition to assert itself above the monarchy, particularly shown in the struggle between Brunihildis and the Austrasian *leudes*, 184 *sq*., 187, 188, 192, 193, 202, 203, 205, 208, 209, 210, 228 *sq*., 230, 231, 232 *sq*., 277 ; ruthless suppression of the king's possible rivals among, 215 *sqq*., 219 ; men of low origin in, 215, 222 *sq*., 226 ; official, 217, 218, 219 *sqq*., 225 ; not hereditary, 218 *sq*., 225, 226, 228 ; entirely dependent on king's will and choice, 218, 219, 223, 226 ; Gallo-Romans in, 220 *sq*., 223 ; landed, 223 *sqq*. ; titles given to, 226 *sqq*. ; growth of its independent power, 228 *sqq*. ; devout households among, 271 *sqq*. ; the appeal of the ascetic life among, and its explanation, 272 *sq*., 311, 313, 318, 359 *sq*., 361, 362, 407, 408 *sq*., 473 ; lawlessness and violence among, 299 *sqq*. ; bishoprics considered a prize by, 316 *sq*., 329, 473, 496, 501 ; health of, apparently precarious, 322

Arles, Aegidius's defence of, 14 ; the plague in, 34, 260 ; besieged by Theuderic, 97, 99 *sq*. ; conduct of the Jews during the siege, 99, 100, 244 *sq*. ; Theudebert repulsed at, 163 ; in the hands of Guntram, 174, 179

Armentaria, mother of Gregory of Tours, 38, 309, 310, 321 *sq*., 323

Asceticism, growth of the influence of, 24, 36, 76, 256, 269, 324, 355 *sqq*. ; its appeal to the nobler spirits of the aristocracy, 256, 272 *sq*., 311, 313, 318, 358 *sqq*., 361, 362, 407, 408 *sq*., 473 ; its practices Oriental in origin, 355, 356 ; its excesses, 356, 357 ; the cult of the ascetics, 407 *sq*., 415 *sq*.

Attalus, Gregory's tale of his escape from the Germans, 312 *sq*.

Attila, invasion of, 9, 10, 11, 13, 17, 27

Audovera, repudiated wife of Chilperic, 134, 173, 184, 284

Aurelian, envoy from Clovis to Clothilde, disguised as a beggar, 83 *sq*.

Ausonius, peaceful scenes depicted by, 71, 236

Austrasia, 171 ; attempt to unite with Neustria under Brunihildis, 124 *sq*. ; Gundobald's conspiracy fostered in, 125, 192, 194, 199, 202 ; under Mayors of the Palace, 140, 212 ; Saxon invasion of, 169 ; causes of distinction and conflict between Neustria and, 171 *sqq*. ; Frank predominance in, 171 ; Neustria invaded by, 179 ; ambitious Austrasian nobles and their struggle with Brunihildis, 182 *sq*., 184, 185, 187, 188, 192, 193, 202, 203, 205, 208, 209, 210, 228 *sq*., 230, 231, 232 *sqq*., 277 ; strife between the factions of the nobles, 186 *sq*., 188, 189, 190, 193, 228 ; proposed alliance with Neustria against Burgundy, 187 *sq*. ; efforts to recapture cities of Aquitaine, 189, 191 *sq*., 193, 196, 197 *sq*. ; Guntram and the Austrasian nobles, 197, 198, 199 ; reconciliation with Burgundy, 199 *sq*. ; the Pact of Andelot, 203, 242 ; vengeance afterwards taken on the rebellious nobles, 203 *sq*., 205 ; Brunihildis driven from, 209, 229 ; Neustria crushed by Burgundy and, 209, 229, 231 ; war with Burgundy ending in death of Brunihildis, 209 *sqq*., 230 *sqq*. ; arrogant Roman governor of, killed, 220 *sq*. ; Auvergne falls under sway of, 320 *sq*.

Austrechildis, wife of Guntram, 133 ; Guntram punishes calumnies on, 133, 135, 178, 284 ; orders the execution of her two physicians, 135 *sq*., 178

Austrigiselus and Sicharius, blood feud between families of, 145, 304 *sqq.*

Autun, legend of ghostly choir of, 412

Autun, Count of, *see* Gregory, Bishop of Langres

Auvergne, Euric's successful campaign in, 22, 24, 314 ; Theuderic's invasion and devastation of, 97, 121, 161 *sq.*, 299 *sq.*, 313, 318 ; career of Chramnus in, 123 *sq.*, 167 *sqq.*, 276, 321 ; remission of taxation in, 129 ; a hotbed of revolt against Merovingians, 159, 160, 308, 318 *sq.* ; Arcadius leads revolt against Theuderic in, 160, 161, 308, 319 *sqq.*; anchorets and monasteries of, 163, 309, 317, 318, 326, 360, 361, 363, 432 *sq.* ; slave rises to be governor of, 222 ; the Jews of, 244, 245 *sq.*, 247, 471 ; a hunter's paradise, 252 ; the plague in, 260, 314, 327; calamities and portents in, 314, 327 ; disputed succession to bishopric of, 314, 316 *sq.* ; history of, in decade preceding birth of Gregory, 318 *sqq.*

Avignon, Clovis marches on, 90 ; custom house at, 126 ; Mummolus besieged in, 195, 196

Avitus, Bishop of Auvergne, 316 *sqq.* ; offers Jews alternative of conversion or expulsion, 247, 471 ; tutor of Gregory, 316, 317, 326

Avitus, Bishop of Vienne, 93 ; fails to convert Gundobad from Arianism, 64, 75, 83, 88, 92, 116 ; letter to Clovis from, 88

Ballomer, Gundobald, 114, 192. *See* Gundobald

Basina, Queen, mother of Clovis, 7

Batavia and the Batavi, 6, 108

Bavarian Code, the, 51

Becco, Count, tyranny of, 132, 162

Beppolenus, Duke, revolt of the Bretons against, 152, 153

Berny, Gregory's trial at, 150, 333 *sq.* ; Chilperic seizes royal treasure at, 171, 227

Berthefredus, leader of Austrasian nobles opposing Brunihildis, 185, 188 ; plots to dethrone Guntram, 203, 204, 228

Berthegundis and Ingitrudis, story of, 344 *sq.*, 500

Bertram, Bishop of Bordeaux, 499 *sq.* ;

alleged relations with Fredegundis, 149, 285, 332, 499 ; immoral life of, 288, 460, 462 ; his quarrel with Palladius, 288, 341, 500 ; at the trial of Gregory, 334 ; his part in the Gundobaldian conspiracy, 340, 479, 499 ; his reception by Guntram after the rising, 340, 500 ; keeps his sister from her husband, 344, 500 ; presides at trial of Bishop Praetextatus, 499

Bibianus, Bishop of Saintes, his visit to Theodoric, 35, 36 ; his intimacy with an Eastern merchant, 244

Bishops, the, 23, 476 *sqq.* ; growth of their power, 24, 116 *sq.*, 145 *sq.*, 150, 198, 472, 476, 496, 502 ; for the most part Gallo-Roman aristocrats, 115, 137, 329, 336 *sq.*, 455, 477, 479, 487, 495, 502 ; disputes between Counts and, 145 *sqq.* ; courts held by, *ib.* ; Chilperic's reverence for, 176 ; the royal power in episcopal elections, 198, 480, 481, 482, 484, 489 *sqq.*, 493 *sqq.* ; powers of the Church extended and royal power limited, by council of seventy-nine, 212 ; their treatment of the Jews, 244, 245, 246 *sq.* ; provision for lepers entrusted to, 256 ; moral tone of, 286 *sqq.*, 461 *sq.*, 463, 488, 496, 497, 498 *sqq.* ; greed for wealth one of their failings, 296, 302 ; different conceptions of the episcopal office among, 316 *sq.*, 336 ; development of their authority over monasteries and convents, 366 *sq.*, 369, 370, 374 *sqq.*, 386 *sqq.*, 392 *sqq.* ; bequests to the Church by, 440 ; their power over the estates of their sees, 440, 441 ; church building by, 444, 461 ; schools maintained by, 474 ; as the defenders of the people, 476, 502 ; their functions, 476, 484 *sq.*, 502 ; as statesmen, 479, 484 ; their freedom from external control, 480 *sqq.* ; not under the authority of Pope or primate, 480, 481, 482, 502 ; their despotic power over clergy and *clerici*, 482 *sqq.*, 485 ; serfs emancipated and captives redeemed by, 484 ; their archpresbyters and archdeacons, 485 *sq.* ; the voice of the people in episcopal elections, 486 *sqq.*, 490, 495 ; bitter rivalry for the episcopal throne, 488 *sqq.*

Bodegiselus, Duke, 225 ; appointed Bishop of Le Mans, 494, 498; villainy of, *ib.*

Bordeaux, trade of, 242, 244 ; earthquake and fire at, 260, 266 ; splendour of its Cathedral, 443, 448

Boso, Guntram, 194, 436 ; charges of sacrilege against, 48, 195, 203, 294 *sq.* ; his misconduct at Tours, 148, 337, 338, 454; his part in the death of Theudebert, 183, 194, 456 ; his consummate treachery, 185, 194, 195, 200, 225, 294, 337, 436, 454, 456, 457 ; agrees to betray Merovech, 185, 194, 456, 457 ; prime mover in the Gundobaldian rising, 192, 194, 195, 197, 198, 199, 201 ; himself the slayer of Gundobald, 201 ; hatred of Brunihildis for, 203, 228 ; his end 203 *sq.*, 225 ; prophecy of pythoness consulted by, 436, 454 *sq.*

Bourges, Chilperic's attack on, 188, 196 ; conversion of Jews at. 245 ; its feud with Tours, 265

Bretons, the, fight for Rome, 13 ; defeated by Visigoths, 14, 15 ; Chilperic's campaign against, 119, 186 ; Chramnus raises revolt among, 124 ; their native princes called Counts, 142 ; rebellion against Guntram's governor, 152 *sq.* ; not under Merovingian control, 206, 336

Breviarium Alarici, 94, 263

Briccius, Bishop of Tours, election and expulsion of, 487 *sq.*

Brioude, shrine of S. Julian at, 25, 161, 255, 320, 322 *sq.*, 396 ; protection from plague sought at, 260, 327 ; sacrilege in, 320, 322

Brivate, 239 ; sacred herds at, 263

Bructeri, the, 6, 108

Brunihildis, wife of Sigibert, 172 *sq.*, 174, 183, 233 *sqq.*, 237, 284 ; afterwards marries her nephew Merovech, 124, 125, 184, 185, 453 ; Gregory on, 172, 233 ; Fortunatus on, *ib.*, 379 ; her struggle for the power of the Crown against the Austrasian nobles, 173, 184 *sq.*, 186 *sqq.*, 193, 202 *sq.*, 204, 205, 208, 209, 210 *sq.*, 222, 228 *sq.*, 230, 231, 232 *sqq.*, 277 ; her courage and statesmanship, 173, 208, 210, 231, 233 *sq.* ; her blood feud with Fredegundis, 174, 191, 205, 226, 229, 233, 285, 329 ; supported by a faction of

Austrasian nobles, 186 *sq.*, 188 *sq.*, 190, 193, 228 ; a party to the Gundobaldian conspiracy, 193 *sq.*, 199, 201, 202, 242 ; the Pact of Andelot, 203, 224 ; inspires vengeance on Boso and his associates, 203, 204, 205 ; attempts upon her life, 205, 225, 226, 464 ; takes refuge in Burgundy, 209, 229 ; revives Gallo-Roman power there, *ib.*, 210, 229, 230, 299 ; opposition and treachery, 211, 212, 230, 231, 232 ; captured, tortured and killed, 211, 232 ; said to have encouraged Theuderic's immoralities, 287 *sq.*

Burgundian Code, the, 38, 62 *sq.*, 65, 66, 70, 126, 141, 239, 251 ; fairness towards Gallo-Romans in, 38, 67, 91 ; capital offences in, 50, 66 ; pecuniary compensation system in, 51, 52, 66

Burgundians, the, penetration of Gaul by, 10, 13, 63 *sq.* ; Roman cause supported by, 20, 63 *sq.* ; as "guests" of Rome, in Eastern Gaul, 20, 36, 37, 64, 68, 79 ; Arianism of, 20, 64, 75, 465 ; condition of Eastern Gaul under, 36 *sqq.* ; character and social life of, 37 *sq.*, 40 *sqq.*, 67 ; Gallo-Romans and, 20, 38, 62, 65, 67, 91 ; sacrilege committed by, 300

Burgundy, position of Gallo-Romans in, 5, 20, 21, 38, 62, 65, 67, 82, 91, 221, 229, 234 ; temporary partition of, 20, 90 ; its kings Arians, 20, 64, 75, 83, 89, 90, 92, 94 ; its queens Catholics, 20 *sq.*, 64, 83, 94; made tributary to Clovis, 64, 91 ; its independence regained by Gundobad, 64, 91, 92, 95 ; movement to hand the country over to the Franks, 78, 83, 88 ; Lombard invasions of, 82, 205 *sq.*, 221, 383 ; embassies between Clovis and, 83 ; Frank invasions of, 90 *sq.*, 95, 121, 158, 160 ; absorbed into Frank empire, *ib.*, 320 ; struggle with Neustria and Austrasia, 187, 188 *sq.* ; Austrasian nobles break with, 187 *sq.* ; alliance with Austrasia to recapture cities of Aquitaine, 189 ; temporarily united with Neustria, 190 *sq.* ; the Gundobaldian conspiracy, 196, 198 *sq.*, 200 *sq.*, 221 ; reconciliation with Austrasia, 199 *sq.* ; the Pact of

Andelot, 203, 242; campaign in Septimania, 205, 242; assists Austrasia to crush Neustria, 209; rebellion of Frank nobles in, 209, 229, 231, 232; Brunihildis flees to, 209, 229; she revives Gallo-Roman power in, 209 *sq.*, 229, 230, 234; war with Austrasia, and internal treason, ending in death of Brunihildis, 209 *sqq.*, 230 *sqq.*; under Mayor of the Palace, 212; the plague in, 260 *sq.*; Latin the official language of, 277

Caesar, foresees danger from the German tribes, 4; on their use of a devastated region as a defensive barrier, 108
Caesaria, sister of S. Caesarius, 99, 101
Camararius, office of, 139
Cambrai, occupied by Chlogio, 8, 30; pagan Franks of, 89
Carcassonne, Clovis besieges, 97, 102, 112; Guntram's attack on, 206, 300
Cassian, reproves desire of monks to take Orders, 369
Cassiodorus, defeat of the Alemanni mentioned in letters of, 93; as minister of Theodoric, 95, 141; his part in making the monastery a centre of enlightenment, 368
Catholicism, of Burgundian queens, 20 *sq.*, 64, 83, 89, 94; its hatred for Arianism, 24, 25, 64, 78, 88, 89, 94, 105 *sq.*, 338 *sq.*, 465; its superior organisation and solidarity, 92 *sq.* *See also* Church
Cautinus, Bishop of Auvergne, 227, 290; disputes the see with Cato, 167, 491 *sq.*; his evil character, 167, 316, 327, 461, 493; his close relations with Jew traders, 245; victim of the plague, 260, 327
Celsus, raised to the Patriciate, 82, 120, 221, 299; plunders Church estates, 221, 299
Châlons, battle of, 9, 10, 64
Chamavi, the, 6, 7
Champagne, German invasion of, 31; Rauchingus plots to make himself ruler of, 151, 295; Childebert's devastation of, 169; Munderic claims allegiance of, 294
Charibert, sent by Chlothar against Chramnus, 123, 168; patron of Leudastes, 147, 223; his death, 147,

179; Gundobald adopted by, 193; his several wives, 223, 233, 283, 287; Gregory on, 280; Fortunatus on, *ib.*; excommunicated, 283, 287; story of punishment of greed of, 296; his death foretold to Guntram, 436; his election of Emerius to bishopric of Saintes, 493 *sq.*
Charity, organisation of, in Gaul, 255 *sq.*
Chatti, the, 6, 108
Chauci, the, 6
Cherusci, the, 108
Childebert I., son of Clovis, 155; his invasion of Burgundy, 121, 160 *sq.*, 320; his part in the murder of his nephews, 131, 159, 219, 282; punishment of plot against, 133; his possessions on the death of Clovis, 155 *sq.*; invited to annex Auvergne in absence of Theuderic, 160, 319 *sq.*; his campaigns against the Visigoths, 160, 166, 279; frustration of his attempts to divide Theudebert's realm with Chlothar, 163, 165, 228; joins Theudebert against Chlothar, *ib.*; defrauded by Chlothar of his share in Theudebald's dominions, 166, 168; supports rebellion of Chramnus, 168, 169; his death, 169; hospice established at Lyons by, 255; Fortunatus on, 280
Childebert II., succeeds Sigibert, 113, 183; made heir to Guntram, 113, 187, 199, 229; his campaigns against the Lombards, 120, 189, 205, 206, 207 *sq.*; Church taxation remitted by, 129, 443; removes an unpopular governor, 152; his minority gives Austrasian nobles their opportunity, 185; Chilperic's attempts to seize his possessions in Aquitaine, *ib. sqq.*, 196; often proclaimed heir of Chilperic, 187, 188; his difficult relations with Guntram, 187, 190 *sq.*, 201, 340 *sq.*, 342, 348; and the Gundobaldian conspiracy, 192, 195, 196, 198, 199, 202; attempts made upon his life, *ib. sqq.*, 225, 226, 295, 391, 464; the Pact of Andelot made with Guntram, 203, 224, 342 *sq.*; assembles council of bishops for trial of Egidius, 204, 346, 391; causes of his military failures, 206, 207; his death, 229;

Gregory's relations with, 239, 340 *sq.*, 342 *sq.*, 344 ; as a hunter, 252, 365 ; his endowment of S. Carileffus, 365, 421 ; episcopal elections controlled by, 495

Childeric, becomes chief of the Franks, 10, 13 ; banished, 10, 11, 13, 30 ; his return, 11, 12, 14, 15 ; supports Roman cause on the Loire, *ib.*, 16, 77 ; legend of S. Geneviève and, 27 ; the father of Clovis, 77 ; sheltered during banishment by the Thuringians, 371

Chilperic I., son of Gundicar, 20

Chilperic II., son of Gundiac, 18, 20, 83 ; seizes sole sovereignty of Burgundy, 20, 64 ; his times described in letters of Sidonius, 20, 21 ; defeated and murdered by Gundobad, 21, 64, 77, 83 ; his kindness to abbot of Romainmôtier, 37

Chilperic, son of Chlothar, 170 ; his struggle with Sigibert, 114, 119, 120, 148, 172, 180, 181 *sqq.*, 225, 280, 329 *sq.*, 331; his campaign against the Bretons, 119, 186 ; attempts to seize sole monarchy, 170 *sq.* ; character of, 175, 186, 190, 281 ; the rebellion of his son Merovech, 124 *sq.*, 134, 149, 184, 337, 454, 456 *sq.*, 458 ; oppressive taxation under, 126 *sqq.*, 130, 175, 186 ; the plague carries off two of his sons, 128, 135, 147, 186, 260, 266, 280, 338, 378 *sq.* ; his jealousy of the wealth and power of the Church, 128, 130, 175, 176, 186, 190, 365, 441, 479 ; his wives and concubines, 134, 173 *sq.*, 179, 284 *sq.* ; Limoges passes from Guntram to, 146 ; Tours devastated by, 148, 180, 300, 329 ; and Leudastes and the conspiracy against Gregory, 148, 149, 150, 331, 332 *sqq.* ; the marriage and murder of Galswintha, 173 *sq.*, 179, 284 *sq.* ; Gregory on, 175, 176, 179, 190, 281, 337, 455 ; his persistent struggle for the cities of Aquitaine, 175, 180, 181, 182, 183 *sqq.*, 188, 189, 196, 197, 329 *sq.* ; his admiration for Roman culture, 175, 190, 277 ; episcopal seats sold by, 175 ; revives the Sabellian heresy, *ib. sq.*, 186, 471, 480; his taste for theological controversy, 175 *sq.*, 186, 471, 480 ; Priscus the

Jew and, 176, 245, 247 *sq.*, 471 *sq.* ; his relations with Guntram, 178, 179, 180, 181, 188 ; in league with Austrasia against Burgundy, 187 *sq.*, 196, 228, 242 ; murdered, 190, 252, 285 ; Fortunatus on, 236, 280, 333 *sq.*, 378 *sq.* ; his attempt to convert Jews of Paris, 247 *sq.*, 471 ; Gregory's vision of the end of his line, 337, 455 ; uses relics to defend him from consequences of perjury, 434

Chlodomer, 86, 155, 156 ; falls in battle against Burgundians, 131, 158, 279, 281 ; his sons murdered by their uncles, 131, 159, 219, 282, 372

Chlogio, first king of a Frank tribe in Gaul, 8 *sq.* ; his successes against Romans, *ib.*, 30

Chlothar I., 155 ; his campaigns against the Thuringians and Saxons, 34, 123, 158, 166 *sq.*, 168, 169, 282, 371, 372 ; his invasion of Burgundy, 121, 160 *sq.*, 320, 372 ; rebellion of his son Chramnus, 123 *sq.*, 167 *sqq.*, 372, 436 ; Church estates taxed by, 126, 443 ; his taxation taken as a standard of fairness, 127, 128 ; murders the sons of Chlodomer, 131, 159, 219, 282, 372 ; original possessions of, 155, 156 ; his attempts to deprive Theudebert of his succession, 163, 165; Childebert and Theudebert combine against, 165 ; his army in Italy destroyed by plague and famine, 166 ; appropriates Theudebald's possessions, 166 ; his death, 170 ; Gundobald disowned by, 192; excommunicated, 271, 478; Theuderic's treacherous attempt on his life, 282 ; Radegund made his unwilling wife, 282, 371 *sq.* ; his wives and concubines, 282, 283, 372 ; allows Radegund to leave him and found her convent, 372 *sqq.* ; his interference in episcopal elections, 492 *sq.*, 494

Chlothar II., 187, 190, 227 ; forced to exempt Tours from taxation, 128 ; Guntram as his guardian, 190, 191, 196, 205, 348 ; his defeat at Dormeille reduces his possessions to twelve cantons, 209, 210, 229, 230 ; offered the crown of Austrasia, 210, 211, 231 ; he defeats and kills

Brunihildis and the sons of Theuderic, 211, 231 *sq.* ; the three Frank realms temporarily united under, 211 ; customs dues reduced by, 243 ; his excessive devotion to sport, 253

Chramnesind and Sicharius, the case of, 305 *sq.*

Chramnus, the rebel son of Chlothar I., 123 ; his misconduct as Viceroy of Auvergne, *ib.*, 142, 167 *sq.*, 276, 458 ; plans to seize his father's possessions, 123, 124, 167 *sqq.*, 321 ; the *Sortes biblicae* consulted by, 124, 169, 436 ; his defeat and death, 124, 170 ; supports Cato's claim to bishopric of Auvergne, 167, 492

Chrodieldis, leader of revolt of nuns at Poitiers, 385, 386 *sqq.*, 392

Church, the, and the decline of Roman power, 5 ; its dignitaries usually Gallo-Romans, 12, 38, 51, 81, 105, 114, 115, 220, 273, 278, 311, 329, 479 ; comparatively undisturbed during period preceding the triumph of the Franks, 25 ; the Frank kingship and, 41, 479, 480, 481, 482, 484 ; its marvellous power shown by the conversion of the Franks, 42, 114, 465 ; the cruelty of the law mitigated by, 50 *sq.*, 52, 131 *sq.*, 367, 452 *sq.* ; its support of the Franks as its champions against the Arians, and its disillusionment, 64, 78, 94 *sq.*, 114, 159, 318-19, 330, 339 ; its growing power shown in legal codes, 75 ; possible design of Arian league against, 92 *sq.* ; its resistance to taxation by the Merovingians, 126, 127 *sq.*, 129, 130, 343 *sq.*, 443 ; its lenity towards the crimes of its benefactors, 170, 177, 178, 234, 269 *sq.*, 425 *sq.* ; ecclesiastical provinces created by, 180 ; lands held by, 203, 224, 363, 364, 441 *sqq.* ; organisation of charity by, 255, 451 *sqq.* ; Gregory's attitude to, 269 *sq.* ; the moral tone of the clergy, 286 *sqq.*, 302 *sqq.*, 459 *sqq.* ; restoration of ancient shrines by, 318 ; its authority in early Middle Ages, 324 *sq.* ; its absorption of ancient and pagan tradition and speculation into its system, 398, 399 ; its spiritual theory of the Universe, 399, 400 *sq.*, 416 ; and the power of the Evil One, 401, 414 ;

condones the pious frauds of hagiography, 421, 422, 423 *sq.* ; the materialism of the religion of the age, 425 *sq.* ; Church life and routine, 439 *sqq.* ; growth of its wealth, 440 *sqq.*, 451 ; its property held to be under divine guardianship, 441, 442 ; and the right of asylum, 452 *sqq.* ; enactments against heretics and Jews, 468 *sqq.* ; decay of culture and learning in, 473 *sqq.* ; not subject to Rome, 480, 481 ; under no primate, 481, 482 ; simony rampant in, 490, 491, 494 *sq.* ; its triumphant state-craft, 503. *See also* Bishops, Catholicism, *and* Clergy

Churches, their aspect and arrangement, 444 *sqq.* ; services in, 445, 446 ; chapels and oratories, 446, 447 ; sacred furniture and vessels, 449 ; as hospitals and almshouses, 450 *sqq.*

Civitates, administrative divisions, 140, 141 ; ecclesiastical provinces corresponding to, 180

Claudius, his murder of Eberulfus in the cathedral of Tours, 435, 452, 458 *sq.*

Clergy, the, moral tone of, 286 *sqq.*, 302 *sqq.*, 459 *sqq.* ; sexual relations of, 460 *sq.*, 464 ; largely recruited from servile class, 462, 480, 483 ; rebelliousness of, 463 *sq.*, 464 ; as hired assassins, 464 ; sport forbidden to, 465, 483 ; their attitude to heretics dictated to, 468 *sq.* ; not educated men, 473 *sqq.* ; absolute power of bishops over, 482 *sqq.*

Clerici, the, functions and position of, 483 *sq.*

Clothilde, wife of Clovis, 20, 21, 64, 83 ; and the building of the shrine of the Apostles, 29, 96 ; Clovis's wooing, 83, *sq.* 85 ; the baptism of her children, and her influence on her husband, 86, 88, 89 ; prefers to see the sons of Chlodomer dead rather than degraded, 159, 282 ; her death, 166 ; her asceticism and deeds of mercy, 256, 407 ; foundations of, 364, 425

Clovis, son of Childeric, 5, 77, 111 *sq.* ; lost original Life of, 29 *sq.* ; S. Geneviève and, 29 ; his conversion and baptism, 30, 32, 85, 87 *sq.*, 89 *sq.*, 94, 114, 364, 465 ; S. Rémi and,

30, 31, 32, 33, 85, 88, 89, 96 ; and the vase of Soissons, 32 *sq.*, 80, 86, 116 ; ancient Salic Law amended by, 43 ; overwhelms Romans under Syagrius, 79, 95, 111 ; lands given to his followers by, 79, 80, 114 *sq.* ; his conciliatory policy towards Gallo-Romans, 80 *sq.*, 112, 114, 115, 154, 215, 217 ; his success as statesman and organiser, 80, 81, 90, 112, 137, 141 ; romantic tale of his wooing of Clothilde, 83 *sq.*, 85 ; the battle of Tolbiacum, 86 *sq.* ; his outburst on hearing the story of the Crucifixion, 90, 398 ; his invasion of Burgundy, 90 *sq.*, 95 ; Theodoric's efforts to restrain, 92, 93, 95 ; his victory at Vouglé, 95 *sqq.*, 111 ; master of four-fifths of Gaul, 95 *sqq.*, 111 ; forced to raise siege of Carcassonne, 102, 103 ; his triumphal entry into Tours, 104, 105, 112 ; Imperial dignities assumed by, 104 *sq.*, 109, 112 ; his army, 118 *sq.* ; unbroken line of his descendants, 122; possible rivals ruthlessly removed by, 131, 133, 215 *sq.*, 217, 219, 281; his deception of the vassals of Ragnachar, 216, 217, 227, 296 ; his grants to churches on his conversion, 364; miraculously cured of fever, 262 ; his relations with the bishops, 489

Clovis, son of Chilperic, 134 ; hatred of Fredegundis for, *ib.*, 332 ; alleged conspiracy of, 134, 150 ; defeated by Mummolus, 330

Cologne, sacked by Franks, 7, 14, 31 ; Frank settlement in, 42, 216 ; pagan tribes of, 89

Comes, the office of, 141 *sq.* See Count

Comitatus of old German nobles, 218, 219

Common people, the life of, as seen in Gregory and Fortunatus, 235 *sqq.*

Convenae, the siege of, 125, 200, 201, 264, 277

Count, the office of, 139, 140, 141 *sqq.*, 151, 263 ; in Salic Law, 54, 55, 56 ; Gallo-Roman counts, 115, 120, 142, 162, 168, 215, 217, 220, 224 ; military duties, 118, 119, 120, 143 ; responsibilities in connection with taxation, 129 *sq.*, 143, 245, 254 ; judicial functions, 131, 132, 141, 143

sqq., 151, 152 ; in palatine service, 139, 140, 142 ; an Imperial dignity, 141 ; family succession to the office, 142 ; terms of appointment, 143 ; disputes between bishops and counts, 145 *sqq.* ; in relation to dukes, 151, 152 *sq.* ; counts appointed bishops, 496

Country life, as seen in the codes of law, 45 *sqq.*, 60 *sqq.*, 68 *sqq.*, 251 ; survival of the old Gallo-Roman estates, 60, 62, 237, 272 ; the *villae*, 60 *sqq.*, 242, 254 ; as described by Fortunatus, Gregory, and other writers, 236 *sqq.*, 249 *sqq.* ; the ravages of plague and famine, 254, 257 ; the isolation of small communities conducive to interbreeding, 257 *sq.* ; lingering traces of paganism, 262 *sq.* ; devout family life on many rural estates, 272 *sq.*

Court, the Merovingian, a shadow of the Imperial, 137 *sq.* ; its officials, 138 *sqq.*

Curia, the, retains many of its powers, 81, 126, 263 ; becomes democratic, 263, 264

Dagobert, relief in customs dues conceded by, 243 ; his foundation of S. Denis, 253, 425 *sq.* ; hospice founded by, 255

Danes, the, raids by, 157, 188 ; crushed by Lupus, *ib.*, 222

Demoniac possession, its probable explanation, 259, 402, 403, 432, 451

Desiderius, Duke, 115, 120, 145, 220, 291 ; wins Aquitanian cities for Chilperic, 185, 196 *sq.* ; in the Gundobaldian conspiracy, 196, 197, 198, 201 ; seizes the treasure of Rigunthis, 197, 297 ; abandons Gundobald, 200

Desiderius the impostor, 436 *sq.*

Deuteria, Theudebert's intrigue with, 163, 289

Dijon, Gregory's description of, 264 *sq.*, 311

Disease in Gaul, 257 *sqq.*, 342, 348, 402, 403, 432, 450 ; epilepsy and demoniacal possession, 259, 402, 403, 432, 451. *See also* Plague

Divorce under the Burgundian Law, 72

Domesticus, the office of, 138, 139, 140

Dormeille, defeat of Chlothar II. at, 209, 211, 229

Drunkenness in Merovingian society, 286 *sq.* ; among Churchmen, *ib.*, 463, 498

Duke, the office of, 140, 151 *sqq.* ; in the palatine service, 140 ; functions of, 151 *sq.* ; military duties, *ib.*, 206; in provincial government, 151 ; in collision with the count, 152 *sq.* ; Gallo-Roman dukes, 220 ; the rapacity of some dukes, 298 *sqq.* ; dukes appointed bishops, 496

Eastern Empire, the, unsuccessful against Vandals, 17, 20 ; attacked by Ostrogoths, 21 *sq.*, 23 ; its nominal sovereignty in Gaul, 104 ; its support of the Gundobaldian rising, 194, 202

Eberulfus, his conduct in asylum at Tours, 435, 442 ; murdered in S. Martin's, 435, 452, 458 *sq.*

Ecdicius, 120 ; defends Auvergne against the Visigoths, 22, 23, 38, 274

Education, at a low ebb in fifth and sixth centuries, 473 *sqq.* ; schools maintained by bishops, 474

Egidius, Bishop of Rheims, opponent of Brunihildis, 126, 184, 185, 186, 187, 188, 190, 192, 193, 210, 222, 228, 233, 422 ; supports Gundobald, 196, 199 ; plots to murder Childebert, 204, 346, 391 ; tried by council of bishops, *ib.* ; escapes severe punishment, 204, 346 ; his alleged intrigue with Fredegundis, 285, 422 ; Fortunatus's Life of S. Rémi composed for, *ib.* ; his moral faults, *ib.*, 460, 462

Eufronius, Bishop of Tours, and S. Radegund's convent, 375, 382, 387

Eulalius, Count of Auvergne, iniquities of, 145, 152, 290 *sq.*

Euric, king of the Visigoths, Gallo-Roman struggle with, 5, 22 ; his conquests, 23 *sqq.* ; Arian persecutions of Catholics under, 24, 94, 339, 465 *sq.* ; his Roman advisers, 65, 81

Famine recurrent in Gaul, 254, 298

Felix, Bishop of Nantes, his great public works, 237, 243, 336 ; his quarrel with Gregory, *ib. sq.*

Ferreolus, Bishop of Uzès, 128, 494 ; his epistles, 474

Ferreolus, Tonantius, Prefect of the Gauls, 7, 12, 494

Firminus, Count of Auvergne, 98, 167, 220 ; removed and maltreated by Chramnus, 168, 458

Florentius, father of Gregory, 308, 309, 321 *sqq.* ; miraculously healed, 322, 361

Fortunatus, Venantius, 38, 138, 220, 308, 317, 336, 377 *sqq.* ; his abbreviated Life of S. Rémi, 29, 31, 422 ; new churches celebrated in his poems, 36, 237, 443 ; on Sigibert and Brunihildis, 172 *sq.*, 280, 379 ; on the wedding of Galswintha, 173, 284, 379 ; a flatterer and a parasite, 173, 237, 279 *sq.*, 281, 333 *sq.*, 378, 379, 380, 384 ; on Chilperic, 175, 280, 333 *sq.*, 379 ; his praise of Lupus, 188, 222, 237, 379 ; his travels in Gaul, 236, 237, 238, 239, 377 *sq.* ; tranquillity of life in Gaul as depicted in his poems, 236 *sqq.*, 249 ; on the public works of Felix, Bishop of Nantes, 237, 336 ; evidence of Frank adoption of Roman culture in his works, 277 *sq.* ; his descriptions of the Merovingians at variance with Gregory's, 279 *sqq.* ; on Charibert, 280 ; on Childebert, *ib.* ; on Fredegundis, *ib.*, 334, 379 ; his friendship with Gregory, 326, 377, 378, 379 ; his stay with Radegund at the Convent of the Holy Cross, 370, 377, 378, 380, 383 *sqq.*, 392 ; his redeeming qualities, 378, 379 *sq.*, 384 ; on the verses of Bertram of Bordeaux, 499

Franci utiliores, the, 227

Franks, the, legends of their origin and early history, 5 *sq.*, 28 ; early conquests in Gaul, 6 *sq.*, 8, 10, 13, 14, 31, 42 ; as friends, defenders, and despoilers of Rome, 6, 7 *sq.*, 11, 15, 16, 79, 274 ; Romans as chiefs of, 6, 11 *sq.* ; their proverbial ferocity and faithlessness, 7, 42, 89, 103, 104, 120, 154, 156 ; in palatine service, 7 *sq.* ; their first king, 8 ; leagued with Romans against Visigoths, 15, 16 ; their conversion to Christianity, 30, 42, 43, 87, 89, 114, 398 ; character and social life as revealed in the Codes, 40 *sqq.* ; their ancient legal usages, 43, 44 ; position of Romans among, 44, 47, 58,

59, 80 *sq.* ; their numbers at the accession of Clovis, 77, 80 ; the Church considers them its champions and gives them its support, 77 *sq.*, 88, 104, 105, 114, 318 *sq.*, 330, 339, 489 ; land settlement among, 79 *sq.* ; their aristocracy not one of birth, 80 *sq.*, 118, 215 *sqq.* ; kingship among, *see* Kingship, Frank ; Rheims pillaged by, 86 ; their defeat of the Alemanni, 86 *sq.*, 93 ; some tribes remain pagan, 89, 122 ; invasion of Burgundy under Clovis, 90 *sq.*, 95 ; struggle with the Visigoths, 96 *sqq.*, 100 *sqq.* ; very different from the Germans of Tacitus, 107, 108, 109 ; their loss of old German representative institutions, 110 *sq.*, 116, 118 ; question of their exemption from land tax, 130 *sq.*; Burgundy invaded and absorbed in Frank empire, 158, 160 ; they frequently show a mutinous spirit, *ib.* *sq.*, 167, 182 *sq.*, 188 ; their devastation of Auvergne, 161 *sq.* ; involved in disastrous Italian campaign, 164, 165, 166 ; relative numbers of Gallo-Romans and, 171, 274 *sq.* ; change in their character, 273, 274 ; tendency to coalesce with Gallo-Romans, 277, 278 ; dukedoms held by, 278 ; their greed for wealth and frequent sacrilege, 296 *sqq.*, 312, 320, 321, 330, 337, 431, 459 ; their reverence for bishops, 477, 478

Fredegarius, 29, 43, 85, 139, 227, 231 ; his story of the banishment and restoration of Childeric, 10, 11, 15 ; the wooing of Clothilde by Clovis, 83 *sq.*, 85 ; Clovis and the tale of the Passion, 90

Fredegundis, wife of Chilperic, 174, 179, 284 ; her fit of penitence on the loss of her sons in the plague, 128, 135, 186, 338 ; appeals to Chilperic to reduce taxation, 128 ; causes the murder of Sigibert, 133, 183, 331 ; her hideous cruelty, 134 *sq.* ; brings about the death of her stepson Clovis, *ib.*, 187, 332 ; tortures the witches of Paris, 134, 135, 402 ; tortures Mummolus, 135 ; her treatment of Leudastes, *ib.*, 149, 265 *sq.* ; Gregory tried for alleged imputations on her virtue, 149 *sqq.*, 332 *sqq.* ; her alleged intrigues with various lovers, 149, 150, 190, 205, 285, 332, 499 ; her treatment of Beppolenus, 152, 153 ; causes the murder of Galswintha, 173 *sq.*, 285, 329 ; her blood feud with Brunihildis, 174, 179, 184, 191, 205, 209, 226, 229, 233, 329 ; places herself and Chlothar under protection of Guntram, 177, 190, 191, 192, 196, 348 ; her persecution of Merovech, 185, 456 ; her husband's murder attributed to, 190 ; her attempts on the lives of Brunihildis and Childebert, 205, 226, 464 ; her death, 208 ; praised by Fortunatus, 280, 334, 379 ; her ability and fascination, 285 ; attempts the murder of her daughter Rigunthis, 297 *sq.* ; orders the murder of Eberulfus, 435

Gallo-Romans, the, divided in the struggle with the invaders of Gaul, 5, 9 *sq.*, 23 ; many prefer to come to terms, 5, 14, 16 ; their comparative tranquillity and security under the conquerors, 5, 12, 25, 38, 62, 80 *sq.*, 110, 114, 115, 153 *sq.*, 159, 168, 196, 224 *sq.*, 310, 319 ; a Roman as chief of the Franks, 11 *sq.* ; the great Churchmen principally drawn from their ranks, 12, 38, 51, 81, 105, 115, 220, 273, 278, 311, 329, 479 ; their position among the tolerant Burgundians, 21, 62, 65, 67, 68, 73, 74, 82, 90 *sq.* ; Gallo-Roman estates as Frank *villae*, 60 *sq.*, 67, 114 *sq.* ; land divided between Gallo-Romans and Burgundians, 68, 79, 115 ; their preference of Franks to Arians, 78, 94, 95, 96, 99, 105 ; under no form of oppression, 80 *sq.*, 114, 115, 153 *sq.* ; their distinguished service in the Merovingian armies, 81, 115, 119, 120, 156 *sq.*, 165, 206, 265, 274; their administrative experience valuable to the Merovingians, 81 *sq.*, 114, 115, 138, 153 *sq.*, 164, 165, 221 ; Frank power never challenged by, 110, 114, 121, 153 *sq.* ; Clovis's conciliatory policy towards, 110, 112, 114 *sq.*, 215, 217 ; as Counts, 115, 120, 142, 162, 168, 215, 217, 220, 224; retain vast possessions and prestige in Aquitaine, 159, 168, 196, 224 *sq.* ; their predominance in Neustria, 171 *sq.* ; by no means free from the evil traits of the Franks, 201, 230, 273 *sq.*, 299, 321; their power in Burgundy revived by Brunihildis, 209 *sq.*, 229, 230, 234, 299; in the Merovingian aristocracy, 220 *sq.*, 223, 229; as physicians, 261; their social life centred in the cities, 265; many live devout lives on their estates, 272 *sqq.*; ascetic movement among, *ib.*, 359 *sq.*, 361, 362; change in their character, 273, 274; relative numbers and influence of Gallo-Romans and Franks, *ib. sqq.*; their tendency to coalesce with Franks, 277, 278

Gallus, Bishop of Auvergne, uncle of Gregory, 308 *sq.*, 313 *sq.*, 325; his funeral, 238, 314, 471; believed to have warded off plague from Auvergne, 260, 314; destroys pagan temple, 263, 313; his election to the bishopric, 314, 491

Galswintha, wife of Chilperic, 173; her wedding procession, *ib.*, 284; Fortunatus on, 173, 284; her murder begins the blood feud between Brunihildis and Fredegundis, 174, 179, 285, 329; her dower of five cities, 179, 203, 329

Gaul, sources of its history for the period, 4, 266 *sqq.*; decline of Roman power, 10, 16, 22, 23; sacrificed by the Empire for a visionary security at home, 22; its social condition obscure, 25 *sq.*; the plague in, 34, 128, 135, 146 *sq.*, 186, 208, 236, 254, 259 *sqq.*, 266, 280, 314, 327, 338, 342, 348, 430, 450; conquest of, a " peaceful penetration ", 37 *sq.*; its social life as revealed in the Codes, 40 *sqq.*; its ancient inhabitants not oppressed by their original conquerors, 80 *sq.*, 114; survival of paganism in, 89, 262 *sq.*, 313; Eastern Empire's shadow of sovereignty in, 104; organisation of its administration after the conquest, 110, 137, 138, 141; partition of, 171 *sq.*, 179, 275, 481; earthquake, fire, and flood in, 186, 259 *sq.*, 338, 347, 348, 438; its country life, 236 *sqq.*, 248 *sqq.*; travel in, 237, 238 *sqq.*; its inland trade, 242 *sqq.*; dues and customs, 243; famine and disease in, 253 *sqq.*, 298, 450; relative numbers and influence of Franks and Gallo-Romans, 274 *sq.*; treated as a whole by Gregory, 275, 276, 279

Genseric, character of, 17; attacks on the Empire inspired by, 23

Germans, the: their pressure on the declining Roman Empire, 4; conquests in Gaul, *ib.*, 6, 10, 12 *sq.*; common action with Romans against Huns, 11; masters of the Western Empire, 18, 23, 24; early character and institutions, 40 *sqq.*, 106 *sqq.*, 110, 116, 118; German critics and their mistaken belief in unchanged German character and polity, 40, 41, 106 *sq.*, 109, 218, 219; ancient legal usages and the Codes, 43, 44, 45, 49, 50, 53, 57; their cherished ideal of female purity, 72; their respect for the tradition and the dignities of Rome, 104, 105, 109, 112, 138, 477; changed since the time of Tacitus, 107, 108, 110; kingship among, 107 *sqq.*, 110, 111; ancient representative institutions lost by Franks, 110 *sq.*, 116, 118; ceremony of election of chieftains, 113 *sq.*; tribes from beyond the Rhine called in by Sigibert and Brunihildis, 172, 174, 182, 211, 232, 280; the fate of their original aristocracy, 218, 219; paganism revived by their settlement in north-eastern Gaul, 263; monogamy usual among, 283

Gesta Francorum on the framing of the Salic Law, 43

Gibbon, 312; on the army of Syagrius, 79; on the conversion of Clovis, 89

Godegesil, 20, 77; his kingdom seized by Chilperic II., 20, 64; Franks and Romans in army of, 65; pact with Clovis, 84, 90; his treachery to his brother Gundobad, *ib.*; defeated and killed, 91, 92

Godomar, son of Gundiac, 20

Godomar, son of Gundobad, 158, 160

Grafio, the office of, 54, 55

Gregory, Bishop of Langres, 309, 310; his career, 5, 38 *sq.*, 264 *sq.*, 310 *sqq.*, 497; as Count of Autun, 5, 38, 42, 142, 224, 311, 497; his asceticism, 38, 311, 497; elected bishop by popular voice, 39, 311, 497; his seat at Dijon, 264, 311; legends of, *ib. sq.*, 412

Gregory, Bishop of Tours, 80, 115, 235, 269 *sq.*, 308 *sqq.*; story of the banishment of Childeric, 10 *sq.*, 15 ; Gundobad's murder of Chilperic, 21 ; his admiration for the anchorets of Auvergne, 26, 163, 200, 267, 272, 317, 318, 356, 357, 358, 360, 361 ; the Life of S. Rémi, 29 *sq.* ; crime and violence in his pages, 46, 49, 81, 289 *sqq.*, 295, 304 *sqq.* ; on the Burgundian Code, 63, 64 *sq.* ; on the surrender of Syagrius to Clovis, 79 ; relations of Franks and Gallo-Romans in his works, 81 ; tales of the early years of Clovis, 85 ; his hatred of Arianism, 89, 338, 339, 466 *sq.* ; on the land tax system, 126, 127, 139 ; defends Tours from taxation, 128, 343 *sq.*, 443 ; on the officials of the Court, 139, 140, 141 ; the enmity of Leudastes, Count of Tours, 147 *sqq.*, 223, 331 *sqq.*, 436, 463 ; his trial for alleged slanders on Fredegundis, 149 *sqq.*, 331 *sqq.*, 463 ; oral tradition as basis of much of his work, 155, 161 ; on the devastation of Auvergne, 155, 161, 181, 320 *sq.* ; on Theudebert, 163 *sq.*, 281, 289, 443 ; his enthusiasm for the miraculous, 166, 239 *sq.*, 258, 261, 269, 291, 316, 322, 323, 327 *sq.*, 346, 350, 395, 406, 418, 426, 433 ; the rebellion of Chramnus, 168, 169, 170, 436 ; condones the worst crimes of champions of the Church, 170, 177, 178, 269, 348 ; Gaul treated as a whole in his work, 171, 275, 276, 277 ; his tribute to Brunihildis, 172, 233, 234 ; on the character of Chilperic, 175 *sq.*, 190, 270, 281, 455 ; his liking for theological debate, 176, 186, 247 *sq.*, 338, 339, 347, 467, 472 ; his favourable estimate of Guntram, 176 *sq.*, 178, 281, 283, 348 ; mentions the dethronement of Chilperic, 179 ; the mutiny of Sigibert's *leudes*, 182 ; his careful account of the Gundobaldian rebellion, 200 *sqq.*; addresses Guntram's generals on their failures, 207 ; his death, 208, 310, 346 ; on the Merovingian aristocracy, 219 *sqq.* ; a Gallo-Roman aristocrat, 220, 269, 308, 309, 329, 349 ; on grants of land by the king, 324 ; the Pact of Andelot given by, 224,

342 *sq.* ; his use of the term "nobiles", 226 ; his travels, 238, 239, 240, 241, 327 *sq.*, 340, 341, 346, 350 ; at the Court of Guntram and Childebert, 238, 239, 340 *sq.*, 342 *sq.*, 344 ; miraculously saved from harm, 239, 240, 241, 327 *sq.*, 341, 431 ; his cult of S. Martin, 239, 258 *sq.*, 261, 267, 292 *sqq.*, 326, 327 *sq.*, 395 *sq.*, 404, 406, 418, 429, 433, 447, 450 ; conscious of his defective literary style, 236, 326, 349, 408, 475 ; and the Jews, 245 *sq.* ; goes to Brioude during the plague, 260, 327 ; his description of the fortifications of Dijon, 264 *sq.*, 311 ; on the fire at Paris, 267 ; compared with Herodotus, 269 ; the morals of the time as seen in his works, 269 *sq.*, 271, 272, 273, 275 *sqq.*, 288 *sqq.*, 296, 460, 462 *sqq.* ; his pessimistic view of the world, 270 ; his vision of the doom of the Merovingians, *ib.*, 337, 455 ; problems not discussed by, 274 *sq.*, 276 ; on Charibert, 280 ; Fortunatus disagrees with his estimates, 280 *sq.* ; on the moral life of the clergy, 286 *sq.*, 462 *sqq.* ; on divine punishment of perjury, 291 *sqq.* ; the blood feud of Sicharius and Austrigiselus, 304 *sqq.* ; his family, 308 *sqq.*, 321 *sqq.* ; materials for his Life, 309 ; his elevation to the bishopric, 309, 310, 328 *sq.* ; on his uncle Gallus, 313 ; on his father, 321, 322 ; on Nicetius, Bishop of Lyons, 315 *sq.* ; Avitus his friend and tutor, 316 *sqq.*, 326 ; restores ancient shrines and builds new churches, 318, 349 ; the religious outlook of his time, 323 *sqq.*, 395, 397 ; his youth, 325 *sqq.* ; his education, 326 ; the troubles of his times, 329 *sq.*, 331 ; quarrels with Felix, Bishop of Nantes, 336 *sq.* ; and the sacrilegious conduct of Merovech, 337 *sq.*, 454, 455 ; the affair of Berthegundis, 344 *sq.*, 500 ; on the election of Gregory the Great, 345 ; improbable story of his meeting with Gregory the Great, 345 *sq.* ; finishes his History, 346 ; as literary and historical artist, *ib.*, 348, 349, 409 ; anxious for the survival of his works, 349 ; at the burial of

S. Radegund, 342, 370, 385 *sq.*; stories of monastic foundations, 360, 361; his relations with Fortunatus, 377, 378, 379; the story of the convent of S. Radegund, 381, 385, 386 *sqq.*; receives deputation of the revolted nuns, 386 *sq.*; his works on the miracles of saints and martyrs, 396; stories of demons, 402; theory of the cult of saints, 406; legend of married purity repeated by, 412; uses relics as charms, 431, 433, 434; his treatment of impostors, 436 *sq.*; his belief in signs and omens in convulsions of nature, 438; his banquets, 445; his consecration of a chamber in the bishop's house, 447; dedicates relics of S. Julian, 451; mentions only one appeal of Gallic clergy to Rome, 480 *sq.*; on episcopal elections, 490, 491, 492, 494, 495, 497; on the morals of the bishops, 497, 498; describes Guntram's reception of Bertram and Palladius, 500

Gregory the Great, Pope, Brunihildis and, 234; suppresses paganism, 263; his election amid calamities and portents, 345; his meeting with Gregory of Tours improbable, 346; distinguishes monastic life from clerical, 369; his theological system, 395, 397 *sqq.*; his *Dialogues*, 401; defends the cult of the saints, 405 *sq.*; encourages sacred art, 448; guards the right of asylum, 452; protests against traffic in Christian slaves, 470; protects legal rights of Jews, *ib.*; a man of little learning, 473

Gundiac, king of Burgundy, 18, 20

Gundicar, king of Burgundy, killed at Châlons, 20, 64

Gundobad, son of Gundiac, 20, 64; Master of the Roman Armies during exile, 11, 18, 21, 64; his kingdom seized by Chilperic II., 20, 64; overthrows and kills Chilperic, 21, 64, 77, 83, 84; Burgundian Code issued by, 62, 63, 65, 66 *sq.*, 91; a devoted but tolerant Arian, 64, 75, 88, 90, 93, 116; plot to call in the Franks against, 78, 83; treachery and defeat of Godegesil, 90 *sq.*; Gundobad nominally tributary to Clovis, 91, 92, 95; invades Auvergne with Theuderic, 97

Gundobald, claims to be son of Chlothar I., 113, 125, 192 *sqq.*, 202; once a painter of religious frescoes, 193, 448; story of his conspiracy, 192 *sqq.*, 277, 297, 301, 330; really a scheme of the aristocratic party to overthrow the old Merovingians, 192, 193, 196, 199, 202, 479; supported by Mummolus and Desiderius, 194 *sq.*, 196 *sq.*, 200, 201, 202, 221, 297; proclaimed king, 197; the rebellion crushed at Convenae, 200 *sq.*, 264, 277; relic coveted by, 244

Guntram, king of Burgundy, 171, 179; allows judicial combat, 50, 133; makes Childebert II. his heir, 113, 187, 198, 229; makes a direct appeal to his people for their support, 113, 117, 121, 177, 191, 446; calls his generals to account for their defeat in Septimania, 120, 207, 300, 301; his cruelty, 133, 135, 178, 198, 261, 435; executes the sons of Magnacharius for slandering his queen, 133, 135, 178; kills her physicians, 135 *sq.*, 260 *sq.*; a complex character with some redeeming qualities, 135, 177, 178, 281, 289, 291, 343, 446; the Breton rebellion against his governors, 152 *sq.*; Gregory's indulgent estimate of him, 176 *sq.*, 178, 281, 283, 348; his generosity to the Church and to the poor, 177, 191, 201; as protector of Fredegundis and Chlothar, 177, 190, 191 *sq.*, 227, 348; as protector of Brunihildis and Childebert, 178, 185, 186, 187, 188; his policy obliges him constantly to change sides in the wars between his brothers, 178, 179, 180, 181, 182, 185, 330; his struggle with Chilperic, 187 *sqq.*, 196; becomes regent of Neustria and guardian of Chlothar, 190 *sq.*, 196; refuses to surrender Fredegundis and the cities of Aquitaine, 191 *sqq.*, 196; his complicated relations with Childebert, 191 *sqq.*, 196, 199, 340 *sq.*, 342, 348; Guntram Boso's insults, conspiracy, and death, 192, 197, 198, 203 *sq.*; the conspiracy of Gundobald, 192 *sqq.*, 201, 264, 277, 297, 301, 330, 500; other plots against him crushed, 202 *sqq.*, 228, 242, 435; the Pact of Andelot with Childebert, 203, 224,

342 *sq.* ; campaign against Lombards, 205, 274 ; his death, 208, 229 ; his Gallo-Roman generals and advisers, 221, 229 ; his relations with Gregory, 239, 340 *sq.*, 342 *sq.* ; his triumphal entry into Orleans, 244, 266 ; a mighty hunter, 252 *sq.* ; his wise action during the plague, 260 *sq.* ; his wives, 283 *sq.* ; his greed of wealth, 296 ; his horror of sacrilege, 300, 301 ; his reception of Bertram and Palladius, 344, 500 ; and the revolted nuns of Poitiers, 387 ; consults a pythoness, 436 ; episcopal elections controlled by, 474, 494 ; his superstitious reverence for bishops, 478 *sq.*, 501 *sq.*

Hagiography, its historical value, 4, 26 *sqq.*, 35, 396 *sq.*, 406 *sq.* ; its copiousness, 396 ; the charm of the Lives of the Saints, 406 *sq.* ; the psychology behind these stories, 413 *sqq.* ; the growth of hagiography, 419 *sq.*, 422 ; the doubtful authenticity of such records, 420 *sqq.*

Hermenefred, king of Thuringia, husband of Theodoric's niece, 92, 157 ; Theuderic's revenge for his treachery, 158, 371

Hermenegild, converted from Arianism by Ingundis, 339, 466 ; killed by his father, *ib.*

Hermits, 23, 409 *sqq.* ; no records left by, 26 ; of the Jura, 36 *sq.*, 76, 273, 358, 360, 407, 410 ; appeal of the ascetic movement, 24, 256, 311, 313, 318, 359 *sq.*, 407 ; monasteries founded by, 36 *sq.*, 360, 361, 362 ; of Auvergne, 163, 309, 317, 318, 326, 432 *sq.* ; often of noble families, 273, 281, 359 *sq.*, 362 ; the system Oriental in origin, 355, 356 ; their excesses of austerity, 356, 357 ; they become objects of a cult, 407 *sq.*, 415 *sq.*

Hincmar, 422 ; his Life of S. Rémi, 29, 34, 421, 422, 423

Hortensius, Count of Auvergne, 168, 220 ; incurs the wrath of Bishop Quintianus, 146, 162

Hospices for poor and sick, 255

Huns, the, their invasions of Gaul, 9, 10, 11, 13, 64, 236

Hunting, the favourite sport of the Merovingians, 251 *sqq.* ; expeditions beneficial to the Church, 253, 364 *sq.*

Inbreeding and the prevalence of disease in Gaul, 257 *sq.*

Ingitrudis and Berthegundis, the case of, 344 *sq.*, 500

Ingoberga, wife of Charibert, 223, 283, 343

Ingundis, her conversion of Hermenegild, 339, 466

Intermarriage between Frank and Roman once forbidden, 278

Javols, pagan rites at holy lake of, 263

Jews, discrimination against, in Burgundian Code, 76 ; in the siege of Arles, 99, 100, 244 *sq.* ; partisans of the Arians, *ib.* ; as bankers, moneylenders, and physicians, 129 *sq.*, 244, 245, 471 ; members of a moneylending firm assassinated by their debtors, 129 *sq.*, 245 ; as traders, 244 *sqq.*, 469, 470 *sq.* ; efforts to convert them, 245, 246 *sqq.*, 470, 471, 472 ; persecutions of, 246, 247, 248, 470 ; their disabilities under Romans and Merovingians, 469 *sqq.*

Jordanes, on the Franks in battle against Attila, 9 ; on Genseric, 17 ; on the conquests of Euric, 23 ; on the Burgundian defeat at Arles, 101

Judex, the office of, 131, 133, 141, 143

Judicial combat, 73 ; allowed by Guntram, 50, 133

Judicial system, Merovingian, in the Codes, 53 *sqq.*, 62 *sq.*, 65 *sqq.* ; its cruelty, 131 *sqq.* ; efforts of the Church to mitigate its severity, 50 *sq.*, 52, 131 *sq.*, 367, 452 *sq.* ; the king as supreme judicial authority, 54 *sq.*, 66 *sq.*, 117, 133 ; the king's council, 56, 67, 136, 140 ; the Counts' courts, 131, 132, 141, 143 *sqq.* ; the *curia*, 145, 263 *sq.*, 276

Julian, invasions of Gaul repelled by, 4, 7

Jura, the, ascetics of, 36 *sq.*, 76, 273, 358, 360, 407, 410 ; famine in, 254 ; laxity in the monasteries of, 366

Justinian, bribes the Franks for their aid, 165

Kingship, Frank, 41, 80, 81, 106 *sqq.* ; its difference from the early German chieftainship, 41, 107 *sqq.*, 111 ; as seen in the Codes, 53, 54, 66 *sq.* ; its supreme judicial authority, 54 *sq.*, 66 *sq.*, 117, 133 ; aristocracy entirely dependent on, 80 *sq.*, 118, 218, 219, 223, 226 ; the institution binding Franks and Romans, 110 *sq.* ; its assumption of Roman titles and dignities, 112 ; hereditary, not elective, 113, 122 *sq.* ; the exclusion of females, 113 ; the system of divided inheritance, *ib.*, 122, 123, 155, 165, 171, 210 ; the ceremony of installation, 113 *sq.* ; military in character, 116, 118 *sqq.*, 122, 153 ; its absolutism, 116 *sqq.*, 120, 121, 122, 131, 133, 136, 153 ; the harem system and the appearance of pretenders to the throne, 123 *sqq.*, 193 ; powers of taxation and, 124 *sq.*, 126, 127 *sq.* ; harshness of judicial system upheld by, 131 *sq.*, 133

Land ownership, system of, 61 *sq.*, 67 *sq.*, 114 *sq.* ; Burgundian laws, 67, 68, 79, 115 ; subdivision of estates, *ib.*, 129 ; grants made by the king, 224 *sq.* ; the estates of the Church, 203, 224, 363, 364, 440, 441 ; not held in return for military service, 224

Land tax, the, 126 *sqq.*, 139, 164 ; the *curia* responsible for collection of, 126, 264; Roman system retained by Frank kings, 126 *sq.*, 263, 276 ; resisted by the Church, 126, 127 *sq.*, 129, 130, 343 *sq.*, 443 ; mode of assessment, 127 ; revolts against, 127 *sq.*, 186, 299; question of the exemption of Frank proprietors, 130 *sq.*

Latin, the language of the Frank court and administration, 277, 278 ; adopted by the common people, 278

Leges Barbarorum, their origin, 43, 44

Leman, Lake, monasteries of, 36 *sq.*, 357 *sq.*

Lepers, the treatment of, 256

Lérins, monastery of, 97, 357 *sq.*, 368 ; S. Caesarius in, 97, 98, 358, 366 ; laxity in its discipline, *ib.* ; distinguished bishops from, *ib.* 357

Leudastes, Count of Tours, career of, 143, 147 *sqq.*, 223, 331 *sq.* ; his cruelty and rapacity, 132, 147, 148, 223, 298, 331 ; ultimately attacked and tortured to death by order of Fredegundis, 135, 265 *sq.* ; Gregory's arch-enemy, 147, 148, 186, 331 ; his feud with Merovech, 148

sq., 331, 456 ; his plot to ruin Gregory, 149 *sqq.*, 186, 331 *sqq.*, 463 ; excommunicated, 334

Leudes, the class of, 53, 227 *sq.* ; their mutinousness, 160 *sq.*, 182 *sq.*, 320 ; the ambitions of the Austrasian *leudes* and their struggle with Brunihildis, 184, 185, 186 *sqq.*, 193, 202 *sq.*, 204, 205, 208, 209, 210 *sq.*, 222, 228 *sq.*, 230, 231, 232 *sqq.*, 277 ; their position under the Pact of Andelot, 203

Lex Alarici, 62

Lex Romana, 62 *sq.*

Liber Constitutionum, 62, 63

Licinianus, failure of his mission to Euric, 5, 22, 24

Limoges, revolts against crushing taxation, 127 *sq.*, 186, 299 ; changing ownership of, 146, 179, 196 ; plague in, 348

Literary culture of decadent Roman aristocracy, 18, 23

Liti (serfs), 227

Lives of the Saints, the, their pictures of the social life of Gaul, 26 *sqq.*, 235, 272 ; harsh justice depicted by, mitigated by the efforts of the Church, 50, 131, 132 ; use of word " nobilis " in, 226 ; copiousness of the collections of works of this kind, 396 *sq.* ; their historical value, 396, 397 ; their charm and importance, 399, 406 *sq.*, 408 ; the whole literature of the time concentrated in, *ib.*, 475 ; the psychology behind them, 413 *sqq.* ; their development, 419 *sq.*, 422 ; of doubtful authenticity, 420 *sqq.* ; episcopal elections as described in, 495 *sqq.*

Lombards, the, their invasions of Burgundy repelled by Mummolus, 82, 120, 205 *sq.*, 221, 274, 330, 383 ; Childebert's disastrous campaign against, 120, 189, 207 *sq.*

Lupus, Bishop of Troyes, 27, 98

Lupus, Duke of Champagne, 151, 188, 220, 222 ; his support of Brunihildis, 186, 188, 222, 228, 229, 379 *sq.* ; praised by Fortunatus, 188, 222, 237, 379 *sq.* ; Saxons and Danes crushed by, 188, 222, 237

Magnacharius, the sons of, executed for slandering Guntram's queen, 133, 135, 178

Major domus, the office of, 139, 140, 230, 231

Majorian, 9 ; his Roman generals, 10, 12, 13 ; loss of his fleet and death, 13, 17, 20 ; Theodoric renounces peace with, 14 ; his murder the real close of the Western Empire, 18 ; Ricimer's hatred for, 19

Mallus, the, in Salic Law, 52, 53, 54 *sq.*, 143 *sq.*

Marcatrudis, divorced wife of Guntram, 135, 284

Marcellinus, Roman general against the Vandals, 17, 18, 19

Marcomanni, the, 108

Marcovefa, wife of Charibert, shows favour to Leudastes, 147, 223 ; Charibert excommunicated for marrying her, 287

Mark system and the organisation of the *villa*, 61

Maroveus, Bishop of Poitiers, his indifference to the fortunes of S. Radegund's convent, 381 *sq.*, 385, 386, 387, 388

Marseilles, custom house at, 126 ; feud between factions of Austrasian nobles begins in, 242 ; struggle for, between Austrasia and Burgundy, 242 ; trade of, *ib.*, 243 ; violence and sacrilege by great officers in, 303 *sq.*

Martius, Abbot, Gregory's father healed by, 322, 361 ; monastery founded by, *ib.*

Maurice, Emperor, finances the pretender, Gundobald, 125, 193, 194 ; subsidises Childebert to attack Lombards, 189, 206

Mayors of the Palace, their rise to power, 140, 212, 233

Meliores natu, meaning of term, 227

Menapii, the, 6

Merovech, son of Chilperic, deserts his command, 124, 184, 453 ; marries his aunt, 124, 184, 337, 453 ; conspires against his father, 124 *sq.*, 184 *sq.*, 194, 337, 453 ; his death, 134, 185, 457 *sq.* ; plunders estates of Leudastes, 148 *sq.*, 331, 456 ; his behaviour while in sanctuary at Tours, 185, 194, 252, 300, 337 *sq.*, 453 *sqq.* ; Fredegundis sends Boso to entrap him, but the plot fails, 185, 194, 252, 453, 456 ; *Sortes* consulted by, 436, 457

Merovechus, king of the Franks, mystery of his birth, 9

Merovingian kings, their success in adopting Roman administration and conciliating conquered peoples, 110, 112, 114 *sq.*, 137 ; their unbroken succession, 113, 122 ; the system of divided inheritance, 113, 122, 123, 135, 165, 171, 179 *sq.*, 210 ; their claim to be " defenders of the people ", 113, 117, 120, 121 *sq.*, 176, 191, 446 ; their absolutism, 116 *sqq.*, 120, 121, 122, 131, 133, 136, 217, 219 ; their armies, 118 *sqq.*, 156 *sq.*, 206, 207, 208 ; Oriental in their relations with women, 123, 172, 193, 223, 283, 287 *sq.*, 289 ; risings against, caused by harsh taxation, 125 *sq.*, 127 *sq.*, 186, 299 ; faithless, cruel, and greedy, 131, 133 *sq.*, 135, 156, 158, 163, 164, 165, 170 *sq.*, 175, 178, 180, 181, 190, 281 *sq.*, 283 *sq.*, 291, 293, 294, 296 *sqq.* ; inhumanity of their judicial system, 131 *sq.*, 133 ; their council, 136, 140, 217 ; their court a shadow of the Imperial Roman court, 137 *sqq.* ; their power passes to nobles and Mayors of the Palace, 212, 232 ; position of the aristocracy under, 215 *sqq.* ; their ruthless suppression of possible rivals, 215 *sqq.*, 219 ; their love of sport, 251 *sqq.*, 456 ; high qualities possibly obscured by their vices, 279 *sq.* ; Gregory and Fortunatus at variance regarding, 280 *sq.* ; devoted sons of the Church, 364, 365, 371, 440, 478, 479, 489 ; monasticism supported by, 364 ; power of the bishops over, 478, 479 *sqq.*, 502 ; their voice in episcopal elections, 480, 481, 482, 484, 489 *sqq.*

Miracles, many of them trivial or selfish, 31 *sq.*, 57, 239 *sq.*, 249, 251, 406, 426, 427 *sq.* ; performed in favour of travellers, 239, 240, 241, 341 ; Gregory's enthusiasm for the miraculous, 166, 239 *sq.*, 258, 261, 269, 291, 316, 322, 323, 327 *sq.*, 346, 350, 395, 406, 418, 426, 433 ; belief in, and the psychology of the age, 395, 405 *sqq.*, 413, 414 *sqq.* ; distinction drawn between Christian and pagan miracles, 434 ; rivalry in, between Arians and Catholics, 468

Monachism, 355 *sqq.* ; Oriental origin of the ascetic movement, 355, 356 ; motives of the monastic life, 358 *sqq.*, 363 *sq.*

Monasteries, the part played by solitary ascetics or hermit communities in their development, 36 *sq.*, 360, 361, 362 ; laxity of discipline in, 98, 358, 366, 367 ; traditions of the endowment of, 362 *sqq.* ; lands held by, 363, 364, 421 ; constitution of, 365 *sq.*, 369 *sq.*, 393 *sq.* ; development of episcopal control, 366 *sq.*, 360, 370, 371 *sq.*, 386 *sqq.*, 392 *sqq.* ; their services to European civilisation, 367 *sq.* ; monastic life distinct from clerical, 369 *sq.*, 393 ; lives of founders composed to establish title to lands, 421 *sq.*

Morals of the Merovingian age, 268 *sqq.* ; example set by the royal house, 279 *sqq.*, 287 *sq.* ; drunkenness, 286 *sq.*, 463, 498 ; sexual immorality, 287 *sqq.* ; prevalence of perjury, 291 *sqq.*, 426, 434 *sq.* ; greed for wealth, 296 *sqq.* ; violence and sacrilege, 302 *sqq.*, 454 *sqq.*

Mummolus, 82, 115, 120, 156, 209, 221, 229 ; displaces his father by bribery, 82, 142, 221, 298 ; repels Lombard invasions, 82, 120, 205 *sq.*, 221, 274, 330, 383 ; supports Gundobald's conspiracy, 120, 194 *sqq.*, 200 *sq.*, 202, 221, 229 ; as Guntram's general in Aquitaine, 185, 221 ; besieged in Convenae and killed, 200 *sq.*, 277

Munderic, revolt and fate of, 123, 294

Municipal government, the Imperial system maintained, 263, 276, 319 ; modified powers of the *curia*, 145, 263 *sq.*, 276

Nantes, tradition of siege of, 82 ; trade of, 243

Neustria, 171 *sqq.* ; Sigibert's conquest of, 114, 182, 183 ; causes of the distinction and the struggle between Austrasia and, 171 *sqq.* ; Gallo-Roman predominance in, 171; invaded by Austrasia and Burgundy, 179, 187, 188 ; invades Aquitaine, 181 *sq.*, 184, 185, 188 ; alliance with Austrasia against Burgundy proposed, 187 *sq.* ; temporarily united with Burgundy, 190 *sq.*, 193 ; Gundobald's conspiracy aimed at, 198, 199, 202 ; Brunihildis attempts to wipe out, 208, 209 ; reduced to twelve cantons, 209, 229, 231 ; under Mayors of the Palace, 212

Nicetius, Bishop of Lyons, 146, 237, 273, 429 ; denounces Theudebert from the altar, 270 *sq.* ; promised bishopric by Childebert, 280 ; miracles at his shrine, 292 *sq.*, 419, 429, 472 ; makes no bequests to the Church, 429 ; struggles for relics of, 432 ; rationalist criticism of his miracles, 472, 490 *sq.*

Nicetius, Duke of Auvergne, 151, 152, 298, 300 *sq.* ; his castle, 237

Oath of compurgation, ritual of, 58 *sq.* ; taken by Gregory at his trial, 150, 334

Odo, Abbot, his Life of Gregory, 309 ; his story of the meeting of the two Gregorys not authentic, 345 *sq.*

Optimates, the class of, 227

Oral tradition, its historic value, 85

Ordeal, trial by, in Salic Law, 57 *sq.* ; ordeal by combat, *ib.*, 73, 133, 252 *sq.* ; recourse to trial by ordeal in theological controversy, 468

Orleans, battle of, 15 ; Guntram's appeal to the people at, 113, 117, 121, 177, 191, 446 ; great fire at, 260, 338 ; Guntram's entry into, 266, 340

Ostrogoths, the, their advance in East and West, 4, 17, 21 *sq.* ; Franks and Burgundians defeated by, 100 *sqq.* ; treacherous policy of the Franks towards both Ostrogoths and East Romans, 164, 165, 166

Pact of Andelot, 113, 203, 224, 342 *sq.*

Paganism, Frank, 78, 86, 87 ; its sentiment not much different from the materialistic Christianity of the time, 88 *sq.*, 395, 397 *sq.*; not wholly discarded, 89, 122 ; its survival in Gaul, 262 *sq.*, 313, 329, 341, 434, 435 *sq.* ; the ascetic movement originating in, 355 *sq.*; its lingering influence, 405, 416, 424, 434, 435 *sq.* ; Christian sanction of certain of its practices, 434, 435 *sq.*

Pagus, meaning of the term, 141

Palace, Merovingian, 137 *sq.*; its officials, 138 *sqq.*

Palladius, Count, 142, 220, 281; his quarrel with Bertram at Guntram's table, 288, 341, 500; charged with licentiousness, *ib.*; his reception by Guntram, *ib.*, 499, 500; Guntram's refusal to hear him say Mass, 341, 500

Pannonia, Vandal pressure on Ostrogoths of, 17, 23; Ostrogothic invasion begun from, 21 *sq.*

Paris, S. Geneviève and Childeric at, 27 *sq.*; Childebert's capital, 156; neutralised, 171; Syrian merchant as Bishop of, 244; attempted conversion of Jews of, 247 *sq.*; shops and booths in, 265; street scenes in, *ib. sq.*; fires in, 266 *sq.*

Parthenius, stoned to death for imposing land-tax on Franks, 82, 164, 220 *sq.*; a glutton and a murderer, *ib.*

Patiens, Bishop of Lyons, 20, 83

Patrician, the office of, 19, 37, 221; held by Gallo-Romans under the Merovingians, 82, 221; German kings proud of the title, 104 *sq.*, 112, 221

Pecuniary compensation, principle of, in the Codes, 44, 47, 48, 49 *sqq.*, 53, 58, 66; not the original old German system, 44, 48; implies a high standard of wealth, *ib.*; varying degrees of, 47, 48; growth of the system from three different roots, 50 *sqq.*

Perjury, its prevalence, and legends of divine punishment of, 58, 59, 291 *sqq.*, 426, 434 *sq.*

Peter, brother of Gregory, 323; murdered, 302

Pharamond, legendary king of the Franks, 8, 43

Physicians of Merovingian times, 261 *sq.*

Pippin the Elder, 210, 231

Plague, the, in Gaul, 128, 135, 146 *sq.*, 236, 254, 259 *sqq.*, 266, 280, 314, 348 *sq.*, 450; the great plague of 580, 128, 135 *sq.*, 146 *sq.*, 186, 208, 260, 280, 338; kills two of Chilperic's sons, 128, 135, 186, 260, 266, 280, 338; physicians murdered on death of Austrechildis from, 135 *sq.*, 261; omens preceding its onslaughts, 259

sq., 338; stories of the efficacy of shrines and relics against, 260, 314, 430; in Rome, 345

Poitiers, 171, 179, 191, 196, 330; misdeeds of Leudastes in, 335; burial of S. Radegund at, 342; revolt of nuns of the Convent of the Holy Cross, *ib.*, 343, 367, 370, 385, 386 *sqq.*, 392

Poverty of the age, 254 *sqq.*, 358; the Church and the relief of, 255 *sq.*, 451 *sq.*

Praetextatus, Bishop of Rouen, 183; marries Merovech and Brunihildis, 124, 185, 453; his trial, 125, 499; attacked while celebrating Mass, 464 *sq.*; collection of sermons by, 474

Priores, class of, 227

Priscus, Byzantine historian, and the birth of Merovechus, 9; on the exploits of Aegidius, 14

Priscus, the Jew, 176, 245; his relations with Chilperic, 176, 245, 247 *sq.*, 471 *sq.*; their theological debate 176, 247 *sq.*, 471 *sq.*; murdered, 248, 472

Probus, German invasions repelled by, 4, 6

Procopius, on the failure of the Franks at Nantes, 82

Property, inheritance of, Salic Law, 52 *sq.*, 67; laws of, Burgundian Code, 66, 67 *sq.*, 72 *sq.*; succession to land granted to women, 175

Prosper, 85; Pharamond mentioned in his chronicle, 8

Protadius, raised to the Patriciate by Brunihildis, 209, 230, 299; avaricious and insolent, *ib.*; murdered, 209

Provence, reorganised by Theodoric, 102 *sq.*; parcelled out among northern kingdoms, 179; Saxon threat to, 181; fortifications of its cities, 264 *sq.*

Quintianus, Bishop of Auvergne, his quarrel with Count Hortensius, 146, 162; in the siege of Cahors, 161; his election to the bishopric, 490

Rachimburgi, their position and duties, 55 *sq.*, 58, 144

Radegundis, Queen, 158. *See under* S. Radegund.

Ragnachar of Cambrai, 79, 122 ; his vassals betray him to Clovis, 216 ; Clovis deceives them with sham gold, *ib.*, 227, 296

Rauchingus, 185, 295 ; his plot against Childebert, 202 *sq.*, 204, 295; his outrages upon his slaves, *ib.*

Referendarius, the office of, 138 ; referendaries made bishops, 496.

Reipus in Salic Law, relic of marriage by purchase, 52, 56

Relics of the saints, their sanctity and miraculous power, 430 *sqq.*, 439, 449; obtained by unscrupulous methods, 432 *sq.*

Religion in Merovingian times (*see also* Arianism, Ascetic movement, Catholicism, Church) ; growth of the religious spirit, 29, 30, 36 ; spread of spiritual ideals in upper classes, 272 ; religious outlook of early Middle Ages, 324 *sq.* ; its superstitious side, 324, 325 ; the ascetic movement, its origin and motives, 355, 356, 358 *sqq.* ; religious impostors become numerous, 347 *sq.* ; the belief in the miraculous, 395, 397, 413, 414 *sqq.* ; the pagan element in, 395, 397 *sq.*, 405, 416, 424, 434, 435 *sq.* ; ancient tradition and mystic speculation, 398 *sqq.* ; its system one of mathematical symmetry, 399, 400 *sqq.* ; the outlook of the age as seen in the Lives of the Saints, 413 *sqq.*, 424 ; the materialism of popular religion, 425 *sq.*, 440, 459

Remigius, *see* S. Rémi

Rheims, 31, 86, 171 ; its sufferings in the days of Charles Martel, 29, 422 ; S. Rémi at, 31 *sqq.*, 86 ; grants made to the church by Clovis, 33 ; the plague in, 34 ; devastation round, in wars of the Merovingians, 169

Richaredus, king of the Visigoths, 189, 205, 242

Ricimer, king of the Vandals, 4, 12, 15, 17, 18 *sqq.* ; campaign of Aegidius against, 12, 13, 20 ; his part in the overthrow of the Western Empire, 18 *sqq.* ; as king-maker, 18, 19, 20 ; his protection of Gundobad, 21, 64

Riculfus, his part in the plot against Gregory, 150, 332, 333, 335, 336, 337, 463 ; his punishment, 151

Rigunthis, Princess, her wedding procession, 189, 196, 225, 227, 297, 301 ; her treasure seized by Desiderius for Gundobald, 197, 199, 297 ; Fredegundis attempts to murder her, 297 *sq.*

Ripuaria, 155

Ripuarian Code, 52, 112, 126, 142 ; later and more scientific than Salic Law, 45, 57 ; civil power supreme in, 45, 66 ; regal power in, 45, 116 ; judicial combat and oath of compurgation in, 58, 59 ; growing power of the Church in, 75

Roman Empire, the Franks both its defenders and despoilers, 7 *sq.*, 11 ; doom of its power in Gaul, 16, 22, 23 ; causes of its decline, 16 *sq.*, 18 ; Teutonic noblesse in its service, *ib.* ; supported in Gaul by Burgundians, 20, 63 *sq.* ; respect felt by German chiefs for its dignities, 18, 19, 41, 79, 81, 104, 105, 109, 112, 138, 477 ; its authority and administrative methods appropriated by its successors, 41, 81, 110, 137, 138, 153, 476, 477 ; its financial and municipal system retained by Merovingians, 81, 125 *sq.*, 127, 243, 263, 276 ; disabilities of Jews under, 469

Roman law, and barbarian usage, as basis of Salic Law, 44, 62 *sq.*, 65 ; pecuniary compensation in, 50 ; its influence on Burgundian Code, 65, 72, 74

Roman roads still open in Gaul, 238

Romans, their decadence, 3 *sq.*, 18, 23 ; some ready to serve the invaders, 5 ; campaign of Visigoths against, 14, 15, 16 ; supported by Franks in this campaign, 15, 16 ; treated among the Franks as an inferior race, 44, 47, 67, 81 ; their position among the Burgundians, 62, 65, 67, 73, 74, 82, 90 *sq.* ; their position under the Merovingians, 81 *sq.* See Gallo-Romans

Rome, 4 ; sacked by the Vandals, 17, 20, 21 ; the plague in, 345

Sabbath-breaking regarded as a crime, 250, 348

Sabellian heresy revived by Chilperic, 176, 186, 471, 480

Sagittarius, Bishop of Toulouse, 198 ; his dissoluteness and violence, 286 *sq.*, 501 *sq.*

S. Aridius, 272 *sq.* ; pleads for reduced taxation, 127

S. Arnulfus, his ascetic life, 256

S. Caesarius, 97 *sqq.*, 357 ; Life of, 97, 420 ; at Lérins, 97 *sq.*, 358, 366 ; made bishop of Arles, 98 ; accused of disloyalty, exiled and restored, 99 *sq.* ; fire at Bordeaux arrested by, 99, 266 *sq.* ; founds hospital, 101, 262 ; generously treated by Theodoric, *ib.* ; the Jews and, 244 *sq.* ; denounces paganism, 263 ; represses practice of leaving church before end of service, 445 ; denounces court vices, *ib.* ; elected to Tours, 487

S. Carileffus, 364 *sq.* ; his Life possibly written to establish a monastery's title to its lands, *ib.*, 421 *sq.* ; story of Childebert's grant of land to, 365, 421

S. Denis (Dionysius), concessions made to Abbey of, 243 ; foundation of Church of, 253, 364, 425 *sq.* ; it replaces the chapel of S. Geneviève, 253, 427 ; hospice of, 255 ; murderous conflict in the Church of, 303

S. Geneviève, 27 *sq.*, 427 ; social life of the time as depicted in the Life of, 27 *sqq.* ; her travels, 28, 239 ; story of Clovis and, 28 *sq.* ; her chapel of S. Denis supplanted by Dagobert's fane, 253, 427

S. Germanus, 115, 183 ; and S. Geneviève, 27 ; excommunicates Charibert, 283, 287 ; intercedes for S. Radegund, 373

S. Julian, shrine of, 25, 161, 255, 260, 320, 322 *sq.*, 327, 396 ; violated by Frank army, 161

S. Martin, Cathedral of, 25 (*see* Tours); Gregory's cult of, 239, 258 *sq.*, 261, 267, 292 *sqq.*, 326, 327 *sq.*, 395 *sq.*, 404, 406, 418, 429, 433, 447, 450 ; his foundations, 357 ; Life of, by Sulpicius Severus, 420; his election to bishopric of Tours, 487

S. Patroclus, 273, 361 ; Gregory's Life of, 270 ; monastery founded by, 362

S. Radegund, 371 *sqq.* ; captured in battle, becomes wife of Chlothar, 158, 282, 372 ; founds Convent of the Holy Cross at Poitiers, 236, 342, 370, 373 *sqq.*, 380 *sqq.*, 391 *sq.* ; her relations with Fortunatus, 236, 380, 381, 383 *sqq.* ; her asceticism and ministry to the sick, 256, 372, 374, 375, 383, 384, 390, 407 ; her death and obsequies, 342, 385 *sq.* ; revolt in her convent, 342, 367, 370, 385, 386 *sqq.* ; sacred relics acquired by, 383, 387, 431

S. Rémi, 25, 30 *sqq.*, 115 ; the Life of, 29, 31 *sqq.*, 421, 422, 423 ; his conversion and baptism of Clovis, 29, 30, 85, 86, 87, 88, 89, 489 ; miracles attributed to, often trivial, 31 *sq.*, 33, 34, 249, 427 *sq.* ; the vase of Soissons restored to, 32 *sq.*, 86 ; his possible part in the wooing of Clothilde, 83 ; foretells victory over Visigoths, 96 ; grant of land made to, 364

S. Sequanus, legend of, 410 *sq.*

S. Vincent, Saragossa saved by relics of, 166, 431 *sq.*

Saints and martyrs as guardian powers, 405, 406, 413, 414, 415, 416 *sq.*, 418, 424, 426 ; the cult of, 405 *sq.*, 424, 426 ; miraculous powers attributed to, 413, 414 *sqq.*, 426 ; a curious tendency to bargain for their favour, 425, 426, 429 ; their punishment of violation of their shrines or estates, 428 *sq.*, 441 *sq.* ; relics of, their sacredness and miraculous power, 429 *sqq.*, 439, 449

Salian Franks (Salii), original home of, 6, 9, 42, 44, 77 ; their conquests in Gaul, 13

Salic Code, 43 *sqq.*, 65, 66, 112, 175, 239, 251 ; Tongres the scene of the life it describes, 7, 45 ; MSS. of, 43, 44, 116 ; traditional origin of, *ib.* ; criminal law, 42 *sqq.* ; civil procedure, 52 *sq.*, 66 ; political and judicial system, 53 *sqq.*, 144 ; its omissions, 53 *sq.* ; no hereditary nobility mentioned in, 218, 219

Salonius, Bishop of Gap, his dissoluteness and violence, 286 *sq.*, 501 *sq.*

Salvian on the sensual life of Aquitaine, 271 ; retires to Lérins, 357

Sanctuary, right of, 51, 444

Saragossa saved by relics of S. Vincent, 166, 431 *sq.*

Saxons, the, support Visigoths against Romans, 15, 35; Chlothar compelled by his army to a disastrous expedition, 121, 166 *sq*., 168, 169; Theuderic's struggle with, 157; Mummolus repels raids of, 181, 221; defeated by Lupus, 188, 237

Sea power, its importance in last years of the Western Empire, 4, 17

Septimania, left in possession of Visigoths, 102, 157, 205; Guntram's army demoralised and disgraced in, 120, 205, 206 *sq*., 274, 300; Theudebert's campaign in, 163; outrages committed by the Burgundian armies in, 207, 300; embargo on entry of Burgundians into, 242; Childebert's campaign in, 279

Sicambri, the 6, 7, 8

Sicharius and Austrigiselus, blood feud between families of, 145, 304 *sqq*.

Sidonius Apollonaris, 308; value of his letters, 4; his pictures of serene Gallo-Roman country life, 5, 81, 139, 249, 271 *sq*., 306; mentions Roman attack on Chlogio, 9; on Burgundy under Chilperic II., 20 *sq*., 37, 67; on the Roman surrender of Auvergne, 22; banished from his diocese, 24; his panegyric on Euric, 24 *sq*.; his picture of Theodoric, 35; on the hermits of the Jura, 36; on Syagrius, 79; his travels, 238; delivers address in Latin, 278; on episcopal elections, *ib*., 316, 488; called to bishopric, 308, 487; on architectural works of his brother bishops, 444

Sigibert, son of Chlothar, 309; his war with his brother Chilperic, 114, 119, 120, 148, 172, 180, 181 *sqq*., 225, 280, 329 *sq*., 331; his assassination, 148, 174 *sq*., 183, 196, 331; uses forces of Auvergne against Guntram, 119, 174; calls in German tribes from beyond the Rhine, 120, 172, 182, 330; Gregory appointed to Tours by, 148, 328; his marriage to Brunihildis, 172 *sq*., 237, 284; his character and abilities, 172, 174 *sq*., 280; and the murder of Galswintha, 174, 178, 179; his territory on death of Charibert, 179, 180; his rebellious *leudes*, 182 *sq*.; sends Gundobald into exile, 193; For-

tunatus and, 236, 379, 381; and episcopal elections, 316, 317

Sigibert of Cologne, murdered, 113 *sq*., 216

Sigismund, king of Burgundy, and the Burgundian Code, 62, 63, 65, 75; Theodoric's son-in-law, 92; monastery founded by, 158; murders his own son, *ib*.; defeated and killed by Chlodomer, *ib*.

Sigiwald, Duke of Auvergne, his violence and rapacity, 162, 252, 321, 322; killed by Theuderic, 162, 164; his reverence for ascetics, 163; punished for attempting to annex Church lands, 428, 442

Slaves, harshness of the law towards, 47, 48, 51, 69 *sq*., 71, 72; prisoners sold as, 104; able to rise to official aristocracy of Merovingian court, 215, 222 *sqq*., 331; regulations as to Christian slaves of Jews, 246, 469 *sq*.; corrupting influence of domestic slavery, 288

Social condition of Gaul, as depicted in the Codes, 7, 40 *sqq*., 53 *sq*., 68 *sqq*.; its obscurity, 25 *sq*.; the evidence of hagiography, 26 *sqq*.; general insecurity and lawlessness, 46 *sqq*., 302 *sqq*., 407; the aristocracy (*q.v.*), 215 *sqq*.; devout life of many landed families, 233 *sqq*.; strange appeal of the ascetic life, 256, 272 *sq*., 311, 313, 318, 358 *sqq*., 362, 407, 408 *sq*., 473; life of the common people, 235 *sqq*.; travel, 237, 238 *sqq*.; inland trade, 242 *sqq*.; appalling poverty of the age, 254 *sqq*., 358; prevalence of disease, 253 *sq*., 257 *sqq*.; morals of the period, 268 *sqq*.; drunkenness, 286 *sq*.; immorality, 287 *sqq*.; perjury, 291 *sqq*.; greed for wealth, 296 *sqq*., 407

Soissons, kingdom of the Syagrii, 5, 10, 12 *sq*., 15, 77, 78, 79, 110; Clovis and the vase of, 32 *sq*., 80, 86, 116; as a Frank capital, 137, 156, 171; church of, 373

Solomon's Temple, sacred vessels of, carried off by Alaric, 97

Sortes Biblicae, practice of divination by, 124, 169, 436, 457

Spain, under the Visigoths, 25, 102; the plague in, 260; Arian persecution of Catholics in, 338, 339, 466

Sulpicius, Alexander, on early Frank *duces*, 8

Sunnegiselus, conspiracy of, 205, 225

Superstition, as a pillar of the law, 57 ; its part in religion of early Middle Ages, 324 *sq.* ; preyed on by religious impostors, 347 *sq.*, 436 *sq.* ; regarding unseen powers, 401 *sqq.*, 413 *sqq.* ; witchcraft, 402, 404 *sq.* ; the guardianship of saints and angels, 405, 406, 413, 414 ; surrounding relics of the saints, 429 *sqq.* (*see under* Miracles) ; forbidden practices still supported by Christians, 435 *sq.*

Syagrii, the, 12 *sq.*, 78 *sq.* ; their kingdom at Soissons, 5, 10, 12 *sq.*, 15, 77, 78, 79 ; maintain last remnant of Roman power in Gaul, 5, 10, 12, 16, 38, 110 ; overthrown by Clovis, 32, 79

Syrian merchants in Gaul, 244 ; one becomes Bishop of Paris, *ib.*

Tacitus, 107 ; pecuniary compensation mentioned by, 49 ; his Germans very different from their Frank successors, 41, 107, 108, 109, 110, 111 ; his idealisation of the old Germans, 107 ; on their kingship, *ib. sq.*, 111 ; on their leaders and aristocracy, *ib.*, 222 ; on their general monogamy, 283

Taxation, intolerably heavy under Visigoths, 35 ; revolts against burdens imposed by some Merovingians, 125 *sq.*, 127 *sq.*, 186, 299 ; the land tax, 126 *sq.* ; resisted by the Church, *ib.*, 128 *sq.*, 130, 343 *sq.*, 443 ; the Roman system retained, 127, 243 ; the Count's position as collector of taxes, 129 *sq.*, 143, 245, 254 ; tolls and customs, 243

Teutonic noblesse in the service of the Empire, 18

Theodoric, king of the Ostrogoths, 21 ; defeated by Aegidius, 13 *sq.* ; Franks and Romans leagued against, 15, 16 ; Ricimer's possible intrigues with, 19 ; supported by Burgundians against Sueves, 20 ; his advance into Italy, 21 *sq.* ; his tolerance and magnanimity, 25, 92, 101, 103, 465, 470 ; his family alliances, 92, 157, 172 ; his attitude and the policy of Clovis, 87, 92, 93 *sq.*, 95,

157 ; assists the Visigoths against the Franks, 100 *sqq.* ; his generosity to S. Caesarius, 101 ; establishes hold on Southern Gaul and Spain, 102, 159 ; his reorganisation of Provence, 103 ; receives Imperial dignities, 104 ; his death, 157

Theodoric II., king of the Visigoths, reduces taxation at request of Bibianus, 34 *sq.* ; Roman culture of his court, 277

Theodorus, Bishop of Marseilles, in feud between factions of Austrasian nobles, 187 ; supports Gundobald, 194, 195, 227 ; imprisoned by Guntram, 195

Theodosian Code, the, 69, 70 ; power of the King in, 112, 117 ; responsibility of *curia* for tax-collection in, 126 ; local dues mentioned in, 243 ; visitation of prisoners ordered by, 255

Thesaurarius, the office of, 139

Theudebald, son of Theudebert I., 166, 167

Theudebert I., son of Theuderic, remits taxation on Church property in Auvergne, 129, 164, 443 ; land tax on Franks under, 130 ; crushes the Danes, 157 ; ordered to kill Sigiwald's son, but saves him, 162, 164 ; in command of attack on Ostrogoths in Septimania, 163, 289 ; his intrigue with Deuteria, *ib.* ; his brothers attempt to seize his realm, 163, 165, 228 ; Gregory on his character, 163 *sq.*, 289, 443 ; his great qualities, 164, 289 ; his generosity to impoverished traders of Verdun, 164, 243 ; his Gallo-Roman advisers, 164 ; puts his own head on coins, *ib.* ; his disastrous Italian campaigns, *ib. sq.*, 274 ; failure of campaign with Childebert against Chlothar, 165 *sq.* ; his death, 166 ; his loose-living followers denounced by Bishop Nicetius, 270, 271

Theudebert, son of Chilperic, his devastation of Aquitaine, 148, 181, 182, 300, 330, 331 ; killed, reputedly by Boso, 182, 183, 194, 456

Theudebert II., son of Childebert, combines with Theuderic to crush Neustria, 209 ; war with Theuderic instigated by Brunihildis, *ib.*, 210, 229, 230 *sq.* ; defeated and murdered, 210, 230 *sq.*

Theuderic I., son of Clovis, 155 ; his devastations of Auvergne, 97, 121, 161 *sq.*, 299 *sq.*, 313, 318, 319 *sqq.* ; orders compilation of Ripuarian Code, 116 ; rebelliousness of his *leudes*, 121, 160 *sq.* ; his treachery to Munderic, 123, 294 ; plans to kill Chlothar, 131, 158, 282 ; his dominions at the death of Clovis, 155, 156 ; raid of the Danes on, 157 ; crushes the Thuringians, 158, 279, 282, 371 ; rumour of his death encourages revolt in Auvergne, 159, 160, 161 *sq.*, 308, 319 *sqq.* ; attacks the Ostrogoths, 163 ; Bishop Nicetius honoured by, 271, 490 *sq.* ; his numerous wives, 287 ; appoints Gallus to see of Clermont, 313, 314, 491 ; episcopal elections controlled by, 314, 490 *sq.*

Theuderic II., son of Childebert, 209 ; combines with Theudebert II. to crush Neustria, *ib.* ; war with Theudebert instigated by Brunihildis, *ib.*, 210, 229, 230 *sq.* ; defeats and murders Theudebert, 210, 230 *sq.* ; dies, 210, 231

Thuringians, the, defeated by Clovis, 95, 111 ; crushed by Theuderic I., 158, 279, 282, 371

Titles of Merovingian aristocracy, 226 *sqq.*

Tolbiacum, Clovis's victory at, 25, 87 ; Theudebert defeated by Theuderic at, 210, 230

Tongres, first settled home of Franks in Gaul, 7, 9, 42

Torture, use of, under Merovingians, 131, 134, 135, 266

Toul, Theudebert defeated at, 210, 230

Toulouse, as Visigoth capital, 13, 94 ; captured by Clovis, 97 ; surrenders to Gundobald, 198

Tournai, seat of Salian Franks, 10, 11, 16, 25, 77, 130

Tours, miracles at shrine of S. Martin, 28, 258 *sq.*, 261, 349, 449 *sq.* ; its special sanctity, 96, 349, 387, 396, 449 *sq.* ; respected by Clovis, 96 ; basilica raised by Perpetuus, 105, 444 ; Clovis invested with Imperial dignities in, 104, 105, 106, 112 ; Gregory opposes taxation of, 128, 129, 343 *sq.*, 443 ; Leudastes as governor of, 148, 331 *sqq.* ; Merovech

in asylum at, 148, 194, 299, 453 *sq.*, 458 ; the district devastated in wars of the Merovingians, 181, 184, 191 *sq.*, 300, 329, 330, 331, 337 ; cattle plague round, 254 ; its feud with Bourges, 265 ; destroyed by fire, 267 ; Pelagius punished for outrages at, 293, 441 ; rising against Cuppa in, 299 ; family blood-feud in, 304 *sqq.* ; former paganism in, 329 ; plague in, 348 ; moral atmosphere of, 387 *sq.* ; desecrated by Eberulfus and Claudius, 435, 442, 452, 458 *sq.* ; council of bishops enacts against violation of Church property, 442 *sq.* ; the Cathedral itself, 444 *sq.* ; right of asylum at, *ib.*, 453 *sq.*, 458 *sq.*

Town life in Gaul, 263 *sqq.*, 319 ; scanty materials for study of, 263 ; municipal government, *ib. sq.*, 276, 319 ; fortified cities, 264 *sq.*, hostilities between cities, 265 ; ravages of disease and fire, 266 *sq.*

Toxandria, Salian Franks established in, 7, 8, 42, 44

Travel in sixth century, 237, 238 *sqq.* ; and rapid spread of news, 16 ; relatively easy and expeditious, 238 *sq.* ; its perils and discomforts, 240 *sq.*, 327 *sq.*, 346 ; miracles performed on behalf of travellers, 240, 241, 328, 341 ; communications interrupted during warfare, 241 *sq.*

Trèves, sacked by Franks and Alemanni, 7, 8, 14, 31, 40 ; oppressive governor stoned in, 220 *sq.* ; Theudebert denounced in cathedral of, 270 *sq.*

Tribune, the office of, 138

Trojan origin of the Franks, legend of, 5, 6, 28

Ursio, leader of Austrasian nobles against Brunihildis, 184, 185, 186, 193, 233 ; insults Brunihildis, 188, 204, 228 *sq.* ; conspires against Childebert, 203, 204 ; killed, *ib.*

Ursus, his revenge on Andarchius, 222 *sq.*

Valentinian III., murdered, 10

Vandals, the, pressure of their seapower, 4, 17 ; defeated by Marcellinus, 12 ; Rome plundered by, 17 failure of Roman campaign against, *ib.*, 20 ; conquest of North Africa by, 24 ; Arian persecutions of Catholics under, *ib.*, 339, 465

Vase of Soissons, the, 32 *sq.*, 80, 86, 116

Verus, Bishop of Tours, intrigues on behalf of Franks, 78, 94 *sq.*

Vicus, the term, 60, 61

Videmir, brother of Theodoric, 21, 22

Villae, 45, 47, 242, 254 ; meaning of the term, 60, 61 ; royal, 137, 139, 217

Viri fortes, class of, 227

Viri magnifici, class of, 227

Visigothic Code, the, 50, 75, 99

Visigoths, the, annex Western Gaul, 10, 13 ; defeated by Aegidius, 14, 15 ; Romans supported by Franks against, *ib.*, 16 ; Auvergne ceded to, 22 ; their power under Euric, 24 *sq.*, heavy taxation under, 35 ; Burgundians and, resist Hun invasion, 64 ; their Arianism, 78, 88, 92, 93, 105, 338 ; Church intrigues against, 78, 88, 94 *sq.*, 99 ; Syagrius surrendered to Clovis by, 79 ; defeated by Clovis, 96 *sq.* ; failure of Guntram's campaign against, 120, 205, 206 *sq.* ; in league with Ostrogoths, 157 ; attacked by Childeric, 160 ; Childebert and Chlothar repelled by, 166, 279 ; Latin the official language of, 277 ; Arian persecutions of Catholics by, 338, 465, 466 ; Jews persecuted by, 469

Vitry, Munderic besieged in, 123, 294 ; Sigibert murdered at, 174 *sq.*, 183, 331

Volusianus, Bishop of Tours, intrigues on behalf of Franks, 78, 94

Vouglé, the victory of Clovis at, 4, 26, 79, 93, 100, 111, 120

Waddo, Duke, escorts the wedding procession of Rigunthis, 189, 197,

225 ; declares for Gundobald, 197 ; protected by Brunihildis, 201 ; outrages by his sons, 240, 391 ; his violence and lawlessness, 301, 391 ; his death, 301 *sq.*

Warnacharius, becomes mayor of the palace, 210, 212, 231 ; his treachery, 211, 231, 233 ; failure of Brunihildis's plans for his murder, 211, 232

Wehrgeld, 49 *sqq.* ; lower for a Roman than a Frank, 47, 81 ; very high for *antrustiones*, 117, 218, 219 ; five cities of Aquitaine as *wehrgeld* for Galswintha, 179 ; not high for *leudes*, 227

Western Empire, the, causes of its decline, 3, 16 *sq.*, 18 ; murder of Majorian marks its close, 18 ; Imperial place only once assumed by a barbarian, 19 ; the sacrifice of Gaul, 22

Wine, legends of miraculous provision of, 31 *sq.*, 239 *sq.*, 249, 426 *sqq.*

Wintrio, Duke of Champagne, expelled by his people, 152 ; in campaign against Lombards, 207 ; slain at instigation of Brunihildis, 209, 229

Witchcraft and sorcery, belief in, 402, 404, 435 ; cruelty of Fredegundis to witches of Paris, 134, 402, 435 *sq.* ; and the use of relics as charms, 434 ; still practised with Christian support, 435 *sq.*, 454 *sq.*

Witigis cedes Provence to the Franks, 103, 165

Women, jealously protected by Frank law, 10, 45, 46, 47 *sq.*, 72 ; relic of marriage by purchase in Salic Law, 52 ; right of succession to landed property refused by Salic Law, *ib.*, 175 ; property rights under Burgundian Law, 72 ; right of succession given by Chilperic, 175

THE END